Scarred Communities

Scarred Communities

PSYCHOSOCIAL IMPACT OF MAN-MADE AND NATURAL DISASTERS ON SRI LANKAN SOCIETY

Daya Somasundaram

$SAGE www.sagepublications.com
Los Angeles • London • New Delhi • Singapore • Washington DC

First published in 2014 by

 SAGE Publications India Pvt Ltd
B1/I-1 Mohan Cooperative Industrial Area
Mathura Road, New Delhi 110 044, India
www.sagepub.in

SAGE Publications Inc
2455 Teller Road
Thousand Oaks, California 91320, USA

SAGE Publications Ltd
1 Oliver's Yard, 55 City Road
London EC1Y 1SP, United Kingdom

SAGE Publications Asia-Pacific Pte Ltd
3 Church Street
#10-04 Samsung Hub
Singapore 049483

Published by Vivek Mehra for SAGE Publications India Pvt Ltd, typeset in 10/12 Book Antiqua by Diligent Typesetter, Delhi, and printed at Saurabh Printers Pvt Ltd, New Delhi.

Library of Congress Cataloging-in-Publication Data Available

ISBN: 978-81-321-1168-9 (HB)

The SAGE Team: Shambhu Sahu, Shreya Chakraborti, Anju Saxena and Rajinder Kaur

To all those who perished, were maimed, traumatized.
To all those families and communities who were separated,
scattered, uprooted, broken.
To all those who suffered and continue to suffer in the silence....

Thank you for choosing a SAGE product! If you have any comment, observation or feedback, I would like to personally hear from you. Please write to me at <u>contactceo@sagepub.in</u>

—Vivek Mehra, Managing Director and CEO,
SAGE Publications India Pvt Ltd, New Delhi

Bulk Sales

SAGE India offers special discounts for purchase of books in bulk. We also make available special imprints and excerpts from our books on demand.

For orders and enquiries, write to us at

Marketing Department
SAGE Publications India Pvt Ltd
B1/I-1, Mohan Cooperative Industrial Area
Mathura Road, Post Bag 7
New Delhi 110044, India
E-mail us at <u>marketing@sagepub.in</u>

Get to know more about SAGE, be invited to SAGE events, get on our mailing list. Write today to <u>marketing@sagepub.in</u>

This book is also available as an e-book.

Contents

List of Tables

List of Figures

List of Boxes

List of Abbreviations

AGA	Assistant Government Agent
AHRC	Asian Human Rights Commission
AI	Amnesty International
APRC	All Party Representative Committee
ASR	Acute Stress Reaction
AWOL	Absent Without Leave
BeCARE	Basic Education for Children in the Affected Areas
BESP	Basic Education Sector Programme
BRC	British Refugee Council
ca.	circa
CBO	Community-based Organization
CBT	Cognitive Behaviour Therapy
CG	Core Group
CHA	Consortium of Humanitarian Agencies
CHC	Centre for Health Care
CNO	Centre for National Operations
CO	Commanding Officer
CPA	Centre for Policy Initiatives
CSO	Community Support Officers
DESNOS	Disorders of Extreme Stress Not Otherwise Specified
DPU	Deep Penetration Unit
DRC	Danish Red Cross
DSM	Diagnostic and Statistical Manual of Mental Disorders
EMDR	Eye Movement Desensitization and Reprocessing
ER	Emergency Regulations
EU	European Union
FDL	Forward Defence Line
GA	Government Agent
GHQ	General Health Questionnaire
GP	General Practitioner
GS	*Grama Sevaka*

GTZ	Deutsche Gesellschaft für Technische Zusammenarbeit (German Technical Cooperation)
HRCSL	Human Rights Commission of Sri Lanka
HRW	Human Rights Watch
HSZ	High Security Zone
IASC	Inter-Agency Standing Committee
ICC	International Criminal Court
ICD	International Classification of Diseases
ICG	International Crisis Group
ICRC	International Committee of the Red Cross
IDP	Internally Displaced Person
IMF	International Monetary Fund
INGO	International Non-governmental Organization
IPKF	Indian Peace Keeping Force
IRC	Island Reconvicted Criminal
ISA	In-service Advisor
JHU	Jathika Hela Urumaya
JVP	Janatha Vimukthi Peramuna
LKR	Sri Lankan Rupees
LLRC	Lessons Learnt and Reconciliation Commission
LNGO	Local Non-governmental Organization
LSSP	Lanka Sama Samaja Party
LTTE	Liberation Tigers of Tamil Eelam
MDM	Médicos del Mundo
MHPSS	Mental Health and Psychosocial Support
MHTF	Mental Health Task Force
MOH	Ministry of Health
NCO	Non-commissioned Officer
NET	Narrative Exposure Therapy
NGO	Non-governmental Organization
NIE	National Institute of Education
ODIP	One-day Induction Process
pers. comm.	personal communication
PGDP	Provincial Gross Domestic Product
PHI	Public Health Inspector
PHM	Public Health Midwife
PIE	Provincial Institute of Education
PLO	Palestine Liberation Organization
POW	Prisoner of War
PST	Psychosocial Trainer
PSW	Psychosocial Worker
PTA	Prevention of Terrorism (Temporary Provisions) Act No. 48 of 1979

PTF	Presidential Task Force for Resettlement, Development and Security in the Northern Province
PTSD	Post-traumatic Stress Disorder
R2P	Responsibility to Protect
RHDS	Regional Director of Health Services
RPG	Rocket-propelled Grenade
SAARC	South Asian Association for Regional Cooperation
SLFP	Sri Lanka Freedom Party
SLMC	Sri Lanka Muslim Congress
SLRC	Sri Lanka Red Cross
STF	Special Task Force
STTARS	Survivors of Torture and Trauma Assistance and Rehabilitation Service
TC	Tamil Congress
TNA	Tamil National Alliance
TOT	Training of Trainers
TPO	Transcultural Psychosocial Organization
TRC	Truth and Reconciliation Commission
TULF	Tamil United Liberation Front
UKBA	United Kingdom Border Agency
UN	United Nations
UNHRC	United Nations Human Rights Council
UNOCHA	United Nations Office for the Coordination of Humanitarian Affairs
UNP	United National Party
USSR	Union of Soviet Socialist Republics
UTHR-J	University Teachers for Human Rights (Jaffna)
UXO	Unexploded Ordnance
Ven.	Venerable
YRT	Yoga and Relaxation Therapist

The Psychiatrist as a Political Critic

A Foreword

Ever since I read Daya Somasundaram's first book in the late 1990s, I have always read his writings with a mix of great anticipation and visceral discomfort. He has a clinical style which, even when dealing with gory violence, brings to his intellectual concerns not the calming touch of the family physician but the practical, robust, this-worldly presence of an engaged physician. Somasundaram works on the long- and short-term effects of mass violence on communities and persons and his gaze remains steadfastly clinical, but that clinical gaze has a clear political and social edge. And the prognosis — perhaps defying Somasundaram himself — will look somewhat pessimistic to most readers.

This pessimism has something to do with the perspective that the psychological disciplines bring to conflict situations in the region from which both Somasundaram and I happen to come. Though there is a rich tradition of exploring the psychological in South Asia, the public culture of the region has come to disdain it as soft, romantic and a hindrance to tough-minded statecraft and political realism. Very few in the more articulate and audible sections in our societies and none of the parties involved in a conflict are willing to even listen to the kinds of analysis Somasundaram has ventured in his work. We in South Asia are becoming, by our own choice, hard-eyed, masculinized devotees of realpolitik and have begun to look at anything psychological or dealing with human subjectivities with suspicion.

As a clinical discipline, modern psychiatry has consistently emphasized the suffering of the individual patient. This is as it should be. Most traditions of healing observe this rule, even when they underline the roles of society and culture in shaping the context and the source of a patient's suffering. In the southern hemisphere such contexts and sources can be formulated more directly and even brashly. One could say, for instance, that cholera in the tropics is caused first by poverty and only then by the cholera bacteria. You and I and our kind do not die of cholera, even if we are careless. Our environment and our class status sanitize and protect us, sometimes even when we are casual or careless about our personal hygiene. People living in slums have to more consciously take care of their personal and family hygiene and be more particular in their food habits and lifestyles.

We also know by now, thanks to Ivan Illich, that no epidemic, except smallpox, has been eradicated by drugs and vaccination. Public health and hygiene and improved quality of life have played a larger role in each case. And Illich, in retrospect, was modest in his claim because, even in the case of smallpox, subsequent research has shown that traditional methods of variolation had kept in check epidemics of smallpox in countries like China and India.

However, if you are a physician facing a case of cholera, your first job is not to enlighten the patient on the subtleties of social epidemiology or social history of a disease but to take care of the suffering in front of you. Somasundaram's work has always been a testimony to this double-edged responsibility of psychiatry, which cannot be shelved by giving a few ritual lectures on social psychiatry to students of medicine the way business schools teach business ethics and the social responsibility of business as trendy subjects with which futures corporate bigwigs must be familiar, so that they can navigate the upper echelons of society with self-confidence.

Those who have read Somasundaram's first foray in the area in 1998, *Scarred Minds: The Psychological Impact of War on Sri Lankan Tamils*, have come to expect from him a heightened sensitivity to the larger responsi-bilities that disciplines like psychiatry bear in conflict zones. The author wrote that book with what many would consider admirable scholarly detachment, but it was nonetheless a powerful testimony to his awareness of the changing nature of mass violence in our times, particularly the pre-dicament in which the non-combatants, trying to live their normal lives and protect their familiar moral universe, get caught. The other name for this predicament is collateral damage and it interests neither the combat-ants nor the political class and the media. The present book can be read as a companion volume to *Scarred Minds*.

The psychiatrist's job, in recent times, has not been a pleasant one, particularly when it comes to the mental health problems that modern warfare triggers. On the one hand, the number and proportion of non-combatants who die in wars and other forms of armed conflicts have begun to rise dramatically all over the world. Some estimates yield figures as high as 85 per cent. In addition, Somasundaram himself has shown elsewhere how civilian populations might be caught in the cross-fire between competing forms of ethno-nationalist ruthlessness, paranoia and systematic onslaughts on a community's way of life. A community can be made to go through multiple experiences of being uprooted when entire villages are resettled and re-resettled, made to walk through corridors of terror, torture, censorship and surveillance, and forced to see the militarization and brutalization of its children through systematic propaganda, hate speeches and politically slanted history.

On the other hand, the diagnosis of post-traumatic stress disorder (PTSD) has become not only more frequent, but also a double-edged instrument. PTSD is no longer only a nosological category or a handy clinical diagnosis that names the psychological devastation caused by war, both among the victims of war and the perpetrators. PTSD can also simultaneously be a means of declaring an afflicted community as socially and culturally challenged and unable to take care of itself. Psychiatrists rarely recognize what is pretty obvious to political analysts and journalists—calling a community traumatized is nowadays also a way of handing over agency to international bodies and outside experts, who are then expected to look after its welfare as professional social workers and political negotiators. As if war-induced trauma was not enough, the diagnosis of PTSD introduces into the theatre of war a new means of infantilization.

This book is a collective effort that offers another form of psychosocial support system for the victim communities whose world has been torn apart by the experience of war—with family and community processes damaged, culture and belief systems altered beyond recognition and daily life marked by suspicion and loss of hope, trust and motivation. War has pushed to them to the margin of despair and sometimes self-destruction. Somasundaram's alternative seeks to go beyond individual psychotherapy, bypass the ornate clinical and psycho-pharmaceutical interventions, and emphasize instead the restoration of the dignity and autonomy of the victims and their networks of human relations, while being sensitive to the cultural, social and psychological needs of the community. At the same time, it seems to be more affordable in resource-scarce societies.

In the post-Second World War period, civil wars have become a rather distinctive form of armed conflict. Even some of the major wars identified with countries such as Korea, Vietnam, Iraq and Iran had a large component of civil war built into them. Over the years, in places like China, India, Cambodia, West and East Africa and the Balkans, civil strife has taken a huge toll on human life, devastating entire communities and cultures. One main feature of such wars is that high casualties are not only seen as collateral damage but also quickly written off as 'normal' sacrifices for state formation and nation-building. Somasundaram himself has shown in the context of the Sri Lankan civil war how civilians were caught between the conflicting demands and competing atrocities of the two sides and were seen as expendable cannon fodder by both sides. They are still waiting for justice and rehabilitation.

Under these conditions, where does the psychiatrist's professional duty end and their responsibility as a citizen begin? Can resistance to war itself be part of a psychiatrist's intellectual self-definition? Or should they consider that an avoidable digression that takes them outside the ken of their discipline and the familiar landscape within which professional ethics and Hippocratic oath work? Does the psychiatrist's responsibility end at the perimeter of the clinic or does it extend to the epidemiology and the political sociology of the patient's suffering? Can psychiatry claim to be a 'total' discipline, for which there is no alien territory, because human subjectivities, the psychiatrist's main preoccupation, recognize no temporal and spatial borders?

These are questions to which there are no simple answers. The disciplines concerned with mental health have seen an enormous expansion in the range of psycho-pharmaceutical drugs. As a result, long-term psychotherapeutic interventions seem to be going out of fashion. The boundaries of the mental health worker's awareness too have widened to include a larger range of social and cultural variables. No psychiatrist can avoid taking a look at the changing nature of human violence, believing it to be primarily the concern of political scientists and sociologists. Yet, one has the nagging feeling that these expansions are accompanied by an abridgement of the intellectual and philosophical self of psychiatrists and in this abridgement a crucial role has been played by a narrow definition of professionalism.

Daya Somaundaram in this respect represents neither the conventional boundaries of clinical psychiatry nor the limits of the narrower professional conventions imposed on the discipline. He represents, I like to believe, the future of the discipline in our part of the world, at a time when violence is becoming endemic, predictable and thoroughly institutionalized as a part of the process of modernization. At this moment of brutalization of our societies, the psychological sciences in South Asia are today richer, better equipped and potentially more self-reflexive by virtue of the presence of this intrepid researcher from Sri Lanka. He has shown that there may still be some life in psychiatry as a critical social discipline in South Asia. The following pages should be read not only as a scientific monograph on mass violence in some distant land but also as a disciplinary testimony on what we ourselves have done to our part of the world.

Ashis Nandy

Prologue

Promise me,
promise me this day,
promise me now,
while the sun is overhead
exactly at the zenith,
promise me:

Even as they
strike you down
with a mountain of hatred and violence;
even as they step on you and crush you
like a worm,
Even as they dismember and disembowel you,
remember, brother,
remember:
man is not our enemy.

The only thing worthy of you is compassion—
invincible, limitless, unconditional.
Hatred will never let you face
the beast in man.

One day, when you face this beast alone,
with your courage intact, your eyes kind,
untroubled
(even as no one sees them),
out of your smile
will bloom a flower.

—Ven. Thich Nhat Hanh, *Understanding Our Mind*

This book is a sequel to my earlier description of individual trauma in Sri Lankan Tamils due to the civil war, titled *Scarred Minds: The Psychological Impact of War on Sri Lankan Tamils*, written largely in 1988–89 in the aftermath of the Indian intervention, eventually published by SAGE Publications in 1998. Much has happened since then—considerable blood has flown under the bridge. But much has remained the same—a sickening repetition of deaths, destruction, displacements, repression, terror and general misery. There has been a cycle of violence and ceasefires, war and peace with low-intensity conflict always simmering in the background and a 'final' battle in 2008–09 that has, one hopes, brought large-scale violence to an end. Then there was the massive natural disaster, the tsunami of 26 December 2004. This book attempts to document the cumulative, collective effects of massive trauma but also looks at some of the background factors and psychosocial treatments.

According to Eastern spiritual traditions, both Buddhist and Hindu, all life, or samsara, is full of suffering and grief. However, it appears to me that the population in Sri Lanka has undergone somewhat more than its share of misery in the last few decades. The country as a whole has faced an increasing authoritarian style of governance characterized by breakdown in the rule of law, judicial system and freedom of the press, electoral malpractices, corruption, clientelism or patronage politics, horizontal inequities (F. Stewart 2001), extrajudicial killings, disappearances, torture and a repressive state apparatus that has become institutionalized (Weliamuna 2012). It has spawned in the process two bloody ultra-left-wing Sinhala insurrections in the south and the ethnic war in the north and east. Perhaps that is our collective karma. This book focuses on what happened in the north and east. This chronic, ongoing conflict situation has been termed variously as an internal, civil or ethnic conflict by most and only a 'terrorist problem' by some politicians. The basis of the conflict is polarized ethnic consciousness that overdetermines events on this island and, to a large extent, in many other parts of the world racked by internal conflicts. Ethno-nationalism could even be considered the zeitgeist of the modern era and world view of present generations. As Benedict Anderson (2006), Edward Said (1995) and others have clearly explained, the growth and influence of nationalism and later, ethnic consciousness, developed from the period of European enlightenment to the colonial and postcolonial, Cold War compunctions to understand, administer, control, rule, classify, categorize and divide vast populations. There can be no doubt that the seeds of ethnic and tribal groupings and belonging have roots extending to the hoary past. However, the current preoccupation with communal identities is a modern development. The focusing and particular configuration of current ethnic groupings and definitions of exclusion and 'othering' are due more to recent historical, economic, sociopolitical, geographic and psychological factors. Sri Lanka is no exception. However, the words 'imagination', 'false consciousness', 'construction' and even 'maya' to describe what are really elements of collective perception or consciousness may not do justice to the phenomena they are trying to describe. For ethnic identity and belonging are not merely 'imagination' or 'false consciousness' but social reality for the vast majority of people who have grown up taking these for granted. The seeds of ethnic consciousness have come from the historical past, literature, folklore, cultural practices, ancestors, socialization and life experiences; modern manifestations though have been shaped by recent developments including political leadership, media, academic discourse and socio-economic factors. The experienced Vietnamese Buddhist monk and peace activist, Thich Nhat Hanh (2008) points out:

> Our society, country, and the whole universe are also manifestations of seeds in our collective consciousness…. The process of mistaking our perceptions for reality is so subtle that it is very difficult to know that it is going on…. In fact, people kill one another over their different perceptions of the same reality…. The way to avoid this is mindfulness.

The context of the poem (on the opposite page) he wrote as advice to his followers, who were sacrificing themselves out of love for victims, was the Vietnam War in the 1960s. One of his students, Nhat Chi Mai, immolated herself as a call to the two warring parties to sit down together and end the war. She read this poem into a tape recorder twice before she set fire to herself. The urgency, compelling nature and desperation the poem communicates fits the Sri Lankan context, a divided nation searching for reconciliation. Similar self-immolations have taken place recently in places as far afield as India, Malaysia, and Switzerland, and an attempt in the United Kingdom, as a form of moral protest asking for an end to the plight of Tamils. The motivational factors that drive desperate sacrifice and altruistic suicide are explored in Chapter 3C. The 'urgency' of the testimonial narrators in the chapters that follow brings out the 'metonymic character of testimonial discourse — the sense that the voice that is addressing us is a part that stands for a larger whole' (Beverley 2005). This book, using qualitative research methodology, attempts to represent 'the polyphonic *testimonio* made up of accounts by different participants' that gives voice to the silenced, powerless subaltern minority to bring out their collective story and trauma as well as a therapeutic mechanism of ventilation and catharsis for the scarred communities.

Mindfulness here is not some esoteric, spiritual practice, but an attempt, a struggle to stay in the here and now, in the present moment, trying to understand what is happening with some clarity, without bias or prejudice.

It is a way of gaining insight into events, the context and environment. This book is basically a desperate attempt to describe the ecology of the current situation in Sri Lanka, particularly for the Tamil community. Of course, it is a coloured, biased account of a Tamil living and working in the war-torn areas, with all the baggage of past experiences and current trauma. However, the hope is that through all this some clarity will emerge to guide us in fashioning a better future for the community and help those already scarred by what has happened. It can also shed some light on what is happening in similar situations around the world, caught in the quagmire of chronic civil conflict and ethnic strife, creating large scarred communities, refugees and internally displaced peoples.

I was given the unenviable task of taking psychiatric care of this share of the misery, the trauma, in the north, in the beginning, almost alone. Part of this book is a sharing of that long journey, a sharing that began with *Scarred Minds*. As described in that book, one of the first steps was to learn about trauma, as my medical training had not prepared me for this. In trying to intervene to treat the traumatized, we soon learnt that purely individual-oriented psychological and medical help was not sufficient. As Ananda Galappatti describes in his contribution, the local realization of the importance of the psychosocial dimension was part of an international awakening to its reality in conflict and post-conflict situations worldwide. In time, we began to appreciate the deeper collective nature of the effects of what was happening and the need to address the problem from a broader, holistic perspective. I was very thankful and I think the community was also fortunate that many started sharing in this journey. We soon had an increasing multidisciplinary team from a variety of backgrounds and skills, mostly trained by us over the years, which took over the burden and responsibility of caring for the affected. There was also welcome help and collaboration from the south, though not officially (which has largely ignored our needs and work), and also internationally by individuals and organizations. This was markedly noticeable in the enormous work after the tsunami. Some of this ongoing support and constructive collaboration is reflected in the special contributions. This book is a record and documentation of that journey, what we found in our developing knowledge of the psychosocial but also our struggle to find the best way to help, the variety of psychosocial interventions we evolved over time from our experiences, and work elsewhere in the world which were found effective. It is an attempt to share the pain and the learning, a necessary ventilation of our trauma and common humanity.

This book tries to bring a collective perspective to the Sri Lankan ethnic conflict in particular, but with broader implications for similar situations elsewhere in the world, in trying to understand the psychosocial causes, the traumatic consequences and community-level interventions. The experience and lessons learned have implications and suggestions for similar situations around the globe. It adopts a research study structure with an introduction followed by the background (Section 1), the psychopathology or psychosocial causes (ethnic consciousness — Chapter 1A) and effects of the conflict (terror — Chapter 1B). Section 2 describes the theory (Chapter 2A) of collective trauma and the methodology (Chapter 2B) used. Results and discussions of the study are given in case narratives, observations and interventions during the Asian tsunami of 2004 (Chapter 3A), Vanni war (Chapter 3B), disappearances (Chapter 3C) and the special case of Tamil militancy (Chapter 3D). A broader perspective is considered, with chapters by guest contributors, to describe the situation among the Sri Lankan military personnel (Chapter 4A) and the Tamil diaspora (Chapter 4B). The final section (Section 5) on treatment looks at psychosocial interventions from different perspectives: what we actually did (Chapter 5A), a reflective description of the evolution of psychosocial interventions in Sri Lanka (Chapter 5B) and an assessment of the post-conflict work and context (Chapter 5C). Each section and chapter can be read on its own by those interested in a particular topic or field. Trauma experts, fieldworkers, academicians and researchers can skip Section 1 and go directly to Section 2 for the theory and methodology, and the results thereafter in the chapters that follow. Those not interested in theoretical considerations or methodology can conveniently skip Section 2. Those from Sri Lanka and those interested in what happened here can read the Introduction and Section 1 from the author's perspective. Readers who are more practical and fieldwork-oriented can go directly to Sections 3, 4 and 5. Nevertheless, there is a thread, a theme that connects all the sections and subsections, to a bigger picture that the book is trying to present: a developing narrative, a descriptive analysis, an argument for prevention, peace and reconciliation, a way to intervene to build functioning families and communities after disasters that would have important lessons and implications for similar situations around the world. Sri Lanka becomes a case study for diverse topics of current concern such as ethnic conflict, modern war, peace, collective phenomena after disasters and psychosocial interventions and qualitative research methods and inquiry.

For the readers' benefit, I have included here two figures. Figure P.1 shows the map of Sri Lanka and Figure P.2 shows a broad timeline of important events in Sri Lanka's history.

Acknowledgements

It would be almost impossible to acknowledge all those who over the years have shared this journey with us, contributing to the ongoing work and helping with the writing of the book. Let me recall a few important

Figure P.1:
Map of Sri Lanka

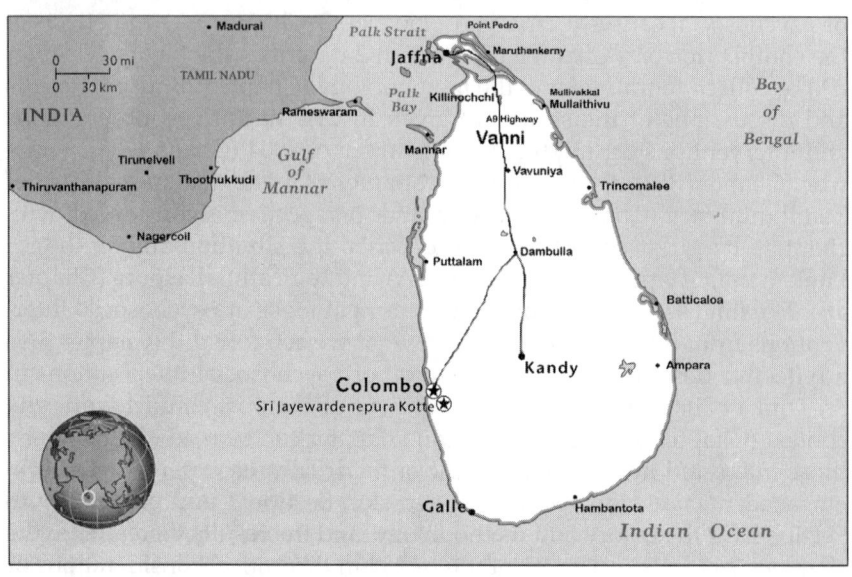

SRI LANKA

Source: Made by author using the National Geographic Map Maker at http://education.
nationalgeographic.com/education/mapping/interactive-map?ar_a=1

individuals who directly made suggestions, critiqued or reviewed drafts of sections from the book: the late Robert Barrett, Michael Roberts, Riaz Hassan, Rajan Hoole, Devanesan Nesiah, Francis Harrison, Norman James, Jeevan Hoole. Sambasivamoorthy Sivayokan and Shankaran Somasundaram worked closely, virtually editing the whole manuscript. The University of Adelaide library and its staff were an immense resource of reference books, papers and articles. Rathakrishnan Sivaneswararajah was responsible for the figures and graphs. Babu (now Dr Naguleswaran) drew the picture of the child soldier. Shambhu Sahu and the editorial team at SAGE Publications have worked hard to bring out the book. Finally, I must thank all my patients, colleagues and friends who continue to be a source of inspiration and support.

Figure P.2:
Sri Lankan Timeline

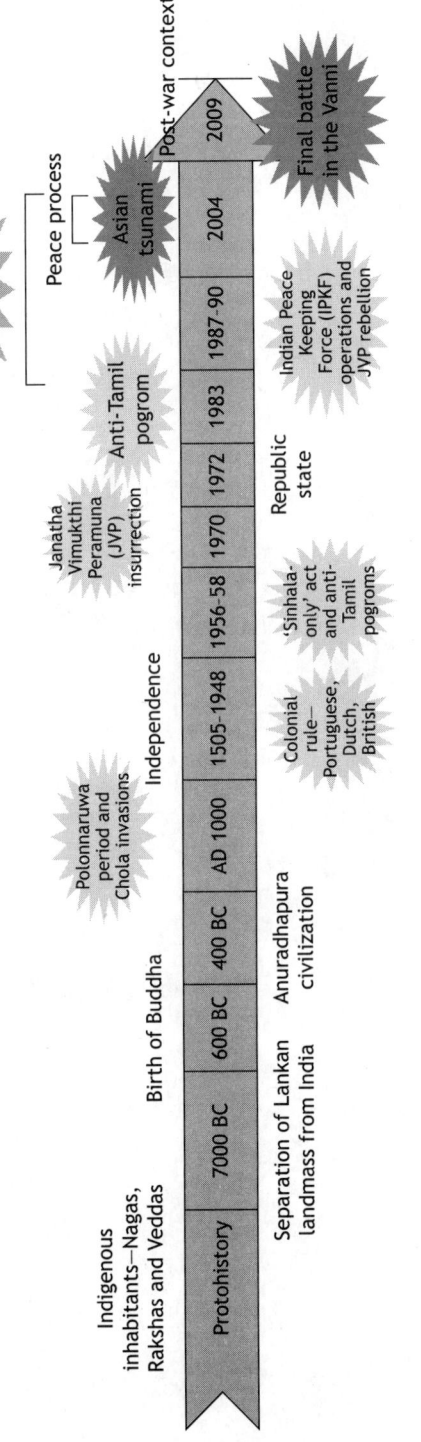

Continuous migration from India and other areas (and outmigration)

Source: Author's representation.
Notes: (i) Time periods not to scale.
(ii) ● indicates potentially traumatic events in history.
(iii) ● indicates traumatic events dealt with in this book.

Introduction

Since the end of Second World War, the numbers of global or interstate wars have decreased while intra-state, ethnic civil wars have increased dramatically. In 2008, twenty-one states were involved in major armed conflicts of which twenty were internal ones (Cordell and Wolff 2010; Marshall and Cole 2008). These phenomena are often attributed to modern developments within nation states in the context of postcolonial or imperial or post–Cold War collapses, for example the break-up of the Union of Soviet Socialist Republics (USSR) and Yugoslavia, and socio-economic or other horizontal inequities between groups (F. Stewart 2001). Sadly, Sri Lanka is often studied as one of the examples of ethnic conflict that progressed to war (Smith 1998; Byman 2002; Cordell and Wolff 2010; Horowitz 2000; Eller 1999; Esman 2004; Jesse and Williams 2011; Ross 2007) with a casualty list of well over a hundred thousand killed, and many more injured, mentally affected, displaced both internally and overseas, and communities, property and ecosystems destroyed (National Peace Council and Marga Institute 2001). Although the actual physical fighting drew to a close in May 2009, it is pertinent to look at what caused the conflict and its psychosocial consequences on communities since the underlying issues remain unresolved. Further, an understanding of what happened in Sri Lanka will help shed light on similar contexts and dynamics elsewhere in the world and perhaps lead to measures to prevent violent ethnic conflict from erupting again in Sri Lanka.

Contrary to popular accounts in the media, portrayals by the political elite and even many superficial or partisan scholarly studies, the causes for the 'ethnic' war in Sri Lanka, as in other ethnic conflicts, are complex and multidimensional, being a result of escalating, interrelated dynamics of different factors. A useful contemporary method to try and understand the underlying play of forces is to undertake what is called the levels-of-analysis approach that considers the local, state, regional and global levels and the interaction amongst them (Cordell and Wolff 2010; Jesse and Williams 2011). At each of these levels (see Table I.1), different actors

Table I.1:
Levels of Analysis

Levels	State Structures and Actors	Non-state Structures and Actors	Issues
Individual	Anagarika Dharmapala, Walsingha Harichandra, Migettuvatte Gunananda, Munidasa Cumaratunga, Bandaranaikes (Solomon West Ridgeway Dias, Sirimavo and Chandrika), Junius Richard Jayewardene, Senanayakes (Don Stephen and Dudley Shelton), Ranasinghe Premadasa, Mahinda Rajapaksa, Vijaya Kumaratunga	Arumuga Navalar, C. W. Thamotharampillai, Samuel James Veluppillai Chelvanayakam, Ponnambalam Ramanathan, Appapillai Amirthalingam, Vettivelu Yogeswaran, Velupillai Prabakharan, Neelan Tiruchelvam	Elite-led nationalism, ethnocentrism, chauvinism, moderation, extremism, gender, *jathika chinthanaya*
Local/ National	United National Party (UNP), Sri Lanka Freedom Party (SLFP), Federal Party (FP), Tamil Congress (TC), Tamil United Liberation Front (TULF), Tamil National Alliance (TNA), JVP, Jathika Hela Urumaya (JHU), ethnic parties, Sinhala community, Sinhala state, structure and institutions, armed forces, police, judiciary, Buddhist sangha	Liberation Tigers of Tamil Eelam (LTTE), Tamil militants, paramilitaries, Sri Lankan Tamil community, Muslim community, Indian Tamil community, media, local non-governmental organizations (LNGOs), civil society, community-based organizations (CBOs)	Ethnic/identity politics, ethnic outbidding, majoritarianism, federalism, consocialism, power sharing, devolution, separation, socio-economic discrimination, resource distribution, territory, violence, extrajudicial practices, terror, security, counter-insurgency
Regional	India, Tamil Nadu, China, Pakistan	Tamil communities, South Asian Association for Regional Cooperation (SAARC)	Regional geopolitics, pan-Tamil nationalism, terrorism
Global	Colonial empires, Britain, United Nations (UN), United States, Israel, European Union (EU), Norway, Japan	Tamil diaspora, Sinhala diaspora, international non-governmental organizations (INGOs), multinationals, World Bank, International Monetary Fund (IMF), international community	Postcolonialism, humanitarianism, human rights, responsibility to protect (R2P), global power balance, 'war on terror', crimes against humanity, sovereignty, globalization, modernization, transnationalism

Source: Adapted for Sri Lanka from Cordell and Wolff (2010).

and structures interact and create a specific politico-historical, socio-economic and psycho-cultural context in which ethnic conflict can escalate into war or de-escalate into peace which is grounded in motivation, means and opportunity. In the Sri Lankan case, an overdetermining motivational factor has been ethnic consciousness (see Chapter 1A) that has coloured perceptions and inflamed emotions. After gaining independence in a postcolonial context, the Sinhala ruling elite, which represented the majority, was unwilling to build a broad-based multicultural political system; the big power rivalry, economic interests and the competition for jobs and resources could have played itself out in healthier ways, as in India (Chandra 2005), if the politics had not been shaped so strongly by exclusive nationalistic ideologies that created horizontal inequities (Stewart 2001). European theories of race, largely discredited by the early twentieth century, gave rise to virulent ideologies, Sinhala, and its mirror image, Tamil, which have driven the ethnic conflict.

Individual Level

Considering the individual level of analysis, of the two types of ethnic conflict (Cordell and Wolff 2010; Kaufman 2001), the Sri Lankan case was clearly elite-instigated rather than mass-led. On the Sinhala side, leaders like Anagarika Dharmapala, Walsingha Harichandra, Migettuvatte Gunananda and Munidasa Cumaratunga were instrumental in laying the foundation for Sinhala-Buddhist nationalism at the turn of the twentieth century. With independence, of the more prominent elite political leaders who played crucial roles on the slippery slope of ethnic party politics, ethnic outbidding and arousing ethnic passions to win elections, S. W. R. D. Bandaranaike and Sirimavo Bandaranaike (Uyangoda 2007), J. R. Jayewardene and M. Rajapaksa stand out. An exception was the charismatic film idol, Vijaya Kumaratunga, who personified an egalitarian, inclusive and conciliatory approach but was killed by the apparently leftist but Sinhala extremist JVP. In fact, most of the left eventually forsook their principled commitments to jump on to the ethnic bandwagon.

On the Tamil side, a child of the bitter ethnic conflict became the central figure in the violence and war, the LTTE leader Velupillai Prabhakaran. Growing up in the seafaring port of Valvettithurai in the aftermath of the 1958 anti-Tamil riots and the rousing rhetoric of Tamil nationalistic politics, he became fanatically committed to the goal of a separate Tamil state, Eelam, as the only solution to the ethnic problem of Sri Lanka. He personified the resistive, defiant and proud spirit of Tamil youth and was the alter ego for many Tamils, locally and abroad. Under him the LTTE became a highly organized, disciplined, fascist organization that did not tolerate any dissent or opposition (Hoole 2001; Swamy 2003) and built up a powerful military and functioning de facto state structures. Prabhakaran had an understandable paranoid, reclusive personality, a tendency in most authoritarian leaders that has survival value in the struggle for power. He was completely dedicated to the Tamil nationalist cause of Tamil Eelam that demanded blind sacrifice and obedience to his objectives (Pratap 2002). His exclusivist and violent methods eventually alienated the Sinhala people, Tamil dissidents, other Tamils, Muslims, India and the international community, which considerably isolated and weakened the sympathy and support for the Tamils in a post-9/11 terror sensitive world. At many opportune moments, he instinctively followed the path of violence and intransience where flexibility, diplomacy and compromise would have served the long-term ethno-national interest of the Tamils and achieved reasonable self-governance (Loganathan 1996). His elimination of all suspected opposition, alternate leadership and totalitarian control that did not allow a viable people's movement left the Tamil community exposed and vulnerable when the LTTE was conclusively destroyed militarily in 2009.

National Level

At the *local level*, while ethnic conflict is said to be inevitable in multi-ethnic societies where different ethnic groups compete for limited resources, status, space (territory), rights and way of life, the incidences of these differences ending in actual war are exceptional. Ordinary people do not want war, and left to their own devices, usually get along with each other, particularly the womenfolk — war being a 'paradigmatic masculine enterprise' (Chawade 2011; de Mel 2007; Manchanda 2001).

It is often said that Ceylon, as it was then called, received its independence from Britain in 1948 on a silver platter. She began on a sound economic footing with a large sterling balance and favourable terms of trade from plantation commodities which earned 90 per cent of its foreign exchange. The agrarian sector had been developed through the repair and restoration of ancient tanks and irrigation systems and Second World War had compelled the colonial government to encourage the local growth of paddy towards self-sufficiency. Health services had improved, following the stationing of allied troops all over the country under the South East Asian command. Notably, malaria had been controlled by the introduction of DDT in 1946 and was directly related to the subsequent population explosion. The antibiotic revolution improved child and maternal care, with infant and maternal mortality rates becoming lowest in the region. Free education had been introduced in 1944. A well-organized system of schools teaching in Sinhala and Tamil covered the whole country, while mission and 'central' schools teaching in English were found in the major towns. Sixty per cent of people were literate at the time. An advanced administrative structure, with a network of roads and railroads connecting the various parts of the country, modern harbours, efficient plantation production and able civil service officers generated a per capita income second only to Japan in Asia. Countries like Singapore looked to Ceylon as a role model to emulate. Victor Ivan (2008) blames the state for the colossal mismanagement of this bright future within sixty years. In 2002, the per capita income of Sri Lanka had declined drastically in relative terms to US$880 while in Japan it had increased to US$25,616; while Hong Kong (US$25,330), Singapore (US$25,330), South Korea (US$16,950), Malaysia (US$9,120), Thailand (US$1,940) and Philippines (US$1,030), to mention a few, had overtaken her.

What went wrong? Although political mismanagement did play a major role in the deterioration, other developments too had an impact on the unfolding tragedy. Unlike India, Ceylon made a peaceful transition from colonial status to independence. There had been no mass agitation, civil disobedience or disturbances, satyagraha and arrest of leaders as in India. The national elite had been extremely moderate in their demands, cooperating with Britain in its war effort and good relations continued into the post-independence period as well. The elite did not involve the masses or build a unified, national consciousness and identity that cut across communal lines. One of the first acts of the newly independent state was the disenfranchisement of the hill-country Tamils who constituted 12 per cent of the total population of the island at that time, by Acts of Parliament. These were acts of structural violence that helped keep this very profitable (to the state and capitalist class), exploited population, who formed the backbone of the economy of the country, in statelessness under slave-like conditions (Caspers 1987) apparently to deprive the then powerful left of a crucial vote bank. They remain the most disadvantaged and exploited group in Sri Lanka, apart from the indigenous Veddas, who have been made extinct as a community.

World economic trends did not favour Ceylon. The plantation commodities of tea, rubber and coconut did not do well on the world market. Belatedly there was some diversification of its foreign exchange earnings with garments, tourism and sending workers mainly to the Middle East who remitted their wages. Sri Lanka lacked easily exploitable natural resources. At the same time the price of essential commodities on the world market increased dramatically. There continued to be heavy spending on welfare measures like health, education, social benefits and subsidies for xxxvi Scarred Communities

agriculture, rice, state-run institutions and state ventures, increasingly funded by foreign aid and loans. Infrastructure or human resources did not develop to keep pace with world trends. With the dramatic drop in death rates from control of malaria, use of antibiotics and improvements in medical health care, the population increased geometrically. The population density, particularly in the crowded south-west of the country, reached uncomfortable proportions for a small island nation that made people naturally look for less populated areas. The tragedy of modern Sri Lanka is that it never produced a great statesman like Nehru, Gandhi or Mandela who could rise above petty sectarian differences and act in the national interest, to plan and lead the country to the much-coveted newly industrialized country status. The promising few that emerged were killed off. Instead the country descended into bitter inter-party feuding, with the two national parties using all their ingenuity and skills to come to power and stay in power. The democratic system implanted by Britain did not thrive unlike in neighbouring India. Increasingly, each election (pre-, during and post-election) became an orgy of threats, abductions and killings of opposition candidates and their supporters, voter intimidation, rigging, ballot stuffing, impersonation, obstruction and destruction of booths followed by violence by the victors against the losers.[1] The goal was to win by any means possible and then remain in power. The charade of democracy, which none of the elite seemed to believe in, was enacted at election times for external and internal consumption. At least, with closer election monitoring by national and international bodies, the level of violence has declined. Those winning have needed the foreign and local legitimacy that the elections bring. On the positive side, there have been periodic elections with a parliament,[2] press, judiciary, police, local government and various committees even at institutional and organizational levels. However, the usual checks and balances that characterize democracy, the give and take of negotiations, debate and discussions and the impartial rule of law have proved illusory. There is no real division of power amongst the executive, legislature and judiciary. Gradually, particularly after the 1970s and the introduction of the presidential system, these powers became concentrated at the top, with the head of state. The freedom and independence of the press were gradually muzzled. Many of the more able journalists left the country, were killed or made to fall silent. The current press has become extremely polarized and inflammatory, aggravating and engendering ethnic passions. The justice system has

---

[1] Post-election curfew is routine practice.

[2] Although with decreasing power, due to the introduction of an authoritarian presidential system, and where most ministers are given lucrative cabinet posts attracting many in the opposition to cross over.

been cowed into partiality, silence and favouritism (Ivan 2003; University Teachers for Human Rights (Jaffna) [UTHR-J] 2006b). More importantly, Sri Lanka has lacked the tradition and practice of democratic institutions, civil organizations, public discourse, respect and belief systems and protection of civil liberties and minority rights that would have allowed democracy to function. Behind the 'democratic' façade, the tendency has always been towards authoritarianism, with absolute, dictatorial control, much like the old feudal kings (Ivan 2008). Corruption (Transparency International 2006), a close nexus between politicians and the criminal underworld, nepotism and 'clientism' or patronage where stalwarts and loyalists were rewarded with jobs and influence in the bloated, inefficient state sector (Tambiah 1986), and short-sighted, poor planning have led the country to economic ruin, to the brink of becoming a failed state. Currently, nearly all the members of parliament belonging to the ruling party are ministers, over a hundred, enjoying all the benefits while wielding hardly any power. Major decisions are taken by a small group surrounding the president, which includes three of his brothers, sidestepping the cabinet and Parliament (Uyangoda 2008). The historic exclusion from governance and access to state resources and opportunities of the disgruntled rural and urban educated Sinhala youth in the south of the country led to the JVP uprisings in the 1970s and late 1980s (Cooke 2011). The state responded with the full might of its repressive apparatus with the help of India and other countries. The death toll in the second bloodletting was variously estimated to be over sixty thousand, with daily reports of disappearances, of men being dragged from their families in the dead of night to be tortured and killed and their bodies destroyed on makeshift pyres of old tyres (Brown 1988). The mental health and psychosocial fallout from the reign of terror in the south by both sides has been largely swept under the carpet and not dealt with. The same repressive measures were then used by the state to squash the ethnic rebellion in the north and east.[3]

Though it could be argued that the Sinhala armed forces (of the state) and Tamil militants were proxy forces of the respective communities doing battle on their behalf, the war itself never reached a popular level where people readily volunteered in great numbers to join the fighting. A

---

[3] A deeply emotional and politically contentious issue is the status of the north and east of the country. Although divided administratively into the Northern and Eastern Provinces, Tamil nationalists believe that the north and east should be merged and consider it their homeland, Eelam. Sinhala nationalists and others on the other hand say that they should be separate. The north and east were merged under the thirteenth amendment to the Sri Lankan Constitution under Indian auspices in 1988 as part of the peace deal but again demerged in 2006 after the fresh outbreak of war when Sinhala nationalists challenged it in court. This book reflects this controversy and debate by using the terms north-east, north and east, northern and eastern, depending on the context.

great deal of inducements, incentives, propaganda and indoctrination was needed for recruitment of fighting forces on both sides (see section 3D and Somasundaram 2009). While most Tamil families went to extraordinary lengths to send their children of eligible age out of the reach of the militants or took desperate measures to avoid recruitment; in the south, it was the economic inducements that led to the poor and socio-economically disadvantaged sections of the community joining the armed forces, which provided the bulk of manpower. A careful analysis of election voting patterns shows that people from all three[4] communities, when allowed to express their preference freely, consistently voted for peace although the winning candidates and party invariably proceeded with the opposite — hawkish policies and war. Public opinion (Social Indicator 2001–08) from 2001 to 2008 indicated that people from all three communities were overwhelmingly in favour of a negotiated settlement and the change in the Sinhala community (while the other communities continued to support a peaceful solution) favouring a military solution reached significant levels only in 2007 after the Rajapaksa regime's concerted mobilization of Sinhala-Buddhist extremism and signs that the military would win the war. The analysis concludes: the 'shift to military means originated from the political elite and government rather than the popular level, but also that the public opinion eventually reflected the shift in policy' (Peiris and Stokke 2011).

The common use of terms like ethnic or civil conflict or war to depict what happened is misleading. It was not the case that the Sinhalese and Tamils were fighting or killing each other. It has been the armed forces of the Sri Lankan state, who are exclusively Sinhala, and the Tamil militants, particularly the LTTE and that too only after 1983, who have been violent. Even the so-called race or ethnic 'riots' of 1956, 1958, 1977, 1981 and 1983 where Tamil civilians were attacked by 'Sinhala' mobs and thugs while the 'Sinhala' armed forces stood by or assisted never reached the state of 'Sinhala' civilians going on the rampage against Tamils. The overwhelming evidence points to the thugs, *chandiyas*[5] (Jeganathan 2000), mobs and 'lumpen' elements being organized, prompted and encouraged by the extreme 'Sinhala' elite leadership with public transport,[6] equipment[7] for destruction, arrack[8] and voters' lists containing information about Tamil homes and businesses (Hoole 2001; Piyadasa 1984; Vittachi 1958). In fact, many ordinary Sinhala people and communities protected and provided for Tamils at great risk to themselves (Kanapathipillai 1990). In all these

---

[4] Sinhala, Tamil and Muslim.
[5] Even modern-day politicians are fond of playing this role.
[6] State-owned buses and trucks.
[7] Swords, axes, machetes, knives, crowbars, sticks, poles, kerosene and petrol.
[8] Potent local alcohol.

instances of periodic violence against Tamils, the state and its elite leadership has mobilized ethnic emotions and heightened a narrow consciousness (see Chapter 1A) to orchestrate mob violence that was covered up as 'racial riots'. There was never any impartial inquiry nor has the state or institutional structures under it been held accountable; no one was charged or sentenced. Rather, the violence has been justified as deserved, a necessary lesson; rationalized as being caused by provocative acts or denied altogether. However, the massive and blatant organized state terror (see Chapter 1B) directed at a minority community was enacted and performed on the world stage with many international witnesses and media coverage.

The brutal violence has left many embittered and polarized, resulting in a hardening of antipathies and opposition that have become more difficult to reverse or resolve. Volkan (2006) describes the

transgenerational transmissions of trauma: shared mental image of massive tragedy that leads to shame, humiliation, helplessness and difficulty in mourning over losses within a large group which decades or centuries later may become the fuel for new infernos that are deliberately started by people in the name of identity.

For example, current politico-military attempts to suppress the memories of the massacre in 2009 at Mullivaikal, during the final battle in the Vanni and inadequate psychosocial processing of the trauma, can sow the seeds for disastrous consequences in the future (see Chapter 3B).

Ironically, sections of the Buddhist sangha have played a significant role in promoting an ethnic nationalist ideology and extremist political course (DeVotta 2007; Senewiratne 2006; Tambiah 1992; Uyangoda 2007). Other factors at the national level, which have gradually gained prominence in civil affairs, are the security forces, the police and military. From being largely ceremonial, the forces have grown, following the JVP insurgency and rapidly with the ethnic war thereafter. After the failed coup of 1962 (which was said to have been a reaction to the Sinhala-Buddhist political resurgence), the forces have become almost exclusively Sinhala Buddhist (Horowitz 1980) and grown to number over two hundred thousand by 2009 with very sophisticated weaponry and organization. With the highest armed serviceman to civilian ratio (currently at ten thousand per million population), highest military spending as a percentage of GDP and highest military holding index (based on number of heavy weapons) Sri Lanka is the most militarized state in the region (Strategic Foresight Group 2006; Sarvananthan 2011). The near complete militarization of civilian life has meant that the military has intruded into every aspect of day-to-day life, transforming society in significant ways into a militarized nation (de Mel 2007). Armed uniformed men with all the paraphernalia of war are everywhere. Ubiquitous checkpoints, where checking is often terse, using intimidating verbal and body language, mass arrests, assaults, executed bodies in public places, being searched, humiliated and pushed around have become normal, day-to-day experiences. Women constantly face sexual harassment, abuse and violation. There are spies, informers, intelligence agents, paramilitaries in civilian clothes, unscrupulous elements and constant surveillance (see Chapter 1B). The military and police being predominantly, if not exclusively, Sinhala were able to carry out actions against Tamil civilians like aerial bombings, shelling and internment camps that could not have been done against Sinhala civilians. Even after the defeat of the LTTE and no obvious security threat, the north and east continue to be occupied, under martial law, with the military in key civilian administrative posts, taking major decisions or supervising civilian administrators (ICG 2012b). In the south, the military has become the largest state employer, with the majority of families in the rural south dependent on the military or paramilitary institutions in some way for their income (Spencer 2011) making them a grateful power base of the government. It also functions as the 'safety valve for potentially disaffected and radicalized youth in the south' (Goodhand and Korf 2011), as well as psychopathic personalities (Somasundaram 1998). As an institution it has taken on non-military roles in development, municipal bodies and training of university entrants, thereby instilling a military mind in the population. These developments could explain the 'government's puzzling insistence on expanding military strength after the apparently conclusive defeat of its main enemy' (Spencer 2011) and increasing the military budget.[9] The military and state, as much as the extreme elements of the Tamil diaspora, have felt the need to keep the ghost of the LTTE alive for their own institutional survival. However, in any demobilization and reintegration into society of combatants who have been traumatized by direct fighting

---

[9] The Defence budget has grown exponentially to reach an official 250 billion rupees annually by 2013 (11 per cent of budget) which is much more than that of Health (4 per cent) and Education (3 per cent) combined (Minister of Finance and Planning, 2012; Ratnayake and de Mel 2012). The defence budget reflects only the declared part of military spending, covert expenses being covered through other votes, departments and the shadow world. 250 billion is estimated from the allocation of LKR 290 billion for the Ministry of Defence and Urban Development for 2013 that includes the expenditures on the air force, army, civil defence force, coast guard, navy, police PLUS urban development. If we subtract the expenditures on urban development the expenditures on defence would be around LKR 240 billion (US$2 billion). The foregoing defence expenditure figure does not include the pensions and disability payments of the police and armed forces personnel which is paid by the Pensions Department of Ministry of Public Administration that could be estimated to be around 10–15 billion (Saravananthan, personal communication). In the total budget, a major portion goes for debt repayment. Of the rest, defence is allocated 17 per cent. Health and Education budgets' calculation should take into account significant allocation through the provincial councils but in actual disbursement these are often cut down (Ratnayake and de Mel 2012).

(see Chapters 3D and 4A), appropriate rehabilitation, vocational training and social support measures will have to be designed.

There has been a common portrayal and uncritical ready acceptance that the Sinhalese and Tamils have been fighting each other throughout history, that there is an inherent 'ancient hatred' between these primordial groups that drive them to fight each other. However, the narrow categorization of current identities and consciousness into Sinhala-Buddhist, Tamil and Muslim may not have accurately reflected the actual lived experience of the people of Sri Lanka. Current antipathies and polarized world views based on modern identities are projected backwards into history, a kind of retrospective reframing of the past in terms of the present (Wickramasinghe 2006). The reality was more a rich blend, overlap and encompassing inclusiveness where people had multiple identities, loyalties, beliefs and common cultural practices (Silva 2002). Clear examples of a shared consciousness can be seen in sociocultural festivals like the Sinhala–Tamil new year celebrations, religious practices at Kataragama, Bellanvilla (Gombrich and Obeyesekere 1988), Madhu church and other countless shrines around the country (Kapferer 1988). It is in the commonalities, the hybridity of the different groups, the shared culture that the possibility for reconciliation can be promoted. Tragically, evolving socio-economic circumstances, media, academics and leaders have pushed communities into convenient, exclusive compartments with rigid, antagonistic perceptions. Rather than emphasize and highlight the common interests, shared beliefs, history and customs; differences, divisions and grievances are accentuated and drawn out. The commonalities and shared similarities are gradually erased from memory and consciousness to be replaced by division, bitterness, fear, hostility and hate. As Taraki pointed out (Whitaker 2007), modern political leaders have found that fanning ethno-national passions is the most effective way to power and manage populations. Thus, despite the consequences and devastations of the war, people are made to support the political system that divide people based on communal emotions and conflict. Leaders have ensured continuing public support by selectively breeding a servile media, using patronage politics to reward the party faithful through jobs and other benefits and maintaining obedient institutions like the military and public sector that remain grateful to them. The people themselves, who are now labelled Sinhala and Tamil, have coexisted in harmony historically, mutually helping each other. The beginnings of what would later develop into the present-day Sinhala-Buddhist nationalism could be traced to the nineteenth-century European racial theories, the zeitgeist of nationalisms and the local needs of the imperial power (Anderson 2006). The colonial administrators and oriental scholars needed to make sense of the bewildering kaleidoscope of subjects they had to rule in their far-flung empires (Said 1995). They introduced racial categories as a means of organizing and understanding the exotic cultures and people they had to deal with. Using numerical enumeration through regular census and other techniques they brought order to their empires (Wickramasinghe 2006). People were compelled to identify themselves as belonging to specific categories, they had to choose to belong exclusively to one or other racial and later, ethnic group. But people had multiple, cross-cutting, inclusive identities and had more complex, interrelated ways of life and world views. While family, extended kin, clan, caste and village identities had been prominent, ethnic identities became more defined, important politically and practically to survive in the colonial and post-colonial world and as a reaction to the Western, modernizing influence. Psychosocially, ethnic belonging was able to draw on the same emotions, loyalty, dedication, sacrifice and passions that family and kinship had evoked (Horowitz 2000).

When we try to understand the situation as it developed in Sri Lanka, we find that the emergence of the modern form of Sinhala-Buddhist identity, described in detail by Gunawardena (1990), Kumari Jayawardena (1986) and Nira Wickramasinghe (2006), was a gradual process but took its current form only from the end of the nineteenth century. It started initially as a reaction to the proselytizing Christianity of the missionaries, in particular and Westernization, engendered by the colonial power in general which threatened Buddhism as practised by the Sinhalese. This developed into a movement led notably by Anagarika Dharmapala and was later taken up by other aspiring Sinhala leaders. The popularization of the Sinhala-Buddhist identity took place through the newly discovered printing press (print nationalism), popular meetings, literature, mass media, political demagoguery and anti-minority conflicts. What we see today as opposed, polarized ethnic consciousness is a result of 'complex political, historical, economical, military, social and religious factors intertwined with large-group psychological processes' (Volkan 2006). Nevertheless, large-scale ethnic violence, after the anti-Muslim riots of 1915, took place against the Tamils only in 1956 at Gal Oya, the state-aided colonization scheme in the east, following on from the Sinhala-only ideology developed that year, and then spread rapidly to the rest of the country (Vittachi 1958).

The popular conception that has been assiduously developed in modern times as a historic truth has it that the Sinhala-Buddhist and the Tamil-Hindu 'races' are primordial and essentialist; that is, intrinsic, biological, in the genes and blood of the groups, have existed from time immemorial and have been inveterate foes down the ages. Unfortunately, respected academics and scholars have been at the forefront of this propagation through supposedly 'scientific research', publications in scholarly and popular literature and public pronouncements that have been widely disseminated by political demagogues, popular media and school text-books. The Sinhala language was typed, with some credible philological evidence, as belonging to the Indo-Aryan family. This was then linked to the Aryan race and by extension the Sinhalese were taken to be Aryan, a claim that was enthusiastically adopted by the intelligentsia of local colonial subjects. The myth of Vijaya as found in the Pali chronicle *Mahavamsa* was taken to explain how the Aryans came to this island from north India to establish the Sinhala race (De Silva 2005). The Tamils are then said to belong to the Dravidian race, the Tamil nationalists claiming their origins from the Mohenjo-daro and Harappa civilization of the Indus valley in the pre-Vedic fourth millennium BC (Indrapala 2007).

It is difficult to realize from the contemporary, rigidified, polarized ethnic categories that they have solidified, 'jelled' (Byman 2002) into their current form due to recent politico-historical and socio-economic processes (Wickramasinghe 2006). They are 'affinity groups whose boundaries, unity and coordination vary across time and space' (Ross 2007). As will be shown in the next chapter, Sinhala and Tamil 'groupness' cannot be assumed to be homogenous, monolithic entities between whom there is conflict, but they themselves contain considerable intra-group variations with porous, vague, overlapping boundaries. This is not to say that the terms Sinhala and Tamil or a derivative (Hela, Demala) as ascriptive characteristics used by people historically have not existed, and clearly strands of lineage can be traced back in history (Indrapala 2007; Roberts 2004), but the meaning of these terms, what they referred to (perhaps the language spoken) and the context of their use would have been very different from modern-day meanings (Wickramasinghe 2006). When histories and analyses are based on such covert assumptions, they unfortunately reinforce ethnic differences and conflict by reifying these terms. But it may be difficult, if not impossible, to avoid using these terms as they have become so much a natural part of the discourse, literature and even thinking. And more importantly, these terms have become the living reality for both communities: how they identify themselves and how others see and treat them.

Ethnic conflicts have usually been analysed in terms of the *underlying* and *proximate* (catalytic or trigger) causes (Cordell and Wolff 2010). The underlying causes for the conflict in Sri Lanka have been understood in terms of the postcolonial development of majoritarian politics in a multi-ethnic society in a country with limited natural resources, soaring population growth, welfare services and stagnant economy. The (Sinhala) historical grievances of colonial suppression of native culture, particularly language and religion, have been used by national elite to mobilize emotive ethnic politics to redress these disadvantages. From the late nineteenth century there has been a resurgence of Sinhala-Buddhist ideology that has resulted in its domination over state power, structures and institutions at the expense of the minorities. Ethnic party politics and electoral outbidding along ethnic lines have resulted in a Sinhala ethnocracy (DeVotta 2004). Tamils as a group have felt discriminated against in higher education, jobs, economic development and demographical representation in their areas, and resentment has increased.

The *catalytic or trigger* events included the exclusion from citizenship and withdrawal of voting rights of Tamils of recent Indian origin (most of them born in Sri Lanka), the watershed Sinhala-only language bill of 1956 and periodic anti-Tamil riots culminating with the 1983 pogrom. Precipitating the beginning of Tamil militancy was the change in admission criteria to universities from merit (as measured in examination scores) to 'standardization' designed to favour district and ethnic balance. The Tamil frustration resulting from successive failures of non-violent agitation for a federal solution to redress some of their grievances through periodic negotiated agreements by the moderate Tamil leadership with the Sinhala elite, like the Bandaranaike–Chelvanayakam pact of 1957 and Dudley–Chelvanayakam pact of 1966, culminated in the 1976 Vaddukoddai resolution for a separate state. The dissatisfied Tamil youth became more restive and militant; they were met with increasingly repressive measures by the state, including arrest, torture and death.

The ambush of thirteen soldiers on patrol in the Jaffna district by the LTTE is often blamed for provoking the 1983 anti-Tamil pogrom. Tamils fled, as refugees, to the north and to south India where there were sympathetic kindred Tamils. Indira Gandhi's government became more involved in training and arming the Tamil militants to offset the increasing Western tilt of Jayewardene's UNP government. The escalating clashes between the Tamil militants and Sri Lankan armed forces with the civilian population trapped in between led to increasing Indian diplomatic efforts at negotiations between the parties and eventually to military intervention with the IPKF in 1987. Ironically, the IPKF soon became tangled in fighting the LTTE with the civilians once again caught in between (Hoole et al. 1988). With the hasty departure of the IPKF in 1990, the LTTE and the Sri Lankan forces went back to battling each other. Meanwhile the LTTE had militarily eliminated other Tamil militant groups and opposition within the Tamil community to establish itself as a formidable guerrilla/conventional fighting force to run a de facto counter state in the north and east. The Norway-sponsored peace agreement of 2002 brought a cessation of hostilities that unwound rapidly due to wrangling over the post-tsunami recovery effort after the massive tsunami devastated the coast (see Chapter 3A). In a concerted military effort with crucial international support, the Sri Lankan state decimated the LTTE in 2009 leaving over one hundred thousand civilians dead, injured and mentally traumatized.

An *underlying cause* for the ethnic conflict was the frustration stemming from relative economic deprivation and inequity in resource distribution (Stewart 2001). The liberal economy ushered in 1977 unleashed market forces and opened up the country to international consumer goods; the concomitant structural readjustments and cutbacks of welfare services have been blamed for the frustrations and anger in those excluded from the benefits (Bastian 1994; Gunasinghe 1984). Social exclusion in a stagnant economy can be fertile ground for the emergence and sustenance of political conflict (Abeyratne 2004). However, inflamed ethnic emotions can lead to group mobilization despite the economic circumstances (Kaufman 2001).

Regional Level

At the *regional level*, India played and continues to play a critical role in the affairs of Sri Lanka, particularly in the current ethnic conflict. In more recent times, its influence with regard to Sri Lanka has extended to the international level, promoting and supporting the actions of the state in defeating the LTTE at the UN and other international bodies. The minority Sri Lankan Tamils share close cultural, linguistic, religious, ethnic and kindred ties with Tamils in southern India, particularly Tamil Nadu. Tamil politics in both countries is intertwined, with Sri Lankan Tamil politicians looking for succour and directions from Tamil Nadu, while the Sri Lankan Tamil situation is often a major emotive issue in the Indian local and central political scene. After the 1983 anti-Tamil pogrom, a sizeable Tamil population fled to India as refugees. As mentioned previously, India's training and arming the Tamil militants was a crucial turning point in the ethnic conflict's escalation into war. The moral support and access to base camps in India where they could train and flee back to when pursued or injured and from which they could smuggle arms and other supplies into Sri Lanka provided the means and opportunity structures for the war. At the same time, India continued to play different roles as mediator, facilitator, host, negotiator and broker, exerting behind-the-scene pressure in resolving the crisis through diplomacy, negotiated settlement, agreements and constitutional amendments, while arming, training and providing crucial military (naval) intelligence to the Sri Lankan state (Gokhale 2009; Swamy 2010). Thus, India has to a large extent determined the balance of power between the contending parties. After the assassination of Rajiv Gandhi by the LTTE however, the balance tilted in favour of the state, covertly not supporting the 2002–06 peace process that gave undue recognition to the LTTE and strongly backed the war that followed

(Keethaponcalan 2011). There is much Sinhala apprehension of being a minority within the large Tamil majority in the region (and the harking back to 'historical memories' of invasions from south India) that is evoked by the Sinhala nationalists. Since colonial Britain brought in Indian Tamil indentured labourers to work in the plantations and other sectors, who in time became a significant population, particularly in the hill country, and constituted up to 12 per cent of the population on the island, India has continued to have an abiding interest in their welfare. Many were repatriated through various negotiated settlements between the two states, while those that stayed back still hold nostalgic ties with India. Situated on India's southern border, with the Trincomalee and Hambantota harbours (now under the Chinese 'string of pearls' strategy) overlooking the Indian Ocean, Sri Lanka has a vital geopolitical importance for the overall security of India (believed to be a major reason for their diplomatic and military intervention in 1987, on account of American interests in the Trincomalee harbour and the Voice of America station). Sri Lanka, particularly during the Rajapaksa regime, has adroitly played on India's neighbourly power contest with China and Pakistan to obtain training and arms as well as funds and support at international forums (Perera 2010a). However, with the destruction of the LTTE, concern over the growing influence of China and growing pressure from Tamil Nadu appears to be changing the attitude and policy of the Indian state (Keethaponcalan 2011). India tilted the dynamics again dramatically in March 2012 by supporting the United States–led resolution at the United Nations Human Rights Council (UNHRC) that asked (perceived by Sri Lanka as censure) Sri Lanka to implement its own Lessons Learnt and Reconciliation Commission (LLRC) recommendations (Commission of Inquiry 2011).

Global Level

At the *international level*, colonial subjugation for over three hundred years under the Portuguese, Dutch and British rules, independence and postcolonial developments shaped the fundamental nature and configuration of ethnic relations. The British had unified the colony under central administrative control, defined and threw various groups together, seemingly favouring some, particularly the low-country Sinhalese and Jaffna Tamils, through opportunity structures such as education, employment, proselytizing and Western cultural influence, and finally handing over rule to a Westernized national elite. It took until 1956 for a mass-based Sinhala-Buddhist resurgence to wrest control of the state.

In the modern era of globalization, different nation states have supported, given recognition, funding, trade, technical support, military training, sold arms and provided vital military information that provided direct and tacit support to the Sri Lankan state and its governance, including its ethnic policies. Similarly, the international network of organizations, like the UN and other multilateral agencies, corporate bodies and companies have played important roles in what happened in Sri Lanka (Nordstrom 2004). Cold-War rivalry, international socialist influences and massive foreign development aid, such as for state-aided colonization schemes, aggravated ethnic relations (Bastian 2007; Esman and Herring 2001). INGOs have been blamed for fuelling the conflict through neocolonial, developmental, conflict resolution and human rights discourse (Goonatilake 2006). Changing definitions as well as hypocritical stands on national sovereignty, terrorism and legitimate liberation struggles depending on a country's perceived interests have characterized international relations.

Ironically, the term terrorism has been perceived and portrayed in different ways, depending on the context and the interests of states, both locally and internationally. When a state or coalition of states carries out bombings and killings (for whatever reason), it is portrayed in legitimate terms as defensive, preventive, proactive or humanitarian action, not terrorism. But when the same act is done by a non-state actor or states not in favour (so-called rogue states), then it is easily labelled as terrorism. Similarly, some actions are described as liberation struggles, such as the American war for independence, others as insurgencies, rebellions or worse, terrorism. Sri Lanka is no exception. The ethnic war, particularly the last phase of the brutal war in the Vanni, has been brought under the rubric of 'war against terrorism', a popular terminology first used by the Bush government in the United States. On the other hand, some, like the former Australian foreign minister and chairperson of the International Crisis Group (ICG), Gareth Evans (2007, 2008), have advocated for the right and duty of the international community to intervene when the state fails to protect its citizens, a principle called responsibility to protect (R2P), a justification that was used in Iraq and Libya, but not in other similar situations.

The increasing role of international actors and structures in Sri Lanka's ethnic conflict was brought into sharp focus during the 2002 peace process and towards the end of the final battle in the Vanni in 2009. The 2002 peace process enabled the 'most internationalized, systematic and sustained' liberal peace building exercise by the international community through 'track-one' peace talks between the protagonists in different capitals of world, provision of 'peace dividend' of generous aid and development projects and 'track-two' conflict transformation at the local community level by workshops, capacity development, civil society empowerment and other peace promoting activities (Goodhand et al. 2011). A major reason for the failure of the peace engineering process was 'overlooking the significance of ethnicity and identity in the long-running crisis of the

Sri Lankan State' (Burke and Mulakala 2011). The next chapter attempts to explore the vital role of ethnic consciousness in the conflict. Towards the end of the final battle, developments in the UN pitched various governments against each other over the way the ethnic war was being fought (De Alwis 2010; Lee 2009). With considerable pressure from the Tamil diaspora in their countries,[10] many Western countries began raising objections to the large numbers of civilian casualties and their predicament, demanding a ceasefire so that civilians could get out. Visits from high-level UN representatives, delegations from the United States, Canada, Norway, Sweden, Germany and other European countries, and even the foreign ministers of United Kingdom and France, could not restrain the Rajapaksa regime. In 2009, attempts to raise the issue at the UN Security Council were blocked by China, Russia and India. Then a resolution by Switzerland with the support of the United Kingdom, France and the United States at the UNHRC, calling for an investigation into human rights violations by both parties, was turned on its head with a counter-resolution brought by Sri Lanka, congratulating itself for defeating terrorism, with the support of China, India and member nations of the Non-Aligned Movement (Perera 2010b; De Alwis 2010; Lee 2009). As mentioned, it was only in March 2012 that the UNHRC adopted a resolution asking the Sri Lankan government to implement its own LLRC recommendations and address alleged violations of international law.

The UNHRC had been turned into a political battleground. There was criticism of the double standards of Western powers in ignoring their own behaviour in countries like Iraq and Afghanistan and in giving trade concessions and loans when it was in their interest to overlook human rights records. Sri Lanka turned to China, which has now become its biggest donor, Pakistan and even Iran (De Alwis 2010; Perera 2010a). Under mounting pressure from Western powers, which were being intensely lobbied by the Tamil diaspora, the UN Secretary General, Ban Ki-moon had appointed a panel of experts which came out with a scathing report (UN 2011). Sri Lanka protested vehemently. The UN's internal review of what happened in the last phase of the fighting candidly exposes the systemic failure of the UN to meet its protection and humanitarian responsibilities in Sri Lanka while being more concerned about diplomatic issues and sensitiveness of the Sri Lankan government in power (UN 2012). The review also indirectly brings out the entire international dynamics and behaviour of member states in the face of this crisis. While India had started

---

[10] There is a large Tamil diaspora in Canada, Britain, United States, France, Germany, Norway and Australia, which is well organized and able to bring pressure on its respective governments through lobbying and voting en bloc in elections. Towards the end of the fighting in the Vanni, the Tamil diaspora held large demonstrations, marches, protests and vigils, including some self-immolations, all over the world. In India too considerable pressure was brought through demonstrations and protests by sections of the population in Tamil Nadu.

training Tamil militants after the 1983 anti-Tamil pogrom, Israel became increasingly involved in Sri Lanka through the special interest section of the American embassy (Israel not having any direct diplomatic relations with Sri Lanka). Military and intelligence advice was given, military officers and others went to Israel for training (Ostrovsky and Hoy 1990) and Israeli counter-insurgency strategy was adopted against the Tamils (see Chapter 1B). Ironically, some Tamil militant leaders were trained by the Palestine Liberation Organization (PLO) in Lebanon at the same time.

One of the major consequences of the Sri Lankan civil war has been the internal and external displacement of Tamil refugees. The Tamil diaspora abroad was estimated to be around one million in 2010, or one quarter of the entire Sri Lankan Tamil population[11] (ICG 2010a). In turn, they have maintained close links with their families and kin back home, helping them also migrate, sending remittances (*undiyal* or hawala) that provided financial and moral support, and the means for the LTTE. Through its overseas financial and transport network, the LTTE was able to procure arms and equipment to continue fighting (ICG 2010a; Karmi 2007). The easy availability of arms, particularly light weapons that could be used by its young, female and child cadres, mortar and handheld missiles from arms bazaars in Eastern Europe, Ukraine, Middle East, Pakistan, Thailand and Cambodia in the post–Cold War period after the collapse of the USSR were instrumental in the development of the LTTE into a formidable fighting force and provided the *means* to challenge the Sri Lankan state to the point of establishing a de facto state. The changing international atmosphere after 9/11 with the war on terrorism, the designation of the LTTE as a terrorist organization by some nations and tightening of arms availability and funding sources were responsible for the decline of the LTTE and its final defeat. The military decimation of the LTTE in Sri Lanka has also weakened the solidarity and cohesion of the Tamil diaspora.

The ICG (2010a) was pessimistic that the opportunity to resolve the ethnic problem and achieve lasting peace by addressing the 'legitimate grievances at the root of the conflict: the political marginalization and physical insecurity of most Tamils in Sri Lanka' would be squandered by the present Rajapaksa regime:

> There is little chance [that] the needed political and constitutional reforms will be offered…. Any significant improvement in the political position of Tamils and other minorities in Sri Lanka will thus come slowly and with

---

[11] Tamil Nadu (200,000); Canada (300,000); United Kingdom (180,000); Germany (60,000); Australia (40,000); Switzerland (47,000); France (50,000); the Netherlands (20,000); United States (25,000); Italy (15,000); Malaysia (20,000); Norway (10,000); Denmark (7,000); New Zealand (3,000); Sweden (2,000); South Africa; Gulf States; Thailand; Cambodia; Singapore. The largest Sri Lankan Tamil city in the world is Toronto (approximately 250,000), outnumbering Colombo and Jaffna (about 200,000 each).

difficulty, requiring significant shifts in the balance of political power within Sri Lanka as well as careful but tough persuasion from outside.

India, Japan, Western governments and multilateral organisations can do much more to assist the political empowerment of Tamils in Sri Lanka and press Colombo to address the causes behind the rise of the LTTE and other Tamil militant groups.

By 2012, its dire predictions had been proven right; a golden opportunity for genuine reconciliation was being lost and ICG's expectations for future developments were even more gloomy: 'Deepening militarization and lack of accountable governance in Sri Lanka's Northern Province are preventing a return to normal life and threaten future violence ... the Tamil-majority north remains under de facto military occupation, with all important policies set by Sinhala officials in Colombo' (ICG 2012a).

Ultimately it is the psychosocial nature of the ethnic problem; polarized identities, perceptions and consciousness; myths, psycho-cultural narratives, interpretations and emotional investment; underlying animosity, paranoia, hatred and hostility; ethnocentrism and chauvinism that would prevent reconciliation, a practical solution in the long-term interest of the different ethnic groups and the nation as a whole (Cordell and Wolff 2010; Horowitz 2000; Kaufman 2001; Ross 2007; Volkan 1997). For example, though a peace poll in 2010 undertaken in line with the Northern Ireland peace process (Irwin 2010) found that there was widespread support from all communities for the proposals made by the All Party Representative Committee (APRC) (appointed by the government), the ruling Sinhala-Buddhist regime is unlikely to implement them in its current mood of triumphalism. The same fate awaits the LLRC recommendations. The next chapter will explore in depth some of these fundamental psychosocial issues driving the ethnic conflict, the motivating passion that makes it so intractable, as in many other parts of the world (Cordell and Wolff 2010; Horowitz 2000; Jesse and Williams 2011; Kaufman 2001; Ross 2007).

Collective Trauma

Although this book is primarily a case study of a specific situation affecting Tamils in northern Sri Lanka, the phenomenon of collective trauma is also happening to other traditional communities around the world that are caught in the context of internal civil and ethnic conflict (see Chapter 2A for the definition and description of collective trauma). The impact of collective trauma on families, extended families, kinship groups, villages and communities includes mass migratory processes as they try to flee from the traumatic ecological context. They try to rebuild their lives in a new environment of safety and opportunity. Individually or as families they may migrate to new places and continue to struggle to bring others across one by one. Those coming from collectivistic societies (Hofstede and Hofstede 2005) remain bound through organic links to those left behind and feel responsible for their welfare. However, the legacy of collective trauma continues to plague them in their new homes, haunting their settlement process (Somasundaram 2011).

Kai Erikson (1976, 1979) was the first to describe collective trauma as 'loss of communality' following the Buffalo Creek disaster in the United States. Although the collective consequences of mass trauma were beginning to be realized after the bombing raids in Jaffna during the early 1990s (Somasundaram 1996), collective trauma first became very obvious to me when working in the post-war recovery and rehabilitation context in Cambodia (Somasundaram et al. 1999). During the Khmer Rouge regime in the late 1970s, all social structures, institutions, family, educational and religious orders had been razed to 'ground zero' deliberately (so as to rebuild a just society anew). Mistrust and suspicion arose among family members as children were made to report on their parents. The essential unity, trust and security within the family system, the basic unit of society, was broken. A whole generation had missed out on basic education. So when we tried to help individuals, it soon became obvious there were deeper, more fundamental problems at the family and collective levels that needed addressing before individuals would recover. Societal and community trust, relationships, structures and institutions had to be rebuilt first.

The concept of collective trauma is being introduced in this book to describe the impact of massive trauma on the family and community. The threat, fear and terror are experienced at the familial and community levels and families and communities respond in a myriad ways. The calamity makes an impact on the family and community structures, dynamics, networks and cohesion. The social fabric is torn asunder; people are uprooted from their familiar habitat. Indispensable members, usually leaders or breadwinners, are killed, made to disappear or separated. The way the family and community function changes. Basic trust and hope is lost, the glue that held the relationships and networks together is destroyed. Often there is family and social dysfunction and problems arise in coping with the situation, but there can be resilience and strength in adapting to the challenges. In responding, in trying to help, it becomes important to understand these wider ramifications and intervene to rectify the adverse changes at the family and collective levels. We have found that if the balance, equilibrium and healthy functioning of the family and community can be restored, individuals also recover within the nurturing environment. It is important to rebuild social capital, trust and collective efficacy. This is the emerging and growing field of mental health and psychosocial support (MHPSS) described in Chapter 5B by Ananda Galappatti and Chapter 5C on interventions.

I have had the unique opportunity of treating refugees from many conflict-affected communities from around the world at the centre for Supporting Survivors of Torture and Trauma Assistance and Rehabilitation Service (STTARS) in Adelaide, Australia for the past six years (Somasundaram 2010c, 2010h, 2011). The Kurd, Palestinian, Shi'ite, Sunni, Sinhala, Tamil, Coptic Christian, Hutu, Tutsi, Uighur, Bosnian, Zaghawa, Pashtun, Tajik, Hazara, Uzbek, Tibetan, Nepalese (from Bhutan), Karen, Eritrean, Somali, Hema, Lendu, Ossetian, Chechnyan, Armenian and other communities have and continue to undergo horrendous hardships. The similarities and parallels to what had been happening in Sri Lanka were remarkable: large-scale destruction, deaths, injuries and subsequent chaos resulting in mass displacements, uprooting from familiar surroundings, deprivations of all sorts, insecurity and social disconnection. Social institutions, structures, leadership, connections and relationships, vital community resources and social capital may be irretrievably lost. In addition, during civil conflicts, arbitrary detention, torture, massacres, extrajudicial killings, disappearances, rape, forced displacements, bombing and shelling become common. Whole communities or villages are targeted for total destruction, including their way of life and their environment (Summerfield 1996).

Much modern warfare is conducted through internal civil wars, where the conflict is more psychological for control of loyalties through intimidation, terror and counter-terror (see Chapter 1B); the fighting occurs within civilian populations, where 90 per cent of casualties are civilians (Machel 1996). Apart from wars for complete extermination, or genocide, the goal of modern warfare is more for absorption and assimilation into one dominant culture and way of life. The minority is expected to forgo its own culture and identity and merge with or become subservient to the dominant culture. When it tries to resist the process, ethnic or civil conflict erupts. Unlike what follows after natural disasters, civil conflict causes community trauma by the creation of a 'repressive ecology' based on imminent, pervasive threat, terror and inhibition that causes a state of generalized insecurity, terror and rupture of the social fabric (Baykal et al. 2004).

Another important casualty in war is the implicit faith in the world order and social justice in particular. Those responsible for what may be called war crimes and the worst types of human rights abuses are rarely punished, except in a few recent examples, under the International Criminal Court

(ICC) in The Hague or other tribunals. A few cases of massacres, disappearances, torture, rape, custodial killings and burials in mass graves have been investigated and brought to light. However, impunity prevails in the majority of cases. The victims usually have to bear it in silence, a silence that is often individual as well as collective.

A well designed and analysed study, sponsored by the United Nations Children's Fund (UNICEF) and Sri Lanka's Ministry of Health in post-war Jaffna in September 2009 by Farah Husain et al. (2011) and published in the prestigious *Journal of American Medical Association*, found that in the general population, the incidence of mental health problems included PTSD (7 per cent), anxiety (32.6 per cent), depression (22.2 per cent), while internally displaced persons (IDPs) had significantly higher rates of trauma, 58 per cent having experienced more than ten trauma events while 41 per cent had faced between five and nine events. Trauma events were bombardment (80 per cent), caught in crossfire (77 per cent), shot at (61 per cent), death of kin or friend (29 per cent), death of acquaintance (29 per cent), missing family (31 per cent), interrogation (37 per cent), forced separation from family (50 per cent), assault (11 per cent), torture (7 per cent), war injury (33 per cent), kidnapping (10 per cent), imprisonment (5 per cent), disability (13 per cent), landmine or unexploded ordinance (UXO) injury (13 per cent). The IDPs' mental health problems were comparatively higher with PTSD (13 per cent), anxiety (49 per cent) and depression (42 per cent). There is a sharp increase in suicide rates in the whole of the north (see Chapter 3D). None of this is being addressed in any appropriate way. Though there has been a massive resettlement and economic development programme with international funding, *uthuru vasanthaya* or *vadakkin vasantham* (northern spring), being carried out by the Presidential Task Force for Resettlement, Development and Security in the Northern Province (PTF 2013), there is a restrictive ban by the military and PTF on carrying out psychosocial and mental health programmes in the north (see Chapter 5C). Unfortunately despite the path-breaking pioneer development in psychosocial interventions from experiences gained during the war and post-tsunami work (see Chapters 3A, 5A and 5B), fear of oral evidence of war crimes leaking out through the process of counselling and the paranoid perception of Western non-governmental organization (NGO) 'conspiracy' (Goonatilake 2006) empowering and promoting a human rights discourse that would embolden and mobilize minority restiveness has made psychosocial programmes taboo to the authorities. Nevertheless, denying psychosocial treatment, counselling and traditional grieving rituals to the traumatized and grieving innocent civilian population is perhaps the most uncivilized aspect of the post-war dispensation. Another was the bulldozing of all the graveyards of the militants (*thuyilam illams*), which uncovered the deep collective emotional scars simmering below the surface. These deeper issues would need to be dealt with if there is to be any real reconciliation. The politico-military establishment appears to be stuck in the post-war mentality and is unable to make the transition to a post-conflict context with civilian administration where genuine reconciliation can take place and psychosocial programmes to heal the wounds of the war can be implemented (ICG 2012a, 2012b). International law recognizes the principle of *restitutio ad integrum* for the redress of victims of armed conflict (C. Evans 2012; Villalba 2009). This justifies the need for rehabilitation as a form of reparation. In these cases, paragraph 18 of the UN General Assembly resolution on basic principles and guidelines on the right to a remedy and reparation for victims of gross violation of international human rights law stipulates five forms of reparation: restitution, compensation, rehabilitation, satisfaction and guarantees of non-repetition (UN General Assembly 2005). This should necessarily include forms of psychosocial rehabilitation (Somasundaram 2010g).

Following the tradition of public health principles and the time-honoured adage, prevention is better than cure, Chapter 1A attempts to disentangle the underlying psychosocial beliefs, perceptions and consciousness that have driven the intractable conflict and thereby create awareness; a humble, preventive intervention towards reconciliation and peaceful coexistence.

SECTION 1

Background

A.

Ethnic Consciousness

When a wise man, established well in virtue,
Develops consciousness and understanding,
Then as a bhikkhu ardent and sagacious
He succeeds in disentangling this tangle.

—Buddhaghosa, *Visuddhimagga* (~500)

The Emergence of Ethnic Consciousness

The fundamental process fuelling, sustaining and driving the ongoing, seemingly intractable and, at times violent, civil conflict in Sri Lanka has been the polarized ethnic consciousness of two groups—Sinhala and Tamil. However, it has not always been this way, though some have said that this is ancient hatred and the two groups have been fighting each other throughout history. Until the recent past, relations between the Sinhalese and the Tamils had been harmonious. They shared many religio-cultural practices, lived side by side as friends, colleagues, neighbours, or in the same house as family, husband and wife or as lovers. The Sinhala and Tamil identities were not so salient, exclusive or polarized: both had multiple, cross-cutting, overlapping, inclusive and hybrid identities (Silva 2002). As Eller (1999: 95–96) describes the Sri Lankan ethnic conflict:

This conflict has not been a continuous or ancient sequence but has resulted from particular and recent action, decisions, and interpretations that have selectively exacerbated certain potential differences between cultural groups while overlooking or even denying other differences or, for that matter, certain levels of similarity. In fact, there may be no place on earth where the 'use' of culture and history is more conspicuous, where present claims and past grievances are couched in terms of the ancient battles and kingdoms and of cultural revival and survival—where history, mythology, archaeology, are all political tools and weapons. We will also see that the cultural picture in Sri Lanka (as in Leach's Burma) is much more complicated than a mere bi-ethnic face-off and that other groups, and groups within these groups, contoured along other cultural or political or economic lines, exist and help to move and shape the overall and dominant national conflict.

Modern political developments, socio-economic factors, increasing population pressures and a stagnant economy (Abeyratne 2004) have created the conditions for the elite to mobilize the population along ethnic lines for their own electoral and power needs. What had been a proto or nascent ethno-national consciousness (Indrapala 2007; Pieris 2010; Roberts 2004), a strand in the multi-textured quilt of myriad possibilities, has been made salient and rigidly defined with clear boundaries set against the 'other'; a condensation, jelling (Byman 2002), crystallization of hostile and exclusive group identities.

Worldwide, nationalism, perhaps partly based on older, historic identities, is a modern psychosocial phenomenon that developed due to a confluence of global, historical, psychological, socio-economic, religious and political factors (Anderson 2006). The appeal of nationalism to a core group identity helped bring communities together, forge a cohesive consciousness, define boundaries and create nation states with 'profound emotional legitimacy and attachment' and 'generate colossal sacrifice', a willingness to kill and die for it (Anderson 2006). During the colonial period, the world witnessed the growth and development of powerful nation states in America and Europe and their subsequent imperial expansion into global empires. The fierce European (and Japanese) nationalistic rivalries resulted in the two destructive world wars of the twentieth century that affected every part of the globe (Chatterjee 2010) and set the stage for what was to follow: the breakup of the colonial empires, superpower rivalry for the spoils (the Cold War) and eventually smaller, intra-state, ethnic civil conflicts. The postcolonial struggles of the twentieth century have seen the growth of nationalism and ethnic differentiation, unparalleled in history. This vigorous affirmation of distinctions and exclusiveness has meant struggles for self-determination and autonomy. However, national and ethnic assertion cannot be constrained to follow just the boundaries wished by those who helped create them. Frantz Fanon (1967) wanted to create a positive black African identity, but what eventually emerged was a host of conflicting national and even tribal identities, a veritable Pandora's box. The dangers of too much differentiation and exclusiveness are only too clear for us to see today — the problems of ethnocentrism and chauvinism. This is the tendency where the positive elevation of group identity progresses to the extreme position of the group thinking that it is special and superior to all others, as it happened in Nazi Germany.

That group identity can arouse ultimate loyalties and sacrifice, particularly when it is felt to be under threat, is abundantly clear from numerous examples of current ethnic conflicts around the globe (in former Yugoslavia, former USSR, Ireland, Rwanda, Kenya, Somalia, Sudan, Burma, Thailand, India, Philippines, East Timor, Iraq, Afghanistan and other countries). It is this mystical feeling of belonging to something greater than the individual self, of belonging to the larger group, a patriotic fervour, that has driven communities to extreme action; 'militant enthusiasm' as Konrad Lorenz (1963) terms it. According to Sivaram (cited in Whitaker 2007), modern ruling elites have found ethno-nationalism to be the most effective principle to organize and run modern nation states. Gilroy (2000) eloquently opposes the 'emergence and entrenchment of biopolitical power as means and technique for managing the life of populations, states and societies'. Biopolitical power is based on ethno-nationalism, a form of 'New Racism' in the modern postcolonial world, arising out of beliefs in discrete and exclusive racial and national identities with genomic undertones. The tragic consequences of creating divisive ethno-nationalistic groupings can be seen from three modern examples, among many. The construction of India from a multitude of princely and chieftaincy regimes through diplomacy, statecraft, conspiracy, cunning, terror and subversion, for economic interest and administrative efficiency, was an achievement of the British Raj and the East India Company. In the process, there arose the need for an overarching concept of 'Hinduism', to make sense of and unify a myriad and kaleidoscope conglomeration of diverse practices and beliefs into the communal interpretation of a two-nation theory. Hinduism was contrasted with Islam and people were compelled to identify with one or the other. This divisive categorization eventually led to partition, with the creation of Pakistan and later Bangladesh, and continuing tribulations within and without (Chatterjee 2010; Frykenberg 1993; Ludden 1996; Pandey 1990; Thapar et al. 1969). The story of Rwanda is more illustrative (Cordell and Wolff 2010; Gourevitch 1998; Volkan 1997). Belgium, and to a lesser extent Germany and the Roman Catholic Church, succeeded during their period of colonial rule in creating racial consciousness and divisions between the Hutus and Tutsis, through racial theories based on such origin myths as the story of Ham from the Bible (Gourevitch 1998) and divisive actions like issuing ethnic identity cards indicating which group people belonged to, whereas in precolonial times, their ascriptions had been tribal, clannish and proximity to power. They had shared the same territory, religion and language and a system that allowed for intermarriage and social mobility between caste and clan (Cordell and Wolff 2010). The resultant political ambitions, mutually exclusive discourses, division, animosity and suspicion erupted in Hutu–Tutsi violence for the first time in their history in 1959 and led to the genocide in 1994, which spilled over into neighbouring countries. The strategy of ethnically dividing Iraqis into Shi'ite, Sunni and Kurd sects for governance—ethnic quotas in the Governing Council, single district electoral law and process (Chandrasekaran 2006) after the invasion led by the United States, conveniently (for Western powers), split the Islamic world in the current 'clash of civilizations' ideology (Huntington 1993). Chandrasekaran (2006) quotes Saad Jawad, professor of political science at Baghdad University, thus: 'We never saw each other as Sunnis or Shi'ites first. We were Iraqis first. But the Americans changed all that. They made a point of categorizing people as Sunni or Shi'iteor Kurd.' These impressions were confirmed by my key inform-ant interviews of Iraqi refugees in Australia from the Shi'ite, Sunni and Kurdish communities. Many of these 'ethnic' groupings are not de novo constructions by any means, but may have already existed as potential or floating possibilities among many in 'proto-nationalistic' form. It is pos-sible to trace the strands of many modern-day ethnic identities back into history. 'Hindu' conceptions can be found in Vedic literature. But there was a broad inclusiveness and universality of vision in the Hindu concept of spiritual insights, discernible from Rig Vedic times, that was able to encompass other religious traditions within its folds (Coomaraswamy 1977). Buddhism had an extremely tolerant tradition, welcoming Jain, Islamic and Hindu practices and beliefs. It is reported that when Christian missionaries first came to Ceylon, Buddhist monks invited them to preach in their viharas. It was only when the missionaries started to actively pros-elytize and rebuke Buddhist practices that antagonism started (Scott 1996, 2000). Saddam Hussein dictatorially ruled Iraq—having a Shi'ite major-ity—using a Sunni minority. Admittedly, the situation is much more complex. The Kurds straddle the current geographic divisions of Iraq, Iran and Turkey, while Shi'ites in Iraq may look to Iran and the Arabic communities in Iran may look to Iraq, all of which became complicated by the Iran–Iraq war. All these loyalties and belongings antedate the Ameri-can invasion. However, ethnic divisions and conflict can be aggravated or engendered by the way policies are formulated, frameworks are adopted, governance and power issues are formulated, blocks and identities are emphasized, configured and drawn out. There are many different ways of analysing or looking at a situation. The tangle starts with trying to carve the world into neat nation states with convenient boundaries, which the imperial powers proceeded to do in a hurry, trying to understand and rule the myriad and esoteric world they had conquered. The modern Western or European predilection for concrete, reductionist categorization (the category fallacy of Kleinman (1977), where one finds all the character-istics of a predetermined category), Orientalism (Said 1995) and recep-tive local conditions have selectively accentuated, reinterpreted, focused, emphasized and objectified (Cohn 1987) certain aspects while ignoring others to bring out, subtly influence, construct and mould or transform (Van der Veer 1994) modern perceptions, consciousness, ways and patterns of thinking and world views into current ethnic groupings. These categories are then propagated as natural and a 'history' found for them. The Western way of thinking and seeing the world (Nisbett 2003) in concrete, reductionist categories with clear divisions has come to dominate the thoughts of not only academicians but also laypersons. John Lennon's (2005) refrain for peace comes to mind: 'Imagine there's no countries, it isn't hard to do, nothing to kill or die for.' A more ancient verse by the poet Kaniyan Poongkuntran in *Purananuru* of Sangam literature sings of the universal concept of being a global citizen, 'Yathum oore yavarum kelir' (To us all towns are one, all men our kin, listen...); it has become part of Tamil folklore. This is not to blame the West for all that is happening, for other imaginations and configurations may have led to different cleavages, fault lines, conflicts and violence. Nevertheless, current conceptualizations and subsequent developments are outgrowths of dominant Western frameworks. At least, if the relativity and contextuality of ethnic consciousness can be realized, it may reduce our fanaticism and enthusiasm for fighting each other!

Unfortunately for multi-ethnic Sri Lanka, which has become a case study for what can go awry, various 'sub-nationalisms' have tended to assert their own separate identities, resulting in ethnic confrontation. Though secular scholars (Bastian 1994; Committee for Rational Development 1984; Jeganathan and Ismail 1995; Obeyesekere 1988; Roberts 1994, 1997; Spencer 1990; Tambiah 1992) have, belatedly, tried to disentangle and deconstruct the divisive consciousness, the nationalisms have already become invested with considerable emotions and are supported by strong mythic beliefs that defy rational arguments. Ultimately nationalisms are, in modern social science parlance, 'constructed' from multiple socio-economic, psycho-cultural and politico-historical contextual determinants. Anderson (2006) termed the process 'imagined', while Marxists criticized the 'false consciousness'—material and class interests, they claimed, should be more progressive determinants of consciousness. Later, under Lenin, they did recognize the importance of solving the 'national question' with the recognition that national consciousness arose out of the more recent development of capitalism, from feudalism as well as anti-colonial struggles (Fanon 2004). Marxists have also described the process of 'interpellation', where the nationalistic ideology would define and constitute the subjective experience of belonging to a particular nation or social group that changes from time to time or conjecture to conjecture (Ismail 2000). Unfortunately for Sri Lanka, most of the left parties, rather than help solve the 'national question', eventually capitulated to the lure of ethno-nationalism for the easy ride to power. Then there is the Buddhist and Hindu metaphysical concept of construction, *vikalpa*, or the illusionary maya, like outer clothing or *kosha* one puts on, the cloth spun as a product of the socializing process from childhood, but becomes strongly identified with. It would take a Buddha to transcend these constricting boundaries (see Figure 1A.1), to liberate oneself by developing better understanding and deeper insight by clearing the misperceptions and compelling hold of ethnic identification, to disentangle the tangle.

This is not to say that ethnic consciousness is not real. Ethno-national consciousness gives rise to cultural diversity, which is the beautiful flowering of the differentiation of humanity. It is when ethnic consciousness becomes exclusive, without respect and tolerance for the 'other', chauvinistic, blinding ethnocentrism that the trouble starts. There have been a few genuine Sri Lankans from different communities who have managed to break away from communalism but their voice for peace and reconciliation is easily drowned by the vociferous clamouring of ethnic entrepreneurs (DeVotta 2004). Current socio-economic realities (Abeyratne 2004; Bastian 1994; Gunasinghe 1984) and powerful myths, legends and passions (Kapferer 1988) shape how the different ethnic groups perceive themselves, interpret what is happening around them and determine herd behaviour with tragic consequences. Group and ethnic identities are linked to self-esteem, dignity and sense of belonging, defended or sacrificed with

Figure 1A.1:
Increasing Group Identification

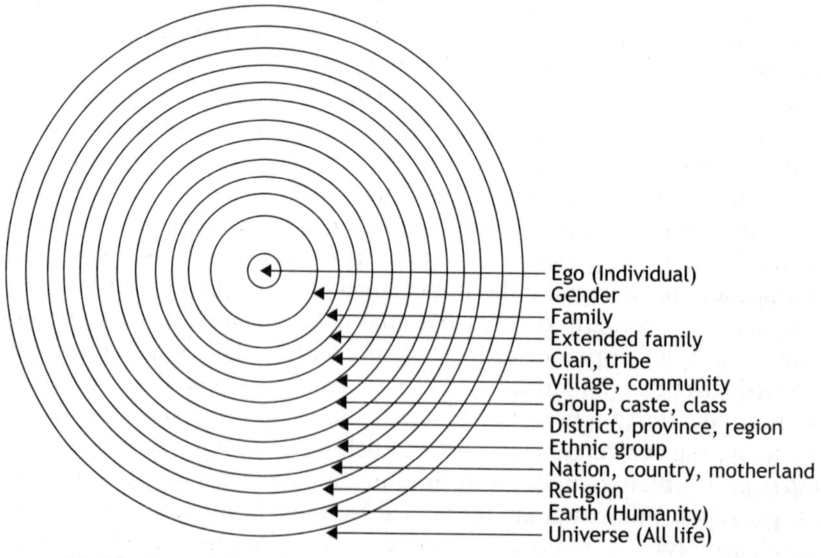

Ego (Individual)
Gender
Family
Extended family
Clan, tribe
Village, community
Group, caste, class
District, province, region
Ethnic group
Nation, country, motherland
Religion
Earth (Humanity)
Universe (All life)

Source: Modified from Allport (1954).

life itself, developing a self-fulfilling, transgenerational, reproductive capacity to pass on to future generations through the socialization process. Unfortunately they harden and become rigidified into polarized, exclusive categories impervious to change after bitter conflict, violence and war (Kaufman 2001; Thiranagama 2011; Volkan 1997). These identifications and belongings become fixed social reality, overdetermining how ethnic groups perceive themselves and how others perceive them. These are collective psychosocial phenomena affecting whole communities that provide the fuel for the ongoing ethnic turmoil capitalized upon by aspiring leaders and ethnic and conflict entrepreneurs.

Ethnic Group Dynamics

Ethno-national consciousness is the way an ethnic or national group perceives and experiences itself, the outer world and other groups. Central to ethnic consciousness is the group or collective identity based on a way of life — culture, language, religion and home territory among other characteristics (which could yet include clan, tribe or caste in some societies) — usually in opposition to other groups. Group identity is given sustenance by strong mythical beliefs about its origin, life, history, 'chosen traumas' (Volkan 1997), and the future. Ethnic identity becomes invested with considerable emotions, a sense of loyalty and belonging felt at the core of the being. Susan Greenfield (2000) explains that emotions, though often subterranean, subconscious and apparently irrational, are the most basic building blocks of consciousness. A picture of concentrically increasing and expanding identities and loyalties is given in Figure 1A.1. Similar concentric circles of loyalties (Allport 1954), applicable to the Sri Lankan situation have been described by Arasaratnam (1979, 1998) and Somasundaram (1998). Smith (1998) describes the 'onion character' of ethnicity, its capacity for forging 'concentric circles' of identity and loyalty, the wider circle encompassing the narrower. Multiple identities can be coextensive, if not symbiotic, as in multicultural societies where there can be harmony, and does not necessarily lead to destructive, violent conflict. Family and group identity and feelings may be more salient in collectivistic societies like many Afro-Asian communities where membership and loyalty to the community are much stronger than in individualistic ones like in the United States and Australia (Hofstede and Hofstede 2005; Hofstede et al. 2008; Nisbett 2003). Within the concentric circles of identities, the narrow inner circle is individualistic self-interest. In the Western world view of the social contract described by Rousseau, egoistic individuals come together to form groups or society out of self-interest, agreeing to conditions of mutual benefit. But unlike the coalescence of individualistic identities, group identity is determined by how the group or community defines itself, who belong and who do not, socially accepted practices, rituals, beliefs, interactions and relationships, collective memories, the past and the present, history, myths, narratives, stories, songs and dances that are passed on to future generations by a socialization process starting from birth. This results in self-effacement, interdependence, cooperative behaviour, relationships and networks, group norms, common goals and motivations where people can act for altruistic reasons, for the common good, sacrificing self-interest (Chun et al. 2006; Heppner et al. 2006). Ethnic consciousness arises from this background, as does the sociocultural context to mould the way the community sees the world. Collective consciousness and unconsciousness of ethnic groups, collective memories, cultural world views and group identity are manifested in their psychocultural narratives (Ross 2007). Collective stories, dramas, songs, art and other creative productions, images, metaphors, rituals and symbols reveal the inner world, chosen memories, deep fears, perceived threats and grievances that determine day-to-day behaviour, choices, motivation and, more pertinent to our purpose here, drive the ethnic conflict. The collective narratives are thus good reflectors, entry points that give insight and access to understanding the inner workings of the group mind.

Group identity is a basic need that determines a community's well-being; its cohesiveness, relationships and networking; its social capital. When it is lost or weakened, the group undergoes loss of dignity, esteem, status, confidence and pride; feelings of inferiority, disempowerment and lack of direction and control over their fate rise to the fore. There may develop various forms of social dysfunction like anomie, suicidality, crime, domestic and child abuse, alcohol and drug problems, amotivation, helplessness, dependence (on outside help), mistrust, paranoia and a host of other social ills. These kinds of adverse social consequences can be seen in indigenous communities that have been destroyed by colonization, as in the Americas (Erikson and Vecsey 1980), Australia (Atkinson 2002; Krieg 2009) and by assimilation among the Veddas in Sri Lanka (Thangarajah 1995). Signs of collective trauma and loss of social capital can be seen today among communities that have faced the brunt of long civil wars, as in Africa (Abramowitz 2005), Cambodia (Somasundaram et al. 1999), among the Tamils (Somasundaram 2007a), which will be described in the sections to come (see Table 3B.1), and other minorities experiencing repression. A strong sense of group cohesiveness, confidence, identity and collective efficacy is positive, leading to resilience and is protective against stress from adverse events. But when group identification becomes extreme, transforming into ethnocentrism and chauvinism, it can lead to difficulties, first for other groups that are in its path and then the group itself, when emotions can turn inwards becoming exclusive, puritan and paranoid. Buddhaghosa's (~500) insightful description about entanglements of the 'I' consciousness (and unconsciousness) can be logically extended to exclusive 'we' consciousness (and unconsciousness). The individual and collective unconscious negatives tend to be projected, as defence mechanisms, attributed onto the 'other(s)', which according to Jung (1931) 'leads to collective delusions, "incidents", war and revolutions, in a word, to destructive mass psychoses'. Jung blames politicians and journalists who 'unwittingly unleash (these) mental epidemics'. Short of mass understanding and awakening, politicians, journalists and educators hold the power to reverse the process. Eastern traditions, Frieir's (1972) pedagogy of 'conscientisation' and psychotherapy (Watts 1973), claim that *vidya* (right knowledge), *vipassana* (insight) and clear perception can be liberating from these entanglements, complexes, bondage.

Although rationally, ethnicity can be understood on the basis of a common way of life, language, religion or territory, membership of an ethnic group usually bases itself in an overpowering and ineffable belief of sharing the same primordial essence (Smith 1998; Isaacs 1989), a sense of solidarity (Smith 1986), having the same origin and descent, an extended kinship[1] network (Horowitz 2000). There is often a deep-seated faith of sharing the same pure blood (Allport 1954; Volkan 1997) or belonging to the same native soil (*bhumiputra*s or sons of the soil). During ethnic identity formation and conflict, appeals to blood and soil become common in the images, symbols, mass media, political rhetoric and rituals as seen in the north and south of Sri Lanka.[2] An important feature of social identity formation is that once committed to a particular group, often a small sub-group, the members of that group become 'tribal and clannish', intolerant and cruel in their exclusion of other groups, while pledging total and blind obedience and loyalty to their own group. Groups have a need to externalize, project their fears, feelings of threats, frustrations and aggressions on to an outer group, the 'other', an enemy to hate (Kaufman 2001; Volkan 1988). This process of in-group formation and exclusion of any out-group was brought out by a series of revealing experiments. When subjects are assigned to a group, any group, even arbitrarily (for example,

---

[1] Tamil co-ethnics were addressed as brothers and sisters by the LTTE.

[2] Tamil militant youth used to cut their fingers with a blade and put *pottus* (mark of different colours applied in the centre of the forehead or between the eyebrows of religious or cultural significance) on themselves and each other as symbols of their loyalty and commitment at political rallies, which had a profound, electrifying effect on the audience. These stories were then passed on in awe by word of mouth. The phrase *raththathin raththham* (blood of our blood) was a common metaphor in political rhetoric and nationalistic songs, as was *sontha mann* (this is our common soil).

at a weekend camp), they immediately, automatically, almost reflexively, think of that group as 'us', as an in-group for them, as better, attributing positive qualities and showing in-group preferences. To them any alternative is an out-group, 'them', the 'other', attributing negative qualities and showing discrimination against them and depriving them of resources even when it is clearly detrimental to their own interests (Brown 1965, 1986; Tajfel 1978). These result in zero-sum games, with competitive and incompatible goals, where both sides lose, the overriding emotional concern being that that the other side loses more (Jesse and Williams 2011). Being social animals, humans seem to have the intrinsic tendency and need to form groups that had survival value when competing for food or security.

Erik Erikson (1968) describes this need for psychosocial identity, both personal and collective, to be of a 'special kind' and to project all the negative qualities on to others which 'in conjunction with their territoriality, gave men a reason to slaughter one another *in majorem gloriam*' (see also Erikson [1963]). Reggie Siriwardena (1984) describes the 'mystical belief in blood' in the racist vocabulary to denote racial purity, saying, 'If you really believe that your blood is inherently superior to that of another race, you will have less compunction about shedding the latter.' Allport (1954) points out:

> Both family and racial pride focus on blood. Race is a fashionable focus for the propaganda of alarmists and demagogues. It is the favourite bogey used by those who have something to gain, or who themselves are suffering from some nameless dread. Racists seem to be people who out of their own anxieties, have manufactured the demon of race. Others, like Hitler, have found racism useful in distracting people from their own troubles, and providing them with an easy scapegoat.

A very important component of ethnic consciousness is perception of 'us' and 'them', the 'other', against whom or in reference to whom the group becomes more clearly defined. As Kapferer (1988) argues, the Tamils have become the demonic, evil 'other' in the Sinhala psyche. Perception of the 'other' includes attitudes and stereotypes concerning the 'other'. Stereotypical labels usually have an associated emotional tone, often negative. Thus, the terms Demala for the Tamil and Cinkalavar for the Sinhalese, though strictly neutral and used in formal writing, can be used in a derogatory way or as means of exclusion by the other group. Labels paradoxically also influence the person labelled, compelling him to fit the mould. The label can become an inner command (Sartre 1963; Solomon 1974), forcing the individual to behave in a way expected by others. Thus, stereotypes can become both self-perpetuating and self-fulfilling by influencing our behaviour towards those we stereotype as well as drawing out the stereotyped behaviour.

These labels and stereotypes are socially supported, continually revived and hammered in by mass media—by novels, short stories, news items, movies, stage, radio, television, Internet, political demagoguery and schoolbooks. For example, early Sinhala novels like *Kalahanda* by W. A. Silva use derogatory terms to refer to Tamil workers (Jayatunge 2011). The late Reggie Siriwardena (1984), in an illuminating study of school textbooks, reports:

> What is more shocking is that millions of school children should be taught, in the name of social studies, through text-books published by the state, the myths of divergent racial origins which will help to divide the Sinhalese and Tamils for more generations to come.

Taking a specific example (from a Sinhalese school textbook) he says:

> What this lesson does is to evoke the child's memories of being frightened by his parents with threats of the mysterious and fearful '*billo*' [a spirit in Sinhala folklore, usually evil in nature] to identify these bogeymen as Tamil agents, and thus to enlist the deep-seated irrational fears of early childhood for the purpose of creating apprehension and hatred of Tamils.

Referring to the exploitation of history as an instrument of divisive ethnic ideologies, he says history text books 'project an image of Sinhala-Buddhist identity which is defined fundamentally through opposition to and struggles against Tamils in past history'. As for Tamil textbooks, he quotes Professor Indrapala, saying that they 'fostered in the Tamil child a special feeling for his or her community and language, and helped to strengthen communal attitudes ... and helped to foster a kind of patriotic feeling, not towards Sri Lanka but towards Tamil Nadu'. He concludes:

> A system of education that encourages and fosters ideas of racial superiority and domination among the majority community is no basis for national unity or even for national peace. To adapt or sanction a two-faced educational policy by giving Sinhala and Tamil school children different conceptions of the relation between the two communities and their place in the national life is in fact to promote continuing discord, conflict and bitterness and to foster divisiveness and separation.

Even after decades of bitter strife have torn the country apart, though a group of dedicated social scientists struggled to point this out, except for some cosmetic changes, the system has not changed in any fundamental way. The National Institute of Education (NIE), which determines national educational policy and programmes, develops the curriculum and syllabi and directs the publication and distribution of school textbooks, continues to function as a Sinhala-Buddhist institution propagating the one-sided views and attitudes (Sivathamby 2005).[3]

The modern Sinhala-Buddhist resurgence started as a reaction to Western colonialism, in particular, imposition of the English language and Christian domination. It began at the end of the nineteenth century under the leadership of the Ven. Migettuvatte Gunananda, the Ven. Hikkaduwe Sumangala, (the Ven. Devamitta) Anagarika Dharmapala, Colonel Olcott and others (Gombrich and Obeyesekere 1988; Tambiah 1992). Though Christians formed less than 10 per cent of the population in colonial Ceylon, the Christian elite dominated the political and socio-economic life of the country. The Buddhist revival led by militant monks like Migettuwatte Gunananda, 'focused attention on the privileges and alleged misdeeds of the Christian minority, instead of on the colonial regime itself, by the use of slogans, public debates (*Pandaura Vadaya*) and pamphlets to mobilize people in anti-Christian agitation' (Jayawardena 1986). Thus, the great Sinhala-Buddhist ideologue, Anagarika Dharmapala wrote in 1902:

> This bright, beautiful island was made into a paradise by the Aryan Sinhalese before its destruction was brought about by the barbaric vandals.... Christianity and polytheism are responsible for the vulgar practice of killing animals, stealing, prostitution, licentiousness, lying and drunkenness.... This ancient historic, refined people, under the diabolism of vicious paganism, introduced by the British administration are now declining and slowly dying away. The bureaucratic administrators ... have cut down primeval forests to plant tea, have i oduced opium, *ganga*, whisky, arrack and other alcoholic poisons, have openea ... '-oons and drinking taverns in every village; have killed all industries and made the people indolent. (Guruge 1965: 482, cited in Jayawardena [1986])

The first ethnic riots directed at the Christian community took place in Kotahena in 1883 and occasional attacks continue up to the present. This

---

[3] The day begins with the playing of the national anthem over a public speaker system and everyone in the campus has to stand in silent attention. Similar to many national institutions, there is no representation from minority communities in the senior administration or academic positions. Books for the Tamil medium schools are often translated from the Sinhala. Translations are of poor quality. Further, textbooks do not reach schools in the peripheral areas on time. The Tamil Teachers Trade Union has objected often but to no avail. There were attempts under the LTTE to set up a Tamil Provincial Institute of Education (PIE) for northern and eastern Sri Lanka.

was followed in 1915 by more significant ethnic violence against Muslims, the Coast Moors, who were recent immigrants from the Coromandel and Malabar coasts of south India. They soon gained control of retail trade in the island, thereby activating the animosities of their Sinhalese competitors — the Sinhalese traders (mainly low-country Sinhalese) — who had no compunctions about exploiting religious and racial sentiments to lend a cloak of respectability to sordid commercial rivalry (De Silva 1981). Fearing a plot against the state in times of war, the British panicked at the anti-Muslim riots, declared martial law and arrested members of the Sinhalese community including the respected country gentleman, D. S. Senanayake; he had actually used his influence to stop the rioting. The agitation for his release led by Sir Ponnambalam Ramanathan resulted in a wave of mass feeling for nationalism, which had until then been not much more than a movement among the elite. The arrest provoked Senanayake to enter the arena of national politics, which eventually resulted in his becoming Ceylon's first prime minister. The events led to the formation of the Ceylon National Congress in 1919, following the model of the Indian National Congress, uniting the major Sinhalese and Tamil organizations. The historian K. M. De Silva (1981) comments:

> At this stage in the island's development (Sinhala-Tamil) ethnicity was not a divisive factor. The divisive forces were religion and caste, especially the latter, and these caused divisions among the Sinhalese themselves rather than dividing the Sinhalese from the other ethnic and religious groups in the island.

There was considerable antagonism between the traditional up-country Kandyan aristocracy and Goyigama caste against the low-country, commercial entrepreneurs of the mainly Karava caste who had taken advantage of the opportunities under the colonial powers. It is a historic irony that the Kandyan Sinhalese felt themselves so threatened by the ascendency of the low-country Sinhalese that S. W. R. D. Bandaranaike, the originator of the present-day ruling SLFP, proposed a federal form of government in 1927 and later to the Donoughmore Commission to safeguard their then distinct interests. The fact that these two groups have now merged into one overarching Sinhala-Buddhist identity is proof of the contextual nature of identity formation. There was also labour competition and unrest in Colombo against the Malayali workers from India (brought in by the colonial British as cheap and compliant labour). At independence, one of the first acts of the new nation was to disenfranchise the Indian Tamils (brought in by the British to work in the hill-country tea estates as cheap, indentured labour). The first ethnic violence against Sri Lankan Tamils took place only in 1956.

Sinhala Buddhist and Tamil Consciousness

According to Kumari Jayawardena (1986), the Sinhala-Buddhist identity is based on:

1. The doctrine of the primacy and superiority of the Sinhala 'race' as the original, true inhabitants of the island, linked to the myth that the Sinhalese were 'Aryan' migrants from Bengal.
2. The concept that the Sinhala race has been placed in a special relationship to Buddhism as its protector. Appeals to save Buddhism from infidels or non-Buddhists calling for a 'dharma *yudhaya*' (holy war) to protect the Buddhist religion.
3. The feeling that the Sinhalese (and also the Sinhala language) are really a minority in the region, with no other country except Sri Lanka, unlike the other minority groups which have ethnic links with other countries, particularly in reference to the fifty million Tamils in south India.

This relatively recent development of the modern Sinhala-Buddhist identity based on 'race, religion and language' within a geographically defined territory, perceiving itself to be threatened by the 'alien' Tamil 'invaders' from south India has had a profound influence on the Sinhalese people, spurring them to action, politically and violently against those they were told threatened this historic identity. History was reinterpreted to create a strong feeling of grievance and historic injustice suffered under colonial, British rule, as in the All Ceylon Buddhist Congress Committee of Inquiry report, *The Betrayal of Buddhism* in 1956 (Tambiah 1992). It was this appeal to the core identity of the Sinhalese by upcoming parochial leaders like S. W. R. D. Bandaranaike that provided the impetus to establish a Sinhalesized state, beginning in 1956. These strong feelings were to grow into virulent Sinhala-Buddhist ethnocentrism, culminating in the 1983 anti-Tamil pogrom, inflaming the ethnic conflict. Anthropologists Obeyesekere (1988), Gombrich and Obeyesekere (1988), Kapferer (1988, 1997) and Tambiah (1992) have elucidated what happened from a deeper, intra-psychic, sociocultural perspective. They studied the myths, legends, common religio-cultural practices and social context for 'an understanding of the current circumstances of state terror and violence that are part of the ethnic conflict' (Kapferer 1988). Ancient chronicles like the *Mahavamsa* and *Dipavamsa*, myths and legends such as those of Duttugemunu and Vijaya in the current socioeconomic and political contextual realities, have been reconstituted and imbibed with new meanings to identify the Tamils as the 'dangerous other' (Nissan and Stirrat 1990), the demonic and evil (Kapferer 1988), as they have been perceived to threaten Sinhala Buddhism by resisting incorporation and assimilation (Tambiah 1992). These beliefs, fear, anger and hate have become deep-seated forces within the Sinhala psyche and were seen to irrupt into visible reality in the periodic mob violence against Tamils and drive the continuing state terror machine. The current version of the extreme Sinhala-Buddhist ideology and politics are represented by *jathika chinthanaya* or 'national consciousness' (Goonewardena 2007), which manoeuvred itself into the driving seat of the Sri Lankan state as the Rajapaksa regime, JHU and JVP.

Paul Gilroy (2000) describes the emergence of a form of ultranationalism or 'New Racism' from ethnic absolutism with authoritarian, antidemocratic and fascist characteristics in the modern postcolonial world. A lasting solution to the current ethnic conflict would require a radical change in ethnic perceptions, challenging internal representations, transforming schemas in the collective psyche that would be painful and 'generate more strife and suffering for Sinhalese, let alone for others, instead of producing Buddhist equanimity' (Kapferer 1988). This arises from a basic psychosocial principle which makes it much more difficult to change internal attitudes, beliefs and narratives, to realize the underlying causes, so much so that it is much easier (less threatening and painful for internal schemas, representations) to project, externalizing and expressing the problem outward, even with aggression and violence at extreme cost to everyone. Tamils have reacted by asserting their own separate identity (Arasaratnam 1998; Wilson 2000) while projecting on to the Sinhalese all that is aversive, and thus the ethnic conflict.

Although a short-lived Hindu revival was led by Arumugam Navalar in the nineteenth century as a response to the Christian missionary activity[4] in the north, particularly loosening of the rigid caste system, modern Sri Lankan Tamil identity developed mainly as a reaction to the increasing dominance of the Sinhala-Buddhist hegemony (Arasaratnam 1998; Wilson 2000). Successive Sinhala leaders rose to power by exploiting emotions relating to Sinhala Buddhism and then proceeded to use the state machinery to enforce Sinhala as the only official language (Official Language Act, 1956), enshrine Buddhism as the state religion (1972 constitution), discriminate in favour of the majority Sinhalese in education (for example, 'standardization' of university admissions), employment, allocation of resources and land (colonization) and organized periodic mob violence (1956, 1958, 1977, 1981, 1983) against the minority Tamils.

---

[4] Christian mission activity undermined orthodox Hindu social structures, particularly caste hierarchy and privileges, by encouraging and empowering the lower castes through awareness, education, economic inducements, opportunities for advancement and conversion.

The Tamils in turn began to fear that their very identity, their cultural existence as a separate and unique group, was threatened. Although the Tamil identity crystallized more in opposition to the threat from the Sinhala state, it was again not a de novo synthesis; strands of it can be traced back to prehistoric times (Indrapala 2007). Language was the vital element of the Tamil identity, with territory, a homeland in the north and east of Sri Lanka, being posited as another, newer aspect. Though not stressed by the secular youth and Tamil nationalist ideologues, Hinduism was also a part of the Tamil identity; perhaps more so as part of the general Tamil culture.[5] Hinduism is a rich blend of Saivism, folk beliefs, cults and elements of Vaishnavism, Tantra, Shaktism, Buddhism and Jainism in varying proportions in different communities and areas. For Tamils, their heritage, culture and literature were a more important part of their identity than history (Daniel 1996; Eller 1999). In fact, there was no sense of history (or time) as developed in modern, Western historiography but cyclical, mythical and karmic beliefs about the past (Rajanayagam 1994). Like the Sinhalese, the Tamils of Sri Lanka, as a group, developed more recently (post-independence), after decades of being discriminated against and facing violent state repression and humiliation, a minority complex of victimhood and persecution, mixed with fear, even terror (explored in Chapter 1B). This has become a part of the lived experience of Tamils, as will be described, a part of their consciousness and collective memory. This has led them to hide their identity in public in areas outside their traditional homeland, avoid being conspicuous and unnecessarily attract attention.[6] In Sri Lanka, those belonging to the minority Tamil community were made to establish their identity at military checkpoints or in house-to-house searches, explain themselves, face unruly mobs and state violence, mass arrests, detention, assault and registration at police stations as during apartheid in South Africa. Many found this intolerable and fled the country, which partly explains the aggrieved viewpoints and attitudes widely prevalent in the diaspora. The Tamil reaction grew increasingly violent after the 1983 pogrom, becoming militant and fascist in turn, adopting methods of terror against the state, Sinhala and Muslim communities, as well as within the Tamil community.

[5] For example, the cultural influence can be seen in many Tamil 'Christian' practices.

[6] For instance, not speaking Tamil (or talking in hushed tones) in public or wearing symbols of their ethnic group such as *pottus*, while avoiding compatriots doing so. They no longer 'performed their Tamilness' in public for fear of being identified as a Tamil (Ismail 2000; Kanapathipillai 1990). According to a UN official who has lived in rebel-controlled areas, there is a qualitative difference between these areas. Children particularly appear to be more carefree and can be seen shouting, laughing and playing more readily, at times jumping into ponds or rivers and having fun; something not seen among Tamil children in government-controlled areas.

The growth of Tamil nationalism and its linkage to a pan-Sri Lankan Tamil nationalism[7] are already apparent worldwide, where there are steps to establish a transnational government. Apart from large movements in Western countries such as Canada, the United States, the United Kingdom, Australia, France, Sweden, Norway and Germany, at a recent (2007) protest rally by Indians in Malaysia, placards of Velupillai Prabhakaran, leader of the powerful Tamil militant group, the LTTE, were in evidence. Significantly, the LTTE was banned in most of these countries as a 'terrorist' organization and even after the demise of the LTTE some members of the Tamil diaspora continue to be vociferous advocates for a separate Tamil Eelam. Tamil nationalism refers to the purity of the Dravidian race, descendants of the ancient Mohenjo-daro civilization, the greatness of a five-thousand-year-old Tamil language and the glories of the Chola empire. The LTTE adopted the emblem of the Chola tiger on its flag (seen waved during international Tamil protests) to represent and appeal to extreme emotive nationalism. The Pongu Thamil mobilization and plays by Sithamparanathan (for example, *Uyirthamanithar koothu*) attempt to celebrate the Tamil spirit while bringing out decades of suppression by the state. However, the dangers of an ethnocentric, exclusive national identity alienating minorities within Tamil-speaking areas was seen in the expulsion of the Muslims from the north of the country and their massacres in the east. Eastern Tamils, who perceive themselves as being traditionally demeaned by their northern brethren and feel that their identity, history, culture and problems are somewhat different, voice fears of being dominated by the Jaffna Tamils (Eller 1999; Reddiar 1997); such fears resurfaced with the fatal, LTTE–Karuna split in 2005. Sri Lankan Tamil nationalism, as it developed, also excluded the hill-country or estate Tamils, southern Tamils as well as the larger Tamil community in India (Wilson 1994; Ismail 2000). Comparatively, the Sinhala identity was progressively more inclusive and assimilative, with the Kandyan and low-country Sinhala identities merging, while absorbing other groups like the Salagama, Durava and Karava of recent south Indian origin, as long as they accepted the hegemony of the Sinhala language and Buddhist religion.

Other minority groups too have recently begun to assert their own identity. One of them is the Muslim community, which has seen a rapid

[7] This is essentially a Sri Lankan Tamil phenomenon not involving the bulk of Tamils in or from India. However, a few Indian Tamil leaders, such as Vaiko and Pazha Nedumaran, have identified with this nationalism. The original pan-Tamil movement based in Tamil Nadu abandoned separation during the India–China war. No major Tamil leader based in India has since advocated separatism in India or Sri Lanka. Even in Sri Lanka, the objectives were federalism, not separation, prior to the Vaddukoddai Resolution of 1976. Federalism has continued to be the objective of the mainstream, moderate Sri Lankan Tamil leaders, which is why many of them were killed by the militants.

political awakening 'in response to exclusionary and increasingly violent Sinhala and Tamil nationalism' (Lewer and Ismail 2011). The electoral success of the Sri Lanka Muslim Congress (SLMC) has led to demands for an autonomous region of their own in eastern Sri Lanka. It is particularly significant to the fundamental thesis being developed here, namely the contextual determinism of ethnic consciousness, that Muslim identity and consciousness are increasingly taking a supranational dimension in the wake of international developments. Muslims are now beginning to identify and perceive themselves as members of the international Muslim community, transcending national boundaries. The other potentially revolutionary group that has been gaining a positive identity under articulate leaders, shedding its negative self-image maintained under years of exploitation, is the hill-country Tamils. It can also be observed that amongst the Sri Lankan diaspora worldwide communities have polarized along ethnic lines; where one would have expected them to be aware of having so much in common compared to other groups in the host country and be influenced by global, modernizing values (Smith 1998) that would transcend narrow ethnicity; some have become even more rabid, hawkish and supportive of ethnic warfare than those left back home. The narrow ethnic identity serves an inherent need to belong, to soothe nostalgia, atone for guilt for leaving kin behind in dire straits and gives purpose, a raft to hold on to in an alienating, anomic, lonely and fragmenting life abroad. However, this is true mainly of the first-generation migrants who have in some way directly experienced the polarized situation in Lanka, and less true of the second generation.[8]

Social comparison takes place only between groups of equal status or with itself at an earlier time. It is important to note that even in the pre-independence era the 'reference group' for the Sinhalese and Tamils was each other and not the British, who were regarded as a dominant, superior group with a positive social identity and thus not comparable. If anger and aggression are to result from the perceived inequity, then the disadvantaged group must not attribute the disadvantage to itself, and must not take responsibility for the inequity. But it may not attribute the cause to the truly responsible group (for example, the British, the ruling elite) or socio-economic conditions. Anger and violence can be displaced from real sources or problems to more available and vulnerable targets such as a convenient scapegoat. Thus, we see the frustration resulting from real socio-economic problems of poverty, unemployment, over-population, unequal distribution of wealth found in Ceylon displaced by the adroit political leadership, first on to Christians from the end of the

---

[8] Some second- and later-generation Tamils have shown a keen interest and active involvement in Tamil national causes that is more mature, democratic and technological.

nineteenth century, Muslims in 1915, then on to the 'Cochins' (Malayalis), Indian Tamils, again the Christians and finally on to Sri Lankan Tamils after 1956.

The Sinhalese and Tamils have gone through a cycle of perceived inequity during the past century. In the beginning the Tamils were perceived as holding an unfair advantage, a position inconsistent with their numbers, in regard to education and state sector jobs (this was also true of the low-country Sinhalese, who were after some initial differentiation compelled[9] to join forces with the up-country Kandyan Sinhalese to make common cause). However, the situation was the reverse in other sectors like the private sector, commercial and business sectors and agriculture as the dry north-east was not developed and did not have resources for agriculture like the rest of the island.

This led to affirmative action to correct perceived historic injustices by successive Sinhala governments, some of which were beneficial to rural, agrarian and deprived communities of all ethnicities (Phadnis 1979). In time this overshot the mark. Tamils perceived themselves to be disadvantaged in terms of costs (discrimination, repeated violence, destruction of property, displacement) compared to benefits (education, citizenship, ethnic proportion) and felt themselves slipping from the privileged position they had enjoyed in certain key areas (see Table 1A.1) to become '2nd class citizens' (Schwarz 1988). Not only the state but even the private sector and even some diplomatic missions discriminated against Tamils; for example, in recruitment, issue of visas and scholarships. Apart from prejudice, there might be an element of 'discrimination without prejudice' (Nesiah 1997) due to current ethnic situational dynamics; while recruiting Sinhalese might bring in state goodwill and resultant benefits (similar to employing Bumiputras in Malaysia), recruiting Tamils might bring trouble and costly intrusion from the police and armed services by way of arrests and detentions of Tamil employees and loss of business (similar to employing blacks in parts of the United States in the past, Jews in pre-war Germany or blacks during apartheid in South Africa); Tamil employees might not be able to visit certain areas or institutions; Tamil (and this applied to low castes until recently) managers might not be able to enforce discipline among Sinhala employees.

The state became an ethnocracy (DeVotta 2004), that is completely 'Sinhalesized', with the government, judiciary, armed forces, security apparatus, institutions and structures all perpetuating the will of the majority ethnic group. In a context of depleting resources, this led in turn

---

[9] By communal mobilization, but interestingly, also by an act of census-making, when this categorization was taken out of the census report of 1981 after having sought this information during the census itself. The Kandyan Sinhalese have continued to be underprivileged as opposed to their elite counterparts.

Table 1A.1:
Decline in the Privileged Position of Sri Lankan Tamils

	(updated from Schwarz, 1988)[10]		
	1956	*1965*	*1970*	*2002*
Administrative Service	30	20	5	8
Clerical Service	50	30	5	9
Professions				
(Engineers, Doctors)	60	30	10	10
Armed Forces	40	20	1	.01
Labour	40	20	5	12

Sources: Figures for 1956, 1965 and 1970 from Schwarz (1988); figures for 2002 from Department of Census and Statistics (2005); figure on Tamils in the armed forces in 2002 from Library of Congress (2013).
Notes: (i) Sri Lankan Tamils represent 12.6 per cent of the population.
(ii) Figures are indicated in percentage terms.

to increasing defiance and militancy among Tamils, ending in the political struggle for separation. It is worth noting that through all this, the (Indian) hill-country Tamils, who were the most deprived, have not reacted due to their negative social identity, acceptance of domination by other groups and lack of a reference group for comparison. The 'concept of deserved-ness' is very important in perceived injustice (Brown 1986). It is easy to see how elevation of social identity is a potentially revolutionary act (by changing comparison groups and perception of justice) as is happening to the Muslims and could happen to the hill-country Tamils. According to Brown (1986), a disadvantaged group works to elevate group identity chiefly by making propaganda in favour of group image, language and abilities, as was seen in the Sinhala-Buddhist and Tamil-Hindu revival of the late nineteenth and early twentieth centuries. The Sinhala-Buddhist resurgence of the late nineteenth century was able to mobilize the Bud-dhist and Sinhala intelligentsia that was being suppressed under the colo-nial regime to the forefront, to slowly right the disadvantaged position they were in, to take control and power into their own hands. During the period of successive colonial rulers, the local religions—Buddhism, Hinduism and Islam—had been repressed by colonial Christianity, and native languages by British English, among the elites. First the Portuguese destroyed all local temples in the coastal belt under their control and built churches from these ruins and sometimes converted people, it is said, at

---

[10] Figures for 2002 may not be exactly comparable with earlier data. The accuracy of fig-ures for the other years is also doubtful; for example, 40 per cent of the armed forces being Tamil in 1956 (Horowitz 1980). The table does, however, show the general trend.

the point of the sword, to Catholic Christianity.[11] The Dutch were more interested in economic profit and were thus more tolerant towards the Buddhist and Hindu religions and customs though less tolerant towards Muslims on account of rivalry with Arab traders operating in the Indian Ocean. They promoted Protestant Christianity more subtly through administrative and socio-economic means. The British proved more thorough in their imperial 'civilizing mission', transforming the local people through education, administration (Colebrooke–Cameron reforms) and socio-economic means. After independence, with universal franchise and mass education, the Sinhala-Buddhist intelligentsia took control of the state machinery through electoral majoritarian means to first unseat the Western-oriented English-speaking ruling elite, beginning with the (Sinhala-only) Official Language Act in 1956 and then reducing the privileges of the Tamils.

Fear, mistrust and perception of hostile intent can set off a spiral of threats and counter-threats, the so-called 'security dilemma' that is said to be one of the causes of ethnic mobilization and violent conflict escalation (Byman 2002; Cordell and Wolff 2010; Jesse and Williams 2011). According to the security dilemma concept used in international relations theory, and now being used in ethnic conflict analysis and peace strategies as well, one side, fearing the other side, will take defensive measures, arm itself and increase its offensive rhetoric which would alarm the other side, who would itself do the same, thus provoking the earlier group to increase its offensive and defensive actions thereby setting off an escalating spiral. Sinhalese have a fear, a minority complex, of living in a region with more than seventy-two million Tamils[12] in south India who they are taught have been invading Sri Lanka periodically throughout history, creating also a 'historical memory', a 'historical fear'. The Tamils in Sri Lanka, fearing the majority Sinhalese after facing repeated mob violence and state terror, have reacted with militancy, violence and separatism, setting off the spiral. One could almost say that the 1983 pogrom was the 'tipping point', though there were developments before that, which sent an unequivocal message to Tamils and drove their youth into militancy. Rather than security dilemma arising out of a state of anarchy, as it is usually conceived in international relations theory, in Sri Lanka, anarchy — insecurity, breakdown of law and order, delegitimization of political authority, refugees and displacement, collective trauma and social chaos, terror and

---

[11] There were exceptions to aggressive religiosity such as Francis Xavier who was invited by the people of Mannar to come and preach to them and many Catholics showed their faith by refusing to reconvert when ordered by the Tamil king Changiliyan, leading to their massacre.

[12] According to Government of India (2011).

counter-terror (see Chapter 1B) — was the result of the bitter contest for political power, control and authority, rather than the cause (Cordell and Wolff 2010).

Multiple Histories

Regardless of how far into the past we trace the origins of the various strands of ethnic consciousness, proto-nationalism or nascent forms remain contentious. Even more so, the continuing acrimonious debate as to which ethnic group came first has political consequences. However, there is no evidence of the claimed mass migration from different parts of India (Sinhalese claim 'Aryan' migration from north India while Tamils claim south Indian origins). The people, who are now labelled Sinhala and Tamil, seem to have evolved from the same basic indigenous stock with considerable infusion from frequent migrations from south India over the years. If the genes of the two groups were studied, there would be few differences except perhaps for some genetic clustering which could be due to the more recent separate cultural evolution. Until recent times, the whole of south India and Sri Lanka formed a single unit, the Palk Strait acting more as a 'unifier' (for easy fishing, trade and travel) than a geographical boundary. The landmasses separated only nine thousand years ago (Indrapala 2007). Even after that event, there was constant movement of people, ideas, language, culture and goods back and forth. There were several centres of power, rises and falls of ruling dynasties and allying with and fighting against each other, what Tambiah (1992) appropriately describes as 'pulsating galactic polities'. Armies were mixed, with mercenaries from different areas granted land after any fighting was over to settle in and merge with the local population. Brides were exchanged, and royal matrimonial alliances were common. Ignoring equal genetic contribution from the female side in racial theories is a clear manifestation of exclusive male chauvinism. What appears to have happened is a gradual process of transformation of the local, autochthonous inhabitants by influences from mainland India, supplemented by the movement of traders, craftsmen, skilled workers, mercenaries, prisoners of war, brides and others in both directions (Indrapala 2007; Wickramasinghe 2006). Some merged into the local population without a trace, others assimilating as a separate group or sub-caste (De Silva 2005). The current ethnic differentiation would have resulted from the physical barrier created by the malarial jungles separating the two centres of power after the collapse of the Anuradhapura and Polonnaruwa kingdoms, and different cultural influences from outside.

Exemplifying this process of 'ethnogenesis' are the Karava, Salagama and Durava castes, relatively recent migrants from south Indian or Dravidian stock, kin to the Tamils, who settled in south-west Sri Lanka and were completely absorbed into the Sinhala social hierarchy by the process of 'inferiorization', that is, assigned to an inferior position (Eller 1999; Roberts 1982). In time, people of the Karava caste became the driving force of the low-country Sinhalese, who adapted well to the colonial conquest, to become wealthy entrepreneurs and leaders of the national elite. Migettuwatte Gunananda, a Salagama bhikkhu, was part of the Sinhala-Buddhist resurgence, leading the debates against Christianity in the late nineteenth century. Throughout Sri Lankan history, people came not only from various parts of India but also from Java, Malaya, Arabia, China and Europe. People also migrated out of and within Sri Lanka, freely switched from one language to another—ethnic, linguistic and religious identities were fluid.

In a context of competing aspirants to the throne, feuding dynasties and potential royal lineages there was a historic need to legitimize a particular ruler or a favoured line as well as to secure political support for particular religious sects. The mythohistorical chronicle, *Mahavamsa*, played this pivotal role and has continued to do so up to the present— President Jayewardene had it updated (Kemper 1990) and President Rajapaksa has recently expressed a similar intention (Gunasekara 2011). It is understandable that the Sinhala-Buddhist credentials of a ruler would have been promoted by the Theravada Buddhist clergy who would have had a vested interest in maintaining their influence in court. As a consequence, the chronicles (other *vamsa* texts, poems and edicts from the royal court) have their favourite kings patronizing the Buddhist religion and clergy, building viharas, maintaining the sangha and nurturing their ideology.[13] Sinhala-Buddhist credentials have become a prerequisite for even present-day rulers (for instance, the repackaging of S. W. R. D. Bandaranaike and J. R. Jayewardene). There is also the historical contest between orthodox Theravada and heterodox Mahayana sects, the

---

[13] It is significant that some of these kings were not Sinhala Buddhist. For example, in addition to a number of Kalinga and Pandyan rulers, Vijayabahu, Vikramabahu, Gajabahu, the Tamil horse-traders Sena and Guthaka, Elara and the last Kandyan kings were 'Hindu', and Mahasena supported the rival heterodox Mahayana sect of Abhayagiri. Even the Sinhala-Buddhist examples had Tamil ancestors. For example, the greatest of them, Parakramabahu's grandfather was a Pandyan prince. Many of the conflicts were between or within dynasties. There was a long-standing, bitter, long-drawn-out feud between the Lambakannas and Moriya clans lasting well into the seventh century. Others included the Kalingas, Tarachchas and Balibhojakas. The 'Sinhala' dynasty or lineage was one of those competing for power until it eventually became ascendant for some periods, perhaps with the backing of the clergy. The last kings of Sri Lanka were of the Nayakkar dynasty from south India.

Mahavihara and Abhayagiri viharas, its bhikkhus, congregation and royal supporters. Historically, it is noteworthy that during the Anuradhapura period, Mahayana may have had more numerous followers than Theravada. Mahayana forms of Buddhist worship, images, rituals, ceremonies and devotion have had a profound influence on Sri Lankan religious practice (De Silva 2005). For example, the deeply psycho-culturally symbolic politico-national ceremonies, rituals and devotion surrounding Buddha's tooth relics are Mahayanist. Tantric beliefs and practices, for example, around the female (Shakti or Devi) principle such as the goddesses Tara and Pattini, have also contributed profoundly to Sinhala-Buddhist and Tamil collective (un)consciousness (Obeyesekere 1984).

The much espoused pure Sinhala-Buddhist identity of today does not seem to have been a feature of the general population in earlier times where identity appears to have been a heterogeneous one. It represented only the royal, official or at least only one strand of ideas, ideologies and influence. It is extremely difficult to access the consciousness, thinking and emotions of common people in the past. Unfortunately ordinary people are invisible in historical accounts. They would have understood events in their own way, inhabiting very different lifeworlds in what Chatterjee (2004) calls 'heterogeneous time', in contrast to the 'homogenising time' of the nationalistic narrative. There can be no doubt that individual elements of what constitute present-day ethnic characteristics have evolved from historic roots. Dharmadasa (1996), Roberts (2004), Pieris (2010) and Indrapala (2007) have traced back Sinhala and Tamil consciousness to precolonial times. Much of the recorded wrangling took place in the centre, capitals and courts. Not much is known about the periphery, the village life and people who existed outside royal courts. What were their experiences, their consciousness? It would be correct to surmise that a significant part of the population lived around the centre, the big cities and trading networks that would have been directly under the control and influence of the kings, or at least his loyal chieftains. However, as one proceeded outward to the villages the amount of control and influence would have decreased markedly. Modern centralized administrative control, strict and clear boundaries of state and a network of reciprocal obligations, responsibilities and relationships would not have existed. Concepts of nation states, sovereignty, independent countries with clear geographical demarcation and subject people are fairly recent western constructs.[14] Borders were porous; outlying chiefs were constantly trying

---

[14] Tamil nationalists would contend that Ceylon was a colonial construct. The unification of the island under one administration occurred when the British finally conquered the Kandyan kingdom, built roads and railways to connect outlying parts and developed administrative mechanisms. Earlier it had been administered from Madras under the

to be independent of central control and frequently switched allegiances. Kings at the centre were always battling to retain control, to establish their rule, have the chiefs acknowledge their suzerainty and pay their tributary taxes. Centripetal forces were always threatening the centre. The situation tended to be extremely fluid, in constant flux, with considerable fighting and bitter rivalry (Tambiah 1992).

Duttugemunu, according to the *Mahavamsa*, had to put down thirty-two chiefs including some of his own family in the south, Ruhuna, before proceeding to defeat Elara and conquer Anuradhapura.[15] It is interesting that Ruhuna, the deep south, is portrayed in the chronicles as a perennial source of challenge to the centre, a hotbed of rebellion that had to be constantly defeated by strong kings extolled in the chronicles and present-day history books.[16] How did ordinary people

---

East India Company. Much of the northern part of the island had been more closely linked to south India, the Vanni jungles forming a more formidable barrier than the Palk Strait. Sinhala nationalists would point to historic periods where the country had been united under rulers like Duttugemunu and Parakramabahu. However, under modern globalization processes, physical state boundaries are becoming less salient in the face of changing international and regional economic, geopolitical and even maritime overlapping boundaries and interconnected networks. Jazeel (2009) has brilliantly explored the evolution of the geographical and spatial imagination of the islandness of Sri Lanka from different perspectives.

[15] In an epic, chivalrous personal combat in lieu of an all-out battle between the armies, which undoubtedly prevented the loss of many lives, Duttugemunu (who ruled from 161–137 BC) killed the ageing Elara. The *Mahavamsa* portrays Elara, a Chola noble from south India, as a just and righteous king who administered Anuradhapura for forty-four years, continuing state patronage of Buddhism and winning the esteem and loyalty of his subjects (Greiger 1964). The politically motivated interpretation of the battle between Elara and Duttugemunu as a racial war between Tamils and Sinhalese is not substantiated by historic or archaeological evidence (Arasaratnam 1964). Tamil generals fought for Duttugemunu while Sinhalese royalty including the brother of Duttugemunu allied with Elara. It is recorded in the *Mahavamsa* that Duttugemunu ordered that Elara's body be given full honours and after cremating it with appropriate rites, he caused a monument (*caitiya*) to be erected. Moreover, he ordered that all music must cease whenever anyone passed the monument, which order was being honoured up to recent times. The legend emphasises that Duttugemunu was a champion of Buddhism ('not for the joy of sovereignty is this toil of mine, my striving has been ever to establish the doctrine of Sambuddha' [*Mahavamsa* 25: 17]) and fought to re-establish the faith, while expelling the Hindu heresy, referring to Damilas (Tamils) as 'unbelievers and men of evil life, not more to be esteemed than the rest' and by slaying them 'rises no hindrance on the way to heaven' (*Mahavamsa* 25: 109–11). The moral of the story is clear. It marks the beginning of Sinhala-Buddhist nationalism and the idea that the island must be preserved as a seat of Sinhalese political power and monopolized by the Buddhist faith (Farmer 1963). The myth built around Duttugemunu is a favourite theme of present-day Sinhala-Buddhist politicians who at times portray themselves as modern-day versions of the warrior hero. National leaders have often re-enacted the symbolic psycho-cultural narrative; the cabinet became involved in the theatrical performance, proclaiming the tomb of Elara as that of Duttugemunu in 1980 (Rutnam 1981).

perceive the periodic taxation, requirement for *Rajakariya* (compulsory labour for the crown), the hard labour that would have been extracted to build the vast public monuments and recruitment into the army to fight and die? It has been pointed out that some of these outward expansionary conquests, for example, by the greatest Sinhala king, Parakramabahu, eventually led to exhaustion of local resources, ruin of the economy and neglect of the vast irrigation works that led to their breakdown, breeding of malaria (Demographic Training and Research Unit 1976) and necessitated the movement of the seat of the kingdom to Polonnaruwa. Yet, the collapse of the Anuradhapura and Polonnaruwa kingdoms has been portrayed as being due to frequent invasions from Tamils from south India, and thus the Sinhalese are said to suffer from a 'historic fear' that explains their present-day anti-Tamil animosity.

The Sinhala language itself evolved historically, perhaps from the second century AD (De Silva 2005), from several sources: Hela, several Prakrits (Indic vernacular dialects), Pali (a more formalized Prakrit), Sanskrit and Tamil. It took its present form with promotion by Anagarika Dharmapala and the print media (the so-called 'print nationalism' or 'print capitalism'). The alphabets of present-day Sinhala and Tamil are amazingly similar if not identical; as are so many words and idioms, and the vocabulary, sentence structure and grammar. The legendary account of the introduction of Buddhism to Sri Lanka has Mahinda, the son of Emperor Ashoka of India, converting the king, Devanampiya Tissa at Mihintale around the third century BC. However, the dramatized version would not represent the slower historical process of a gradually increasing influence and acceptance of the religion in the island. Some idea of the new religion would have been introduced by commercial travellers, immigrants and emissaries. The actual work of conversion and implantation of concepts and practices among the common people must have been carried out over a long period by a succession of devoted missionaries, many of whom would have come from south India, where Buddhism flourished in this early period, but was later persecuted and driven out by Hindu revival and extremism to find safe refuge in Sri Lanka. There was rich reciprocal exchange with south Indian Buddhist centres like Kanchi, Badaratittha, Nagapattinam and Nagarjunakonda and much of the early writings and development of Buddhism, particularly the original Pali texts, were done by south Indian (likely Tamil) bhikkhus like Buddhaghosa, Buddhadatta

---

[16] This 'particularism' and 'separatism' (De Silva 1981) appears to have continued until the recent uprisings of the JVP in the 1970s and 1980s. JVP's power base is the deep south, and their call on anti-foreign, anti-centre sentiments has evoked a sympathetic response, leading to their eventual co-option into the ruling elite in the 2000s.

and Dhammapala among others (De Silva 2005). Buddhaghosa wrote the *Visuddhimagga*, the basic *Abhidhamma* text of Theravada Buddhism in the fifth century AD at the Mahavihara in Anuradhapura. Ven. Nanamoli, a British bhikkhu, translated it into English as *The Path of Purification* at the Island Hermitage in Dodanduwa, Ceylon and it has now run into five editions (Buddhaghosa 1991).

The 'discovery', translation and publication by the British of the *Mahavamsa*, the reconstruction of the ruins of what was later to be called Anuradhapura and Polonnaruwa and the particular 'historical' interpretation and narratives constructed at that point of time must be understood in the prevailing colonial context (Jeganathan 1995). Significantly, the *Mahavamsa* was first translated into English from Pali before it was translated into Sinhala and that was from the English translation. It was clearly not widely known at the time of its 'discovery' among the people of the time (Rogers 1990), though the narrative accounts would have been part of common folklore kept alive by the Buddhist sangha.

Discussing Nissan's (1989) important work on Anuradhapura, Jeganathan (1995) shows how the British 'discovery' and step-by-step construction of the ancient Anuradhapura civilization from 1868 met an immediate need of the colonial power to transport a large number of indentured labour from south India through the North Central Province (a jungle territory that had to be claimed, developed and legitimized for which naming and making Anuradhapura the capital served the colonial project) to the coffee and later tea plantations in the hill country to offset the rebellious tendency in the Kandyan region. These colonial constructions of an 'ancient civilization' were later, towards the end of the nineteenth century, to be appropriated in remarkably similar detail by the Sinhala–Buddhist resurgence as the foundation of their identity.

It is interesting that the low-country and Kandyan Sinhalese were considered different groups only a century ago, more so than the Sinhala–Tamil demarcation, which shared many caste overlaps and were not in opposition (Wickramasinghe 2006). The low-country Sinhalese had been exposed to colonial influences from 1505, first the Portuguese, then the Dutch, followed by the British in 1796. Many had converted nominally to Catholicism and later Protestantism, to later revert to their original 'religious' system. The idea of masks that can be removed and others substituted in their place has been suggested in the case of Tamil Hindus who became nominally Christian. A form of 'double consciousness' has been described by Du Bois (Du Bois 1989; Gilroy 1993) that allows oppressed people to live in two worlds simultaneously. However, there may not have been a need for the different 'religious' systems to be exclusive of each other as in Western categorization. Religion as a 'demarcated system of doctrines-scriptures-beliefs' that one affirms and owes allegiance to in opposition to rival religions are modern European constructs (Scott 2000). It may have been possible for non-European communities in earlier times to experience hybrid 'religious' beliefs, fulfilling different needs and explaining different parts of life and the world. Scott (1996) shows that the modern Sri Lankan conception of religion(s) is something that has developed in response to how Christianity defined and projected itself. 'Religious cultures' may have been transformed into rival systems of doctrine, faith, practices, beliefs, propositions, truth claims and subject positions. It is interesting that present-day Buddhism and Hinduism, sometimes called Protestant Buddhism (Gombrich and Obeyesekere 1988) and Protestant Hinduism, in opposition to the challenge of Christianity, adopted the same methods used in Christian proselytization. Thus, the practice of sermons, preaching, regular services, prayers and observance of religious festivals—for example, Vesak—catechistic nature of teachings, Western-style organization, Young Men's Buddhist Association (modelled on Young Men's Christian Association), production of tracts, pamphlets, holy books, conversion, Sunday schools for children and mission schools were taken from Christianity, often by enthusiasts like Arumuga Navalar and Anagarika Dharmapala who had first studied in Christian mission schools.

Gombrich and Obeyesekere (1988), Mendis (1963) and Kapferer (1988) have documented that the majority of common Sinhala people practise a mixture of folk religion, Hinduism, Tantra and Buddhism. This would have been more so when we proceed backwards in time (the current ethnic conflict and pressures for racial purity compelling more prescribed, orthodox practices). Hindu gods were domesticated and incorporated into the Buddhist pantheon, drawing their *varan* (authority) from the Buddha (Gombrich and Obeyesekere 1988; Kapferer 1988; Roberts 2004). Both Buddhist and Hindu practices appear to have coexisted peacefully and satisfied the complementary needs of the people who propitiated the Hindu gods for their immediate needs and for devotional worship including folk, Tantra and Mahayana practices while they looked to Theravada Buddhism for their next life, accumulation of merit and for intellectual and moral edification (De Silva 2005; Mendis 1963).

Buddha and more so, Uppalavanna, mentioned in the *Mahavamsa* as being sent by the king of the Gods, Sakka, to protect the island, Saman, Vibhishana, Skanda or Kataragama Devayo and Pattini have been added to the pantheon of gods of the Sinhalese, often within the same temple. In addition, the Christian Jesus, Mary and saints as well as some symbols of the Islamic faith have found their way into the pantheon of the island people, as can be seen hanging side by side in a row in buses and the ubiquitous three-wheel taxis, as guardian deities to secure their safety on the roads (Walters 1995). The temples in Kataragama, Bellanvilla,

Koneswaram, Thiruketheeswaram, Madhu church and smaller shrines attract thousands of worshipers from all communities who find no incongruence in the common practices. There is an extraordinary syncretism of religious and spiritual practices that is uniquely Sri Lankan, which is being lost in the purist orthodoxy of the present-day ethnic conflict. Similarly, the overarching concept of Hinduism invented by the British covers a conglomeration of ritual practices, supernatural events, sorcery and beliefs that includes a plethora of gods, deities, good and evil spirits, ghosts and assorted supernatural beings (Somasundaram and Sivayokan 2005). Apart from all this variety in the Tamil and Sinhala religious beliefs and practices, there are popular charismatic movements common to Sinhala, Tamil and Muslim followers like Sai Baba, Aulia Rahman and Muhammad Raheem Bawa Muhaiyaddeen. It is significant that the dominant Tamil militant group had the most difficulty with the unorthodox, charismatic Christian movements when they engineered the mass exodus of people from Jaffna in 1995 (UTHR-J 1995a). Their defiance and resistance was so strong that they had to physically beat up a pastor and forcefully evict the sect from Jaffna. In contrast, I had the opportunity to interact closely with a group of young Tamil mainstream Christian seminary students and pastors (and observe many others) in Jaffna. I found that in their mindset, private conversations and actions, they were much more enamoured with, loyal to and in awe of the LTTE leader, Prabhakaran, than Jesus Christ although they continued to preach the customary sermons and lead community prayers. The militant leader was easily much more prominent and present in their consciousness than the remote god. In the current politically charged situation, for most people, ethnic consciousness tends to intrude into consciousness with an imperative force. Mainstream Christian churches such as the Catholic and Protestant churches, straddling both ethnic groups, could have played a constructive role in unifying and bridging divisions, but have tragically failed to do so. In some instances, they have reversed harmonious relationships into splits along ethnic lines.

While the low-country Sinhalese engaged with the colonial enterprise and thereby improved socio-economically, the Kandyan Sinhalese resisted. They preserved the more 'pure' form of Sinhala Buddhism, falling to the British only in 1815. Yet, the last ruling dynasty in the Kandyan kingdom was the south Indian Nayakkar, and some Sinhala chieftains even signed the treaty with the British in Tamil. In all probability, Tamil was the court language. Court and formal practices were Brahmanical Hindu rituals, which continue to the present day in modified form (such as official state functions). It is ironic that many patriots who opposed the British and rebelled violently in 1817–18 and 1848 were banished and slipped into historic oblivion while those who cooperated with the British (and were considered 'traitors' then) rose to positions of power and formed the lineage to the present-day elite, ruling class and political leadership. They have managed to suppress their history of collaboration in their political rhetoric and claim patriotic credit in place of those who resisted and had to escape, to eventually become forgotten peasants in the east (Hoole 2001).

There had been considerable intermarriages between the Sinhalese, notably among the nobility, and south Indian women. It is said reliably that both groups considered themselves as 'sons of the soil' (Nissan and Stirrat 1990). In relation to the Sri Lankan Tamil identity formation, Indrapala (2007) has traced the origins to as far back as 300 BC as the Demala group who would have evolved from the indigenous Nagas in the north. South Indian influences from the Telugus, Kannadigas and Keralites, the people of the Coromandel and Malabar coasts as well as the various Pandyan, Pallava, Chola, Chera, Kalinga and Vijayanagar empires and the evolving local Sinhala population would have all made contributions. Many areas in the north had been inhabited by Sinhala-speaking people as can be seen by names of places, and many Tamils were Buddhist until the Hindu resurgence after the seventh century. The evolving Sinhala- and Tamil-speaking people themselves did not appear to have been in conflict.[17] Considerable interaction, intermarriages and mutual relationships, boundary crossing and assimilation seem to have been common. Perhaps it was with the growth of the dense, malaria-infested forests that separated the north from the rest of the island that separate developmental trajectories took place. With the advent of the Portuguese in the region from the 1500s and their control of the sea routes, the close relationship that the Tamils, particularly in the north, had with south India was effectively cut off, leaving the Sri Lankan Tamil identity to develop independently.[18] Thus, the Sri Lankan and Indian

---

[17] This is not to say that there was no conflict between different rulers and dynasties. The rich intertwining of modern-day 'ethnicities' can be seen, for example, during the 'last glorious period of Sinhalese history' (Paranavitana and Nicholas 1961), when Parakramabahu VI became king of Kotte with Chinese assistance (China actually invaded Sri Lanka twice during the Ming dynasty) to repulse an invasion by a Kannadiga army from the Vijayanagar empire and sent Prince Perumal (Sapumal in Sinhala), son of a Chola nobleman, north to conquer Jaffna, the Vanni and the east. Jaffna fell in 1450 despite a bitter hand-to-hand struggle led by a Muslim warrior, Yon Vadakra. When Sapumal had to return to Kotte to ascend the throne as Vanni Bhaveneka Bahu VI after putting down the 'Sinhala' rebellion, the deposed king of Jaffna, Arya Chakravati Kanakacuriyan, was able to return from India to regain his throne. The image of Sapumal Kumaraya is evoked in relation to modern-day 'conquerors' of Jaffna, for example, in 1995 by the Defence Minister General Ratwatte, during symbolic ceremonies in Colombo.

[18] The link of the north with the south of the island had been already effectively blocked by the growth of the dense malaria-ridden forests across the centre, with the collapse of the Anuradhapura and Polonnaruwa kingdoms.

Tamil identities are said to be different as shown by the tendency for the Sri Lankan Tamils to dissociate themselves from the recent migration of Tamils from south India to the central plantation areas under the British. This was apparent by the indifference shown by Sri Lankan Tamils to the plight of the hill-country Tamils when the newly independent state disenfranchised them by an act of the Sri Lankan Parliament. The hill-country Tamils formed 12 per cent of the total population[19] of the island at that time. They were brought as bonded labourers from 1820 onwards from south India to work for the British colonial plantation system and had to survive an extremely perilous overland journey, with large numbers perishing on the way, to be crowded into 'line rooms'[20] with hardly any sanitary, recreational, cultural, educational or medical facilities. They were made to work without adequate rest or nutrition on very poor subsistence wages, paying back their *kanganies* (foremen) for bringing them here and were restricted to the plantations, amidst the surrounding, resentful Sinhala villages. Their lot has not improved much over the intervening years. The predominantly Sinhala state has continued to be wary of this large Tamil population with potential power and has sought to repatriate them back through repeated negotiations and agreements with India.[21] Their leaders, like Thondaman Sr., have managed to win some concessions through adroit political practices, aligning with the party in power. Many were granted citizenship, and wages and conditions in the plantations have improved. However they remain the most disadvantaged and exploited group in Sri Lanka (Minority Rights Group International 2011). Although politically, some leaders have attempted to forge links between the Sri Lankan and Indian Tamils, there continues to be cultural distance between the groups as shown by pejorative nicknames and perceptions (Daniel 1996). However, when the Indian Tamils faced starvation under the state nationalization policies and violence in 1977, and again after the pogrom of July 1983, they sought refuge in northern Tamil areas, settling in the Vanni (UTHR-J 1993b) to be displaced once again by the fighting in 2009 into the Vavuniya internments camps.

The historical development of the Tamils in the east is less clear. But Whitaker (1990) has described it as a compound of many histories with a string of conflicts at the regional, village, inter-caste and intra-caste levels.

[19] At one point the Indian Tamil population was more than the Sri Lankan Tamil population.

[20] Accommodation built in lines on hillsides with one small room per family (Minority Rights Group International 2011).

[21] The Indian Tamil population has been halved since independence through repatriation to India under the Sirimavo–Shastri pact of the mid-1960s and other agreements with India.

There was considerable migration from the Malabar coast of south India, giving rise to the Mukkuvar caste. The indigenous Veddas who, facing extinction, seem to have sought sanctuary in the east, have developed a consciousness of victimhood on the margin of other identities (Thangarajah 1995). There also seems to have been suzerainty by the Kandyan kingdom and migration of persecuted people to settle in the east via Kandy. Thus, when the Muslims were persecuted by the Portuguese, they found sanctuary in the Kandyan kingdom and settled down in the east. Some Sinhalese who rebelled against the British in 1818 and 1848 escaped to settle in Gomarankadawela in Trincomalee and Uhana and Panama in Ampara (Hoole 2001). These movements and history may have contributed to the multi-ethnic, plural identity of the eastern polity. Trincomalee being a natural port has attracted the Mahayana Buddhists, Cholas and under the colonial rulers a more cosmopolitan mix including the Chinese. There are communities in the east who are very conscious of being mixed and even sport Sinhalese names, but have suffered like the Tamils and have contributed to the Tamil militancy.

In more recent times, particularly in the twentieth century and after, the Tamils and Muslims perceive themselves as having separate political and ethnic identities. Both speak Tamil as their mother tongue and seem to have come mainly from the same parts of south India though at different times; the Muslims are also partly of Arabian origin. The Muslims from the east and north appear to have shared much of the same culture with the Tamils and are said to have lived in the east like the *puttu* and *thengai pu* in the *puttu kullal* (cheek and jowl) without much (relatively) animosity down the ages. Though McGilvray (2008) does report some limited Tamil–Muslim *kullapams* (turmoil) in the twentieth century, these conflicts appear to have been on a minor scale and, more likely, less problematic than the intra-group, particularly inter-caste, conflicts among the eastern Tamils reported by Whitaker (1990). A telling historic event illustrates how administrative acts may determine the process of ethnogenesis (Nissan and Stirrat 1990). In the 1880s, when the representation in the Legislative Council was under review by the British, Sir Ponnambalam Ramanathan, contriving to represent the entire Tamil-speaking population, insisted that Tamil Muslims were ethnically Tamil, arguing that Muslims were emigrants from southern India, spoke the same language at home, had similar customs and physical features and were in reality Tamils who had adopted Islam. However, elite Muslims of that time, wanting representation of the mercantile interests of the trading class from Colombo (Ismail 1995), maintained that although there had been much intermarriage with Tamil women, since their male ancestors had originally come from Arabia, they were a separate racial entity (Rogers 1990). The British accepted this position, perhaps as their usual strategy of divide and rule, thereby institutionalizing Muslim differences and helped 'create' a Muslim identity (Ismail 1995). The more current actions of Tamil militants like the LTTE and the Sri Lankan state have driven the two groups apart, though many still recognize their common ecological situation, grievances and needs. The more commercial contextual situation of the Muslims in the south-west may be different and so would their consciousness. Much of the Muslim leadership which had come from this sector has tended to mould Muslim consciousness in their direction until the eastern Muslims asserted themselves under the SLMC. Similarly, the Tamils of the east have always been suspicious of their Jaffna counterparts (McGilvray 2008) and felt a strong eastern identity, which was highlighted when the LTTE–Karuna split occurred.[22] Further, the Tamils living outside the north-east having lived more closely with other communities and, having been more exposed to modern cosmopolitan influences, possess a wider consciousness. However, the resurgence of a strong Sinhala-Buddhist chauvinism, majoritarian state policies and violence directed against these Tamils have driven them together. Since independence, the state has promoted colonization, which introduced a large number of Sinhala settlers and forced the expulsion of entire Tamil and Muslim villages. This has completely changed the demographical pattern of the east (Manogaran 1994).

The fighting during the ethnic war resulted in the displacement of Tamil, Muslim and Sinhala communities some of whom have not been allowed to return. Despite the destruction of the LTTE, the north and east remain heavily militarized, with the state employing earlier ethnicity-based counter-insurgency strategies of selective colonization in areas such as Ampara and restricting access to return in Muthur and Sampoor while approving projects for multinational companies; all this portends ominously for the future (Minority Rights Group International 2011).

In the past, up to the present elder generation, caste considerations and disputes took primacy, particularly in the more caste conscious Tamil community. Personal affronts, family insults and boundary infringements generated considerable emotions and violent group reactions. Social relations, marriage alliances and institutions functioned along caste lines. However, modernization with its economic mobilization, liberalization and the prolonged civil war has frequently forced different castes together in displaced and refugee populations. Significantly, the more egalitarian policies of the Tamil militants (Sivathamby 2005) and consequences of ethnic conflict (Somasundaram 2007a) have resulted in the lowering

[22] There were a few Sinhala and many Muslim militants in the LTTE during its early stages but its exclusive practices, like the massacre of Sinhala and Muslim civilians, have driven them out.

of caste barriers. During the conflict though ethnic consciousness overshadowed and in many ways replaced caste consciousness,[23] it appears to be making a post-war comeback (Somasundaram and Sivayokan 2013).

Even within present-day ethnic groups, there is considerable variation among members, particularly at the psychosocial borders. There are considerable numbers who are in the process of assimilating from one group into another, thus retaining some aspects of the old consciousness while adopting the new. This is the case with the fishing community in Negombo who are relatively recent migrants from south India. In my practice as a psychiatrist, I have come across individuals who having belonged to another group, for example, who were born Sinhala, with Sinhala parents and brought up as such, moved to the north for a variety of reasons (marriage, daughter's, son's or other kin's marriage, work, alienation from their original group) several decades ago and have adapted to living incognito amidst the Tamil community as one of them without the community being aware of their original identity, particularly in these polarized times. It is only through in-depth interviews that these confidential details became known. Then there are the mixed marriages, Sinhala and Tamil, for example. In Trincomalee I came across numerous such cases during my work and likewise in cities like Colombo, where identities become very complicated, confused, vague and sometimes tragic, particularly among the children. Some of these families migrate overseas to escape the toxic environment at home.

The cases of so-called 'miscegenation', where an occupying army would have covert relationships[24] that produced mixed offspring who grow up as belonging to the mother's ethnic group are examples of hybridity. This could be quite obvious as in the case of the Portuguese miscegenation, where even today their contribution can be seen in people with brown or blue-green eyes. The Portuguese and Dutch left behind the vibrant Burgher community, which migrated out to countries like Australia after the Sinhala-only movement. But in the case of the current occupying Sinhala army, offspring born within wedlock, that is, where the soldier takes advantage of a married woman while the husband is

---

[23] Interestingly, the original Sanskrit term, jati, is used in Sinhala and Tamil for caste, but in Sinhala, has been made to cover ethnicity, and it now even encompasses the national as *jathika chinthanaya*.

[24] Sometimes forced, but often consensual (even then containing an element of coercion due to fear and potential use of the power they had over their victims, often lonely housewives). This has been true all over the world at all times. More recent examples are from South East Asian countries like Thailand and Philippines; as a legacy of the American war in Vietnam, the GIs used to go on their R & R leave to the capitals of these countries where a complex 'red light' industry sprang up to service them.

away at work and visiting on the pretext of routine checking,[25] the child may be brought up like the proverbial cuckoo (never to be thrown out or disowned), unknown to everyone, especially the child. Only the mother would know and even she may have some doubt which 'fades in memory' over time. This child shares the ethnic consciousness of the group that she grows up in. Another situation has developed in the post-war Vanni resettlement process. An estimated ninety thousand widows in the north-east, many of them who lost their husbands to the war, have to rebuild their shattered lives as single-headed families. Ostracized by traditional Tamil society and in dire economic straits, they are compelled to depend on the military, which controls most needs, whether housing, rations, allowances, subsidies and/or schooling. They are then placed in a vulnerable and helpless position (ICG 2011). They are also lonely and in need of help to complete masculine tasks. Soldiers help out by lending a hand in rebuilding their houses in remote villages. They are able to get the land and housing loan, materials and other benefits with their military influence. Natural albeit temporary friendships and liaisons are struck out of mutual need and attraction. A child follows who would eventually inherit the house and land but the soldier moves on. The practical arrangement results in mutual benefit. The ICG (2011) report also mentions that some returning Muslim men engaging with the socially marginalized widows. The children of mixed relationships are living proof that ethnicity is not something intrinsic or in the blood but completely extrinsic, constructed by upbringing, the socialization process. People belonging to each ethnic group have multiple identities — gender, caste, occupation, socio-economic class, village or residence, family, extended family, social groups (societies, clubs and organizations) — which would overlap and intersect with their language, religion and ethnic identities in varying and fluid ways. Then there would be 'anomalies' like Sinhala Christian further divisible into Catholic, Protestant, various sub-sects and so forth. As people begin to identify, define and experience themselves as these categories they become 'objectified' (Cohn 1987).

Belonging to a specific geographical territory, a homeland, is a fundamental aspect of ethno-national identity. In *The Territorial Imperative*, Ardrey (1967) attributes most of man's ills to his drive to conquer and maintain a geographical territory. The problem of territoriality is at the centre of the Sinhala–Tamil ethnic conflict. The majority Sinhala-Buddhist ethno-national consciousness has been built up to identify itself with the

---

[25] According to a reliable, Sinhala human rights worker, some of these instances were part of a deliberate counter-insurgency strategy (see Chapter 1B) used by the army intelligence for gathering information. 'Handsome' and charming '007's would be let loose in the community for this purpose.

whole island (*Sinhadeepa*). They strongly feel that the other ethnic groups inhabiting the island are migrants whose home territory is elsewhere. The *bhumiputra* theory holds that they are the legitimate sons of the soil and have all rights procuring from it. The Tamils on the other hand, also regard themselves as heirs to the land, a well-demarcated but restricted area—the north and the east of the island—and claim to have been living in their homeland from historic times. There is further disagreement as to whether the north and east are to be merged and whether the Muslims have a right to a territory of their own. Even India's intervention can be seen as a defence of its 'geopolitical' territory—India now expanding its territoriality to include the whole of South Asia (which Nehru (1985) once dreamed of) and taking action to maintain its permanent position and security in the region.

Bastian (1994) argues:

> Control over land in the Northern and Eastern Provinces can be termed the major issue in the ethnic conflict of Sri Lanka. This control has a political and economic dimension and an identity dimension as far as the Sri Lankan Tamil minority is concerned. As a result, settlement of people in these provinces through state-sponsored 'colonization' schemes in the past has been the most controversial issue in the ethnic conflict of Sri Lanka. The possible changes of the ethnic composition in these areas through such programmes and its implications for political power have been a bone of contention. These programmes also threaten an economic resource base of the Tamil minority and, finally, they undermine the basis of their ethnic identity.

Conclusion

The current ethnic polarization appears to have evolved from colonial and postcolonial experiences which have tended to divide people along racial lines. Before those times, it is doubtful whether people experienced themselves in modern ethnic categories and people who spoke different languages appear to have coexisted in relative harmony though there was dynastic feuding, intense rivalry among kings and inter-caste conflicts. When one analyses the various factors that are preventing a lasting solution to the ethnic strife, it is the polarized ethnic consciousness of the two groups—Sinhalese and Tamil—more than anything else that comes in the way of an amicable resolution. It is only by making people more aware that this polarization can be overcome.

Another way to break the vicious cycle of conflict would be to address the genuine grievances of the minorities (Minority Rights Group International 2011). However, the emotional investment in the Sinhala-only ideology, consequent unconscious resistance and lack of political will, as with many similar issues, make it difficult. According to Jayadeva Uyangoda (1994) what is fundamental is the 'unwillingness of the leading political forces of the majority Sinhalese society to come to terms with the democratic requirements of an ethnically pluralistic political order'. A change in attitude and state of mind to reconciliation, compassion and mutual understanding could take advantage of the opportunity created by the ending of the direct fighting in 2009 to usher in a new beginning. Unfortunately, polarized ethnic consciousness continues to direct state thinking and policy. There has only been more hardening and entrenchment of polarized ethnic consciousness; the Gordian knot becomes more entangled day by day. And that is the karma of violence. This book is a plea for resisting the narrower, exclusive, nationalistic interpellation; towards more enabling conditions of being, reimagining and experiencing wider, more inclusive notions of community (Ismail 2000), a disentangling of the tangle.

Tragically, in Sri Lanka, we have seen that when harmony, conciliation and amity breaks down between groups due to ethnic polarization, it leads to conflict, violence and ethnic strife. Ethnic civil war, with modern techniques of terror and counter-terror, results in untold misery for civilians.

B.

Heart of Terror*

... by terror thereof, he [government] is enabled to form the wills of them all, ...

—Thomas Hobbes, *Leviathan*

The prophetic dream of Marx and the over-inspired predictions of Hegel or of Nietzsche ended by conjuring up, after the city of God had been razed to the ground, a rational or irrational State, which in both cases, however, was founded on terror.

—Albert Camus, *The Rebel*

But faced with the endemicity of torture, terror and growth of armies, we in the New World are today assailed with a new urgency. There is the effort to understand terror, in order to make others understand.

—Michael Taussig, 'Culture of Terror—Space of Death'

How does one become socialized to terror? Does it imply conformity or acquiescence to the status quo, as a friend suggested? While it is true that with repetitiveness and familiarity people learn to accommodate themselves to terror and fear, low-intensity panic remains in the shadow of waking consciousness. One cannot live in a constant state of alertness, and so the chaos one feels becomes diffused throughout the body. It surfaces frequently in dreams and chronic illnesses.

—Linda Green, 'Living in a State of Fear'

* An extract of this chapter was presented as a paper at the conference on Globalizing Religions and Cultures in the Asia Pacific, organized by the University of Adelaide from 1 to 5 December 2008 and a modified version published in the *Journal of Asian and African Studies*; see Somasundaram (2010e).

Terror has been an instrument of statecraft, diplomacy and political advocacy for centuries.... The mainstream global culture of statecraft insists that
the true antidote to terror is counter-terror.

— Ashis Nandy, 'Narcissism and Despair'

Technology and the strategy of total war have resulted in civilians becoming
the overwhelming casualties of war. Warfare is no longer something which
happens far away on the front, an empty space functionally differentiated
for conflict. In South Asia's internal conflicts, as elsewhere, modern organ-
ised political violence rests on creating institutional terror which penetrates
the entire fabric of grassroots social relations as a means of control. The
sites for confrontation with the enemy are the market-place, the community
water tap and bathing space, sites largely visited by women. The counter-
war objective is to undermine the social fabric of society, psychologically
demoralise the community and alienate their support for the 'enemy' as a
viable alternative.

— Rita Manchanda, 'Where are the Women in South Asian Conflicts?'

It was Thomas Hobbes who in 1651 first pointed out that behind the
veneer of states is the spectre of violence and threat of terror, which is
used to control and rule subject populations, for example, through the
police, military, paramilitary, armed forces, or, increasingly in the modern 'security states', through intelligence agencies and other covert operations. Conventionally, a state rules by retaining a monopoly on violence
which it rarely has to exhibit. When this control and rule is challenged,
comes under question or is weakened, the covert violence becomes more
overt, manifesting as techniques of terror. When the power to rule is contested by other parties, they may vie for control, loyalty and legitimacy
through practising terror and counter-terror tactics on the populace.

The ethnic war in Sri Lanka was a good example of the modern use of
terror on a mass scale. All parties to the conflict resorted to a dirty war
(Nordstrom 1994) with the use of terror tactics in the bitter contest for
power. The Sri Lankan state, the various Tamil militants, in particular
the LTTE, the Sinhala JVP and India, during its short intervention in the
island (1987–90) to impose peace, used mass terror to control the population, compel obedience to their dispensation and suppress dissent.
But in the scale, duration, sheer numbers of victims and in the vast
resources, national and international, available to it, it is the Sri Lankan
state that was and continues to be most guilty of the misuse of power
and the privileges that accrue to it as a state (Cooke 2011; Hoole 2001).
Though critical at times, the international community, its many organizations, diplomatic missions, the UN and aid agencies giving technical support, military hardware and training, and the global network of

socio-economic ties and mutual relationships that give covert recognition, legitimacy and tacit sanction are also indirectly implicated in what was actually going on in countries like Sri Lanka (Nordstrom 2004). While the use of external and internal terror (against its own community) by Tamil militants, particularly the LTTE, the Indian intervention and the JVP and counter-terror by the state in the south has been described (Cooke 2011; Hoole 2001; Hoole et al. 1988; Somasundaram 1998), the extent and subtle ramifications of state terror on the Tamil population have remained hidden (Somasundaram 2004). The description of the long-term psychosocial consequences of mass terror will be the main goal of subsequent sections of this book.

The conventional understanding of war does not apply to situations like that in Sri Lanka. Modern, internal, civil or ethnic wars are largely the result of postcolonial and post–Cold War forces. Decolonization, with the break-up of colonial empires and the transfer of power to urban elites, the rise of new nation states and ethno-national consciousness; concepts of freedom, liberty, democracy, capitalism and Marxism; dynamics of majoritarian politics and socialist transformation; struggles for survival amidst rapidly increasing populations and diminishing resources; and a host of other complex factors have determined the nature of power and conflicts.

War was understood as either a contest between two sovereign states or power blocks that could no longer resolve their differences through diplomacy or mutual agreements, or a glorified territorial conquest. The goal was mutual destruction or reciprocal killing and injury to the opponent (or the convincing display of such capacity) until one side 'gives in', surrenders or succumbs (Scarry 1985). With the increase in military technology, the ability to destroy and kill has also increased enormously, particularly the capacity to kill at a distance without seeing the victim(s) or experiencing the act of killing. Thus, in addition to the social sanctioning and military training to kill, natural inhibitions preventing intra-species killing are further neutralized in the ordinary soldier who carries out the business of war for his nation (Somasundaram 2009).

The number of civilian casualties has also increased dramatically; from being considered 'accidental' or 'collateral damage', they have become central. During the First World War, civilian casualties were much fewer than combatant casualties. This trend was reversed in the Second World War. Ratios of civilian deaths to combatant deaths range at around 10:1 (Machel 1996). According to Scarry (1985), in war, the desired outcome is victory, that is, the losing side is permanently deprived of the capacity to injure (by being either annihilated or enslaved or permanently occupied and policed), unable to resume fighting or recreate its power base and carries with it the power of its own enforcement of the winner's version of victory. The destruction, deaths and injuries substantiate that war has taken place and become permanently objectified and memorialized in the disposition of post-war issues.

The overarching issues that are exterior to war or form the framework for conflict are nationalistic constructions that are portrayed in terms of ideology, justice, basic rights, resources, political freedom, defensive or pre-emptive strikes, territorial legitimacy, national sovereignty or assertion of authority in a given area. As a result, the vanquished have to radically change their perception, consciousness and memory to adapt to the changed circumstances, they would need to reconstitute their schemas, constructs and ideologies to come in line with that of the victor.

The nature of modern warfare has changed to more internal, civil or ethnic issues. Violent conflicts are asymmetrical contests fought over legitimacy to power, ideologies, loyalties and identity politics in the minds of subjects using unconventional means such as propaganda, guerrilla, subversive or insurgent tactics. These conflicts rarely reach the complete, total war situations of all-out battle between two conventional armies, but tend to become chronic, 'low-intensity conflicts' of organized violence (Schauer et al. 2005). There is pervasive sociopolitical repression or merely elite power struggles. Often, there is a complex mixture of many of these elements. Bracken and Petty (1998b), in a Save the Children (UK) publication, describe the nature of current conflicts:

> Civilians are no longer 'incidental' casualties but the direct targets of violence. Mass terror becomes a deliberate strategy. Destruction of schools, houses, religious buildings, fields and crops as well as torture, rape and internment, become commonplace. Modern warfare is concerned not only to destroy life, but also ways of life. It targets social and cultural institutions and deliberately aims to undermine the means whereby people endure and recover from the suffering of war.

Summerfield (1996) adds, 'A key element of modern political violence is the creation of states of terror to penetrate the entire fabric of economic, sociocultural and political relations as a means of social control.'

Wars may never be officially declared and authorities may continue to deny that there is a war going on, admitting only to an internal security or terrorism problem. Yet, there could be thousands of civilian casualties, massive displacements, massacres, slaughter and genocide. It may not be clear who the enemy is, and who the citizen(s). Conflicting ideologies and those who profess it; socio-economic issues; in ethnic terms, a way of life, a religion or language; political and social definitions, subtle distinctions and issues may shift over time. Enemies and friends may change over time or suddenly with shifts in political power and fortune. Elimination or co-option of leaders as well as control and coercion of groups, media, governance structures and institutions and in the final analysis, the minds of ordinary people may become covert goals.

It would be instructive, as an illustrative example of other similar developments in the modern world, to inquire from a (Tamil) ethno-national perspective—granted, a one-sided view—how the situation in Sri Lanka deteriorated into the kind of civil war that has torn the country apart for the last three decades.

Historical Development of State Terror

Since its independence, the Sri Lankan state has gradually become Sinhalesized through majoritarian politics, that is, an ethnocracy (DeVotta 2004). The first act of structural violence of far-reaching significance by the new state was the disenfranchisement and further marginalization of the socially weak hill-country or plantation Tamils,[1] who were the mainstay of the Sri Lankan economy. As a result, a large number of them were forced to move to India, including the commercially powerful Chettiar community. Next, the 'Sinhala-only' Official Language Act, 1956 was a momentous introduction of structural violence into the state machinery whereby discrimination against the minorities was enacted into the very laws of the country. Dr Colvin De Silva, leader of the left Lanka Sama Samaja Party (LSSP), prophesied in Parliament, 'Two languages—one nation; one language—two nations!' The imposition of the Sinhala-only policy and concomitant discriminatory practices that were entrenched with it sharply undermined opportunities for minorities in the state sector. Under the socialist policies adapted by successive Sinhala governments, many private enterprises, including plantations and utilities, schools and other large-scale programmes were nationalized and taken over by the state. Thus the public services, armed forces, administration and public enterprises became Sinhalesized (see Table 1A.1). Large numbers of minorities led by the enterprising Burgher community, who were hybrid descendants of European migrants during four centuries of colonial rule, began leaving the country. This first wave of emigration, resulting from institutionalized discrimination, depleted the minority communities of their professional and entrepreneurial class. In response to the state's Sinhala hegemonic approach, Tamil elite politics became less pragmatic and embraced a parallel millenarian nationalism looking back to lost glory. This affected the remaining Tamils in two principal ways.

[1] Sometimes contemptuously called 'Indian Tamils', referring to their recent transport from South India as indentured labour during the British Colonial period.

With the luxury of a relatively stable future in their new homes, the expatriates emotionally financed and encouraged youth at home into separatist violence, which once monopolized by the LTTE, became fascistic and narrow-minded. Second, those who remained felt more isolated from the state and helpless, leaving them with no hope but militancy.

Another debilitating structural discrimination that made the Tamil community powerless was that it was gradually deprived of decision-making positions in the state service, while most public service positions assigned to the north and east were neither advertised nor filled, creating severe shortages in human resources.[2]

When the Tamil FP protested the passing of the Sinhala-only statute in 1956 by non-violent satyagraha in front of the Parliament, protesters were assaulted and humiliated while the prime minister, ministers and police looked on approvingly. The anti-Tamil violence soon spread in the capital and then to Gal Oya in the Eastern Province, a state-aided colonization scheme. This was the first anti-Tamil mob violence. The same pattern was to repeat itself in 1958, 1977, 1981 and finally in the 1983 pogrom, with increasing political organization, support, complicity and covert sanction from the state and armed forces (Hoole 2001; Piyadasa 1984; Vittachi 1958). Each time, in addition to the large number of Tamils killed and injured, and destruction of property, massive numbers of people were displaced; some were in refugee camps in the south and some fled to the north-east. In 1961, the Tamil FP launched a non-violent satyagraha campaign in the north-east but Sirimavo Bandaranaike,[3] the world's first woman prime minister, responded by sending in the army and declaring an emergency. This violent repression by the state of what the Tamils felt was a peaceful and legitimate struggle for their rights left many embittered. The cry for Eelam, a separate Tamil state, was first made by Chellappah Suntharalingam, a former professor of mathematics, but found no response among the Tamils at that time.

A long-standing deep fear and grievance of the Tamils is the continuing state-sponsored colonization of the north-east that has been gradually

[2] Furthermore, appointments for these vacancies were made in the south so that total numbers met budget requirement. In effect, human resources needed in the north and east were diverted to the south. The staffing positions so distorted were then frozen. Further compounding the problem was that regular upgrading of staff needs (cadres) was not done for the north and east, as it was in the south. Thus the cadre for the north and east actually declined from 1983, with severe shortages in most areas (Somasundaram 2005a). Basically, there was an unequal distribution of all grades of staff—less in the north and east and more in the rest of the country. Even within the north and east there was unequal distribution among the districts depending on political links to the ruling powers.

[3] She had taken over from her husband, S.W. R. D. Bandaranaike. He had projected himself as the champion of Sinhala Buddhism and architect of the Sinhala-only statute, but was slain by a Buddhist monk for being too moderate.

changing the demographic character in that area (Manogaran 1994). In what were predominantly Tamil-speaking areas, the influx of Sinhala settlers was radically altering the ethnic balance. For example, whole divisions like Weli Oya (earlier Manal Aaru), Seruwilla (from Kanthalai, Pankulam, Muthalikulam, Panankattimurippu, Nochchikulam, Eachilampathu) and Ampara had already become Sinhala-dominant areas. As a result, the Sinhala population in Trincomalee rose from 4.2 per cent in 1881 to 33.6 per cent in 1981 and would be higher now. Vast state resources with heavy international funding like the Mahaweli scheme[4] (Hoole 2001; UTHR-J 1993a) were mobilized to accomplish this demographic transformation using poor Sinhala peasants and armed ex-convicts (so-called island reconvicted criminals or IRCs). Tamil and Muslim inhabitants of these areas were driven out by the state's armed forces and so-called home guards. For example, the whole of the outlying fifty-two Tamil villages in the Trincomalee district, the inhabitants of Manal Aaru and more recently large tracts of the Batticaloa district have been depopulated, to be replaced often with Sinhala settlers or declared no-go high security zones (HSZs).

The Sinhala youth insurrection of April 1971 by the JVP was the 'first large-scale revolt against the government by youth in this country, and also perhaps the biggest revolt by young people in any part of the word in recorded history, the first instance of tension between generations becoming military conflict on a national scale' (de Silva 2005). The Che Guevara-style insurrection with strong elements of Sinhala nationalism was put down with considerable state terror. Between ten and sixty thousand Sinhala youth were killed, thousands detained without trial and Sirimavo Bandaranaike declared a 'state of emergency' that was to continue for six years. This was the beginning of a trend towards abuse of legal powers and authoritarianism that was to characterize Sri Lankan politics after 1977. The extension of the state of emergency was more out of political expediency to rule easily than from necessity.[5] The emergency regulations

---

[4] Mahaweli is the longest river in Sri Lanka. A human settlement and vast irrigation scheme based on the historic hydraulic system 'to restore the old glory of the Sinhala kingdom' is being developed.

[5] For example, the state of emergency continued well after the fighting with the LTTE ended in May 2009 and there was no security threat. The state continued to raise the spectre of the LTTE, alarming the Sinhala south of dangers of a LTTE regrouping or resurgence and the threat from the Tamil diaspora. The Sinhala ruling elite needed to keep the LTTE alive for its survival. The Sinhala and Tamil nationalists were mirror images. The LTTE had earlier engineered Rajapaksa's election victory in 2005 as it was more comfortable and familiar with his brand of extremist politics. In 2010, former BBC journalist Frances Harrison was present at the annual 'Heroes Day' celebration in London. She observed (Frances Harrison, pers. comm.):

I was horrified. You would have thought the war wasn't over and there hadn't been a defeat of the LTTE. It was complete denial. They had speakers from India on tape

in effect suspended normal political processes, conferring extraordinary powers on the state which found it useful in dealing with dissent and political opponents of all types.

The regime in power proceeded to 'use the machinery of the state and administrative regulations to harass and intimidate its political opponents' (de Silva 2005). This discrimination on political grounds also extended to preferential treatment of supporters of the state. Political patronage in the form of preferential recruitment and promotion within the state service became widespread and 'institutionalized'. De Silva (2005) says:

> Politicization of the public services was not restricted to key appointment at the policy-making levels, but extended through the service and intruded into the judiciary as well. The basis of appointments was political affiliation, personal connection, or still more dubious considerations. It led to both inefficiency and corruption.

The media (broadcasting, press) and later the judiciary were brought under state control. The state ownership, state industries and state involvement in all aspects of national and village life, including the cooperatives, was described as 'statism' (Balakrishnan 1992). And this state had become essentially Sinhala-only (DeVotta 2004).

A key state structural action that was to precipitate the birth of Tamil militancy in the beginning of the 1970s was the government's decision to determine university admission by a process called standardization in early 1971.[6] A high number of Tamil students had traditionally been entering the medical and engineering streams, one of the few avenues open to them due to their particular geographical context, through educational achievement to coveted professions and employment. Subsequently, the number of Tamils gaining admission to these streams plummeted. Forty-two Tamil youths were arrested in 1972 and held for two years for putting up posters peacefully against the standardization of university entrance. The 1972 republican constitution (and later, the 1978 constitution) effectively made Buddhism the state religion, confirmed the official position

---

saying Prabhakaran and Pottu Amman were still alive and things like, 'the Sinhala soldiers drink the blood of our youth'. This gave false hope to the thousands of families seeking news about the disappeared. I found the sheer delusion very disturbing — especially as there was an absolutely huge crowd. At some point there needs to be an honest revision of why the LTTE lost so badly but it seems that point has passed and there's growing polarisation and anger.

[6] A more equitable district quota system for university admissions was introduced later, around 1975.

of the Sinhala language and did away with the minimum protection of minority rights provided in the British Soulbury constitution. The state renamed itself Sri Lanka.[7]

In 1974, at the International Tamil Research Conference held in Jaffna, the police opened fire when the speeches became inflammatory, and accidentally electrocuted (by hitting the overhead cables) nine participants. In 1981, following the killing of a policeman and a Sinhala political candidate, the police retaliated with violence, including by burning the Jaffna public library that contained numerous culturally important and irreplaceable, old palm-leaf manuscripts. This burst of state terror, classed by some as cultural genocide, left a grievous hurt in the collective memory of the Tamil people. During the ethnic war in the subsequent years, many community institutions like temples, churches and schools were destroyed or damaged. Whole communities and villages were displaced, forced to leave their way of life and cultural foundations behind. Articulate leaders, intellectuals and socially motivated resources were killed (by different armed parties, state and militant) or forced to flee. Damien Short (2010) defines cultural genocide after Lemkin as destruction of the 'cultural pattern of a group, such as the language, the traditions, the monuments, archives, libraries, churches; in brief: the shrines of the soul of a nation', a form of social murder. This threat and attack at the collective heart, at its way of life, would perhaps be the most subtle terror felt by the Tamil community. Militancy (see Chapter 3D) could then be understood, as in many other parts of the world today, as the response of the youth to this threat to the life of their community.

There were other incidents during that time where the state played a direct role in the violence against Tamils on a massive scale. One was in Trincomalee during the month of June in 1983 (and again during May–September 1985) where, after the imposition of a curfew, the Sri Lankan navy went about systematically burning Tamil houses, street by street, house by house and shooting the inhabitants as they tried to escape. Another

---

[7] The colonial name had been Ceylon, from the Portuguese Zeylan. Lanka was an old name found, for example, in the Ramayana as, ironically, had been Ila, now appropriated by the Tamil Eelamist. Other names had been Hela and Taprobane. Sri was added more as an honorific to the older term Lanka used in Sinhala scriptures (Jazeel 2009). Christopher Hitchens (2007), discussing the 'grotesque' renaming of Burma as Myanmar, says,

> You can tell a lot from this sort of emphasis. Lanka is the Sinhala word for Ceylon, and sri means holy, so the name Sri Lanka expresses the concept that the island is both Sinhala and Buddhist. Tamils tend to call it Ceylon still, or to demonstrate their own nationalism by calling it Eelam. Lives are lost on the proposition.

Other symbols of ethnic contention were the lion flag (the lion coming from *Mahavamsa* Vijaya myth) and national anthem, which Tamil schoolchildren are now compelled to sing in Sinhala by state decree (which they earlier sang in Tamil).

was the massacre of Tamil political prisoners in the maximum security Welikada prison on two separate occasions in July 1983 (UTHR-J 2007b). In 1978, following a spate of terrorist attacks, the Tamil 'Tigers' (LTTE) were proscribed by an Act of Parliament and President Jayewardene sent his nephew Brigadier 'Bull' Weeratunga to Jaffna in 1979, with orders to wipe out terrorism in six months. Soon afterwards six Tamil youths disappeared after being taken into custody — the bodies of two of them, Inpam and Selvam, were later found near the beach in Jaffna. Reports of torture of those detained began to surface. Brigadier Weeratunga was to be rewarded with an ambassadorship to Canada when he retired, a practice of state reward in diplomatic missions for terror services rendered that continues to the present day.

The Prevention of Terrorism Act[8] (PTA), enacted as a temporary provision in 1979 and made permanent law in 1982, and the Emergency Regulations (ER), passed every month in Parliament in accordance with the Public Security Ordinance, have been used by the security forces to arrest persons without a warrant or due process, detain without access to attorneys or relatives for prolonged periods and use torture to obtain confessions under duress or as a method of social control (Bastiampillai et al. 2010). Torture became widespread (Somasundaram 2008). Torture victims stated that they were stripped and beaten, had pins pushed under their fingernails, struck on the knees, neck, face and feet with iron rods, bound in chains and lowered into wells, suspended from the ceiling and beaten, tormented with hot chilli powder rubbed into the eyes and genitals, burned with hot rods and cigarettes and subjected to electric shock and mock executions (Somasundaram 2008). Tamil youths, usually between fifteen and thirty years of age were arrested en masse. Many detainees disappeared (AI 1993) without a trace or were killed outright. A number of mass graves have been discovered all over the killing fields of the northeast where it is believed these bodies may have been buried. Case histories of such disappearances now run into the thousands (HRW 2008). In one case that came to light, a schoolgirl returning home after exams was gang-raped and killed at an army checkpoint and her family who went looking for her also disappeared (UTHR-J 1999). The accused corporal revealed the existence of the Chemmani mass graves adjoining the checkpoint.

After 1983, as the violent Tamil militancy grew phenomenally and the Sinhala armed forces expanded, the state was able to affect reprisals by responding to attacks by the 'terrorists' with raids using the air force, navy and/or army on the Tamil civilian population in the northeast. People learnt to routinely expect a bombing raid or increased shelling in the north-east with Tamil civilian casualties whenever there was a 'terrorist'

[8] Prevention of Terrorism (Temporary Provisions) Act No. 48 of 1979.

attack. This appeared to be part of the state's counter-insurgency strategy where Tamil militant terror was countered with state terror, a mirror of terror and counter-terror.

Gradually, with increasing 'terrorist' attacks, state counter-terror became institutionalized into the very laws of the land (AI 1993; HRW 2008), structures of society and mechanisms of governance. The PTA and ER provided legal sanction, impunity, protection and thus encourage-ment to perpetuators of mass human rights abuses (Bastiampillai et al. 2010). It led to the establishment of a culture of violence, intimidation and state terror. Arbitrary detention, torture, massacres, extrajudicial kill-ings, disappearances, rape, forced displacements, bombings and shelling became common. When compared to similar developments elsewhere in the world, for example, in Latin America or in South Africa some time ago, the pattern of state terror appears to be similar. Further, in trying to violently suppress defiance and rebellion, particularly when it takes a militant or 'terrorist' turn, the response of states appears to follow a similar pattern of what is often diplomatically called counter-insurgency.

Counter-insurgency

Understanding the counter-insurgency paradigm provides a good per-spective on what happened in the ethnic conflict in Sri Lanka and perhaps elsewhere in the world. From the outset, the state appears to have opted to suppress the grievances of the Tamil minority through violence, that is state terror, instead of addressing them through negotiations and com-promise. As discussed in Chapter 1A, compulsions of an ethno-national consciousness would not emotionally allow the Sinhala leadership to grant equality despite the economic and developmental cost to the nation. It found arousing communal passions an effective way to win elections through ethnic outbidding (DeVotta 2004), and then staying in power.

Though initially, there was a period between 1956 and 1983, when the minority Tamil political leadership struggled to obtain redress through various non-violent means, since the 1983 anti-Tamil pogrom, Tamil militants took increasingly to violent armed guerrilla warfare. Tamil militancy grew to the dimensions of a counter state with a conventional army able to challenge the very existence of a unified nation (Whitaker 2007). The Sri Lankan state invested increasing resources to fight the Tamil insurgency—what was a ceremonial armed force numbering a few thousand soldiers grew to include a modern trained and equipped army of over two hundred thousand soldiers with Russian T-55 tanks, BMP armoured personnel carriers, 137 mm guns, 127 mm howitzers, 120 mm mortars, multi-barrel rocket launchers; navy and air force with the state-of-the-art carriers like the Russian MiGs, Mil Mi-24 (Hind) gunships, HIP Mi-17 troop carriers, Israeli Kfir fighters, Bell helicopters, Israeli and Chinese fast gunboats, Dvora class patrol boats, hovercrafts, naval craft equipped with weapons of massive destructive power[9]; and a police force of eighty thousand with a paramilitary wing called the Special Task Force (STF), trained in counter-insurgency techniques (Vijayasiri 1999).

The LTTE for its part put up a stiff resistance with some spectacular military successes of its own: 'The combat varies from conventional battles to the classic guerrilla hit and run tactics .... Some battles rage to such an extent that a well defended brigade of 1,200 soldiers supported by artillery and air support can perish in just three days' (Vijayasiri 1999). At the same time, the state became more sophisticated and professional, sending its men and women for advanced, state-of-the-art counter-insurgency training in some of the best military schools in the world. In keeping with world trends and military advice from experts in Israel, United States, United Kingdom, India, Pakistan and other countries, the state adopted modern counter-insurgency techniques in its fight against the LTTE as pointed out by Sivaram (Whitaker 2007). With the successful defeat of the LTTE, countries with their own internal insurgencies are being advised to emulate the 'Lanka model' (BBC 2009; HRW 2011; Sri Lanka Army 2011). But there have been 'models' of insurgency and purportedly successful counter-insurgency elsewhere in the world, such as in Malaya and Kenya (Kitson 1971, 1977) and in the Sri Lankan past.

In the twelfth century, following Parakramabahu's reign, the rapid disintegration of the Anuradhapura and Polonnaruwa kingdoms saw fourteen rulers toppling each other in quick succession in a destructive struggle for power. Internecine conflicts, insurgent activities and sabotage of irrigation tanks became common. The culmination of all this turbulence was the reign of Maha of Kalinga (1215–36) who took advantage of the opening created by the instability to adopt a policy of blood and terror to grab power (de Silva 2005). Historically there had always been insurgent activity from the south, Rohana, which challenged control from the centre at Anuradhapura, Polonnaruwa and later Kotte. There is a more clear record of fairly successful guerrilla activity against the Portuguese, who captured Jaffna in 1560, by the Tamil king Sangili from the Vanni together with Nikapitiya Bandara from the low country and the king of Kandy. Another very successful guerrilla campaign against the Portu-

---

[9] Incredibly, all this costly equipment is for the efficient killing of 'other' human beings! Much of this was obtained as outright loans from other countries or through shady deals with shadowy arms dealers and corrupt Sri Lankan officials. Lanka Logistics & Technologies Limited is a company with monopoly for procuring arms that involves high state officials.

guese was waged by Wimala Dharmasuriya who eventually became king of Kandy in 1594. Perhaps the greatest skill in guerrilla (as well as conventional) warfare was shown by warriors like Mayadunne and Rajasimha of Sitavaka against the Portuguese, Kandy, Kotte and Colombo.

The British used counter-insurgency tactics to suppress the Kandyan rebellions from 1817 to 1848. The British answer to the skilful guerrilla tactics of the Kandyans was to starve into submission those villages that were suspected of harbouring the guerrillas and generally terrorize the population in the hope of cutting off support for the rebels. The scorched-earth tactics and 'search and destroy missions eventually sapped the morale of the people' (de Silva 2005).

The most recent guerrilla fighter against Dutch and British colonial powers was Pandara Vanniyan (or Wanni Bandara in Sinhalese), the last king of the Vanni (Logeswaran 1982; Selladurai 2007). In alliance with the Kandy kingdom he drove Lieutenant von Drieberg and his garrison from the Mullaithivu fort, capturing their canons and 'overran the whole of the northern districts (Vanni) and [had] the boldness to penetrate as far as Elephant pass into the Jaffna Peninsula' (Lewis 1895). From conventional warfare, he resorted to guerrilla attacks and was finally defeated by Lieutenant von Drieberg when the British organized a three-pronged attack from Jaffna, Mannar and Trincomalee around 1803. This was followed by 'burning of all his houses and his people were dispersed into the jungle, and eventually out of the Vanni. The power of the Vanni Chiefs was thus finally and effectually extinguished' (Lewis 1895). Interestingly, folklore has it that Lieutenant von Drieberg was originally with the Dutch forces when he was humiliated by Pandara Vanniyan, who had defeated him several times, including in a personal combat, and had been chivalrously permitted to withdraw. He had stayed on after the Dutch were ousted by the British to fight on to defeat Pandara Vanniyan.

The similarity between Lieutenant von Drieberg and General Sarath Fonseka, who developed a passionate zeal for defeating the LTTE and Prabhakaran after being trapped in the early 1990s at Pompamadu near Chettikulum in the Vanni by the LTTE when he was a lieutenant colonel and later surviving a near-fatal suicide attack, is striking. He led the war in the Vanni and was responsible for systematically and relentlessly pursuing the LTTE until they were completely destroyed. He became a Sinhala national hero of epic proportions. Pandara Vanniyan was declared a national hero by the prime minister and a statue of him was opened in 1982 with much fanfare in Vavuniya at the main junction where the A9 highway between Jaffna and Kandy (and Colombo) meets the road to Mannar (and further down the road to Trincomalee) (Logeswaran 1982). The LTTE leader, Prabhakaran, was compared to him by present-day

Tamil nationalists such as Muthuvel Karunanidhi, the former chief minister of Tamil Nadu in his book *Payum Puli Pandara Vanniyan* (The Leaping Tiger) (Sivaram 1990) and Pazha Nedumaran. The historical parallels to what happened in the Vanni recently are remarkable except that then, ordinary civilians were not used as hostages.

Modern Counter-insurgency

The current doctrine of counter-insurgency is rooted in the colonial experience of administering far-flung empires. Native populations often rebelled against the imperial powers using insurgent methods and they were met with counter-insurgency techniques. According to Sivaram, the original counter-insurgency manual was written by Frank Kitson (1971, 1977), a British army commander in charge of counter-insurgency operations in Kenya, Malaya, Cyprus and Oman. According to Whitaker (2007), Kitson described the use of penetration agents, the mounting of psychological operation (or 'psyops' — propaganda, misinformation, public relations), the making of fake political concessions to split the opposition, the wielding of army counter-terror, the cordoning off of communities, the deployment of informers in hoods (to cover their face) and, somewhat less forthrightly, the rough interrogations and 'wetwork' (that is, the hooding, torture, 'turning', disposal or dispatching of captives) that are being used in Sri Lanka by the state in its counter-insurgency operations. The most current and state-of-the-art counter-insurgency manual is that of the American army (United States Army 2006) which was tested in Iraq and later in Afghanistan by one of its authors, General David Petraeus. After emphasizing the essentially political components of counter-insurgency, all these experts (Amato 2002; Kitson 1971, 1977; United States Army 2006; Vijayasiri 1999; Whitaker 2007) assert that counter-insurgency, when practised properly, is effective.

However, apart from temporarily suppressing the immediate rebellion, it is not clear how far counter-insurgency is effective in solving the underlying problem(s) that are the source(s) of the insurgency. As recent uprisings in Kenya and stirrings in Malaysia show, the underlying inequities are left simmering in the postcolonial milieu. Amato (2002) and Vijayasiri (1999) were quick to point out that counter-insurgency had not been carried out properly in Sri Lanka and if used correctly it would have been successful. They mentioned lack of clear political will or policy as the cause of the failure of counter-insurgency in Sri Lanka and give suggestions for improving counter-insurgency operations. President Mahinda Rajapaksa, with his brothers, advisers and General Sarath

Fonseka mounted their own 'home-grown' brand of no-holds-barred counter-insurgency campaign to defeat the LTTE in 2007–09, setting a model for the rest of the world.

The Sri Lankan state and military received considerable support from many countries around the world. Support included training, military hardware and equipment; real-time vital information, for example, about LTTE ships carrying arms; and sometimes direct personnel assistance. Apart from United Kingdom, India, China, Pakistan, Iran and Israel, the United States have continued to support the Sri Lankan military through heavy financial aid (over US$ sixty million in 2007), agreements, equipment and training (Arulanantham 2007). Amato (2002) also refers to American interest in counter-insurgency and learning from other conflicts. He writes: 'Continuing US commitment to engagement ensures that sub-state conflicts will remain relevant to policy-makers and military leaders of the future. Analysis of the conflict in Sri Lanka may help frame further questions US doctrine writers need answer about counter-insurgency.'

In the post–9/11 world with the global war on terror, terrorism and counter-terrorism have become very closely associated, if not synonymous, with the discourse on counter-insurgency. Another term used is asymmetrical warfare, where a less resourced and weaker force will use unconventional, guerrilla or subversive techniques in the conflict against stronger and more established states and those helping them. Essentially it is a struggle for power, for legitimacy to rule from the target populations. Both parties will vie for the support and allegiance of the civilian population using whatever technique they think will work. Thus, though officially denied, terror and counter terror become one of the accepted methods of the dirty war, of trying to win over, frighten or coerce the population to their side. Instead of the traditional violence, it is now thought more effective and efficient (cost-effective) in the long term to use the 'stick and carrot' method to psychologically win over the population.

Sivaram reports a discussion with a retired Sri Lankan army general, which is quoted by Whitaker (2007: 153):

> [T]hat a population targeted by CI is actually like the body of a prisoner who has been taken under the Prevention of Terrorism Act. He is beaten out of his wits in the first phase of his detention. He is tortured. He is deprived. He loses track of normalcy. The focus of his whole being after a few days of this kind of abuse would be to hope that when the door opens he won't be assaulted. His whole focus is on not getting beaten. His life's sole aim would be focused on that—he would lose track of everything else ... this general was talking about how the target population is like the prisoner under the Prevention of Terrorism Act. So you treat the target population as a prisoner: break its will, reduce its expectations to bare minimum, so Tamils who set out to demand a separate state would end up just arguing for not

being tortured. So your aspirations are depressed from separatism to being allowed to travel without being shot.

Fundamentally, counter-insurgency is aimed at re-establishing the legitimacy of the state while cutting off the target population's support and sympathy for the insurgents (United States Army 2006). According to Sivaram (quoted in Whitaker [2007]),

> Another aim of counter-insurgency is to induce war-weariness in the target population ... the state is always focused on destroying the political will of the target population, and the art and science of doing that is counter-insurgency ... and the way it does that is: 'Massacres and terror; Arrest, detention, torture, all indiscriminate, and interrogation to destroy the basis of civil society; Checkpoints, constant checks; Promote vigilante groups [who] create an atmosphere of terror and collapse the social fabric (Patricia Lawrence's thesis becomes important here [see Lawrence (2000)]): people lose their psychological moorings and so become unable to make any kind of politically cohesive statement, so the vigilante groups become a regime of terror within a regime of terror; Promotion of numerous political and interest groups from within the target population to dilute and obfuscate the basic issue in question that in the first place gave rise to the insurgency.

Massacres (see Table 1B.1) of innocent civilians by all the parties to the conflict were relatively common. Apart from individual, targeted, political abductions, disappearances and extrajudicial killings (HRW 2008), these mass executions can only be called crimes against humanity that keep the population in abject terror. They easily qualify for prosecution under criteria set out for war crimes by the International Criminal Court (ICC 2002). The various contending authorities, the state, paramilitaries, LTTE and even the Indian army as the IPKF, appeared to believe that use of these terror tactics would keep the population under their control and counter similar tactics of the opposing party by winning over the 'hearts and minds' through fear, an attempt at outbidding by terror.

Table 1B.1 gives illustrative and representative examples of civilian massacres involving more than fifteen civilians with a clear, planned intent, carried out in a deliberate, organized way to cause terror and/ or as a lesson or retaliation, with no clear military target. Disorganized mob killings[10] or where soldiers have gone 'berserk' or where it could be argued to be accidental, unintentional or 'collateral damage' have been left out. Numbers of people injured have been left out (they are not available or reliable in most cases).

---

[10] Significantly, this has been exceptionally rare or non-existent.

Table 1B.1:
War Crimes in Sri Lanka—Civilian Massacres

Date	Place	Number of People Killed	Description	Possible Perpetrator(s)
July 1983	Welikada prison	53	Tamil detainees	State officials, prisoners
24 July 1983	Jaffna	60	Tamil civilians	Sri Lankan army
April 1984	Jaffna	70	Our Lady of Refuge church	Sri Lankan army
20 November 1984	Dollar and Kent Farm, Mullaitivu	62	Sinhala ex-convicts and settlers	LTTE
2 December 1984	Iraperiyakulam army camp, Vavuniya	100	Young Tamil men	Sri Lankan army
4 December 1984	Mannar	107	Tamil civilians	Sri Lankan state forces
May 1985	Valvettithurai	70	Tamil civilians and schoolboys	Sri Lankan state forces
14 May 1985	Anuradhapura	146	Bus stand and vihara	LTTE
May 1985	Thambiluvil, Eastern Province	60–63	Tamil youths	Sri Lankan state forces
15 May 1985	Northern seas off Delft	34	Passengers on the boat Kumuthini	Sri Lankan navy
3 June 1985	Pankulam	85	Civilian bus passengers	Lankan state forces
3 May 1986	Katunayake airport	16	Passengers including foreign tourists	Tamil militants
May 1986	Central telegraph office	14	Civilians	Tamil militants
April 1987	Colombo	113	Car bomb in the central bus station	LTTE
2 June 1987	Aranthalawa	31	Buddhist monks and civilians	LTTE
22 October 1987	Jaffna hospital	70	Patients, doctors, nurses and staff	Indian army (IPKF)
August 1987	Trincomalee	100	Sinhala villagers	LTTE
April 1989	Trincomalee	51	Car bomb	LTTE
2 August 1989	Valvettithurai	63	Tamil youths and boys	Indian army (IPKF)
1 August 1990	Akkaraipattu	14	Execution of Muslims	LTTE

(Table 1B.1 contd.)

(Table 1B.1 contd.)

Date	Place	Number of People Killed	Description	Possible Perpetrator(s)
4 August 1990	Kathankudi mosque	103	Muslim men and children in prayer	LTTE
18 August 1990	Eravur	121	Muslim men, women and children	LTTE
5 September 1990	Vantharumoolai	158	Tamil civilian refugees	Sri Lankan state forces
10 September 1990	Saththurukkondan	184	Tamil civilian refugees	Sri Lankan state forces
12 June 1991	Kokkaddicholai	82	Tamil civilians	Sri Lankan state forces
October 1991	Palliyagodella	109	Muslim men, women and children	LTTE
09 August 1992	Mylanthanai, Batticaloa	32	Tamil civilians including children	Sri Lankan state forces
02 January 1993	Killaly sea	52	Fleeing refugees	Sri Lankan navy
18 April 1995	Nachchikuda	30	Civilians	Sri Lankan state forces
25 May 1995	Kallarawa	42	Sinhala men, women and children	LTTE
October 1995	Border villages in the east	120	People hacked	LTTE
January 1996	Colombo	100	Truck with explosives at the Central bank	LTTE
11 February 1996	Kumarapuram	24	Civilians	Sri Lankan state forces
20 April 1996	Killaly sea	42	Fleeing refugees	Sri Lankan navy
24 July 1996	Dehiwala	56	Train bombing	LTTE
11 August 1997	Mullaitivu (Manthuvil)	40	Tamil civilians	Sri Lankan state forces
10 June 1998	Suthanthirapuram, Mullaitivu	32	Tamil civilians	Sri Lankan state forces
17 September 1999	Gongala	52	Sinhala men, women and children hacked	LTTE
25 October 2000	Bindunuwewa	31	Surrendered child, youth soldiers	Lankan mob, police officials
15 June 2006	Kebithigollewa, Anuradhapura	64	Mine attack on a civilian bus	LTTE

(Table 1B.1 contd.)

(Table 1B.1 contd.)

Date	Place	Number of People Killed	Description	Possible Perpetrator(s)
7 August 2006	Muttur	17	French action against hunger workers	Sri Lankan state forces
2 April 2007	Ampara	16	Bombing of civilian bus	LTTE
28 November 2007	Colombo	18	Bombs	LTTE
5 December 2007	Anuradhapura	16	Bombing of civilian bus	LTTE
16 January 2008	Buttala	27	Bus passengers	LTTE
29 January 2008	Palampiddi	20	Schoolchildren	Lankan state forces Deep penetration unit (DPU)
2 February 2008	Dambulla	20	Bus passengers	LTTE
August 2006– May 2009	The Vanni	40,000	Tamil civilians	Sri Lankan state forces and LTTE

Source: University Teachers for Human Rights (UTHR-J), various reports (http://www.uthr.org, retrieved on 8 October 2013); Tamil Centre for Human Rights—TCHR (http://www.tchr.net, retrieved on 8 October 2013); Illankai Tamil Sangam (http://www.sangam.org/2007/11/Killed_1956_2007.php?uid=2619, retrieved on 8 October 2013).

Indian Counter-insurgency in Sri Lanka

Among the massacres, the one carried out by the Indian army on the holy Deepavali day in 1987 during their intervention in Sri Lanka as the IPKF had a fateful impact on the morale of health staff working in the area (Somasundaram 1997a):

> On that Deepavali day (22 October), over seventy civilians including patients, two doctors, one paediatric consultant, and three nurses died in the massacre that followed. The Indian army made no apology; no inquiry was held and effectively blanketed any news of the hospital massacre getting out.

Every year, on Deepavali day, the staff and community hold a ceremony at the Jaffna hospital to remember those who died and were injured. A picture of the staff killed hangs in the vicinity of the massacre.

The hospital massacre happened during a period of complete war, when the Indians launched the so-called Operation Pawan to wrest Jaffna from LTTE control (Hoole et al. 1988) between October and December 1987. Terror was widely prevalent in the months of October and November and appears to have been a deliberate policy (Somasundaram 1998: 230–31, 244, 255):

> The local population was pushed, shoved and beaten up with extreme callousness and brutality. Status, age, sex ... nothing mattered. Lawyers, doctors, engineers, the old, the young, the sick and disabled were humiliated, assaulted or shot even after being identified; whole families were pulled out of their houses and shot.... The decision to use terror may have been to wrest control over the civilian population and force them to relinquish their sympathy and support for the LTTE .... The meaning behind the military term *pacification*[11] became clear only after the war when the army officers made subtle differentiations between areas.

The role of India in the Tamil insurgency and later in the counter-insurgency operations is a strange and paradoxical one. After initially arming and training the Tamil militants, it took on the self-proclaimed role of trying to disarm them, mainly the LTTE, which resisted this. Then came the counter-insurgency operations against the LTTE within the Tamil population, a bitter learning experience for the Indian army and state, that was to come in useful when it had to carry out its own counter-insurgency operations within India in Punjab, Jammu & Kashmir, Assam, Nagaland and Andhra Pradesh. According to interviews with Tamil militants that surfaced at that time, it was alleged that the Research and Analysis Wing, the covert intelligence agency of the Indian state, had a hand in instigating the LTTE to carry out the first attack on Sinhala civilians at Anuradhapura in 1985 to put pressure on the Sri Lankan state which led to the Thimbu talks. This line of reasoning provided a rationalization, a justification for violence against civilians, the instrumental use of terror. The often-stated belief was that the state would only understand the language of violence.

---

[11] The American army manual on counter-insurgency defines pacification differently (United States Army 2006): Pacification is the process by which the government asserts its influence and control in an area beset by insurgents. It includes local security efforts, programmes to distribute food and medical supplies and lasting reforms (like land redistribution). Sivaram, quoted in Whitaker (2007), defines it as:

> The main aim of pacification in modern counter insurgency techniques is the closure of the political space from which a rebellion derives its staying power and ability to spread its influence with ease. The military drive against a rebellion can consolidate its successes ultimately only if it can achieve a near total closure of the political space in which a rebellion is brought forth and thrives.

Israeli Counter-insurgency in Sri Lanka

A country that determined Sri Lankan counter-insurgency strategy in the 1980s was Israel (Hoole 2001; Ostrovsky and Hoy 1990). Its intelligence agency, Mossad, advised on counter-insurgency policies to match the strategies used by Israel against Palestine and provided training aircraft like the Kfir and naval gunboats like the Dvora and arms. There are credible reports that Mossad agents were physically present in some of the ground, sea and air operations. Mossad was directly implicated in the violent eviction of Tamil settlers in the area north of Trincomalee and the planting of Sinhala settlers in areas ethnically cleansed of Tamils in 1984 (Hoole 2001; Sabaratnam 2004). For the Sinhala Sri Lankan government, this served multiple purposes, splitting up contiguity of the Tamil population, separating the population from insurgent groups and weakening the Tamil support base of the insurgents. Sabaratnam (2004) observes that a special institution called the Joint Services Operation (JOSSOP) was created, with headquarters in Anuradhapura, whose task was to implement Mossad's counter-insurgency plan to destroy the base for Tamil Eelam:

> MOSSAD's plan was nothing but the classic counterinsurgency program — complete evacuation and destruction of villages supporting the insurgents along with destruction of crops and prevention of cultivation ... MOSSAD advised Athulathmudali to do the same: plug the routes and dry up the supplies. Israeli advice suited Athulathmudali's mission of destroying the territorial base of Tamil Eelam and his ambition of becoming Jayewardene's successor.

Lalith Athulathmudali, as the national security minister, announced in Parliament his grand design based on the Israeli model to solve the terrorist problem once and for all by herding all the Tamil population in the north into camps and then settling two hundred thousand Sinhalese ex-convicts (IRCs) and fisherfolk in villages throughout the north (Hoole 2001). It was also under Athulathmudali that the air force bombed civilian targets in Jaffna using napalm-like incendiary material in barrels.

A key figure groomed by Israel was the son of President Jayewardene, Ravi Jayewardene. He was instrumental in the creation of the counter-insurgency unit within the police called the Special Task Force (STF). The STF operated in the east and was responsible for civilian massacres, torture, disappearances and killings, which later spread to Colombo. Mutilated bodies of Tamils who had been held at STF headquarters were found dumped in Bolgoda Lake.

Sri Lankan Counter-insurgency Practice

Sivaram described 'levels of terror' during a lecture on counter-insurgency at Palmerstone North, New Zealand, in 1999 as something that can be turned on and off, and increased or reduced as the situation necessitated (Margaret Trawick, pers. comm.). It would be like fine-tuning a population to keep it under control, like the use of the friendly and 'bad' interrogator, which would cause the population to start yearning for periods of less terror and they would do anything to avoid the increase in terror levels.

Sivaram argues that one of the main strategies of counter-insurgency is to 'divide the target population — to prevent them from coalescing into one body' (Whitaker 2007). One ongoing strategy has been systematic, state-aided colonization with Sinhala settlements in traditionally Tamil-speaking areas in the north-east, starting with the Gal Oya scheme where the first anti-Tamil violence erupted in 1956. Another was the entire Mahaweli programme, especially the accelerated version with the 'L' scheme (UTHR-J 1993a), which was part of the state's overall military strategy. Tragically, the Sinhala settlers cynically used by the state were poor peasants from the south, who suffered immensely, showing increased suicide rates (D. de Silva and Jayasinghe 2003). The families settled at Weli Oya and in other so-called 'border villages' provided security for army garrisons by functioning as early warning systems, buffers and soft targets for attacks by the guerrillas (UTHR-J 1993a) and other questionable purposes. International development and rehabilitation aid and material such as for the massive accelerated Mahaweli programme were used for military purposes or have favoured the dominant ethnic group.

However, at the same time, the ethnic war brought all economic development in the north and east to a complete halt. Further, it led to the utter devastation of the land, buildings, institutions, resources and property; contamination with landmines and large-scale displacements made the north and east look like ancient ruins of some long-lost civilization. The contrast with the south, where modern developments have kept pace with the rest of the world, for example, in technology, communication, media, electronics and so on, is striking. The north and east had gone backwards, to candlelight and bicycles. With the fighting over, there is a belated effort to catch up with the world. The LTTE's armed struggle, apart from having exposed people under its control to the violence of the state, has given the state the excuse to push ahead with its colonization schemes with extra vigour and with the protection of the army as well.

Abductions and disappearances were and are strong components of counter-insurgency operations. Challenging leaders, dissidents and suspected enemy sympathizers are extrajudicially eliminated by being disappeared. This gives the powers an easy of way of disposing of problems without involving the long and messy route of arrest, detention and legal process. Abduction and disappearances of not only opponents but also ordinary civilians create a social climate of terror, pervasive insecurity and helplessness that helps the powers to control the community. A Human Rights Watch (HRW) report (HRW 2008), gives a very clear description:

> Hundreds of enforced disappearances committed since 2006 have already placed Sri Lanka among the countries with the highest number of new cases in the world. The victims are primarily young ethnic Tamil men who 'disappear' — often after being picked up by government security forces in the country's embattled north and east, but also in the capital Colombo.... Most are feared dead. In the face of this crisis, the government of Sri Lanka has demonstrated an utter lack of resolve to investigate and prosecute those responsible. ... Government security forces are believed to have been responsible for tens of thousands of 'disappearances' during the short-lived but extremely violent insurgency from the left-wing Sinhalese nationalist Janatha Vimukthi Peramuna (JVP) from 1987 to 1990, and the ongoing two-decades-long civil war between the government and the Tamil-nationalist LTTE....
>
> In the great majority of cases documented by Human Rights Watch and Sri Lankan groups, evidence indicates the involvement of government security forces — army, navy, or police. The Sri Lankan military, empowered by the country's counterterrorism laws, has long relied on extrajudicial means, such as 'disappearances' and summary executions — in its operations against Tamil militants and JVP insurgents. The involvement of the security forces in 'disappearances' is facilitated by Sri Lanka's emergency laws, which grant sweeping powers to the army along with broad immunity from prosecution .... Also implicated in abductions and 'disappearances' are pro-government Tamil armed groups acting either independently or in conjunction with the security forces....
>
> The LTTE has been implicated in abductions in conflict areas under the government's control ... the LTTE prefers to openly execute opponents, perhaps to ensure a deterrent effect on the population. LTTE abductions may also be underreported because the family members of the victims and eyewitnesses are often reluctant to report the abuses, fearing LTTE retribution. No matter who is responsible for the 'disappearances', the vast majority of the victims are ethnic Tamils, although Muslims and Sinhalese have also been targeted.

Apart from the state and its allied paramilitary forces, the internecine warfare among various Tamil militant organizations competing for the loyalty of the community has resulted in the elimination of many of its own ethnic, more able, civilians — a process of self-destruction, auto genocide (Hoole 2001). Those with leadership qualities, those willing to challenge and argue, the intellectuals, the dissenters and those with social

motivation have been weeded out (*kalaieduthal* or weeding—those elimi-
/ nated are labelled antisocial elements or traitors). At critical nodal shifts in
power, recriminations, false accusations, revenge and retribution become
very common. It happened in 1987 (IPKF, the Indian intervention), in 1990
(LTTE takeover), in 1996 (Sri Lankan army control) and in 2005 with the
collapse of the ceasefire. The loss of leadership, talented, skilful, resource-
ful persons, the professionals, technocrats and entrepreneurs from the
community has had devastating consequences. Many have left over the
years due to increasing difficulties, traumatic experiences and social pressure from family and colleagues, the so-called 'brain drain'. Those who
remained have been targeted by those aspiring to rule the community.
Two examples from those I have worked closely with come to mind.

One example was the brutal murder of Rajani Thiranagama in the
north on 21 September 1989, which illustrates the situation among Tamils.
An intellectual who was the only lecturer of anatomy at the University of
Jaffna Medical Faculty, Rajani was at the same time a deeply concerned
human working tirelessly for the very survival of the community. She had
courageously chosen to work at the grass roots, helping those affected,
particularly women and young students, highlighting their problems and
exposing human rights abuses, painfully building a society that would
determine its own future with dignity. But in their struggle for power
and control, the Tamil militants, here the LTTE, wanted a spiritless and
submissive society terrorized to obedience, and thus killed off one of the
most valuable resources that the Tamil community had. Rajani, just before
she was killed, had written (Hoole et al. 1988) in her characteristic style,
showing her total commitment to the plight of the community, describing
the *collective trauma* that is the theme of this book:

> Living under the long shadow of the gun for more than a decade and a
> half, holding hope against hope for the survival of our children, dominated
> by violence from all directions without a purpose or meaning, but on the
> other hand observing the *glazed faces of people accepting it all with a sense of
> resignation*—to be objective or analytical seems to be a major effort like try-
> ing to do something physical in the midst of a debilitating illness; whenever
> we write we are dogged by *this reality, fearing losing the thread of sanity and
> the community submerging without resistance into this slime of terror and violence.*
> The community is bereft of all its human potential. Every 'sane' person is
> fleeing this burning country—its hospitals have no doctors; its universities
> no teachers; its crumbled war-torn buildings cannot be rebuilt because there
> are no engineers or masons or even a labour force; its families are headed
> by women; the old, the sick and the weary die without even the family to
> mourn or sons to bury the dead. It was important for us to arrive at a synthe-
> sis in analysis, seek for an understanding, find spaces to organize, revitalize
> a community sinking into a state of resignation. Objectivity was not solely an
> academic exercise for us. Objectivity, the pursuit of truth and the propagation

of critical and honest positions, was not only crucial for the community but was a view that could cost many of us our lives. It was only undertaken as a survival task. (Emphasis added)

A similar killing of another irreplaceable resource of the Tamil community was that of Neelan Tiruchelvam, an internationally recognized constitutional expert. His crime, in the eyes of LTTE's counter counter-insurgency strategy, had been cooperating with the 'enemy' in drafting a federal constitution without its consent, during which he struggled, using all his experience, skills and knowledge, for a document that would be acceptable to all communities, a product that was to be later acknowledged by Anton Balasingham of the LTTE as the best so far. Many other socially minded leaders and ordinary civilians were killed in the long war by all parties; this created an irreplaceable vacuum and sense of helplessness.

Bronfenbrenner (1979) warns of the destructive consequences to a society which experiences the systematic degrading and debilitation of its most talented members. This is the loss of vital resources (Hobfoll 1998), the destruction of social capital, the nodal points of vibrant relationships and essential networks which is a prominent cause of *collective trauma*. Without leadership and organization, vital networks and working relationships have collapsed, leaving the community easy prey to competing propaganda, authoritarian control and suppression. Many have observed that ordinary people in Jaffna have become passive and submissive. These qualities have become part of the socialization process, where children are taught to keep quiet, not to question or challenge and accept the situation, as assertive behaviour carries considerable risk. The creative spirit, the vital capacity to rebuild and recover, which is be critical for any kind of recovery, is being suppressed.

Torture was used as a routine counter-insurgency procedure on Tamil detainees (Doney 1998). Apart from the stated attempt to obtain information, it was used to break the individual personalities of those who tried to resist, as well as an encompassing method to coerce a community into submission. Many individuals did not survive torture, but those who did were released in a broken condition; when dead, their maimed bodies were conspicuously exhibited to act as warning to others. Torture, according to Elaine Scarry (1985), is used by a regime in crisis when its power is contested, questioned and challenged, when a 'central idea or ideology or cultural construct has ceased to elicit a population's belief'. Agonizing pain is inflicted on the body as a way of inscribing, translating the insignias of power on to individuals who represent the collective. When we see that around 1 per cent of the Tamil population has been tortured (Somasundaram and Sivayokan 1994), the extensive, endemic nature of torture becomes apparent. A whole sub-population becomes branded. The torture and interrogation break downs the world, voice and consciousness of the victims. Their forced confessions then become the objectification of that process of deconstruction (Scarry 1985). Torture became one aspect of institutionalized violence and laws such as PTA and ER, which legitimized the use of torture (and death) in custody. It was similarly used by the militants but without the legal veneer. The project team who worked on the Istanbul Protocol to the manual on investigation and documentation of torture speaks of community trauma by the creation of a 'repressive ecology' based on 'imminent, pervasive threat, terror and inhibition that causes a state of generalized insecurity, terror and rupture of the social fabric. Collective fear that is based on this massive threat of being tortured has long-lasting effects on the forms of collective behaviour' (Baykal et al. 2004). According to Bracken (2000), the systematic use of torture by a regime undermines social cohesion where community leaders are not killed outright but tortured, broken and sent back as symbols of the community's vulnerability leading to terror and social fragmentation.

Another counter-insurgency technique was mass displacement of people from their habitat and home environment (see Table 1B.2) as a way

Table 1B.2:
War Crimes in Sri Lanka—Mass Displacements

Date	Place	Number of People Displaced	Description	Possible Perpetrator(s)	Comments
1956	Gal Oya; spread to other places	3,000	Widespread anti-Tamil violence	Mobs directed and organized by politicians	Followed protests against the 'Sinhala-only' Act
1958	Colombo, outstations	35,000	Mass displacement of Tamils following widespread anti-Tamil violence	Mobs directed and organized by politicians	Followed Bandaranaike–Chelvanayakam pact and its abrogation
1977	Hill-country, Colombo	15,000	Mass displacement of Tamils following widespread anti-Tamil violence	Mobs directed and organized by politicians	Followed UNP's victory in the 1977 elections
1983	Colombo, south-west, central	250,000	Mass displacement of Tamils following widespread anti-Tamil violence	Mobs directed and organized by politicians	

(Table 1B.2 contd.)

(Table 1B.2 contd.)

Date	Place	Number of People Displaced	Description	Possible Perpetrator(s)	Comments
Post-1983	All over Sri Lanka	500,000– 1,000,000	Mostly Tamils	Lankan state forces	Asylum abroad
August 1987	Border areas	Not available	Sinhala villagers	LTTE	
October 1987	Jaffna	300,000	Indian army; Operation Pawan	IPKF	
1988	North-east	253,000	IPKF operations	IPKF	
October 1990	North	100,000	Muslims ordered to leave	LTTE	Fear of the fifth column
October 1995	Jaffna	400,000	Sri Lankan forces advancing on Jaffna	LTTE	Engineered by LTTE
1996	North	335,000	Operations of Sri Lankan forces	Sri Lankan forces	
1997	North	255,000	Operations of Sri Lankan forces	Sri Lankan forces	
1999	North	51,000	Operations of Sri Lankan forces	Sri Lankan forces	
2000	North	192,000	Operations of Sri Lankan forces		
2001	North	67,000	Operations of Sri Lankan forces	Sri Lankan forces	
December 2006	North and east	520,000	Tamils	Conflict	
April 2007	East	301,000	Tamils	Conflict	
June 2007	Colombo	376	Tamils	Sri Lankan authorities	Deportation to Vavuniya
August 2007	North-east	460,000	Tamils	Conflict	
January– May 2009	The Vanni	300,000	Tamils	Military operations	Internment in camps

Sources: Internal Displacement Monitoring Centre (2007); UNHCR (2006).

of cutting off support for the insurgents but also cutting off the sustaining roots of resident populations. Displacement from familiar surroundings causes a fundamental disruption in life and relationships, a disorganization and confusion that breaks the cohesiveness and spirit of communities. There had been mass displacement of Tamils after each episode of the anti-Tamil violence in the south, that is, in 1956, 1958, 1977, 1981 and 1983. During the war, people belonging to all three ethnic communities,

Sinhala, Tamil and Muslim, have been displaced. However, the overwhelming majority of those displaced have been Tamils and Muslims. Over a million Tamils have fled abroad through precarious and devious routes as refugees to India, Europe, Canada, Australia and other countries, seeking asylum and forming a worldwide diaspora. The current population of the Jaffna peninsula in the north is around six hundred thousand, while the projected population sans violence would have been around 1.2 million. This indicates the level of depopulation of one of the areas. Similarly, all the outlying villages in Trincomalee, fifty-two in all, have been emptied of their Tamil inhabitants by the security forces. A similar fate befell Manal Aaru Tamils in 1985. The LTTE for its part depopulated the whole north of its Muslim and Sinhala civilians. These are forms of territorial ethnic cleansing (Clarance 2007) and minority management strategy, by keeping the percentage of their population below certain governable levels (some say 10 per cent, others claim the unofficial goal is 7 per cent). Leading academicians had predicted that with the present rate of depopulation of Tamils, very soon there would be few Tamils left in the country (S. R. H. Hoole 2007a, 2007b)! Of course, the largest minority population successfully managed in this way was the hill-country Tamils where large numbers (over 50 per cent) were made stateless and sent 'back' to India. India, although already overburdened with large populations in poor economic circumstances, has always been magnanimous in hosting large refugee populations not only from Sri Lanka but also from other neighbouring countries.

It was a Sri Lankan army strategy to empty an area of its inhabitants before launching an attack, perhaps to reduce civilian casualties to make it easier for military action (making it more difficult for the guerrillas to merge and hide within the civilian population). However, once the area has been secured, the counter-insurgency strategy was to deny a base for reorganization. This was done through no go HSZs (with eventual Sinhala colonization or permanent military settlements), saturating the area with army camps, posts (the Indian army had a post every hundred yards) and 'points', a detailed list of residents, entry and exit procedures, identification papers, frequent checking, arrests, assaults, detentions, disappearances and paramilitary and home guard surveillance with simultaneous 'hearts and minds' operations by distributing relief items, settlement programmes and other activity to win over the people. Exactly this strategy was and currently continues to be enacted in the east (UTHR-J 2007a) and the Vanni (Minority Rights Group International 2011).

The mass exodus from Jaffna in 1995 engineered by the LTTE as a counter-insurgency strategy was another type of experience (UTHR-J 1995a). Apart from the forced breaking of bonds with their homes and villages, the trek by over four hundred thousand people in the middle of the night with rain and shells changed everyone. They left in terror and not by choice, with few possessions, roads clogged with crowds moving slowly, step by step, the less able, the elderly, falling by the wayside; and finally arriving in makeshift, inadequate accommodation with very poor facilities or none at all. People lost their identity, pride, dignity and hope. Apart from the strategic withdrawal of all their military assets to fight another day, the removal of almost the entire Tamil population to areas under their control and presentation to the Sri Lankan security forces an empty city bereft of civilians was a temporary counter counter-insurgency victory for the LTTE. Sivaram describes it as the 'fish taking the ocean with it' (quoted in Whitaker [2007]) as the LTTE also needed the captive population for its recruitment base, protection and sustenance. It was the same population that was to face the trauma of the all-out final battle (see Chapter 3B). It is interesting that at that time there was considerable resentment among the Tamil population against the LTTE for having forced them to undergo this ordeal but in time the LTTE and the continued alienating actions of the state managed to transform the collective memory of what happened to one in which the LTTE was no longer held responsible[12] and the blame was shifted to the state.

The total eviction of nearly one hundred thousand Muslims from their traditional homes in the north in 1990 by the LTTE, was ostensibly a counter-insurgency exercise to eliminate an alleged fifth column in their areas for which there was scant evidence. Many of these Muslims still languish in refugee camps, a forgotten and rejected people (Citizens' Commission 2011). When frequent mass displacement of people from their natural habitat is looked at from the counter-insurgency perspective, it appears to be a strategy to remove the support base, sustenance, information and assistance given to the 'enemy'. It would also appear to be a policy designed as a method of punishment for aiding and abetting the 'enemy', inducing weariness, hopelessness, helplessness, rootlessness and despair that would make them ready to accept any conditions, break their cohesion and fighting spirit, a form of pacification. It is a destruction of the vital resources of a community, their homes, property, traditional way of life, occupation, employment, earnings and source of livelihood, so that they become completely dependent on handouts, at the mercy of authorities and under their power and control. It is also about ethnicity-based territoriality, a strategy to retain land under one ethnic group by driving out another or for resettlement with tight military arrangements in place, as is happening in the east and the Vanni.

---

[12] The transformation in memory may be partly explained by how the state insulted Tamil sensibilities by celebrating the 'conquest of Jaffna' in glorious, historic and royal style despite the empty city and hollow 'victory'.

A consequence of ongoing counter-insurgency security operations was the saturation of public space with the military. In Jaffna, the atmosphere created a feeling of entrapment, of being besieged. The conditions were compared to being in an 'open prison' by some community leaders, the Bishop of Jaffna (Savundaranayagam 2006) and the surgeon of the Jaffna hospital, Dr Thayalan Ambalavanar (Partners 1999) among them. There was also the more pervasive 'counter-control' by Tamil militants through social pressure, intimidation, killings, abductions and internal terror, trapping the civil population between the two forces. This atmosphere and tense situation created a sense of apprehension, a constant state of alertness, a 'low intensity panic', a pervasive background of terror that did not allow people to relax and go about their ordinary life. This was exactly the feeling that made people yearn for a respite, a period of peace that counter-insurgency operatives wanted to create. A photographic record of this terror can be seen in the faces of the army identification cards issued to those returning to Jaffna after the army took control in 1996.

Despite all this, people learnt to manage their terror and life went on in the surreal atmosphere so well described by Trawick (2007). On the one hand there would be massive killings, disappearances, 'encounters', search operations while at the same time there would be schools with children in uniforms, festivals, weddings, celebrations, village markets, entertainment, sports meets. Sometimes these events occurred simultaneously. In April 2000, the day that Elephant Pass army camp fell, with over one thousand casualties, the local army commander at Marathanamidam (probably not quite aware of what has happening forty kilometres away) was organizing a sports meet and variety entertainment evening with loudspeakers and food for the civilians at the Ramanathan College grounds (a counter-insurgency 'hearts and minds' operation), with soldiers trying to herd the locals, who were trying their best to avoid going there by escaping along the by-lanes, into attending the fanfare.

When the war was going on, the atmosphere gradually permeated all aspects of daily life, family and community processes. It was not certain that a person going to work would return in the evening. A home could be suddenly searched, someone brutally killed, a mother raped or a father taken away. A shell could land anywhere, destroying everything around. Sounds of gunshots, machine gunfire, exploding shells, diving planes and circling helicopters were ever present. This kind of pervasive atmosphere of violence, rather than breaking down the resistance and spirit of the population, in time creates resistance and defiance (Nordstrom 1994), particularly in the youth. Thus, within each breast would grow, small at first, a counter-anger and hate, which could transform into militancy. Thus, these kinds of counter-insurgency policies and strategies would spawn a whole generation of rebellious youth. The apparent need of the Sri Lankan state to continue to use the overwhelming presence of the military and threat of terror to rule the north and east meets the American army's counter-insurgency manual criteria, 'illegitimate states (sometimes called "police states") typically cannot regulate society or can do so only by applying overwhelming coercion' (United States Army 2006).

Parallel Governments—Parallel Worlds

An extraordinary situation existed in the north-east from 1983 to 2009 where the writ of the official government was challenged by various Tamil militant groups contesting the state(s), each other and themselves in internecine fighting for power, control and the legitimacy to rule. For a short period between 1987 and 1989, the Indians too joined this fracas. From over thirty-six Tamil militant groups the LTTE emerged dominant, ruthlessly eliminating other contenders by 1986 (Hoole et al. 1988) until it was decimated in May 2009 (UTHR-J 2009). However, other militant groups regained some power by aligning either with the states (Sri Lanka or India) or LTTE. The LTTE managed to establish at different times, varying degrees of military control over different territories, what the government termed 'uncleared areas' where the state continued to pay government salaries, provide rations and materials. The LTTE established a parallel government of its own with police, army, navy, air force, legal codes, courts, prisons, taxes, customs, immigration, administration, local government, planning, development programmes, social services, NGOs, financial systems, trades, shops, commercial ventures, medical services, educational services—all trappings of a counter state in these uncleared areas. It also had considerable control and power over the local Tamil population in state-controlled, 'cleared areas', as well as abroad among the Tamil diaspora through sympathy, terror and infiltration of various institutions and organizations.

The Tamil population faced two types of terror—one external and the other internal. They faced the external violence of state terror more readily. However, the second form of terror from within, exerted by the LTTE over the Tamils, made them silent or avoid criticizing the LTTE in any genuine way and led to a completely totalitarian regime. Keenan (2007) describes the internal terror of the LTTE thus:

> The political closures of the state, however, are matched, if not exceeded, by those of the Tamil Tigers, who are more ruthlessly and fully antidemocratic and are easily labeled as 'terrorists' by foreign states and by local critics. More important than their use of standard terrorist forms of violence such

as attacks on civilian targets is the terror produced by their desire for total control over the 'Tamil nation'. This desire for control is evidenced by the human-rights violations committed over the course of the peace process, including the murder and exile of dissenting voices, the elimination of rival political groups, the forcible recruitment of child soldiers, and the effective control over the activities and statements of organizations ostensibly part of civil society.

Legitimacy, power and control in the whole of the north-east was under intense, violent contest on a daily basis through terror and counter-terror. Extrajudicial, revenge and reprisal killings, abductions, disappearances, torture, intimidation, threats, assaults, extortion and robberies were daily occurrences that the civil population faced. Often, it was not clear who was responsible for what. There were economic blockades, sanctions, embargoes, restrictions or quotas for essential and other goods, transport barriers, frontier closures, wholesale battles, curfews, hartals or strikes, hoarding, shortages, lack of food, water, electricity, shelter, exorbitant prices, multiple taxes, extortion, paralysis or poor quality services and chronic understaffing.

People were caught between multiple powers competing for their obedience, allegiance and legitimacy. It became a risky, nuanced game of going through the motions and play-acting for the benefit of each side. When one side called for a hartal or strike, the other side would want the shops open and transport operating. Shopkeepers would compromise by keeping one door open, or sometimes loosely closed doors which could be pushed open. When the state wanted the Independence Day or the LTTE its Heroes Day observed, people would comply by hanging out appropriate flags or cleaning their compound. Each side understood the situation and would usually not be too strict. Of course, when it came down to the line, people were more terrified of the LTTE and would obey its diktat more closely.

Authorities and those in administrative positions were those most caught up in the dilemma. Some senior government agents (GAs) like district administrators were killed by the LTTE for consorting too much with the other side or not complying with an order. The situation was fluid and could change easily. For example, there were periods when the state (Sri Lanka or India) and LTTE were on good terms and it would be 'allowed' to be friendly with them, but there were other times when it would be considered treason. Even a barber giving a haircut to those from the opposing side, or a school principal agreeing to a cricket match with the army, was shot during a particularly bad time. Terminology, terms of reference and connotation would also change. Times of change of power were extremely dangerous periods when even personal vendettas and revenge considerations could result in being denounced, betrayed or killed. LTTE called it the time of *kalaieduthal* or weeding out of unwanted elements. People who were killed were displayed publicly, with accusatory placards hanging on their bodies or mutilated, as warning to others.

Between the terror and counter-terror of the Sri Lankan state, paramilitaries and the LTTE existed the shadow world (Nordstrom 2004). This was the grey area beyond the legal, formal, overt world where civilians had to survive when the official government collapsed around them. Nordstrom (2004) describes the

> ground zero of the (shifting and fluid) front-line intersections of war and invisible economies that ultimately extend worldwide. In the shadows, beyond public scrutiny, commanders may partner with international wildcatters who move consumer items, from weapons to cigarettes, into a war zone while moving valuable resources out to the cosmopolitan centers of the world in less than legal ways. More visibly they may partner with international state-sponsored vendors to procure expensive weapons and goods .... Systems of partnership, alliance, coercion, dependency, and outright violation variously mark these transactions.

Sarvananthan (2006) estimated that the informal economy formed 30 per cent of the provincial gross domestic product (PGDP) of the northeast. The PGDP for the north was the lowest in the country (the east being also low) due to lack of economic activity, but was compensated by the informal economy. The informal economy included the extralegal trade of goods across the various borders into the north-east, various small commercial ventures, foreign remittances and the income and expenditure of the LTTE. The illicit movements of goods across various borders and from India were quite extensive, particularly when the state imposed various embargoes or blockades. The costs of the risky transport across jungles, borders or the sea and payments to various authorities at borders and elsewhere as bribes to let them through as well as other expenses such as multiple taxes and profits fell ultimately on the civilians. Thus, the exorbitant prices in the north-east increased the cost of living for a population already displaced and deprived of regular income. But the extraordinary fact was that most goods were available at a price! During the severe embargo by the state on all types of essential goods to Jaffna after 1990, when the land route was cut off, a whole range of essential goods were available on the pavements of Jaffna town. From the ubiquitous Panadol,[13]

---

[13] Counterfeit, out-of-date, state pharmaceutical corporation drugs, which should legally be in state hospitals where there is chronic shortage for the same drugs, and banned drugs (not hard, narcotic drugs but ordinary medical drugs long withdrawn from the market due to adverse effects) were freely available over the counter or on pavements. Most of the cheaper varieties were from India where the pharmaceutical industry had suddenly taken off.

which people believed mitigated all kinds of ills,[14] to petrol which was selling at thirty times the normal rate, almost everything people needed for their daily living was available. During the twenty-four-hour curfew that lasted almost a month in October 1987 when the Indian army shot people on sight, enterprising traders moved through internal by-lanes (*olungays*) to keep the small, informal shops in the interior supplied with essential goods (Somasundaram 1998).

Thus, as Nordstrom (2004) maintains, the informal economy is vital to sustain a civilian population during hard times in war zones. Due to fighting, and subsequent collapse of most traditional occupations and income, most people in the north-east became dependent on outside remittances. As Sarvananthan (2006) points out, this was not a new phenomenon in Jaffna where traditional breadwinners, due to lack of resources and harsh climate, had ventured out to the south and abroad for employment and earnings which they remitted back to their families. This was one of the causes for increasing hostility against the Tamils in the south when competition for jobs became more acute due to population pressures. However, the remittances are now more from abroad. In the east, a good number of women have gone to the Middle East as housemaids, to earn for their families, causing severe family problems in their homes. In the north also, migrants, refugees and asylum seekers in Western countries send back part of their earnings or meagre welfare payments through *undiyal* or hawala, and this has kept the home fires burning. It is said that most families have at least one member, if not more, abroad who support their family back home. Families of asylum seekers would have sacrificed considerable money as payments to human smugglers and unscrupulous agents (transactions where they are easily cheated), and as expenses involved in complicated passages through inhospitable routes to get their family member to safety.

A dominant part of the informal economy of the north and east was the LTTE's financial empire. Although it is difficult to estimate the extent of the LTTE's finances, *Jane's Intelligence Review* (Karmi 2007) and Sarvananthan (2006) have estimated that the LTTE generated between US$ two hundred and three hundred million per year through their earnings in Sri Lanka, from both uncleared and cleared areas including Colombo, and abroad. Locally, the LTTE earned through numerous direct and indirect taxes, commercial ventures, extortion, siphoning from government organizations and NGOs and various other sources and means. Taxation included a fixed income tax on salaries and earnings (Saravananthan estimates this

---

[14] I was treating an old lady with somatoform disorder who used to swallow Panadol on hearing bomber planes overhead (see details of the case history in Somasundaram [1998]). Perhaps it would prevent the subsequent headache?

as 8 per cent), including state employees both in the cleared and in the uncleared areas of the north and east, for example, as an almost 'semi-official', regular deduction before monthly salary payments through the finance section. There were also special 'deductions' for various reasons such as a defence levy, Pongu Thamil celebrations and LTTE special days like *Maveerar Nal* (Heroes' Day).[15] All businesses, occupations and produce were taxed varying amounts. According to Saravananthan (2006) the daily tax collection from the A9 highway was US$ one hundred thousand. In fact, many foreign diplomatic experts believed that the LTTE would not go back to war, as it did not want to forgo this 'gold mine'. However, the LTTE perceived nationalistic imperatives as overriding its financial interests. The LTTE also, incredibly, had earnings in Colombo through various business ventures, taxation including a regular rate per passenger for flights to Jaffna and goods transported by sea, ransom, protection money and extortion. Others, like the paramilitaries, military and ex-military deserters, also took advantage of the terror induced by the LTTE by pretending to be the LTTE for extortion and ransom (HRW 2008). However, it was LTTE's foreign financial network that was most lucrative. The LTTE was said to earn considerable amounts through collections (both voluntary and compelled) from the Tamil diaspora (HRW 2006), extortion, contraband, narcotic and human trafficking, shipping and credit-card fraud (Karmi 2007). *Jane's Intelligence Review* estimated that the LTTE spent around US$ eight million for its operation within Sri Lanka and after spending for arms procurement, the money remaining was profit saved and invested abroad as a thriving multinational corporation. Most of LTTE's overseas financial empire is said to have survived its elimination within Sri Lanka in May 2009. However, there is struggle for control of this rich bounty with several factions competing with each other (Jeyaraj 2010) and the Sri Lankan state applying pressure on foreign governments.

Although not directly related to the terror and counter-terror, there was a close nexus between illicit arms' dealings, profiteering, corruption, racketeering, smuggling, the underworld, politicians and militants in the dirty war. They were closely interrelated and the ongoing war, terror and murky atmosphere were needed for maintaining power, interests and investments. At the same time, unofficial funds, illegal transactions and money laundering, fraudulent accounting and resources were needed to finance the terror machine. Sri Lanka has been frequently cited for its high rate of

---

[15] I faced several tense moments when I refused this payment, claiming conscientious objector status due to being a pacifist, and despite some dire warnings the LTTE leadership grudgingly acceded.

corruption (Transparency International 2008). According to the head of Sri Lanka's parliamentary committee on public enterprises, 'Kick-backs and crooked deals cost Sri Lanka over 100 billion rupees [US$911 million], amounting to about a fifth of tax revenue [in 2006]' (Transparency International 2006). However, such events in the shadows happen beyond public knowledge, in an invisible world with its own logic, system and processes (Nordstrom 2004). Thus, it is extremely difficult to obtain a clear picture of the extent of corruption due to the risks and the secrecy involved. For example, Iqbal Athas, an eminent journalist who reported on the enormous corruption in arms procurement was threatened, intimidated and placed at high risk (Reporters Sans Frontières 2007). J. C. Weliamuna, a respected human rights lawyer and investigator for Transparency International, was forced underground. Several journalists have disappeared after revealing underground and shady arm dealings.

Apart from corruption in arm deals, the state has bought arms from the United States, United Kingdom, Russia and former USSR countries, Poland, former Czechoslovakia, India, China, Pakistan, Iran, Israel and other countries on easy payment terms or outright grants. When the United States or United Kingdom expressed concerns about human rights abuses or India about Tamils, Sri Lanka turned to Pakistan, China and Iran for arms. The LTTE procured (also stolen and captured) arms from the Sri Lankan and Indian states, as well as from various illicit arms' bazaars and dealers in Cambodia, Thailand, other South East Asian countries, North Korea, Afghanistan, Pakistan, Lebanon, United States, Turkey and Ukraine and shipped them using its deep sea shipping fleet (Karmi 2007).

Tighter controls by the United States and other Western countries after the 'war on terror' and Indian naval surveillance made it almost impossible for the LTTE to obtain supplies, particularly anti-aircraft missiles, and this critically tipped the military balance in favour of the well-supplied Sri Lankan security forces. Several LTTE attempts to procure or bring in arms' supplies were interdicted in mid-sea. American officials charged six individuals of diverse nationalities, including men from Singapore, a retired Indonesian marine general and others with arms trade and money laundering for the LTTE. Another international network was unearthed in Canada with the intent to purchase between fifty and hundred Russian-made surface-to-air missiles (Karmi 2007).

Transparency International reported on the breadth and depth of corruption in the judiciary and the political control over the judicial process by dismissing, intimidating or transferring judges who do not toe the political line while those who do are shielded from disciplinary action despite evidence of corrupt practices (Ivan 2003; Jayawardena and Weliamuna 2007). There have been rackets which involved arrest, abduction and detention of Tamils, particularly in Colombo but also elsewhere, who then are released only on payments of varying but exorbitant amounts of money (Fernando 2008; HRW 2008). The police, military, intelligence and paramilitaries, alone or in combination, have been implicated.

International Community

A countervailing power against the terror and counter-terror has been the humanitarian programmes, human rights advocacy and pressure for negotiation and peace from the international community. In the post–Cold War world, conflicts have become increasingly intra-state, civil and ethnic in poor, developing parts of the world that are being managed and contained in the periphery. Wealthy nations have used diplomacy and a policy of 'distributing carrots through economic aid and deploying sticks by withdrawing recognition and legitimacy to influence regimes and obtain particular outcomes – altered economic policies, democratiza-tion, relief of suffering from catastrophes' (Esman and Herring 2001). As Bastian (2007) points out, the influence of foreign development assistance 'has permeated all corners of the Sri Lankan economy, state and society. It has become a decisive political factor in key areas of Sri Lankan political and economic life ... promoting democracy and human rights and resolv-ing conflicts.'

Yet, in the case of Sri Lanka, large external funding has inadvertently exacerbated the ethnic conflict by buttressing and legitimizing the ruling regime through indirect support for its discriminatory policies, patronage system and politics to promote mass appeal among recipients, influence, corruption and iniquitous distribution of resources – the massive accel-erated Mahaweli programme is a glaring example (Herring 2001). Apart from direct military hardware, training and advice, provision of massive amounts of aid allowed the state to freely use budgetary manipulation to divert more funds to cover defence spending (Bastian 2007). However, there are also important and successful projects and programmes that have worked for ethnic harmony and created better relationships (Uphoff 2001).

In more recent times, the international community, at least the Western and bilateral donors, have become more directly involved as important stakeholders in the political equation, insisting on good governance, negotiation and peace process as conditions of aid. Multilateral donors like the World Bank, IMF and the Asian Development Bank, and countries like Japan and China, the largest donor, have always focused on economic growth while ignoring the conflict and the politics of governance, even avoiding altogether development projects in the north-east. Indeed some state and international reports, assessments and statistics completely left out or ignored the north and east—a kind of de facto separation or relegation to oblivion. Yet, some donors and UN bodies were able to obtain permission from the state, albeit with official and unofficial restrictions, to carry out limited relief, rehabilitation and, to a lesser extent, reconstruction in the north-east, particularly after the tsunami. As a major counter-insurgency strategy, the state had always carefully monitored and restricted the resources, be they aid, funds or materials, reaching the north-east.

It was under considerable international pressure and direction from Norway and the co-chairs, United States, EU and Japan, with India in the background that the ceasefire and peace process between the Sri Lankan state and LTTE took place from 2002 to 2008 (though it started unravelling from 2005–06, the tsunami having actually postponed the return to hostilities by one year). It was mainly the ultra-Sinhala nationalism of the Rajapaksa regime and his close allies, JVP and JHU, as well as the LTTE's preference for military logic that were primarily responsible for the demise of the peace process. The ouster of Norway and the abrogation of the ceasefire agreement were basic conditions of the JVP's support for Rajapaksa. The LTTE for its part had also clearly shown that it was more comfortable in a war situation and actually initiated this slide to war by ensuring the election of Rajapaksa (Bastian 2007). The strategy of bringing Rajapaksa to power was a fatal blunder of LTTE statecraft, like the blunders with the Muslims, India and with several of the peace processes, and this was another unmitigated disaster for the Tamil-speaking people.

In many critical situations during the conflict, INGOs and LNGOs have functioned as an alternative to the government, providing invaluable humanitarian supplies, assistance and support. Even in more 'normal' situations, they have initiated and carried through much-needed programmes which the government, whose prime responsibility it was, failed to do. They have also been impartial witnesses to the terror and counter-terror described earlier, horrors and atrocities of an inhuman war, human rights abuses and neglect of whole populations. There was an increasing involvement of the international community in Sri Lanka; some have even argued that it is the responsibility of the international community to intervene when the state fails to protect its own citizens, a principle called R2P (Evans 2007, 2008). Traditionally, nation states have respected each other's sovereignty, not questioning what they did within their own borders. There have been various international treaties and conventions like the Geneva conventions, principles of humanitarian law, the Universal Declaration of Human Rights, the International

Covenant on Civil and Political Rights, the International Covenant on Economic, Social and Cultural Rights, the International Convention on the Elimination of All Forms of Racial Discrimination and the United Nations Convention against Torture and Other Cruel, Inhuman or Degrading Treatment or Punishment that countries have ratified and adopted into their own laws. Yet these conventions and agreements did not prevent atrocities and human right abuses on a massive scale from taking place, as the international community was reluctant to interfere in the internal affairs of states and moreover, states easily resisted such diplomatic pressures. International watchdogs like Amnesty International, International Alert, Human Rights Watch, Asian Human Rights Commission and their local counterparts could only monitor and expose violations, but did not have the mechanism to act.

However, more recently after international scandals as in Cambodia, Rwanda, Bosnia, Somalia and Darfur and possibly with the opening up associated with globalization, there has been a growing readiness on the part of the international community, through multinational bodies such as the UN Security Council and General Assembly, or through regional bodies such as the EU, to bring diplomatic pressure or apply economic sanctions and, where that fails, to send in peacekeeping forces to intervene in the internal affairs of the nations that are facing humanitarian crises or failing to protect their citizens (R2P). There have also been efforts and some success in trying to hold wayward leaders accountable for their past actions against civilians through the mechanism of charging them for crimes against humanity or war crimes at the ICC at The Hague. See for example, Table 1B.1, which lists some massive massacres of civilians in Sri Lanka by all sides, which would easily qualify as war crimes. After what happened in the final phase of the war in the Vanni in May 2009, there have been allegations of war crimes, and crimes against humanity raised at the highest levels, calling for investigations and prosecution (BBC 2010; Centre for Policy Alternatives 2009; HRW 2009b; Philp 2009; Philp and Evans 2009; Stein 2010; UN 2011; United States Department of State 2009; UTHR-J 2009; Wax 2009).

Nevertheless, the Sri Lankan state has more recently viewed the involvement of foreign organizations and nations with alarm, perceiving it as a form of recolonization (Goonatilake 2006) and interference in the internal affairs of a sovereign nation. The state has resisted calls for an international investigation into the allegations of war crimes and strictly restricts foreign projects or involvement within Sri Lanka. Paradoxically it is possible that development assistance and humanitarian aid from the international community can promote conflict and war. Bastian (2007) points out that 'development assistance strengthens the structures and relationships responsible for violence and conflict'. For example, in Sri Lanka, as in the example of the accelerated Mahaweli scheme (Herring 2001) mentioned earlier, foreign aid through the state and the dynamics of the relationships of the Colombo-based missions, UN[16] and international agencies with the ruling elite perpetuates the very inequities and structures that are the source of the ethnic conflict (Somasundaram 2000). Moore (1990), quoted by Bastian (2007), describes the 'mutual dependence among donors and the regime, which in the final analysis amounts to a strategy of protecting the regime' in Sri Lanka.

Arulanantham (2007) argues:

> In the conflict in Sri Lanka, counter-insurgency is the method used by the Sri Lankan government to fight the LTTE, which is claiming for some of the power of the state. As the LTTE is perceived to be supported and thus strengthened by the Tamil community, in Sri Lanka and in diaspora, the community also becomes a target for counter-insurgency operations.

A part of the concerted counter-insurgency effort by the state to reduce the international support base for the LTTE was a successful campaign led by the late Lakshman Kadirgamar, the Tamil foreign minister in the SLFP government, a strategy carried on later by the UNP government, to have the LTTE declared a terrorist organization in several countries like the United States, United Kingdom, Canada and EU (India and Malaysia had already banned it), interdict its international financing as well as arms supply and build an 'international network' against the LTTE. Kadirgamar was subsequently killed by the LTTE at his home in Colombo. The state continued its campaign against diaspora who are perceived to be pro-LTTE.

The role of India has been decisive in the ethnic conflict despite its more aloof posturing following the failed IPKF intervention and the assassination of Rajiv Gandhi by the LTTE. India always manipulated a delicate equilibrium in the balance of forces between the Tamil insurgents and Sri Lankan state, dictated by its own internal politics in Tamil Nadu and regional superpower concerns. From initially training, supporting and providing sanctuary to the Tamil insurgents following the anti-Tamil pogrom of 1983 and later attempting to disarm them in its attempt at a peaceful solution in 1987, India armed and trained the Sri Lankan forces. Later India covertly restricted arm supply to the LTTE by closely monitoring and reporting to Sri Lanka ship movements while overtly promoting

---

[16] For example, in the 1980s and 1990s most of the UN organizations in Colombo had exclusively Sinhala staff, sometimes partners of the military hierarchy, who directed most of the humanitarian aid to the south, such as the Mahaweli scheme. The UNICEF had to go through a painful internal review and reorganization in the mid-1990s to try and get its balance right. Now it is being accused by the state of supporting the LTTE!

the now-failed Norwegian peace process (Swamy 2008). Thus, the LTTE was starved of vital arms like the multi-barrel rockets and surface to air missiles, shifting the military balance very much in the favour of the Sri Lankan state.

The lack of surface-to-air missiles meant that the Sri Lankan air force had the freedom of the skies to bomb as they pleased, something they had not been able to do before the peace negotiations. With more training and technological sophistication it has also meant more precise, targeted bombing though there has been considerable (so-called) 'collateral damage'. One example was the bombing of the girls' orphanage on 14 August 2006 where fifty-one girls died (Senewiratne 2006). An earlier mass bombing in 1995 was at the St Peter's Church in Navaly where over 120 refugees died. Another killed thirty-nine schoolchildren at Nagar Kovil. Large district-level hospitals that would have been clearly discernable from above with large white-on-red crosses on their roofs, like the Jaffna General Hospital in the early 1990s and Kilinochchi General Hospital more recently, were bombed. The state always denied these incidents and civilian casualties and severely reprimanded international organizations like the International Committee of the Red Cross (ICRC), UNICEF and ceasefire monitoring bodies for exposing what had happened.

Rehabilitation and Conflict Transformation (Peace Building)

Given the shortcomings of the international community, its complicity, at least indirectly, in the global system attempting to contain internal conflicts to the periphery, its generalized war on terror, support to local states and the vast global interrelated network linking the informal economy, arms and drug trade into the shadow war, an alternate countervailing force would be to mobilize local civic society (Nordstrom 2004). Doing that 'allows allegiance to basic democratic rights and principles to reclaim the fundamental right of average, unarmed citizens to speak freely and engage in independent political activities, against the deliberate destruction of political space by the violence and arbitrary rule' (Keenan 2007).

However, this is easier said than done! The report of UN special rapporteur on extrajudicial summary or arbitrary executions clearly describes the risky environment and the purpose of political killings: 'to repress and divide the population for political gain. Today many people—most notably, Tamil and Muslim civilians—face a credible threat of death for exercising freedoms of expression, movement, association, and participation in public affairs' (Alston 2006).

The real aim of terror and counter-terror is destruction of communities, their cultural heart and spirit of resistance, to cow them into submission, which is part of the collective trauma described in the chapters to come. As Nordstrom (1994) points out:

> The physical violence produced by socio-political conflict is a staggering enough figure. But what happens when we consider the destruction to identity, community, society, and culture that accompanies physical violence — the common targets of 'dirty war' specifically intended to destabilize both people (the generalized opponent) and political process (the threat of resistance)? As war strategists recognize: a physical casualty reduces the opposition by one, while the violence of terror can undermine the political will of an entire population. Yet political will is never successfully quashed, and we know little of the creative resources people employ in overcoming cultures of violence set into play by war.

Thus, in attempting to rekindle the creative spirit of communities to restore peace, one obvious strategy has been to rebuild the communities devastated by war. Psychosocial rehabilitation will be examined in Section 5 of this book, but physical rehabilitation efforts in Sri Lanka have become an intrinsic part of the context. The current relief and rehabilitation programmes for war-affected areas and people, particularly in the north and east, have been brought under the direct control of the government of Sri Lanka for various reasons (ostensibly for fear of resurgence of the LTTE). This is mainly done through the PTF headed by the brother of the President, Basil Rajapaksa and the Ministry of Defence (see Chapter 5C). All INGOs LNGOs working in these areas and all foreign aid have to be channelled through the government. There is considerable monitoring and suspicion of Western countries and NGOs, with restrictions on their activities.

The plans for rehabilitation have tended to be Colombo-centric — drawn up by authorities in Colombo and implemented with close monitoring by the military. As usual, there is corruption and influence involved in these dealings. Lack of political will or basic mistrust can be seen by the non-appointment of a Tamil to any meaningful position of authority in the rehabilitation process. The target population rarely participates in the drawing up of the plans and programmes. Local leadership is often side-lined and made to fall silent by competing political forces. Instead, the military is given an authoritarian role in the decision-making process and the north and east remain under virtual martial law. INGOs have faced considerable difficulties in carrying out their humanitarian work. Unfortunately many internationally supported programmes and structures tended to collapse when the funding is stopped or INGOs pull out. The local partners and government were not able to maintain the momentum.

This raises the question of long-term sustainability. The national discrimination and inequity in distribution of resources and programmes continue to be insurmountable hurdles. This is particularly so when it comes to psychosocial rehabilitation, which is not being permitted (see Chapter 5C). The skills and capacity in psychosocial programming that had been developed during the war and after the tsunami are gradually being lost. In addition, whole populations that have been traumatized by the chronic war do not have the recourse to healing opportunities that would help them participate actively in recovery, physical rehabilitation and development. When planning and undertaking mental health and psychosocial interventions, it is important to reflect on what we have been doing, the experiences and lessons learnt, and consider the developing literature in the field of disaster studies to understand the theory so as to make what we do more effective.

SECTION 2

Theory and Methodology

A.

Theory

Worldwide, disasters like earthquakes, floods, cyclones, landslides, technological accidents and droughts occur daily. On average, there are seven hundred natural and technological disasters which kill 100,000 people and affect 255 million people each year. Most tend to occur suddenly, without much warning, and cause massive destruction, sometimes killing or injuring large numbers of people within a short time. The cost has been estimated at US$ one hundred thousand million each year (McClean 2010). In addition, the man-made[1] disaster called war raging in many parts of the world today as complex political emergencies produces countless deaths and injuries of civilians as well as combatants, and displacement of massive populations. It can be estimated that there have been over 320 wars and armed conflicts in 162 countries since 1946 (Marshall and Cole 2008), mainly internal, civil wars, producing over 378,000 deaths annually (Obermeyer et al. 2008), many more injured and 43.3 million displaced, including fifteen million refugees and twenty-seven million IDPs (UNHCR 2010). It has been found that disasters disproportionately strike the poor, socially deprived, minorities and marginalized, and that their consequences may be more serious and long-lasting for these groups. Similarly, disasters affect developing nations more adversely than developed nations. However, these groups and nations may have the least resources or facilities to cope with the aftermath of disasters.

It is recognized that disaster survivors need food, shelter, other immediate relief measures and long term rehabilitation facilities. Survivors need financial and developmental aid to recover. However, the need for mental health care is not as widely appreciated. Yet short- and long-term mental health problems can hamper rehabilitation efforts. Mental health problems cause difficulties in normal functioning, working capacity, relationships

[1] The word man-made is purposefully chosen with a male gender bias, as wars are typically male projects (de Mel 2007) showing their aggressive, assertive nature while females are more nurturant, tending towards peaceful, negotiated coexistence.

and family life, as well as in recovery and rehabilitation. As much as we work to provide emergency relief and look after survivors' basic needs, we also need to provide mental health care alongside physical health care (The Sphere Project 2004).

Beginning with an immediate acute stress reaction, survivors can develop the whole spectrum of mental responses following massive trauma. Anxiety, depression, PTSD and alcohol or drug abuse can occur in a significant number of survivors, although most people recover remarkably well (Green 1994; Green et al. 2003). Chronic long-term trauma can lead to complex PTSD (Herman 1992), enduring personality changes (WHO 1992) or disorders of extreme stress not otherwise specified (DESNOS) (de Jong et al. 2005). Complex PTSD as a diagnostic category is being introduced for the first time in the new (eleventh) revision of WHO's International Classification of Diseases (ICD-11) (Maercker et al. 2013). In addition, disaster-stricken communities often experience disruption of family and community life, work, normal networks, institutions and structures. Loss of motivation, dependence on relief, hostility and despair can sometimes develop in members of the community exposed to disasters.

Currently, there are a number of recommended interventions that can be used following disasters (Green et al. 2003). Cognitive behaviour therapy (CBT) and pharmacotherapy for post-trauma consequences like PTSD, depression and anxiety are now used in Western countries (Australian Centre for Posttraumatic Mental Health 2007; National Institute for Clinical Excellence 2005; Nutt et al. 2000), but other experts have been critical (Institute of Medicine 2008). Once popular and routine methods like debriefing have been shown not to be helpful, even harmful (Hobfoll et al. 2007).

There is less understanding of the effects that disasters have at the supra-individual family and community levels. Less is known about appropriate interventions at collective levels (The Psychosocial Working Group 2003). There are two principal reasons for this relative deficiency. First, the field of disaster studies is itself rather young. For example, the diagnosis of PTSD was accepted only in 1980 by the American Diagnostic and Statistical Manual of Mental Disorders (DSM)-III (American Psychiatric Association 1980, 1994), following extensive experience with Vietnam war veterans.

Second, modern psychology and psychiatry as it has developed has had a Western medical illness model perspective that is primarily individualistic in orientation (de Jong 2004). Geertz (1983) describes the Western concept of the individual self as

> a bounded, unique, more or less integrated motivational and cognitive
> universe, a dynamic centre of awareness, emotion, judgment, and action
> organized into a distinctive whole and set contrastively both against other

such wholes and against its social and cultural background ... is a peculiar idea within the context of world cultures.

The 'Kantian concept of an autonomous self' (Flood 2006) and 'Enlightenment values of individualism' (Kostelny 2006) have come to mould Western ways of experiencing the self, set against the world and events. Here, the 'self' actually refers to the Freudian ego (*ahangkaram*), the mundane or reality principle which is the coordinating, experiential centre of the individual identity, personality, cognitive, emotional and behavioural components. Losi (2000) describes the contrasting worldviews:

> The term 'egocentric self' refers to an understanding of the individual being as a self-contained, autonomous entity. Psychological normality and abnormality are therefore seen as internal processes also limited to the self. This idea disregards the social origins of mental illness. Most of the world's populations, however, hold a more sociocentric conception of the self, where individuals exist within networks of social relationships from which they derive self-worth, self-fulfilment, self-control and other attributes. In this model, reciprocal and interpersonal privileges or obligations are more important than the rights of individuals.

Significantly, the central teaching of Buddhism is *annatta*, that there is no self, no essential, underlying substance, while Hindu metaphysics points to a different perspective of the self, that it is a reflection of the universal self (Haritayana 2008).

PTSD has been constructed as a condition that afflicts the mind (*manas*) of the individual self (*jiva*), the traumatic event impacting the individual psyche to produce the PTSD. The core symptoms of traumatization become the re-experiencing, reliving of the traumatic event in the present, avoidance of reminders and hyperarousal (Maercker et al. 2013). There is evidence of a neurobiological basis to PTSD that is reflected in changes in brain structures such as the amygdala, hippocampus and prefrontal cortex and their functioning; memory networks, neurotransmitter systems such as noradrenalin and serotonin; and the endocrinal axis that can manifest as somatic symptoms (Somasundaram 1998). However, it is being increasingly recognized generally that we need to go beyond the individual level, to the family, group, village, community and social levels, if we are to more fully understand what is going on in the individual, whether it be the individual's development, behaviour, perceptions, consciousness, experiences or responses to stress and trauma, as well as design effective interventions to help in the recovery and rehabilitation of not only the affected individuals but also their families and community (Harvey 1996; Hoshmand 2007; Landau and Saul 2004; Macy et al. 2004a).

When the family and/or community regain/s its equilibrium and healthy functioning, there is often improvement in the individual member's well-being as well. Family and social support, networks, relationships and the sense of community appear to be vital protective factors for individual and their family and important in their recovery. Cultural rituals and practices, like the North American sweat lodge ceremony (Wilson 1989), *thuku kavadi* in northern Sri Lanka (Derges 2009, 2013) and the eastern Sri Lankan oracle tradition (Lawrence 1999), can heal and provide meaning to suffering after trauma. It is also becoming clear that social and cultural values, beliefs and perceptions will shape how traumatic events impact the individual, family and community and the way they respond (Wilson and Tang 2007; Wong and Wong 2006). The meaning attributed to the event(s), the historical and social contexts, as well as community coping strategies determine the impact and consequences of trauma. For example, strong religious or political beliefs and convictions about what is happening may attenuate the impact. The suffering and distress due to civil conflict experienced as part of a legitimate freedom struggle would be less deleterious than when perceived as afflicting innocent and hapless bystanders. Similarly, firm religious beliefs and organization has been shown to be a protective factor against the effects of trauma. Equally, community coping and resilience help individuals and families deal with and recover from the destructive effects of disasters.

The *World Health Report 2001*, while pointing out that there is considerable mental morbidity among those exposed to severe trauma, warns that there is controversy regarding the cross-cultural validity of PTSD (WHO 2001). It has been argued that PTSD is a recent Western construct that does not apply to non-Western societies (Bracken et al. 1995). However, in my experience I have found that it is a universal, etic phenomenon, appearing across different cultures in a variety of post-traumatic situations including torture (Doney 1998; Somasundaram 2008, 2010h) and landmine victims (Gunaratnam et al. 2003; Somasundaram and Renol 1998). A multi-site survey by the Transcultural Psychosocial Organization (TPO), a WHO collaborating centre, in low-income post-conflict situations using culture sensitive methodology found significant prevalence rates of PTSD in Algeria, Cambodia, Gaza and Ethiopia (de Jong et al. 2001). However, there can be differences in the prevalence and significance of the various criteria. For example, survivor guilt may not be that important or prevalent as in Judeo-Christian cultures where guilt has strong religious meaning. The emotions of shame, humiliation, blame (outward), mistrust and explanations based on karma may be more relevant in Asian cultures. Somatization and somatoform symptoms, though not part of the current PTSD criteria, are often a prominent complaint in those with PTSD (Somasundaram 2001; Somasundaram and Sivayokan 1994). At the same time, PTSD and individual reactions may not be perceived as the most pressing problem in many non-Western cultures.

These differences have clinical implications for assessment and psychotherapy. There can be also a variation in severity from what can be considered a normal reaction to an abnormal situation to degrees of increasing incapacitation and dysfunction. Nevertheless, the diagnosis of PTSD is often clinically helpful in cases that have presented to health care with somatization and other non-specific complaints (Somasundaram 2001). Often the specific history of traumatization is not disclosed or elicited while individuals are treated and investigated without much benefit. When they finally reach mental health services after a long course of help-seeking behaviour that has taken them through traditional healers and other community resources, a detailed history reveals the past traumatization and explains the link between their complaints, suffering and their past experiences.

The theoretical framework of PTSD (Horowitz 1986) provides a reasonable way of understanding the suffering of the patient and doing something for them. However, as Damani de Silva (2001) points out in regard to torture, PTSD is an important but insufficient diagnosis to explain the whole of the reaction to torture. Even psychologically, the survivor often has depression and anxiety in addition to PTSD (American Psychiatric Association 1980, 1994). The effects on the personality, long-term functioning capacity and their family and community go far beyond this. Chronic, severe trauma over several years, particularly of an interpersonal nature in childhood, can have a devastating and permanent effect on personality development. In contrast to a one-off, single exposure to a traumatic event that is called Type I trauma, long-standing or repeated exposure to extreme external events is termed Type II trauma by Lenore Terr (1991). The person is left with an absence of feeling, a sense of rage or unremitting sadness coupled with an underlying terror.

Herman (1992) describes complex PTSD in victims of totalitarian control who develop alterations in affect regulation, consciousness, self-perception, relationships and systems of meaning. I prefer the term malignant PTSD (Somasundaram 2002a), first described by Rosenbeck (1985). A report by the South African National Medical and Dental Association states that such victims develop mistrust, smouldering bitterness, resentment and a thirst for revenge (Browde 1988).

In my clinical experience, I found such disorders in those who had taken to militancy when very young and had been exposed to massive trauma: they had themselves been badly injured or witnessed gruesome deaths and mutilating injuries to many of their comrades (Somasundaram 1998). They had frequently been involved in atrocities, having been responsible for many cruel deaths and torture. They present very disturbed, aggressive outbursts when they re-experience traumatic events. Many expressed an intense death wish, saying that they hoped to be sent off for battle and be killed in action or volunteer for a suicide mission. My observation has been that children are particularly vulnerable during their impressionable formative period; their developing personalities are permanently scarred. Their eventual demobilization, rehabilitation and reintegration into civil society will pose a formidable challenge for the community and post-conflict reconstruction. Though there is the danger of medicalizing what is essentially a politico-social problem (Young 1980), the diagnosis of PTSD helps identify those who will benefit from special care and treatment to alleviate their individual suffering. The recognition of their suffering itself goes a long way in reassuring and supporting them. Further, the diagnosis of PTSD is an internationally recognized standard to document and describe the psychological cost of war. Thus, it becomes an effective tool that contributes towards ending the politico-economic causes of war as well as in humanitarian campaigns, for example, those advocating the banning of landmines and torture.

In Sri Lanka, it has been very difficult to bring out the suffering of civilians. The authorities and even the medical mental health establishment here had been very adverse to any such exposure (Sumathipala and Mendis 2002). It was only after the 2004 Asian tsunami that the post-traumatic psychosocial consequences, the so-called 'tsunami wisdom', become acceptable and programmes to alleviate the distress were permitted (Sundram et al. 2008). There has also been increasing acceptance of the deleterious effects of the war on the state's military combatants and some help has been organized for them (Jayatunge 2004). But again, after the Vanni operation of 2009, there is state denial for political reasons (Somasundaram 2010a).

Thus, the concept of PTSD has been useful in bringing about awareness and understanding of the mental health and psychosocial consequences of disasters. However, it does not adequately capture or explain the extent or wider ramifications of traumatic events on families and communities. These impacts and consequences may have more significance in non-Western collectivistic cultures (de Jong 2004; Hofstede and Hofstede 2005; Nisbett 2003). Psychosocial interventions to alleviate these systemic, ecological repercussions would have to be designed to work at the family, community and societal levels to be effective.

Collectivism

Collectivistic or socio-centric communities are composed of interdependent selves (Markus and Kitayama 1991) where relationships, harmony, solidarity and cooperative spirit with shared goals and sacrifice for the common good are valued. On the other hand, individualistic societies privilege the individual and foster independence, autonomy, competitive spirit and the pleasure principle with personal gratification and consumerism protected by concepts of human rights, democracy and individual freedom. Collective events and consequences may have more significance in collectivistic communities than in individualistic societies. In collectivist societies, the individual becomes embedded within the family and community so much so that traumatic events are experienced through the larger unit and the impact will also manifest at that level. The family and community are part of the self, identity and consciousness. The demarcation or boundary between the individual self and the outside becomes blurred. Thus, 'interdependent selves experience themselves, others and the world around them in an overlapping space–time continuum consisting of an interconnected, interwoven fabric of common environmental, familial, social, and contextual elements' (Yeh et al. 2006).

Tamil families, due to close and strong bonds and cohesiveness in nuclear and extended families, tend to function and respond to external threat or trauma as a unit rather than as individual members. They share the experience and perceive the event in a collective way. During traumatic experiences, the family comes together with solidarity to face the threat as a unit and provide mutual support and protection. The family acts to define and interpret the traumatic event, give it structure and assign a common meaning, as well as evolve strategies to cope with the stress. Thus, it may be more appropriate to talk in terms of family dynamics rather than individual personalities. Traditionally, it is customary to refer to events, impacts and responses in terms of them happening to the family, for example, 'this happened to the so-and-so family and they reacted by doing such and such'. There may be some variations in manifestation, depending on the individual's responsibilities and roles within the family and personal characteristics, and some individuals may become the scapegoat in the family dynamics that ensue. Familial relationships would encompass the extended family, kith and kin as well as ancestors from the past.

The family unit and its functioning have been undergoing rapid changes due to modernization and globalization (Winter 2000). It could be said that the extended family had become less important and functional. Even the nuclear family has become increasingly fragmented (Smith 2006). In the modern, Western world of increasing individuation, where divorce and separation have become the norm, with one-parent families, and individuals having their own lifestyles and choices, some claim that the nuclear family has become an anachronism.

However, in traditional Tamil communities, the village and its people, way of life and environment provided organic roots, a sustaining support system, nourishing environment and network of relationships (*uravu*). The village traditions, structures and institutions were the foundations and framework for their daily life. In the Tamil tradition, a person's identity was defined to a large extent by their village (*uur*) of origin (Daniel 1984). The person's *uur* more or less placed them in a particular sociocultural matrix. Although, modern changes had affected the traditional Tamil families and communities to some extent, the impact of disasters has been more acute and disruptive, accelerating processes that were already happening. Some of these changes could be positive, for example, the salutary effects on female roles, responsibilities, empowerment and emancipation (Chawade 2011; Manchanda 2001; Rajasingham-Senanayake 2001). It may have also made family and community members less exclusive, clannish and family- or group-oriented, compelling them to seek and depend on outside help. However, by and large, the negative impact of disasters has been more salient (Green et al. 2003). It is noteworthy that Tamils as a community have taken their cultural beliefs, practices, structures and institutions with them in the worldwide diaspora, albeit in an attenuated and changing form, where family, extended family and village (*uur*) still play an important organizing, belonging function (Cheran et al. 2007).

A word of caution is necessary; in trying to romanticize or idealize the traditional family, neighbourhood, village, collective and community, it must not be overlooked that in reality they are vague, amorphous terms and include considerable variations among members as well as negative dynamics like scapegoating, marginalization, exclusion, ostracism, silencing and stigmatization of some members, families, castes or groups while others seek power and privilege. The social institution of a traditional *uur* has also undergone tremendous breakdown with the chronic war and displacements as well as modernity. It also proves very difficult to define community and collective very precisely; there are considerable overlaps and borders invariably break down (Van de Put and Eisenbruch 2002). It may also be important to bear in mind that societies are in flux, changing. With modernization and globalization, collectivistic societies are also increasingly becoming individualistic, consumer-oriented, with relationships based on mutual benefit and networks, broader and outward looking. There may also be subcultures within the bigger society with their own, different characteristics.

There will always be debate, tension, a contest in emphasis between the individualistic and collective perspectives. Conventional approaches, assumptions, modern knowledge systems, clinical, academic and research discourses have been individualistic. For example, there has been concern for and attention to individual human rights, the protection of vulnerable individuals, such as in cases of domestic and child abuse. Education, training, legal systems, services and programmes have tended to be individual-oriented, introducing an individualistic world view into collective communities. There can be no doubt that this has been a progressive development, a historical process that has evolved into protecting and empowering vulnerable and excluded individuals who were traditionally suppressed and exploited by the community. However, this positive development can be at the expense of recognizing and understanding the role and dynamics of families and communities that traditionally ensured the well-being of individual members. More recently there has been a growing appreciation and advocacy for collective and social rights, a more community-based approach from non-Western (Wong and Wong 2006) and even some Western workers for Western contexts in the aftermath of 9/11 and Hurricane Katrina (Saul and Bava 2008). Obviously, there needs to be a balance, a more comprehensive and complex conceptual framework to take into consideration the different and at times, competing interests and needs as well as systemic level processes.

Dimensions of Psychosocial Well-being

A better understanding of the supra-individual effects can be sought through the ecological model of Bronfenbrenner (1979) with the micro, meso, exo and macro systems or the individual nested in the family nested in the community (Dalton et al. 2007; Hobfoll 1998). The Bronfenbrenner model fits the WHO definition of health, which also emphasizes the need to look beyond the micro or individual level (see Table 2A.1). According to WHO (1948),[2]

> Health is a state of complete physical, mental, [familial,][3] social, [cultural,] [spiritual] and [ecological] well-being, and not merely an absence of disease or infirmity.

The family unit (and other elements in square brackets indicating my additions) has been included as it is paramount in traditional Tamil society while the spiritual dimension is an essential part of the Tamil culture. The spiritual dimension has been put forward at various WHO forums but has not been formally accepted yet. Culture is increasingly recognized as an important dimension of mental health (Bhugra and Bhui 2007). The ecological dimension arises from Bronfenbrenner's and environmental models and systems theory that emphasizes an overall holistic approach,

[2] See the preamble. The constitution was adopted by the International Health Conference, New York, 19–22 June 1946, and came into force on 7 April 1948.

[3] The words within square brackets are my additions, the reasons for which are explained in the text that follows.

Table 2A.1:
Dimensions of Health—Some Examples of Ill Health

Dimensions of Health	Causes	Symptoms	Diagnoses	Interventions
Physical	Physical injury infections, nutritional deficiencies, excesses	Pain, fever, disability, somatization	Physical illness, psychosomatic, somatoform disorders	Health education, drug treatment, physiotherapy, relaxation techniques, massage
Psychological	Shock, stress, fear, terror, loss, trauma	Tension, fear, sadness, learned helplessness	Acute stress reaction (ASR), PTSD, anxiety, depression, alcohol and drug abuse	Psychoeducation, psychological first aid, psychotherapy, counselling, relaxation techniques, CBT, testimonial therapy
Family	Death, disappearance, separation, disability, poverty	Role vacuum disharmony, negative dynamics, violence scapegoating	Family pathology	Psychoeducation, family therapy, marital therapy, family support, family unity, cohesion, mutual understanding, relationships
Social	Unemployment, displacement, poverty, war, 'repressive ecology', genocide	Conflict, suicidal ideation, anomie, alienation, withdrawal, loss of communality, substance abuse, empty rituals	Parasuicide, suicide, violence, collective trauma	Psychosocial education, group therapy, *testimonio*, trust, rehabilitation, community mobilization, participatory methods, empowerment, social engineering, social cohesion, building social capital, collective efficacy
Cultural	Racism, colonization, majoritarianism, cultural genocide, assimilation, domination, culture shock, acculturation stress	Depression, suicide, anger, violence, helplessness, despair, demoralization, crime	Fractured communities, drugs and alcohol, suicide, cultural bereavement, domestic violence, violence	Strengthening communities, cultural traditions, practices, healing rituals, ceremonies, traditional healers, elders, narrative therapy, recognition of the culture
Spiritual	Misfortune, bad period, spirits, angry gods, evil spells, karma	Despair, demoralization, loss of belief, loss of hope	Possession, dissociation	Logotherapy, rituals, traditional healing, meditation, contemplation, mindfulness, middle way, harmony

(Table 2A.1 Contd.)

(Table 2A.1 Contd.)

Dimensions of Health	Causes	Symptoms	Diagnoses	Interventions
Ecological	Disasters, pollution, climate change, loss of biodiversity, exploitation of resources, deforestation	Epidemics, malnutrition, starvation, stress, conflict, migration, loss of communality	Pandemics, disaster syndromes, ecocide	Sustainable development, conservation, renewable energy, environmental protection, holistic and integrative methods, equilibrium, homeostasis

Source: Author.

looking at how the different levels, dimensions and systems with different temporal trajectories of their own influence each other to produce an interactive, dynamic (dys)functional whole. The disaster itself has an impact on these systems and their interaction, and moreover has a temporal trajectory of its own (Sims 1983, Kinston and Rosser 1974 ; see Figures 2A.1 and Table 2A.3). More recently a growing consensus has been emerging on the need to look at these wider dimensions to understand the dynamics of the effects of disasters and to design effective interventions (de Jong 2002; Landau and Saul 2004; The Psychosocial Working Group 2003).

Though the WHO definition of well-being artificially divides into the physical, mental and social dimensions for the sake of elucidation, they are in reality interdependent and interconnected systems. When one dimension is adversely affected it causes disturbances at all the other levels. Table 2A.1 provides an expanded interpretation of health, with examples of causes, symptoms, diagnoses and interventions for illnesses or disorders.

The primary treatment in the West for individuals with minor mental health disorders due to psychosocial problems is counselling or psychotherapy and more recently, CBT. However, people from non-Western countries may find modern psychiatric methods of treatment like psychotherapy quite strange and unacceptable. Although traditional forms of counselling do exist (Van de Put et al. 1997), both the counsellor and the clients usually find the modern method of counselling uncomfortable. Thus, it was not unexpected that the outcome of Western counselling methods was also poor (Geevathasan 1995). Further, the very assumptions on which psychotherapeutic interventions are based may be culturally flawed and thus the issues one takes up in psychotherapy might be erroneous. According to Bracken et al. (1995), '[H]elping to alleviate distress by the exploration of intrapsychic cognitions, emotions and conflicts is a form of healing somewhat peculiar to Western societies and of doubtful relevance to societies holding different core assumptions about the nature of self and illness.' It is very important to work through peoples' cultural beliefs and explanations, if psychological forms of treatment are to succeed.

Nevertheless, people feel relief after expressing their distress verbally or otherwise. There is evidence that disclosing traumatic experiences is psychologically and physically beneficial. Inhibition of trauma-related thoughts or feelings appears to require a physiological and psychological effort that acts over time as a cumulative stressor that can lead to health problems like hypertension, weight loss and skin rashes (de Jong 2002). Expressing traumatic material can be done in more culturally appropriate ways to community resources like confiding in respected elders, traditional healers or priests, and through creative arts like drama, narratives, dance, music, drawing and writing. Trauma experts John P. Wilson (2007) and Joop de Jong (2002) emphasize that modern methods such as CBT are not appropriate in non-Western settings. There is some evidence emerging that alternate forms of CBT such as narrative therapies may be more appropriate in non-Western (Schauer et al. 2005) and indigenous populations (Australian Centre for Posttraumatic Mental Health 2007).

Stress leads to many physiological changes in the body (particularly activation of the sympathetic division of the autonomic nervous system and the adrenal medulla and cortex of the endocrinal system) that in turn maybe lead to a host of physical diseases. The lifesaving role of the hypothalamo-pituitary-adrenocortical axisto secrete corticosteroids under stress was first recognized by Selye (1976) who described the exhaustion of the general adaptation syndrome under extreme situations. In trauma, on the other hand, there is a chronic state of hyperactivation to this system leading to hyperarousal. Western biomedicine realized that one of the best ways to relieve stress is through relaxation exercises. Jacobson (1938) first introduced relaxation methods into Western medicine in the 1930s. Jacobson's exercises produced a state of relaxation which was hypothesized to be incompatible with a state of tension due to stress.

However, physiologically similar traditional methods have been used for centuries in Asia. The yogic pranayama and Buddhist form of mindful breathing (*anapanasati*) are culturally well-known breathing exercises that produce conscious, deep, regular abdominal (diaphragmatic) breathing. The yogic shanti or *savasana* produces progressive muscular relaxation. Similar to Benson's relaxation response, the Hindu *jappa*, Catholic rosary, prayer beads, Islamic *dhikr*, Buddhist *pirit* and chanting are culturally familiar and acceptable. For meditation, dhyana, *samadhi*, *vipassana*, contemplation and other methods are in use. In addition, traditional oil massage used in Ayurvedic and Siddha medicine can induce states of relaxation. A worldwide panel of trauma experts on the treatment of those exposed to disaster and mass violence have identified promoting and producing a sense of calming as an important empirically supported intervention principle to counteract the increase in emotionality, hyperarousal, anxiety, distress, fear and avoidance found in these post-traumatic situations. Significantly, they recommend deep, diaphragmatic breathing; deep muscle relaxation; yoga; and mindfulness techniques drawn from Asian culture and meditation methods (Hobfoll et al. 2007).

It is becoming evident that physical symptoms, the experience of these symptoms or illness itself, health-seeking behaviour and explanation and beliefs about causation are culturally determined (Kirmayer 1996; Kleinman 1980). Social processes may actually influence the pathophysiology to change bodily processes. Thus, a therapy that works through culturally accepted practices and beliefs systems could be of immense benefit. It may be able to use or reverse the very psychosocial processes that were responsible for the original problem or complaint. But more importantly, traditional methods that co-opt cultural processes can be used to address widespread problems that have taken on a social dimension. One good example is trauma. Trauma in war-torn societies tends to be pervasive, massive, chronic, complex and multilayered. Given the widespread nature of the traumatization due to war (Somasundaram and Sivayokan 1994), a community-based approach will be most effective (Somasundaram 1997b). A community-based revival of using traditional relaxation methods could act as a calming, countervailing force against the social chaos and violence of a chronic war. One way would be by teaching the traditional practices to large groups in the community, in temples, pagodas, churches, community centres, and as part of the curricula in schools. This will be promotive, preventive and curative. When people come together to learn and practise these methods in a temple, church or pagoda under a senior priest, pastor, nun or monk, the atmosphere will be very therapeutic and socially healing. Apart from the actual practice of the methods, people will interact in a healthy way, support each other, find meaning for their problems and suffering through the religious doctrines on karma and suffering as well as structure their time and energy in a constructive, non-detrimental way (such as not drinking or gambling). Family life too would improve. Researchers have shown that when 1 per cent of the population in a city starts practising transcendental medication, the crime rate begins to reduce and other social parameters start improving (Borland and Landrith 1976; Dillbeck et al. 1987). Apparently, the calmness, tranquillity and ways of responding to frustrations are passed on from the practitioners to others. They have even reported reduced conflict in war-torn areas (Orme-Johnson et al. 1988).

Spiritually, the benefits of these originally spiritual practices are not confined to producing relaxation. When methods are culturally familiar, they tap into past childhood, community and religious roots and thus release a rich source of associations that can be helpful in therapy and the healing process. Mindfulness and meditation draw upon hidden resources within the individual and open into dimensions that can create spiritual well-being and give meaning to what has happened. Although these techniques do no formal psychotherapy, they may accomplish what psychotherapy attempts to do by releasing cultural and spiritual restorative processes.

Ecological perspectives are gaining importance with modern concerns about climate change, environmental exploitation, pandemics and ecological degradation. Systemic methods to promote conservation, sustainable development, holistic and integrative approaches to maintain psycho-ecological equilibrium, homeostasis and peace have relevance to psychosocial principles, planning, interventions and prevention. In rebuilding communities after disasters, these principles are particularly important and approaches to community reintegration, reconciliation, relationships, contexts and processes have to follow these same principles if they are to be effective.

Collective Trauma

The phenomenon of collective trauma first became very obvious to me when I was working in the post-war recovery and rehabilitation context in Cambodia (Van de Put et al. 1997). The Khmer Rouge had deliberately targeted basic social structures, institutions, traditional privileges, hierarchies, roles and responsibilities, all to be reorganized and made ostensibly more egalitarian. Feudal, educational and religious structures were systematically destroyed. Large communist-style communes were organized and everyone was expected to contribute their labour and allegiance. Any shirking or opposition was put down violently. As such, this 'social experiment' clearly brought out how families and communities respond and act in extreme situations in culturally resonant ways (Hinton 2007).

Previous researchers had already drawn attention to the community-level problems caused by disasters. Kai Erikson (1976, 1979) gives a graphic account of collective trauma as 'loss of communality' following the Buffalo Creek disaster in the United States. He and his colleagues describe the 'broken cultures' in North American Indians and 'destruction of the entire fabric of their culture' due to forced dispossession from traditional lands into reservations, separations, massacres and loss of their way of life, relationships and spiritual beliefs (Erikson and Vecsey 1980). A similar tearing of the 'social fabric' has been described in Australian indigenous populations by Milroy (2005):

> [I]t implies things have to be woven together properly for strength, what a shame our fabric was torn to shreds through invasion, what we have left now is in tatters, repairing fabric can make it weak or sometimes stronger

depending on how it is done. It is important to repair the holes and not just cover them over so that when some tension is applied it doesn't fall apart. What kept our fabric strong was spirituality, the invisible thread that binds us all.

The National Strategic Framework for Aboriginal and Torres Strait Islander Health, according to the National Aboriginal and Torres Strait Islander Health Council (2003), states:

> The sense of grief and loss experienced by generations of Aboriginal and Torres Strait Islander peoples in relation to dispossession, to the disruption of culture, family and community and to the legislated removal of children has contributed to ongoing problems in emotional, spiritual, cultural and social well-being for Aboriginal and Torres Strait Islander individuals, families and communities. (Emphasis added)

Atkinson (2002) describes how the legacy of historical trauma and consequent cycles of ongoing stressors impact indigenous families and communities, making them dysfunctional, and how to heal using cultural practices like *dadiri* (an Australian indigenous cultural practice of deep listening), dreaming, narratives, family and community story maps, dance, art and drama.

Maurice Eisenbruch (1991) uses the term 'cultural bereavement' for the loss of cultural traditions and rituals in Indo-Chinese refugees in the United States. More recently, a number of discerning researchers in the field are drawing attention to the importance of looking at the family (Landau and Saul 2004; Tribe 2004; Tribe and Family Rehabilitation Centre Staff 2004) and cultural dimension (de Jong 2002, 2004; Landau and Saul 2004; Miller and Rasco 2004; Silove and Steel 2006) following disasters. Abramowitz (2005) paints a moving picture of collective trauma in six Guinean communities exposed to war.

The concept of collective trauma is being introduced for the first time in a modern mental health diagnostic classification in the draft of the WHO ICD-11 guidelines[4] for PTSD under cultural considerations:

> Large-scale traumatic events and disasters affect families and society. In collectivistic or sociocentric cultures, this impact can be profound. Far-reaching changes in family and community relationships, institutions, practices, and social resources can result in consequences such as loss of communality, tearing of the social fabric, cultural bereavement and collective trauma. For example, in indigenous and other communities that have been persecuted over long periods there is preliminary evidence for trans-generational effects of historical trauma.

---

[4] This is an unpublished document of the WHO ICD-11 Working Group on the Classification of Disorders Specifically Associated with Stress.

Supra-individual effects can manifest in a variety of forms, including collective distrust; loss of motivation; loss of beliefs, values and norms; learned helplessness; anti-social behaviour; substance abuse; gender-based violence; child abuse; and suicidality. These effects, as well as real or perceived family and social support, can also impact on individual resilience and outcomes.

Though both the American DSM and WHO ICD classification systems have traditionally been exclusively individual-based, it is argued that a collective approach becomes paramount from a public mental health perspective where large populations are affected and where resources are limited.[5] Further, community-based approaches may be more effective and meaningful in collectivistic societies.

Jung's concept of the 'collective unconscious' (Jung 1969; Read et al. 1954) is convenient to metaphorically[6] denote the repository of the mass-scale impact of major catastrophic events on the group mind (Bloom 1998), the collective memory. Jung (1947) describes the psychological concept of collective guilt in relation to Germany after the Second World War. Looking back, it is intriguing to speculate on the power of collective guilt and other collective phenomena to influence (and explain) post–Second World War developments in Germany (and by extension in Japan): the remarkable economic revival, compulsive restraints in military development and generous, international humanitarian aid programmes. Similar collective reactions to the Second World War can be discerned in Europe and elsewhere: the creation of the United Nations (and the earlier League of Nations after First World War), the four Geneva and other conventions, humanitarian law and the ICC.

John Wilson (2004) talks of the unconscious manifestation of collective trauma as the 'trauma archetype' that is universal, common to all cultures. Yael Danieli (2007) writes eloquently about the transgenerational transmission of trauma:

> [M]assive trauma shapes the internal representation of reality of several generations, becoming an unconscious organizing principles passed on by

[5] Though I am a member of the WHO ICD-11 Working Group on the Classification of Disorders Specifically Associated with Stress, reporting to the WHO International Advisory Group for the Revision of ICD-10 Mental and Behavioural Disorders, the views expressed here are mine and, except as specifically noted, do not represent the official policies or positions of the International Advisory Group or the WHO.

[6] It is possible that the inspiration for Jung's model for the collective unconscious came from Eastern thought, particularly Buddhist and Hindu tantric yoga, or he was merely describing parallels. He considered the *sahasrara chakra* as the seat of the collective unconscious (Jung 1996).

parents and internalized by their children' … the multigenerational, collective, historical, and cumulative psychic wounding or 'soul wound' over time, both in their victims' life span and across generations.

The trauma can be transmitted through possible epigenetic mechanisms, parent–child interactions, family dynamics, sociocultural perpetuation of a persecuted ethnic identity based on selective, communal memories (Wessells and Strang 2006) or 'chosen traumas' (Volkan 1997), narratives, songs, drama, language, political ideologies and institutional structures. The long-lasting impact at the collective level — some have called it tearing in the social fabric — would then result in the social transformation (Bloom 1998) of a sociopathic nature that can be called collective trauma (see Table 2A.2). Table 2A.2 explores the characteristics of collective trauma across seven dimensions: disasters; causal conditions; ecological context; symptoms; coping strategies; consequences; and community-level interventions. The 'x' sign between causal conditions and ecological context is to indicate the interaction between psychosocial effects of the disaster and what are sometimes called the indirect psychosocial effects that are subsumed under the psychosocial ecological context. The systemic nature of traumatogenic forces and their impact on family, community and societal systems has been described (Hoshmand 2007). Families and communities cope with the disaster in a multitude of adaptive and non-adaptive ways which can result in a variety of psychosocial problems or in positive resilience and growth. Community-level interventions (Harvey 1996; Macy et al. 2004a), particularly MHPSS, can be used to help communities affected by disasters (see Section 5).

The impact of catastrophic events on the individual has been well established internationally (American Psychiatric Association 1980, 1994; WHO 1992) and was quite clear in northern Sri Lanka (Somasundaram 1993c, 1998). There have been some observations on the family level too in northern Sri Lanka (Jeyanthy et al. 1993). However, it was when it came to addressing mental health problems that the impact on the community became evident. Conventional interventions at the individual level were inadequate. The problems at the community level too had to be understood and addressed if the individuals were to be fully helped. Further, families and communities had to recover if any meaningful socio-economic rehabilitation programmes were to succeed. In fact, in time, most long-term programmes, as in other post-disaster settings around the world, began to include a community-based psychosocial component, what is now being termed MHPSS, within the larger socio-economic rehabilitation and reconstruction efforts (IASC 2007; The Sphere Project 2004; WHO 2003).

Table 2A.2:
Collective Trauma—Theoretical Model

Disasters	Causal Conditions	Ecological Context	Signs and Symptoms	Coping Strategies	Consequences	Community-level Interventions
Man-made (for example, war)	Displacements	Social chaos, uprooting	Insecurity	*Negative* Silence, withdrawal, isolation, benumbing;	*Negative* Dependency, learned helplessness, passivity;	Psychosocial education, awareness; Training of community workers; Community interventions, family; Groups encourage indigenous coping strategies, cultural rituals and ceremonies; Expressive (emotive, creative) methods; Psychosocial rehabilitation, multi-sectorial collaboration, networking; Promote resilience; Prevention
	Separations	Breakdown of social structures and institutions	Terror	Suspicion	Loss of trust, paranoia	
	Massive destruction		Impunity, social injustice		Despair, disbelief, amotivation, hopelessness;	
Natural (for example, tsunami)	Multiple deaths	Unemployment or under-employment, poverty	Breakdown of law and order	'Fight, flight or freeze', survival, escape, suicide	Loss of communality, decrease in social cohesion, tearing of social fabric, Loss of social capital	
	Injuries	Starvation, hunger, malnutrition	Inequity, discrimination	*Positive* Cultural practices, rituals;	*Positive*	
	Losses	Lack of medical care, diseases, epidemics	Helplessness, hopelessness	Adaptation, facing the challenge, problem solving	Adaptive changes in memory, reframing, meaning, realism; Resilience, forbearance, new networks, friendship, relationships, hope; Regeneration, development, progress	
	Cultural and social bereavements	'Repressive ecology', violence, torture, abductions, detentions, disappearances, extrajudicial killings	Rumours, disinformation			

Source: Author.

Social Capital

The construct of social capital is becoming increasingly recognized as an important factor in mental health (Cullen and Whiteford 2001; McKenzie and Harpham 2006). Disasters such as a chronic civil war can lead to depletion of social capital (Kawachi and Subramanian 2006; Wind and Komproe 2012). According to Bracken and Petty (1998b) and Summerfield (1998) modern wars deliberately destroy social capital assets to control communities through terror (see Chapter 1B). Understanding the destruction of social capital by long-term civil conflict is crucial for describing collective trauma. However, contemporary social analysts caution against a simplistic or superficial view of social capital and call for a deeper, detailed, fine-grained analysis of social transformation at the community level to look for positive, negative and 'perverse' changes (Goodhand et al. 2000). Social capital encompasses community networks, relationships, civic engagement with norms of reciprocity and trust in others that facilitate cooperation and coordination for mutual benefit (Cullen and Whiteford 2001).[7] Fundamentally, it encompasses social institutions, structures, functions, dynamics, the quality and quantity of social interactions; it is a reflection of social cohesion, the glue that holds society together. Theoretically, positive social capital would increase the community's capacity to withstand disasters, its resilience and respond constructively.

From a collectivist social capital perspective, the root cause of civil conflict stems from the lack of bridging social capital, that is, competitive and antagonistic inter-ethnic relations as a result of polarized and exclusive ethnocentric perceptions (see Chapter 1A). This could arise from a myriad of further sub-causes like horizontal inequalities (Stewart 2001) in opportunity, income and economic resources (poor linking), ethnic suspicions and tensions (poor bridging), group exclusion, disparities in political access and participation, weak civic engagement with the government leading to weak community links with the state, polarization between ethnic communities and experiencing discrimination and humiliation based on ethnicity.

Although Tamil communities had high levels of social capital, this was mainly in the form of social, family and intra-ethnic bonding. In the past, there had been inter-ethnic relationships and bridging bonding with other

---

[7] Current conceptualizations of social capital contain the Western bias of social analysis from a Western, individualistic paradigm. Social relationships are viewed from the perspective of mutual benefit, Rousseau's social contract, stemming from individuals acting out of their own self-interest. However, in non-Western contexts, social relationships usually are for their own value, people act for the benefit of the family or group, even when detriment to their own interest. These acts are often termed sacrifice or altruism (see Chapter 1A).

communities (see Chapter 1A). The driving force for the modern conflict was ethnic identity (Somasundaram 1998). The insecurity, fear and strong feelings aroused when the group's identity, culture and way of life, its access to resources and survival were perceived as being threatened, were mobilized into collective actions, defiance, resistance, militancy and violence. The sources of growing frustrations and rebellion were the power differentials between the rulers and the governed in a hierarchical society, the poor or absent access to sources of power and decision-makers, lack of control over opportunity structures and resource distribution and discrimination as a group — these were also indications of the lack of vertical or linking social capital among the minority Tamils.

A consequence of the long-drawn conflict, say Goodhand et al. (2000), was a redrawing of ethnic boundaries in the north and east of Sri Lanka with ethnic enclaves and a constantly changing geography of security and insecurity between so-called cleared and uncleared areas. The social capital in these differing contexts may vary enormously. In more secure areas where the state or LTTE has/had a monopoly of violence, there was more stability and predictability where mono-ethnic communities had a reassurance of being among one's own people and thus had more positive social capital. Networks and organizations thrived with more civic engagement, trust and participation. However, in contested, grey areas like the border villages but also in many parts of the north-east with frequent changes in power and patterns of displacement of multi-ethnic communities, constant insecurity and instability due to violence from the state, paramilitaries, LTTE and home guards, there was competition for resources, a survival economy, breakdown of social capital, deep suspicion and polarization between groups. In these circumstances, the 'common community coping strategy was to fall back on group based networks and family ties. The most resilient sources of social capital are socially embedded networks and institutions, particularly those based on caste and religion' (Goodhand et al. 2000). This resulted in strengthening social bonding within groups while weakening bridging social capital between groups. The goal of psychosocial rehabilitation and national reconciliation is to rebuild these bridges.

Conflict entrepreneurs, that is, social actors with a vested interest in creating and arousing ethnic tensions, socially engineered 'perverse' social capital gaining power, legitimacy and social control. The resulting social transformation led to the emergence of a new leadership, it altered gender and generational hierarchies and created a 'new rich', entrepreneurial class in a 'dirty war' context (Nordstrom 2004; Somasundaram 2010e) (see Chapter 1B). However, in the long term with competing regimes of control and terror, even the bonding social capital eroded, the bridging social capital between groups was consistently undermined and people lost trust in social institutions, structures and governance. Thus, according to Goodhand et al. (2000):

> [S]ocial capital may represent a powerful social glue when there is a clearly defined enemy, but when conflict becomes protracted, the fault lines become less clear and bonding may break down. Conflict entrepreneurs on either side are aware of these tensions and exploit them accordingly. Political and military support for the Tamil paramilitary groups, for example, represents an attempt to harness tensions within Tamil civil society and so undermine LTTE attempts to create an ideology which transcends local loyalties. Therefore, social capital may be manipulated and strengthened for perverse outcomes. While a political economy perspective points to the primacy of 'interests', rather than 'passions', one should not ignore the importance of the 'emotional economy' of violence, and the processes through which hate is constructed and mobilized. Conflict entrepreneurs appear to have an intuitive understanding of such processes and how to destroy social capital and create 'anti-social' capital. The LTTE for instance have either co-opted or destroyed pre-existing institutions and created new ones to win hearts and minds. Propaganda and violence have been used to nurture an emotional economy based on a currency of fear, victimhood and a sense of grievance. Showcase killings and 'theatrical' violence have been used strategically to cow populations, provoke reprisal killings and deepen ethnic fault lines. Another important element of the affective economy is the mythology of the 'heroic death'. Its most extreme version is the LTTE's female suicide bombers which draws on this symbolism of valour to recruit and mobilise young men.

Communities under stress manifest social disorganization, unpredictability, low trust, fear, high vigilance, low efficacy, low social control of antisocial behaviours and high emigration which lead to anomie, learned helplessness, thwarted aspirations, low self-esteem and insecurity. With the breakdown of social capital, social pathologies like substance abuse, violence, gender-based and child abuse increase, and health problems like heart disease, depression, stress-related conditions, behaviours contributing to chronic illness and reduction in immunity to infection and cancer develop (Cullen and Whiteford 2001).

According to Colletta and Cullen (2000):

> Unlike interstate conflict, which often mobilizes national unity and strengthens societal cohesiveness, violent conflict within a state weakens its social fabric. It divides the population by undermining interpersonal and communal trust, destroying the norms and values that underlie cooperation and collective action for the common good, and increasing the likelihood of

communal strife. This damage to a nation's social capital — the norms, values, and social relations that bond communities together, as well as the bridges between communal groups (civil society) and the state — impedes the ability of either communal groups or the state to recover after hostilities cease. Even if other forms of capital are replenished, economic and social development will be hindered unless social capital stocks are restored .... Such an understanding could enhance the abilities of international actors and policymakers to more effectively carry out peacebuilding — relief, reconstruction, reconciliation, and development.

There have been more recent developments towards community-level interventions for massive trauma (de Jong 2002; Somasundaram 1997b; The Psychosocial Working Group 2003). The Inter-Agency Standing Committee (IASC), set up under a UN General Assembly resolution in 1992, used the experience of over two hundred organizations working worldwide in situations of mass trauma, to collaboratively prepare the IASC Guidelines on Mental Health and Psychosocial Support in Emergency Settings (IASC 2007). The guidelines recommend considering the sociopolitical and cultural context to maximize the participation of local population, building on available local resources and capacities and integrating close collaboration between support systems when responding. An excellent conceptual framework for building community resilience as a process of dynamic adaptation with a positive trajectory to buffer the adverse effects of disasters and promote community well-being has been developed (Norris et al. 2008). Among other principles, the guidelines suggest ensuring commitment from the community; engaging the entire system of the community in an inclusive process; identifying scripts, themes and patterns across generations and community history, fostering creativity as the central process of healing; maintaining sensitivity to issues of culture, gender and spirituality; encouraging access to all natural and ancillary resources; building on existing resources; collaborating and networking across all systems; relating programme needs to goals, future and best interests of the community; encouraging natural change agents and leadership within the community; empowering families and communities; and developing ownership by the community. The strategies for reconstruction and revitalization of social capital after conflict include (Lochner 2000):

1. Strengthening social networks.
2. Building social organizations, for example, CBOs.
3. Strengthening community ties, that is, bridging groups normally divided along grounds of class, caste, race, ethnicity or religion.
4. Strengthening civil society.
5. Bringing about macro-social policy reform while increasing community access to external resources and power.

It becomes vital to take into consideration the complex effects of civil conflict on social capital and address programmes to repair the damage if reconciliation and development are to succeed in the current post-war situation.

Coping and Resilience

Community resilience can be seen as positive, collective adaptability despite high levels of adversity. Instead of looking only at pathological negative outcomes, resilience looks at adaptation and withstanding adversity. Community resilience has been defined as the '[c]ommunity's capacity, hope and faith to withstand major trauma and loss, overcome adversity, and to prevail, usually with increased resources, competence and connectedness' (Landau and Saul 2004). Community values, beliefs and traditions can provide bulwarks against mass trauma (Harvey 1996). Adversity-activated development describes salutary social transformation, post-traumatic growth and progressive changes following challenging circumstances (Papadopoulos 2007). The analysis of social protective and risk factors, the social dynamics of coping and growth can help understand social processes and identify collective competency factors that can be built upon.

Important characteristics of resilient communities include availability of family, extended and neighbourhood support systems and networks, that is, bonding social capital, community resources like respected and functioning elders, traditional healers and cultural practices, religious leaders and organizations, institutions like schools, health facilities, governmental organizations and NGOs, community-level conflict resolving mechanisms and functioning structures like judiciary and judicial system, democratic practices and access, free media and reliable information. Economic and income stability, employment, occupations and traditional vocations, food, shelter, security and other essential needs being met would help communities cope with adversities and shocks to the system. Norris et al. (2008) identify four primary sets of adaptive capacities for community resilience — economic development, social capital, information and communication and community competence. Community competence refers to the capacity, resources and skills within the community to act together, cooperatively and effectively, to meet challenges. Unfortunately in disaster situations, particularly chronic war contexts some or many of these resources and support systems would be affected, dysfunctional or not available. Community responses and coping may thus become compromised. A vicious resource loss cycle (Hobfoll 1998) with breakdown of social support, networks, leadership, economic resources and material goods creates a downward spiral of a deteriorating situation of increasing needs and dysfunction, one lacks feeding the other deprivation.

Yet, critical challenges and adversity may just provide the impetus, catalytic stimulus for change and social transformation. Thus the breakdown of traditional forms of oppression and rigid hierarchical structures like caste, feudal ownership and patriarchal female suppression could lead to more positive emancipation and development. New organizations, networks, relationships, friendships, forgetting of old quarrels and conflicts, shared memories and experiences could lead to community growth and enhancement. Motivated and vibrant leadership may emerge while older, ineffective and anachronistic methods are shed. There can be radical and revolutionary alteration in the social trajectories due to critical challenges. A common enemy can forge social unity and cohesion. Common people, oppressed and excluded minorities could gain more power and access to resources due to shifts in the social system or out of collective action. Collective consciousness can be awakened, leading to more awareness and knowledge. In the tradition of Friere's (1972) 'conscientization', the breakdown in social structures and institutions creates an opportunity for empowerment, collective transformation and re-alignment of social dynamics, 'challenging existing structures of power and achieving a shift in power relations, ultimately resulting in the transformation of the existing social order' (Psychosocial Assessment of Development and Humanitarian Interventions [PADHI] 2009).

Conventional understanding of stress and coping has been Western, individualistically oriented, emphasizing a sense of personal agency and internal locus of control, focus on problem solving, meeting challenges and overcoming obstacles through individual effort. However, Asian collectivistic values and coping styles may be fundamentally different. Thus, Chun et al. (2006) say:

> [C]oping strategies that confront and modify external stressors (for example, behavioural or approach-focused coping strategies) are expected to be more common in individualistic cultures, whereas coping strategies that avoid external stressors and instead modify internal psychological states (for example, cognitive or avoidance-focused coping strategies) are expected to more common in collectivistic cultures.

Self-transformation through reframing and spiritual practices is possible in Asian communities (Chen 2006). Asian values that have been identified include salience of family, avoidance of family shame, conformity to family norms and expectations, deference to authority figures, filial piety, self-control and restraint, maintenance of interpersonal harmony, placing

other's needs ahead of one's own, reciprocity, respect for elders and ancestors, holistic world view, collectivism and self-effacement (Heppner et al.
2006). Understanding the Asian style of coping needs to consider family
support, religion–spirituality, forbearance, karmic belief system, respect
for authority and avoidance–detachment strategies (Hoshmand 2007;
Yeh et al. 2006).

Thus, what may appear as maladaptive coping from a Western point
of view, for example, avoidance, passivity, silence and non-engagement,
may, in an Asian setting, be adaptive and appropriate for the context.
However, what may be adaptive, aiding survival in a conflict situation,
like silence and avoidance, can become maladaptive, inhibiting recovery,
rehabilitation and development in a post-conflict setting. It would be as
important not to undermine these traditional ways of coping by importing inappropriate Western concepts and methods, as it is to consider the
context.

The Western tradition of seeking help from a counsellor or psychologist would be culturally inappropriate in a collectivistic community
(Yeh et al. 2006). Equally, CBT, the most validated psychotherapy for PTSD
in the Western world, may not be applicable in non-Western communities
(J. P. Wilson 2007). However, it should be appreciated that in a rapidly
changing global world, people are dynamic and complex, often holding
multiple realities shaped by different world views that might collide
and overlap with one another. It is equally important to 'distinguish collective strategies (that is, mobilizing group resources) from collectivistic
coping style (that is, normative coping style of collectivistic individuals)'
(Chun et al. 2006; emphasis in original). Individuals from collectivistic
communities may not necessarily adopt collective coping such as seeking
social support. They may be more concerned with the impact of social
consequences (relationships, group harmony, shaming the family). Strong
family bonding may preclude community engagement. Interdependent
individuals tend to define in-group members more narrowly and with
more overt impermeability than independent individuals. They maintain tighter and longer bonds with in-group members, increasing the distance between in-group and out-group members (Yeh et al. 2006). Thus,
family or community members may join together in collective coping to
pool resources, act cooperatively, sharing the burden to resolve a single
or common problem at the family (extended family) or community levels
respectively, exclusively or in combination.

These complex processes and ways of coping have to be taken into consideration when undertaking community-level interventions in a collectivistic culture. It would be useful to do a systemic and comprehensive
assessment using a trauma grid (Papadopoulos 2007) to look at the functioning of the community in the context of different levels: individual,

family, community and society/culture, as these may be affected in different ways, positively, negatively or varying combination of both. It is good to keep in mind that communities may find 'meaning in their suffering and are able to transmute their negative experiences in a positive way, finding new strengths and experiencing transformative renewal' (Papadopoulos 2007).

Community-level Interventions

Traditionally, post-disaster interventions have been conceptualized and categorized into rescue, relief, rehabilitation, reconstruction and development, depending primarily on time course after the disaster (see Figure 2A.1 and Table 2A.3). Different organizations, government departments and international bodies like INGOs and the UN have been responsible for the implementation of interventions depending on the phase of the disaster. However, a chronic war situation may not lend itself to temporal divisions into neat phases, but be a series of continuing, complex (political) emergencies going on for years with overlapping, periodic acute disaster situations. Typical emergencies could present as an episode of intense fighting for control of a region, a bombing raid, ambush or a skirmish in the background of long-term displacement.

In the immediate aftermath of natural disasters or traumatic events, emergency rescue and relief efforts would be directed towards safety, basic needs, family reunion, reliable information and mobilizing social support. As mentioned, Hobfoll et al. (2007) propose that the best practice in situations of disasters is promoting a sense of safety, calming, a sense of self- and community efficacy, connectedness and hope. It is noteworthy that Silove (2007) also emphasizes the fundamental need to re-establish a sense of safety and security in his ecosocial model of trauma. Though this may be possible after a natural disaster, the lack of community safety and security is the psychosocial ecology of an ongoing civil conflict. The only option may be to flee the area as IDPs or refugees. The WHO (2003)

Figure 2A.1:
Time Course of Psychosocial Interventions after Disasters

Rescue ----▶ Relief ----▶ Rehabilitation ----▶ Reconstruction ----▶ Development

Time ──────────────────────────────────────▶

Source: Author.

Table 2A.3:
Temporal Dimension of Disasters

Feature	Threat	Warning	Impact	Recoil	Post-trauma
Duration	Time Months	Minutes–Hours	Seconds–Minutes	Hours	Months–years
Cognition	Expectation, anticipation, worry, threat, preparation	Warning messages Emergency/denial	Shock	Relief	Inventory, loss, reality sense, coping
Emotion	Fear, anxiety, insomnia	Apprehension, arousal, panic	Panic, shock, helplessness	Daze, inhibition, numbing, euphoria, emotional release	Grief, sadness, anger, hostility, despair
Behaviour	Preparatory activity	Protective action, seeking safety, displacement,	Self-preservation, survival, flight or fight	Hypo or hyper activity rescue/relief	Organized reconstruction, adaptation
Mental Reaction	Generalized anxiety disorder	Panic	Shock	Acute stress reaction	Phobic, Anxiety, depression, alcohol & drug abuse antisocial personality developmental disorders, suicide
Social	Family & friends support and help. Long-term plans	Rumours, herd-instinct, gathering together, evacuation	Family unity, clinging, Hierarchical roles	Therapeutic community, Social unity, breakdown of social barriers, loss of communality, social chaos	Refugees, rehabilitation, reconstruction, recovery, restitution, resettlement, social & cultural changes

Sources: Modified from Kinston and Rosser (1974) and Sims (1983).

and other organizations have formulated the Sphere Project humanitarian charter and minimum standards to deal with mental and social aspects of health (The Sphere Project 2004) and the IASC guidelines.

A comprehensive and useful conceptual model for longer term psychosocial and mental health interventions is an inverted pyramid with five overlapping and interrelated levels of interventions for UN and other disaster workers prepared by the UN and the International Society for

Traumatic Stress Studies[8] (Green et al. 2003). As shown in Figure 2A.2, at the top of the pyramid are *societal* or macro-level interventions designed for an entire population (regional, national or international), such as laws, public safety, public policy, social justice and a free press. Descending the pyramid, interventions target progressively smaller groups of people. The next two layers are *community* and *neighbourhood*, or meso-level interventions, which include public education, support for community leaders, reconstruction of social infrastructure, empowerment, cultural rituals and ceremonies, service coordination, training and education of grass-roots workers and capacity building. The fourth layer from the top is *family* or micro-level interventions that focus both on the individual within a family context and on strategies to promote well-being of the family as a unit. The bottom layer of the pyramid concerns interventions designed for the *individual* with psychological symptoms or psychiatric disorders. These

Figure 2A.2:
Conceptual Model for Psychosocial Interventions in Social and Humanitarian Crises

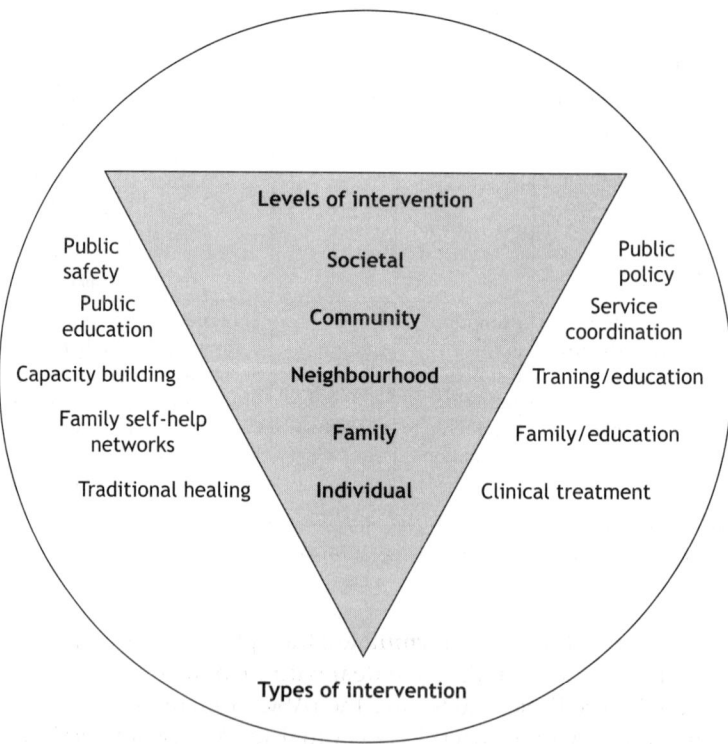

Source: Adapted from Green et al. (2003).

[8] The author was part of this team.

Box 2A.1:
Therapeutic Interventions for Disaster Survivors

- Psychoeducation
- Psychological first aid, crisis intervention
- Psychotherapy
- Behavioural–cognitive methods
- Relaxation techniques
- Pharmacotherapy
- Group therapy
- Family therapy
- Expressive methods
- Rehabilitation
- Community approaches

Source: Somasundaram (1997b).

include counselling or mental health treatment, which are the most expensive and skilled labour intensive. Therefore, they should be reserved, particularly in the poor, developing world settings, for the small minority of individuals who cannot benefit from the larger-scale interventions at higher levels of the pyramid. Theoretical, practical, empirical and treatment considerations suggest a holistic, integrated, expanded psychosocial synthetic approach, with multiple levels of interventions (Assagioli 1975).

Another conceptual approach in this complex field is to use the WHO definition of health mentioned earlier to address the physical and psychosocial needs of survivors, families and communities through physical and psychosocial interventions (see Table 2A.1). Theoretical, practical, empirical and treatment considerations suggest holistic, integrated, multiple levels of interventions (de Jong 2002). Among therapeutic interventions in post-disaster situations (see Box 2A.1), perhaps community-level interventions are best suited for resource-poor, developing countries.

Community Approaches

The widespread problem of collective traumatization or 'loss of communality' (K. Erikson 1976) following disasters is best approached through community-level interventions. Further, community-based approaches will reach a larger target population as well as include preventive and promotional public mental health activities at the same time (see Box 2A.2). As described earlier, individuals can be expected to recover and cope

Box 2A.2:
Community Approaches

- Psychoeducation—awareness
- Training of community workers
- Public mental health promotive activities
- Encouraging indigenous coping strategies
- Cultural rituals and ceremonies
- Community interventions
  - Family
  - Groups
  - Expressive methods
  - Rehabilitation
- Prevention

Source: Author.

when communities and families become functional, activating healing mechanisms within themselves. An extensive research for the cause of well-being—in terms of markedly reduced rates of death from all causes (30–50 per cent lower than normal in the United States), cardiac diseases, peptic ulcer, other social ills like suicide, alcoholism, drug addictions or crime and no one on welfare—in a closely knit Rosetan community (originally migrants from Italy) in Bangor, Pennsylvania, compared to other communities found that it was the communality, extended family clans, egalitarian ethos, *paesani* culture and social cohesiveness that was protective (Gladwell 2008). Thus, it may be more beneficial to consider strengthening and rebuilding the family and village structures, as well as finding a common meaning for the immense suffering than to treat individual traumatization per se. For this purpose, the protocol developed by Joop de Jong of the TPO, working around the world to relieve the psychosocial problems of people affected by internal conflict and war (de Jong 2002, 2011), which I had the opportunity to implement in Cambodia (Van de Put et al. 1997) and Jaffna (Somasundaram and Jamunanantha 2002), is very effective.

Psychoeducation

Basic information about what has happened, where help can be obtained, instructions about available programmes and assistance is essential. Psychoeducation about trauma for the general public, what to do and not to do, can be accomplished through the media, pamphlets and popular lectures.

Training

Training grass-roots community-level workers in basic mental health knowledge and skills is the easiest way of reaching a large population. They in turn would increase general awareness and disseminate knowledge, as well as do preventive and promotional work. The majority of minor mental health problems following disasters could be managed by community-level workers and others referred to the appropriate level (see Figure 2A.3).

Figure 2A.3:
Referral Structure for Management of Post-Disaster Mental Health Problems (At District Level)

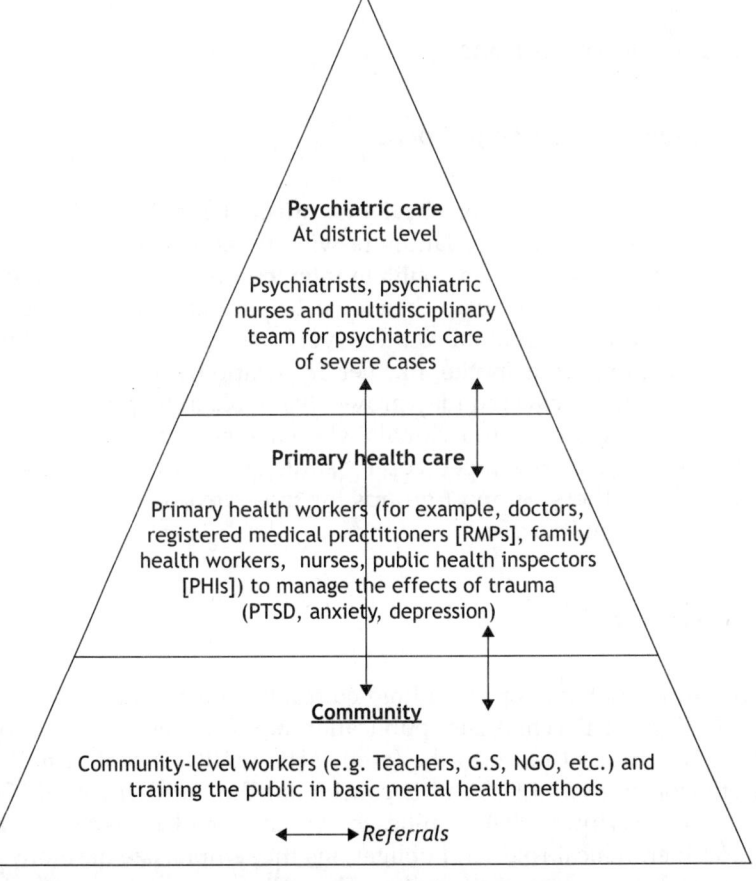

Source: Author.
Notes: (i) Multidisciplinary team—psychiatric social worker, clinical psychologist, counsellor, child therapist (includes art, play, drama), relaxation therapist and occupational therapist.
(ii) The arrows indicate referral.

Primary health workers including doctors, medical assistants, nurses, family health workers, school teachers, village resources like the village headman, elders, traditional healers, priests, monks and nuns, governmental organizations, NGOs, volunteer relief and refugee camp workers are ideal community-level workers for training. Trauma and mental health should become part of the normal curricula of health staff and teachers. A manual based on the WHO and UNHCR (1996) booklet, *Mental Health of Refugees*, can be prepared and adapted to the cultural context for this purpose. A training of trainers (TOT) programme in community mental health using this manual can be undertaken. The trainers will in turn train the community-level workers mentioned earlier. In this way, the necessary knowledge and skill can be disseminated to a wider population.

Community Interventions

Group Support or Self-help Groups

The formation of groups for survivors, affected families, widows, ex-detainees, torture survivors, landmine victims and others can be very helpful. A therapist can then facilitate interactions within these groups, which in time should develop their own healing and caring processes. Experiences of one individual could be very useful to another and more acceptable coming from another like her. In addition, the services of those who have already recovered may prove invaluable in helping others and running the programme. Individuals who have survived severe trauma would have already developed coping strategies that could be used for the therapy of others. Support groups for those involved in helping the clients can prevent 'burnout'.

Family Support

The recommendations for providing 'culturally competent services' in a Royal College of Psychiatrists' publication authored by Patel and Stein (2007), give pride of place to the family. The family is central to Asian 'collectivistic communities' and is considered the 'fundamental form of social capital' (Winter 2000). Families tend to think and act as a unit. There are strict hierarchical roles and obligations that emphasize harmony and support each other during difficulties. The individual submerges the individual 'self' within the nuclear and extended family dynamics. Family cohesion should be strengthened (see Box 2A.3). The principles of family

Box 2A.3:
Family Support

- Promoting unity and cohesiveness
- Sharing burden and responsibilities
- Increasing mutual understanding, communications and inter-
  actions
- Filling roles and respect
- Encouraging positive family dynamics
- Mobilizing extended family support

Source: Author.

dynamics can be used to facilitate supportive and healing relationships
while counteracting damaging and maladaptive interactions. Communication of individual problems leading to an awareness of each other, one's
role and encouragement towards mutually interdependent functioning
can be used to build family unity. These considerations can hold true for
the extended family as well.

Expressive Methods

Artistic expression of emotions and trauma can be cathartic for individuals, groups and the community as a whole. Art, drama, storytelling,
writing poetry or novels (testimonies), singing, dancing, clay modelling
and sculpturing are very useful emotive methods in trauma therapy
(Wilson and Drozdek 2004). The traumatized individual or group is able
to externalize the traumatic experience through a medium and thereby
handle and manipulate the working through the outside without the associated internal distress. Children in particular, who are usually unable to
express their thoughts or emotions verbally, will benefit from the above-
mentioned expressive methods and play therapy.

Testimony method was used in Latin America and elsewhere in the
context of state terror with political oppression, torture, disappearances and killings (Agger and Jensen 1996) very similar to the repressive
ecology of Sri Lanka. In Sri Lanka, it has been used as a component of narrative exposure therapy (NET) in the north and in torture survivors in the
south (Puvimanasinghe and Price 2010). The testimonies help survivors
ventilate and experience through telling and sharing what happened to
them in a supportive and caring environment. Further, their narratives
can be documented and used in human rights work, advocacy and to seek

justice. By using the 'metonymic character' of *testimonio* to represent the whole (Beverley 2005), the community can benefit through the collective expression of trauma.

Traditional Coping Strategies

Indigenous coping strategies that have helped the local population to survive should be encouraged. Culturally mediated protective factors like rituals and ceremonies should be strengthened. Wilson (1989, 2007) describes the sweat lodge purification ceremony among Native American nations to heal altered maladaptive states following war trauma. In traditional cultures, funerals and anniversaries can be very powerful ways to help in grieving and finding comfort. They can be a source of strength, support and meaning. Social attitudes can influence how traumatized individuals are treated, their response and eventual recovery. Cultures and villages have their own rituals and traditional functions to deal with trauma. Funeral rites like *eddu chelavu, anthyetty, andu thuvasam, thuvasam* and similar anniversary observances are powerful social mechanisms to deal with grief and loss. The gathering together of relations, friends and the community is an important social process to share, work through and release deep emotions, define and come to terms with what has happened and finally integrate the traumatic experience into social reality.

In addition to funerals, religious and temple rites, cultural festivals, dramas, musical fares, exhibitions and other programmes, meetings and social gatherings provide the opportunity for people to discuss, construct meaning, share and assimilate traumatic events. In war, when due to the disturbed situation these rituals are not possible or improperly performed, the trauma is never fully accepted or put to rest, as in the cases of 'disappearances' where there is no finality about death. Patricia Lawrence (1999) describes the psychosocial value of the traditional oracle practice of '*vakuu choluthal*' in Batticaloa, particularly in cases of disappearances, where the families are told what has happened to the disappeared person in a socially supportive environment. In cases of detention by security forces the relatives may take vows (*nethi kadan*) at temples in front of various gods, which they will fulfil if the person is released. The practice of *thuku kavadi*, a propitiatory ritual involving hanging from hooks, has increased dramatically after the war and may be especially useful after detention and torture (Derges 2009, 2013). After resettlement, *Kovalan Koothu* (a popular folk drama) was performed all over the Vanni with large attendances and community participation. In the traditional folk form of *opari* (lament), recent experiences and losses from the Vanni war were incorporated into community grief performances (Duran 2011). Religious festivals, folk singing and dancing as well as leisure activities like sports can be ways of meeting, finding support and expressing emotions.

Ideally, the social processes should work to promote feelings of belonging and participation, where the group is able to give meaning to what has happened, adapt to the new situation and determine its future. It is noteworthy that the worldwide panel of trauma experts referred to earlier (Hobfoll et al. 2007) also identified restoring connectedness, social support and a sense of collective efficacy as essential elements in interventions after mass trauma. Cultural rituals and practices are well suited to do just that (see Box 2A.4).

Box 2A.4:
Healing Effects of Cultural Rituals

> * Purge, purify and heal physical and psychological wounds of war
> * Provide supportive and caring milieu, communal participation
> * Aid continuity of culture, meaning and hope
> * Create solidity, integration, social cohesion, group identity
> * Restore communality, relationships, networks, interpersonal bonding
> * Are familiar, access childhood associations, spiritual strengths

Source: Author.

Teaching of the culturally familiar relaxation exercises like *jappa*, *dhikr*, *anapanasati*, rosaries or yoga (see Box 2A.5) to families, large groups in the community and as part of the curricula in schools can be both preventive and promotive of mental health. Their practice can produce the calming sense of collective efficacy and social and cultural connectedness that trauma experts recommend (Hobfoll et al. 2007). Although these techniques are not formal psychotherapy, they may achieve what psychotherapy attempts to, by releasing cultural and spiritual restorative processes and mobilizing social support.

Psychosocial Rehabilitation

Attempts can be made to rebuild social networks and sense of community by encouraging and facilitating formation of organizations (for widows), rural societies (CBOs), schools and other groupings (Cullen

Box 2A.5:
Cultural Relaxation Techniques

These techniques can be practised individually, as a family, group and/or community

- Regular repetition of words:
  - Hindu — *jappa* of *pranava* mantra 'om'
  - Buddhist — *pirit* or chanting *'buddhang saranang gachchami'*
  - Islam — *dhikr, takbir, tasbih,* 'subhanallah'
  - Catholic Christianity — rosary, prayer beads, the prayer 'Jesus Christ have mercy on me'
  - Cambodia — *Keatha, angkam, puthoo*
  - Vietnam — *mophit*
  - Scientific — transcendental meditation, Benson's relaxation response
- Breathing exercises: Pranayama, *anapanasati* or mindful breathing
- Muscular relaxation: Shanti or *savasana,* mindful body awareness, t'ai chi ch'uan
- Meditation: *Dhyanam,* contemplation, *samadhi, vipassana*
- Massage: Ayurvedic or Siddha oil massage and the Cambodian *thveu saasay*

Source: Author.

and Whiteford 2001; PADHI 2009; Silove and Steel 2006). Rehabilitation programmes should include education, vocational training, income generating projects, loans and housing that are tailored to the needs of the survivors and the post-disaster situation. Close liaison, cooperation, collaboration and networking with governmental organizations and NGOs involved in relief, rehabilitation, reconstruction and development work will be very productive (see Figure 2A.4). The network can be used to refer needy survivors for socio-economic and rehabilitation assistance.

What needs to be stressed here is that such a design includes due consideration for the psychological processes that promote individual, family and social healing, recovery and integration. It is important that any such programme take into account the wishes of the local population concerned, that they be given an active and deciding role rather than a dependent, 'victims' role, as it promotes their overall sense of participation and thus their eventual psychological recovery. To achieve this, emergent self-help groups and local leadership should be encouraged to resume traditional and habitual patterns of behaviour, re-establish social

Figure 2A.4:
Networking

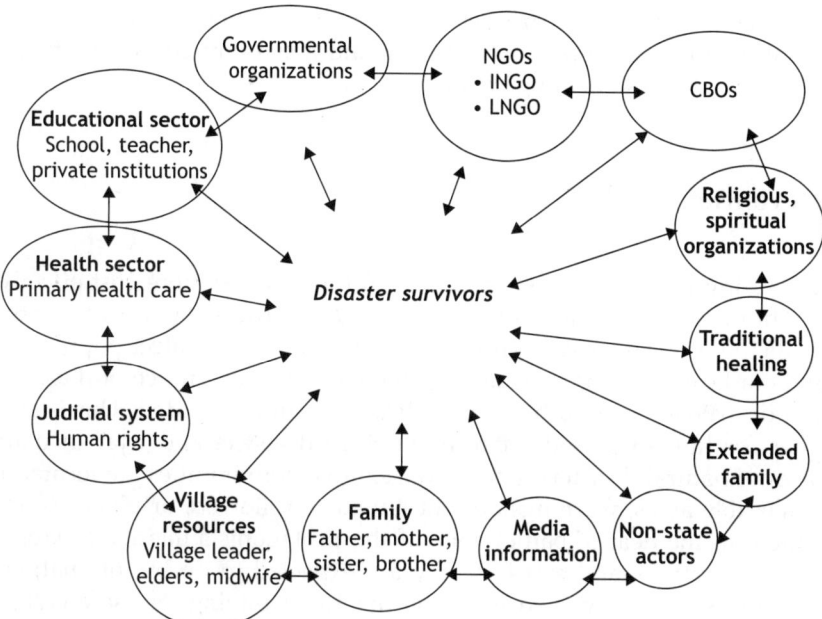

Source: Author.

networks and community functioning at the grass-roots level (Raphael 1986). Local skills and resources have to be tapped and utilized if the community is to gain a sense of accomplishment and fulfilment in the recovery process. Provision for non-partisan cultural working through shared traumatic experience in the form of periodic reminders of the loss and reiteration of its meaning, and of the heroism of those who suffered expressed in media, arts, public works, monuments, special museums and occasions of public mourning have been found to be useful in post-disaster situations (Kinston and Rosser 1974). Community monuments that would help focus and express emotions after mass trauma have been called traumascapes (Tumarkin 2005). For example, a civil monument at Mullivaikal[9] to all who died there (military, militant, civilian) by a sensitive sculptor and national ceremonies to be observed there annually would go a long way towards reconciliation. Community gatherings, meetings and religious ceremonies will allow for communal release of feeling, reviewing and coming to terms with the collective trauma, socially define and interpret

[9] The scene of the final Vanni battle in May 2009, where thousands perished.

their experiences, as well as re-establish social relationships and plan for the future. In rebuilding community resilience, it is important to promote the re-establishment of trust between members of the community and in social institutions, hope for the future and a sense of collective efficacy that they can do something about it.

Prevention

In treating medical diseases it has been found to be more cost effective and humane to prevent them from happening in the first place. Preventive medicine uses large-scale public health measures to protect populations and eradicate or mitigate causative agents. Tragically, much of the death and destruction caused by natural disasters can be avoided. This is even truer for human-caused (or technological) disasters and war. In many cases of natural disasters, poor and excluded communities are located in vulnerable areas, warnings are not issued or followed, or plans are forgotten. In the heat of battle, none of the protagonists maintain maps of where they laid landmines as they are expected to do by international conventions, making it so much harder for demining and safe civilian resettlement. Serious attention should be paid to prevention in the future as we develop better understanding of disasters, how and why they occur, their effects, and how best to manage their short- and long-term mental health consequences. Wars and conflict can be prevented and psychosocial well-being ensured by appropriate conflict resolution mechanisms, equitable access to resources, power sharing arrangements, social justice and respect for human and social rights (PADHI 2009).

It is worthwhile planning beforehand to prevent or mitigate the impact of disasters at the community and family levels. In fact, there should be plans at the local, provincial, national, regional and international levels for disaster preparedness and emergency response because many disasters affect multiple communities or regions or even countries. Such plans are typically formulated by committees at the appropriate level and may involve collaborative efforts between formal emergency management agencies, public health agencies and citizen groups. There should be regional and international mechanisms to protect civilians in times of conflict and/or when powerful leaders and states overstep boundaries of good governance and observation of basic rights. Increasing powers to the UN Security Council and General Assembly to intervene with sanctions and peacekeeping forces, international conventions, establishment of the ICC and the principle of R2P (Evans 2007, 2008) are promising developments.

In the long term, there is a need to create a 'culture of peace' by social peace building (Large 1997). There were concerted efforts, particularly during the peace process from 2002–06, to develop and educate the public in Sri Lanka about peace building, conflict resolution and transformation by an array of INGOs and programmes. It was assumed that for peace to be sustainable it had to come from the bottom. However, they failed to take into the account the peculiar governance process in Sri Lanka. Although nominally a democracy with periodic elections where theoretically the people can choose their leaders and policies, in practice it has been ruled by ethnic leaders seeking power for family patronage, earnings, resources and influence (Frerks and Klem 2005). Imtiyaz and Stavis (2008) argue:

> [E]lite political leaders believe they can win support and strengthen their positions by mobilizing along ethnic cleavages. They anticipate that appeals to ethnicity are particularly effective in expanding their power. Leaders sometimes encourage followers to use crude violence — pogroms or ethnic cleansing, or exploit ethnic tensions in electoral politics. Outbidding opponents along ethnic lines is one of the strategies to win votes in (fragmented) societies that hold elections. This process frequently results in a polarization of the political system into ethnic divisions and a possible breakdown into violence. Marginalized minorities may suffer, emigrate, or fight back with the weapons of the weak — terrorism and/or guerrilla activities. Elites manipulate ethnic identities in their quest for power, and these processes can either deliberately or unexpectedly trigger ethnic conflict.

Political leaders have always been able to manipulate public opinion to suit their power aspirations and rule according to their agenda. Even in so-called functioning democracies, political leaders have been able to convince and mobilize an unwilling populace to go to war and then train military recruits to do the killing (Somasundaram 2009; Woodward 2002, 2004) The education and training in peace building and conflict resolution in Sri Lanka failed to address the crucial political leadership. A few inconsequential members of parliament and LTTE leaders were taken on tours of European capitals and attended seminars there.

The Centre for Policy Alternatives (CPA) had regular social indicator surveys and measured the peace confidence index before each election which clearly showed that the electorate from all communities wanted peace (Peiris and Stokke 2011; Social Indicator 2001–08). A poll of the recently concluded APRC meeting with proposals to resolve the conflict showed that the overwhelming majority of all communities were in favour of constitutional reforms (Irwin 2010) but the government in power appears to be implementing something entirely the opposite, for example, expanding presidential power. The LTTE was always a fascist organization believing in 'realpolitik' and viewed the so-called NGO 'peace industry' with contempt, only to be used for purposes that suited it. There were also regular and systemic seminars and workshops on human rights for the military, police and other security forces by the ICRC, Human Rights Commission of Sri Lanka (HRCSL) and other organizations, but it did not prevent any human rights abuses when the war started again in 2006.

Thus, preventive measures would have to address those at the top, the governance processes and culture and the polarized ethnocentric perceptions that drive them. Jung (1947) though acknowledging political, social, economic and historical reasons for war, describes war as an epidemic of madness, as an animation of the collective unconscious where the inherent evil is projected onto the neighbouring tribe, the 'other'. The only way to prevent 'outbreaks of the collective unconscious' is to bring it into consciousness, to develop insight and understanding, to untangle the tangle (this is the aim of books such as this).

At the community level in situations of disasters, adequate warning and evacuation procedures are particularly important. Such actions not only save lives but also protect mental health by reducing exposure of the public to the most traumatic elements of disasters (injury, threat to life and bereavement). Almost any community can benefit from developing strategies and procedures for warning and evacuating people when it is appropriate. There is no one simple formula for how to do this because any plan must take into account the probable threats (such as tsunami, battle, shelling), resources (such as transportation, shelter), attitudes (such as understanding of risk, fear of looting, trust in authorities), social networks (such as informal communication channels), economic realities and communication infrastructures (such as ability to reach people by television or radio) of the area involved. Though disaster preparedness is difficult to promote, beliefs that people can influence their own chances of surviving can lead to precautionary acts and a sense of collective efficacy. Like other behavioural interventions, campaigns to educate the public about disaster preparedness must focus on specific behavioural messages.

Another area of intervention, both for prevention and promoting recovery after the catastrophe, is at the national level by influencing policymaking, rehabilitation and international aid programmes. In post-conflict situations, procedures used elsewhere like healing of memories, truth and reconciliation councils and transitional justice can be helpful. WHO has developed the concept of using health as a bridge for peace. More recently UNICEF has developed

> peace education as the process of promoting the knowledge, skills, attitudes and values needed to bring about behaviour changes that will enable children, youth and adults to prevent conflict and violence, both overt

and structural; to resolve conflict peacefully; and to create the conditions conducive to peace, whether at an intrapersonal, interpersonal, intergroup, national or international level.

(Fountain 1999)

UNICEF's more recent publication edited by Bush and Saltarelli (2000), *The Two Faces of Education in Ethnic Conflict* is a powerful critique of the way education can be an aggravating factor in ethnic conflict and how it can be used more positively for solving such problems.

One of the most effective collective preventive actions would be to create resilient communities. According to Colletta and Cullen (2000):

> Resilient communities rely on all forms of responsibility and social capital: bonding primary ties for protection and survival in time of crisis; bridging links for action and development in time of hope; efficient and functional bureaucracies and transparent norms and rules; and synergistic government-community relations that allow civic engagement to thrive as the ultimate guarantor against violent conflict. Development needs to nurture and transform social capital in order to create and maintain the mechanisms and institutions necessary for strengthening social cohesion, managing diversity, preventing violent conflict, and sustaining peace and reconciliation.

Sadly, powerful political forces may act to undermine these resilient community actions.

It would be possible to influence policy by making use some of the conclusions mentioned in the above analysis under such headings as the causes of the disaster, context, assessment, planning and preparedness. Considerably more research needs to be done on the effects of disasters and especially on processes that influence community mental and psychosocial well-being. Disasters are difficult to study well because they occur suddenly and create chaos. Initially, attention must be directed at meeting basic physical needs such as providing food and shelter. Mental health is usually not considered a high priority at this stage. Research gets a very low priority, if it can be carried out at all. However, it is possible to retain the capacity to observe, reflect, analyse and document while actively engaged in the recovery and rehabilitation work following disasters. Qualitative methods particularly suit these kinds of complex emergency situations to improve the types and nature of interventions and provide important lessons for similar contexts elsewhere.

B.

Methodology

Overview

The study in this book uses qualitative ethnographic methods to explore and describe the causes, effects and interventions in disasters, both man-made and natural, at the community level in northern Sri Lanka during the period from 1980 to 2011 but with particular emphasis on the later years. An earlier book, *Scarred Minds* (Somasundaram 1998), described the effects of war at the individual level through in-depth case studies and quantitative data. This attempt is to understand the ecological context and phenomenologically interpret from a cultural, collective perspective the long-term sequelae of war and the Asian tsunami of 2004 on Sri Lankan communities, the Tamil community in the north in particular, but with contributions from the south and internationally to provide a more holistic picture. My observations and data were collected while I was privileged to work as a medical officer and psychiatrist, for long periods as the sole psychiatrist, in the Northern Province. There are some quantitative data from questionnaires and analyses reported here, making it technically a mixed-method study.

The impetus for this form of critical inquiry arose from my experiences in Cambodia during a sabbatical (1996–98), as I tried to set up a community mental health programme (Somasundaram et al. 1999; Van de Put et al. 1997) from scratch. Incredibly, except for the informal, traditional sector, there had been no mental health services in Cambodia for over two decades after the Khmer Rouge had dismantled them. During the Khmer Rouge regime, all social structures, institutions, family, educational and religious orders were razed to 'ground zero' deliberately (so as to rebuild a just society anew) (Vickery 1984). Mistrust and suspicion arose among family members as children were made to report on their parents. The essential trust and security within the family system, the basic unit of society, was broken. A whole generation had missed out on basic education. So when we tried to help individuals, it soon became obvious there were deeper, more fundamental problems at the family and collective levels that needed to be addressed before individuals would recover. Social and community trust, relationships, structures and institutions had to be rebuilt first. When I returned to work in northern Sri Lanka in 1998, I was able to discern similar collective-level phenomena, perhaps not to the extreme degree seen in Cambodia, but still deteriorating in that direction. It appeared that considering and understanding the broader family and social processes would help in designing and implementing more effective community-level interventions. There was always a comparative aspect: comparing the post-conflict, rehabilitation phase in Cambodia with the situation in Sri Lanka.

Attempts were also made at a participant- and peer-review process through feedback and discussion of findings, analyses and conclusions with participants, local leaders, scholars and peers. For example, the concept of collective trauma was discussed and debated at various individual and group meetings, forums[1] and publications. This process included going through case histories, key informant interviews, literature survey, focus group discussions and regular reviews. I have also tried to document in detail the procedural aspects, how the data, observations, analyses and conclusions were collected or reached in a transparent way without endangering others in a politically charged and risky environment. The self-censorship observed even by patients owing to the ideological constraints of the civil war was a severe handicap to a study of this nature. There was a 'culture of silence' (Crotty 1998; Taussig 2004) imposed through intimidation, extrajudicial killings, abductions, torture and indoctrination or brain washing. My colleague and co-author of *The Broken Palmyrah* (Hoole et al. 1988), Rajani Thiranagama, was killed by the LTTE for her dissenting views and community enabling activities. I have struggled to maintain an apolitical and neutral position throughout, nevertheless realizing that everything becomes politicized in these circumstances (Denzin and Lincoln 2000, 2005). The mere living and working in the north was a political act, a resistance of sorts. On hartal days, one party

---

[1] Including international forums (Somasundaram 2002c, 2003a, 2006, 2007b, 2010b), following which there were lively discussions and feedback, and as peer-reviewed papers (Somasundaram 2007a) and chapters (Somasundaram 2011). The late Professor Robert Barrett at the University of Adelaide provided a constructive sounding board for developing this concept further. In 2011–12, as part of the WHO ICD-11 revision subcommittee responsible for stress-related disorders, where I was the co-chair responsible for PTSD, I was able to submit, after much discussion and reservations, the concept of collective trauma as part of the characteristics of PTSD after mass trauma.

threatened the public with death if they go for work while the other party wanted everyone at work or in school.

Though living in that environment, I was, by degrees and not by original intention, driven into what seemed to me an inconspicuous, unobtrusive role of addressing this 'culture of silence', through writing and giving voice to what could be liberating or emancipating in the sense of Freire's *Pedagogy of the Oppressed* (1972). Much of the work described in the sections to come was with the underprivileged: women, widows, children, elderly, families of the disappeared, victims of torture, rape and landmines and the mentally ill, a socially stigmatized population. We had special programmes targeting these vulnerable and excluded groups specifically. Thus, there is an important critical inquiry into the politics of power underlying this whole situation. However, the practical effects cannot be overestimated. The access of ordinary people to unbiased information is extremely limited. There is considerable official and unofficial censorship in operation in addition to a situation of extreme political repression and military logic, what has been aptly described as a repressive ecology (Baykal et al. 2004).

Naturalistic Study

This naturalistic study follows Bronfenbrenner (1979):

> [A]n effort to investigate the progressive accommodation between the growing human organism and its environment through systematic contrast between two or more environmental systems or their structural components .... There are instances in which a design exploiting an experiment of nature proves a more critical contrast, insures greater objectivity, and permits more precise and theoretically significant inferences—in short, is more elegant and constitutes 'harder' science—than the best possible contrived experiment addressed to the same research question.

My documentation, descriptions and interpretation are the result of studying and reflecting on the situation that I found myself in as a psychiatrist in pre-conflict, conflict, post-tsunami and post-war settings. The war and post-tsunami situations were hardly conducive to controlled, planned research. It was a series of acute emergencies and responding to ongoing deprivations. This book is a result of gathering data on the go, amidst the pressing need to find immediate solutions to desperate problems, a moral and therapeutic project (Denzin and Lincoln 2000, 2005) done side by side with significant contributions from other workers who I had the privilege to work with in these difficult times.

In many ways, the methods adopted here were very similar to Brandon Hamber's (2009) research into the post-apartheid experience of the Truth and Reconciliation Commission (TRC) in South Africa:

> The research … is built on active participation in the area under study. I was an observer, a participant, a researcher, an activist, and an action researcher. My position in relation to the area under study and the research that flowed from it cannot be divorced from my role in the process. Furthermore, the research produced and presented here was undertaken in a dynamic context of political and social upheaval in the country at the time. Valuable evidence of how the social world operates can also be generated by observation and participation in interactive situations and social settings. Broadly I adopt a perspective that might be described as 'emic'; that is understanding phenomena on their own terms, with insights flowing from inductive processes, and building general accounts from pieces of experience and research. Actors immersed in the context know what the experience of that social setting feels like … and in that sense they are epistemologically privileged.

There were several ecological contexts that presented themselves for observation and intervention (see Table 2B.1). The first was pre-conflict Jaffna, before 1983, and the more traditional, Tamil community which was already being affected by modernization and globalization. Then, the rapid escalation of hostilities following the 1983 anti-Tamil pogrom that changed the atmosphere to an ongoing civil war situation. The Tamil community before the conflict became a control group to compare with the community at other times. However, there were other confounding variables like the process of modernization, globalization[2] and demographic changes due to displacement. In many ways the war accelerated many changes that were already there due to modernization, globalization and movements of those seeking employment abroad, in the Middle East and elsewhere, for better economic prospects. The breakdown in caste barriers and the phenomena of the nouveau riche were examples of social processes already happening. The ethnic depopulation of the north-east, for example, the population of Jaffna was reduced to about half its expected number, creation of a large Tamil diaspora and shift in gender balance and responsibility (power) towards a more female preponderance were consequences of the war described in this study. The massive Asian tsunami of 2004 presented another natural disaster and post-disaster environment. I was put in charge of the psychosocial rehabilitation efforts in the north by those in power (both state and militant) and was given direct access to study materials. The post-war situation evolving after the final Vanni

---

[2] Part of the global influence on the home society was the influence of those who had migrated abroad, such as the change in values and economic standing they brought back.

Table 2B.1:
Jaffna in Different Ecological Contexts (1980-2011)

	Pre-conflict	*Conflict*	*Post-tsunami*	*Post-conflict*
Family	Home (*veedu*), nuclear, extended, united, under-reported child abuse and domestic violence	Separations, deaths, fragmentation, female-headed households	Multiple deaths, injuries, women and child casualties, destruction of home and property, camp life	Female-headed families, widows, broken homes, homelessness, grief, reunification, returning combatants
Community	Village (*uur*), caste and hierarchical structures, networks, traditions, rituals	Fragmentation, displacement, refugee camps	Whole villages washed out, displacement camps	Fragmentation, resettlements, demobilization
Social Processes	Cohesion, communality, patriarchy, modernization, globalization	Loss of communality, repressive ecology, female empowerment	Loss of communality, massive trauma, humanitarian help, support, breakdown of barriers and hatred, NGO culture	Repressive ecology, powerlessness, fragmentation, female empowerment
Social Effects	Changing values, loosening of traditions, family system, village, cast, gender roles, nouveau riche	Collective trauma, worldwide diaspora	Collective trauma, male alcoholism, remarriages, fostering	Collective trauma, despair, helplessness, cultural bereavement
Psychosocial Interventions	Psycho-education, participation, development, empowerment, basic mental health	Psychological first aid, psychosocial interventions (see Section 5), conflict resolution, peace building	Psychological first aid, grief counselling, return to earlier life patterns, psychosocial interventions (see Chapter 3A and Section 5)	Grief counselling, re-establishing traditional structures, cultural practices, rituals, psychosocial interventions (see Section 5), reconciliation, rehabilitation, vocational training, income generation

Source: Author's compilation.

battle and the military decimation of the LTTE in May 2009 is a contrasting ecological context that will be described in Chapter 3B. This is the setting that needs to be taken into consideration for any future psychosocial interventions (see Section 5).

Another similar and contrasting situation was Cambodia in 1996–98. The country was in a post-conflict rehabilitation phase when I worked there as community mental health consultant. The situations in northern Sri Lanka and Cambodia gave a unique opportunity to contrast and compare two Asian communities with different demographic, socio-economic, cultural and geo-historical factors in a broad and general way. Observations and studies from a southern Sri Lankan perspective (see Chapters 4A, 5B and 5C), the Tamil diaspora (see Chapter 4B) and by other contributors in the north (see Chapters 3C and 5A) complement these ecological contexts to bring out the myriad impacts of the chronic war on different communities. These contrasting contexts give a naturalistic opportunity to study comparatively the effects of disasters, natural and man-made, on communities. There is no attempt to tease out individual variables or factors and in-depth analyses, which are left for further studies.

Participatory Observation and Critical Inquiry

The basic methods adopted were participatory observation or, more accurately, observation of participation (Tedlock 2000) and critical inquiry. I lived and worked in northern Sri Lanka and was physically present during most of the years in the period 1980–2011. My sampling frame was the whole Tamil population of the north, mainly in Jaffna, but I was conducting clinics in the district hospitals and visiting the other districts, Killinochchi, Vavuniya and Mannar, on a regular basis. There were some quantitative studies where random sampling was done that have been reported in previous publications (Somasundaram 1998) while newer data are reported in the following sections. Generally the sampling has been more purposive and convenient of those affected psychosocially, such as clinic patients, displaced and refugee populations, and those identified or referred during community work.

The fieldwork was primarily done during the three decades when I lived and worked in the north. The general observations were collected from the lived experience, observing the day-to-day life of the Tamil community, their gatherings, activities, cultural practices and celebrations, responses to adverse events like the ongoing war and the tsunami, and conversations and discussions with a wide variety of people. However, it was risky to share or debate some of the more politically sensitive or incorrect conclusions with participants. Yet, identification and collaboration at a deeper empathetic level were possible for me as a member of the community (Foley and Valenzuela 2005). In this respect it became more of a cultural, constructivist inquiry into the historical, social and political structures of power underlying the conflict situation (Saukko 2005). There is always (one hopes) a creative tension between having to represent the interpretation of the personal lived experience and the beliefs and world-views of the study population as well as the social reality, compelling nature of ethno-nationalism, the power play and vested interests underlying the context.

An interesting characteristic of the ethno-national discourse is that the majority and minority ideologies are mirror images of each other. If the majority Sinhala-Buddhist ideology defined the 'other' minority identities by exclusion or in opposition, they act to reinforce each other. War then becomes a contest between hegemonic ideologies for supremacy, subjugation of one by the other, an attempt to impose a particular construction of social reality. However, they all operate within the same paradigm of ethno-nationalism, producing a master narrative that is hegemonic within the group, totalitarian in nature. Paul Gilroy (1993) describes this modern ultranationalism or neo-racism well: 'However, where racist, nationalist, or ethnically absolutist discourses orchestrate political relationships so that these identities appear to be mutually exclusive, occupying the space between them or trying to demonstrate their continuity has been viewed as a provocative and even oppositional act of political insubordination.' In a politically contested, polarized and violent situation these attempts can be misunderstood as treason: the 'if you are not with us, then you are against us' mentality.

Sharika, the daughter of Rajani Thiranagama, has written insightfully (Thiranagama and Kelly 2010) about treason (*throham*), traitors (*throhi*) and the

> technologies of terror ... that attempt [total] political and social control ... through fear and suspicion ... the patrolling of inner life ... to penetrate/colonize the intimate thoughts and dreams ... the monitoring of emotions ... to mark out the boundaries of acceptable behaviour and stake out claims to ultimate authority.

I hope this book will be a testimony of what I actually did, in defence against the accusations of treachery by different actors at different phases of the conflict. It was a struggle to resist the daily brainwashing and peer pressure, to maintain an ethical and moral compass, or evolving perspective, that sought to preserve basic humanistic values, care for victims and communities with their best interest at heart and a way out of the tangle of ethnic conflict. Day-to-day life, research and writings were coloured by the accusations of treason, informing and analysing from scientific, moral and ethical principles that defied the party/group/state line of loyalty and blind obedience. Writing was always a fine-tuned, tightrope balancing act, acutely aware of the rapidly shifting political and power contexts; the prerogative to speak, to give voice tempered by what could be said and what expressed in veiled terms, what tolerated and what best avoided altogether; treading a fine line, a razor edge that could end in misinterpretation, for a misunderstanding would mean the maximum penalty.

Ironically, in the post-war context, with a change in the power equilibrium, these accusations are turned on their head, with many shifting their allegiance to the victor and where the same writings could still be misconstrued as treacherous to those left standing. 'Positions that at one moment seemed the epitome of patriotism and loyalty can be transformed to be seen as disloyal and duplicitous [and vice versa], as historical conditions create new frames of evaluation' (Thiranagama and Kelly 2010).

Case Studies and In-depth Interviews

Many of the interviews and case studies were with patients and clients that I saw as part of my work or those referred to me. The interviews were therapeutic in providing support and empathy (Ellis and Bochner 2000). Many felt better after having ventilated their inner feelings and the journey of discovery and understanding the interview led them on. At times, it was possible to promote positive skills, responses, resilience and coping.

However, in this book, I have tried to concentrate not on the individual, but more on how families and the community were affected. A problem arises in trying to define exactly what a community is, or attempt to delineate its exact boundaries (Van de Put et al. 1997). Some would define ethnic membership by asking which group one belongs to. Many people start defining their ethnicity by answering ascriptive questions during census, statistical surveys or interrogation. Some are compelled to adopt an ethnic identity by force of circumstances like ethnic riots or conflict. It is at the boundaries, for example, in mixed marriages and children, that such clear definitions significantly start to blur and break down. However, a dominant ethno-national ideology imposes, maintains and sustains fundamental ethnic identities and membership. In times of ethnic conflict, there would be polarizations, and boundaries may become more rigid and exclusive. Political and ethnic leaders may promote and engineer more exclusive definitions of membership, strict observance of boundaries, restrict relationships and movements between communities and create suspicions, paranoia, fear and antagonism for their power interests. Some of the peace-building interventions tried to bridge and reconnect communities, to bring them together to build relationships and understanding. The methodology employed here will look at some of these boundary conditions, their creation, maintenance and possibilities for dissolution.

Focus Groups

During my work as the person in charge of mental health care in northern Sri Lanka, I had opportunity to participate in a number of groups that were formed for the specific tasks of addressing psychosocial and mental health issues. Other groups discussed these issues as part of their broader mandates. Some groups were formed in response to immediate emergencies and needs such as after the tsunami (Mental Health Task Force) and displacement during the war. The focus group discussions and debates on mental health and psychosocial needs, interventions and programmes have included participants from the community, village, local government (village headman, teachers, social workers, priests); displaced camp and relief workers; district (GAs, district authority, NGO, militant) committees; national government (Ministry of Health, PTF); and INGOs (UN). The groups and committees functioned and represented different levels, from the local—community to village—to district, division, region, national and international levels. Groups included camp groups, women's groups, extended family groups and community groups (adolescents, religious, mothers, teachers, doctors, health staff). There were attempts to make these participatory and representative of issues and groups involved. For example, the child protection committee in Jaffna had students from the different district schools. It was usual practice to routinely have their voice heard. The meetings often lasted an hour, detailed notes were kept and official minutes circulated, to be revisited at the next meeting. I also kept my own notes.

Despite all this apparent democratic and representative practice, the control and dominance of competing political powers could be discerned and felt. There were clearly certain lines that no one dared to cross or topics into which no one trespassed. Often, views and complaints reflected accepted and allowed rhetorical positions. In these circumstances, comments made as asides, whispered reactions, tone of voice, body language like facial expressions, what was left unsaid and smaller, informal discussions after the meetings were more meaningful.

Key Informant Interviews

In the course of my work, I had the opportunity to meet and interview a variety of individuals from various positions of leadership and responsibility. Many of these were frank, open and confidential discussions. Others pertained to specific topics or special needs. My informants included government officers (assistant government agents [AGAs]), *grama sevaka*s (GSs), officers from social services, women affairs, child rights departments and other officers from AGA offices; INGO and NGO workers; doctors, health staff (nurses and primary health workers); teachers; priests; community leaders (chairmen, presidents and other members of committees and organizations); military and militant leaders; administrators in a variety of positions both internationally and locally in Colombo and the north; counsellors; dramatists; artists; psychosocial workers (PSWs); traditional healers; refugee camp leaders; women leaders; organizers and public representatives.

Narrative Inquiry

The collected stories and interviews from a variety of ecological contexts (see Table 2B.1) are presented to describe traumatic events and capture emotions, responses and consequences first hand. The attempt was to 'extract the meaning and implications, to reveal patterns or [and] to stitch together descriptions of events into a coherent narrative' (Corbin and Strauss [2008], quoted in Liamputtong [2009]). They become the testimonies of victims and survivors that give an idea of what they had gone through and what has happened to their families and communities. The testimonies were selected to represent common experiences of the community in general, eschewing the extremes and more sensational accounts, so that a collective narrative emerges. Thus the 'epistemological and ethical authority of testimonial narratives' gives rise to their authentic metonymic property to reflect the whole community (Beverley 2005). The transcripts of interviews were translated into English by the authors but the original meaning, tone, emotion and descriptive language was preserved as far as possible.

Qualitative Analysis

The narratives, drawings, letters and poems, as well as data from observations, key informant interviews, extended family, focus group discussions and media reports were analysed for impact at the family and community levels. Qualitative analysis of data used standard qualitative techniques like narrative analysis (content, idioms and structure analysis to locate common epiphanies, contexts, themes, processes, unique features and semiotics); phenomenology (personal and family experiences in essence, meaning and experiential description); grounded theory (selective coding and interrelated categories to develop propositions, conditional matrix, alternate interpretations, themes, hypothesis and theory); ethnography (cultural, religious and social contexts, events, actors, themes and patterned regularities to interpret how the culture worked in this situation); and case studies (using categorical aggregation to establish themes and patterns, direct interpretation and natural generalizations to extract in-depth pictures of cases).

Researcher

I was given the rare and unique opportunity to carry out this naturalistic study while involved in psychosocial and mental health work in the Northern Province during this period. Towards this end, the researcher functions as a bricoleur (Denzin and Lincoln 2000, 2005), being descriptive, interpretive, narrative, critical, theoretical, moral, ethical and at times political, using multiple methodologies and perspectives. The hope is that the result is an 'emergent construction', a quilt or montage that creates understanding but at the same time is pragmatic, strategic and self-reflexive (Denzin and Lincoln 2000, 2005).

Of course, I bring my own baggage, my personal history, biography, gender, education, training, experiences, social class and ethnicity to the task at hand. Towards a better disclosure of the several stands of background factors shaping the interpretive process, I have included some minimal personal history, experiences and responses where appropriate but have tried not to overdo it. The study is in many ways an autoethnography (Denzin and Lincoln 2000, 2005), where I am an ethnic Tamil (who grew up in Colombo and practised in different parts of the country and overseas but mainly in northern Sri Lanka), observing my own community, a native or insider looking critically into his own milieu. However, most of my secondary and tertiary education was completed abroad, in various countries, and my professional training was in the field of Western medicine and science, also much of it abroad, particularly in the West. Thus, I am a 'professional stranger', providing an 'outsider's' viewpoint as well. This enabled a process of 'disidentification', to hopefully escape the 'powerful lure of the readily available national(ist) explanation of these same events' (Ismail 2000). There were significant tensions and conflicts in accommodating what were, at times, contradictory stances, but it did provide a way of triangulation where different perspectives and methods were used to develop an in-depth understanding of the phenomena and add rigour, breadth, complexity and richness to the study (Denzin and Lincoln 2000, 2005).

There is also the reflexive, subjective element of the participatory observation, that is, observing myself caught up in the ongoing situation, as a refugee or experiencing the war first hand. The techniques of psychosocial introspection (Ellis 1991) were used to take account of how I was reacting and the effects the situation and events were having on me. There was no doubt that the events and what I had witnessed affected me deeply as they have most of those living in the north and east and would be reflected in my writing. Those in the south have been exposed to different ecological contexts. At the same time, interviewing, treating, assisting, researching and documentation were therapeutic for me, as it provided a way out of the traumatization and the constraints of the environment while providing a sense of purpose, of doing something constructive in an otherwise hopeless situation. In many ways, the book is a record, a documentation of my journey, begun with Broken Palmyrah, Scarred Minds and other publications and is a cathartic expression of my experiences.

Epistemology

The theoretical framework informing the study, the way of understanding the world and particularly what is being studied, guides the interpretations, analyses and results. Thus, it becomes imperative to tease out the underlying assumptions, clarify the ways of knowing embedded in the study (Crotty 1998) and make explicit the theoretical foundations and perspectives being employed.

Basically, the first part of the book on background is from a constructionist viewpoint (Crotty 1998), and critically interpretive or hermeneutic (Holstein and Gubrium 2005; Kincheloe and McLaren 2005). The foundations of the ongoing ethnic conflict are deconstructed from a historical and current sociopolitical and economic context (see Chapter 1A). The polarized ethno-nationalism that drives the war is a social construct. This study is also a critique of the hegemonic power relations and interests that battle to maintain their privileged positions, both Sinhala and Tamil, over the subject populations. The use of terror and counter terror-tactics show how far they will go (see Chapter 1B). In the modern tradition of Paulo Freire's (1972) *Pedagogy of the Oppressed*, conscientization can lead to praxis or mass action for potential liberation from the current system of ethno-nationalistic conflict.

Participatory Action Research

The final part of the book will describe the community-level interventions (see Chapter 5A) that grew out of participatory action research, that is, psychosocial interventions grew out of pressing needs and what was feasible given the ground situation and available resources, but were continually modified depending on the feedback and outcome.

Conclusion

The theory and methodology developed is a dynamic and reflexive process, as part of the actual work during the war and post-tsunami context. Due to the immediate needs and lack of prior training or experience, we had to first learn about trauma (Somasundaram 1998) from the available literature, by attending various conferences, seminars, through discussions with experts and colleagues and from sheer experience. The concept of collective trauma developed from having to deal with large populations that had undergone massive trauma, in Cambodia and Sri Lanka. We realized that our initial individual-level theory and intervention were not adequate or effective. The methodology that we used to understand the processes involved grew out of the actual work, a naturalistic, mainly qualitative, observatory and participatory technique that we documented and analysed as we dealt with the effects of different disasters, natural and man-made. One of the biggest natural disasters in the last century, the Asian tsunami of 2004, affected several countries in Asia and even reached Africa. One of the worst affected was Sri Lanka.

Collective Trauma: Causes and Consequences

A.

Tsunami

Mother, most gracious fountain of endless energy
You're Nature, renewing itself in the form of Fire, Water, Wind, Earth and Ether
Mother, most gracious I salute you!

You, the full moon drawing patterns on our compound
The gentle rain and the surging sea are my parents
You my mother, I your child
This life's your boon, my sole force
My mind is drenched with thy love

Thoughts of you sway my dreams

The morning sky your eyes compassionate
The hot sun and the cold windy rain
Are but manifestations of thy infinite care for us
Your radiant glance and your loving closeness
Your days and your nights the nourishing sap coursing through the roots

Thoughts of you sway my dreams

The days change like the ceaseless surge of waves
The spark lights the wick, the lamp sheds light

Thoughts of you sway my dreams

—N. Sivasithamparam, 'Alaparang Karunai' (Boundless benevolence)[1]

[1] Set to music for post-tsunami healing work.

Introduction[2]

The gigantic Asian tsunami of 26 December 2004 was generated by one of the worst earthquakes on record, measuring nine on the Richter scale, with an epicentre just off the coast in Aceh, Indonesia (see Figure 3A.1).

A series of massive tidal waves sped across the Indian Ocean, killing more than 220,000 people in twelve countries spanning South East Asia, South Asia and East Africa and displaced more than 1.6 million people in addition to colossal damage to property and infrastructure. In Sri Lanka, over a million of its people were affected; over 800,000 people were displaced, their homes and belongings destroyed, and 36,000 killed from the coastal communities of the north, east and south (ADBI 2007; WHO 2005b) (see Figure 3A.2). Ninety per cent of those killed were from the fishing community and belonged to the lower socio-economic class (Frerks and Klem 2005). Kilinochchi, Jaffna and Mullaitivu districts in the Northern Province of Sri Lanka were affected by the tsunami, and as of April 2005, 6,200 people had lost their lives (see Figure 3A.2), 961 were still missing,

Figure 3A.1:
Asian Tsunami—Map Showing Countries Affected

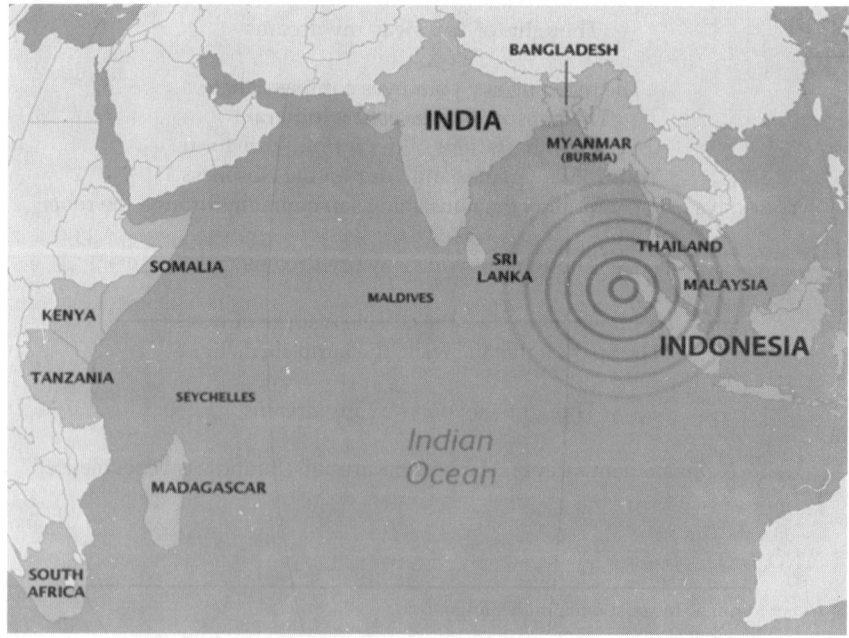

Source: Wikipedia (2013). Last modified 26 July 2013, last accessed 28 July 2013.

[2] Expanded and modified from Sundram et al. (2008).

Figure 3A.2:
Impact of the Tsunami on Sri Lanka

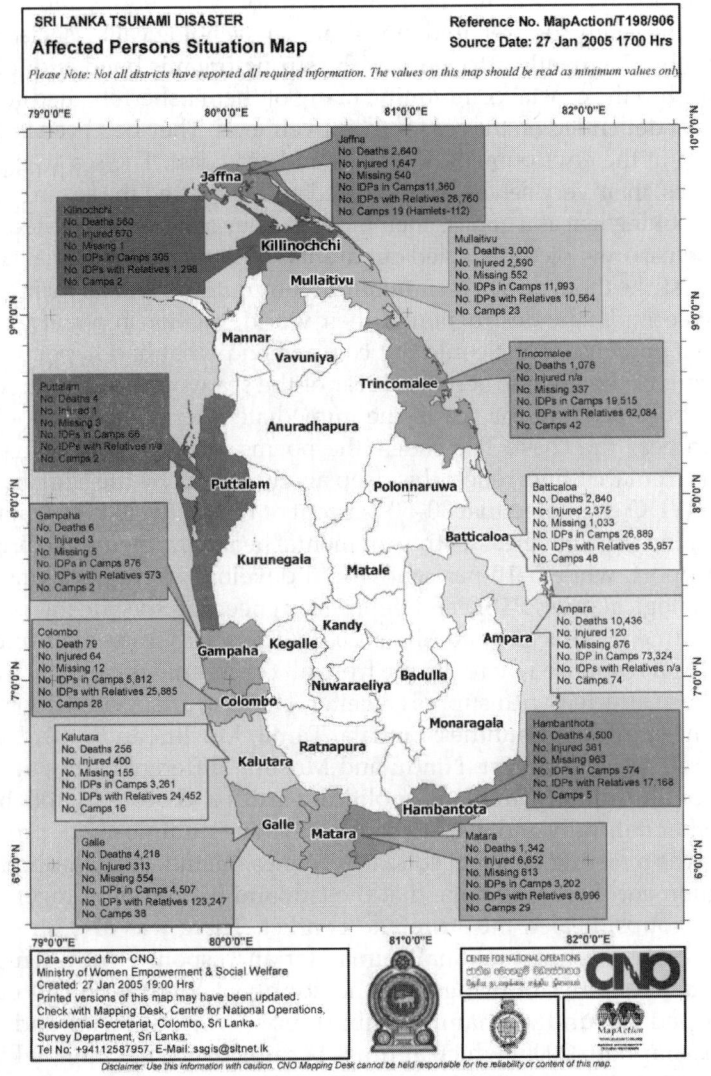

Source: Centre for National Operations (CNO). Available online at http://www.cnosrilan-ka.org/. On completion of the immediate recovery phase after the Tsunami, the CNO was closed by the Government of Sri Lanka. Figure reproduced with the permission of the director of CNO, Dr Tara De Mel.

19,618 people were still housed in welfare centres and 45,548 people were housed with relatives and friends (Government of Sri Lanka 2005).

The suddenness and massive nature of the wave(s) overwhelmed and surprised everyone. The deaths, injuries, destruction and chaos were unprecedented. The concept of a tsunami or possibility of the sea rising from the ocean bed was unknown to the majority of people, and it caught them completely unprepared physically, psychologically, socially and spiritually. Poignantly affected was the strong organic bond and intimate relationship the coastal community, many of them fisherfolk, had with the sea. Most depended on the sea for their livelihood. They had been born and grew up in the environment of the sea and sea coast. The sea was part of their lives, their very selves. They adored and respected the sea in spiritual terms, looking it at as a god, as their mother. They sang songs, recited verses and poems, drew pictures, acted out dramas and prayed to the sea. When it arose to strike them down, their families, communities and all their belongings in seconds, the destruction of their world, relationship and imagination was immense. Most could not comprehend what had happened. The rupturing of the organic bond and fear of the sea would take time to heal. Many could not face the sea in the immediate aftermath and would not venture near the coast. The songs, the poems, drawings, narratives and dramas from that time reflect this deep agony caused by the tsunami.

The WHO estimated that 30–50 per cent of those affected were at risk of developing psychological distress or mental health problems needing help and support, while 5–10 per cent would develop severe problems (such as pathological grief, PTSD and depression) needing specific intervention and treatment (Saraceno and Minas 2005). There was immediate and generous local response where people from all communities came forward to help those affected with support, shelter, clothing and food. People from different ethnic communities: Sinhala, Tamil, Muslim and others, of different religions: Buddhist, Hindu and Muslim, different castes, ages and walks of life: military, militants, political parties and ordinary folk helped each other naturally and warmly without barriers, animosity or prejudice. There was a feeling of social solidarity, cohesion and comradeship. For a brief moment there was hope that the tsunami had brought together the ethnic groups, healed the strife and conflict. There was also an unprecedented massive international humanitarian response with sympathy, aid and personnel pouring into the country. A whole NGO culture developed around tsunami rehabilitation work (Frerks and Klem 2005; Galappatti 2005) which at times became overwhelming, taking on a carnival atmosphere (Wickramage 2006). For the first time, the need for psychosocial work was recognized at the national level. However, no coordination mechanism existed and at that time there were no IASC guidelines (2007). At the local level, the pre-existing and experienced primary health care and militant structures proved most effective in organizing services during the acute emergency. At the district level, spontaneous formation of committees to coordinate psychosocial efforts, for example, the Mangrove (2006) in the east, Centre for Health Care (CHC) in the Vanni and the Mental Health Task Force (MHTF) in Jaffna (Danvers et al. 2006), was seen. Efforts were taken to organize mental health and psychosocial relief, recovery and rehabilitation at the national level through the Centre for National Operations (CNO) — Psychosocial Desk (and later, Task Force to Rebuild the Nation, TAFREN), Ministry of Health, Sri Lanka College of Psychiatrists, WHO, Consortium of Humanitarian Agencies (CHA) and many other organizations. However, links from the national level to the periphery, particularly in the north and east, for post-tsunami activities did not develop and responses in the north (and east) were undertaken in isolation from the well-resourced and funded programmes at the national level. The state response was tardy and discriminatory, marked by politics, favouritism and corruption (Frerks and Klem 2005; Goodhand 2005; Grewal 2006). In fact, Goodhand et al. (2005) say:

> The tsunami accentuated rather than ameliorated the conflict dynamics described above. In spite of initial hopes that the tsunami response would provide a space to re-energize peace negotiations, it had the opposite effect, deepening political fault lines. Protracted negotiations about the institutional arrangements for delivering tsunami assistance to the North-East mirrored earlier peace talks and exposed the deep underlying problems of flawed governance, entrenched positions, and patronage politics.

The impact in the north was immense (see Figure 3A.2). I was appointed by the Ministry of Health to coordinate the psychosocial response in the north. This chapter is based on that experience, describing the psychosocial impact and interventions used in the north.

Impact

Narratives

The narratives of what happened were taken from survivors along the northern coast by PSWs during their interventions in the immediate aftermath, starting within days of the tsunami, and with ongoing support and care. Most of the cohort were in hospital after sustaining injuries or were in IDPs camps with identified psychological distress for which they had been referred or selected by the PSWs. All the names have been changed from the original to de-identify the survivor.

Yesuthasan, six years old, Manalkadu:

> Some friends and I were playing when we heard a loud *iraichal* (high pitch sound). We thought a big ship was coming and ran into the house. When we looked we saw a flood. We *kathinom* (screamed). My friend and I climbed

a coconut tree. We saw our other friends being swept away by the flood. Later, when the tree fell, we were also dragged away and battered by the flood. On the way, my mother who was hanging on to a pole, caught hold of me. I do not know what happened after that. We were brought to where the army was. The *armykaran* [army man] bandaged my injured head and took us to the Manthikai [Point Pedro] hospital. Now I am frightened to close my eyes, it feels like the wave is coming. My heart is beating *padapada* (palpitation). I am scared to go to the seaside.

He was given a mantra *uchadanam* (chant) after which he reported that his fear had reduced. On the next day, he said he had experienced fear only once and when he chanted, 'baby Jesus, baby Jesus,' (being a Catholic Christian), the fear subsided. There was a picture of the sea on the wall. He was staring at it with eyes wide open. When asked, he said when he saw the picture, what had happened came to his mind. He was asked to repeat the mantra (*uchadanam*) whenever he experienced fear. When his case was followed up, it was found that he was attending the school at Manthikai.

Jeyarani, thirty-six years old, wife of fisherman, with five children, Thikkam, Point Pedro : They had been worshipping in the temple when everyone was *vellam addithuthalla* (swept away by the flood). She thought she was going to die and that the flood had taken her children away. She had, at that time, counted her children again and again to confirm that they were all there. That counting her children continued, and she did it frequently. She was embarrassed by this tendency but was unable to control herself. She also complained of numbness all over her body and said she talked loudly. She was sobbing as she talked.

Thangeswaran, twenty-six years old, fisherman, married with wife four months' pregnant, living with extended family—parents and four siblings, two of whom are married with children, Andhriayan North, Thalaiaddy. He said, crying:

I had just returned from fishing in the sea, eaten and gone to the market. I heard a big noise and the wave coming, that is all I knew. I fell and was swept away for 'miles'. I collided with barbed wire which split my legs open. I lost consciousness. I was taken by volunteers to the nearest (Maruthankerny) hospital and from there to Jaffna Hospital where I had surgery. The house was levelled to the ground and all my fishing equipment was lost. The home people thought I had died and only learnt yesterday that I was alive. At that time of the tsunami, I saw my wife being swept away. I could not save her. What would have happened to her? She was pregnant and alone! I could not help her when she needed me. My Father and mother were also injured. My father-in-law and mother-in-law and their son died. I do not know what happened to others.

Ritamma, forty-six years old, married to a fisherman, with five children, displaced in 1996, living in a rented house, Point Pedro:

I was with my youngest child [eight years old] in the house when my son shouted from the seashore that a big wave was coming. I grabbed my child and started to run when the wave overwhelmed us. We fell and were rolled on the ground. My daughter screamed that she was going to die. I held on to her as much as I could. At one point we were caught up in barbed wire. Without realizing it, I let go of my daughter. At once I thought she had died. I thought about why I should live any more. I was lying in the barbed wire with all my clothes torn when my eldest came and rescued me. I had injuries all over. They had saved my last child also. We have lost everything.

Nimala, thirty years old, married to a fisherman, with three children, Killappady, Mullaitivu:

My husband came running from the shore shouting that a *suravalli* (cyclone) was coming. I took hold of my youngest son and tried to get out when our palm-leaf house collapsed on top of us. The other children were also inside. I do not know what happened after that. When I came to later, I was one kilometre away, having been swept there by the water. Then others came to my rescue. When the next wave came, they put me up on a tree. I learnt that my husband was in hospital. My three children had died. I was informed by my relative that their bodies had been buried. My sister and her children who had come to visit us for Christmas also died.

Just after the tsunami, on being rescued and placed at a refugee centre, she recounted what had happened without any emotion in a dazed state. Weeks after the tsunami, she remembers what happened with fear and emotional distress.

Ariyabalan, fisherman, Mullaitivu: He lost his wife, two children, seven grandchildren, brother, sister and other relatives; a total of thirty-one people in his family died. He would not talk to anyone but when he saw the others telling their stories, he forced himself to talk for more than three quarters of an hour. He wept inconsolably as he recounted what happened. He said he had gone to the local tavern to forget his sorrow but then thought of his wife and cried without drinking. Later, he said that he felt that his grandchildren were hugging and biting him playfully. He felt he was going mad. He wanted sleeping tablets. He declared that he was going to go back and look at the sea at Mullaitivu and sleep on top of his broken-down home. Then he said he was going to commit suicide. After the PSWs spent a long time with him, he calmed down and went to sleep.

For many, the tsunami was an additional disaster, having already been affected by the civil war. Some had just begun to recover from the war, during the recent peace process, rebuilding their homes and lives when the tsunami struck. Some had already lost loved ones during the war, been displaced many times or suffered in other ways. The tsunami reminded them of the earlier travails, reopening old wounds.

Vijyakanthan, sixteen years old, Uduthurai, Thalaiaddy: His *amma* (mother) had died in 1996 due to shelling and *appa* (father) was a fisherman who looked after the family and two younger sisters. He said:

> I had just risen and come to the veranda; other family members were still asleep inside. Suddenly water started coming into the house. I did not know what was happening, I could not comprehend it. Out of fear I shouted, '*Appa*! Get up, there is water in the house!' They came running out of the house just as the house collapsed. After that I do not know what happened. Someone brought us to the hospital. Only after that did I regain consciousness. There is a big wound in my chest and leg. Both my eyes are red. Something has pierced my eye and my eyesight is affected. Both sisters are injured; an iron rod that has pierced one in her thigh and the other has injuries on her hands and legs. Father is in the Kilinochchi hospital. My uncle and aunt have died.

He was eager to see his father. 'Without *amma*, only *appa* is bringing us up with great difficulty,' he said, with tears in his eyes. He did not know where he would go after being discharged from the hospital. 'Who will come for me?' he wondered with apprehension. He was searching the environment for known people. 'Will my eyes become alright?' He did not know where to go and looked lost. (It was later learnt that one of his sisters had died but he did not know the details.)

Kandamalar, forty-seven years old, husband had been killed by the navy at sea in 1990, with three sons and two daughters—one had attained *veerachavu* (LTTE term for heroic death while fighting for them), Uduthurai, Thalaiaddy:

> When I was at my sister's home, the ground trembled, '*kidu, kidu*'. I wanted to run towards the back of the house but before I could run, water started coming in. I held on to a palmyra tree. The tree tilted, crushing me. When the next wave came, the tree straightened. The floodwater rolled and rolled me along. Later I was rolled into a Hindu temple. I screamed, 'Mayava, Mayava, save me!' At that time, I had no clothes on my body. My relatives heard me moaning and put me on a plank to bring me back. My younger brother and his children all died as a family. The sea took my sister's baby.

Summary of Narratives

The narratives are graphic descriptions of what happened that Sunday morning. The fishermen had just returned from the sea, given their catch at the market and returning home or were at home having breakfast or resting. The families were just waking up, cooking or playing outside. It was raining lightly, drizzling. The first intimation at that something was amiss was a loud hissing sound. Due to their past experience with events during the war, some mistook it for a diving Kfir bomber and thought the war had begun again. Some looked outside or up to see a big wall of water, the height of a palmyra tree (twenty to thirty metres) bearing down on them at great speed. Nothing from their previous experience or folklore had prepared them for this. Many appeared to be bewildered, unable to comprehend what was happening. They had just enough time to scream to others or pick up a child and start running when it swept them away. Most appear to have lost consciousness at that point. Some only saw the water flooding their homes or sweeping away everything in their path. Some saw their homes being filled with water, houses collapsing, family and friends being swept away, some plucked out from their grasp. Many were thrown by the waves against walls, barbed wire or other objects injuring, fracturing and penetrating them, tearing their clothes. Many became tangled in the extensive barbed wire surrounding the pervasive state military establishments on the north-eastern coast, which tore their clothes and skins and separated them from children who they were clinging to. Some held on to a raft, a tree or climbed aloft a floating object. Some could swim and this helped them feebly navigate the rushing water. They often found themselves miles from their original homes. Families, relatives and friends were separated, killed, injured, without clothes, in a daze. Recovered bodies were hurriedly buried in mass graves to preserve sanitation. There was little opportunity to identify bodies, carry out traditional funeral rituals and in many cases bodies were never recovered.

Though told by individuals, the narratives, without exception, were always in the context of what happened to the family: where each person was and what they were doing when the tsunami struck, what happened to each person, their whereabouts when they regained consciousness, the search for family members, concern for their well-being and guilt when they had died. The impact and consequence of the trauma depended on what happened to the family, going beyond the individual level, to affect the relationships and the family dynamics. When the mother died, the father took over her role and the children responded appropriately, compensating and filling in. When this did not work well, the father took to alcohol and this in turn affected the family dynamics adversely, which affected him further.

At the community level, village structures were destroyed and institutions stopped functioning. There was total displacement. Because of this, the usual community support was not available. However, people from different communities came to the rescue. Injured were taken to hospital. Displaced were found shelter; clothes and cooked food were distributed. Social barriers were broken, as people from different groups, ethnicities, religions and castes helped others with an outpouring of humanity. Soldiers and militants alike were at the forefront of rescue and support. They took people to hospital, gave assistance and were openly helpful and friendly. The dead bodies were buried and sanitation measures were undertaken. Soon people from other areas and regions—national and international—started to respond with all manner of help, support and personnel. Massive aid poured in. But within weeks divisive politics took over, taking control of the aid and funds, claiming authority and responsibility for relief efforts. Discrimination and corruption became rampant.

Qualitative Assessment in the Immediate Aftermath[3]

In the immediate aftermath of the tsunami, survivors were overwhelmed, in shock, with an acute feeling of having lost everything. ASR was common, and typically lasted for a few days. People were seen to be in a daze and highly emotional. Grief was the predominant psychological symptom. Factors which complicated grief reactions included:

1. Guilt: Commonly, survivors felt that they could have saved family members. Many had repetitive mental images of immediate family members, kin and friends being swept away, being snatched from their hands, being unable to hold on. Some had to make agonizing choices, holding on to one while letting go of another. Some had saved themselves without looking out for others.
2. Anger and hostility: These emotions were directed towards nature or the gods, at family members (for example, one parent blaming the other for the deaths of children), or at outside agencies such as the government or staff in welfare centres. Despair, anguish, tears, desolation, inability to accept what had happened, disbelief and other emotional expressions were seen.
3. Missing people: In cases where no body was recovered, unanswered questions and ongoing hope of survival were common. Those involved in recovery efforts, relief workers and volunteers experienced severe and acute stress reactions in response to traumatic experiences such as witnessing the aftermath of the tsunami or disposing of dead bodies.

[3] Adapted from Danvers et al. (2006).

4. Suicidal ideation: Guilt was a risk factor for suicidal ideation, as was losing a large proportion of close family. There was one case of suicide due to property loss in the first few weeks.
5. Alcohol abuse: This was especially common in men who had lost their wives and were struggling to cope with young children.

Fear of the sea and nightmares were initially common, as were fears about the future and returning to coastal areas. Most of the affected were from fishing communities, and mistrust of nature was expressed as 'she, who gave everything, also destroyed everything'. An assessment of seventy-one children (aged between eight and fifteen years) carried out about three weeks after the tsunami in Manalkadu by trained teachers showed that 40 per cent were at risk of developing PTSD (Neuner et al. 2006).

In the first few months, minor mental health conditions like depression, anxiety-related conditions including phobias, PTSD, somatoform disorders, traumatic grief reactions, alcohol abuse and suicidal ideas and attempts were observed and treated with a combination of reassurance, mobilization of support networks, listening, counselling, group work, opportunity for creative expression through art, narration, drama, play (for children), music, encouragement to return to habitual routines and social activities, medication where necessary and follow-up. They were observed to be expressive of their losses, wanting to talk about it and showing signs of distress. These basic psychosocial interventions helped them recover over time. The majority did not show overt mental health disorders but continued to have sleep disturbances, nightmares and a sense of loss for varying periods over a few months.

However, there was an increase in relapse of schizophrenia, exacerbation of symptoms and failure to follow regular treatment routines. Some individuals lost their medical records and medications, and defaulted clinic appointments and treatments. Some cases of schizophrenic illness or other psychotic episodes were not identified, or misidentified as reactions to the disaster, and managed only with psychological methods.

Some aspects of the systems put in place after the tsunami to deliver aid seemed to lead to more difficulties for the affected people. There was a complex official registration process to receive aid, which many found stressful. Initially, agencies were poorly organized and coordinated, and there were some cases of political interference in the supply of aid and provision of psychosocial support. Many felt this led to aid and psychosocial interventions not reaching all those in need, which caused resentment and anger amongst the affected people. Initially, only a few structured activities were available in the welfare centres, and this particularly affected children and adolescents who had lost parents. As time went on, there were reports of a lack of sensitivity and sympathy shown by some authorities dealing with tsunami survivors, including school principals and government officials who expected them to get back to normal functioning.

Previous experiences of being displaced (due to conflict) and dealing with trauma appear to have prepared those affected and the relief workers to deal with the effects of the tsunami. Local traditional healers and religious and community leaders already had experience in helping people who had suffered traumatic experiences. The combined effects of resilience due to previous coping experiences with trauma and quickly mobilized community psychosocial programmes might have prevented some from developing problems needing referral to hospital-level psychiatric services. The widespread availability of community psychosocial support may also have prevented some from accessing appropriate psychiatric support for their mental health problems. Some workers doing psychosocial support had insufficient training, and misidentified severe mental health problems needing professional help, attempting rather to manage them on their own. After the tsunami, some services (particularly community-based programmes) were diverted to the tsunami-affected areas, and away from areas which have a high level of psychosocial need as a result of other factors including poverty and conflict.

Surveys and Results

In the north-east, there were 126 schools that had children directly affected by the tsunami and 235 schools that had children indirectly affected; a total of 49,150 students affected by the tsunami.

The author and team of trained teacher counsellors (see section 5A) carried out an epidemiological survey of schoolchildren (in the age group of six to nineteen years) and found that 48 per cent of those who had been exposed directly to the tsunami (within three hundred metres) compared to 15 per cent of matched children not exposed fulfilled the DSM-IV criteria for PTSD (see Table 3A.1). It should be noted that all of them had been living in a war context. It was found that 18 per cent of those directly affected had depression while 8 per cent of those not exposed to the tsunami were depressed.

The common behavioural (see Box 3A.1), emotional (see Box 3A.2) and cognitive (see Box 3A.3) changes found in the students have been set out accordingly.

Those who were identified to have psychosocial problems were given help by counsellors in the form of a variety of psychosocial interventions

Table 3A.1:
Psychiatric Diagnosis According to Distance from Shore When Exposed to Tsunami

Diagnosis	*Within 300 m* *N = 122*			*Beyond 300 m* *N = 86*		
	Male *N = 57*	*Female* *N = 65*	*Total* *N = 122*	*Male* *N = 43*	*Female* *N = 43*	*Total* *N = 86*
PTSD	29	29	58 (48%)	06	07	13 (15%)
ASR	16	20	36 (30%)	02	05	07 (8%)
Depression	12	10	22 (18%)	01	06	07 (8%)

Source: Author's findings.

Box 3A.1:
Common Behavioural Changes

- Being startled at small sounds
- Restlessness
- Slow activity, slow response
- Aggressiveness
- Phobias (about the sea)
- Avoiding being alone
- Unhappiness when separated from parents
- Lack of concentration when separated from family members
- Lack of interest in activities

Source: Author's findings.

Box 3A.2:
Common Emotional Changes

- Malaise
- Getting angry easily
- Sadness
- Crying easily and/or frequently
- Feeling of having lost something
- Grief about loved ones lost
- Unwarranted fear
- Feel unhappy when separated from family members
- Unusual fear for the sound of waves

Source: Author's findings.

Box 3A.3:
Common Cognitive Changes

- Lack of concentration
- Decreased learning performance
- Increased interest in family activities
- Increased interest in God and/or worship

Source: Author's findings.

they had been trained in, including NET. Those with more severe problems were referred to mental health professionals or other appropriate services in the local region.

A survey of tsunami-affected families in the north of Sri Lanka after six to nine months using the General Health Questionnaire (GHQ-12) was undertaken by WHO-supported community support officers (CSOs) in two geographical clusters, Mullaitivu and Maruthenkerny (see Figure 3A.2). The majority were in camps for IDPs while some had moved in with relatives or friends. The LTTE did not allow the survey to continue in areas under their control due to their probable concern that some of the statistics would be used by state intelligence to ascertain the demographic situation in their area. In Maruthankerny, 901 people out of a local population of 16,153 died due to the tsunami. It was found that 50 per cent of families had lost one or more member, over 65 per cent of those dead were female and survivors had an average GHQ score of

Table 3A.2:
Analysis of GHQ Scores in Cluster 1 (Mullaitivu) and Cluster 2 (Thalaiaddy)

| | Cluster 1: Mullaitivu | | Cluster 2: Thalaiaddy | |
Analysis of GHQ Score	*People Who Lost Family Members*	*People Who Did Not Lose Family Members*	*People Who Lost Family Members*	*People Who Did Not Lose Family Members*
GHQ Score Range	10–33	9–35	9–30	6–34
Mean	13.4	12.9	17.3	15.7
Median	14	12	16	13.5
Mode	10	9	15	8
Variance	59.21	86.76	47.26	10.45
Standard Deviation	7.69	9.31	6.87	3.23

Source: Author and psychosocial team.

Table 3A.3:
Post-tsunami Psychiatric Disorders in Maruthankerny Psychiatric Clinic (total patients = 72) (January-November 2005)

Post-Tsunami Psychiatric Disorders	Numbers (Percentage) n = 72
PTSD	24 (53)
Depression	11 (24)
Traumatic grief	6 (13)
Anxiety (including panic and phobia)	4 (8)
Acute psychosis	2 (4)
Post-tsunami disorders	45 (63)

Source: Author's findings.
Notes: (i) Total number of patients seen: 72.
(ii) Period of observation: January–November 2005.

around 14 (see Table 3A.2). Although a cut-off score of 3 or 4 is considered an indication for 'caseness' or mental health problems in European samples, in Asia a score of around 12 is usually taken as the cut-off. Based on the mental health problems and distress in the post-tsunami context, CSOs were asked to actively intervene if the scores were above 15 and those with scores greater than 20 were to be referred for mental health assessment. Though GHQ scores were higher among those who had lost a family member it was not statistically significant in both clusters. It would thus appear that the majority of the tsunami survivors in general had high GHQ scores irrespective of whether they lost their family members or not. This means that in addition to personal loss, the tsunami caused widespread mental health problems (or distress) in the community.

In general, it was found that more women and children had been killed in the Asian countries affected by the tsunami (Oxfam 2005), there were multiple deaths in the same family (Samarasinghe 2006), the tsunami had been sudden, unexpected and overwhelming and many had witnessed the agonizing deaths of close kin or friends, leaving a deep sense of helplessness and guilt (see narratives above).

An analysis of the cases I saw at a fortnightly outreach psychiatric clinic at Maruthankerny hospital, from January to November 2005, showed that out of a total of seventy-two new patients, forty-five were diagnosed with post-tsunami psychiatric disorders (63 per cent) (see Table 3A.3). The major psychosocial problems identified in the IDP camps were traumatic grief (with severe guilt), phobias (fear of the sea), PTSD, depression, suicide, alcohol abuse, anger and psychotic illness (pre-existing, exacerbation, relapse or new).

Interventions

The psychosocial interventions were multidisciplinary, consisting of psychoeducation, crisis intervention, psychological first aid, behavioural–cognitive methods, traditional healing, rituals, relaxation techniques, pharmacotherapy, group and family work, expressive methods, rehabilitation, networking and community approaches. Psychoeducation and awareness was created through pamphlets (dos and don'ts, basic information), media (writings through popular media, interviews for television and radio), lectures (small target groups and popular), discussion and dramas (including traditional street theatre). Considerable training of grass-roots workers such as camp and relief workers, teachers, primary health staff and governmental officers was undertaken.

Advising and Coordinating: MHTF[4]

The urgent need to coordinate psychosocial activities became clear in the immediate aftermath of the tsunami. There was an immediate outpouring of local and international aid and humanitarian workers who responded rapidly for relief and recovery work. Due to the pressing practical needs, a mechanism for coordinating psychosocial activities evolved organically in the Jaffna peninsula. Within three days after tsunami, local and international agencies involved in psychosocial work, eighteen in total, came together to form the MHTF and coordinate the responses (Danvers et al. 2006; Krishnakumar et al. 2008; Somasundaram 2008; Van der Veen and Somasundaram 2006). The purpose was to coordinate and direct mental health and psychosocial activities. I was appointed as the chairperson. Initially the MHTF met daily to share their experiences and lessons learnt in their fieldwork. Organizations discussed the needs of the affected population and ways to help the survivors psychosocially. During that critical period there was no competition or rivalry; indeed there was an overwhelming spirit of urgency, comradeship and cooperation. Particularly affected geographical areas and tasks were allocated to different organizations and volunteers, schedules and timetables of visiting and work prepared, transport, food and other needs of workers arranged and catered for. Workers and volunteers reported back on what they had observed and done. Information was collected and disseminated appropriately. Resources were shared. The task force was quickly recognized

---

[4] Modified from Krishnakumar et al. (2008), Sundram et al. (2008) and Danvers et al. (2006) with additional information from Thedsanamoorthy Vijayasangar.

and representatives from the MHTF participated at the local and district-level inter-sectoral meetings chaired by governmental administrators and LTTE to highlight psychosocial issues, advocate interventions and contribute to planning.

There were training programmes on needs assessment, psychological first aid, support and handling acute grief for counsellors, psychosocial and other workers. They were given direction on how to identify and refer individuals at risk. Regular supervision and peer group meetings were held. Primary health-care workers were given a similar training programme and asked to look into psychosocial issues as well as their normal work. After the tsunami the MHTF carried out eighteen awareness programmes for 568 relief workers and others. Over a nine-month period in 2005, there were thirty-six different training programmes for eleven agencies with a total of 732 participants. The WHO developed a national strategy of training CSOs to address the mental health needs of the affected families throughout the areas devastated by the tsunami. In the north it was decided to select the CSOs from previous health volunteers who had worked in the health department's 'well baby' clinics and been involved in the immediate relief work after the tsunami in the camps. The senior primary health-care staff supervised their work. They were given training in basic mental health and psychosocial work. CSOs then visited each family affected by the tsunami and identified families and individuals needing help. They attended to simple problems using a variety of psychosocial interventions and referred more difficult cases to the local mental health clinic. Community interventions were also carried out.

Pamphlets and booklets on simple dos and don'ts were published by the forum in Tamil. The pamphlet was printed for the people affected by the disaster and the booklet was for workers in the community. Media briefings (*Tamilnet* 2004) and public awareness programmes were carried out regularly. The MHTF coordinated articles in the local papers, gave interviews and a press conference and also produced information leaflets for affected people and aid workers to give information to the public about normal reactions to trauma. Information was provided to the media about different stress-related issues. The task force disseminated information about normal psychological reactions, with an emphasis on the expectation of natural recovery (WHO 2003), while also ensuring that a system for psychiatric referral was in place for the minority with more severe or abnormal psychological reactions. Through contacts with the media, the MHTF hoped to encourage social agencies to promote normality and resettlement as soon as possible, and to influence newspapers' reporting style to avoid increased public distress.

In the first four weeks after the tsunami there was an influx of organizations, consultants and individuals who for humanitarian reasons felt the need to help. Both local and international organizations showed a great interest in psychosocial activities, even when they had no expertise in the field. Many consultants and individuals offered training in psycho-social issues. It soon became clear that some programmes, probably in their ill-conceived enthusiasm to help, did not meet minimum standards of training or psychosocial work, were culturally inappropriate and did not provide for continuing follow-up or support. Many new and inex-perienced people were given brief training about similar subjects by dif-ferent people and there was no real coordination about what was being taught. As a result MHTF was requested to process all the psychosocial programmes. A subcommittee was selected to go through the proposals and provided necessary advice and guidelines for their implementation. However, the MHTF had no real authority to take administrative action, its role being to persuade, suggest and coordinate.

Once the emergency and relief phase were over, some ten months post-tsunami, the MHTF wound down. In the latter part of 2005, the gov-ernment of Sri Lanka wanted to streamline the tsunami activities at the district levels. The GA of Jaffna requested the Regional Director of Health Services (RDHS) to organize a coordinating mechanism for psychosocial activities. It was in this context that the district-level psychosocial forum was established as a continuation of the MHTF to enhance the coordina-tion between various governmental, non-governmental and international organizations involved in psychosocial activities in Jaffna district. It is officially chaired by the RDHS, Jaffna, technically supported by the dis-trict psychiatrist and has over 20 organizational members that continue to meet regularly.

Long-term Interventions

Once the immediate emergency situation had been dealt with, many organizations closed up and left. Some implemented longer-term resettlement, rehabilitation and development programmes. Few focused on psychosocial work as such. With UNICEF's funding support, the MHTF allocated the villages of Valvettithurai, Athikoviladdy, Erinthakoviladdy and Vadamarachchi West in the Vadamarachchi area to Shanthiham for long-term psychosocial rehabilitation work. In addition, in Maruthankerny area (Vadamarachchi East), Shanthiham was asked by the Kilinochchi CHC to work in the villages of Kudathanai, Chempiyanpattu and Thalaiaddy. The overall aim of psychosocial interventions was healing, recovery and social empowerment. Rebuilding the destroyed community was undertaken by re-establishing and strengthening the village institutions and structures that had stopped functioning. Women's, elders' and children's groups, and core groups (CGs)[5] were established with regular ongoing support and facilitation for meetings, discussions, informational seminars, training and self-help activities to rekindle the social dynamics. Specific training in mental health and psychosocial subjects were carried out for teachers and members of core groups. Assistance for family reunions as well as encouragement and support towards unity, cohesion and positive relationships helped to re-establish healthy family dynamics. Social and cultural practices, rituals and remembrance ceremonies were arranged and supported. Although the displaced in camps had initially been helpful to each other with sympathy and compassion, in time, misunderstandings, conflict, alcoholism and deterioration in social norms, sexual behaviour, ethics and morality were seen. To counter these, psychosocial awareness, information sessions and training for the camp leaders and inmates were undertaken. Problem solving, conflict resolution, income generating activities and other interventions were also undertaken.

Training

Shanthiham was requested by both governmental organizations and NGOs to train their workers in post-tsunami psychosocial work. Various levels of training depending on the needs of the organizations were carried out in that period. In the government sector, village headmen (GSs), Samurdhi officers and health staff working in the tsunami-affected areas were given basic training for a minimum of ten days. In the NGO sector, the Danish Red Cross (DRC) organized Sri Lanka Red Cross (SLRC) volunteers from Batticaloa, Ampara and Trincomalee from the east who were trained as four groups of thirty each for ten days. They were then given follow-up support, training and supervision for six months in the field. There was an opportunity to work with members from all three communities — Sinhalese, Muslim and Tamil. In addition, training was provided for workers from Seva Lanka, Médicos del Mundo (MDM), Care International, ICRC Kilinochchi, CHC and Jaffna Social Action Centre (JASAC), Vanni. During 2005 and 2006, fourteen governmental agencies and twenty-two NGOs were given fifty-two trainings for a total of 512 workers. Finally, a one-year counselling training was carried out at Shanthiham for candidates with aptitude (previous experience, recommended by organizations) selected from Jaffna, Vavuniya, Mullaitivu, Kilinochchi and Mannar

[5] Members for the CG were selected from those in the affected community who showed special interest and psychosocial aptitude, such as through previous experience with social work. Mainly they were youths with an active and altruistic spirit.

using WHO funding support. Twenty-five candidates successfully completed the training and are currently[6] working as counsellors in their areas. Regular follow-up was provided. Some projects that were already in operation were able to extend their work for post-tsunami work such as the Transcultural Psychosocial Organization-Child Thematic Project (TPO-CTP) and Widows Support Programme (WSP).

Lessons Learnt

Although there was considerable experience in addressing the mental health and psychosocial needs of people affected by the conflict, the tsunami was the first experience in post–natural disaster work. Running the MHTF, organizing a large variety of workers, giving them basic training and sending them to separate affected geographical areas in a systematic way to carry out relevant psychosocial interventions was a unique experience. Although very similar mental health and psychosocial consequences upon individuals, families and communities were observed after conflict-related traumas, the effects of a massive natural disaster had some special characteristics. Particularly the extraordinarily massive, unexpected impact within a short time period that caused destruction of whole villages was unprecedented. Everyone was affected. There was a temporary state of helplessness. The PSWs learnt how to work in a situation of massive natural disaster with affected individuals, families and communities.

Community-based Psychosocial Work
with *Vijayasangar*
(Shantiaham PST)

Maruthankerny is a cluster of remote fishing villages about fifty kilometres south-east of Jaffna town, off the A9 highway (see Figure 3A.3), which was at the time of the tsunami under LTTE control. It lacked most basic facilities. It was situated very near the forward defence lines of the Sri Lankan army separated by a strip of no man's land of about three hundred meters from the LTTE stronghold and was subject to shelling and gunfire during times of conflict. Access was also difficult with poor roads and transport. The tsunami totally destroyed the small coconut-leaf huts that families

[6] One died in the Vanni war, one or two left the country and two are not working. But the majority of them are still working as counsellors in different places.

Figure 3A.3:
Maruthankerny with Three Villages

Source: Created from Google Earth by authors.
Note: The three villages are Mamunai, Chempiyanpattu and Vaththirayan.

lived in and other village structures. Many of the injured were transported to the nearest hospitals that had facilities to deal with them. Dead bodies were taken to the Maruthankerny rural hospital and other locations and then buried in mass graves. Some bodies were not recovered. All the survivors were displaced; the majority were given temporary shelter in camps and then later settled in small huts some distance from the coast (see Figure 3A.4). The LTTE and organizations operating under it such as the medical unit, CHCs and the state institutions like the local government, primary health care workers from the Ministry of Health and other volunteers were at the forefront of rescue and relief activities.

As part of the immediate psychosocial support organized by the MHTF, Shanthiham sent a team of ten experienced PSWs to Maruthankerny. Unlike in the other areas, due to the remoteness and difficulties of travel, the team stayed for several days at a time in rotation. In view of the extreme heat during the middle of the day in these areas, they worked early mornings (between six o'clock and ten o'clock) and late evenings (between four o'clock and seven o'clock). By living close to the affected population, the psychosocial workers were able to build a close relationship and trust that they were always available. It gave them an opportunity to understand and make a more comprehensive assessment of the conditions by being able

Figure 3A.4:
Resettlement Huts

Source: Shanthiaham with permission.

to observe behaviours and expressive manifestations directly. The PSWs carried out the variety of psychosocial interventions described above. At the same time, I was able to visit[7] the local Maruthankerny hospital and camps on a periodic basis (weekly to fortnightly) to review, discuss and manage those referred for more severe mental health problems (see statistics in Table 3A.3). Other organizations under the direction of the CHC also sent PSWs and counsellors to the area on a regular basis but generally Maruthankerny did not receive much attention and support in all forms of assistance due to its remote location and logistical difficulties. An art exhibition by students was organized at Uduthurai Mahavidyalaya by the Kilinochchi Medical Association (Sivathas 2006). A significant psychosocial activity that was undertaken was to build memorial sites at locations of mass burials. It was observed that survivors had taken to visiting these sites and spent long periods grieving and carrying out various rituals like laying flowers and praying in the hot sun (see Figure 3A.5).

---

[7] Significantly, I was denied access to Mullaitivu by the LTTE, although I managed to sneak in a couple of times.

Figure 3A.5:
Mass Burials

Source: Shanthiaham with permission.

Long-term Work in Maruthankerny

Long-term psychosocial work with the survivors was carried out by Shanthiham with financial support from the Finnish government and the Dutch agencies, Cordaid, Achmea and HealthNet–TPO. Three villages were selected for psychosocial interventions: Mamunai, Chempiyanpattu and Vaththirayan (see Figure 3A.3). Fifteen youths from the area were trained as PSWs and ten as yoga and relaxation therapists (YRTs). The scope, aims and objectives of psychosocial work were introduced to community leaders, government and non-governmental agencies and other service providers in Maruthankerny. Social mapping of the villages was done and statistics data were collected (see Table 3A.4).

There were many INGOs and LNGOs working in the project area on reconstruction and rehabilitation but few were involved in psychosocial work. The post-tsunami psychosocial work done is summarized in Table 3A.5.

The objectives of psychosocial work were basic information and psychoeducation, sharing of experiences and narratives, group activities,

Table 3A.4:
Pre- and Post-tsunami Population Data of Maruthankerny

Category of People in the Community	Mamunai	Chempiyanpattu	Vaththirayan
Total number of families	161	435	426
Total population before the tsunami	623	1,778	1,406
Deaths[8] from tsunami	26	51	133
Total population after the tsunami[9]	597	1,593	1,308
Disabled	7	54	38
Widows	12	61	49
Wives deserted by husband	10	17	13
Widowers	8	32	31
Children without mothers	10	58	35
Children without fathers	2	81	44
Children without father and mother	1	6	13
Total number of children	180	515	335
Total number of elders	22	122	57

Source: Shanthiaham with permission.
Note: Data is as of 10 March 2006.

relaxation exercises and for children, play and creative productions; strengthening the communities to inculcate a sense of belonging and rebuilding traditional social networks. Debates were held within groups on specific topics where arguments were put forward for and against a given concept using *padi mandram* (musical debate following traditional format) with the whole community participating. PSWs and YRTs acted as catalysts for gender-based attitudinal changes, which they hoped would have a cascading effect within the community, especially the youth. Elders were encouraged to relate stories (folklore) to children. The services of the Child Thematic Project of HealthNet–TPO were obtained to teach cooperative games structured for children to have fun safely and calmly, ensuring all children were involved with a sense of equality and connected to others in a win-win atmosphere.

YRTs worked along with PSWs to deal with clients having various psychosocial problems. They worked at the Maruthankerny hospital during psychiatric clinics to provide relaxation and yoga therapy to clients. They also provided yoga training to the various groups. These traditional healing methods were found relevant and supportive even in

[8] Does not include people missing.
[9] Some families were displaced or migrated after the tsunami.

Table 3A.5:
Psychosocial Intervention Reports from Maruthankerny

Activities	Target Group	Number of Programmes	Number of Participants or Beneficiaries
Health education and awareness	Community	32	1,402
Yoga and relaxation	Identified beneficiaries	256 sessions	102
Backup training	PSWs and YRTs	06	31
Befriending	Psychosocially affected	495 sessions	256
Group activities (Six groups)	Children, elders, youth, widows, widowers and women	87 sessions in total	977
Referrals	Traumatized	Counselling sessions	10
Supervision	Field staff	25 sessions	105
Total Number of Beneficiaries	Mamunai, Chempiyanpattu and Vaththirayan communities		**2,779**

Source: Shanthiaham with permission.
Notes: (i) Report is as of March–April 2006.
(ii) Field location: Mamunai, Chempiyanpattu and Vaththirayan.

addressing illnesses induced by post-war trauma. Befriending sessions were held for clients identified during home visits by providing active listening and empathy (see case below), mobilizing home and community support, and referred for social support to relevant service providers for skilled counselling or to the psychiatrist.

Kamala, aged 48, was married with four children. Her eldest son, Selva, aged twenty-four, was an able fisherman supporting the family. He used a *kattumaram* (three hollowed wood pieces tied together) for fishing. From his earnings he had bought a new out-boat engine and nets which he intended to start using at an auspicious date and hour. (Unfortunately this happened to be on the day after the tsunami.) This was his long-cherished dream from boyhood. On the day of the tsunami he was at the beach admiring this new acquisition, which was to be launched into the sea after a religious ceremony the following day, when the tsunami struck at 8.50 a.m. taking away Selva and his boat. Kamala was unable to trace the whereabouts of Selva. Meanwhile, someone had told Kamala that Selva was seen running away from the tsunami and she lived in hope until his body was recovered. It was Kamala who searched for Selva and found the body the next day in the evening about three quarters of a kilometre away from the beach. She said that she had used a makeshift stretcher and summoned her brother and son to take the body for burial.

Kamala said that Selva was an able-bodied youth, respected within the community as someone who could bring in a good income. Moreover, she was grieving that her son could not enjoy or benefit from of his long-cherished boat. Kamala loved this lad the most as he was the eldest son and brought prestige to the family and in turn this son loved her dearly. Selva had planned to launch the boat on the day after he bought it (before the tsunami) but it was Kamala who had advised him to wait for an auspicious day and time, which happened to be the day after the tsunami. Selva wanted to buy a motorcycle with the money left over after the purchase of the boat but it was Kamala who dissuaded him from doing so as people would cast an evil eye on his (relative) wealth and requested Selva to postpone the purchase of the motorcycle. Kamala had severe guilt that she prevented the launching of the boat on the day her son had wished. If Selva had launched the boat on that day he had planned, he would have been at sea at the time of the tsunami and would have been alive (those at sea survived). Kamala prevented her son enjoying the use of a motorcycle. The money for motorcycle was at home and was lost to the tsunami. She was frustrated that she could not reciprocate the enrichment he brought to the family. During the first home visits her children complained that she was constantly crying, mindless, sleepless and not eating. The family was provided with psychoeducation and Kamala was taken to hospital for treatment by psychiatrist for loss of sleep and depression. PSWs and YRTs made regular home visits and encouraged her to ventilate her thoughts and feelings while listening actively and empathetically. The family was unable to support her, as they too were grieving. The family as a whole received psychological support. Kamala was provided relaxation at home by the YRTs. The counsellor dealt with Kamala's guilt feelings.

During supervision, the befrienders' (PSWs and YRTs) personal problems were dealt with as many of the befrienders themselves have lost their loved ones and belongings to the tsunami. As a result of the training, those from within the community (PSWs and YRTs) are able to identify mental health problems, deal with minor mental health problems or refer them for specialized intervention.

At the time of commencement of the project the security situation was relatively stable. However, over time, the ceasefire agreement began to unwind and there was an escalation of skirmishes across the border. The villages of Mamunai and Chempiyanpattu were completely evacuated on 16 May 2006 following heavy exchange of artillery fire and shelling across the border. Most of them moved out to live with relatives and friends around Vaththirayan, the project area, where the psychosocial trainers

(PSTs), PSWs and YRTs regrouped. This displacement further stressed the facilities in the temporary shelters in Vaththirayan. With a temporary reduction in armed confrontations, families moved back to their villages. The simmering conflict escalated into a fully blown armed confrontation across the border on 11 August 2006, with the exchange of artillery and motor shelling, use of multi-barrel rocket launchers and Israeli Kfir jet bombers. The villagers mostly resettled in the coastal villages of Kalaru in the Kilinochchi district and Ambalavanpokkanai and Matalan in Mullaitivu district. PSWs and YRTs too moved along with them and engaged in crisis intervention. The confrontation then escalated into the final Vanni battle and everyone was displaced several times, ending up in the Vavuniya internment camps (see Chapter 3B).

Cultural Interventions

Affected schools were encouraged to have regular ceremonies to commemorate those who died, to have pictures, flowers and candles for the students who had died. Support was sought for communities which sought to build memorial structures at sites of mass burials. It was found that sites where mass trauma had occurred become sacred, imbibed with community meaning (Tumarkin 2005). All over Sri Lanka, every year on 26 December, anniversary day memorial ceremonies are held in tsunami-affected areas.

Post-tsunami Politics
continued by *Daya Somasundaram*

Malathi de Alwis (2009) while discussing the 'double wounding' due to the post- tsunami aid raises the urgent need to 'interrogate the political via more affectual categories such as grief, injury and suffering' as a means to address the 'deepest, darkest and most desolating laceration of our land — the ethnic conflict'. As Frerks and Klem (2011) sadly point out,

> [H]uman suffering and victims are not just the humanitarian source of a moral appeal; they are also highly political commodities. The ability to respond to these appeals is vital for political credit (legitimacy) and to control (over resources and who gets them). The competition over 'victims' manifested itself in different arenas: among aid agencies ('competitive humanitarianism'), among militias (the LTTE and the government forces), between the state and the non-state (the LTTE, but also to some extent the

Janatha Vimukthi Peramuna, JVP) and among the sub-state political parties and individuals.

The politics surrounding post-tsunami reconstruction showed in stark relief the ethnic, minority and other fault lines in Sri Lanka. The tsunami occurred during a lengthy period of ceasefire when people were getting back to their normal lives, but had a heavy impact in the north and east on people already affected by the conflict, some living in IDP camps on the coastal belt. Some associated the calamity with the war. The tsunami first appeared to have actually postponed the return to ethnic hostilities by one year. The war clouds were gathering when the tsunami struck, putting all plans into disarray and creating a civilian catastrophe that was difficult to ignore. Even more, it created a window of opportunity, an opening for possible joint action by the warring parties, a forgetting of old wounds in the recovery and rehabilitation of the tsunami victims. As described above, the immediate aftermath of the tsunami brought out the best in all communities and people, local, national and international. People helped each other without even considering the traditional barriers of ethnicity, religion, language, class, caste, colour, gender or age (Lock 2006). Soldiers helped ordinary civilians, rescued them from the waves, dressed their wounds and took them to hospital. Religious institutions and priests gave shelter, food and clothes to people of other faiths. Sinhalese, Tamils and Muslims helped each other without barriers. Rescue volunteers, national and international, poured into affected areas. Aid and assistance were overwhelming. Militant organizations like the LTTE and JVP used their efficient structures to respond to immediate needs like shelter, food, disposal of bodies and sanitation. In general, the immediate rescue operations were highly successful (Frerks and Klem 2005; Goodhand 2005; Shaw et al. 2010). Displaced families were provided shelter, fed and clothed. Outbreaks of epidemics predicted by the WHO did not materialize due to effective preventive measures. Soon, activities for children, support and consolation for the bereaved, counselling for the traumatized and training for volunteers were underway. However, once massive foreign funding started arriving and politicians stepped in to control the lucrative flow; corruption, discrimination, divisions, misunderstandings, frustrations, anger and conflict arose.

Tragically for Sri Lanka, unlike in Aceh, the opportunity created by the tsunami for addressing a humanitarian need in an equitable, neutral way through building trust and faith in peaceful rehabilitation by bringing warring parties to work together was lost. As de Alwis and Hedman (2009: 9–10) note:

> In both Aceh and Sri Lanka, the devastation of the tsunami and rehabilitation and reconstruction in its aftermath, also intersected with and shaped

the politics of ongoing civil wars leading to militant groups and government forces launching new battles over control of people, land, livelihoods and humanitarian/development aid ... pushing the Indonesian government to lift the civil emergency in Aceh, in June 2005, and most importantly, enabling the Helsinki-brokered peace talks which led to the signing of a Memorandum of Understanding to end the conflict between GAM and GoI, on August 15th 2005 .... In Sri Lanka, in contrast, a tenuous ceasefire, between the LTTE and Government of Sri Lanka, which had been in place since February 2002, broke down soon after the tsunami around the issue of the disbursement of tsunami aid.

There were marked regional and ethnic inequities in the post-tsunami reconstruction process (ADBI 2007; Frerks and Klem 2005; Grewal 2006; Mulligan and Nadarajah 2010), which aggravated the ethnic conflict. Shaw et al. (2010) observe:

> For example, more new houses were built than needed in Hambantota while more than 400 Muslim families at Sainthamarathu were left to 'rot' in cynically named 'welfare camps' when the national government announced that all the aid money had been expended. The inequitable distribution of tsunami aid in Sri Lanka has exacerbated some pre-existing tensions at both national and regional levels. This study showed there is far less confidence about the future within the case study communities in the Ampara District compared to those in the southern province.

There were allegations of mal-distribution and patronage—Goodhand (2005):

> A third effect of central government involvement was that aid became subject to patronage. The Prime Minister [Mahinda Rajapaksa] gave a particularly egregious example, concentrating his efforts on his own constituency, the Hambantota district. He stands accused of directing 83 million rupees (approx. 685,00 Euros) of international donor money into the private 'Helping Hambantota' fund (BBC, 2005). Generally, national politicians are focusing on the South coast, because most of their constituency comes from the Sinhala majority in the South of the country.

It appeared that the poor, socially disadvantaged and marginalized, widows and landless and ethnic minorities were left out. Only a few permanent houses had been completed in some parts of the north such as Maruthankerny and Mullaitivu while progress was very slow in other parts of the north-east compared to almost full completion in the south (ADBI 2007). It was more difficult to work in some areas than others (Shaw et al. 2010). Logistic and administrative restrictions prevented many of the aid agencies working in the north. Even when Kofi Annan, then secretary general of the UN, visited Sri Lanka after the tsunami, he was prevented from visiting affected areas in the north, clearly for political reasons (Frerks and Klem 2005). Goodhand (2005) notes:

> The slow, ineffective, overcentralised and corrupt response from the state had various consequences. Firstly, international donor agencies soon lost trust in the state as a mechanism for disbursing tsunami relief and reconstruction funds, and channelled primarily to NGOs and UN agencies. Secondly, it caused a very different post-tsunami situation to emerge on the ground in South, East and North. Thirdly, this differential response in turn caused each region to feel disadvantaged and hard done by in comparison to the others.

In comparison to the central government favouring the south in post-tsunami reconstruction, there was said to be higher presence of INGOs in the east and more generous donations from the Tamil diaspora in the north. All aid in the north had to be effectively channelled through the Tamil Rehabilitation Organization (TRO) and LTTE. It was not clear how much reached the people themselves and how much was diverted to the LTTE coffers. Grewal (2006) says:

> There is some evidence to suggest that in Northern LTTE-controlled areas, increased efforts on community consultation, the provision of early and consistent beneficiary lists, stronger NGO coordination and the setting of maximum standards for housing yielded some positive results on equity for the post-tsunami IDP group. However other reports have suggested that preferential access to relief and rehabilitation assistance has been provided to families and groups within tsunami IDP communities that have demonstrated loyalty toward or been of strategic importance to the LTTE.

Senanayake (2005) argues that raising unrealistic expectations and delays in providing permanent housing and other rehabilitative measures prolonged the psychological trauma and generated aid dependency among those languishing in transitional shelters.

Thus, unlike in Aceh, the post-tsunami work in Sri Lanka did not become the means to long-term reconciliation and peace. Almost half a year after the tsunami, through a long-drawn, acrimonious process in June 2005, the state and LTTE finally reached an agreement over joint Post-Tsunami Operational Management Structure (P-TOMS) that was intended to facilitate a fair distribution of tsunami aid and reconstruction (Goodhand et al. 2005). However, this agreement was not allowed to be enforced by ultra-Sinhala forces and was stayed by the Supreme Court of Sri Lanka (ADBI 2007; Grewal 2006). Political and military conflict soon overtook the entire post-tsunami rehabilitation and reconstruction effort.

Another important actor in the post-tsunami scene and politics was the international sector. Unlike in India, where international aid and assistance was limited as a national policy, in Sri Lanka there were no initial restrictions; in fact, it was encouraged through various incentives, tax breaks, lowering of entry and funding requirements, media access and worldwide publicity. 'Over 500 aid agencies participated in the relief and recovery operations in Sri Lanka and many of these had no prior experience in long-term social recovery after a large-scale disaster' (Shaw et al. 2010). Their contributions were acknowledged to be beneficial and helped to fill in the gaps due to the tardy and lack of organized response by the state in north-east (Goodhand 2005). However, there was considerable unhealthy competition between them 'with a rat race for victims' (Frerks and Klem 2005) and pressure to show results to their donors back home (Goodhand 2005). Their overwhelming presence and role also led to a distorting effect on the local economy by increasing land prices, wages and salaries, culture (by introducing foreign practices), values and lifestyles. Emphasis was placed on 'asset replacement' and micro enterprises but long-term community development with local knowledge and sensitivity was lacking (Shaw et al. 2010). Creating more resilient local communities needed adequate public space for community activities to promote the re-emergence of new social networks, re-establishing 'community level enterprises' capable of generating incomes for a range of people. A further observation was that the affected population rarely participated in the drawing up of the plans or programmes or when they were asked their views were ignored when the final plan was made or implemented. They had no input or say in what was to be done for them. However, for the first time, there was wide acceptance of psychosocial problems, the so-called 'tsunami wisdom', and there were considerable effort to address psychosocial and mental health needs by the state, militants, NGO and INGO sectors. Constructive long-term programmes were supported through international goodwill. Locally, Shanthiham was strengthened by inputs from TPO and the Dutch agency Achmea's funds to develop its administrative structure, set up a training unit and establish an office. Vavuniya benefitted from a psychosocial centre, wards and intermediate care units. The Centre for Addiction and Mental Health from the University of Toronto ran a capacity-building programme for mental health staff.

Using the conducive post-tsunami atmosphere and generous international aid, the WHO was able to push through considerable reform including a National Mental Health Policy and Plan (WHO 2005a), decentralization of mental health services and building up of the peripheral mental health services and infrastructure. The WHO introduced an effective community-based mental health strategy nationally through the CSO programme (Kakuma et al. 2011; Mahoney et al. 2006; Psychosocial Forum of CHA 2008). UNICEF worked with the Ministry of Education to develop counselling and psychosocial capacity within the school system. A national council and committees on disaster management, planning and preparedness at various levels were constituted.

Unfortunately, the larger post-tsunami politics aggravated the ethnic conflict in Sri Lanka rather than helping to resolve it as in Aceh, leading to a resumption of hostilities and eventually an all-out war to the finish, leaving people reeling from the double blow.

B.

Vanni

Vanni War Narratives[1]

Introduction

What happened in the Vanni and to its people from August 2006 onwards, particularly from January 2009 to May 2009, has been described in apocalyptic (in Tamil, *pralayam*) terms (Centre for Policy Alternatives 2009; Harrison 2012; ICG 2010b; Swamy 2010; UTHR-J 2009; Weiss 2011). The total destruction of civilian infrastructure that ensued in the bitter fight to the end between the Sri Lankan military forces and the LTTE, with an estimated civilian population of around three hundred thousand trapped in between, is an ineffable human calamity. A common refrain from people who were there is, *varthayal varnicca mudiyathavai* (it is beyond description by words) (Anonymous 2009). There are several contested versions and discourses battling to establish their perspective. The Sri Lankan state and military have actively striven to suppress the truth of the ensuing carnage for fear of investigations of war crimes (BBC 2010; ICG 2010b; Stein 2010; UN 2011; United States Department of State 2009). There also appears to be a more long-term effort to frame and reconstruct collective memories and historical record in line with the political agendas of different actors. The Sri Lankan state and Sinhala nationalists would like to paint it as a war against terrorism (Chandraprema 2012; de Silva 2012), while many Sri Lankan Tamils depict it as the *irithi por* (final battle),[2] or simply *mudivu* (finish) in a long liberation struggle (Malathy 2012).

---

[1] Modified from Somasundaram (2010a).

[2] *Irithi por* was a periodic 'mobilizing metaphor' (Goodhand and Korf 2011) used by the LTTE to depict a looming major battle for recruitment, prepare the population for sacrifices, a call to arms, a rhetorical device for its propaganda and fund collection locally and abroad. It was heard first in 1987 during the war against the Indian army and periodically thereafter,

However, the psychosocial and mental health impact on the civilian population and interventions for their recovery remains a major concern that has been neglected.

The Tamil community needs an acknowledgement of what happened, to make others understand their losses and extent of suffering, for their own grieving process and to carry on with their lives. For the nation, for the eventual process of reconciliation needed for future progress, the stories of ordinary people have to be told. Social justice has to at least appear to have been carried out for people to regain trust in the world and its institutions, which have been effectively destroyed. Under international law and humanitarian considerations, victims of armed conflicts also have a right to reparation and rehabilitation so that they can reconstruct their 'life plan' (C. Evans 2012; UN General Assembly 2005; Villalba 2009).

In the world today, in many countries that are trying to recover from internal, civil conflict, a well-known method is to promote acknowledgement of past atrocities and a 'healing of memories' towards national reconciliation. It is hoped that when people come to realize and understand what has happened, they will be in a better position to reconcile, forgive and reform relationships. The TRC in South Africa was formed with the purpose of promoting 'national unity and reconciliation in a spirit of understanding which transcends the conflicts and divisions of the past' during the 1990s (Hamber 2009). Although later studies show that testimonies are not sufficient to restore healing, there was some satisfaction with sharing, catharsis with emotional expression and relief when there was empathy. Survivors, their families and community needed continuing psychosocial support, community rebuilding and reparation and a sense of social justice. At a social and national level there was some evidence that the process employed by the TRC had caused some positive attitudinal changes, repaired relationships and brought people together, and developed a shared vision, making the country more democratic and participative (Foster 2006; Hamber 2009; D. J. Stein et al. 2008). There have been more than fifty truth commissions in the last two decades, that is, about half the countries undergoing post-conflict transition have employed this approach: Rwanda, former Yugoslavian countries, East Timor, Sierra Leone, Uganda and Philippines to mention a few. In Sri Lanka, the LLRC attempted to address some of these needs and make recommendations (Commission of Inquiry 2011) (see Chapter 5C).

---

announced over loudspeakers, during speeches, by the media, in notices and publications. The motif meant it was either going to be total defeat or victory with the promise of Tamil Eelam. Though in each previous case the LTTE had withdrawn to fight on as a guerrilla force, this time it stayed (or was trapped) to fight to the finish, turning out to be indeed the final battle.

Where it was not possible to have public truth commissions, testimonies and stories were collected and published as *Nunca Más* (Never again) reports in Latin American countries (Commission for Historical Clarification 1998; National Commission on the Disappearance of Persons 1984). In Brazil, Argentina, Chile, El Salvador and Guatemala the *Nunca Más* stories were photocopied for circulation and published as cheap paperbacks in book stalls and street corners that sold quickly in their hundreds of thousands. The publication of these testimonies completely changed public awareness and brought about a radical opening in public discourse and eventually, social transformation in those countries. Towards this end, a collection of Vanni narratives were published in newspapers of all three languages in Sri Lanka. The Tamil original version was serialized in *Virakesari*, the Sinhala translation in *Ravaya* and the English version in *Lakbima News*. It was also posted on several websites. The original qualitative study with the narratives was published in the *International Journal of Mental Health Systems*, a peer-reviewed, online, open access journal, where it soon gained 'the highest accessed' status for articles published in that journal (Somasundaram 2010b). The study was also submitted to the LLRC (Commission of Inquiry 2011) and UN Secretary General's Expert Panel on Accountability in Sri Lanka (UN 2011). Initially many concerned colleagues opposed the publication, reasoning that it would hamper the reconciliation and put psychosocial work at risk. Only limited psychosocial support had been allowed in the IDP camps, while counselling or cultural healing practices either in the camps or resettlements was severely restricted (Ruki 2010a, 2010b; UTHR-J 2009). The authorities appeared to be fearful that the stories of what had happened would get out. After trying to convince the state, including the governor for the north, about the need for psychosocial support and when the detailed mental health plan designed by the Mental Health Consultative Forum[3] was ignored, the paper was published. Gradually, with the publication and production of accounts from a variety of sources including from within the UN system (UN 2011, 2012), former BBC reporter (Harrison 2012), United Kingdom's Channel 4 (Macrae 2011, 2012) and Sri Lanka's refutation (Ministry of Defence 2012), there has been increasing awareness of what happened, such as the reversal at the UNHRC asking the Sri Lankan state to implement its own LLRC recommendations (see Introduction).

[3] The Mental Health Consultative Forum for the Northern Province consisting of mental health professionals and health administrators from the health department was formed in November 2009 to deal with the mental health needs in the resettlement process of IDPs. The forum had formulated a plan to mobilize those already trained and skilled in community-level mental health to form a network of psychosocial support at the periphery — divisional (AGA) or district (GA) levels.

Taken as a whole, the narratives sought to represent what happened to the community at a collective level, the metonymic character of testimonies (Beverley 2005). Thus, the telling of their stories, the documentation and publication becomes a conduit for collective catharsis, a therapeutic method of addressing the collective trauma, a way to break out of the silence and repression. When the stories are shared and others come to understand, empathize and (it is hoped) extend solidarity and support, that process in itself becomes a powerful healing process.

Memories can change over time depending on internal and external conditions. This is always a challenge in psychoanalysis and narrative ethnography. Child abuse, trauma, depression, grief, fear, wishes, desires and other strong emotions can repress or distort memories. Similarly, the external political environment or sociocultural milieu can determine what can and what cannot be said. Silence in a situation of 'repressive ecology' (Baykal et al. 2004) is a survival strategy that can become ingrained and permanent. As Scarry (1985) so eloquently describes, for the defeated, 'a world deconstruction takes place in the collective consciousness to an altered reality and reconstitution of constructs'. Thus peoples' memories can become a field of intense contest, memories can be erased and others created or changed. Complex situations that follow war and natural disasters have a psychosocial impact on not only the individual but also on the family, community and society. The qualitative study explored the long-term psychosocial and mental health consequences of exposure to massive, existential trauma at the individual, family and community levels.

Context

The area called the Vanni comprises mainly the districts of Kilinochchi and Mullaitivu and adjoining parts of Vavuniya and Mannar districts in northern Sri Lanka (see the map of Sri Lanka in Figure P.1 and Figure 3B.1). With the more recent migrations, an estimate of the total population would have been between three hundred thousand and four hundred thousand, consisting exclusively of Tamils. Due to conflicting political compulsions the exact number remains controversial (UTHR-J 2009).

The LTTE had gradually built up an alternate administrative structure in the Vanni amounting to an autonomous, separate de facto state (Balasingham 2004). There were separate police, judicial, financial (tax, bank), administrative, medical, social and other services. When the major A9 highway was opened up after the 2002 peace accord, there were tight custom, immigration and emigration controls at the crossing points on the border. With the resumption of hostilities in 2006, the A9 highway

Figure 3B.1:
Map of the Movement of IDPs in the Vanni

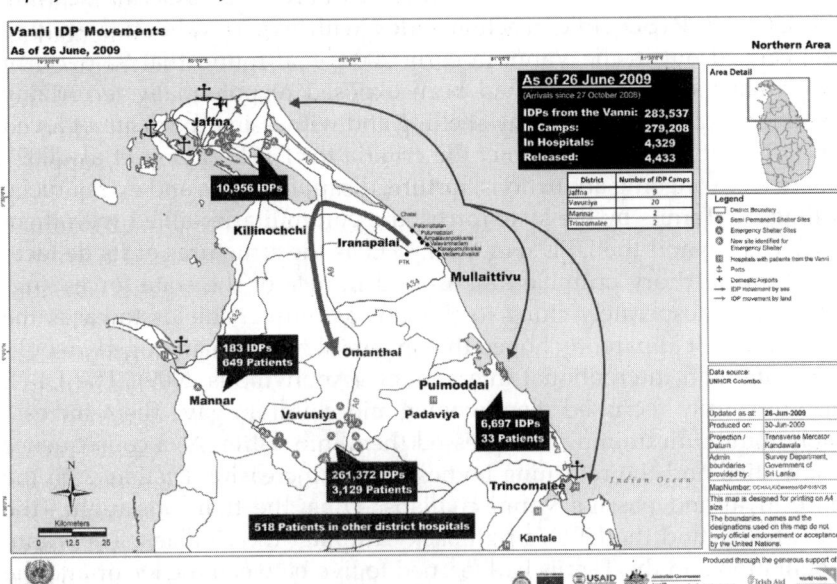

Source: United Nations Office for the Coordination of Humanitarian Affairs (UNOCHA) (2009).
Note: The boundaries and names shown and the designations used on this map do not imply official endorsement or acceptance by the UN.

was closed in August. However, the Sri Lankan forces concentrated first on eastern Sri Lanka and brought it under their control before moving to retake the Vanni. For the Sri Lankan state there was the historic opportunity to destroy the LTTE once and for all, a designated terrorist organization that had been challenging the country for over a quarter of a century in a long-drawn, debilitating civil war. The Sri Lankan state (and military) marshalled all its resources, prepared, planned well from past lessons and apparently garnered international sanction in the post–9/11 'war against terror' climate.

According to reliable health workers in the field and civilian testimony, the maximum damage, both civilian deaths and injuries, was from the massive, relentless shelling of the civilian population, declared safety zones and hospitals. The Vanni population had already experienced the full brunt of state terror (see Chapter 1B) and had every reason to be afraid of the advancing army (Hoole 2001; Somasundaram 2004). There had been many massacres of civilians by state forces (see Table 1B.1) in the living memory of the Vanni people, some of which they had barely survived.

Many had lost a relation or faced the wrath of the forces. An epidemio-logical survey by a team from the University of Konstanz, Germany, using the UCLA's PTSD child reaction index with expert validation (Kappa .80) carried out in the Vanni in early 2000s had found that 92 per cent of primary schoolchildren had been exposed to potentially terrorizing experiences including combat, shelling and witnessing the death of loved ones. Twenty five per cent met the criteria for PTSD (Elbert et al. 2009). There were ongoing abductions, torture, disappearances and extrajudicial killings of Tamils by the state forces, the paramilitaries allied with them (HRW 2008) and the DPU. For the LTTE, as the structures of its de facto state and territory crumbled all around in face of the state forces' jug-gernaut, it desperately clung to civilians as human shields towards the later stages. It apparently hoped that the unfolding human tragedy would precipitate an international intervention (Anonymous 2009). The LTTE also forcefully recruited men, women and children, gave them increas-ingly minimum training and pressed them into battle. As a consequence many died and the returning bodies caused increasing friction with the once loyal and passive Vanni civilians. Thus, the twin onslaught—the state forces and the LTTE's fightback—trapped the civilians. The Vanni population and the Tamils had learned to live between the terror and the counter-terror, the parallel authorities and violence of the LTTE and the state (Somasundaram 2010e), but nothing had prepared them for what was to come.

The forces launched well-planned, concerted attacks from multiple fronts but the main advance was from the west. As the Sri Lankan forces advanced using heavy artillery shelling and bombing from the air, people fled eastwards and then towards the north-east, through Killinochchi to Mullaitivu to end up in a sliver of land on the east coast. Food became scarce and expensive—there were reported deaths due to starvation—clean water was difficult to find and medical help and supplies became non-existent as people fled from one place to another seeking some respite from the continuous shelling and firing. People lay dead on the streets and in hastily dug bunkers. Some twenty thousand to forty thousand people are estimated to have died in the apocalyptic carnage (Philp 2009; Stein 2010; UTHR-J 2009; Wax 2009). The injured cried for help while bleed-ing to death; no one stopped to give them a lending hand though, every-one was desperate to escape. The elderly and disabled were left behind. Orphaned children wandered aimlessly amidst the chaos of blocked roads and desperate humanity.

Those who managed to escape this unfolding human tragedy were fired upon by both sides, were injured or killed, waded through deep waters, became separated from family and friends and lost all their belongings. Once on the army side, they were checked, some separated and never seen again. They were then herded into buses and taken to temporary shelters and finally interned in barbed-wire camps for months without access to the outside world (*transCurrents* 2009). The total number of people thus interned in various IDP camps in Vavuniya, Mannar and Jaffna was just under three hundred thousand (UNOCHA 2009) (see Figure 3B.1).

Narratives

There were many stories (Somasundaram 2010a) of multiple displacements. Eventually everyone was displaced several times with shorter periods in one place, increasing pressures from all sides, devastation and hardships. People kept just ahead of the direct fighting (Jeyaraj 2008), taking long, convoluted journeys. The stories usually began with the family described metaphorically as living happily in their village. It was significant that the happiness or well-being was perceived and experienced in terms of the family and community. The war was seen as an imposition from the outside, disturbing this atmosphere of contentment where the family and community was progressing, getting on with life. The war was invariably described in very negative terms, *por arrakan* (war devil), *kodumai* (horrible), *per avalam* (great calamity). As the narrative unfolds, it is the family that is the focus. When the shelling and fighting approached their homes and their villages, it impelled them to start the displacement process. They described how they left as a family, as a community—whole villages taking whatever they could load onto vehicles, hoping to return in a day or two. The dispersion began. They were separated from the supportive context of their community, extended family and village. How the new conditions began to affect the family, how each member suffered, the deaths and injuries, the separation from those who were injured, having buried the dead without the customary rites, the guilt of having left relations behind and the strong yearning to know what happened to other members is described below:

> Funerals were ubiquitous with smell of corpses. Bodies were buried day and night. Witnessing all this, many became mentally deranged. People were stricken by the loss of their belongings, struggled without basic facilities, grieved for the deaths of kith and kin. Many died unnecessarily from the shelling. Dead children and elders lay around orphaned. Air bombings increased. Some succumbed to army firing.

On the other hand, recruitment and forced conscription by the LTTE drove desperate families to hide their young in any way they could:

> Youngsters were caught and taken away at night, at midnight. In the name of conscription, some were beaten up, some were taken away and tied to poles. Young men and women were hidden. Some became frustrated and

joined. There was no one to give comfort to the people; they became desolate. They were broken by shelling and gunshots. Some were taken away for border duty and other work. Some dead youths were returned to the families in coffins with their faces concealed. Everywhere there were funerals. Everyone talked about death. Youths spent their time in hiding, away from their studies.

The impact of the disaster was felt acutely within this living fabric of the family and community and as utter hopelessness, helplessness and devastation when the fabric was torn:

There was no drinking water; people dug holes and drank the water they found there. Shelling was particularly heavy. People were bewildered. On one side there was forced conscription, on the other there was continuous shelling. People lost everything, did not know where to go, what to take, what to do. Shelling was heavy even in what had been declared as the safety zone. Children had lost their parents, parents had lost their children. It was a scene that one could not look at. Bodies were buried in bunkers as it was not possible to bury them properly. Some bodies were wrapped in clothes and buried two or three feet deep. Some could not bury the dead, they simply left them and ran. Some had lost their hands or other limbs, bodies were shattered, people suffered greatly. In the hospital, there was a shortage of medicines and medical workers. People starved without adequate food. Rice and dhal was the only food. Some broke into the stores of cooperative societies, service organizations and shops to meet their needs. There was no clean drinking water. At the same time, the LTTE shot those trying to escape into army-controlled areas. Hospitals were crowded. They suffered without medical facilities. Some days were spent entirely in bunkers. Only for short intervals was it possible to come out. It was in this place that they faced many difficulties. People gave up, leaving things to God's will. Nobody knew who will look after whom, who would provide comfort. We experienced suffering here that cannot be described. Many were widowed. Most people, beyond age differences, were physically and mentally affected.

Eventually whole population was driven into an ever-decreasing area, ending up on the beaches of Mullivaikal. The population was exposed to incessant shelling (*shell malai* or shell rain) and heavy weaponry. Many died in their bunkers or while trying to escape. The injured were left to lie where they were or carried by able-bodied relatives. The final days at Mullivaikal are described in apocalyptic terms:

Mullivaikal was where the Vanni *Thamilan* (Tamil persons) had their hair shorn and mouth gagged while nails were driven through their hands and legs like the scene at Calvary while eighty million [the world] Tamils looked on. In their national interest, the ruling regime washed its hands off Tamils, to kill and destroy using attractive slogans such as 'war for peace' and 'humanitarian action'. Three hundred thousand Tamils were rained with shells causing rivers of blood to soak that land. Every day, I try to forget those days but the memory of the thousands who died makes me want to show the outside world what happened there. That would give the dead souls *athmashanthi* (paying respect, letting them rest in peace).

Civilians who escaped Mullivaikal made it across the lagoon to army positions from where they were taken in buses to internment camps in Vavuniya. A Medecine Sans Frontieres nurse, Karen Stewart, described them (2009):

Wounded, shocked and distressed. After fleeing heavy fighting in the Vanni, people arriving in Vavuniya hospital need both medical care and counselling. People arrive here in a state of extreme anxiety and fear. They have been separated from their families and often have no news about their fate. Young children and elderly travelling with their caretakers claim they were separated at a checkpoint. The caretakers or family members who were healthy were forced to go to camps, whilst those wounded and sick had to go to the hospital. Children at the hospital are unaccompanied. They scream and call out for their mothers. Elderly people are on their own. Some people have bad wounds, some have been amputated or badly hurt by shrapnel.

In the process of escaping, many family members were separated. Upon reaching the internment camps, they began searching for their family, not knowing what had happened to them, whether they had died or were injured. But for long periods, people in a certain camp were confined to that camp, did not have information about the rest of their families. Many of the families were eventually reunited but a good number still do not know the whereabouts of their relatives. The resettlement process out of the camps started towards the end of 2009.

Interviews

Key informant, family and extended family interviews and focus group discussions regarding family and community-level changes indicated mostly negative but also positive developments. Generally, there was consensus that family and community life had suffered due to deaths, separations and deprivations. Relationships, trust, cohesion, beliefs and ethical values had declined, some said deteriorated and destroyed. Instead, there was an increase in misunderstandings, conflict, selfishness, suspicion, anger, bitterness, *virakthi* (disinterest), *veruppu* (state of detestation), *soham* (sorrow), alcoholism and sexual laxity. Expression of survival guilt was common, particularly after the experiences in the internment camps.

After losing so many of their relatives or not knowing their whereabouts, many said they would rather have died in the shelling. Outward blame for what happened was common, some blamed the government, others India (*vaddakathiyar* or northerners) and some the LTTE. There was anger towards the LTTE and some felt betrayed by it. In the immediate aftermath, many were distraught, dazed and disoriented; there were strong feelings of disillusionment, bewilderment, disbelief, bitterness and utter devastation. Some said it was the fate (*thalaivithy*) of the Tamils 'for having been born Tamil in this country'.

Most felt that there had been a decline in religious beliefs and practices, loss of faith and motivation. One widow described how she and her children had left her husband who had been shattered by a shell but still alive and struggling on the road. She was haunted by this memory and blamed God for creating the terrible situation (*pallaipona kadavul*). But others said that it was only religion and faith in God that had sustained them when everything else failed. Their only trust was that God would find a way out for them. Some mentioned an increase in new relationships, mutual help and cooperation, a sense of unity, comradeship and togetherness by being thrown together against adversity. These feelings were marked during the last days of the 'final war' and for a short period thereafter but had progressively decreased.

A common observation was that people had become dependent on handouts, used to welfare and that there was a decline in efforts to work and earn. People had betrayed (*kaddikodduthu*) others for benefits and privilege from the army and authorities. But, with the resettlement process, motivation to rebuild their lives and livelihood was strong. There was a sense (with some exceptions among those who had suffered and lost the most) that their situation was improving and that there was hope for the future compared to how it was a year ago. There were some positive stories of resilience and post-traumatic growth. A senior government officer and writer said that they had gone through great hardship (*peravalam*), but that they now only needed to get back their infrastructure, resources, occupational opportunities and jobs to rebuild and restart their lives. He denied any ill effects like poor sleep, bad dreams or loss of motivation. He appeared in good health and committed to contribute to the resettlement and rehabilitation process.

A recent observation by Narendran (2010) of what is happening in the Vanni echoes this positive hope:

> The spirit of the Tamils in the north has not been extinguished by the long years of war and its brutal end. All indications point that the Tamils will rise again to play a meaningful role in Sri Lanka and prosper. The spirit that is manifesting itself in numerous ways all over the north, despite the all too

obvious adversities and disadvantages, is definitely a harbinger of a bright future for the Tamils and Sri Lanka. If they are helped and guided, they will advance faster. If not, they will yet become a great people, though at a slower pace. The Tamils will emerge from their prolonged tragedy and the associated misery, despite their politicians, bureaucrats and malcontents — both within and the diaspora, to become what they deserve to be in the land of their birth and life. I may not live to see this happen, but will die convinced, it will happen. Tamils are not a species destined for extinction in Sri Lanka, as many, including me had feared six months back. They are proving that they have what it takes to rebound from adversity and hurdles, to survive and prosper.

A young doctor who had served through the last days of the fighting said that he had seen terrible injuries and deaths, struggled through the heavy shelling and firing at the different hospitals, working without rest. At one stage he had lost all fear and was able to continue working amidst all the chaos. He was ready to do anything. He was seen to be extraordinarily dedicated, motivated, a tireless worker and administrator appreciated by all. An expatriate medic also described the last days of fighting as harrowing, but

[a]fter looking at the people dying and dead bodies everywhere, it is like nothing threatens me anymore, it is like I have had the hard time in my life and I think I am prepared to take up whatever happens in life now. I'm not that old Vany that sits down and cries for little things. I'm stronger now after going through and seeing all that problem. My mind is clear now. (Chamberlain 2009)

Discussion

There are several themes that emerge from accounts of what happened. A striking theme to emerge from the narratives is the collective nature of the trauma. All the stories describe what happened to people as a family or in some cases, to the community. The narratives clearly show the impact of the war on the family and community. The exclusively individual perspective characteristic of Western narratives is completely lacking here. There are hardly any spontaneous complaints of individual symptoms or suffering. Even where a person talks of their personal agony, it is framed in general terms, reflecting what happened to the family or community. Undoubtedly, individual symptoms, how the trauma affected each member, can be elicited with direct questioning (Somasundaram 1998). In these circumstances, the best approach to restore the psychosocial and mental health of the IDPs of the Vanni, according to mental health professionals working in the internment camps as well as clearly recommended in the IASC guidelines on mental health and psychosocial support in emergency settings (IASC 2007), would have been to reunite the survivors with their families, give information on the members' whereabouts. The second best strategy would have been to release them to find their own way and reunite with their families and community. However, the state strictly resisted these well-meant efforts. If one could extrapolate from the decisions and restrictions placed by the authorities, discern the pattern behind the policies from past analysis (Hoole 2001) and experience to understand the mindset (Sackur 2010), the operating paradigm, it would appear that the state still fears a regrouping of the destroyed LTTE, but more than that, it harbours a deep paranoia based on ethnocentric perceptions of the 'other' (Somasundaram 2010d) and wants to prevent any future minority mobilization.

In the post-conflict, militarily and politically sensitive situation, dealing with the mental health and psychosocial needs of the Vanni's IDPs was a difficult and challenging task. A small team of mental health professionals and a few NGOs with limited resources attempted to address the immediate and urgent needs. The priority was given to severe mental illnesses, particularly psychosis, which needed medication and intensive care. Some chronic patients had relapsed or developed exacerbation in their symptoms when they had run out of drugs or had simply stopped taking them. A large number had been displaced from long care institutions in the Vanni, Vetti Mannai and Santhosam, which had been caring for over 150 chronic patients. Some had developed psychotic illness anew. Regular psychiatric services were available at the district hospitals in Vavuniya, Mannar and Jaffna. In addition, clinics were arranged in the camps with additional staff. However, when it came to addressing psychosocial needs, access was limited. Ingenious strategies had to be adopted to gain access and provide support despite the military presence.

A group of community-level workers, CSOs, who had been trained after the tsunami under a Ministry of Health/WHO programme (Mahoney et al. 2006; Wickramage 2010) to work with the affected population in the Vanni were among the IDPs in the camps at Vavuniya. They were again mobilized by a Ministry of Health/WHO programme to work among the IDPs. Some other psychosocial NGOs did yeomen service under trying circumstances. Nevertheless, consistent and systemic long-term programmes were not allowed.

Other community-level and governmental workers can be trained. Training grass-roots community-level workers in basic mental health knowledge and skills is the easiest way of reaching a large population. They in turn would increase general awareness and disseminate the knowledge as well as do preventive and promotional work. The majority of minor mental health problems could be managed by community-level workers, with the remaining referred to the appropriate higher levels. The main effort of community-level workers would be directed towards strengthening and uniting families; rebuilding and regenerating community structures and institutions; encouraging leaders; facilitating self-support groups; village and traditional resources; using creative arts; cultural, ritualistic practices; and linking up with other service sectors like education, social service, local and regional government. Trust, a sense of collective efficacy, social capital and cohesion need to be rejuvenated if the community is to regain its functioning capacity.

The Vanni's IDPs must be given an opportunity to mourn for the dead, grieve for the losses and practise cultural rituals for collective consolation. What happened cannot simply be erased from individual and collective memory. A broader and long-term psychosocial intervention for collective catharsis and a healing of memories for traumatized families and the community would be an acknowledgement of what happened. The politics of memory and history writing are linked to power. Those with the power to impose their version can change memory traces and perceptions of what happened. The LTTE managed to enforce its account of the 1995 exodus in the memory and imagination of Tamils as resulting from state action, when in fact it engineered a movement of over four hundred thousand people from Jaffna (UTHR-J 1995a). Around forty thousand civilians appear to have been killed and many more injured in a short period, with large-scale, repeated displacements, shortages and neglect of basic needs such as food, shelter and medical care. There have also been heavy casualties in the Sri Lankan army. According to reliable reports around five thousand soldiers died while many more were injured in the final push (Fonseka 2009a, 2009b). Perhaps seven thousand LTTE militants died or were executed in 2009 alone. Many were raw conscripts pressed into battle with a few days' training to become cannon fodder. From past experience with such battles and casualty figures, a conservative estimate for the whole Vanni battle may be well over ten thousand killed on each side.

The stories of ordinary soldiers and militants also need to be told; their sacrifices, suffering and agony recognized and accepted for their memories to heal, and ultimately, for national reconciliation. It becomes abundantly clear that both the Sri Lankan state and the LTTE are responsible for serious human rights violations on a large scale.[4] Though indictments or establishing moral responsibility may not be realistic in the current international, regional and local political context, at a minimum, reinstituting a

---

[4] As discussed elsewhere in the book, the international community (including India), which did not intervene despite the unfolding humanitarian tragedy and the Tamil diaspora, which had encouraged the war all along, protesting only towards the end, and those supporting the LTTE (continuing to wave the tiger flag and not asking the LTTE to allow the civilians they were holding hostage to leave or ask that the shooting of Tamil civilians be stopped) are also complicit in what transpired.

belief in social justice would be an important psychosocial intervention for communal harmony and well-being as well as the future of the country.

However, another interesting theme that emerges from the narratives is the contest for the loyalty or obedience, the so-called 'hearts and minds' exercise, that operated to a large extent at the unconscious level. Evidently the Vanni civilians had some allegiance to the LTTE up to the beginning of the last phase of fighting in 2006. Under the totalitarian control of the LTTE, any kind of dissent or counter-views had been eliminated. People had adapted to this state of affairs despite embargoes, restrictions and attacks by the state, showing considerable resilience. They were content in many ways, as expressed in the narratives metaphorically as being 'happy'.

Criticism of and antagonism towards the actions of the LTTE start creeping into the narratives much later. Many show a strong reluctance to name the LTTE directly, always using indirect terms. Some completely leave the actions and atrocities done by the LTTE out of their accounts (Chamberlain 2009; Christy 2009). Apart from its more overt repression and terror, the LTTE had succeeded in establishing this kind of collective internal censor that prevented people seeing their negative side, and more insidiously, even thinking or speaking about it. This was partly due to terror and a survival strategy, but it was also a result of the discriminatory policies of the state and the harsh actions of its security forces that had made them share the ideology of the struggle. But as the price for this loyalty mounted, with increasing death, injuries and conscription, the tide turned and people became disillusioned with the actions of the LTTE and tried to escape.

It would appear that this was a deliberate 'psyops' military strategy of the state to drive a wedge between the civilians and the LTTE, as they increased the harsh conditions: shelling causing death and injuries even in hospitals and state-declared safety zones, restrictions on food, medicine and other basic items (Suntharalingam 2009). The counter-insurgency strategy appeared to have worked, with people becoming more overt in their resistance to the LTTE, more open in criticism and defiance, at times breaking out into direct clashes (Anonymous 2009; UTHR-J 2009), finally escaping over to army-controlled areas. Some narratives expressed gratitude to the state forces for having saved them from the LTTE. The state has continued to use this counter-insurgency strategy to completely wean the people of the Vanni from the LTTE after the conflict by interning them in IDP camps with callous restrictions. They have sought to impose their version of the discourse in contrast to the ideas of liberation, Tamil homeland and separation.

Instead of using the historic opportunity for national reconciliation, this repressive ethnocentric approach, which does not deal with the underlying grievances, will in the long term only alienate the minorities once again. Apart from the political implications, at stake is the contest between the different discourses and the need to heal the trauma of the Vanni IDPs—if not provide them social justice. Also, the whole national reconciliation process needs, at the very least, some acknowledgement of what really happened. If there is no healing of memories, merely a repression, the untreated collective trauma could well turn into resentment and rekindle the cycles of violence once more.

Post-war Vanni Community

When thirty years of civil war came to an end in May 2009 in the Vanni, roughly three hundred thousand people ended up in internment camps. Many of these people have since moved on, some resettling in the Vanni. Muslims who were forcibly evicted from the north by the LTTE and some Sinhalese have returned to the Northern Province. There has been a massive resettlement and development programme carried out the by the PTF (2013). However, people have not been allowed to resettle in areas around major army camps, so-called HSZs. Most people had lost everything by the time they entered army-controlled areas at the end of war. They had lost their homes, personal belongings and livestock during the multiple displacements. According to a poet from the Vanni,

> I never liked this war. This was imposed on us and there was no way we could avoid it. During the final months I was among the crowds, fleeing. We passed through Kilinochchi, Visvamadu, Vallipunam, Iranaipalai, Matalan, Valaiyarmadam, Mullivaikal. We hastily built makeshift houses with much effort, then we removed the houses and belongings with tears and loaded everything into tractors, landmasters and motorbikes. We carried all these things to start with but by the time we reached Mullivaikal, towards the end, we had nothing. We left our things in one place after another and in the end we carried only a bag of clothes. For me this was not the great loss, losing possessions, but we also lost invaluable lives. We will carry injuries we cannot heal as long as we live. I lost my leg. I lost my younger brother and his children. I saw so many deaths of people I knew—the deaths of my relatives and neighbours.

Many returned to find their old homes flattened with the village atmosphere entirely changed:

> Last month we went back to the Vanni. Everything was flattened. There was nothing to identify our place. Everything was overgrown like a jungle and *paladainthu poy kidanthathu* [in ruins]. It would be *verrupu* [despair] to stay there. Everywhere there is only the army. They have razed the *maveerar maythanam* [heroes' (LTTE) cemetery] to the ground and ploughed it. The place

of my son's [LTTE combatant] tombstone cannot be recognized. Before, one day of every month, I would go and cry at his tombstone. This time we were not even aware that *maveerar* day had come and gone. When we lived there before, the boys with my son would come often, addressing me as *amma* [mother]. Now who is there for me?

We went to over fifteen places [for assistance] to repair our houses. To whom shall we ask? When we see what has happened to the Tamils, it creates a great sense of despair. How many people were sacrificed, hands and feet lost, houses and property destroyed, ran around as people without a country, bearing so many hardships for liberty, only to come again to a life of subjugation? God has also become blind. I do not repeat the rosaries like before, do not have the heart to go to church. I feel only anger and sorrow. Before, we would celebrate Christmas and New Year in a big way. This time they just came and went. Cake was not made, nor *palaharam* [sweets]. Whom to give them to? Before, all our neighbours and members of our community would come home. I only go to church on Sundays because my children insist. What have we done to anybody? We have sacrificed so many people asking for freedom but only ended up with not even a *kachai thundu* [loincloth]. We could have gone in contentment, been killed by a shell rather than see this end. Prabhakaran has gone, having created a situation where to see our own house we have to get permission from the army. When I think of everything, anger wells up in me. I feel like burning up. There is no sleep. All the difficulties we faced keep running like a movie in my head. I keep tossing and turning; there is no sleep.

When they were resettled, the government gave them five thousand LKR and promised them twenty thousand LKR later. For their shelter, they were given some tarpaulin sheets, sticks to hold up the sheets and a few household items. As most of their homes had been badly damaged without roofs, walls or other protection, people used the sheets as cover which hardly protected them against the weather or afforded security.

Vadivel, a paddy farmer with a silver head of hair and a bit of silver stubble, is in his sixties. Formerly, his house had about seven rooms and was constructed with thick walls with red tile roofing. Now a flimsy blue nylon tarp was strung up to keep out the rain, since all the tiles were gone and most walls had been blasted by the army to detonate any booby traps that might have been set up by the LTTE. Various demining teams had uncovered all sorts of booby traps and thirteen different types of landmines in the Vanni. With a sweeping gesture towards his demolished house and farm, Vadivel said, 'Avungkal engkalai alitthu onrumillamal akkividdangkal' (They [the LTTE] have completely destroyed us and effaced our rights).

Most people used the money to buy utensils and materials to earn an income but it was hardly adequate for this purpose. As many were famers or fishermen, they had difficulties in restarting their traditional occupation.

Some areas had been demined but other areas were still cordoned off by yellow tapes as unsafe. People were left to fend for themselves. LNGOs and INGOs are given severely restricted access to carry out projects. Permission has to be first obtained from the PTF and Ministry of Defence (ICG 2012b; Minority Rights Group International 2011). There continues to be a heavy military presence despite the fighting having come to an end in May 2009 and in the absence of any tangible security threat. Many expressed relief that killings and overt violence had been greatly reduced though they have not completely stopped. But administrative and policy decisions and implementation are largely influenced by the military or under its supervision (Valkyrie 2011). All civil activities and movements of people need permission and are closely monitored. For example, even religious rituals and community events to remember those who died were interfered with and disallowed. Basic psychosocial work or counselling are generally not permitted but have to be done indirectly without attracting attention. Thus, many of the traumatized and those suffering from grief are left without support. In the view of a local psychosocial worker,

> They are affected by psychosocial problems such as no income, unemployment, alcoholic problems, violence, culture related problems, school drop outs. Most of them have experienced trauma. Good counselling will help them to regain faith, hope, cheerfulness and to be active. These may help them to lead a normal life like other people.

There is an ecology of fear, distrust and control (Valkyrie 2011). It can be surmised that authorities fear a resurgence of LTTE activities if tight control is not maintained. However, civilians seem to be overwhelmingly against a return to the LTTE type of ideology or violent conflict. Most wanted to get on with their lives for the first time in decades after all they had been through.

Kutty is a young man in his early twenties, who sustained multiple injuries during the war. While he was a patient in hospitals at Kilinochchi, Tharmapuram, Mungilaru, Puthukudiruppu and Matalan, each of these hospitals came under attack, resulting in injuries and deaths of patients, medical staff and assisting family members. As a result of several attacks during the war in the Vanni, he has injuries to his head, shoulder, abdomen, kidneys and left leg, and his right leg was amputated high above the knee. Kutty was living temporarily with several of his younger sisters, and he expressed anxiety about repeated interrogation by army intelligence personnel who often intruded into his home to interrogate him. He lamented,

> The government fought with LTTE—that's over—Kilinochchi belongs to Tamil people but the government is settling Sinhalese and building Buddhist

temples there. It is not fair. We have nothing to lose anymore. We have lost everything. Now there is no freedom for the Tamil people, and everything has become only loss.

More insidiously, there appears to be a concerted attempt to suppress the collective memory of what happened and transform the collective narrative. Civilians expressed concern over attempts to introduce Sinhalese settlers, businesses, language and Buddhist religious symbols through the state machinery.

Thomas had horrendous memories of the past that he was struggling with, which disturbed his sleep. He was bitter and clearly emotionally upset. It had happened more than one and a half years ago but the memories were still vividly fresh and disturbing. He needed to ventilate and share what he had witnessed and experienced. But this was not officially allowed. Over time, the repressed memories and trauma built up, manifesting as anger:

> When we surrendered to the army they made us remove our clothes and they checked us when we were naked. After this strip search, we were taken to a hall where they told us, 'We have killed your leaders but some are still alive and are among you. Those who are LTTE must come and register your names.' No one came forward to register. After that, we were taken by bus to Chettikulam and we had to stay in the bus for a long time without food.
>
> While we were going in the bus we saw many corpses along the road. During the first week of internment at Menik Farm we had hardly any food or water and no toilet facilities. No one was allowed into our camp, which was just called the 'LTTE Camp' or 'Zone Four', and it was as though the people in our camp were just going to be killed. We felt our lives were in danger there. There were about forty thousand in our camp. They gave one blue tent from China for sixteen people to sleep in. So the women slept in the tents and the men slept outside. They treated us like animals.
>
> Any dissenting opinion against the government is stopped. The government and military intelligence is bringing back the fear or phobia. Tamils strongly feel they are not allowed to be a people anymore. The billboards along the road to Jaffna saying 'one country one nation' is propaganda that makes Tamils angry. They are constructing houses for Sinhalese military families. They will bring in people and it is their idea to maintain the national ethnic ratio in each town, so it is their plan to alter the demography of the north.

A teacher was nostalgic about Iranamadu tank that is now under military control, people can visit the area only with military permission. A Buddhist temple and an army camp were built in that area and people are allowed to fish only in a limited area. But

Kannaki Amman is a Hindu *kovil* [temple] on the riverbed of Iranamadu. Every Friday many Hindus used to gather there, nowadays the *kovil* is empty. We can't go to the *kovil* according to our wishes; we have to take permission from the military. We are not familiar with the Sinhala language and so we avoid the *kovil*. Why do we need to take such a risk to worship?

Although some large-scale projects in road building, industries and commerce are being planned, there is minimal local consultation or participation. Though there was some expectation of benefit from the large-scale development efforts, people report corruption in the awarding of contracts and importation of Sinhala workers, ignoring local priorities, knowledge and workers. Some infrastructure in terms of governmental departments, civil administration, police, law courts, banks, electricity, telephones, communications, postal services, hospital and schools has started to function though there is a severe shortage of buildings, equipment, staff and transport. The state has been unwilling to give priority to the re-establishment of infrastructure and staff shortages and wary of allowing foreign countries or INGOs to do it. Many school classes are still being held under trees or makeshift classrooms. Teachers report high levels of trauma in their students with difficulties in learning, concentration and attention and emotional dysregulation but have no means to address the problems.

When asked about their present life a civilian said,

At present we are leading a wretched life. We have had the worst experience in the past three decades, mainly due to the ethnic war and we were affected by the tsunami also. The shock, trauma and the psychological scars in our conscious and subconscious minds still persist; perhaps, these scars may persist until our death. Yes, we feel so. Especially, our children are the most affected, at least we had a good life in our childhood. But our children have lost everything in their childhood. We could not offer them a continuous education; it was affected by the displacements which happened from time to time in the past. We lost not only our homes, possessions, properties and incomes, but also several lives. We were in a pathetic state. Now also we are very uncertain about our future. However, the sounds of guns have been silenced and we have been resettled and we have started a new life, we have a faith that we may have a good life, but experience in the past throughout the war and displacement is blocking our motivation. This is because of our fate, all these misfortunes.

About thirty thousand men and women were previously employed under the LTTE administration, and they are almost all without work now. A former lawyer who practised in the LTTE civil court said,

I studied up to A/L. The continuous war and related problems prevented me from sitting the A/L exam a second time. I got 2B, C, S in commerce in 1999. The LTTE law college called for candidates and I concentrated on their education for three years. I then practised as a lawyer in the LTTE civil courts. My husband is an ex-combatant who surrendered to the military. He is now at Boosa for rehabilitation. My two children and I face a lot of hardship in our day-to-day life. Once, I took agrochemicals to commit suicide but vomited it out. I thought about the state of my kids and stopped. Every month I need five thousand LKR to visit Boosa to see my husband. I find no meaning in living.

There is an air of hopelessness among the youth and ex-combatants who were rehabilitated and released. Many LTTE members are struggling with guilt and the difficulties of reintegrating with their family and community. Some have committed suicide.
An ex-combatant confided:

I was with the LTTE for twenty years and was injured five times during combat. I surrendered to the army in the end at Mullivaikal. They didn't torture me much and overall treated me well. I was reunited with my family after three months of rehabilitation. I do not have children and my wife died in the shelling in Mullivaikal. I stayed with my sister in Madduvil but I had no company there. It would have been better if I had died during one of those occasions when I was injured. It would have been better than going through all this suffering.

Most people do not want to hire those who were earlier formally employed by the LTTE, which only adds to the latter's burden of frustration. People are afraid to associate with them due to potential repercussion from the state forces. Women ex-combatants particularly are facing difficulties in re-assuming family and social roles. Shamanthi is a mother of three young children in her thirties and she is a former LTTE cadre. She joined the LTTE in 1990 and left in 2004 after her marriage to an LTTE leader. Her husband surrendered to the army. Shamanthi needs assistance with livelihood and she still hopes her husband is alive but there has been no trace of him. Shamanthi's vibrant and bright personality, community awareness, discerning parenting skills and intelligence needs to find a place in a constructive social group. Studying the last photograph of her husband that was on the table, Shamanthi spoke softly,

Because the army caught them, they definitely tortured them. My husband wanted our children to have a good education, because he lost his own education during the fighting. He also wanted our children to have a sense of Tamil nationalism. I named our children pure Tamil names. In Vavuniya hospital when my third baby was born, I also named him that way. Each of the Tamil parties has a different direction now; they should cooperate with each other. I don't know if there is any leadership to coordinate and lead the people now. As Tamil people we have lost many lives, properties and livelihoods. If we want to rebuild there must be strong leadership for Tamils. Most of the women whose husbands disappeared are facing many problems in raising their children and they are facing dire economic difficulty. All the people who were displaced in the Vanni have been forced into poverty. With such problems they can't raise their children with a positive attitude. I am very careful with my children.

I don't know if my husband was killed or if he is alive. This is why for two years I have refused to go to Canada where my father is living. Until I know more about my husband, I don't want to go there. On *Maveerar Nal* [Heroes Day], my daughter wished to light the lamp of her own accord. I didn't stop her because she is used to this culture as a Tamil. She can follow our traditions. I should raise my children with good education, then they can decide for themselves. We will support the Tamil people.

At first people were very friendly with us when we came back to the village, but once the killings started, people began to avoid us. The killing and abductions create fear. Murders and abductions are taking place in the neighbourhood where I am living, and most of those killed came from the Vanni, or supported the movement, so my neighbours won't talk with me now. Sometimes I feel lonely.

Another female ex-combatant struggling to keep her head above water reflected,

Now the greatest problem faced by severely wounded Tamil women fighters is psychological injury. Many ask, 'What is the point of living? What is my reason for being alive?' The Tamil word *virakthi*, which means a lack of motivation or desire to live, describes their condition. They have lost hope.

Many *maveerar*[5] and combatants' families were given land during the LTTE administration. Most of this land belonged to the Tamil diaspora who have since reclaimed them, leaving some of these families without a place to live. Several people in the Vanni do not have deeds for their lands and or houses, making it difficult to obtain loans necessary for repairs. As a mother of two *maveerar*s said,

Two of my children are *maveerar* and my husband also died in the 2000 bombing. We lived on land donated to us by the LTTE. After the resettlement, the

---

[5] Families of militants who had been killed were given privileged treatment in the LTTE-controlled areas like preferences and priority in queues, rations, projects, land, houses and admission.

owner of the land came from Germany and has reclaimed it. Now we have no place to live. If our children were alive, we wouldn't have to go through this.

The military can be seen to be keenly involved in sports while most civilians show little interest in games of any sort. The military are mingling with the people and learning some of the Tamil language. People are not talking about the ethnic problem or solutions. They appear determined not to have another war. However, they say,

> Despite a relaxing of restrictions like ID cards and road checks, there are no cultural celebrations, or spiritual festivals. People keep to their homes after sunset, but tourist and military vehicles pass throughout the night. People are more focused on rebuilding their own lives, but the previous happiness is not there.

LTTE monuments, *maveerar* cemeteries and administrative buildings have been destroyed and replaced with the military's victory monuments and parks in prominent locations at Kilinochchi and Elephant Pass. Military offices are functioning in the semi-structured houses donated by the Chinese government. Areas around Thirumurugandy have also been overtaken by the military. They have started to construct roads by destroying the forests and seem to be paving the way for the creation of permanent military camps.

Hundreds of buses and other vehicles are going to Jaffna along the A9 highway. Many of the passengers are Sinhalese fresh after the war, full of the spirit of victory than concerned about the suffering of the Tamil people. In the words of a Sinhala official, 'Our youths sacrificed and liberated the places from the terrorists. Our president and military did a marvellous job to unite the country after twenty years. Now Tamil people haven't any problem they can live peacefully with us; this is my first trip to Jaffna.'

People are still looking for their lost and disappeared relatives and several have lost their money to fraudsters in this process. A wife of a missing person grieved,

> My husband was part of the LTTE leadership for five years. At the end, we surrendered him to the army and ever since have had no knowledge of his whereabouts. We have checked everywhere and made many complaints to no avail. Children are crying for their father, what should I tell them?

A qualitative study undertaken three years after the end of fighting found continuing, complex psychosocial and mental health problems that were impeding recovery (Somasundaram and Sivayokan 2013). The findings were presented as a trauma grid (see Table 3B.1). There

Table 3B.1:
Trauma Grid

Levels	Negative Effects		Positive Effects	
	Ordinary Human Suffering	*Distressful Psychosocial Reactions* / *Psychiatric Disorders*	*Resilience*	*Adversity Activated Development*
Individual	Sorrow, worries, normal grief, fear, stress, anger, uncertainty, magical thinking, psychological trauma, injuries, handicap, losses, low educational attainment	Intense and extreme levels of suffering, complicated grieving, adjustment disorders, maladaptive coping, alcohol and drug (including non-prescription medication) use, somatization, help-seeking behaviour, change in ideology/ faith, fear of future, suicidal thoughts/ behaviour PTSD, depression, anxiety disorders, prolonged grief disorder, alcohol and drug abuse, complex PTSD, DSH (deliberate self harm), brief (reactive) psychosis, dissociative episodes, personality disorders	Independent, mature personality, adaptive coping mechanisms, flexibility, establishing and maintaining relationships, planning for the future, socialization and networking skills, entrepreneurship	Post-traumatic growth, female leadership, empowerment, liberation, creative activities, non-traditional thinking, innovativeness, involvement in non-traditional jobs
Family	Displacements, separations, deaths, handicap, loss of properties and structures (buildings), disappearances, orphans, single parents, family disharmony, break-up of extended family system	Grief, family conflicts, domestic violence, separations, divorces, extramarital relationships, unwanted pregnancies, child and elder abuse, poor parenting, scapegoating Dysfunctional family units, morbid jealousy, family pathology, child psychiatric disorders or emotional and behavioural problems among children, homicide–suicide pack	Unity of nuclear families, cohesion, extended family ties, support system, new relationships, continuous goals and aspirations	Functional female-headed households, diversity in marriages, split families

(Table 3B.1 Contd.)

(Table 3B.1 Contd.)

Levels	Negative Effects			Positive Effects	
	Ordinary Human Suffering	Distressful Psychosocial Reactions	Psychiatric Disorders	Resilience	Adversity Activated Development
Community	Displacements, uprootedness, separations, destruction of normal systems and structures, dysfunctional structures and institutions, loss of buffer systems, reshuffled neighbourhood, depleted social capital, poverty and unemployment/ underemployment	Denial, rationalization, intellectual dissonance, hopelessness, helplessness, powerlessness, herd instinct, silence, suspicion, distrust, uncertainty, breakdown of ethical and moral values, catharsis, sexual abuse	Collective trauma, suicide, mass hysteria, impulsiveness and antisocial behaviours	Rituals, revival of traditional arts (*koothu*), ceremonies, remembrance observations, monuments and gravestones, social functions	Acceptance of female leadership, female empowerment and liberation, new ways of thinking and breaking of traditional boundaries, entrepreneurship, awareness of global trends, emerging new form of arts (cinema, short films), meaningful narratives, practical (problem solving) support, microfinance schemes and economic development
Society/Culture	Depleted social capital, dysfunctional structures and institutions, patronage, authoritarian personalities, corruption	Hopelessness, helplessness, powerlessness, silence, suspicion, distrust	Collective trauma, suicide	Rituals, ceremonies, remembrance observations, social functions, increasing tolerance about others' views, culture and lifestyle	Reduction of caste barriers, female leadership, empowerment, liberation, multicultural milieu, rights-oriented thinking and behaviour

Source: Adapted to the Sri Lankan context from Papadopoulos (2007).

was a sense of loss of communality and agency. People were resigned, passive and silent. The state and military were in control, determining all matters. People felt beholden and dependent. The general consensus was that if psychosocial problems could be addressed adequately communities would recover. One conclusion of this study was that the ecological context was not conducive in the post-war setting for community recovery, development and growth. Despite this adverse environment[6] some individuals, families and communities were surviving and coping creatively. The study found some resilience and adaptation that should be encouraged and promoted.

---

[6] See the ecology of repression described in Chapter 1B, which includes such phenomena as disappearances, described in greater detail in Chapter 3C.

C.

Disappearance

The Hidden Reality*

With *Sambasivamoorthy Sivayokan*

> The relatives will yearn for information about the missing person—a clue, a phone call, some hope. As time passes without any information forthcoming, doubts will arise: 'Is he alive?' It is this uncertainty and dilemma that cause great pain of mind to the next of kin.
>
> —Shanthiham, *Waiting*

Introduction

Disappearance could be seen as one of the worst agonies known to mankind. It usually happens when a person suddenly loses contact with their family or other concerned people and their whereabouts remain unknown. In normal civilian life, disappearances can occur in different contexts. For example, people can disappear due to natural disasters. The number of disappearances in the 2004 Asian tsunami was estimated as forty-five thousand and in the 2011 tsunami in Japan it was thirteen thousand. In countries where there are internal armed conflicts and extreme human rights violations, illegal migration takes place. In Sri Lanka many people sought asylum abroad. Some disappeared during this process. However, during civil unrests, armed conflicts and wars, internal disappearances become known sequelae, occurring unnaturally and sometimes systematically (ICRC 2003a). In war situations, disappearances can occur

---

* Much of the material in this chapter is taken from the dissertation by Sivayokan (2010), with his permission. I was his supervisor for the dissertation.

in battlefields or during massive attacks when the bodies of all soldiers cannot be recovered, identified or collected. In these circumstances the disappeared combatants are labelled as missing in action. Similarly during times of social unrest, insurgency or militant movements, many civilians just disappear without any evidence of their whereabouts, leaving behind doubts about whether they joined the militants, were killed or kidnapped by rival groups or unaccounted for other reasons.

But there are times where disappearances happen in an organized and systematic manner. In these cases, disappearances are a political strategy used to suppress opponents and terrorize the community at large. Information is withheld as a weapon against enemies, opponents (ICRC 2003b) or communities. These types of disappearances are collectively called 'enforced disappearances'. According to Article 2 of the International Convention for the Protection of All Persons from Enforced Disappearance, adopted by the UN General Assembly resolution 61/177 on 20 December 2006, Article 2, the term enforced disappearance is defined as:

> The arrest, detention, abduction or any other form of deprivation of liberty by agents of the state or by persons or groups of persons acting with the authorization, support or acquiescence of the state, followed by a refusal to acknowledge the deprivation of liberty or by concealment of the fate or whereabouts of the disappeared person, which place such a person outside the protection of the law. (AI 2007)

The phenomenon of enforced disappearance helps the perpetrators stay outside the legal boundaries and obligations (HRW 2008). This extra-judicial strategy protects many participants of this inhumane act—from the person/s who give/s permission to the person/s who carry/ies it out. In countries like Sri Lanka where the law itself gives permission to deal with dead bodies without conducting inquests, creating records or medical reports, enforced disappearances have become institutionalized (Weliamuna 2012).

The disappearance of a person creates an ambiguity about his whereabouts and survival. Hence, disappearance is seen as a special type of loss and is categorized as an ambiguous loss (Boss 2004). Disappearance produces bewilderment, where the family members strongly believe that the disappeared person is still alive but they have absolutely no information about their whereabouts. In other words, the disappeared person is physically absent at home but emotionally still present. The family knows that there is no evidence that their beloved one is alive. However, there is no evidence of death either. 'The disappeared are denied a place among the living and also denied a place among the dead' (Blaauw and Lähteenmäki 2002). Hope that the missing relative may be alive somewhere is smouldering all the time. From time to time it is replaced with fear that she might be dead (Pojskic 2002). Often, there is ambiguity, with a varying mixture of lingering hope, uncertainty, fear, dread and grief. This is really a painful experience. Some writers even consider enforced disappearance of people as one of the cruellest forms of psychological torture for the victims and their relatives (Conte 2002). Hence, the disappearances cause much anguish and agony to the families and loved ones (Monin 2007). The family members are often left in misery and distress. It has been found that a disappearance in a family can generate enormous stress on the family members (Jensen 1996) and invariably affects the well-being of family members as well as dominating the dynamics of family life. The family members suffer from physical, psychological, familial, social, economical and legal problems (Blaauw and Lähteenmäki 2002; Dharmadasa 2002).

There are speculations and rumours about what could have happened to the disappeared persons. There are tales about the possibility of mass graves. Stories about the recovery of unidentified bodies or release of someone who was considered as disappeared years earlier lead the family and community to live in a state of dilemma between hope and despair. This hazy situation with enormous uncertainty disturbs the family dynamics and affects all the family members. The parents and wives suffer silently. The children are kept ignorant of reality for a long time.

The effects of disappearances can go beyond the families. Even a single disappearance can create panic and terror in the community. In cases of natural disasters where many people may disappear without any trace, the acceptance of such disappearances and the possible fate of disappeared persons become part of the community's history, though there is intense psychic pain and grief. But when the 'disappearance' becomes a significantly widespread event, with human agency and some system in it, stories spread, expectations mount, the fear of 'who is next?' encroaches, nights become sleepless, roaring noises of vehicles and barking dogs create terror. At times, those who believe they are at increased risk tend to go into hiding, leaving their families, jobs and social life. On the whole, the community lives in a state of terror. The society loses its cohesion and sovereignty.

Context

Though enforced disappearances were first described in the Latin American context (Kernjak and Lauritsch 2009), it is now happening all over the world in countries such as Algeria, Colombia, Nepal, Russia, Sri Lanka and the former Yugoslavia—to name but a few (AI 2007). Enforced disappearances (or involuntary disappearances) have become a well-known phenomenon in Sri Lanka for more than three decades (HRW 2008). From time to time, Sri Lanka experienced large-scale disappearances, connected to the politico-military situation and in different locations of the country.

In Sri Lanka, people come to know about mass disappearances for the first time during the 1971 JVP insurgency which was violently crushed by the Sri Lankan forces (with the help of the Indian government). Thousands of youths were killed, arrested and reported missing (Cooke 2011). Then the same thing happened to many Tamil-speaking youths during the early 1980s, which increased after the 1983 riots and the escalation of armed conflict (HRW 2008). Initially those disappeared youths were seen as having connections with militant organizations. Since then, like in many parts of the world, 'disappearance' has become a known strategy of counter-terrorism (see Chapter 1B). As the scope of the active armed conflict expanded, with on-and-off large-scale battles, either on land or in sea or in secret missions, many warring combatants disappeared. During the late 1980s disappearances were reported both from the north of the country where the IPKF was engaged in combat with Tamil militants and in the south where there was a JVP uprising. Thousands of youths from southern Sri Lanka were reported as having disappeared during that period (HRW 2008; Rangani 2009).

During early, middle and late 1990s disappearances continued in different parts of the country, at times occurring on a large scale and with groups of people. During these periods there were changes of control in the local areas and with every change of power many people disappeared (HRW 2008; UTHR-J 1999): people of different ages, religions, social status, employment and ethnicity (HRCSL 2003). This could be illustrated with the example of over six hundred disappearances which were reported in the Jaffna peninsula during 1996, just after the Sri Lankan forces wrested control of the Jaffna peninsula from the militants.

Ironically, since 1980s, militant organizations have adopted the very same technique to deal with their opponents, suspected informants, their own 'traitors' (Thiranagama 2010) and community (Somasundaram 1998). Initially they had a policy of openly executing their opponents, other 'unwanted' enemies and elements in the communities mainly under their control. Sometimes they also carried out executions in places where they did not have any direct control. However, as they grew to become an alternate state structure vying for political control, they too started adopting the practice of disappearance. Disappearance is a ploy to say 'don't know'. In cases of disappearances of in-group members, they were later accounted for as if they had died in a battle or the war front.

This phenomenon continued in the new millennium and disappearances became a part and parcel of life for many Sri Lankans. In addition to the above-mentioned purposes and as a strategy of terror and/or counter-terror, 'disappearance' was also used to obtain ransoms or seek other financial gains as well as to eliminate ordinary opponents under the general cover of 'disappearance'. Disappearances once again reached the zenith when the peace process failed in 2006 and large numbers of people were made to disappear not only in the conflict zones but also in the capital (AHRC 2007).

During and after the final battle in the early months of 2009, it is believed that many thousands of combatants and civilians disappeared (UTHR-J 2009) and until now no reliable data is available to confirm either their deaths or their whereabouts. Even in the post-war milieu, enforced disappearances still continue, often dubbed the 'white van'[1] phenomenon (Weliamuna 2012). It appears that civilians and ex-combatants who have been 'rehabilitated and released' continue to disappear into 'thin air'.

Ascertaining the exact number of disappearances in Sri Lanka and how many of those that 'disappeared' have returned is a difficult task. According to the ICRC, thousands of disappearances have occurred in Sri Lanka since 1983 (ICRC 2003b). By 1991, the UN Working Group on Enforced or Involuntary Disappearances had transmitted information about 4,932 cases of disappearances to the government of Sri Lanka and had received reports from various reliable sources of about approximately further 9,000 cases that had not yet been processed (AI 1998). According to the delegation from the European Parliament, the estimated number of disappearances and killings was around sixty thousand in the 1988–90 period (Rangani 2009) while the Asian Human Rights Commission (AHRC) reported that about thirty thousand people were officially recognized to have been disappeared during this same period (AHRC 2007). It was reported that based on information from local and international human rights organizations, a person was abducted every five hours in Sri Lanka at that time (AHRC 2007). The actual number may be much higher than reported cases.

The Phenomenon

The majority of disappeared persons are young, energetic and productive males. Although one study found that the majority of disappeared persons were unemployed (Sivayokan 2010), employment status does not reduce the risk of disappearance, as teachers, engineers, even a vice-chancellor,

---

[1] 'The unmarked white van is the ubiquitous symbol of disappearance and abduction' (Spencer 2011).

have disappeared. Similarly, persons who were with the target have also disappeared as in the Krishanthy Kumarasamy case (UTHR-J 1999). There are incidents where a group of people or multiple family members disappeared at the same time. Females too were reported missing though their numbers were fewer. Many young children and school-going students have also gone missing. In some incidents these children disappeared along with adults (HRCSL 2003).

In many circumstances, the location of the disappearance was unknown, though there was speculation that it happened at a particular place (usually on the roads and close to the checkpoints). At the same time, in contrast, quite a good proportion of 'disappearances' have happened in front of identifiable witnesses (HRCSL 2003), usually the person's family members or friends. The greatest impact was on those left behind when persons were taken away from their homes, in front of family members, and who later 'just disappeared'. This is a horrible experience for the family members. When the survivors are confronted by complete denial by the authorities and are expected to continue life as before, their sense of reality, their sanity, foundations of their belief systems and faith in the orderly functioning of life is shaken.

The majority of disappearance occurred without any anticipation by the victims or their close family members or friends. But there were cases where the event was anticipated to some extent by the disappeared person/s and their family members. When 'disappearance' occurs in an epidemic manner, there will be certain assumptions about who is carrying out the act and who is being victimized. Based on the risk people rank themselves and take precautions, which may fail at times. Further there are 'premonitory' signs — such as the presence of unidentified people in the surroundings, presence of the notorious white vans in the surroundings or confiscation of national identity cards and asking the persons to report to a place — which are often reported by the family members. A woman whose son disappeared lamented:

> They had taken our son's identity card a few days before and did not return it. Because of that our son avoided staying at home, he stayed with relations. One night they came and searched the whole house. When they realized that he was not there, they took our son-in-law and shot him at the front door. Within a few days, our son disappeared. Now we don't have our son nor do we have our son-in-law. My husband has become desolate and disabled. Our family is breaking down (*seeralliyuthu*).

Since the disappearance occurs suddenly and the families have never faced such realities in the past and there are no directions widely available to guide the families on what to do and what not to do, families are left in a dazed state. Many lodge a complaint with the Human Rights Commission of Sri Lanka (HRCSL), ICRC[2] or the nearest police station and then start waiting for their family member's return (Rangani 2009). A few may go beyond this to start communicating with various authorities and human rights organizations. Some make the event more public, thinking that it will put pressure on the perpetrators. On the other hand, many fear that this sort of publicity may endanger the life of the disappeared person and minimize the chances of their return. Others file a case in the court, applying for a writ of habeas corpus, after producing some evidence of the disappearance. Many spend their time and effort in searching and making inquiries, going from place to place, camp to camp, authority to authority, from politicians to traditional healers. They get confusing messages and signals from these places. They tend to follow up on scant news or hearsay, sometimes just a mention of a possibility by a person just released.

The paradox of the phenomenon is that in almost all cases the authorities in power deny such events. They conceal matters from inquiring commissions. The commissions too are established after many years of the occurrence, by which time people tend to forget the exact details of the incident, creating an opportunity for the perpetrators to escape their legal liabilities. Further, repeated inquiries by different authorities and commissions without having a solution or solid answer to the issue create cycles of unrealized hopes and disturb the equilibrium and mindset of the affected people.

The Consequences

The after-effects of disappearance are enormous and can affect individuals, families, communities and the society at large. It is not like a Type I trauma where the traumatic event/s happen once and for all. It is an ongoing, everlasting, never-ending stressor with waxing and waning effect. It infiltrates all parts of individual and community life. The sections below describe some salient features of these consequences amongst different groups.

Victims

What is often unknown is what has happened or is still happening to the disappeared persons. The stories of the primary victims of disappearance are often unheard. But that does not mean that everything is not known.

---

[2] The ICRC has now been asked to leave Sri Lanka, as there is no longer a war going on.

Some survivors have revealed their experiences; perpetrators have also later revealed what happened. Remains of disappeared persons have been unearthed that told many stories. The majority of the victims were targeted by the perpetrators because of their possible past and present involvements and activities. But as mentioned before, there were many incidents where even innocent people were victimized randomly or because they were in the company of targeted persons. It is believed and evident to some extent that the victims were initially tortured before their final disappearance. Their suffering, pain, horrifying experiences and their final words have never been heard by the outside world. What is generally understood is that the acts of disappearance are carried out by specialized groups and the only chance to save the victims is to intervene before they are handed over to those death squads. In the words of a woman whose husband disappeared:

> He was an unassuming human being. He would not even talk back to me. He would not get involved in the usual community gossip (*choli surudukal*). He just kept to his own affairs (*than undu than padundu*). He left that morning saying he was going to visit his sister at Chavakachcheri. They say he went there and left but he never reached home. Somebody said that his motorcycle had been stopped at the (army sentry) point at Chemmani. We could not understand it. We searched everywhere. They showed their empty hands saying they did not know anything about him. We complained everywhere. We have prayed to every god without omission .... He is still missing. It is now four years. My children do not remember his face ...
>
> My chest heaves just thinking of what they may have done to him. He could not tolerate even a slap. He would not argue back. At least I have my children here. Alone there without anyone, I do not know what difficulties he would have gone through. For how long are we to continue like this?

Families

What is apparent is how immediate families are affected by the disappearance of a member, usually the breadwinner. As described by Jane Durgom-Powers, 'in a split second, your life is forever changed' (2002). Responding to disappearance is itself a great challenge for the families. Having no previous experience, the families suffer without knowing how they should respond to the event. Families are particularly devastated when the person was taken away in front of them. The traumatic effects of the loved one's absence are often further exacerbated by the fact that the needs and priorities resulting from it are neglected or denied (Nesiah 2002).

The families live in a state of limbo, with mixed emotions of hope and despair, without knowing their beloved ones' fate. Culturally, the ambiguity of the loss is very significant and the family members are confused about the role they have to adopt. For example, a wife of the disappeared husband is in a dilemma about her role—a waiting wife or a widow? Obviously these two roles are very different in the cultural context. Society is not prepared to accept or not able to understand (Dharmadasa 2002) the nature of ambiguity in cases of disappearance. It expects the victim's family to behave in an 'all-or-none' manner, which creates considerable pressure on the family members. This may reflect in situations like attending cultural ceremonies and festivals, forming new relationships, taking part in different forums, behaviour in school or community gatherings.

In the Tamil culture, the *thali* (a sacred gold symbol attached to a necklace, which functions much like an engagement ring) and *kungumap pottu* (a red mark on the forehead) are the two symbolic representations of a woman's married state and that her husband is alive. In general, an unmarried woman does not wear these until she weds a man; similarly, a divorced or widowed woman is not allowed to wear these symbols. Women without these symbols are 'inauspicious' and hence are not allowed to take part in any cultural event or ceremony, whether in their home or in the community. A widow can adapt to her expected stigmatized cultural role. But the wife of a disappeared person vacillates between the two roles since her loss is ambiguous and is thus put in a quandary in social situations.

The parents of the disappeared also suffer (Dharmadasa 2002). Their expectations, hopes, future, security and peace of mind, all disappear with the disappearance of their son or daughter. Many have to face emotional and economical instability for the rest of their lives. Some parents search for their children by meeting authorities, forming self-help groups, representing themselves in different forums, advocating and reporting. Some others continue to live with the memories of their disappeared son or daughter, which never let them enjoy life again. Their struggle in their late adulthood or when they are elderly is pathetic. In due course, some find ways of coping but many continue to experience 'living corpse' kind of life.

Children of disappeared persons are often told false or fabricated stories, which create additional confusion in their minds, particularly when they have to confront the reality of a missing parent at schools and playgrounds. Adults think that children may not understand the reality or may not withstand the pain of the truth. But children do understand what has happened in the family and tend to suffer silently (Shanthiham 2008). Many children tend to respond to their stress indirectly through behavioural manifestations like outbursts of anger, aggressive behaviour and social withdrawal. Some show regression in their developmental stage and present symptoms of nocturnal enuresis, thumb sucking and loss of abilities. In some others, the unspoken suffering is reflected in their educational performances, socialization skills and dreams (Somasundaram 1998). Others develop somatic complaints.

Generally, family members left behind are expected to take the missing member's role in the family (Jones 2008; Rivero 2000). In many instances, all of a sudden the family is headed by a woman (and a majority of the women are young). The wife, in addition to her personal suffering, has to take on the additional burden of earning a livelihood, dealing with different authorities, looking after their children's educational and other needs, taking care of parents while struggling against family conflicts and social marginalization (Robins 2009). The parents suffer without having a person to help at home.

It has been observed that the family members' reactions after a disappearance are similar in many ways to a grief reaction (Blaauw and Lähteenmäki 2002; Sivayokan 2010). In cases of disappearance, the family members go through various stages of the grieving process. The initial shock, benumbed state and emotional upheaval are later followed by pangs of sorrow, sadness and intense searches for their loved ones. Family members of the disappeared also seem to experience high levels of physical and psychological morbidity (Jensen 1996; Weinstein 2002). They have depressive and anxiety symptoms (Sivayokan 2010). Some may even have significant feelings of guilt (Blaauw and Lähteenmäki 2002) thinking that it was they who were directly or indirectly responsible for the disappearance. Preoccupied with the thoughts of the lost members, keeping their belongings and gifts as memorials (Jurcević and Urlić 2002), thinking about their positive qualities and idealizing them have all been observed in many parts of the world (Weinstein 2002). But, unlike in the grieving process after death, in disappearance, people continue to have hopes of return (ICRC 2009; Sivayokan 2010) and believe that one fine day the disappeared member will come back and knock on the door.

This hope of return is very powerful, keeping the grieving process going, thus preventing any closure. Seeing the dead bodies, having rituals and a chance to say goodbye to the loved one, finding a meaning for the death, believing that the dead soul has reached its final destination and developing a goal and meaning for the rest of their life can facilitate closure in natural mourning (Keiner 2002). However, these are not possible for family members of the disappeared. The death is not confirmed. The body (or its remains) is not found. Without a body the family members cannot do any rituals. It is difficult to find a meaning to the incident which is totally unexpected, unnatural and sometimes perplexing. These factors invariably influence the closure of distress among the family members. Further, anniversary days, news about the fate of disappeared persons, facing inquiries and interviews, hopeful signals or messages and politicized promises may also affect the process of closure. In short, the suffering of the family members is endless (Dharmadasa 2002).

In a study done in northern Sri Lanka (Sivayokan 2010), it was found that the wives of the disappeared, even though they retain strong hope of their husbands' return, suffer from grieving experiences similar to those by wives who have lost their husbands due to natural deaths. In fact, they tend to have more separation anxiety and traumatic distress than their counterparts. Traumatic grief (Prigerson and Jacobs 2002) with functional impairment was seen in 23 per cent of the wives who lost their husbands to disappearance while traumatic grief without functional impairment was seen in 65 per cent of them. The grief did not end within one year and the ITG[3] scores did not correlate with the post-loss period. Similarly, 50 per cent of the wives fit into the 'caseness' of anxiety on the hospital anxiety depression scale (HADS) scale while 80 per cent of them fit into the 'caseness' of depression. Another study done in southern Sri Lanka (Rangani 2009) used GHQ-30[4] and identified that 57.8 per cent of the wives in her sample who had lost their husbands due to disappearance were affected by psychological distress. The anxiety and depression rates were greater than in the general population. Hence, the loss of the husband creates high levels of anxiety and depression among the wives, which in turn can affect their physical, psychological, familial, social and economical well-being.

Many families suffer from severe economic downfall after the disappearance of their family members, usually the earning members of their families. This can be seen from the diagram in Figure 3C.1, in which the majority of the wives of the disappeared husbands perceived economical problems as the main problem in their current life (Sivayokan 2010).

In cultures similar to Sri Lanka, the family generally gets positive support from their relatives, neighbours or friends. However, in some instances, out of safety-related concerns the survivors and witnesses have to flee from the area or country. Similarly, if the politico-military situation is tense, people feel unsafe identifying themselves with the disappeared persons or with their families. In situations where the person was disappeared by the LTTE during their reign, social support and understanding was not forthcoming from within the Tamil community. The family was ostracized. In time, the family had to adopt measures to 'forget' the disappeared, as if he never existed or develop more acceptable narratives of the person to continue to live in the community. A widow whose husband had been disappeared by the LTTE, who attended a psychiatric clinic, was found to gradually lose the memory of her husband. Initially, she

[3] Inventory of traumatic grief.
[4] 30-item version.

Figure 3C.1:
Perceived Problems among Wives of Disappeared Husbands

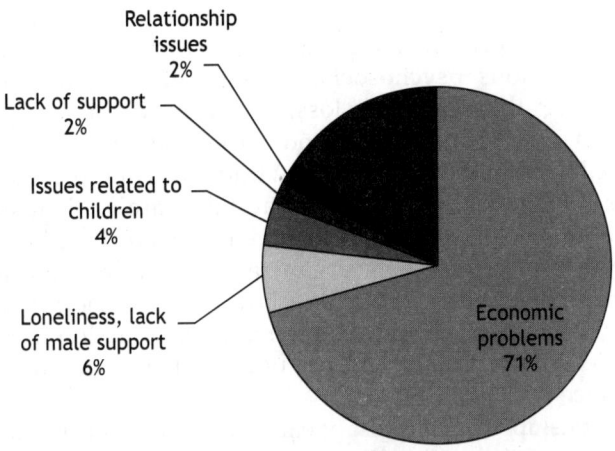

Relationship
issues
2%

Lack of support
2%

Issues related to
children
4%

Loneliness, lack
of male support
6%

Economic
problems
71%

Source: Sivayokan (2010).
Note: n = 52.

removed reminders like photographs and belongings from their home. Then she began to avoid talking about him to her child or others. Over time she had to suppress his memory to maintain her mental equilibrium, long-term survival of her family and social life. In the therapy sessions, she began to show subtle adverse facial and body language to reminders of him and so the therapists had to handle the topic tactfully. Traces of his memory actually faded from her mind and her life. This extraordinary phenomenon can be understood as an adaptive response in a closed community so that she and her child could survive. The perpetrators had even succeeded in disappearing the person from the memories of their beloved relations!

At times, the families do not want to talk about the disappearance or support each other. There could also be differences in perception among family members as some want to continue life as if nothing has happened and the disappeared person would come home soon. A wife of one disappeared person came to the mental health clinic after six years of the event, saying that she wanted to cry aloud and express her sadness, which she was unable to do at home in front of her daughter (who was six, had never seen her father and was not aware of her father's disappearance) and mother-in-law.

For long periods of time, running into years sometimes, families continue their visits to various traditional or ritual healers (Lawrence 1999). They keep on waiting for news about their loved ones. Their yearning for justice and redress becomes infinite. Nevertheless, with time, the families become tired of these procedures and rituals. They start readjusting their life, with deep-rooted uncertainty and pain in their hearts and minds.

Though the family members experience a special kind of trauma and express various psychosocial manifestations, a fair proportion somehow work through their loss. Many move on with their life and develop new relationships and social networks. Since women become the heads of the families, they find ways and means of getting an income. They cook, they work, they take care of their dependent members and they participate in different social forums including the disappeared family member's organization. Children continue their growth and school life. In 2008, the boy who got the highest marks in the Tamil medium year five scholarship examination in Jaffna was able to achieve it even in the absence of his father, a victim of enforced disappearance (Uthayan 2007).

The relationship with the disappeared persons too can influence the ability to cope with the loss. The suffering of a young wife of a disappeared man is different from the suffering of a sibling. The adjustment of a child is different from that of a mother. The women, especially wives, show many differences, additional responsibilities and culturally conditioned dilemmas. Somasundaram (2003b) notes:

> They looked after their families single-handedly, filling in for the absent male in what had been up to then, traditional male roles. They rode bicycles in greater numbers, went to the shops, met and argued with authorities, took their children to schools and temples, and generally 'kept the home fires burning' during this crisis in our society. They were thus under considerable stress and more vulnerable to breakdown. This may have been the price women had to pay to save our society from collapse.

Friends and Associates

The disappearance of a close companion reverberates in that person's close associates because they too start thinking and worrying about their safety in the near future. They may be aware of or be partly involved in the (possible) reason for the disappearance of their close mate and suffer from anticipatory anxiety. Many close associates initially experience shock and later, continuous fear and apprehension. They tend to scan the environment for possible threats and the presence of perpetrators. Some of these associates may move in order to avoid 'trouble', whereas others may even flee the country thinking that they too will be targeted soon. In a few instances, friends and relatives were disappeared when the perpetrators were unable to find their target. The associates may be blamed by their own families for having connections with the disappeared person/s. On the other hand, sometimes the close associates are blamed by the families of the disappeared for their loved one's disappearance. No studies have been done on close associates of disappeared, unlike studies and observations done on the experiences of family members. They are silent sufferers, crying hidden tears.

Community

It has been observed that more than sporadic or isolated occurrences, from time to time, there were mass-scale disappearances occurring in a particular community, like an epidemic. During such epidemics different authorities were involved with disappearances. In most cases, the community knows the perpetrators but is unable to respond or raise its voice against the disappearances or arbitrary extrajudicial killings. The stories of the incidents and witnessing the killings or mutilated bodies evoke panic and terror within the community. Perhaps that is the primary objective of these enforced disappearances. Though the communities are generally supportive of family members of disappeared persons, they sometimes avoid associating with those families and behave as if nothing has happened.

Generally, the storm of disappearances was accompanied by terrifying experiences like killings, robberies and demanding ransoms, which pushed the communities into a state of silence. They could only murmur in a low tone within a close circle. They had to live continuously in a state of fear, older members taking responsibility to protect the youngsters. Any noise of the sudden braking of a vehicle, a white van spotted or seeing unknown people in the vicinity could create fear. In fact, clinical experiences show that some of the community members developed a frank paranoid psychosis during these periods. The whole range of psychological reactions of the community may fit the popular terminology of 'fear psychosis'.

It is important to understand the reactions in the community, since with time the community becomes silent and obedient. The community observes that the various law-enforcing and human rights organizations are 'handcuffed' during these situations. They see that these organizations too have limited capacity to trace their disappeared members, other than registering cases and attending to other paperwork. On the whole, communities experience 'learned helplessness' and are unable to express their opinions or show any dissatisfaction about the events happening around them. Community participation was and is largely restricted in the northern part of the country for more than one simple reason. Those who were in power and who were responsible for the disappearance did not allow the community to actively organize themselves. Often, any community leadership is under constant pressure and monitoring. They themselves become vulnerable to be disappeared. However, even with this ground reality, communities try to organize few support groups and attention-seeking protest marches. Sometimes there are exchange visits with similar groups of people from the other parts of the country. This is an important phenomenon to understand the collective helpless and voiceless experiences, which are part of the root causes of collective trauma this book is trying to describe.

> This war has made us see so many things. In earlier wars, warriors would fight showing their martial qualities. They would fight it out. That was another time. Now small ones are going about fighting with guns. On the streets and junctions there are pictures and memorials of children who have died fighting. There was shelling, bombing, bunkers. We were asked to leave our homes. Then we were told to come back. We were told to stand in straight lines. Get down, they said…. We did all that. We have now come down.
>
> There will be periods in-between. Young ones, boys and girls, those seen and standing will suddenly disappear. Mysteriously they will vanish. Though this person says that person was taken by that group, the group says no.
>
> When these things happen left and right, the community will be scared. Just seeing a white van is enough, the whole community will become subdued. It could just be a van selling fish. If dogs bark at night, we tremble inside.
>
> We first believed that only people with some connection were taken away. But afterwards it did not look that way. The people here know who is doing this and who is having it done. But how can I tell you about it. They are still here. Afterwards, I will be shot even if I am an elderly person.
>
> You see, we are all terrified. We will not open our mouths for anything. We will survive only by being silent. I tell you all this because I know you well.

When communities are silenced, they depend on external agencies to talk for them or to protest on their behalf. Generally, the external agencies receive information from the affected communities to advocate on their behalf. Ironically, sometimes the covert perpetrators too pretend to overtly act on behalf of the communities. Some political organizations make use of the affected families and communities for their own agendas. The sad aspect within the community is that it lacks an empathetic understanding of the family's suffering.

Society

One sinister feature in the phenomenon of disappearance is that it spreads in all spheres of society. No one escapes from the phenomenon. The Sinhala, Muslim and Tamil communities of Sri Lanka have been affected by disappearances. The act of disappearance has gone beyond the systematized counter-terrorism strategy. Many began copying that strategy for their own benefit, like demanding ransom or silencing troublesome media. It has also become a way of obtaining large amounts of money. Many people have been directly or indirectly involved in the disappearance business. However, society has not responded to the massive number of disappearances, which have been happening not only in war-affected areas, but also in the capital and the other major cities of Sri Lanka (Weliamuna 2012).

The society's silence has given encouragement to the perpetrators. Why society has failed to respond adequately to disappearances is an interesting question to think about. One possible answer is that the war and the continuous stressors and the strategies of terrorism and counter-terrorism have changed the organic, native, innovative, responsive nature of traditional Sri Lankan society. Weliamuna (2012) believes it is fear, the terror of a similar fate, that prevents society from protesting. The perpetrators thus achieve their goal of controlling society and silencing dissent.

Remedies

The phenomenon of disappearance needs adequate recognition as a special phenomenon with unique characteristics. The victims, their families and their communities need special attention, care and intervention. The public needs to be adequately informed about the nature of the event and how best they could respond to such situations. The legal issues as well as the psychological and social suffering need to be addressed. Some ground-level counsellors are confused with the fact and struggling to 'force' a decision about whether the disappeared person is alive or not on the victims' families. In reality, it is a decision that the victim's family members have to take and the counsellor's role is to support the family. Sometimes, families may think that the person is unlikely to return but they will not act due to issues like remarrying and/or settling into a new life. The families and communities are unable to take the decision that the disappeared persons may not come back alive. They want to have some evidence to believe in. It could be a testimony of a survivor or perpetrator.

It could be a general statement and declaration by the authorities. Some kind of acceptance, an apology, a magic word: *sorry*.

Sri Lanka as a country has not adequately acknowledged disappearances and often it flatly denies them altogether. On the one hand, the government maintains a stand that it has nothing to do with disappearances. But on the other hand, it will not take adequate steps to find out about it or redress the suffering of the affected families and communities. One positive achievement, however, has been the state agreeing to issue a certificate of death after one year of disappearance, of course, after certain paperwork is completed. In the past it was only considered after seven years of disappearance. But at present, the period has been reduced to one year, which indirectly recognizes the phenomenon of disappearance. However, many family members have not accepted these death certificates. They think by accepting the death certificates, they become responsible in some way for the fate of their loved persons.

Exhumation processes are known to help the victims' families and communities to accept and come in terms with the loss of their family members. They may identify something of the victim, like a piece of cloth, a broken tooth or an earring. Finding and identifying the remains of their loved ones helps the families accept the reality, however sad, and enables them to move on with their life. Some may like to go ahead with a funeral rite to satisfy their belief system and console their mind. It is essential that adequate precautions are taken, preparations are made and psychosocial support is provided to the family members and communities of the disappeared persons during exhumation. But unfortunately in Sri Lanka, there were hardly any exhumation processes because of the state's reluctance to accept the phenomenon. However, there were three planned exhumations, two in the south and one in the north—Chemmani. In other circumstances there were accidental findings of human remains in an abandoned well or lavatory pit or underneath the ground. In the Chemmani exhumation there was no psychological support provided to the families during the exhumation process. That one and only exhumation done in the north was mainly organized by the judicial system, supported by the government and involved local and international agencies, including forensic experts and the media. Few remains were identified by relatives, who were in a heightened emotional state. There was no constructive outcome. All the three exhumations were supported, sponsored and politicized by the government of that time. Afterwards the state neglected these issues.

From time to time, the state has appointed many commissions and inquiry boards, mainly to collect information and evidence. Though the commissions and inquiry boards functioned in good faith and released reports of their findings and recommendations, including families' needs and expectations, unfortunately many of these reports were not taken very seriously. They gather dust in government shelves. Iqbal (2011) from the last government-appointed commission of inquiry (COI) concludes,

> Successive governments continued to ignore the recommendations of the commissions with regard to the perpetrators and steps needed to be taken to prevent such re-occurrence in the future. This promoted the culture of impunity that pervaded the police and security force personnel. It has been said in a lighter vein that the COIs have helped the successive government to identify those in the police and arms who could be used to cause disappearance effectively. By this time causing the disappearance of a person had become a useful weapon in the hands of whichever government that came to power. Even the current incidents of disappearances can be by persons who have by now become adept in the technique.

One of the main issues is the safety of those families and witnesses since most of the inquiries were held in a non-confidential manner. In some incidents, the survivors and witnesses had to flee from the area or country. On the other hand, of the cases filed, almost none of them have moved. A depressing reality is that the alleged perpetrators were sometimes released, honoured and promoted not only within their establishment, but at national and international levels. All these developments and occurrences were keenly observed by individuals and the community, who then lost their belief in morals and justice.

There were and are organizations working with families of disappeared members and most of the time they work without making much noise and publicity. Mostly the organizations confine themselves to their locality for reasons of feasibility and safety. This may have prevented the emergence of national-level organizations and a strong network among the existing organizations. Further, ethnic barriers, majority–minority issues, identification (with the perpetrators) issues have played a role and are proving to be major obstacles in sharing and networking. These organizations have been involved with many activities including advocacy, production of educational films, representing and presenting their problems in conferences such as the one in Geneva in 2003 organized by ICRC and the one in Manila in 2010. However, many organizations which emerged in the north were either misused or politicized and died a natural death, with the possible exception of self-help groups. There was little communication between the organizations from the two sides of Sri Lanka in view of strengthening their relationships and fighting for a common cause.

The common cause or demand is 'the truth', nothing but the truth. A statement; a genuine inquiry; a legitimate attempt to search for the disappeared or at least their remains; justice or an action against the perpetrator; accountability; redress for suffering; and an acknowledgement are needed. For this to become a reality, many things need to happen in parallel.

Conclusion

Disappearances are often denied rather than acknowledged. At present the legal system and human rights organizations do not offer adequate information and services to the victim's family members. Though considerable psychosocial support is needed for the families and communities, available psychosocial support is very minimal. Further, as a result of the politico-military context of disappearances, many organizations and individuals are fearful of working in this area. Everything is done while keeping a low profile. The affected families are continuously suffering from their loss. Some are coping well; some are not. Communities remain in fear and silence.

The long-term response of a community exposed to terror (Chapter 1B), the continuing threat to its collective way of life and security can be one of violence, which in time becomes organized, leading to militancy.

D.

Militancy

Beings manifest when conditions are sufficient.
When conditions lack, they no longer appear.

— Based on the 50 verses of Vasubandhu (Hanh 2008)

Introduction[1]

The Tamils, until recent times, appeared relatively peaceful people. Although there was considerable internal violence, for example, domestic violence, child abuse, caste violence and suicide, the incidence of external aggression, killings and large-scale civil violence were not seen. In fact, only a few decades ago, before the onset of the armed conflict, a single homicide would bring on a general paralysis, extreme fear and apprehension, so much so that people would avoid going outdoors for weeks or even months on end. A single killing would become a major issue, discussed in the media and people would talk about it for weeks. The conflict with the Sri Lankan state brought about a gradual habituation to violence and killing that became part of the day-to-day social climate. At the political level, once the compact between the Tamil and Sinhalese elite was destroyed by communal violence, the structures of elite social control broke down and the Tamil elite began looking for alternatives to buttress their position.

The Tamils had been often stereotyped as somewhat submissive. Thus the term, Demala, used by Sinhalese to describe Tamils had a derogatory tone to it. I can still remember the humiliating label of being routinely called *para demala* during my school days at the Royal College hostel in

---

[1] Modified and updated from Somasundaram (2002a, 2005b, 2010i).

Colombo in the early 1960s. The 1983 pogrom (Piyadasa 1984; Roberts 2003) can be seen as an attempt to teach the Tamils a lesson, to send them running with their tails between their legs.[2] It is only more recently, after the militant reaction to the violent suppression, where the term *kotiya* has replaced this stereotype and with it some grudging respect that the Tamils can stand up and fight!

So the question arises: how could the Tamils, the youth in particular, have become militant so quickly? It would appear that social sanction for a group to behave violently could bring out aggressive acts they have learned or seen, for example, in the media (Ilfeld and Metzner 1970). Although it is generally accepted that certain ethnic groups have special martial abilities (in the Indian subcontinent, the Gurkhas, Sikhs and Rajputs are famed for their fighting prowess), this may as well be a subcultural influence, depending on how the males are brought up in the community, their expectations and training. Thus, it is remarkable that an overtly peaceful people, the Tamils of Sri Lanka, have been able, when motivated and suitably mobilized, to develop quite competent (a competency artificially bolstered by modern easy-to-use light weaponry) military capacities rapidly, and were able to stand up to the aforementioned regiments during the ill-fated Indian intervention in Sri Lanka (1987–90) and the Sri Lankan forces for over two decades. The manner in which this confrontation and the longer running conflict with the Sri Lankan forces played itself out shows that between two well-trained and equipped fighting units, an important factor could be motivation. In the end, the Tamil militancy lost its momentum and morale, and fractured with internal splits and discontent that made it easy prey to a more motivated, organized and superior (in numbers and fire power) force (UTHR-J 2009).

Causes of Militancy

The development of Tamil militancy can be understood in terms of the sociocultural and politico-historical conditions. One way to try and understand the complex contexts under which youth and children become militants is to use of push–pull categorization (see Figure 3D.1) that has been used in relation to child labour by the International Labour Organization's

---

[2] Sinhala leaders, including President Jayewardene, have expressed this view publicly. However, the Tamil militancy had its origin in the early 1970s, as a result of increasing state discrimination, particularly the university standardization of admissions, and frustration with the perceived failure of the Tamil moderate politics to find suitable redress. Many Sinhalese blame the killing of thirteen soldiers by the LTTE for provoking the pogrom.

Figure 3D.1:
Factors Contributing to Creation of Militants

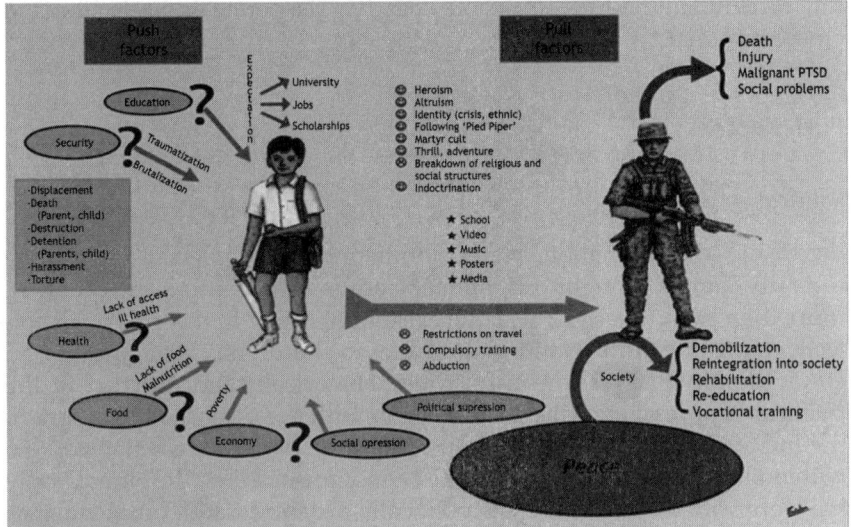

Source: Bapu or Dr Naguleswaran.

International Programme on the Elimination of Child Labour[3] and more specifically child soldiers[4] (Brett and Specht 2004; Somasundaram 2002a). Use of children as soldiers is an example of child labour par excellence, exemplifying most of the underlying socio-economic conditions and mechanisms of recruitment. They are often exploited in situations where there is shortage of adult fighters. Moreover, it is a form of child abuse by the people who conscript; they use children to do their fighting, get killed or injured for them (de Silva et al. 2001). However, push and pull factors often overlap and may oversimplify the context that can be quite complex, particularly in situations of internal civil war and violence (Honwana 2005). In discussing the motivation of the Tamil militants in Sri Lanka and the causes for their militancy in general (there being several Tamil militant groups), even shedding some light on the militancy among discontented youths of various disadvantaged ethnic groups that we are seeing today as a worldwide phenomenon is useful; this section will, however, focus in particular on the Tamil Tiger militant movement. The causes were clearer and more valid at the beginning of the war, but the complex picture

[3] See their website: http://www.ilo.org/ipec/lang−en/index.htm (retrieved on 17 June 2001).

[4] See: http://www.child-soldiers.org/conference/confreport_asiawgc.html (retrieved on 17 June 2001).

changed with time and the same factors were not operative towards the end when the motivation became more muddled. At the end of the fighting, recruitment had become more coercive, desperate and selection and choice minimal.

Push Factors

Political

Increasing discrimination, state humiliation and violence against the minority Tamils brought out militancy among the youth (see Section 1). More than individually, it was the existential threat to the group felt collectively, to the culture and way of life, to the dignity and pride of an ethnic identity that was the prime cause. Historically and structurally, the political suppression of the Tamils began with the disenfranchisement of the Indian Tamils soon after independence in 1948. The election of 1956 with mobilization of Sinhala Buddhist consciousness and the Sinhala-only bill were watershed events. The politically organized anti-Tamil violence of 1956, 1958, 1977 and particularly the 1983 pogrom were provocative. The constitutions of 1970 and 1977, which gave the Sinhala language and the Buddhist religion prominence in the state with cultural trappings, were the structural framework of the Sinhala ethnocracy that marginalized other minorities (DeVotta 2004, 2007). But it was perhaps the standardization of university admissions that effectively restricted access to higher education for many Tamil youths that was the precipitating cause of the birth of Tamil militancy. The role of the frustrated Tamil elite in promoting, encouraging and instigating violence among youth was another critical factor.

One example of an outstanding grievance, the use of the Tamil language, remains inadequately addressed (Nesiah 2012). For example, the legal processes in the country operate virtually entirely in Sinhala and English (Samaraweera 1997). What is true for the legal system is similar to all other areas of public functioning in Sri Lanka today. A Tamil speaker invariably faces humiliation.

In time, with the rise of Tamil militancy and the dynamics of increasing state repression with violent insurgent counter-attacks, laws such as the PTA and ER were passed, which institutionalized and encouraged the arrest, detention, torture, extrajudicial killings and disappearance of suspects (Bastiampillai et al. 2010). By providing legal sanction, impunity, protection and implicit encouragement to perpetrators of mass human rights abuses, the PTA and ER led to the establishment of a culture of violence, intimidation and state terror (see Chapter 1B). As a result, when a Tamil youth was checked or detained, he were often harassed, beaten or tortured. In a study of former Tamil detainees in Vavuniya, all were found to have been tortured (Doney 1998). The greatest impact of this kind of structural violence and oppression was on the younger generation (Somasundaram 2005b).

In these circumstances, it would be easy to understand why youths, children, women and adults joined the militancy. It would have been much more cost-effective in the long term and a more permanent solution for the state to have dismantled the political oppression that the Tamils faced. The raison d'être for the Tamil militancy would have been eliminated and there may not have been any war. Ultimately, militancy is a political message, a signal of frustration by those without access to power; a method, however misguided, misdirected or exploited, resorted to when other alternatives appear to fail; a communication about perceived injustice and inequity.

Social

The Hindu society in Jaffna before the war was very much under the influence of the caste system and the lower castes were suppressed by the higher castes, mainly the Vellala caste who held authority. The caste system has been responsible for considerable covert violence throughout history. For many from the lower castes, joining the militant movement became a way out of this oppressive system. Some of the other militant groups, the Eelam People's Revolutionary Liberation Front (EPRLF) and Eelam Revolutionary Organization of Students (EROS) in particular, were more egalitarian, attracting recruits from the lower castes. The LTTE cadres, particularly the leadership, have been drawn from the Karaiyar caste (traditionally fisherman living along the coast but with a reputation of being seafarers, warriors, mercenaries and smugglers). It is noteworthy that the LTTE developed a fairly powerful naval wing, Sea Tigers, and suicide Black Sea Tigers who would ram their explosive laden crafts into the bigger Sri Lankan navy boats. Similarly, for younger females who had experienced the widespread sociocultural oppression against their sex, it was a means of escape and 'liberation' in a traditional, patriarchal society (Hellmann-Rajanayagam 2008; Trawick 1999). The LTTE used a large number of female suicide bombers, believed to be around 35 per cent. The circumstances for the LTTE recruiting increasing number of women and children arose when it began to run out of youths and men willing to join and fight. According to Neloufer de Mel, the phenomenon of female suicide bombers has raised issues of 'autonomous choice, agency, feminist politics, cultural role models, and the gendered nature of sacrifice/martyrdom' (quoted in M. Bloom [2005]).

Economical

Many of the youths and children who joined the militant forces were from the lower and disadvantaged or deprived socio-economic classes. Economical pressures within the family, lack of opportunities in the wider society drove many youths to join. Many youths felt that their avenues for advancement had been blocked by the discriminatory acts of the state. As described below, many were not able to find employment, opportunity for higher education or vocational training, economic assistance in the form of loans or schemes, or other openings that they saw were available to youths from the majority ethnic group. Under the dowry system, parents having girl children for whom they could not provide a dowry sometimes encouraged their children to join.

It is ironic that the vast majority of the state forces involved in the direct fighting was also from similarly disadvantaged socio-economic classes. However, there were noticeable differences in motivation levels, which appeared to depend on degrees of mobilization, indoctrination and morale. The beginning of Tamil militancy did show that fanatical belief in a cause or perceived threat to group identity could override economic motivation.

Food

Lack of food, especially nutritious food, is another important indirect stressor but perhaps not a direct motivating factor. The gradual deterioration in socio-economic conditions like decreasing employment and income opportunities, poverty, inequity in resource distribution, hunger, chronic shortages, state blockades and ill health created an ecology of deprivation that caused frustration and smouldering anger. Studies in Jaffna General Hospital showed that there had been a statistically significant increase in low-birth weight (below 2.5 kilograms) babies from 19 per cent in 1989 to 23 per cent in 1991 to 25 per cent in 1992. The cause for this can be found in the malnutrition of pregnant mothers. R. Theivendran (pers. comm.) in his 1987 unpublished study on refugees found that all the pregnant mothers, and also lactating mothers, examined in twelve refugee camps within the Jaffna municipality, were anaemic. He also found that 41 per cent of infants and 73 per cent of children between the ages of one and five were below the third percentile expected weight for their age, showing chronic protein calorie malnutrition by two or three degrees. Similar malnutrition (68 per cent below the third percentile in children of ages between one and five) was found in the Ketpeli refugee camp by Save the Children Fund (Council of NGOs 1992). Deprivation of food and chronic hunger are themselves stressors that cause apathy, listlessness, irritation and failure to thrive. Furthermore, low birth weight and malnourishment in infants increases the risk of immediate and long-term morbidity and mortality. Protein malnutrition in the critical period of development of the nervous system, that is, from conception to about two years after birth, leads to permanent brain damage, causing mental retardation. According to a report by the Council of NGOs (1992) and Sivarajah (1993), the reasons for this widespread malnutrition are attributed to the shortage of proteins due to the fall in productivity of the fishing and poultry industries, and perhaps also due to poverty caused by unemployment, loss of working equipment, agricultural fields and savings, as well as shortages, blockades and high prices of food—all indirect effects of war.

Parents have been known to send one or more of their children to join the militants when facing difficulties in feeding the family. They have expressed a satisfaction that at least one child would have enough to eat. At the same time, the LTTE used its ability to feed its cadres good food in its propaganda for recruitment and was mindful of their regular diet.

Health

Another indirect stressor is ill health due to reduced resistance as a consequence of malnourishment and psychological stress, poor sanitation and overcrowding in the refugee camps, epidemic spread of communicable diseases, poor health services, shortage of drugs and uncontrolled multiplication of disease vectors, like mosquitoes, due to a lack of spraying. Diseases on the increase in children included respiratory tract infections, gastroenteritis, dysentery, typhoid, resistant cerebral malaria, tuberculosis, rheumatic fever and carditis, and the so-called fatal 'septicaemia'. Lack of quality healthcare in the north and east was appalling (Somasundaram 2005a). The lack of access to health and malnutrition may produce a milieu of lack, a perception of horizontal inequity (Stewart 2001) that could turn into a direct motivating factor.

Displacement

Displacement is the source of several stresses as Professor Raphael (1986) describes. In children:

> The loss of home, a strange environment, the breakdown of family ritual, separation from parents, from familiar neighbourhood and environment, and from school and friends, the loss of toys and treasures, and crowded and strange accommodation are all likely to be stressful for the child.

Almost all families were displaced during the 1995 exodus (UTHR-J 1995a), and a high proportion had been displaced at other times, particularly during the Indian intervention in October 1987 (Hoole et al. 1988). It was found that all the indices of psychological disturbances were more marked in displaced students (Arunakirinathan et al. 1993). Refugee camps become breeding grounds for recruitment.

Education

Disruption in regular schooling and education was a prominent stressor in the war: inability to attend schools due to displacements; unavailability of schools due to destruction or use as camps; indefiniteness about the national exams; lack of a secure, calm, lighted (no electricity), quiet environment for learning; irregular attendance due to transport difficulties and disturbed situation, students being detained, conscripted, indoctrinated or forced to partake in political activities; seeing the emigration of fellow students; lack of opportunity to continue their education (refugee children being unable to go to school due to lack of uniforms, exercise books and the like); shortages and delays in receiving school text books and materials.

The beginnings of Tamil militancy were a reaction to the discriminatory state policy in education. Developments in the educational system turned this once-cherished endeavour into a big question mark as even the national examinations were not held in the north regularly. The non-attendance and dropout rates increased dramatically in the north, becoming the highest in the island (Wickramasinghe 1996). A study of the performance of students in basic skills such as in language and mathematics showed the north-eastern region placed last in the island (National Education Research and Evaluation Centre 2004). Ironically, what started out as a struggle for better educational opportunities had the opposite effect, to the point of being classified as a 'deprived' district. Under these circumstances, militancy became an alluring alternative to the once-cherished dream of education. If that push factor is to be reversed, there will have to be radical changes in the educational system with opportunities for relevant education, further advancement and more technological training in modern fields.

Death of Parent(s) or Relatives

Death or disappearance of one or both parents left many children orphaned or as members of one-parent families (Thiranagama 2011). Some left to join the militancy when they directly witnessed the brutal killing of their parent(s) by the state; others left later when other pressures builtup. Some reported a burning desire for revenge as a reason for joining.

Destruction

During the fighting, many structures were destroyed including homes, schools, temples, churches and other social institutions. Seeing the destruction of one's home, social or religious institution, can be the collapse of everything secure and strong, of the known world, and create a vacuum that can never be filled. A variety of emotions can result: from anger, resentment and devastation to hopelessness and indignation. The 1983 anti-Tamil pogrom was the turning point for many Tamil youths. Thiranagama (2011) describes the role of state-led riots and violence creating political subjectivity using the example of Ranjan:

> I was emboldened to go and join because of the government. Because of their racism. Because of ethnic discrimination. I had lived in Anuradhapura, I didn't understand Tamil; sometimes I may have said that I didn't know any Tamils. I only knew Sinhalese. If I had stayed there, who knows, I may have even joined the army! Become a commander. Because my basic language was Sinhalese. I would have become a Sinhalese. The reason I am here speaking Tamil to you and thinking of myself as a Tamil is because of the country's ethnic problems. I would not have had the opportunity to go to the LTTE otherwise.

Brutalization

Tamil youths were specifically targeted by the security forces during their checking, cordon and search operations and generally detained for interrogation, detention, torture, execution or even rape. During the so-called Operation Liberation in 1987, youths were either summarily shot (Hoole et al. 1988) or shipped off in chains to the Boosa camp in the south by the army en masse. So many youths would rather join than face, in their eyes, certain detention and death. Fifteen per cent of the six hundred disappearances in 1996 within Jaffna were those of children. An example of the direct cause and effect was in May 1999 when a senior school prefect of a leading school in Jaffna was detained after his parents had taken him to the camp. When he was not subsequently released, all the schools in the Jaffna district went on strike. Finally, he was released without any charges. Contusions and abrasions were found on his body. While he was in detention, five other students from the same area left to join the militant movement. Many were humiliated by the manner in which they or their families were treated at checkpoints, search operations or in dealings with state officials. Women were particularly at risk of harassment in their daily life. This left a burning resentment just below the surface that could easily be tapped by recruiters. Once recruited, the organizational structure of the LTTE was able to harness and direct this emotion against a perceived enemy through indoctrination and training (Arnestad and Daae 2007).

Traumatization

During the civil war in north-east Sri Lanka for almost two decades, people were traumatized by such experiences as frequent shelling, bombing, helicopter strafing, round-ups, cordon and search operations, deaths, injuries, destruction, mass arrests, detention, shootings, grenade explosions and landmines, all of which were common. A study in the Vanni found that over 90 per cent of students had undergone a direct war experience (Vivo 2003). A detailed Canadian study of children in the Eastern Province of Sri Lanka (in addition to studies in Yugoslavia, Palestine and Iraq) found considerably greater exposure to war trauma and psychological seque-lae in the ethnic minority Tamil children (Health Reach 1996). In north-ern Sri Lanka, extensive epidemiological surveys in 1993 of twelve Vaddukoddai cluster schools (Arunakirinathan et al. 1993), adolescents in Jaffna (Geevathasan 1993) and Killinochchi schools showed widespread war stressors and consequences (Somasundaram 1998). According to the senior community medicine professor Sivagnanasundaram, the impact of the war and the resulting traumatization and brutalization would have been a motivating factor for militancy among youths and children.

Future (Employment, Education)

As mentioned in Chapter 1A, opportunities for and access to further edu-cation, sports, foreign scholarships or jobs (see Table 3D.1) in the state sector were progressively restricted by successive Sinhalese governments, despite the lip service paid to maintaining ethnic ratios. According to Stewart (2001) horizontal inequities between groups, in this case the polit-ically privileged Sinhalese and minority Tamils, were a powerful cause for ethnic violence and rebellion.

Pull Factors

Belief

In the beginning youth joined the militant movements out of altruistic beliefs to safeguard their threatened ethnic identity (Somasundaram 1998).

Table 3D.1:
Employment of Minorities

Ethnic Group	Percentage of Population	Percentage in State Service	Percentage in Provincial Services	Percentage in Semi- government Service
Sri Lankan Tamils	12.7	5.9	7.1	8.2
Hill-country Tamils	5.5	0.1	0.2	0.5
Muslims	7.37	2.0	4.2	1.0
Total	25.6	8.0	11.3	9.7

Source: Nissan (1990).

For example, when in the 1983 riots Tamils as a group were humiliated, the youth took up arms to prevent a complete eclipse of the group's identity. They joined any Tamil militant group that was available. That they did so in thousands with complete dedication, determination and resourcefulness is a mark of the deep threat that was felt at the core of their beings, a fear for their identity as a group. It was left to the youth to redeem the Tamil identity and honour, to take up the mantle and meet the challenge for group survival with a violent defiance. It could be said that this was the prime motivating factor at the beginning of Tamil militancy.

> I joined the LTTE in 1990, when I was fifteen years old, of my own volition. I was motivated by Thiyahi Thileepan's speeches. He was a medical student; he left that position and joined to serve the people. He delivered speeches at our school. Although parents made arrangements for our family to emigrate to Canada, I didn't want to go into exile. Just before our family travelled abroad, I chose to join the LTTE. I was young and I had a lot of enthusiasm. At a time when many people were displaced from Jaffna to the Vanni in 1995, I went to the Vanni. That was when the Army captured Jaffna.

Konrad Lorenz (1963) describes such strong motivation as 'militant enthusiasm'. Due to the powerful emotional charge involved, challenges to group identity often end in confrontation and conflict, particularly when obstructed or suppressed violently in situations of inter-group tensions, perceived injustices and inequities. Unfortunately power hungry leaders and demagogues are well versed in the art of cleverly exploiting this reservoir of potentially explosive energy and turning it to their own purpose by appealing to patriotism, language, religion and such mystical concepts as soil and blood. Such appeals have the power to strike deep chords in one's being, evoking ultimate loyalties and emotive passions. With time, the early motivating factors changed to more mundane ones.

After eliminating other Tamil militant groups, taking complete totalitarian control and the subsequent Indian intervention in 1987, the LTTE started using children and females, as the older males no longer joined. In time, the older youths had matured enough to become disillusioned with the way the struggle was being directed. The intra- and inter-group internecine warfare soon disenchanted most. The vast majority of youths fled aboard, using complex routes and all their family resources and ingenuity to find asylum in foreign countries. However, this widespread Tamil diaspora continued to support financially, vocally and even emotionally the violent nationalist project back in their erstwhile homeland. Yet, neither they, nor their children came back to join the militancy and sacrifice themselves for the cause.

The difference between voluntary and compulsory conscription is not all that clear-cut, as this chapter attempts to show through the push and pull factors. It is crucial for a fighting force to have some degree of self-motivation, a will to fight and bear hardships. This is a motivational game that states and rebel forces have to play to have enough cadres to fight and carry out killings (Somasundaram 2009). To a large extent, under the LTTE, recruitment had been 'voluntary' up to the last stages of the Vanni battle. Earlier, for a very short transient period, the Indian army-backed EPRLF (another Tamil militant group) forcefully conscripted youths for its makeshift Tamil National Army, many of whom were later killed by the LTTE. Child recruitment by the LTTE was to become institutionalized after 1990. Although LTTE denied that it used child soldiers, it has been variously estimated that out of a fighting force consisting between seven thousand and ten thousand soldiers, 50 per cent may have been females and 20–40 per cent may have been children (UNICEF and SCF 2000; UTHR-J 1995b, 2000). In specialized units such as the Leopards, children formed an effective fighting force in difficult battles. It is those who were unable to find a way to flee aboard, those from the lower socio-economic class trapped in the north and east with no other avenue of escape that became the catchment population for the militants. The LTTE had also been careful to keep this recruitment source in its control, restricting their travel outside its areas of control and herding them with various degrees of compulsion when it became necessary, for example, during the 1995 exodus and then the 2006–09 Vanni battle.

Once in the LTTE, the atmosphere within the group, trauma from repeated battles and a heightened sense of dedication resulted in some volunteering to become Black Tigers (Arnestad and Daae 2007). The Black Tigers were an elite, highly trained and indoctrinated, specialized suicide squad within the overall militant organization that also included air, sea, anti-aircraft, anti-tank, artillery, demolition, women, young, special units, political and other units. The Black Tigers showed a high degree of commitment, singleness of purpose, devotion to cause, allegiance to the leader, motivation, clarity of mind about day-to-day functioning, skill and loyalty maintained over long periods of time (over three years in the case of President Premadasa's killers) in adverse environments and without the need for regular support, ritualistic practices or encouragement. Very rarely was there seen any wavering, fear, signs of doubt, misgiving or uncertainty and their attacks were carried out with extraordinary precision.

In joining the LTTE, the cadres committed themselves to die, wearing a *kuppi* (cyanide capsule usually on a necklace) at all times, which was to be used in the event of imminent capture, ostensibly to avoid giving information under torture. This pattern of suicide was similar to what the sociologist Emile Durkheim (1951) called 'altruistic suicide', in which the individual so closely identifies with a group and the cause, that he is willing to sacrifice himself for the greater good, or 'fatalistic suicide' where there is high degree of control and indoctrination. An estimated one-third of the LTTE's combat deaths up to 1992 can be attributed to these forms of suicides (Schalk 2003). Among the veteran cadres that I have interviewed or treated over the years (admittedly those with psychological problems), there is a strong death wish (perhaps a result of the harsh realities of battle, death of comrades and hopelessness of fatal outcome). Almost all of them had a strong desire to join the elite Black Tigers; in fact, it was seen as an honour and opportunity to be worthy and useful. The recruiters are looking for able and skilled combatants to be used as instruments in the war, precision weapons of high effectiveness by the weaker party in an asymmetrical war (Hassan 2008a). Though the term 'suicide terrorism' is commonly used, these acts cannot be regarded as suicide in the way it is usually understood, nor as homicidal killings (Hassan 2008b). According to the LTTE and its sympathizers, these were not suicide (*thatkollai*) but self-sacrifice (*thatkodai*). Roberts (2007) has described it as sacrificial devotion (*thiyaham*) with deep cultural roots.

Psychological Methods

Youths and children, because of their age, immaturity, curiosity and love for adventure, were susceptible to a 'Pied Piper' enticement through a variety of psychological methods. Public displays of war paraphernalia, funerals and posters of fallen heroes; speeches and videos, particularly in schools; heroic, melodious songs and stories; drawing out feelings of patriotism and creating a martyr cult all created a compelling milieu. A whole subculture grew up around the Tamil militancy, in particular the LTTE, which claimed to take up arms to defend the Tamils, their honour, dignity, homeland (Eelam) or Tamil motherland (*Thamil thaiyaham*) and culture. The LTTE cadres swore an allegiance to the leader, Prabhakaran, with their life, with the *kuppi* worn around their neck as a symbol of their complete sacrifice (*thiyaham*).

When they died in battle or in service, they were eulogized as *maveerar* (heroes), bodies taken by vehicles all over the region with lamentations and funeral music wailing over loudspeakers in street corners and buried (*vithaikapaduthal*, sowed as seeds) or as memory stones (*natukal* or *nina-ivukkal* when their bodies were not available) in special cemeteries called *thuyilam illams* (literally, sleeping homes). Their pictures appeared in posters pasted all over the north-east, in the media (including daily papers, periodicals, publications and Internet sites), in specially built structures (pandals) on periodic remembrance days, as statues and glorified in songs, poems, stories, drawings, dramas, videos, statues, loudspeakers and speeches. *Maveerar* families were also given special status in LTTE-controlled areas[5] with privileges in accessing services, respect at ceremonies and exemption

---

[5] This was a liability in state-controlled areas and so people would hide their *maveerar* status.

from giving further children to the LTTE (increasingly ignored in the final months). Annual commemoration celebrations were held all over the north-east with massive public participation and among the Tamil diaspora on special days, such as *Maveerar Nal* (27 November, when the first martyr died) and 5 July (Black Tiger Day) with ritualistic practices and cultural performances. LTTE songs were played over loudspeakers and flames (*theepam*, signifying the flame of the eternal spirit or soul) were lit at auspicious times. A pride of place was given to acknowledged Black Tiger martyrs at these ceremonies. This great public drama and spectacle obviously helped in the LTTE propaganda, its public image, control over the populace and recruitment.

Velupillai Prabhakaran, the LTTE supreme leader himself, was reported to have a last supper with the cadres before their suicide mission, a picture of which was released posthumously. It is said that meeting the reclusive leader who inspired awe and reverence befitting a living god (UTHR-J 2000) could itself be motive enough for volunteering for such missions. Although the LTTE claimed to be secular, there was a 'sacralisation of the national'. All these ceremonies and manifestation contained rich cultural, religious and historical symbols and motifs, a syncretism of Hindu and Christian beliefs and practices (Natali 2008; Roberts 2005). This martyr cult gave inspiration, beliefs, purpose, zeal and meaning to LTTE cadres and Black Tigers, which would encourage and sustain them in their sacrificial actions and death. The anticipated power of this cult is seen by the compulsion of the Sri Lankan state forces to destroy and bulldoze the *thuyilam illam*s when they captured that territory and suppressed the ceremonies. However, the real test of the long-term survival of these religio-cultural practices and beliefs would be seen by whether they revive when the grip of the state relaxes and for how long it continues. There is some evidence for continued observances in the Tamil diaspora, but suppressed by the state in the Tamil community in Sri Lanka itself.

The severe restrictions placed by the LTTE on people leaving areas controlled by it, which applied particularly to those of a younger, recruitable age group, created a feeling of entrapment, while it ensured that there was a continuing source of recruits. The LTTE had compulsive military-type training in areas under its control, instilling a military thinking. Everyone, beginning from class nine, was compelled to undergo training in military drill, use of arms and mock battles as well as made to carry out military tasks such as digging bunkers and manning sentry posts. Government rations, other benefits and travel were allowed only to those who had been trained (UTHR-J 2000). The same inducement was used in the cadet system, military drills and even marching bands for adolescents in schools. Once trained they also became compromised, liable if the state forces came in, as they would be identified as possible cadres. This possibility made many join when it became inevitable the army was advancing.

Sociocultural Institutions

The Tamil society had prided itself as belonging to an ancient, cultured civilization. However, when children started being used in the war, the social structures and religious institutions failed to protest. In fact, they remained silent and passive. This was in part due to the environment created by the actions of the Sri Lankan state in its indiscriminate bombing, shelling, detention and torture. The Tamil community had learnt to be silent, non-involved and stay in the background, simply attend to their immediate needs and survive until the next day. Any involvement or participation carried considerable risk. Those with leadership qualities, those willing to challenge and argue, the intellectuals, the dissenters (labelled *throhis*) and those with social motivation had been weeded out. Gradually people were made very passive and submissive. These qualities became part of the socialization process, where children were gradually taught to keep quiet, not to question or challenge, accept the situation, as a forward behaviour carried considerable risk. Thus, there was no social resistance to recruitment or the total control of the militants. As a result, the Tamil militants were allowed to function freely within society in order to attract recruits for their fighting units through their propaganda and psychological pressure exercised within the vacuum left by the abdicating social institutions. However, there was also popular and social sanction for the martyr cult, including the Black Tiger suicide missions. They became revered heroes. As Mia Bloom (2005) argues, it is when the suicidal terror and violence resonates with the public (for whatever reason, be it state suppression or terror) and finds social sanction, that it is likely to sustain itself successfully. The Tamil public and social leaders perceived[6] that the LTTE chose 'legitimate' military or political targets for elimination using weapons of war. In an unequal contest, where the weaker, non-state actor does not have the same resources or heavy weaponry, the LTTE saw using a human bomb as a precision instrument, as a means of delivering the payload to inaccessible but strategic targets. Civilians developed admiration for cadres who dedicated themselves as live weapons (*uyir ayutham*) for this type of altruistic sacrifice (*thatkodai*). A potential countermeasure then would have been to look at the reasons for this popularity or sanction and work to reduce it. In the Sri Lankan example however, the state chose instead to destroy the LTTE organization militarily and use social

---

[6] Perception is a complex act, where indoctrination, media and actions by the state would play an additive, reinforcing role.

repression thereafter, rather than solving the underlying root causes. The state is not in a psychosocial position to resolve the issue of ethnic origins as it is too emotionally entrenched (see Chapter 1A).

Thus, it raises the intriguing question of whether, given sufficient preconditions, that is, violent repression of the Tamil minority, a denial of their legitimate rights (ICG 2012a), the religio-cultural context where there is sanction and honour for violence, and perhaps the most vital, militant organizational capacity for training, the phenomenon of Tamil militancy will again manifest itself.

Alternative Behaviour

At a generalized level it is said that suicide rates are remarkably constant for each society, but show a marked fall during war (Durkheim 1951). Suicide rates in Jaffna have shown the same trend during the war (see Figure 3D.2), with a marked fall during periods of intense fighting (Somasundaram and Rajadurai 1995) and an increase during cessation of war or peace. War is said to increase social cohesion against a common enemy and this gives meaning to live. However, those who may commit suicide during normal times may die from other causes during war, such as fighting and dying on the battlefield or carrying out suicide attacks. Neeleman (2002) described the phenomenon of 'contextual effect modification' within the context of war, modifying the expected suicide risk by opening up other ways of dying. Thus, the drop in suicide rates could be due to war providing an alternate channel for suicidal behaviour (Burvill 1980) or an opportunity to externalize aggression (Lyons 1979). This psychodynamic explanation describes suicide as similar to depression, as a form of aggression turned inwards towards the self, whereas war provides an outlet for the aggression to be turned outwards towards a common enemy (Lyons 1979).

Although Burvill (1980) rejected the hypothesis that war may provide an alternate opportunity for suicidal behaviour based on the figures from Australia, some support for the view comes from clinical observations during the war in Sri Lanka. Adolescents in a suicidal mental state caused by intense frustration or interpersonal conflict who would have attempted suicide in normal times often said that they would rather join the militants and die in combat, for it would have some meaning for society and they would be honoured on public posters and media. The director of a counselling centre in Jaffna, during a seminar for medical officers, described the social ethos as one where adolescents or youths faced with severe family conflict or environmental stress will at times threaten or carry out

Figure 3D. 2:
Suicide Rates in Jaffna (1979-2011)

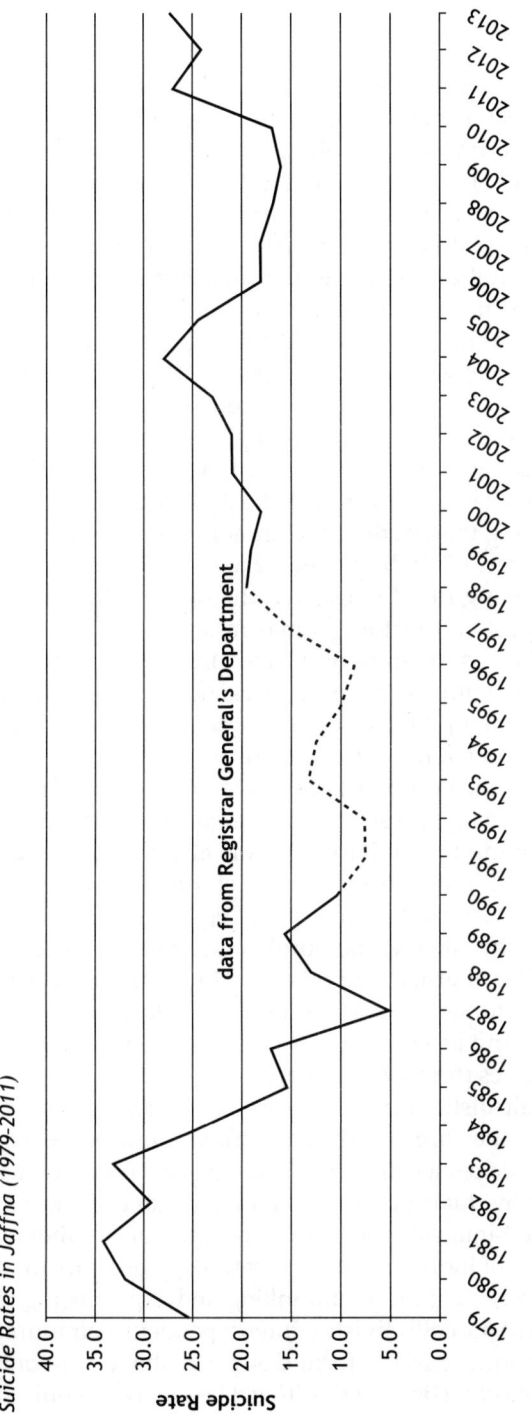

Source: Jaffna District Courts. 1990–97 figures from Registrar General's Department, Sri Lanka. Available online at http://www.rgd.gov.lk/web/ index.php?option=com_content&view=article&id=64&Itemid=41&lang=en

two possible alternatives—one is suicide and the other, joining the militants (Anandarajah, pers. comm.). The 'cult of martyrdom' and sacrificial devotion have become increasingly attractive to frustrated and rebellious youth in the modern world, resulting in 'suicide terrorism' (Roberts 2007).

Whereas suicide is common among the elderly elsewhere in the world (Durkheim 1951), a study of suicide in Jaffna showed highest risk in the group of people aged between twenty-five and thirty-four (Ganesvaran et al. 1984). The authors conclude that this phenomenon may be related to ethnic violence and revolt among the youth. Dissanayake and De Silva (1974) find a similar high risk for suicide and attempted suicide among the youth (those between the ages of fifteen and thirty-four) for Sri Lanka as a whole and attributed it to unemployment and unrest among the youth, as manifested in the 1971 JVP insurgency. It is noteworthy that the suicide rate for Sri Lanka as a whole was the highest in the world, as it was in Jaffna before the war (Ganesvaran et al. 1984). Attempted suicide in Jaffna is also high among the youth and commonly follows stress (Ganesvaran and Rajarajeswaran 1989). Both suicide and attempted suicide rates were seen to be increasing rapidly again in the north with the end of the war due to various post-war factors (Somasundaram 2012).

One study (Somasundaram and Rajadurai 1995) shows that the drop in the suicide rate with war is more marked for males (300 per cent) than females (180 per cent), and is more marked for those in the age group between fifteen and twenty-four years (from 62.4 to 25.4 per 100,000) than for those in the age group between twenty-five and thirty-four years. Males in the adolescent age group are in an overwhelming majority among those joining the militants. This is also the age group which had the highest suicide rate before the war started. However, if we look at the *maveerar* statistics for Jaffna (Natali 2008) and assume that one-third would be deaths by suicide, the numbers far exceed those that would be expected from the alternate hypothesis. Thus, we would have to review the additional factors discussed earlier for the large numbers joining the militancy and dying as *maveerar*. Of these, a select number would be the Black Tiger suicides from 1987 onwards.

Durkheim's altruistic form of suicide or self-sacrifice (*thatkodai*) to the greater cause of the threatened community could be better understood from a collectivistic perspective. Suicidal terror arouses feelings of aversion and horror in individualistic societies and may not be possible in individuals who value self-interest. There could be attempts to understand suicide bombers in terms of individual psychopathology or as arising from hate or revenge. However, the pattern of thinking and experiencing the world are radically different in collectivistic, interdependent communities (Nisbett 2003). Altruistic suicide in the form described above may only be seen in the context of collectivistic societies (Riaz Hassan, pers. comm.).

Demobilization

Now that the fighting is over, there is the immense problem of demobilization and reintegration into society. The same problem faces the Sri Lankan armed forces with over two hundred thousand soldiers mobilized for the final battle. Opportunity structures in the form of jobs, positions and functions in society commensurate with their previous roles in the military or as militants are needed. They will need social recognition and respect for the sacrifices they have made. They should be given the opportunity to put to use, for the benefit of society, the motivation and ideals that made them join the fighting in the first place. If the demobilization, rehabilitation and reintegration into society are not done properly, there will be considerable problems in the long term as has been found in similar situations worldwide.

Suffering from chronic PTSD, depression, suicidal ideation, alcohol and drug abuse, with relationship difficulties (see Chapter 4A) may continue. Family members may find them irritable, withdrawn and given to violent outbursts. Women cadre will face particular difficulties in marriage and reassuming a more subdued role in a traditional patriarchal society. Some develop long-term personality changes, described as complex or malignant PTSD. I have had to treat militants with very disturbed, aggressive outbursts when they re-experience traumatic events (Somasundaram 1998). Death scenes and battles repeatedly overwhelm them in the form of flashbacks and vivid hallucinations. During these periods they completely lose control over themselves, becoming very violent and destructive.

The condition of malignant PTSD was first described by Rosenbeck (1985), where American Vietnam war veterans came to feel the most alive when they are in a situation of intense conflict or potential danger, and feel bored or depressed in the absence of such a situation. Many were anxious or paranoid in crowds or public places and could get irritated or argumentative in such situations. Herman (1992) put forward the concept of complex PTSD with alterations in affect regulation, consciousness, self-perception, relationships and systems of meaning. She further describes how to institute a recovery process through healing, reconnecting, restoring social bonds and commonality. The new category of complex PTSD is being proposed for ICD-11, characterized by alterations in regulating affective arousal with difficulty in modulating anger, self-destructive and suicidal behaviour and impulsive and risk-taking behaviour. In addition, chronic characterological changes with alterations in self-perception — chronic guilt and shame, feelings of self-blame, or ineffectiveness, and of being permanently damaged, a tendency to victimize others — and alterations in systems of meaning such as despair and hopelessness or loss of previously sustaining beliefs have been described as characterizing the new category of complex PTSD (de Jong 1997). The ICD-10 (WHO 1992) included permanent hostility and distrust. These problems will need sensitive handling to prevent long-term consequences for the individual, family and community. Large numbers of soldiers and militants discharged without adequate psychosocial support and rehabilitation could spell disaster for society with antisocial personality developments, violence, broken families, crime, alcohol and drug use and suicide.

The following case history illustrates some of the problems that could arise.

I joined the LTTE at sixteen years when they didn't force recruitment; instead, they gave speeches at schools and I was motivated by Ilamparithi's description of the Tamil struggle. Ilamparithi described the injustices of the government against Tamils and explained why we must have a separate nation. After a group of us joined we went to Manalaru. My mother searched until she found me, but I wouldn't return with her. Upon completion of our training we followed educational courses. I then was trained in communication and IT [information technology] in which I worked for some two years, before being sent to battle.

I was injured from an explosion of the LTTE arms store when it was hit by a K-bomber in February 2009. I was taken to Matalan hospital where they amputated legs without anaesthesia due to shortages. Both civilians and LTTE who were injured were treated there. There was such an enormous crush of people and it would take a day before the patient would be taken inside the hospital. About seventy injured people were lying on the ground outside the hospital without any shade....

On 16 May we went into the army-controlled area after 5 p.m.... On 22 they took us to Pampaimadu Rehabilitation Center. They brought in some medicine and identified those who had experience with the LTTE medical unit, and they used those people to give medicine. Sometimes even the army came in and received medical treatment from them. Rarely did a doctor come from outside. They trained me in sewing for three months only. Mainly they just tried to keep everyone busy, and they taught sewing to say they were giving training. Once in a while we saw a film, and we read books and newspapers. We played volleyball and cricket at 4.00 p.m. when they allowed free time outside. Sisters (Catholic nuns) gave us carom boards and there was a television that we were allowed to watch anytime.

Five or six of the women were mentally disturbed. They broke the television. One day Major General Daya Ratnayake [Commissioner General of Rehabilitation] came to the camp and gave a speech in which he said things like, 'It will take five years to release all of you,' and one woman was so disturbed she swallowed many Piriton tablets without anyone's knowledge. She was admitted to hospital, and afterwards she looked normal but if you spoke harshly to her she would definitely hit you. She hit army women also. In the next year she tried twice to jump over the wall and gate. Then the army added razor wire across the top of the gate. She was released, but I don't know where she went. The others who were mentally disturbed didn't eat well, and were always distracted by their thoughts. Former women fighters, who had no relatives, were handed over to Catholic sisters by the army. A woman who was in Pampaimadu told me she came with her husband into the army-controlled area, and he surrendered when they made the announcement to come forward and surrender; since then there has been no information about him. The persons who surrendered in army-controlled areas in Mullaitivu have all disappeared. The army took one of the priests in Mullaitivu, Father Francis, and there is no information about him either.

Conclusion

Sri Lanka has been subjected to chronic military violence for over twenty years. The rise of Tamil militancy can be understood from the ecological context as an interaction of pull and push factors. By understanding the myriad causes that motivate youths towards militancy and self-sacrifice, it should be possible to address the basic needs and issues involved so that we have a more equitable, just and peaceful society and world. At the same time, similar problems can be seen in the Sri Lankan soldiers who fought the Tamil militants. They have also been scarred by the war which in turn affects their families and communities.

Other Communities

A.

War Trauma in the Military, Their Families and Communities*

By *Ruwan M. Jayatunge*

Combat Trauma Experienced by Soldiers

War is particularly traumatic for soldiers (Hendin and Haas 1984). The thirty-year armed conflict in Sri Lanka has produced a new generation of veterans at risk for chronic mental health problems following prolonged exposure to the war. Over two hundred thousand members of the Sri Lankan armed forces and police were directly or indirectly exposed to combat situations during these years. There were nearly twenty-three major military operations conducted by the armed forces from 1987 to 2009. A large number were exposed to hostile battle conditions and underwent traumatic battle events outside the range of usual human experience. These experiences include seeing fellow soldiers being killed or wounded, seeing unburied decomposing bodies, hearing screams for help from the wounded and helplessly watching the wounded die without the possibility of being rescued. Following combat trauma in Sri Lanka, a number of combatants were diagnosed with PTSD but the majority of these reactions are undetected and untreated.

During the thirty-year war, 23,327 Sri Lankan soldiers and police officers and 1,155 Indian soldiers were killed. According to the LTTE, it lost 27,639 members. As a result of the prolonged conflict, tens of thousands of civilians lost their lives and in the last phase of the war nearly 280,000 people (UNOCHA 2009) were internally displaced.

* The case studies described in this chapter are based on interviews with 824 combatants referred to the psychiatric unit of the Military Hospital, Colombo, between August 2002 and March 2006.

The wounds that they received from war are not confined to the battlefield; they frequently transform their domestic environment as well. Although studies are needed to systematically assess the mental health of members of the armed services, very few studies were conducted during the last thirty years.

The most common mental health issue for soldiers is PTSD and related symptoms of depression, anxiety, inattention, sleeping difficulties, nightmares and survival guilt.

The dedication and the courage of the armed forces cannot be underestimated and Sri Lankan combatants fought one of the longest and deadliest armed conflicts in the world and were able to gain a clear victory. Sri Lanka paid an immense price for this victory. As a result of the three-decade war, many soldiers became physical and psychological casualties. Unfortunately, the society is gradually forgetting the sacrifices made by these people.

Although many see war as a heroic effort, there are thousands of untold traumatic stories from the Eelam war. Some soldiers shared their traumatic stories with us[1] (the author and his colleagues at the psychiatric unit in the Military Hospital, Colombo) and these stories reveal the magnitude of their suffering. They illustrate the true nature of combat trauma in Sri Lanka.

During the 1987 Operation Liberation under the command of the late General Kobbekaduwa, Corporal A faced many battle stresses. He was physically and mentally exhausted. He suffered nightmares, intrusions, hyperarousal and flashbacks. He avoided people and places that reminded of his traumatic experiences and became emotionally numb. In 2003, Corporal A was diagnosed with PTSD. He recalled:

One of our soldiers died in front of my eyes as a result of a booby trap. I can still recall his face, filled with blood. It was a horrific incident. I was terrified by this event. Even after many years, I still see these events in my dreams. To avoid the nightmares I used to take alcohol and go to sleep. I cannot stand any loud noises, I become frightened and my heart starts pounding. Often I try not to think about past events. When I watch television, if I see any combat-related story or pictures, I disconnect myself from it. I hate to talk about past events, especially those related to the war. I have no strength in my body now. My joints are aching. I cannot even walk a mile. Prematurely I have grown old. My mind is full of melancholic feelings. I am unable to feel happiness. For many years, I have never experienced cheerfulness. I am unable to concentrate and I am very forgetful. I have forgotten the names of my fellow soldiers who served with me in the same unit. Sometimes I feel that I have no reason to live. My family members avoid me because of my

---

[1] The author and his colleagues the Psychiatric unit of the Military Hospital, Colombo.

hot temper. I have been turned into an irritable, cold person. Several times, I have thought of disappearing from this world. But according to my religion it is a sin. Therefore, I have resisted the idea of committing suicide.

There is a higher incidence of depression in veterans who had been in combat and had lost a friend. Survival guilt is an especially powerful depression-invoking symptom.

Private K saw his buddy shot in front of his eyes, who fell and lost consciousness. Although Private K wanted to help his friend, he could not reach him due to heavy fire. Eventually when he reached him he was dead. This incident made him very upset. He felt guilty that he could not help his buddy. He often experienced headaches, intrusive thoughts about his dead friend and showed marked depression. He became irritable and was startled at the slightest sound. Private K wanted to avoid military situations. He was referred to the Military Hospital, Colombo, where he was treated with medication and cognitive restructuring. He gained insight and realized he was not responsible for the death of his friend.

Private L was ordered to bury the body of his friend who had died from a sniper's shot. When he touched his friend's body, he could still feel the warmth of the body. He dug a pit and buried his friend's body in the midst of his sorrow. Then they advanced towards Omanthai. After several days, he developed an irrational and guilty feeling that he had buried his friend alive. He suppressed this painful feeling for a long time. Gradually it became a distressing thought that he could not bear anymore. He was treated with rational emotive therapy, during which his irrational and illogical ideas were confronted via a friendly and therapeutic mediation.

Private RS recounted,

I was born in a small village in Polonnaruwa that was often attacked by the LTTE, slaughtering men, women and little children. We had mass funerals after these attacks and most of the villagers felt utterly sad and insecure. At night, we did not sleep in our houses; for security, we slept in the jungle. I did not see a way out of these tremendous problems except joining the military. Due to financial hardship I could not study further and I joined the army. In 1997, I participated in Operation Jayasikuru [Victory Assured] and we were given the task of capturing the Mankulam highway. We fought the enemy face-to-face, with Sergeant L, my senior NCO [non-commissioned officer] behind me. He taught me many combat skills. We always fought the enemy together. He used to cover me and I used to cover him. He was hit by a bullet and bled profusely. I carried him while praying for his life. His breathing became shallow. I could not reach the medics, and half way, he died in my arms. After his death, my conscience blamed me for not saving him. I felt guilty. I was troubled by this guilty feeling and combat-related nightmares and various intrusions. My life came to a standstill. I was filled with sorrow and repulsion for combat. I was disgusted with all these issues and once I wanted to shoot myself and end the suffering. Somebody or some power saved me from self-harm and showed the way towards life. Again, I saw light.

Private RS was found to have PTSD with co-morbid depression. Following intensive treatment, he was able to recover.

Rifleman SN revealed his story:

Operation Yal Devi was my first combat experience. We faced the enemy with courage. I witnessed a lot of traumatic incidents there. Our fellow soldiers died in front of my eyes, leaving us in sorrow. On one occasion, the enemy made a surprise attack, scattering us. I jumped into a pit and waited all night long. It was a dark night. I saw the enemy collecting weapons from our bunkers. I was alone and feared for my life because I knew that the enemy had no mercy. I had seen dead bodies mutilated by the enemy. I had vivid mental pictures of my funeral and I saw my parents crying. The entire night I was praying for my life and by dawn reinforcements rescued me. Although I had no physical injuries, my mind was deeply wounded. Nevertheless, doctors said I was okay. I was sent to the battlefield again but experienced fear and saw the same horrible dream every night. I saw myself trapped in a pit and the enemies were everywhere. My mental health was deteriorating and I decided to go AWOL [absent without leave]. I went home a completely changed person. The innocence of youth and affection towards family members had gone away. They saw me as a frightened, cold soul. My parents thought that some evil spirit had got into my body and they did *thovilaya*, the ancient ritual to chase dark spirits to heal me. But it did not help. My memory was fading and I couldn't sleep. Nightmares ruined my sleep. My family arranged a marriage for me, thinking that it would help me to get away from alienation. My emotions became numbed and I was not interested in marital life. I became more and more hostile and physically abused my wife. Since I couldn't have a sound sleep, I started indulging in alcohol. Practically day and night, I was drinking secretly. But it made me worse. It made me a monster. My wife was afraid of me. When I came home, she would be shivering in fear. When I was angry, I destroyed property in the house. Nothing gave me relief.

Eventually I was treated at the psychotherapeutic unit at the Military Hospital, Colombo. Counselling and medication helped me. Today I am a new man who does not abuse alcohol and I love my family.

Lance Corporal S described his military experience:

At the Weli Oya camp, the enemy attacked us with heavy weapons, killing my fellow soldiers. I saw how they were lying on the ground with bullet or shrapnel wounds. I collected the dead bodies and put them into body bags. I was utterly devastated when collecting human remains.

I had various intrusive images of the battlefield and my dead buddies. I recalled the dead soldiers at Weli Oya, how they were lying on the sand. Some with opened eyes. For many weeks I could not sleep.

I had nightmares and was afraid. I became more irritable and sexually inactive. My body became a source of pain. Every joint in my body started aching. When I experienced an unbearable headache, I could not stand noises. I decided to commit suicide inside the camp. After my unsuccessful suicide attempt, I was treated with medication and psychological support. After months of treatment, my condition improved.

Private R shared his experiences:

My memories are still filled with the events that took place on 24 August 1993. I was guarding a bunker at the Janakapura north camp with two of my buddies, when a group of LTTE cadres attacked our bunker. The enemy came towards us like an unceasing wave. I attacked the enemy with my LMG [light machine gun], killing a dozen of them. One of my buddies was shot and fell down. Suddenly they attacked my bunker with a RPG [rocket-propelled grenade] and the bunker collapsed. A large palmyra log fell on my head and I became semi-conscious. My ears became blocked and I was bleeding from my head. Knowing we would be killed if we stayed there, we came out from the wreck and crawled towards the centre of the camp. In the morning, I was sent to the hospital for treatment.

I still recall how my friend in the bunker fell like a log after being hit by a bullet to the head. We fought while he was gasping and we had no time to pay attention to him. He must have died within a few minutes. These memories hound me at nights. When I am half asleep I see shadows, and I become vigilant. I always get a feeling that the enemy is crawling towards me. I fear that the enemy will attack with an RPG. Then I open my eyes and my heart starts to beat like an accelerated machine. Afterwards, for several hours, I am unable to sleep. Awake at night I think about my friends who died in the battle. Then I feel that it was so unfair that I am alive and they are no more.

Sometimes I see battle events in my dreams. Often when the enemy attacks I am unable to return fire, my gun is jammed. Since I am unable to shoot the enemies, they are approaching me little by little. I can hear their voices scolding us in Tamil, '*Punde army, punde army*'. I become helpless. I hear someone throw a grenade. My fear increases and I shout. Then I realize that it was another nightmare. My family members are now used to my screams at night. My great fear is that when I am sleeping I might harm someone who is near me. Therefore, I often tell my wife and children not to be near me when I am sleeping. My life has changed dramatically and I am not the same person anymore. My emotions are numbed and I cannot cry for my dead friends.

Private UG suffered a blast injury in 1997 near the Thaladi camp. He was wounded and psychologically shattered by the blast. Several months after the injury he complained of severe headaches, insomnia and fear. Gradually he developed PTSD symptoms. Private UG found it difficult to sleep and experienced nightmares related to the blast injury. He experienced fear and always wanted to avoid places and conversations related to the blast injury. The slightest sound made him jumpy. He became irritated and could not control his anger. He often experienced sexual dysfunction and as a result of family turmoil, his wife left him. Owing to family problems and overwhelming anxiety, he tried to commit suicide. When Private UG was referred for psychological therapy, he was treated with CBT and eye movement desensitization and reprocessing (EMDR) which minimized his PTSD symptoms. Today he is able to sleep without nightmares and intrusive thoughts hardly bother him. The final follow-up revealed that his wife had returned and that Private UG was leading a productive life.

Rifleman M said,

> The night of 27 September 1998 was the most terrible of my life. I was at the FDL in the Paranthan area when the LTTE attacked. I was trapped, facing enemy fire. I crawled and found a pit and I hid in there. I heard the enemy's movements and a lot of gunfire. I saw child soldiers moving towards the FDL [forward defence line] with heavy weapons, then LTTE female combatants with AK-47s in their hands. Luckily, no one saw me. I was trapped there for several days. I had no food and my water bottle was empty by the second day. On the third day, I was thirsty and I was compelled to drink my urine. By the fourth day, I had no alternative. I decided to move towards the FDL. Then they recognized me. It was a miracle that I evaded death, lucky to be alive. But this happiness lasted only for a few days. Often the fear and isolation that I experienced inside the ditch bothered me. I could not rest, every moment I was on guard, anticipating an invisible enemy. Days went by and I was still feeling fear that the enemy was behind me, I looked back, and no one was there. I could not concentrate. It was a terrible mess and became an obsessive ritual to look in every direction for the enemy. My head started aching and often I forgot things. At nights, I was practically awake. The slightest sound made my heart ooze with fear. My heart started pounding, giving me aches and pains. I had terrible nightmares. In my dreams, I saw I was trapped in a hole in the ground and surrounded by the enemy. I hated to go to sleep.

Rifleman M was diagnosed with PTSD and treated with medication and psychotherapy. On follow-up he experienced no major PTSD symptoms.

The story of Lance Corporal AS:

> I was happily married but things changed when I became wounded. In 1990, I was at the Thaladi camp, Mannar. There I saw fierce battles. The LTTE attacked us with heavy weapons killing nearly forty soldiers. With utmost difficulty, we were able to defeat the enemy. My heart cried when I saw the dead bodies of our fellow soldiers. We were like one large family. Prior to the attack we used to have meals together and made jokes about odd things. They have gone forever. When I put their bloodstained bodies into the body bags, I cursed the enemy. After this event I became more isolated and had

intrusive memories. There was no one to speak about my anguish. I became alienated. When I came home, my wife often asked what was wrong with me. However, I did not tell her anything. Because it was a pointless effort to tell her my sorrow and she would never understand what happened in the battlefield. Therefore, I silently lived with my grief. But I became more and more irritable.

During these years, I saw many dead soldiers as well as bodies of the LTTE. Some bodies were decomposed or mutilated. I saw large monsters eating dead bodies. The things I have seen confirm to me that there is no glory in war. Once I saw a dead body of a staff sergeant (he was known to me), the enemy had shot his eyes. It was a horrible image to see, a dead body without eyes and instead of the eyeballs, I could see the deep bullet wounds. For many years, that image was deposited in my mind. I even had bad dreams. When I came home, these battle events started roaming around my mind. I wanted to be left alone. But my wife wanted to know what was wrong with me. I was not interested in sex. I was avoiding my wife. She thought I was having an illegitimate affair. I could not stand her accusations. I became depressed and could not tolerate noise. When my children played and shouted, I became extremely angry. I punished them severely. When my wife protested, I used to beat her too. One day I smashed the television and chased everybody out of the house.

My family was suffering with me. When I came home, I used to physically abuse my wife for the slightest argument. She felt uneasy during my presence. Even the children feared me as if I were a monster. Little by little, I was losing my family. When the physical abuse escalated, my wife went to her parents' house with the children. I was all alone and I started abusing alcohol.

My nights became more and more disturbed. I experienced battle events in my dreams and relived painful moments. Sometimes I could hear gunshots, artillery fire and helicopter sounds. I was trapped between reality and illusion. I had a deep loathing when I saw military vehicles and uniforms. I never knew what fear was but now my body shivers even at the sound of a firecracker.

I wanted to end the suffering by shooting myself. I took a weapon to take my life but a senior NCO jumped and grabbed the weapon. Instead of punishing me, they sent me to the Military Hospital. There I was treated and the doctors were kind enough to arrange an open interview with my family. The doctors convinced my wife to come back and finally she agreed. With treatment, I was able to control my anger. My intrusive thoughts and nightmares diminished and gradually I became a productive person. Now for over two years, I have lived with my family and I do not abuse them.

There were many soldiers who lost their voices in the Eelam war, without any organic factors. These soldiers mainly had overwhelming combat stress, which led to their aphonic condition. Lance Corporal W described how he lost his voice:

In 2000, I went to serve in the Pallai camp where the LTTE attacked us with mortars. I was shattered by the sound of this mortar fire. I felt a profound breakdown inside my body. Every time I took cover from incoming mortars, I could feel the shockwave. I saw how our soldiers sustained injuries. I still recall one event in which a soldier succumbed to a mortar blast. His bowels came out and blood splashed all over. It was a cruel and painful death. I was always on guard for incoming mortars. When I heard that 'zooooo...' noise I always took cover. I knew what was going to happen in the next moment. The Pallai experience was a horrendous experience for me. I was not sure of my life and often lived in uncertain situations. I frequently had nightmares. My fellow soldiers did not like me because I used to scream at midnight with fear. Some thought that I was smoking ganja. One night when I was sleeping, I saw an incoming mortar. I cried for help but there was no sound. I became speechless.... Ever since, I could not speak and I lost my voice.

Lance Corporal W was aphonic for several weeks and underwent psychotherapy. He was treated with hypnotherapy and was able to regain his voice.

Private SK admitted,

I was confused and did not know what I was doing. I had walked to the enemy lines. Luckily, a team of special forces saved me. When they found me, I had dropped my weapon and was wandering towards the enemy lines. I don't remember how I left my defence point or where I dropped my T56 [assault rifle]. I was taken to the camp and produced before the Colonel. I was heavily questioned. Later they blamed me for abandoning my post and losing the weapon. I was severely punished for that offence.

Private SK had gone into a psychogenic fugue state following overwhelming battle stress. He could not recall what really took place on that day. He served at Nedunkurni and witnessed the death of four soldiers as a result of an artillery fire. He saw how their bodies had been blown into pieces and instantly he was shocked. After this incident, he gradually became a victim of combat-related PTSD which was undiagnosed and untreated. His symptoms had dissociative features as well. Several times, he went into fugue states and during the final event, he had walked to the enemy lines. After he was rescued Private SK was referred to the psychological treatment centre at the Military Hospital, Colombo. At the centre, he underwent a series of psychological assessments and the cyber testing method was used to elicit autonomic arousal. With the treatment, his mental state improved.

There are a number of prisoners of war (POWs) of the Eelam war who still carry psychological scars.

During Operation Balawegaya, Lance Corporal U sustained a gunshot injury to his leg and became immobile. When the enemy advanced, he could not move and became a prisoner. When he was captured, he was severely beaten and threatened with death. But one of the LTTE's regional leaders stopped the beatings and sent him for medical treatment. When the medical treatment was over, he had to undergo vigorous interrogations. He was tortured to get information about his camp and its inner structure and guard points. He was handcuffed and kept in painful positions for long periods. Frequently his guards physically assaulted and humiliated him. However, Lance Corporal U admits that there were some members who were kind to him and sometimes brought him food. He was kept in a very small cell with forty other prisoners. They had no space to move. The prisoners were allowed to take a bath once in two weeks. Many suffered skin infections. Meals were not served regularly. Following these intolerable conditions, the prisoners launched a hunger strike and eventually he was released through the mediation of the ICRC. Although Lance Corporal U became a free man, he often suffered from an unexplainable fear. The memories of his POW days hounded him severely. Some nights he used to wake up in fear, thinking that he was still in the LTTE prison cell. He was depressed and surrounded by guilty feelings. In order to avoid nightmares, he indulged in alcohol. The more he drank alcohol, the more he became depressed. He often physically abused his spouse. He was suspicious about his surroundings. He lost the ability to trust and feel intimate. He was affected by emotional anaesthesia. He had flashbacks and sometimes he could not distinguish reality from fantasy. His physical strength was weakening and the slightest exertion gave him immense body pain.

Mr N, a civilian, worked as a cook in the Poonari camp. When the LTTE attacked the Poonari camp in 1993, he was captured. He was subjected to considerable physical and mental torture. Eventually the ICRC intervened. For nearly nine-and-a-half years, he was a prisoner under the LTTE. He was homesick and practically every day prayed for his freedom. For a long time he lived with uncertainty, without knowing what his future would be. When the air force attacked the LTTE camps, their guards used to ill-treat the prisoners severely. His condition significantly improved when he met another POW, Captain Boyagoda from the navy. Along with the other POWs, he spent the time discussing their release and writing letters home via the ICRC. After his release, he gradually developed stress-related physical symptoms, like headaches and backaches, which did not respond to painkillers. He was unable to sleep. At nights, he was awake and thinking of the past. He often had melancholic feelings, and was troubled by emotional anaesthesia. He could not feel the happiness of becoming a free man. His emotions were dead. Mr N was losing the will to live. Several times, he planned to commit suicide. He responded however to psychological and drug therapies.

Corporal T was a member of the army's special forces, engaged in a number of military operations. He often worked with the long-range reconnaissance patrols. On one occasion, they had deeply penetrated the enemy area. He was with a five-man team and they operated silently. Suddenly he met two LTTE female combatants face-to-face and none of them fired. Corporal T faced a dilemma; if he had fired his team would have been in great danger. Unbelievably, the two women disappeared into the jungle. He was confused and dazed for a while but was able to return safely. For many years, this incident stuck in his mind. He always questioned himself, 'Why didn't they shoot?' With these intrusive thoughts, he re-experienced combat events that occurred in the north. He was startled by any loud noise and became vigilant all the time.

Private SN, who was shattered by war stress, expressed his experiences in the following manner:

> At Mallakam (1995) the LTTE attacked us with RPGs. I saw my CO [commanding officer] wounded and bleeding heavily. His uniform was soaked with blood. Then another mortar exploded near me. I too sustained injuries. Blood came from my left ear. I had no strength to help my CO. While he was lying on the ground I crawled towards the rear side. I had severe guilt feelings for abandoning him on hostile ground. I could not crawl anymore. I lost my energy. The world was trembling in front of my eyes. I could hear the gunfire, artillery explosions and sounds of the incoming mortar. My eyes were covered with a dark strip. I lost consciousness. When I opened my eyes, I was at the Palali Hospital. I was treated at the hospital for nearly one-and-a-half months. When I was discharged from the hospital, I went back to my unit. I realized that my personality was changing, little by little. I was previously a daring soldier. But the events at Mallakam changed my life. Day and night, my mind was full of these events. Gunfire, black smoke, incoming mortars, images of the enemies and the wounded CO were vivid mental pictures that kept running inside my mind. I became more vigilant. I could not sleep at nights. I used to wake up at the slightest sound. These sounds caused me fear and a burning sensation in my chest. I used to get up in the middle of the night with fear and sweat. Gradually I became depressed and felt that my life was wasted. I wanted to commit suicide. One day when I was at the bunker alone, I tried to release the pin of a hand grenade. Then I saw my wife's eyes. I put the grenade aside.
>
> My world was upside down. I was about to explode. Finally, I told my fears to one of my unit leaders. He listened to me for a long time and said, 'You need medical treatment.' I received drug therapy and psychotherapy. But I have not been completely freed from the Mallakam events. Occasionally I see the face of my CO.

Private H became a victim of an anti-personnel mine in the north and underwent a below-knee amputation. He became shocked when his foot was blown off the ankle, and for a long period of time he relived this traumatic incident. After his injury, his life fell apart. The girl who had promised to marry Private H left him. He could not adjust to life with a prosthetic foot. He became more and more alienated and stopped associating with people. His life was limited to a wheelchair. Once he made an unsuccessful attempt to jump into a pool with his wheelchair. He was given drug therapy, counselling and rehabilitation. He selected handicrafts for a profession—shoemaking—and successfully completed it. A two-year follow-up revealed that Private H was free of PTSD symptoms.

The Elephant Pass debacle that occurred in 2000 due to poor leadership and inefficient strategic evacuation planning led to the loss of many lives. It was a tactical withdrawal of a camp, carried out on a hot sunny afternoon. Many soldiers died of dehydration and heatstroke. During the debacle, 359 military personnel were killed, 349 were listed as missing in action and some 2,500 were injured.

Corporal K described the events that took place on 22 April 2000.

I was at the FDL[2] of the Elephant Pass camp when the enemy attacked the Elephant Pass camp with heavy artillery. While the enemy was attacking, our soldiers withdrew towards Kilalli lagoon. There we met Brigadier Fernando who was a brave officer. He tried to reorganize and launch an attack, to permit a safe withdrawal. We attacked the enemy and moved towards Pallai. The LTTE counter-attacked us with mortars and their snipers targeted our officers and signalmen. I saw Brigadier Fernando sustain a gunshot injury. It was a disastrous moment. Brigadier Fernando did not abandon us. Some cowardly senior officers saved their skin and got away, leaving us to the enemy. But Brigadier Fernando stayed with us and showed leadership until the end. When he fell down, I knew that we were doomed. We were tired and exhausted. Many of our soldiers could not walk. The hot sun and dry wind sapped our energy. I felt thirsty but my water bottle was empty. We were walking like zombies in the hot sand. Some drank salty water from the lagoon. Some began to sing songs as they lost their minds. Many fell down with exhaustion and never got up. While we were moving, the enemy attacked us with mortars. There was no air cover for us. Some fainted in front of my eyes. I knew they would never return home. One soldier became insane. He was singing and dancing, asking for a cup of tea. Wounded soldiers asked us to carry them. But we all were worn out and had no energy to carry a fellow soldier. We were on our own and every man was for himself. My energy was ending. I could not carry the ammunition pack. I had to throw my belongings. Finally, I threw my weapon which had been my saviour for a long time. I was dizzy and fell down. Many soldiers passed me by but no one helped me. I knew if I stayed there, I would be dead soon. I gathered my energy and again started to crawl avoiding enemy

[2] Forward Defence Line.

attacks. Panicked soldiers trampled me and ran towards Pallai. On my way, I saw many dead bodies. One soldier grasped my boots. He was wounded and bleeding. He pleaded with me and those very words still echo in my mind. He said, 'I am dying and I don't want you to carry me.' Then he gave his name and address and asked me to convey his death to his parents. I still cannot forget this incident. By the time I came to Pallai I was unconscious. I too suffered a heatstroke and later recovered. I have forgotten his name and the address. But I still remember his face, filled with utter despair.

Sergeant S served nearly ten years in the operational areas and exposed to heavy combat. He faced a fierce battle while defending the Jaffna Fort. The Jaffna Fort was under siege and the enemy attacked them with heavy weapons. The operation Midnight Express was launched to rescue troops that were trapped inside the fort. During the confrontation, he killed five of the enemy combatants. After some years, he became preoccupied with thoughts related to these killings. Although they came to kill us, they too were human beings, said Sergeant S:

They were poor village boys like us who didn't have many options in life. They were indoctrinated, poisoned with hatred and directed to attack us. We had no alternative except firing at them. In a war, things are intense, either you or the enemy. If you don't kill him, he will kill you. Anyhow, these Tamil youths had parents like us; they too had expectations. All ended sadly. Someone, somewhere may be still missing them. I know killing is bad. It is a violation of the first Buddhist precept. I was compelled to do that act.

Sergeant S feels that one day he has to face the karmic repercussions. His conscience was shattered and he became more religious. Sergeant S wishes to be a monk after his retirement from the army.

Lieutenant Colonel K shared his experiences on the final days of the Eelam war:

When we liberated Thoppigala we knew we were invincible. So we advanced further. The last days of the Eelam war were hectic. The LTTE built large sand walls that were difficult to penetrate. They were among the civilians, making them a human shield. We had to be extra cautious not to harm civilians. However, in a war civilian casualties are inevitable. For instance, how many civilians died in Iraq and in Afghanistan when the US forces retaliated? But I remember several events, when the enemy attacked, our soldiers did not attack back due to the civilian factor. The outside world would never know about these facts. I remember when the enemy fired from a bunker, one of our soldiers tried to attack the bunker with a Tomba gun. Another soldier stopped him saying that there were civilians near the bunker. They had to find other means to destroy the bunker without causing civilian casualties. In another event, I saw soldiers carrying little Tamil children when the civilians broke the sand wall and came towards us. These humane acts were never talked about and only negative points were highlighted. I agree, in a war atrocities are often committed and in every army you see people like William Calley who committed the My Lai massacre. I personally think that the media should comment on atrocities as well as humane acts from the war. Otherwise, there will be no reconciliation at any point. After all, man is not pure evil. I have been living with the war for many years. I have seen perished soldiers, and dead LTTE combatants. All these people were the children of this land. The final days of the war were traumatic. I saw human suffering. I have seen enough blood. Those who cry for war and glorify the war from Colombo should have been there. Then they would know what the war is really like. I felt sorry for the Tamil civilians who followed a mirage. When I first came to the north as a schoolboy at the age of 16, I was touched by the kindness of the Tamil people. The Jaffna people were cultured and educated. They had a great civilization that cherished non-violence. When the conflict erupted in early seventies, things changed drastically. Then I had to come to the north in combat fatigues. Tamil people in the north paid an immense price for the war. Their properties were destroyed, children were forcibly recruited. They faced death and destruction. They lived in poverty. What happened to the millions of dollars that was pumped by the NGOs and by the Tamil diaspora into the North? The people of the Vanni had no infrastructure, people were malnourished. If this money was used to develop the north, they could have built a little Singapore. I am glad that the war is over. We must rebuild the north and work for the ethnic harmony. We must forget our petty racial differences and work for peace with our Tamil brothers. Otherwise, within twenty years there will be another bloody war.

Functional Impairment Following Combat Trauma

Combat can produce long-term consequences involving affective (anxiety, depression, irritability), motivational (low productivity), cognitive (confusion, poor attention and memory), interpersonal (conflicts and withdrawal) and biological (associated with somatic complaints) dimensions, causing maladaptive behaviour.

Difficulties in Parenting

Many of the skills children acquire are fundamentally dependent on their interactions with their parents. Parent–child interactions are crucial in child development, especially self-esteem, academic achievement, cognitive development and behaviour. Traumatized combatants find difficulties while parenting. Many combatants with PTSD are unable to express love since there are troubled by emotional anaesthesia.

Sergeant KP with PTSD described his inability in his role as a father:

Since I became ill, my eight-year-old daughter is detached from me. She is frightened when I have tantrums and quarrel with my wife. Once I broke plates and cups. She started crying and hid under the bed. In the past years, she used to sleep with us, but I wake up for the slightest sound with terror. I have fears that I might harm her when I experience flashbacks of the battlefield. I am unable to express my love for her and my feelings may be dead. I have become a cold father.

Domestic Violence

Family violence is a widespread problem that occurs among combatants with PTSD. They inflict injury, either emotional or physical, upon their spouses. Domestic violence is a form of displacement of anger. Based on our study, out of fifty-six Sri Lankan soldiers with PTSD, thirteen of them frequently physically abused their spouses. Beatings and property damage were commonly seen. Their anger and rage were focused towards their wives. They were irritable and hostile towards family affairs. They had gradually withdrawn from day-to-day activities. There are marked personality changes which affected their functioning as an active member of society as well as in family circles. Often they broke family commitments, both major and minor. They became impulsive, numbed and inhibited. These features destroyed a successful family life and positive parenting. Men with PTSD commonly have sexual dysfunctions. Some males become suspicious and have sexual jealousies. This factor too escalates family violence. Many combatants with PTSD admit that when they have tantrums they over-punish their children. Children often live in fear and despair. The physical abuse takes place inside the family system and rarely do women admit that they were beaten by their husbands. When the children are hospitalized for physical abuse, mothers always conceal the physical beatings in order to evade child protection laws.

Once a soldier with PTSD went in to flashbacks and strangulated his little daughter. The girl was choking when luckily neighbours came and rescued her. In another incident, a father with PTSD became annoyed when his eight-year-old son could not solve mathematical sums and he beat his son with a cricket bat. Later the child was admitted to the hospital and treated for three weeks.

Lance Corporal P served seven years in the combat zone. He sustained a gunshot injury to the right leg. After he came home he could not sleep soundly. He had nightmares with startled reactions. To avoid his sleep-related difficulties and intrusions, he consumed alcohol practically every night. He became depressed and aggressive. He used to physically abuse his spouse and children. Several times he went AWOL. For nearly three years he was undiagnosed and untreated. Subsequently, he was referred to the psychological unit in Military Hospital, Colombo, and diagnosed with combat-related PTSD. After six months of successful medication and psychotherapy, Lance Corporal P was free of his PTSD symptoms. Today he is living a productive family life.

Other combatants convert their rage into more productive activities like social service, religious practices, creative productions, farming, carpentry and other skills, recreation and sports. This helps them, their families and communities.

Occupational Problems

Soldiers with combat stress have occupational problems. Their productivity is weakened. They are detached from co-workers and have dysfunctional interactions at workplaces. Traumatized soldiers develop their own peculiar defences to cope with intrusions and increased psychological arousal. One officer who was diagnosed with PTSD felt uneasy and often manifested startled reactions when soldiers come and halted with a salute. The noise frightened him. Therefore, he used to stay away from others. Another soldier who developed a phobia of uniforms felt uneasy when he went to the camp. The irritability and spontaneous rage make them more socially isolated. They deliberately keep away from people in order to avoid confrontations. They easily get provoked. Some have homicidal tendencies.

Private W, who sustained a gunshot injury to the face in Operation Ranagosa in 1999, became more and more dysfunctional. He had intense rage, suspicion and homicidal ideas. He frequently had conflicts with other soldiers and officers in his unit. In 2002, following a dispute, Private W planned to kill six of his platoon members, including the sergeant. His movements aroused suspicious and he was not issued firearms. Later, Private W was referred for psychological counselling, thus avoiding a major disaster.

Compulsive Exposure

Some traumatized individuals have a compulsive urge to expose themselves to situations reminiscent of their trauma (Van der Kolk et al. 1996). Many Sri Lankan combatants believed to be suffering from combat trauma have joined private security firms, working with politicians and engage in violence during election periods, or join mobs.

Corporal F was psychologically devastated when he witnessed the deaths of three of his platoon members in Silawathura and later developed symptoms of PTSD. He left the military prematurely and joined a local politician. During the infamous Wayamba Provincial Council election in 1999, Corporal F, at the instigation of his political master, engaged in many acts of election-related violence.

Private A experienced numerous traumatic combat events from 1996 to 2001. He went AWOL and joined an underground criminal gang that committed several bank robberies. For several years he evaded the civilian and military police. In 2005, when the criminal gang attempted to rob a bank in Matara district, they were arrested by the police. Today Private A is serving a prison term.

Captain K lost his leg in the northern territory as a result of an anti-personnel landmine called Johnny Batta. He underwent a below-knee amputation and was transferred to a non-combat unit. After serving several years in a non-combat environment, he became distressed and wanted to go to the war front. He had marked post-traumatic features with intense rage. He was affected by severe hyperarousal and traumatic reminiscences. After leaving the army, he joined a private security firm and worked for several years. His occupational difficulties intensified. Once he had a severe conflict with the police and was arrested for assaulting a police officer.

Suicide and Deliberate Self-harm

Studies estimate that patients suffering from PTSD have up to a seven-fold increased incidence of suicide, and four-fold increased risk of death from all external sources (Bullman and Kang 1994). A significant number of soldiers have committed suicide during the Eelam war. In addition, a considerable number of attempted suicides has been recorded. Of 824 combatants referred to the psychiatric unit, Military Hospital, Colombo from August 2002 to March 2005, twenty-two had attempted suicide. These combatants had used various methods such as poisoning, shooting, hanging and in one case a planned road traffic accident.

Sergeant L witnessed a number of traumatic events in the north. He witnessed the death of his platoon members and handled human remains. By 2002, Sergeant L had no life interests. He had an intense death wish. Once he went to the armoury, took a T56, and placed it under his chin. The soldiers who were on duty grabbed the weapon. Subsequently he was referred for psychological therapy. Sergeant L was treated with selective serotonin reuptake inhibitors (SSRI) antidepressants and CBT. After the treatment, he became free of suicidal ideation.

Alcohol and Substance Abuse

Alcohol and substance abuse is an observable condition among combatants, especially those who suffer from combat stress. Among Vietnam veterans seeking treatment for PTSD 60–80 per cent exhibited concurrent diagnoses of drug or alcohol abuse or dependence (Kofoed et al. 1993). These negative coping methods are often used to numb intrusions and negative thoughts, to suppress traumatic war-related memories, escape flashbacks and to achieve sleep free of combat-related nightmares. Alcohol and other substances provide temporary sedation, but in the long term cause enormous damage to the soldier, both physically and psychologically, with significant areas of dysfunction. Chronic alcoholism has serious consequences on a person's health and personal life, on family and friends and on society.

Traditionally, alcohol is part of the military culture. Alcoholic beverages are offered in the officers' messes and sometimes the officers are indirectly encouraged to have alcohol.

When we interviewed fifty-six Sri Lankan combatants with full-blown symptoms of PTSD, we found that 8.9 per cent of them were severely addicted to alcohol. They also had alcohol abuse–related symptoms and their liver functions were seriously affected. They consumed a large amount of alcohol in order to avoid sleep disturbances and eliminate frightening nightmares, to relieve anxiety and block out intrusive memories associated with combat events. But alcohol can disturb the natural sleep process, interrupting REM sleep dream patterns, and the veteran may become more vulnerable to the symptoms of PTSD.

Captain N served in the army for over sixteen years with heavy combat experiences. In an incident near Paranthan, his team was ambushed by the enemy. He saw the death of fellow soldiers and heard their final cries. One soldier was shot in the abdomen and his bowels came out. After they made an unsuccessful attempt to resuscitate him, the soldier died in Captain N's arms. For a number of years he blamed himself for taking his men into the enemy's jaws. He was disturbed over the incident and he increased his alcohol intake in order to sleep better and forget the horrific combat event. He neglected his official duties and senior officers could not trust his capabilities anymore. Several times, he was reprimanded for being drunk during working hours. In 2004, he was diagnosed with harmful use of alcohol.

Tobacco addiction is an unacknowledged factor that has serious health-related consequences. Nicotine produces physical and mood-altering effects and frequent use can increase the risk of numerous health problems. Velde et al. (2002) found that cigarette smoking was more prevalent in those with current PTSD. The researchers hypothesized that in trauma survivors current substance use is associated with peritraumatic patterns of psychological tension-reduction modes.

Lance Corporal R experienced traumatic combat events at Mandativu. He was troubled by the war trauma, becoming more and more isolated and took to smoking. He became a chain smoker and could not be without a cigarette. According to his wife, Lance Corporal R smokes about thirty or forty cigarettes a day.

Warrant Officer A joined the military in 1973 and participated in combat operations until 1999. During this time, he witnessed numerous traumatic events, especially in 1988–89. He smoked over thirty cigarettes a day, which caused serious vascular obstruction in his lower extremities. In 2003, he underwent a below-knee amputation.

Our study (Jayatunge 2005) revealed that cannabis was the most frequent illicit substance used by Sri Lankan combatants.

Corporal W, who was an experienced combatant diagnosed with cannabis intoxication, described how he became addicted to cannabis:

> I was first posted to Nadenkerni. We knew our days were numbered; death was several inches ahead of us. To evade nostalgic feelings and homesickness we smoked ganja. When you take the puff inside, you feel that you are disconnected from reality. No enemy, no bullets, no mortar attacks frighten you. In an attack, you can advance like the wind. You don't feel the heaviness of your backpack, you don't feel pain even when you sustain a gunshot injury.
>
> The supply was a problem. We used to buy the stuff in Colombo. We used several methods to traffic it. The popular method was to put the stuff in to a condom and then insert it inside the anal cavity. When we did bunker duties ganja cigars kept us awake. Thus, we were on guard all night long.
>
> We often used *madana modaka* (an Ayurvedic cannabinoid product) as well. It's like a toffee. When some of our group mates went on operations, they kept it in their wallet. You can run, jump and move your body like a rubber when the effect comes. We feel no pain even we sustain injuries. Some said it delays your ejaculation and we used to take it home when we got duty leave.

After a long use of cannabis, Corporal W had low motivation, aimlessness, apathy and sluggishness in mental and physical responses. He presented with poor self-care and transient disorientation, as well as impaired memory. Today he knows the negative effects of cannabis.

Heroin usage was rare among the Sri Lankan combatants. From 2002 to 2005, we systematically interviewed 824 soldiers and we found only three heroin users. Due to strict rules and regulations soldiers in the army camps find it extremely difficult to obtain and use it. Often they go AWOL to continue their use of heroin.

Effective measures have to be taken to prevent alcohol and substance abuse among the combatants. In the post-war era, there is a real risk. There are many examples from other countries that indicate the excessive use of alcohol and other substances among veterans. According to the 2000 and 2001 National Survey on Drug Use and Health reports[3] on American veterans, an estimated 6 per cent of all veterans had used an illicit drug in the year prior to the survey.

Untreated and Undiagnosed PTSD

As pointed out by Lipkin et al. (1982) many cases of PTSD are under-reported because many primary health workers, general practitioners (GPs), psychiatrists and psychologists fail to ask about military experience or what happened to the person while in the military. We have found a number of combatants who had manifested dissociative reactions in the heat of battle, but were not treated or referred to psychological therapy. When the symptoms aggravated to malignant PTSD they were referred to the psychiatric unit, Military Hospital Colombo.

Corporal T had nightmares, intrusions and disorientation during Operation Jayasikuru in 1997. He became distressed and asked for medical attention. He was taken to the nearest medical dispatch station (MSD) and treated with analgesics. He was sent back to the battlefront. After two weeks he lost his voice, a dissociative reaction of psychogenic aphonia. Still he was not prescribed any kind of treatment. After many months, he became depressed and threatened to commit suicide. Then he was posted to Anuradhapura where there was no active combat, but he had to handle dead bodies and human remains. Only in 2002 was he referred for psychological therapy. By this time, Corporal T had developed chronic PTSD with severe functional impairment.

PTSD and Psychotic Reactions

Some researchers have speculated about the potential links between trauma and psychosis. Ellason and Ross (1997) suggest that psychosis may emerge as a reaction to trauma.

[3] See http://www.oas.samhsa.gov/factsNSDUH.htm (retrieved on 8 October 2013).

Private S was actively involved in combat and on one occasion, he and a small team of soldiers were trapped behind enemy lines for over three days. By 2003, his mental condition was failing and he experienced feelings of passivity, ideas of reference, thought broadcasting, thought insertion and disorganized thinking patterns. He was diagnosed with schizophrenia at the North Colombo Teaching Hospital, but on reassessment he was found to have key symptoms of PTSD such as hyper vigilance, avoidance and nightmares.

Recruit S developed an abnormal reaction after being wounded by a mortar blast injury) to the left shoulder. His flashbacks were wrongly interpreted as visual hallucinations and distress reaction as manic features. After a detailed assessment, this soldier was diagnosed as having PTSD.

Delayed Reactions of PTSD

Currently the definition of delayed-onset PTSD encompasses symptoms that surface only up to six months following an event. Sometimes PTSD can emerge many years after the original trauma. According to Ruzich et al. (2005), large numbers of older veterans present with nightmares and intrusive memories of the war. For some Second World War veterans, memories of the war can still be upsetting more than fifty years later.

Late-onset trauma plagues war veterans in a devastating manner. The delayed reaction could be triggered by a subsequent stressful event. In a study of 147 Dutch veterans who had fought in the Resistance against the Nazis in Second World War, it was found that over half of them were still suffering from PTSD and only 4 per cent showed no symptoms at all (Hovens et al. 1992). New Yorkers exposed to 9/11 who had pre-existing emotional or social problems were found to develop PTSD two years after the event (Boscarino and Adams 2009).

Some Sri Lankan veterans too have shown delayed-onset PTSD reactions. They manifested post-traumatic features many years after the original trauma.

Sergeant T was an experienced combatant who participated in numerous combat operations in the north. During the 1988–89 insurgency, his platoon was deployed in the southern part of Sri Lanka to fight the left-wing Sinhala rebels who launched attacks against the government. In 1989, Sergeant T and his group arrested some of the suspects and eliminated them. Sergeant T tortured one of the suspects who was believed to have masterminded an attack on soldiers. He shot the suspect, poured petrol while the victim was alive, then set him on fire. When the victim was on fire, he made an unsuccessful attempt to grab Sergeant T. Sergeant T narrowly escaped the fire and he became shocked and terrified. Then he aimed his firearm towards the blazing man and fired several shots. The suspect died instantly. After a few weeks, he completely forgot the incident.

In 2002, thirteen years after this incident one night Sergeant T's wife tried to light the kerosene lamp while they were having dinner. Then she accidentally dropped it and the lamp exploded, the fire spreading to her clothes. Immediately Sergeant T poured water on his wife and extinguished the fire. She was unharmed. But Sergeant T was utterly devastated. When he saw his wife on fire, the 1989 incident came into his mind immediately. Instead of his wife, he saw the JVP suspect who tried to grab him a moment before death. From that night on, he had nightmares of the original incident and continuous intrusive memories. Sergeant T startled easily and he gradually turned into a different person. He became depressed and started abusing alcohol. He lost interest in his life. Once he planned to commit suicide. He went to the railway station and walked along the railway track. When the train was a few metres away, he changed his mind and jumped off.

Sergeant T was diagnosed with PTSD in late 2002 and treated with medication and psychotherapy. By 2003, he was free of most of the PTSD symptoms.

Lieutenant Colonel X participated in the Operation Balawegaya in 1991 and faced heavy fire by the enemy. In front of his eyes, several soldiers died by sniper fire. He sustained a gunshot injury to the leg and thought he would die. While lying on the battlefield his thoughts turned to his home, parents, wife and children. He was bleeding profusely and the other combatants made a great effort to evacuate him immediately. He was transferred to Palali hospital and then airlifted to Colombo.

It took the doctors a massive effort to save his leg. He recovered from his physical injuries soon and went back to his unit. In 2003, he suffered deep-vein thrombosis and experienced unbearable pain. While he was in physical pain he had flashbacks of the 1991 Operation Balawegaya events, how he sustained a gunshot injury, how he was lying on the ground, he even saw the late General Kobbekaduwa in his flashbacks. He became restless and had a dissociative attack. After he was treated for the deep-vein thrombosis, his pain subsided, but he was hounded by the battle events. He experienced intrusive memories, flashbacks and startled reactions. His sleeping pattern changed and in order to avoid nightmares he started to work until late in the night. He became a workaholic to evade disturbing ruminations. After sometime, he was physically and mentally exhausted. His system could not cope any more. Then he had a second dissociative attack, which manifested as an aggressive fearful reaction. He was treated with medication and relaxation therapy for a long time and gradually his post-traumatic symptoms subsided.

War Widows

One harsh reality of war is that the every soldier killed in war leaves behind a grieving family and relatives. The women who were left widows as a result of the Sri Lankan conflict are facing radically altered circumstances. There are thousands of war widows and war-affected families of the armed forces who still experience grief reactions. Many widows are in the age group of twenty-two to thirty-five years; with the death of their husbands these women have become a psychologically and socially vulnerable group. Most of the women who underwent severe emotional pain still have not completely recovered. Many have become the victims of prolonged grief. They are unable to work through their grief despite the passage of time. With widowhood, they experience identity change, role adjustment and change in social status. Prolonged grief is associated with other psychiatric disorders like clinically distinct PTSD, generalized anxiety disorder, major depressive disorder as well as suicidal ideation (Gray et al. 2004; Silverman et al. 2000). Many researchers concur that the mental trauma of the war widows can last for long years. In 2005, eighty-six Sri Lankan war widows were clinically interviewed based on the Beck's depression scale and depression was diagnosed in twenty-three of them (27 per cent). Ten war widows said that they had contemplated suicide after they lost their husbands (12 per cent) (Jayatunge 2005).

In conservative Asian societies, widows face social, economic and legal handicaps. Widowhood is associated with sociocultural stigma and humiliation. Widows are considered bad omens in many Sri Lankan rural areas. They are marginalized by their own communities. These factors affect their self-esteem. In some events, they were accused by their in-laws of causing their husbands' deaths because they were 'unlucky'. They experience lack of social support in their own family circles. They are often subjected to extreme forms of discrimination and physical, sexual and mental abuse. Therefore, widowhood represents a form of 'social death' for these women. Their plight and vulnerability lead to numerous psychological ailments.

Common symptoms include intrusive memories about their dead husbands, fear and uncertainty about the future, self-pity, low self-esteem, sleep disturbances, irritability, displacement of anger, emotional numbing, feelings of guilt and psychosomatic complaints like persistent headaches and backaches which do not have any medical basis and do not respond to painkillers. Young war widows, who have suppressed their biological needs following cultural pressure and family honour, often manifest conversion reactions.

The following is the experience of a war widow whose husband died in Operation Jayasikuru in 1997.

When I heard of the death of my husband, my entire world collapsed. He was a lance corporal in the army and we were living in his house with his mother and two unmarried sisters. I still have a fragmented memory of the funeral. Some events I cannot remember. My three-year-old daughter who had no clue about her father's death asked various questions. I did not know what would happen to my daughter and me after my husband's death. After several months, my mother-in-law and husband's two sisters started passing negative comments. They blamed me for his death. They implied that I was unlucky and since I came to their house, things changed negatively. Even the neighbours avoided me. I had to go to Panagoda army pension branch to get my dead husbands' pension. I asked my cousin brother to help me with the paper work. My mother-in-law accused me of seeing men soon after my husband's death. She humiliated me and demanded the full pension saying that I had no financial rights. I had no place to go as my parents had died. I had no other option but to live with my husband's relatives, facing humiliation every day. When I received my husband's pension, my mother-in-law took it. We were given only food. Every month I have to go to the *Grama Niladari* to confirm that I am still a widow and had not remarried. When I once went to get his signature on the document he used to pass inappropriate jokes and once tried to touch my hand. I scolded him and left the office. Ever since, he has delayed signing my papers. I am depressed and when my daughter goes to sleep, I cry alone. If not for her, I would have committed suicide, ending this suffering. My mind is preoccupied with the events of my husband's funeral. I have mental pictures of the coffin, his dead body, ceremonial uniform and many more things. Constantly I have feelings of fear and uncertainty about the future. My memory has started fading and I cannot concentrate. Gradually I have become the living dead.

Mrs A had this story:

When my husband went missing in action, I was thirty years old. We had been married for seven months. I waited for him for many years but he did not return. Every day was a painful anticipatory day for me. I went to many army camps, to the ICRC and even went to the north during the ceasefire in search of my husband. There was no news about him. My relatives urged me to marry again but I refused. I still cannot believe that he is dead. I hope one day he will come back.

Mrs H faced severe hardship with the death of her husband who was a full corporal in the army. She was driven out of home by her husband's family who accused her of being unlucky. She was living in a small house with her four-year-old son. Her neighbour — a middle-aged man — tried to help her, but he had motives in his mind that were not entirely altruistic. When his intentions were revealed, Mrs H stopped speaking to him and avoided him. Then he started spreading malicious rumours about her in the village. The villagers, especially the women, humiliated her publicly.

Some nights, stones were thrown at her house. When the trouble intensified, she decided to leave the village, but she had no place to go.

The conflict in Sri Lanka has generated a large number of war widows in the north and east. Widows in provinces in the north and east totalled some eighty-nine thousand in 2010 (*IRIN* 2010). Many women are living in abject poverty and despair. Many women are faced with the main responsibility for caregiving in the family, with the destiny of their husbands unknown and new and unfamiliar duties placed on them. If the household is facing hardships, this may overload women's capacity to cope, as preoccupation with the needs of the family may lead to neglecting their own needs, especially if they become widows.

The late Air Chief Marshal Goonetilleke conducted a valuable psychosocial assisting project for the war widows of Sri Lanka under the Ranaviru Family Counselling Association. This project helped the war widows reconstruct their lives and gain confidence. He believed that there should be a permanent rehabilitation policy for war widows at the national level. Until his death in 2008, he was actively engaged in the rehabilitation of Sri Lankan war widows.

Mrs K was able to face her destiny with courage and determination:

When I heard the terrible news of my husband's death in the war front, I was utterly devastated. For many months, I could not believe that he would never come back. Somehow, I had to gather strength for the sake of my two little children. I knew that being a widow in a deeply conservative society is not easy. But I had no alternative and with courage I faced the consequences. Ranaviru Family Counselling Association offered me strength and guidance. At the meetings, I saw women like me who were struggling to survive. I learned new skills and started to work in an income-generating project. While working and attending to my children's needs, my emotional trauma was reduced. But the deep sorrow was always with me. I had to be the sole breadwinner of the family; I had to be responsible for my children. I was determined to live a life with dignity. During the ceasefire in 2002, a group of war widows from the north visited us. Their husbands were LTTE combatants who died in the battle. When I saw them, I had angry feelings. I thought for a while one of the husbands of these women had probably killed my husband. My heart stated beating rapidly. I saw they were looking at us. Simultaneously I thought they might be having the same feelings about us. That moment I realized that anger and hatred offer nothing but destruction. My anger dropped to zero level. We welcomed them, women from the opposite side but who share the same grief as us. We all are victims of the war no matter the racial differences. After all, our tears and suffering had no ethnic difference. We spoke with these women and exchanged ideas. Soon we became friends. We cried together for the memories of our dead husbands who left us so unexpectedly. At the end of the day, we parted like sisters. Some of these women still write to me and we are good friends.

Mrs G lost her sense of purpose in life when she underwent a pathological grief reaction following her husband's death in 2001 during the Operation Agni Kheela. She was extremely focused on the loss and became upset when anything reminded her of her husband. She had problems accepting the death, was preoccupied with sorrow, unable to enjoy and move on with life, had trouble carrying out normal routines and was withdrawn from social activities. She was treated with medication and EMDR, which gave optimal results. Today Mrs G is facing her life rationally. She is self-employed and building a house for herself and her children.

Tribe and de Silva (1999) highlight the importance of integrating coping strategies, and self-help principles, and changing perceptions, attitudes and stereotyped beliefs, when improving mental health issues of the Sri Lankan women who were widowed following extreme traumatic events. As they recommend, cultural and sociopolitical issues should be taken into consideration.

Welfare and rehabilitation of widows is essential, along with teaching coping strategies, and facilitating education and job training for the socially shunned widows. These measures are needed to help women transform their skills into financial independence and sustainability. At the same time as strengthening women's existing skills, new skills should be introduced in traditional and non-traditional fields. There must be a permanent rehabilitation policy for war widows at the national level that helps widows build a new life, regain confidence and gently adjust to a new life. The children of these war widows should have a secure and dignified future as their fathers always desired. It is the duty of the nation to pay their dues to these families who have become the invisible victims of the Eelam war.

Children Affected by the Eelam War

UNICEF estimates that over 90 per cent of the victims of modern warfare are women and children (Machel 1996). Children who are a vulnerable group, have suffered severe traumatic events during the Eelam war. Worldwide studies indicate that children in war zones undergo severe psychological trauma. Research in Gaza, Rwanda, Mozambique and Cambodia reveals that children who are exposed to war and atrocities are at a high risk of developing PTSD. Thabet and Vostanis's (2000) study of Palestinian children who experienced war trauma found that 72.8 per cent reported PTSD reactions of at least mild intensity, while 41 per cent reported moderate/severe PTSD reactions.

Organized and institutionalized violence like war can affect children in many ways. K was nine years old when she became a victim of a crossfire between the armed forces and Tamil militants in the north. She sustained a gunshot injury to her left arm. She underwent a traumatic amputation of the left hand. After the operation she was taken to an orphanage in Mulangavil in the Killinochchi district. She has feelings of fear, night terrors, bed-wetting, hyperarousal and alienation. Traumatized children from the war zone like K carry the psychological scars throughout their lives.

Children who have experienced or been exposed to war trauma often have anxieties and insecurities that can cause them to perceive every aspect of the world as being unsafe and frightening. They grow up with a genera feeling of fear and hostility which affects their future lives. S was twelve years old when the 1983 communal riots erupted. The attackers burnt his house while S and his sister were hiding under a bed in their Sinhalese neighbour's house. He could hear the shouting of the mob and the screaming of the victims. S had feelings of fear and he thought that the mob would kill him. These fears lasted for many years as he grew older. The following day, their neighbour, with the help of the police, took them to the refugee camp at Bambalapitiya Kadirashan Kovil. Before going to the camp S took a quick glance at their house; it was completely destroyed by the fire. After spending several months in the refugee camp, his father managed to get asylum in West Germany. For many years S had nostalgic feelings and also feared that a group of people would come and attack him unexpectedly.

After coming to West Germany S underwent a prolonged cultural shock and frequently felt a misfit in Western society. He became more isolated and neglected his studies. As a teenager he became more and more hostile and frequently had conflicts with his parents. After spending twelve years in West Germany, S moved to Canada and got married. But he always felt the empty space and became emotionally numb. On some occasions, he could not control his temper and engaged in acts of domestic violence. One such violent outburst resulted in an injury to his wife and S was charged by the Canadian authorities. Today he is serving a prison term.

As Osofsky (1995) indicates, the differential responses to trauma depend, in part, on the child's age and level of psychological maturity. Some suffer from fears and terrifying memories immediately after the event, which dissolve with time and emotional support. Other children are more severely affected by trauma and experience long-term problems. Children of the war zone may exhibit regressive behaviour such as bed-wetting, thumb sucking or fear of the dark. They may have increased difficulty in separating from their parents. Also they can have attention problems and learning difficulties at school. Many of these affected children can have somatic complaints, irrational fears, sleep problems, nightmares, irritability and angry outbursts. They may appear to be depressed and more withdrawn. Adolescent (from ages twelve to eighteen) responses are more similar to those of adults and they are at increased risk for problems of substance abuse, peer problems and depression.

Child soldiers are exposed to events beyond the normal boundaries of human experiences. This is a story of a child soldier:

SE was eleven years old when he was forcefully recruited by the LTTE. During the training period he was beaten and threatened that he would be killed if he did not obey orders. Once he saw the killing of a rival member by the LTTE. Along with other children he had to take part in a number of attacks against the Sri Lankan army. Called the Baby Brigade, they were a support team for the adult fighters. They never had the opportunity to go to school once they became child soldiers. Instead of books they carried AK-47 rifles and grenades. Their childhood was stolen.

SE witnessed a number of horrific events which changed his psychological make-up drastically. He was forced to observe torture, then forced to practise it on victims. Today SE is in a rehabilitation centre but his horrendous psychological scars have not left him completely. He has intense rage, suicidal urges and alienation. Once a bright and innocent student, he has now become a victim of the Eelam war.

P was terrified when air attacks took place in Jaffna. During this attack his neighbours' house was destroyed and some of them were critically injured. P becomes anxious when he hears aircraft sounds. He has startled reactions, intrusive memories of the air attacks and sometimes nightmares.

Children's well-being and development depend very much on the security of family relationships and a predictable environment. L was thirteen when the LTTE attacked her village in the North Central Province of Sri Lanka. The attackers shot the adults and killed the children and women with knives. She was lucky to be alive. When the village was attacked she managed to escape with her uncle. But her parents and younger brother were killed. L could not continue her education after the tragedy. She became more depressed and had constant feelings of being threatened, nightmares of the attack and psychosomatic ailments.

During the Eelam war some Sinhalese and Tamil children witnessed the deaths of their parents or other family members. These children have undergone severe grief and some have developed pathological grief reactions. Obviously the majority of them have not received adequate treatment and rehabilitation; they will become adults with unhealed trauma. Their trauma will be projected on to society and a vicious cycle will ensue.

D (aged ten) was a bright student who suddenly showed learning difficulties and behavioural problems when his father died in the Rivirasa operation. He became aggressive and started bed-wetting. He lost interest in social activities and showed positive features of the paternal deprivation syndrome. He was not a happy child after his father's death.

Living with a father affected by combat trauma is another predicament faced by some children. B was an eight-year-old boy who was beaten by his father, an ex-combatant, in a sudden fit of rage. The boy was hospitalized and received treatment for his physical injuries.

M (aged fifteen) and L (aged twelve) are sister and brother, from the same family. They often had to spend nights at a neighbour's house when their father became aggressive and had tantrums. He was a combatant, suffering from PTSD. When he experienced combat-related flashbacks, he became extremely violent. Their mother left the house following continuous physical aggression by their father.

The Eelam war caused displacements of civilians at large. Many are still living in refugee camps.

M (aged nine) and his family had to flee from his village with the other neighbours when the LTTE ordered Muslims to leave the north. Their family came to Puttalam and lived in a small hut without basic facilities in Alankuda, Kalpitiya. M became isolated and showed features of anxiety and depression. He was nostalgic for his native village in Mannar. His education was disrupted and today M works as a driver of a three-wheeled vehicle in Puttalam town. M feels like an alien in Kalpitiya. He is addicted to cannabis and has no long-term life plans.

During the Eelam war, the LTTE launched a number of suicide bombings, sometimes targeting civilians. N (aged fifteen) was a psychological victim of the dreadful Central Bank bombing by the LTTE. When the blast occurred they were in a car. They sustained minor injuries, but L was psychologically shattered. He had feelings of fear, startled reactions, intrusive memories and nightmares for nearly a year.

Time does not heal all trauma. Therefore, active measures are needed. Social support should be given to the children who were exposed to war trauma. Children's resiliency to traumatic events is influenced by the degree of social support and positive community influences (Garbarino and Kostelny 1996). Parental support is highly essential to heal the emotional scars experienced by war zone children. As experts point out, children with adequate family cohesion manifest less stress in reacting to trauma and are better able to recover from the initial impact of the trauma.

Cultural factors and traditional healing systems play a vital role. Community ideology, beliefs and value systems contribute to resilience by giving meaning to traumatic events, allowing children to identify with cultural values, and enabling children and adults to function under extreme conditions (Melville and Lykes 1992). In treating war zone children family therapy, group therapy, CBT, art therapy, music therapy, EMDR and school and community interventions have been used. Coping skills are also beneficial.

War trauma in Sri Lanka has created a critical situation. A large number of children have been affected by the prolonged armed conflict in Sri Lanka. This has become one of the crucial problems that will affect our future, considering that significant numbers of our next generation are traumatized and unhealed. There are also Sri Lankan communities who have migrated or fled abroad to escape the war situation back home who suffer from mental health and psychosocial problems.

B.

Collective Trauma in the Tamil Community in London*

By *Andrew Keefe*

Introduction

The Tamil community in London is extensive and well established, the legacy of successive waves of migration since the 1940s. There are estimated to be almost one hundred thousand Tamils in London (Majumdar 2007), including refugees who settled in the United Kingdom to escape earlier phases of conflict in Sri Lanka. Between 1 January 2005 and 31 March 2009, the period leading up to the breakdown of the 2002 ceasefire and the subsequent two years of fighting between the Sri Lankan army and the LTTE, there were 3,605 applications for asylum from Sri Lankan nationals in the United Kingdom (UKBA 2010). There were 396 applications in 2005 and 500 in 2006, the two years before the breakdown of the ceasefire. In 2007, the first year of the renewed fighting, there were 875 and in 2008, 1,470.

* The assessments and treatment of the clients discussed in this chapter were carried out by the BRC's specialist team, including Hermela Chassme, Alanna Maycock, Elena Hage, Alan Javid and Anne Abeja Akaki. Two other members of the team also worked on the project but declined to be mentioned in this chapter. I am indebted to Elena Hage for her observations concerning the significance of cigarette burns. I was the operations manager for the service at the time of the study and provided psychodynamic counselling to some of the clients.

The ongoing casework with the Tamil women who had been raped or exposed to sexual violence was funded by the Comic Relief charity in the United Kingdom, as part of the BRC Vulnerable Women's Project between December 2006 and December 2009. The specialist team staff were ably assisted by a group of Tamil-speaking interpreters (all of them of Tamil origin themselves), but who have declined to be named in this study.

Of this group of 3,605 applications, 38 per cent (1,364) presented to the British Refugee Council (BRC) in Brixton, South London, for assistance and passed through the one-day induction process (ODIP). ODIP is a service funded by the United Kingdom Border Agency (UKBA), which assists newly arrived asylum seekers who have accommodation in London to apply to the UKBA for financial assistance and receive an orientation briefing covering life in the United Kingdom, the asylum process and their rights and entitlements. The United Kingdom's Department of Health, together with the UKBA, funded a health screening process as part of the ODIP contract, operated by the BRC's specialist health team and known as 'ODIP Health'.

All of the group either described themselves as Tamils or asked for Tamil-speaking interpreters, leading us to consider them as Tamils, rather than as Sri Lankans of Sinhala origin. Four hundred and fifty one (33.06 per cent) of the clients presenting to the BRC were referred to the specialist health team and underwent a holistic assessment of their physical, emotional and psychological health, social and family circumstances and history of trauma, where indicated. Of these 451 clients, 55 per cent were male and 45 per cent female. Service users ranged in age from their late teens to late fifties, though the majority were in their twenties and thirties. Through the assessment interviews, we gathered detailed information about the nature of the torture and violence inflicted upon them (as reported by service users themselves) by both Sri Lankan security forces and, to a lesser extent, the LTTE and Karuna (these were the two groups named by service users).

The information provides an opportunity to study the nature of the violence inflicted on a significant percentage of the Tamil asylum seekers arriving in the United Kingdom during the period. As noted, service users passing through the ODIP programme were staying in London with a friend or relative and have in many cases, commented on this experience. The impact on the broader Tamil community of the arrival of 3,605 compatriots direct from the fighting and oppression which they reported in Sri Lanka could also therefore be considered.

Can We Believe What We Hear?

It was difficult to obtain independent corroboration of the reports of violence and persecution we heard. However, it was explained to clients that ODIP Health was a health screening and access service and was not connected with the decision-making process on clients' applications for asylum. BRC is an independent charity and our service is completely confidential, so we do not share information with UKBA officials. The charity does, however, receive funding from UKBA and the Department of Health and is recognized by the British government for its objectivity and impartiality. Clients wishing to obtain medico-legal reports were advised to request their legal representative commission for a report from a medical practitioner. There is little to be gained by exaggerating or fabricating claims of torture in ODIP Health assessments. As noted below, staff were able to observe physical injuries, scars, bullet wounds, burns and clients' distress during assessment interviews.

A range of reports of human rights abuses and torture by independent international bodies (AI 2009; Doney 1998; HRW 2008, 2009a) lend further credence to their accounts (see also Chapter 1B).

Trauma and Collective Trauma

Papadopoulos (2002: 27) notes that the literature on trauma is 'enormous and the debates endless'. This chapter is not an attempt to add to these debates (about the existence or applicability of PTSD for instance) but offers an explanation of the concepts employed by the team to make sense of the experiences described by service users.

We do not find it helpful to use PTSD to describe the condition of the clients we assess, partly because it is a medical diagnosis and we are not a medical team (team members are from counselling, psychotherapy and community health backgrounds). Also because the descriptions of the causes of their distress that clients give us often include the stress of negotiating the United Kingdom's asylum system, as well as the after-effects of violent incidents. Nonetheless, as can be seen from Table 4B.5, many clients do report nightmares, flashbacks and sleep disturbance, symptoms considered part of the criteria for PTSD as described in the DSM-IV. They describe being deeply shaken and terrified by violent experiences such as torture and rape, memories of which constantly intrude upon them and we need a language to understand and seek to reduce this distress.

There is a tendency in contemporary discourse on trauma to use the term to describe both events and their impact. The original psychoanalytic discourse distinguished between the word *trauma* meaning 'any totally unexpected experience which the subject is unable to assimilate' (Ryecroft 1995: 187) and *traumatic neurosis* or symptoms developing after a 'shocking' experience which included 'either stereotyped actions or spells in which parts of the traumatic experience are repeated and/or stereotyped dreams repeating the experience' (Ryecroft 1995: 189). We now prefer 'traumatic experience' to describe the event or events and 'trauma-related distress' to describe the service users' feelings and condition in response to the event.

Somasundaram (1998: 152) observes that the closeness and 'cohesiveness' of their society leads Tamil families to respond to threat or trauma as a *unit* rather than as individuals. 'Traumatisation due to war' (1998: 154) is widespread and has become a 'part of normal life' making it 'more appropriate to talk of *collective trauma*' (1998: 154). We, therefore, consider that for a community to be *collectively* traumatized by a series of events, for the whole community or a large percentage thereof to have been shaken and affected and to be left struggling with the memories of the events, two factors must necessarily be present: First, that violent, trauma-inducing experiences must have directly affected a sufficiently large percentage of the population. And second, that circumstances exist for sufficient numbers of the population not directly affected by the incidents to be indirectly or vicariously traumatized for the trauma to pass through and into relationships.

The following section examines the evidence gathered to consider whether these two factors can be regarded as currently present within the Tamil community in London.

Detention, Torture, Rape and Violence

Abuses by Sri Lankan Security Services

Of the clients we assessed, 36 per cent (162) disclosed they had been tortured in detention. Forty-four clients had been detained and tortured on more than one occasion. One hundred of the two hundred and four women interviewed (49 per cent) disclosed they had been raped and twenty-one that they had been sexually assaulted. Twenty five per cent of the women who had been raped became pregnant as a result. Three women had already had terminations at the time of assessment and one had given birth. Eleven men disclosed that they had been raped while in detention by the security services and thirteen said they had been sexually assaulted. An earlier study by Peel et al. (2000) also found evidence of sexual assault against Tamil men.

Twenty-three clients stated they had relatives who had been killed by government forces, sixteen had relatives in detention and twelve relatives who had been 'disappeared'. Eighteen clients described being assaulted outside of detention. Other clients described being forced to watch other prisoners being tortured, being caught up in bombardments, shot, witnessing violent events or seeing dead or seriously wounded bodies. Twenty clients had lost contact completely with their families in Sri Lanka and eleven had made the difficult decision to leave children behind when they escaped.

Abuses by the LTTE

Although on a much smaller scale, some clients did disclose being subjected to human rights abuses by LTTE members: seven stated they had been detained and tortured by the LTTE, four had relatives killed and four had received death threats. Five clients had been forcibly conscripted and forced to fight by the LTTE and six had left Sri Lanka as they were being pursued by the group.

Seven clients told us they were caught between the army and the LTTE and had been abused by both forces, who accused them of collaboration with 'the other side'.

Table 4B.1 gives a full breakdown of the disturbing life events described by the clients assessed.

Table 4B.1:
Clients Affected by Abuse by the State, LTTE or Other Sources

	Number	*Percentage*
State		
Multiple Detentions with Torture	44	9.75
Detention and Torture	162	35.92
Detention without Torture	5	1.10
Detained with Family	2	0.44
Detained with Baby	1	0.22
Paid Bribe to Escape	23	5.09
Violence by State Forces	18	3.99
Rape by State (Women)	100	49.50 (of women clients)
Rape by State (Men)	11	4.43 (of male clients)
Pregnant after Rape	25	25 (of women who were raped)
Termination of Pregnancy	3	12 (of women pregnant after rape)
Child after Rape	1	4 (of women pregnant after rape)
Sexual Assault by State (Women)	21	10
Sexual Assault by State (Men)	13	7.5
Attempt or Threat of Sexual Assault	6	1.33
Relative Killed	23	5.09

(Table 4B.1 Contd.)

(Table 4B.1 Contd.)

	Number	Percentage
Relative Disappeared	12	2.66
Relative in Detention	16	3.54
Lost Contact with Family	20	4.43
Left Children Behind	11	2.43
Death Threats by State	1	0.22
Witnessing Violent Events	10	2.21
Forced to Watch Torture	2	0.44
Exposure to Dead or Serious Wounds	3	0.66
Exposure to Bombardment	6	1.33
Shot	9	1.99
Internal displacement	1	0.22
LTTE		
Detention and Torture	7	1.55
Detention without Torture	2	0.44
Violence	5	1.10
Death Threats	4	0.88
Caught between Army and LTTE	7	1.55
Forced Conscription	5	1.10
On the Run from LTTE	6	1.33
Relative Killed by LTTE	4	0.88
Natural Disaster		
Affected by Tsunami	3	0.66
United Kingdom		
Assault	1	0.22
Immigration Detention	13	2.88
Denied Access to Healthcare	8	1.77

Source: Materials related to BRC staff during ODIP Health assessments.

Methods of Torture: Pain and Humiliation

For the purpose of the study we used the definition of the United Nations Convention against Torture and Other Cruel, Inhuman or Degrading Treatment or Punishment (UN 1984). Tables 4B.2–4B.4 list the techniques

Table 4B.2:
Torture Methods Used by Sri Lankan Security Forces

1. *Beaten:* with rifle butt; round head on body; on soles of feet; on soles of feet with spiked stick; on legs below the knee; unconscious with plastic bag on head; with stick with hard ball on the end; on hand with hammer; with plastic pipe filled with sand; with cricket bat.

2. *Burnt:* with hot iron rods, front and back; on feet; on back with hands and feet tied together; with cigarette.

3. *Chemicals:* cloth soaked in chemical substance stuffed in face; exposed to; burnt with on face; sprayed on face; burnt by liquid on skin; plastic bag soaked in petrol put over head, tied at neck; injected with drugs.

4. *Blindfolded:* then exposed to sun, eyes forced open; blindfolded, so unsure of what torture being performed.

5. *Other:* interrogated with gun to head.

6. *Bones broken or crushed:* arm broken, leg broken; two men placed iron bar on legs, then stood on it.

7. *Suspended:* hung upside down for long periods; 'Palestinian hanging' rope dropped by guards, crashing to floor.

8. *Stabbed:* slashed with knife; in back with spiked iron bar.

9. *Kicked:* in head; in eyes.

10. *Forced to watch:* other detainees being killed.

11. *Chilli:* powder placed in orifices; head forced into bucket of water with chilli powder; head forced into plastic bag with chilli powder; forced to breathe fumes of burning chillies.

12. *Water:* head forced into bucket of water for long periods; water forced into nose; hosed with freezing water; placed in water tank, piece of wood with nails placed on head to prevent rising out of water; placed in water tank, head just above water, stomach stamped on; submerged in water tank; forced to lie on ice blocks for fifteen minutes at a time; salt water thrown on bleeding wounds.

13. *Stamped:* on fingers with boots.

14. *Sleep deprivation:* for three days.

15. *Conditions of detention:* solitary confinement; kept in room with forty other men, chains on wrists and ankles; kept in dark room; prevented from using the toilet; deprived of food; only given sewage water to drink.

16. *Insertions:* pen pushed into ear; nails hammered through feet; drawing pins stuck all over body.

17. *Whipped:* whipped with barbed wire.

18. *Eyes:* hot light held in front of face in dark room.

19. *Electric shocks:* given electric shocks.

20. *Restricted movement:* tied to pole; suspended from ceiling; suspended from ceiling, head in a tank of water and whipped; suspended from ceiling; knees and elbows twisted.

21. *Mock execution:* beaten unconscious, woke up in makeshift grave.

22. *Head and/or hair:* dragged by hair until unconscious; dragged by hair; head beaten against wall repeatedly.

23. *Toes:* crushed with rifle butt.

24. *Forced to eat and/or drink:* unknown liquid; alcohol until sick; to eat rotten food.

Source: Materials related to BRC staff during ODIP Health assessments.

used by the Sri Lankan security services to inflict pain, humiliation and terror, according to what the clients we interviewed told us they had experienced. Further, separate techniques of sexual violence against men (see Table 4B.3) and women (see Table 4B.4) were reported. These techniques have been listed to explain what the clients interviewed meant when they stated they had been tortured. These acts meet the criteria of 'severe pain or suffering' required by the Convention.

It should also be noted that thirteen of the clients interviewed were placed in immigration detention by the UKBA.

Table 4B.3:
Methods of Sexual Violence Used by State Forces against Male Detainees

Testes crushed, chilli powder rubbed on penis
Anally raped with bottle, sticks or pipes
Forced to drink other men's urine
Burnt on genitals with cigarettes
Penis clamped
String tied round penis so cannot urinate
Tortured in underwear
Petrol injected into penis
Wire inserted into penis
Burnt on penis
Forced to perform oral sex on several other men at a time
Touched on genitals

Source: Materials related to BRC staff during ODIP Health assessments.

Table 4B.4.
Methods of Sexual Violence Used by State Forces against Female Detainees

Watched on toilet by male guards
Ice cubes forced into vagina
Raped and green chillies place in eyes so could not see perpetrators
Repeatedly raped with bag over head
Raped by three men at a time on repeated occasions
Raped daily by one man
Chillies placed in vagina, then raped
Touched all over body by male guards

Source: BRC's findings during ODIP Health assessments.

Impact on Clients

Psychological and Emotional Impact

Table 4B.5 gives a full breakdown of the psychological and emotional symptoms described by clients in assessment interviews or observed directly by the specialist team staff. One hundred and ninety four (43 per cent) complained of significant disturbance in their sleeping patterns. One hundred and sixty (35 per cent) disclosed regular and highly distressing nightmares about traumatic events and 25 per cent described regular flashbacks. Eighty clients described high levels of anxiety and fifty-three noted a reduction in appetite. Eighty-four clients disclosed low mood or depressive symptoms, thirty complained of memory or concentration problems, eighteen disclosed feelings of shame and eighty clients became distressed during the interview. Some clients complained of feelings of shame and

Table 4B.5:
Clients with Psychological Symptoms at Assessment

Symptoms	Number	Percentage
Nightmares	160	35.47
Flashbacks	115	25.49
Anxiety	80	17.73
Fear	35	7.76
Disturbed Sleep	194	43.01
Loss of Appetite	53	11.75
Intrusive Thoughts	10	2.21
Hyper-vigilance	3	0.66
Distress in Session	80	17.73
Separation Anxiety	22	4.67
Bereavement	4	0.88
Isolation	14	3.10
Impaired Memory or Concentration	30	6.65
Low mood or Depressive Symptoms	84	18.62
Shame	18	3.99
Suicidal Ideation	27	5.98
Suicide Attempts	7	1.55
Panic Attacks	9	1.99

Source: Materials related to BRC staff during ODIP Health assessments.

anxiety related to being apart from their families. Twenty-seven clients disclosed suicidal ideation and seven had actually attempted suicide prior to assessment.

Physical Impact

As can be seen from Table 4B.6, a number of women complained of gynaecological issues (including pain, malodorous discharge and heavy menstrual bleeding). Men and women who had been raped also reported urinary infections, passing blood and pain on passing stools or urine. Clients also reported dizziness (thirty-five) blurred vision (twenty-one) fainting or fitting (fifteen), hearing problems (seven) and headaches (one hundred and two) and there appeared to be at least some correlation

Table 4B.6:
Clients with Physical Symptoms at Assessment

Symptoms	Number	Percentage
Gynaecological Issues	31	15.34 (of women)
Urinary Infections	13	2.88 (of all clients)
Pain on Urinating	30	6.65
Pain Passing Stools	7	1.55
Passing Blood with Urine	4	0.88
Passing Blood with Stools	13	2.88
Dizziness	35	7.76
Fainting or Fits	15	3.32
Vomiting or Nausea (on eating)	10	2.21
Blurred Vision	21	4.65
Hearing Problems	7	1.55
Headaches	102	22.61
Bodily Pain	103	22.83
Mobility Issues	33	7.31
Physical Injuries	15	3.32
Shrapnel Wounds	5	1.10
Bullet Wounds	9	1.99
Physical Illness	21	4.65
Scars	42	9.31
Burns	54	11.97

Source: Materials related to BRC staff during ODIP Health assessments.

between these reports and the experience of being beaten around the head. One hundred and three clients complained of bodily pain since being tortured, fifteen reported physical injuries, fourteen described bullet or shrapnel wounds. Forty-two clients bore scars which they stated had been caused by torture and fifty-four had burns on the skin, caused by cigarettes, hot iron rods or chemicals.

Outcome of the Assessment

Post-assessment, clients were assisted in a variety of ways, depending on their needs: 155 were referred out to specialist providers of psychotherapy and counselling in London, including the Medical Foundation for the Care of Victims of Torture, the Helen Bamber Foundation, the Mapesbury Clinic, Women's Therapy Centre and the Multi-Ethnic Counselling Service. Clients were also assisted to access GPs or sexually transmitted infections clinics.

Fifty clients (10 per cent) were given 'therapeutic casework' at BRC. Therapeutic casework (Keefe 2008; Keefe and Hage 2009) is a model of psychosocial intervention developed by the BRC's specialist team specifically for asylum seekers with emotional well-being needs. The model combines counselling skills, emotional support and practical advice and advocacy. Clients are allocated to a 'therapeutic caseworker' who will assist them practically and emotionally with their needs, thereby building a helping alliance within which the deeper symbolic meanings of the symptoms they present with can emerge. This model is particularly suited to clients presenting as distressed due to a combination of psychological issues and practical, social pressures. Clients whose difficulties related more specifically to trauma or loss, for example, would be referred for more formal psychotherapy. There is a high demand for the services of the agencies mentioned earlier, which often have long waiting lists. Clients are then offered six months of therapeutic casework to stabilize them while they wait for a vacancy at a specialist therapeutic agency.

Discussion

The figures shown earlier indicate that a high percentage of the Tamil asylum seekers assessed had been subjected to violent events (49 per cent of women assessed reported being raped for instance) and were experiencing traumatic type symptoms as a result (43 per cent experiencing sleep disturbance, 35 per cent nightmares and 25 per cent flashbacks, for example). This would indicate the first condition for the presence of collective trauma (that violent, trauma-inducing experiences must have directly affected a sufficiently large percentage of the population) has been met. Furthermore, the accounts given by the clients themselves suggest the Sri Lankan security forces were using detention, torture and rape to traumatize and intimidate the broader Tamil society, not just those people they were able to target directly: women reported to us that they would be burnt with cigarettes when they were first detained, on their arms, back and abdomen (areas of the body which would be exposed when wearing a sari). Cigarette burns were understood in the Tamil community as a form of *branding*, as a sign that a woman had been detained and raped. This would therefore be a source of shame for the woman's family who would then try and arrange for her to be sent abroad. Rape can therefore become an impetus to migrate due to its specific cultural meaning.

The claims appear to be supported by the high number of clients presenting with cigarette burns as noted earlier. The high frequency of women who had been raped found in this study and an earlier BRC (2009) study (50 per cent of all women presenting to the BRC Vulnerable Women's Project, a specialist service for survivors of rape and sexual violence from 2006 to 2009, were Tamils). This suggests widespread use of rape in Sri Lankan prisons and detention centres. Rape in this context becomes a message from one group to another, of humiliation and of conquest. Women and men not only suffer immense physical and emotional distress but the *message* is written in the emotional and physical scarring in their minds and bodies. The sexual violence against men described earlier, particularly the assaults on genitals and penises, is evidence of attempts to emasculate. In Freudian terms, this is the *castration* of the Tamil male (Freud 1991).

Trauma in the Community in London

As noted, the second factor required to be present in a situation of collective trauma is that circumstances exist for sufficient numbers of the population not directly affected by the incidents to be indirectly or vicariously traumatized. To explore this, references to where clients were living with were noted, to see how much contact this group had with the wider Tamil community in London. The occasions where clients referred to feelings of trauma *in relation to others* were also noted to examine the extent to which *trauma* would have been visible to the people around them.

When asked, during assessment, about living arrangements and quality of support networks, clients described living with uncles, sisters, cousins, friends of friends and distant relatives. Many clients described the people they lived with as supportive and some stated they felt 'safer' or 'brighter' since moving in with them. Others talked of feeling isolated as they did not know their relatives very well or complained of overcrowding. Clients felt ashamed of not being able to contribute to the bills and there were disagreements about 'fair' shares of food. One woman had to clean the house in return for lodgings and another felt she could not speak to her relatives about her experiences as they had left Sri Lanka a long time before and did not understand what she had been through. Existing tensions in families made some of the people interviewed feel uncomfortable living in their space. Others felt more religious members of the community might judge them for their misfortune, which could be seen within Hinduism as karmic punishment for indiscretions in earlier lives.

Thirty separate comments regarding the expression of trauma or distress in relation to others were recorded; some relate to overt behaviour which would have an obvious impact on others in the house. A woman had to sleep with the light on and became hysterical when her relatives' children watched violent films on the television; another woke at night feeling frightened, but could not remember anything the next morning. A woman's brother heard her shouting at night. A man became distressed when he heard a helicopter at night but remembered nothing in the morning when his relatives told him what happened. Another hid in a cupboard when the doorbell rang. Men in uniforms triggered flashbacks. A wife was woken by her husband's nightmares. A woman's relatives heard her screaming at night.

Other comments relate to more internal feelings which nonetheless impact how people relate to those around them: a young woman worried the community would think she is 'impure' because she had been raped; another worried she would find it difficult to form relationships with men in the future. Clients talked of wanting to beat people who spoke too loudly or who laughed and joked. A woman struggled to care for a child due to her own pain while another worried her daughter would see her scars. Clients talked of spending their time alone in their bedrooms and of being unable to tell their relatives what had happened to them. Some spoke of living with people who were also grieving or had been abused. A mother struggled to cope with her daughter as she is in constant pain.

Women spoke of their feelings of being pregnant through rape, of fear but also of the need to keep the baby and nurture the child. Some feared friends would ask them to leave once they learned of the pregnancy. Clients spoke of missing their families and fears that relatives had been killed. Parents expressed the need to protect children from their own grief and feelings that children 'know there's something wrong'.

Some of the clients were seen as couples: a woman nursing her depressed husband; a couple who were both abused struggled as one was ready to move on, the other was not. A husband and wife who escaped together were both scared. Clients also commented on feelings about engaging with professionals involved in their care: one woman felt ashamed at talking about her body with a male GP. Another felt shame at giving birth without her husband who was 'missing'.

Trauma between Communities: The Diaspora and Those at Home

All of the 451 clients interviewed and indeed all of the 1,364 clients seen by the ODIP were staying with relatives or friends in London. Not only can high levels of trauma be detected in this population but the circumstances for transmission of this trauma to a wider population also exist. The examples noted earlier show how the people sharing houses might see, hear or otherwise witness the distress experienced by the survivor. Where the relative has their own pre-existing history of trauma such experiences can trigger distressing memories and feelings. Even where the people witnessing such occurrences do not have a history of trauma, *vicarious* traumatization can still take place through repeated exposure to such events (Figley 1995; Pearlman and Saakvitne 1995; Satkunanayagam et al. 2010). These studies concentrate on the impact on mental health professionals of exposure to traumatized clients; the impact on the housemate of a traumatized person, exposed to their distress for much longer periods of time and without the security of professional boundaries, could be much more serious. The issue of vicarious trauma among the relatives of survivors of trauma could be a useful subject for further study.

Clients frequently spoke of their fears for the safety of relatives and friends still in Sri Lanka or described feeling their loss: as noted, clients reported having relatives who had been killed, 'disappeared' or who were being held in detention in Sri Lanka. Others reported having lost contact with their families or having to leave children behind. These worries about individuals would be reinforced by discussions with and between housemates concerning the latest news from Sri Lanka about the progress of the war or the latest atrocity. Clients, and some of our interpreters, reported attending the regular demonstrations against the Sri Lankan army offences, held in Trafalgar Square in the centre of London during the fighting and later memorial events for the dead. These events were highly emotionally charged and demonstrated the intense feelings generated in the community in London by events in Sri Lanka.

On 7 April 2009, the BBC reported that police had arrested six Tamil protestors at a demonstration outside the Houses of Parliament in London, for violent disorder, breach of the peace and public order offences. One protestor had jumped into the River Thames but had been recovered safely by the police (BBC 2009). On the same day, the website of the *Guardian* newspaper (Bowcott 2009) reported the police had decided to close both Westminster Tube station and Westminster Bridge (both iconic London landmarks close to the Houses of Parliament), so concerned were they that the demonstration, attended by several thousand Tamils, would spill out of Parliament Square and affect surrounding areas.

The BBC (2009) piece notes UN reports that 150,000 Tamil civilians were trapped by the fighting in the north of Sri Lanka at the time and quotes one community activist as saying of the demonstrators: 'These are people who have relatives and friends in Sri Lanka; people who have lost brothers and fathers and sisters'.

Such reports are consistent with the argument that there is a link between the suffering of Tamils in Sri Lanka and the anger of Tamils in the UK. Suffering and anger are both elements of the same experience of trauma. One wonders whether the response attributed to the Metropolitan Police by the *Guardian* report was a further element in that the police were struggling to contain the overwhelming feelings of anger and fear of the demonstrators and not just their physical presence, hence their need to close off the streets. So strong is the collective experience of trauma that it affects those the community comes into contact with as well as the Tamil diaspora itself.

The Tamil community in Sri Lanka and its fate is constantly *held in mind* by the community in London and in that sense, the pain and fear generated by the traumatic events at home are *shared* by the diaspora: one can think of a circularity of trauma—the new arrival screams at night, reminding the older refugee of their own trauma, heightening tension in the house and adding to the new arrival's stress. News from home of a massacre or the bombing of a village adds further stress to both and the cycle starts again. Trauma becomes a shared experience.

A further factor in these dynamics is the concept of *survivor guilt* (Bettelheim 1979: 29–35): host relatives may struggle with their own feelings of guilt at having survived or escaped earlier experiences of violence. Bettelheim (1979: 32) notes the use of defence mechanisms such as repression and denial amongst Jewish survivors of Nazi concentration camps as a method of coping with the deeply unsettling experience of feeling this guilt. The survivor, who operates such defences in lieu of attempting a full integration of their traumatic experiences, can appear 'relatively symptom-free' (Bettelheim 1979: 33). However, he says, 'theirs is a house of cards existence ... any strong wind of serious trouble may collapse their integration.'

Under such circumstances, the arrival in one's house of a relative, who screams at night due to nightmares of torture, could undermine one's psychological defences and trigger a regression to an earlier traumatized state. This is in addition to feelings there may be between the host generation and the recent arrivals concerning who has borne the brunt of the demands of the struggle and the subsequent repression.

As it was not within the scope of this study to interview the friends and relatives the clients lived with, it is not possible to comment with any certainty about how they responded to visible signs of distress. It is, however, possible to observe and discuss the impact of working with this client group on the interpreters the team worked with, all of whom are themselves Tamils. BRC offers group clinical supervision to interpreters in recognition of the pressures this work places them under. Caseworkers and therapists in the team routinely offer short debriefing support to interpreters at the end of sessions. Interpreter colleagues have disclosed that they find the material discussed by clients upsetting, that it can remind them of their own experiences of loss or violence and that clients can induce powerful feelings of anxiety in them.

Non-Tamil members of the team, especially those involved regularly in the assessment and casework of this group, also reported high levels of distress in response to the material they were exposed to and time and resources needed to be invested in the clinical supervision and training of the team. Several colleagues reported a phenomenon whereby clients' stories and clients themselves would merge into one, making it difficult to distinguish between them. This may have been partially a defensive response to the horror of the material (protecting oneself from the consequences of relating directly to the client as an individual to avoid the full impact of their story), but also perhaps a *countertransferential* (Ryecroft 1995: 28) response to the collective nature of the Tamil clients' culture and of their experience, in that so many had passed through similar stories of abuse. The war and the violence they have lived through have perhaps served to wear away their individuality until they are seen only as traumatized asylum seekers, rather than the *people* they were before and continue to be.

Several writers have identified forms of countertransference which appear to be experienced particularly by therapists working with refugee clients: Bustos (1992: 341–2) refers to 'culturally determined countertransference', where the therapy is adversely affected by the therapist's value system, 'colonial countertransference' where the lack of a common language can lead to refugee clients being regarded as 'not sophisticated enough' for insight therapies and 'ethno-identificative countertransference', where therapist and client are from the same cultural background but working together in a country of exile. Therapist and client can collude unconsciously to avoid traumatic material which both may find distressing. Thomas (2000: 151) refers to Andrew Curry's (1964) concept of *pre*-transference, the 'ideas, fantasies and values ascribed to the black therapist and his race by the white patient long before the two meet for the first time in the consulting room'. Thomas notes that in the reverse situation, the white therapist expecting a black client for a first meeting would also need to address this issue. Arnold (2000: 172) states that white professionals working interculturally usually live in isolation from the client group concerned and only experience people from that group when they are under stress, which can in itself lead to the development of negative stereotypical images.

Danieli (1980), cited in G. van der Veer (1992: 161) describes specific countertransferential responses in therapists working with 'war victims', including 'guilt, repugnance and shame' and a sense of 'powerlessness' which can be transferred into the helping professional as they assess the client, leaving a feeling that there is nothing that they can do for the client, except perhaps to prescribe medication. Guus van der Veer (1992: 242) also notes the phenomenon of therapists being unable to integrate impulses triggered in them by the horrible stories they hear from their refugee clients, which can trigger defences such as repression, splitting, projection or denial. Fassin and Rechtman (2009: 15) refer to the phenomenon of 'cultural trauma', a term employed in the United States to describe the impact of events such as the Holocaust, slavery or 9/11. Cultural traumas are 'wounds in the collective memory that contribute to the construction of identity in different social groups'. They note that the term 'historical trauma' (Fassin and Rechtman 2009: 15) has been applied to the civil war in Sri Lanka, along with other seemingly intractable conflicts.

Despite providing diverse explanations (the therapist's racism, the commonality of the client's experience or the therapist's need to protect themselves from the full horror of what they are hearing), these authors all seem to acknowledge that countertransference can be a response to a group, not just an individual. The feeling of Tamil clients merging into one, noted earlier, can perhaps now be understood in the light of this work as both a defensive reaction to the horror of the material (G. van der Veer 1992: 242) and related to Curry's (1964) concept of *pre*-transference: long experience of assessment of Tamil clients had led the team to *expect* to hear horrific stories. But it is also the echo in the therapist of the collective, cultural experience of trauma which Tamils have lived through: clients' stories appear to merge into one because they really are part of one story, the suffering of the Tamil people.

Limitations of the Study

The study participants were assessed on presentation to the specialist team's assessment, referral and casework service as described earlier, rather than *interviewed* as part of a research project. This meant that although all participants were assessed using the specialist team assessment tool, this is not a set series of questions, but an aide-memoire to ensure caseworkers ask clients about their history of trauma (if any), family history, physical and emotional health, mental health (if indicated), accommodation issues, support networks, daytime activities, legal and financial issues and coping mechanisms. This helps build a holistic picture not just of how the client is (the symptoms they present with), but also of the historical and current stressors (such as anxiety about passing through the asylum system) which may be causing the client distress, which then informs the plan of intervention. The assessment is left deliberately semi-structured to find a balance between the client's need to discuss matters of importance to them and the caseworker's need to gather information to make an informed assessment.

The study participants were not therefore all asked exactly the same questions, although the advantage of this is that the resulting answers may be considered to be spontaneous, rather than in response to specific questions. As noted earlier, the study did not include a survey of the relatives and friends with whom the participants actually lived (and those left behind). We, therefore, only have the comments our clients made about them upon which to base our hypotheses concerning the impact on the wider group. We recommend that further research does concentrate on the wider group of the Tamil diaspora who are now established in the United Kingdom and hosting the latest asylum seekers to arrive.

Conclusion

Notwithstanding the limitations noted earlier, this study identifies a large population of Tamil asylum seekers reporting exposure to violent experiences including rape and torture. Evidence from HRW, AI and the United Kingdom's Foreign & Commonwealth Office raises concerns about respect for human rights among the Sri Lankan security services and armed opposition groups. The population studied exhibit high levels of trauma-related distress and opportunities exist for the transmission of this distress to the wider Tamil community in London, as demonstrated by participants' reports of the manifestation of their trauma in the domestic

setting. The evidence for *collective trauma*, while perhaps not fully conclusive, is compelling and further research, involving the families our clients
are living with is indicated to explore the impact on them of receiving
recently arrived refugees into their homes and living spaces, as well as the
impact of news reports of atrocities and fighting in Sri Lanka. Although
this latter aspect was outside the limits of this study, the news reports
referred to above indicate high levels of anger among the broader Tamil
community and a desire to show their feelings publicly and the feelings
of this group during the period of conflict and subsequently merit further
exploration.

Forward Note

Though the trauma of war and other types of disasters can be widespread,
affecting individuals, families and communities, there are no established
ways of addressing these problems. In Sri Lanka, due to the recent disasters, there have been pioneering developments in mental health and
psychosocial interventions that are of value for countries facing similar
situations.

SECTION 5

Interventions

A.

Psychosocial Interventions

As discussed in Chapter 2A, in addition to individual treatment for affected victims, community-based approaches are more suited in developing, resource-poor countries and would reach larger populations. This chapter will describe some of the community-level interventions that were undertaken in northern Sri Lanka to help those affected by the man-made disaster called war and the natural tsunami of 2004.

Community Approaches

The mental health programme in northern Sri Lanka used a public health approach in combination with MHPSS intervention strategies (see Chapters 2A and 5B). As part of the community-based approach, we adapted the protocol developed by the TPO, a WHO collaborating centre (de Jong 1997, 2002, 2011), to the conflict, post-conflict and post-tsunami situations in northern Sri Lanka. The main principles of the community-level approaches (see Box 2A.2) were to empower the community to look after their own problems not only through psychoeducation to transfer basic psychosocial knowledge and skills, but also through encouragement, support, affirmation and re-establishing community processes, traditional practices, rituals, resources and relationships. On a collective level, communities were strengthened through creating awareness, training of community-level workers, cultural rituals, social development and cohesion. Most important in a post-war context was to rekindle trust between members, in the community and its institutions. Trust is the glue that holds the social fabric together. Difficult though it may be in a militarily controlled environment, it was as important to redevelop a sense of agency, collective efficacy, faith in the power of communities to solve their own problems, belief that their efforts will bear fruit, that they can make a difference and fashion their own future.

Psychoeducation

Basic information about what has happened, what to do and not to do and where help can be obtained was disseminated through the media, pamphlets and popular lectures. Over the years, several pamphlets were produced in Tamil to create awareness and educate the public about simple practices. In the beginning, leaflets from other parts of the world such as those used in the Ash Wednesday fires in Australia were translated (Somasundaram 1998), but were eventually designed and produced to suit the local situation and culture.

Lectures and seminars were held for school students, the general public and a variety of grass-roots workers from the government and NGO sectors. One such popular programme was carried out through the Extra Mural Studies Unit of the University of Jaffna, where several batches of around a hundred participants each were given basic introduction to psychosocial issues over a five-week period. Another major psychoeducational effort was carried out immediately after the tsunami by the MHTF in Jaffna using the media, pamphlets and lectures (see Chapter 3A). There were regular advocacy programmes with the government and militant organizations and NGOs. World Mental Health Day was commemorated each year with activities appropriate to the theme usually ending with a special dramatic, musical or cultural celebration. Art, storytelling and writing competitions on various topics and musical, cultural and dance programmes were organized regularly. Cultural and religious festivals and celebrations were observed and organized throughout the year for mental health patients and their families.

Training

Over the years, many local community workers such as teachers, primary health workers, priests, village headmen (GSs), traditional healers, youths and elders received basic theoretical and practical training on psychosocial issues. They were asked to refer more difficult problems to mental health professionals (see Figure 2A.3). Towards this end, at the primary health level all medical students, nurses and primary health workers (or family health workers) in Jaffna underwent teaching and training in basic mental health as part of their regular curricula each year. Several texts were written in Tamil; for example, *Ula vallathrurai* (Counselling) (Damian 1994), *Mana vadu* (Trauma) (Somasundaram 1993b), *Muthumai* (Elderly) (Sivayokan and Somasundaram 2001) and others mentioned below. A Tamil module based on the UNICEF manual, *Helping Children in Situations of Armed Conflict* (Nikapota and Samarasinghe 1995), was used to train all family health workers and other health staff. Annually, batches of counsellors were trained at Shanthiham, some who have now become trainers themselves. They were given theoretical lectures, demonstrations and role play exercises for six months. They then practised counselling under supervision and met for case supervision and discussion. At the end of one year they underwent an examination and were then certified as counsellors. This process was repeated each year for new batches of trainees. Some practised as counsellors at Shanthiham; with the psychiatric unit at General Hospital, Jaffna; Base Hospital, Tellippalai; Base Hospital, Point Pedro; Base Hospital, Chavakachcheri; and other outreach centres, while others used the skills in conjunction with their work in a variety of organizations. Counselling supervision was done through weekly case conferences at General Hospital, Jaffna and Shanthiham. A batch of twenty-five counsellors was trained following the tsunami with the help of WHO funding for one year for all districts in Northern Province (one died in war and another left the country, but all the others are working in the field). A batch of students was trained as diploma holders in psychosocial work. Several teams were trained to work in the mental health and psychosocial field at the request of MDM in Trincomalee; Sewa Lanka in Vavuniya; DRC and SLRC in Trincomalee, Batticaloa and Ampara; ICRC in Kilinochchi; and Deutsche Gesellschaft für Technische Zusammenarbeit or German Technical Cooperation (GTZ) and VIVO in Mullaitivu.

In view of the demand for the large number of trainings at a variety of levels and to different groups of workers, it became necessary to develop capable trainers who could carry out the task in a professional and competent way as well as be available for regular follow-up of the trainees in the field. It was realized that much of valuable practical and effective learning happened when dealing with real problems and clients in actual field situations. For this purpose, the protocol developed by the TPO (de Jong 1997) for TOT was implemented. Initially, the WHO supported the adaptation and publication of the WHO and UNHCR (1996) book, *Mental Health of Refugees*, for Tamil culture: *Mental Health in the Tamil Community* (Somasundaram and Sivayokan 2001). A TOT in community mental health using this manual was completed with UNICEF support in 2001. These trainers in turn have trained a variety of community-level grassroots workers as mentioned earlier. In this way the necessary knowledge and skill was spread to a wide population. Another TOT (later the trainers were renamed psychosocial trainers) was carried out in 2004.

TOT

With contributions from *Thedsanamoorthy Vijayasangar* and PSTs

The first training programme consisted of three phases.

Phase One—Adoption of Culturally Appropriate Training Manual

In order to train community-level workers in mental health and psycho-social issues, an appropriate manual that addressed the specific needs of the population in simple and lucid language was developed. The manual had to be ecologically valid and culturally sensitive (Bernal et al. 1995) to be practically useful in a community setting. Ecological validity as developed by Bronfenbrenner (1979) attempts to capture the environment and experiential world of the target community, to fit their cultural and psychosocial situation. The Tamil community had their own beliefs, explanatory systems and practices regarding psychosocial, mental and spiritual well-being, limited exposure to Western mental health concepts and scarce human resources trained in such approaches. In addition, the community had been exposed to a chronic war situation with the consequences of trauma, displacement and disruption of community networks and processes.

The manual was purposefully designed to be relevant in this specific context. The aim was to develop an instrument that could transfer the appropriate knowledge, skills and attitudes as well as recognize, create awareness and empower beneficial local practices and resources. In pursuance of this goal, the WHO and UNHCR (1996) manual *Mental Health of Refugees* and its adaptation to Cambodia *Community Mental Health in Cambodia* (Somasundaram et al. 1997) were used as guides and frameworks to develop the *Mental Health in the Tamil Community* (Somasundaram and Sivayokan 2001). I had already worked on the adaptation to the Cambodian post-conflict context (Van de Put et al. 1997), which was the inspiration to undertake a similar exercise in war-ravaged Jaffna. In writing the manual, a balance between the etic (standard, universal principles and theory represented by the WHO manual, DSM and ICD categories) and the emic (local, contextual, cultural epistemology and practices) perspectives had to be struck; or more ambitiously, an integration or meaningful synthesis was sought.

Considerable effort was put into finding local idioms of distress, terms and explanatory models. In time, with field experience we were able to develop a figure with common idioms of distress attributable to each part of the body from head to foot (*pathathikesam*) that was introduced in the third edition. Another innovation in the third edition was a table comparing the description of the stages of development from childhood to old age in the Western models of Erikson, Freud and Piaget and the local tradition. An index was included which was rare in Tamil books. A glossary of terms in Tamil and English had been developed in another publication, *Mana vadu* (Somasundaram 1993b).

To make the manual more user-friendly and easier to understand, illustrations, figures, paintings, drawings, photos and boxes on special topics, main points and examples were introduced. The artwork included paintings and drawings by the locally renowned artist, Rasiah, and a medical student (now doctor), Naguleswaran. The Tamil adaptations were then field-tested to train various PSWs, particularly during the first TOT. The experience, feedback and suggestions were used to modify and correct the text. Then it was translated back to English and each chapter sent for comments to international experts in that field, some being the original authors of the WHO manual chapters. Their responses were used to correct the Tamil and English versions. Several thousand copies have been distributed and sold, several prints, hundreds of trainings based on the manual successfully completed, and with continuous feedback, it has now gone into its second (post-tsunami) and third (post-war) revised editions.

Phase Two—Training of Psychosocial Trainees

A batch of twenty trainees was selected for a nine-month full-time training course in July 2001, supported by UNICEF. Out of 130 applicants, 78 were chosen for a written examination.[1] Forty-three of those who sat for the examination and reached an acceptable standard were interviewed and twenty selected. However, only eighteen completed the training. Most of the trainees were university graduates (psychology, sociology, bioscience and fine arts). Some were non-graduates with experience in social work. Gender balance was considered during the selection process. The training was done in three phases, as described below.

Theory (Two Months)

I taught ten core subjects corresponding to each chapter from the *Mental Health in the Tamil Community* along with other material such as *Muthumai* and *Mana vadu*. Subject specialists from the University of Jaffna taught

[1] Compromising tests for psychosocial aptitudes, intelligence quotient, attitude and problem solving capacity.

special subjects such as basic psychology, sociology and anthropology, and community medicine was handled by traditional resource persons. Basic counselling principles also were taught to the team in detail with practical counselling and supervision later.

Hospital-based Training (One Month)

For three weeks, trainees visited psychiatric units in Tellippalai Base Hospital, Manthikai Base Hospital and Jaffna Teaching Hospital and other institutions for the disabled, handicapped, elders and orphanages for practical training, which included identifying various types of severe psychiatric disorders, particularly psychotic illnesses, interacting with patients and their relatives, learning multidisciplinary work and home visits.

Field-based Training (Six Months)

Three vulnerable villages (Anaikoddai, Punnalaikadduvan South and Kopay Centre) were selected[2] from three divisional secretariat areas in Jaffna District for fieldwork. Trainees were divided into three groups and assigned for each village under supervision of the trainers. Trainees were in the field for three days in a week where they were trained in community-based psychosocial work (see Table 5A.1). One day of the week was spent at the psychiatric outpatient clinic at General Hospital, Jaffna for clinical work: recording histories, case presentations, observing multidisciplinary team treatments and discussions. One day was spent in case presentations by the team to the trainers, with discussion and teaching.

One of the key objectives of the field-based training was to identify local resources and work through them. The traditional sector was sought out and basic knowledge and experience was gained about their working methods by collaboration with them. Particular emphasis was placed in gaining experience from working with vulnerable or marginalized people and advocating for them. Various psychosocial interventions were taught and carried out under supervision (see Table 5A.2).

---

[2] Selection of villages was undertaken after consulting the divisional secretaries, medical officer of health and traditional healers, information available on attendees at the psychiatric and other clinics in Jaffna based on those severely (in relation to others) affected by war trauma (high number of deaths, injuries, amputations, disappearances, torture, sexual abuse, IDPs in refugee camps, collective trauma), poverty, alcoholism, child abuse, domestic violence, low educational status, suicide and parasuicide. This was followed by a feasibility study, keeping in mind the safety of the trainees due the ongoing war, vulnerability of youths, landmines, transport (bicycle was the only form of transport as fuel was rationed to those of importance such as doctors and high government officials) and the financial resources of Shanthiham.

Table 5A.1:
Steps for Community-based Psychosocial Work

Step	Title	Description
1.	Village assessment	Information from GAs, GS, divisional secretaries, psychiatrists, counsellors, psychiatric social workers, health workers, PSWs and the representatives of the organizations from that region (statistical data)
2.	Selection of villages	Based on poverty, affected by war (death, injured, missing), displacement, resettlement, socio-economic problems, domestic violence, alcohol and drug abuse, natural disasters (for example, tsunami), child abuse
3.	Obtaining permission	Permission from the government authorities (GS, divisional secretaries) to work in the selected villages
4.	Integration with people	Introduction to villagers about the worker, organization and the intent of activities
5.	Meeting with resources	Discuss objectives with important resources from the village to get their wholehearted support
6.	Cross walk	Looking around all the nooks and corners of the village
7.	Learning about the society	Getting to know the local language, idioms, culture, traditions, rituals and occupations with the help of the important resources living in the area
8.	Data collection and documentation	Basic demographic data about the village
9.	Social mapping	Ecosystem of society, the house of the community leader, temples, CBOs, traditional healers, places where trauma occurred
10.	Identifying and analysing problems	Through key informant interviews, focus group interviews, case studies
11.	Planning	Based on the above-mentioned identified problems and their priorities
12.	Community meetings and creating awareness	First with the key resources, then for the whole community, explaining plans, benefits, psychosocial well-being and prioritized problems of the community, for example, alcohol awareness, awareness of child abuse, domestic violence, etc.
13.	Selection of the core group	A local group made up of teachers, university students, farmers, youth; contains 8–20 people with gender balance depending on circumstances
14.	Core group training	Based on the manual, *Mental Health in the Tamil Community*; focused on psychosocial well-being and psychosocial problems at the village level, referral and networking
15.	Working with core group	Trainer works with core group in social mobilization, community awareness, children's group activities, identification of psychosocial problems in the community, psychosocial interventions for individuals, families and community, facilitate women groups, following up past cases, doing referral and network for new cases, etc.

(Table 5A.1 Contd.)

(Table 5A.1 Contd.)

Step	Title	Description
16.	Psychosocial interventions	See Table 5A.2
17.	Core group follow-up	After work in the village is handed over to the core group, they continue but under supervision and further updating training
18.	Referral	Problems which the core group is unable to handle referred to mental health professionals
19.	Networking	Collaborating with governmental organizations and NGOs for socio-economic and other needs
20.	Monitoring and evaluation	Feedback to modify planning stage and programme implementation; design of new programmes

Source: Constructed by authors from field work experience.

Table 5A.2:
Psychosocial Interventions at Different Levels

Individual	Family	Community
Case identification	Psychoeducation	Awareness
Psychoeducation	Family counselling	Training
Counselling	Strengthening the family dynamics, for example, talking and eating together	Interventions for special groups (children, widows, widowers, youths)
Other psychotherapies	Family reunification	Encouraging religious activities and rituals
Yoga and relaxation	Social support	Encouraging cultural activities
Traditional practices	Yoga and traditional practices	Yoga and relaxation
Family and social support	Capacity building and income generation	Forming and reactivating CBOs
Referral and networking	Follow-up	Re-establishing relationships, social networks
Capacity building and income generation		Networking with other NGOs
Rehabilitation		Encouraging networking with other communities
Follow-up		Follow-up

Source: Constructed by authors from field work experience.

Trainees presented their experiences in psychosocial interventions at the weekly presentations.

One of the more successful village-level programmes completed by the PSTs during their fieldwork was the initiation and facilitation of a widows' support group at Chavatkaddu (see the subsection titled 'Group Therapy').

The TOT included training in training methodology such as learning theory, learning environment, curriculum development, lesson planning, presentation and demonstrating skills, teaching skills, facilitating skills and usage of audiovisual aids. Weekly peer group support meetings, facilitated by Guus van der Veer, an international expert in counselling in conflict areas and Father Damian, senior counsellor, were held. Apart from local resources, there were periodic visits from international experts like Nancy Baron, Rachel Tribe, art and drama therapists, VSO[3] experts, NIPU[4] and others to train and discuss with trainees. A final trainee evaluation was done in May 2002 by Nancy Baron, Dr Soren and local assessors. In the evaluation sixteen out of eighteen passed as PSTs. The following is a description of a trainee's experience of the training.

Psychosocial Trainee's Field Experience[5]

By *Thedsanamoorthy Vijayasangar*

Situation at the Time of Training

A training session is being conducted in the lecture hall of Shanthiham. The army and rebels are in the battlefield at Ariyalai, a village five or six kilometres away and 'rounds' (bullets) are falling in the vicinity. Ambulances and armoured trucks are passing by; people are moving away from the area of battle. One trainee rushed into a training session sweating and said that on his way to Shanthiham through the alleys (main roads were avoided due to several army checkpoints), when he crossed a main road, he came across two people shot dead. The army stopped him and he produced the identity card given by Shanthiham and was allowed to proceed. He said that the identity card saved him.

---

[3] Volunteer Service Overseas.
[4] National Integration Programme Unit, Sri Lanka.
[5] Translated by C. Wijeyaratnam.

Field Activities

The first task when visiting a chosen village was to meet the governmental and NGO sectors present in the village and persons of importance to introduce ourselves and the activities we intended to undertake. We were to collect as much information about their culture, values, local language and subdivisions by way of caste.

Social Mapping and Need Assessment

Social mapping was done through participatory rural approach to identify physical resources, such as agricultural land, water, roads and transport, geographical and human resources and local organizations such as community centres, women's societies and cooperative societies. Constraints and risks such as landmines as well as recent disastrous events, both natural and man-made, were mapped. This exercise helped people identify their own strengths, weaknesses and unidentified resources and helped us to build a good rapport and understanding. But it was risky because of the delicate political and security situation.

Key Informant and Focus Group Discussions

We met people of importance in the village individually and in groups on several occasions to learn psychosocial and mental health problems in general and those peculiar to the village. At first, they found the language of psychosocial and mental health difficult to comprehend and it took some time to find common ground. Before we went there, many organizations had been working in areas of socio-economics, such as livelihood, vocational training, water, sanitation and housing. Hence, it took some time for the people to figure out our area of work. Social stigma attached to mental health had to be reckoned with. Many trainees felt that in the beginning we needed to provide economic help to support the villagers materially by way of handouts, which would win their cooperation. With time many in the village realized the benefits of our services and were cooperative. We decided to initially work with those who were able to comprehend the need of our services and gradually expand to include others.

Social Mobilization

One day the trainees planned a street drama at one of the villages under study and left Shanthiham with banners, traditional musical instruments and costumes. The trainees went out on the streets with music and songs, moving along bylanes, to arrive at an identified spot for the event, with mostly children, but also a few women and men following. At the central spot the trainees performed roles and cajoled the onlookers to participate in anything they thought fit. One mother enacted the violence she experiences at home from a drunken husband, brawls and beating. The programme ended with all participants pledging determinedly to resolve violence towards children and women. This was a powerful exercise to win their hearts and minds, to understand unwholesome social values and to sow the seed of thought to practise non-violent means. Selection of the trainee teams with diverse areas of interest and study made such creative activities possible.

Experience with Traditional Healers

During our training we visited several traditional healers. In the war milieu, families sought the help of traditional healers in tracing and finding out about those who had disappeared, were missing or were abducted. Families were faced with the uncertainty of whether their missing members were dead or alive (see Chapter 3C). Daily visits to camps, helping organizations such as UNHCR, ICRC and HRCSL for information about their loved ones was psychologically and physically exhausting. Though some institutions provided counselling services for such victims, it did not provide much relief nor were they sought after to a great extent. In this backdrop the traditional healer was of comfort; he sought divine help. In one case, the traditional healer consulted the missing person's horoscope and said that the planetary positions are such that he would be separated from his family for over ten years or so. 'You are sad that he is not at home. Should he be at home, according to the horoscope, he will have deleterious effects on the father. Thus being away is the best option.' He assured them that 'though he is separated there is no danger to his life'. He also gave the direction of where he was, and said that he was in prison. Mostly he provided positive information. He then gave instruction on rituals for the victims' comfort.

We found that interventions by traditional healers, like psychosocial interventions done by us, followed a certain pattern. For example, there were individual interventions (exorcising devils, tying of threads), and at the family (*vasthu sasthiram* [traditional science of architecture], matching horoscopes for marriage, guarding families, *seivinai eduthal* [removing evil spell(s)]) and social (*thee mithitthal* [fire walking], conducting festivals, *yaham* [religious sacrifice], *vellvi* [religious sacrifice, worship] to ward off natural calamities) levels. These interventions followed certain codes of conduct where rituals are conducted at astrologically determined days and times.

The traditional healers maintained confidentiality and clients felt free to confess to them. Healing was done on a specified day and time while the healer was in a trance. Should one later ask the healer as to what was said, he would answer that he is not able to recollect as he was in a trance. It may be a ruse adopted to maintain confidentiality. Going to the healer in the village was considered safer, in a war milieu, than going to other institutions.

In gathering psychosocial information at the village level, governmental Ministry of Health (MOH) PHIs, PHMs and non-governmental sectors gave common information. But the healers were specific and they prioritized areas causing distress to the community. The villagers sought the traditional healer to alleviate distress. However, at times some caused more harm to the clients when dealing with those with major mental disorders by using torturous procedures and charged them exorbitant fees as well.

Presentation and Supervision

During the field phase, all trainees from the three teams met every Friday to present a summary of their weekly activities and case studies to a panel of supervisors. It was a learning experience where the three teams shared their experiences with the guidance of the supervisors. Challenges encountered were collectively discussed. The supervisory panel comprised psychiatrists, heads of the Department of Community Medicine, University of Jaffna and senior counsellors among others. It is noteworthy that the supervisors appreciated and encouraged the trainees, which in turn boosted trainees' self-esteem and was an impetus to bring forth one's best.

Monitoring and Evaluation

Monitoring and evaluation was done at two levels: field and office.

Subject matter specialists visited the village to observe first hand and participated in our interventions, met beneficiaries and got their feedback. Monitoring and evaluation was more a learning exercise than looking for faults and gaps. Their involvement at the grass-roots level greatly motivated the trainees.

Observations in the Villages

The villages of Selvapuram and Yogapuram in Kopay were observed. IDPs from Kurumbasiddy, Vasavillan, Tellippalai and Palali displaced in

1990 due the declaration of these areas as HSZs lived in temporary shelters amongst the permanent residents. Most of the permanent residents were educated high caste Hindus involved in farming. The IDPs were mostly of a lower caste and less educated; they had mostly been fishermen.

The IDPs were labelled refugees and discriminated on the basis of caste. Though they lived in close proximity there was little interaction between people of lower and higher castes. The permanent residents looked at the IDPs as troublemakers, with unacceptable behaviour such as abuse of alcohol and extramarital relationships. The IDPs were employed as manual labourers in the agricultural lands of the resident high caste families.

Psychosocial Needs in the Village

The main aim of the IDPs in this village was to get back to their own villages.

Traditionally a village had its own festivals and rituals with the temple as the focus in addition to the main Hindu festivals which gave them a sense of identity, ownership and collectiveness. As IDPs they lost this collective identity which had its own psychosocial consequences. They felt the need for its revival. In normal situations it was customary for elders to meet in a common place for a chat and to reminisce. So did male youths. There was a lack of basic needs. Training and livelihood assistance were needed.

Psychosocial Problems

During this period of time, there was a constant threat on life. One client quipped, '*Epoluthum naam uyirai kaiya piddichukonndu than vallurum* (we constantly hold onto life with our hands'. Behavioural problems that were identified included anger, aggression, alcohol abuse, domestic violence and antisocial behaviour. There was an increase in theft, cheating and lying. They lost interest in family and societal well-being and lived for the sake of living. They had no vision or faith in the future and suffered from loss of self-confidence, motivation and creativity. The community was experiencing a social upheaval — early marriages, unwanted pregnancies, multiple partners and uncontrolled births.

One IDP leader said: 'When we were in our own village we adhered to our cultural norms and lived amicably and with respect. This war made us refugees and we lost our identity, self-respect and others look down upon us.'

Lack of livelihood induced distillation and sale of *kasippu*,[6] which created problems not only within the village but affected adjoining villages as well. Distillation of local brews by fermenting fruits was a traditional practice. However, with time, yeast meant for bread and sugar was used for illegal distillation under unhygienic conditions. The alcohol content in *kasippu* was above 40 per cent.

Some adapted well and survived. To some degree they developed resilience, having being displaced many times over and having gone through many forms of stress. One said that he was unable to sleep if he did not hear shots being fired at night.

Minor and Major Mental Problems

The communities we worked in had a slightly higher rate of minor and major mental problems. Many of those suffering from major mental disorders had stopped taking medication and had no support from the family. There was a high incidence of attempted suicide.

Some community responses encouraged suicides, such as if a girl committed suicide upon being jilted, the community would praise the girl by saying that she did the right thing and taught the boy a lesson.

During our field training we came across some common expressions and idioms being used by villagers in situations of what we would call psychosocial problems. Some examples are categorized under certain headings for the ease of presentation though there is considerable overlap and they do not fall neatly into these general categories (see Table 5A.3). We found that using them appropriately during our psychoeducational and other interventions when interacting with villagers improved their understanding of the meaning of what we were trying to convey as well as helping us build rapport.

An Overview of Problems in Relation to Gender and Age

Children

The majority of children were suffering from malnutrition; they were unhygienic, without sufficient clothing and unable to have three meals a day. Families with many children, abuse of alcohol and lack of livelihood were the major causes of neglect. In general, the children were mentally and physically lethargic. Child abuse such as sexual exploitation, labour and beatings were rampant.

---

[6] Illicit alcoholic brew.

Table 5A.3:
Common Idioms of Distress

Individual Level

Manathai kaividdittar – He has lost power over his mind

Petravairu pathieriuthu – The womb that gave birth has burst into flames

Yosikka visarvaruguthu – I get mad when I think of it

Nadakurathu nadakkadum – Let what has to happen happen, come to pass

Enkadai thalaivithy – This is my fate

Aatho erukiram – Existing for the sake of living

Naan enna pavam seithean – What sins have I done

Ellam maraththup poachchu – Every part is insensitive (numb)

Enakkendu oru manusarum illai – There is no person to call my own

---

Family Level

Nadutheruvukku vanthutam – We have been thrown to the streets

Kudumbam kulenchupochithu – The family is in disarray

Enkada wamsame alinchipochuthu – Our generation has been lost

Veedu verichchodipocchidu – The home is desolate

Ambilai ellatha veedu – Home without a man

Vedu viruthi illai – The home is not propitious (auspicious)

Atrayo naurru – Somebody's evil eye

Vitanenaichalai kowam kowama varuguthu – When I think of the family I get angry over and over again

Kudumbathodai sethuralam poola irrukku – I feel like dying along with the family

---

Community Level

Uure urenchipochuthu – Whole village is frozen

Uur verichchodipochuthu – The village is desolate

Uur mayana pumiyaga katchiallikudu – The village resembles a cemetery

Sabikkapatta pumi – Cursed land

Kadu urenchipochchuthu – Taken over by forest

Uur redupattu pochithdu – The village is divided into two

Umaikalai valkiroom – Living as mutes

Mannaiya viranduradhu – Scrape the soil for a living

Patterns of Survival

Kaluvira meenuka naluwera meen mathiri – Like pieces of fish that slip while being washed

Odum puliyam palam poola – Relationships like the tamarind fruit sheath and the pulp

Thustanai kandal thuravilagu – Distance oneself on seeing a harmful person

Kaluthai neetitan, enna seivathu, kadiasivarai valaththane venum – I have stuck out my neck, what shall I do, I will have to live till the end

Ellam vithi palan nadakkuithu – Everything is in accordance to my fate

Nadakurathu nadakkatum – Let what happens happen

Enkalukum oru kalam varum – We will also have our day

Etho pillaikalukkaka valukuroom – Somehow we are living for the sake of our children

Etho padaithavan padi allaka thane venum – Somehow my creator will have to measure out for me

---

Source: Compiled by psychosocial trainees during field training.

Lack of living space, living in one thatched hut without any form of privacy, lack of space and lighting for learning had its consequences on the normative development of the child. Newly married couples, living with their parents without privacy for sex, had its toll as well. However, this aspect did not receive the attention of the many state and non-sate actors (LTTE) in these villages.

A father was living away from his family, but visited on and off to meet his wife but avoided meeting his fourteen-year-old daughter. The child was depressed because of her father's behaviour. On speaking to the mother it was discovered that the daughter had seen the father and mother having sexual relations. Since then the father was ashamed to face his daughter. Such incidents may lead the children to indulge in sexual relationships.

Common Psychological Problems Presented by Children Children commonly exhibited behavioural disorders such as aggression, anger, violence, being withdrawn and lack of interest in education. Children were inducted into smoking, taking alcohol, involvement in petty theft and sexual exploits. School dropout was a major problem. Children manipulated and threatened their parents saying that they would join the militants or commit suicide when reprimanded or when their demands were not met. State and non-state actors presenting many projects for the well-being of these IDPs failed to identify and address such behaviour. In general, society labelled them incorrigible and ostracized them. Many such vulnerable children over the age of fourteen were manipulated by militant organizations and were shot, recruited into fighting, abducted or went missing.

Box 5A.1 highlights some traditional methods of alleviating children's fear, which we observed during our fieldwork in the villages.

Women

Most women in the villages we worked in were trapped in the culture and took a compliant role in the family and the community. Internationally

Box 5A.1:
Traditional Methods of Handling Sudden Fear in Children

Traditionally, when children felt sudden fear, mothers would spit thrice on the left side of the chest followed by three light strokes. This was practised during times of shelling and bombing. When a child awoke at night, startled, the mother would apply holy ash and place an iron object under the bed or mat.

Source: Observations of psychosocial trainees during field training.

established women's rights are culturally violated and accepted as the norm. Values and role models carried over through generations and praised in folk songs, drama and ancient literature have persuaded women to be subservient. In this respect elderly women, more than the male members, force younger women to follow the norms.

Loss of male members due to the protracted war forced changes in the roles of women. Especially poignant was the grief for the loss of a male member. My personal observation was that this grief was prolonged, experienced by reliving the loss and its associated pain, which may be a cultural influence. Moreover, repeated losses such as the unnatural death of a husband followed by the abduction of a son or a young family member joining the militants did not provide the necessary opportunity for recovery. The confinement of females to the immediate neighbourhood compared to the exposure of males to a wider society may be another reason. Moreover the men had avenues of escape, such as consuming alcohol.

During normal times it was the male householder that gave protection to the women, but the war reversed this role. It was the mother, sister or wife and elderly women who protected young adults from the armed forces.

The women's problems we encountered and dealt with may be broadly categorized into three areas:

1. *War-related widows and female-headed families*: The villages we worked in comprised mainly war widows and women deserted by their husbands. These women were burdened with many roles: being the breadwinner and raising many children. Many of these women found employment as unskilled workers in small farms but were paid less than their male counterparts. They were subject to sexual harassment and exploitation. Malnourished and worn out, they easily succumbed to illnesses. The children at home, without parental care, were exposed to many forms of exploitation, especially sexual abuse.

2. *Spinsters and the burden of dowry*: Generally a girl child is considered an unwelcome member of the family, mainly due to the dowry system and inability to generate an income. The war aggravated this attitude. Marriage by falling in love does happen, where dowry is not demanded. People in the villages we worked in, however, had little and nothing to give as dowry because they were displaced. Thus, there were many *muthirkannikal* (spinsters). The house and property left behind on being displaced is not considered of value as dowry as it is within the HSZ and occupied by the armed forces.

3. *Domestic violence*: In the villages where we operated, domestic violence was taken for granted. So much so that if a wife was not beaten on and off, the womenfolk assumed that the husband was odd and atypical. Use of alcohol was another causal factor. About 70 per cent of men consumed alcohol and drank until they staggered. Domestic

violence occurs at three levels. One is physical abuse, at times leading to hospitalization. The second is verbal abuse; using unacceptable language. The third is causing pain by manipulating topics very sensitive to the wife. Chastity is a virtue highly valued by women in the Tamil culture. A husband could cause immense pain by questioning her chastity, which at times even led to suicide. The wife takes full responsibility for the well-being of the family from providing emotional support, preparation of food, meeting educational needs, to nursing. The husband adopts a means of flight (escape), saying he is the breadwinner and is tired from working. The cumulative effect was a higher incidence of minor mental disorders such as anxiety, mild depression, somatoform disorders and suicidal tendencies in women.

Elders

Most elders, even in their dotage, were engaged in work due to poverty and to avoid being forsaken by the family. They appeared severely malnourished, with little medical support. Many suffered from eye defects, undiagnosed diabetes and hypertension. Food, clothing and emotional support were lacking, they ate leftover food and wore used clothes. If an elderly man became bed ridden, he was allowed to 'go beyond' with scant attention. On inquiring about the neglect, the response we got most of the time was that he was suffering owing to the injustice and abuses he had meted out to his wife and others in the family. Generally it was the female children who cared for the elderly parents.

Most of the elders suffered (unlike the young) from being uprooted, loss of freedom, lack of belonging and inability to adapt to the new environment. Their dreams were often about living in their own home and village: 'We do not need any support from you all, if you can only arrange for us get back to our villages all our problems will be solved.'

The ultimate aspiration of the elders was to breathe their last and be buried or cremated in their own soil.

Behaviour

Individual Level

Lack of motivation, creativity and helplessness was commonly observed in the village. Women exhibited somatic complaints while the men resorted to abuse of alcohol and violence. Fear about decision-making due to uncertainty was pervasive. Women gave vent to their feeling and emotions following a disaster or loss by wailing and beating their chest and head (*maradithaal*), which in normal times was practised at a funeral.

Another traditional practice was to spread the hair and refrain from wearing the *pottu* (dot on the forehead) called *thalaiviri kolum*.

Family Level

Increase in disputes within the family, family separation, divorce, multiple partnerships, lack of family cohesion and child abuse were common. Some families were marginalized from the community. Brewing of illicit alcohol as a family business involving the children was a common practice.

Community Level

Organized group violence was widely prevalent. There was an increase in deceit, cheating, theft, lack of respect for the elders, lack of concern for the well-being of the community (*namakenna*); those who took leadership in CBOs had to put up with many violent groups, thus endangering their life. Hence, there was hesitance in taking leadership.

Much time was wasted in blaming the war situation and the villages we worked in had a dependent mentality. People expected regular hand-outs, rations and fought over the distribution and sharing of it. There was a marked indolence in socializing, apathy towards traditional cultural festivals and temple-based events.

Box 5A.2 describes community support systems that were observed in the villages studied.

Box 5A.2:
Community Support Systems

Looking at psychosocial problems in totality, in a community disintegrated by three decades of protracted war and disruption of the traditional support systems, did not mean that every individual or the entire community was afflicted. The communities we worked in did have some support mechanisms such as help from the extended family, traditional healers and cultural events. It was observed that not all individuals in the society thought of the well-being of only themselves but were concerned about the welfare of the family, neighbours and the community at large. If a child in the neighbourhood was crying due to hunger, it was customary for neighbours to meet the need of the child in any way possible. If one individual in the community was abroad, it was not only the immediate family that benefited but their remittances trickled down to the extended family, friends and beyond.

Source: Observations of psychosocial trainees during field training.

Analysis of Psychosocial Problems Encountered in the Field over Time

Figure 5A.1 is a diagrammatic representation of the different stages of psychosocial problems presented to the trainees.

First Stage

When we entered, the terms psychosocial and mental health were alien and unfamiliar to the community. They were only anticipating material support. We also were of opinion that their immediate need was food, shelter with some privacy and security. Hence, we debated about what to prioritize. However, with the guidance of our supervisors, we undertook awareness programmes and advocacy on psychosocial issues and mental health. The community and community-based organizations learnt of our role through this exercise. Meanwhile, we were aware of the need for basic facilities, for which we networked with the government, non-state actors and NGOs.

Second Stage

Having educated the community on psychosocial issues and mental health, those with major mental disorders, mental retardation and dementia were referred to us. This was to measure our competence and service delivery. Initially, it was a Herculean task to bring about an attitudinal change due to the stigma attached to mental illness. Most of those identified by the community required psychiatric care. We arranged for appropriate treatment and some were provided occupational therapy. On recovery, the

Figure 5A.1:
Stages of Psychosocial Problems Encountered in Fieldwork

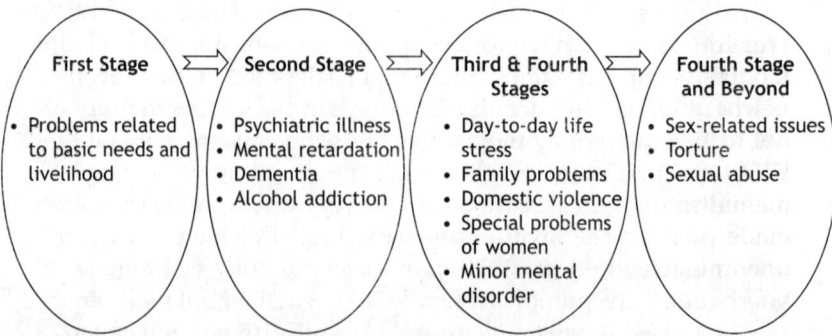

Source: Compiled by psychosocial trainees during field training.

caregivers were given psychoeducation for reintegration into the family and the society. We helped some of them with income generation activities by networking with NGOs. Our close follow-ups and the interest we showed in their well-being instilled in them a confidence and trust in our interventions.

Third Stage

The trust and confidence built during the second stage had a cascading effect, with the community coming to us with problems hitherto hidden within the family, such as minor mental health, marital and psychosocial problems encountered in daily life. With time, the number of people seeking our help increased and as trainees stumbled upon grass-roots psychosocial issues, the guidance of our supervisors was most useful. Case studies were discussed every Wednesday at the psychiatric unit at the Teaching Hospital, Jaffna where mostly those with mental issues were discussed in the context of the family and the society. At one point, the psychiatric unit could not cope with the number of patients and clients we referred, and we were requested to go slow on referrals.

Fourth Stage

The fourth and the last stage took us to psychosocial areas hidden deeply within families and the society due to cultural taboos, stigma, shame, shyness and fear such as sex-related issues, torture and rape. When looking at the four stages in totality, the first stage was the tip of an iceberg.

Box 5.3 discusses the realization by the trainees of the complex psychosocial impact of war on 'normal' day to day issues.

Box 5A.3:
Normal and War-related Issues

> War impacted on every aspect of daily life, causing an adverse modification in 'normal' issues. For example, the abuse of alcohol became much more complex, as men started to use alcohol to alleviate the consequence of war related trauma such as PTSD, anxiety and depression. There were dissimilarities in the mental state of those who were poor before the war and those made poor by the war. Again mental states of those normally unemployed could not be compared with those who lost livelihood due to the war.

Source: Observations of psychosocial trainees during field training.

Psychosocial Interventions

Psychosocial interventions could be conceived of as being undertaken at three levels: individual, family and community. Our observation was that there was potential within the community to resolve their own psychosocial issues. In reality there was an informal structure and resources to address common problems which they were unable to recognize. All that was required was to train selected members in the community with skills such as befriending and communication to identify and resolve psychosocial problems within their capacity or to refer them to mental health professionals. There were members in the community who would respond constructively during times of crisis in a family, conflict within groups, illness or death.

Some elders entertained children by relating folk stories, drama and songs. However, these systems were disrupted with the breakup of the village due to the war. Hence, our task was to reconstruct these structures and provide them the necessary skills. There were also numerous issues related to reproductive health in the community; while they had appropriate resources such as the public health inspector and family health worker, they were not aware or were unable to take advantage of their services.

Community-level Interventions

Advocacy and Awareness The expression 'psychosocial' was alien to the community. Hence, much awareness and advocacy had to be undertaken at all levels. Appropriate tools were used get across the idea and our role in the community. Awareness and advocacy were tailored to suit the target groups. We were able to identify many problems in specific groups during the awareness programmes. This in a way was a screening process.

CBOs had an essential role to play within a disrupted community. The predicament was that prospective leaders were hesitant to take over managerial positions. Our role was to reconstruct these institutions. Some villages did not have these structures at all and it was necessary to establish CBOs to respond to the needs of the community. Survival was the need of the hour and local organizations like CBOs were needed to seek support from the state and non-state actors and NGOs. CBOs were strengthened by providing training in leadership, CBO management, resource mapping, fund raising and community development.

Group Activity Those with similar psychosocial problems, needs and interests were clustered and space was created to meet, discuss and share problems and solutions as a group for their common well-being. These groups were facilitated by trainees. Activities depended on the target group. For example, youth undertook creative activities such as folk dramas and plays. Children were involved in play activities. Group activities aimed at providing psychoeducation, addressing health-related issues, identifying livelihood programmes and promoting life skills, capacity building and empowerment were undertaken. Individual needs were identified and appropriately supported. It also provided a platform for people to share their losses and sorrows and ventilate their feelings. There were no rigid rules to be followed at these meetings. However, some ground rules were specified such as listening with empathy when a person was sharing their distress or grief, and maintaining confidentiality. This was therapeutic group interaction where one tried to help another through their own experiences. Trainees intervened when there was an outburst of emotions.

Encouraging Rituals and Cultural Events   Rituals and cultural events were not being performed owing to the war milieu, displacement and camp life. Hence, the community was persuaded to pursue such events wherever and in whatever scale possible.

Core Group   Individuals who by nature had a helpful attitude were identified and brought together to form a core group comprising 8–20 members, the exact number being determined by the ground situation, to match needs, resources and who is available. They were individuals who were already in some way involved in promoting the well-being of the community. Gender balance and representation of all sectors of the community was ensured. They were provided basic training in psychosocial practices using the manual for over sixty hours, at times that suited them. The core group members participated in all activities of the trainees and they were provided with supervision and guidance.

Family Intervention

Domestic violence was a common problem to be reckoned with in all the communities we worked in. Trainees undertook psychoeducation, family counselling, information on reproductive health and fostered positive family dynamics, emphasizing on the well-being of children and importance of their education. Efforts were taken to bring about reconciliation among separated families. Networking with organizations to provide livelihood support became an important part of our work. On many occasions the family as whole was in misery and needed multipronged support.

Individual Intervention

Individual intervention was mainly for minor and major mental disorders. Those suffering from normal life stresses were befriended and provided psychoeducation, counselling, yoga and relaxation, family and social support and networking for vocational training and rehabilitation. Some with major mental health problems were referred to the psychiatric unit.

Box 5A.4 illustrates an intervention undertaken at the individual level.

Box 5A.4:
Case Study 1

> Theepan was a twenty-seven-year-old labourer, married with a one-year-old daughter. As he worked hard, he was very much in demand. Once when he was digging and clearing a piece of land that had been fallow for a long time with a spade, he hit a landmine. The explosion injured his eye and many parts of his body. The other labourers working with him took him to hospital. After treatment at the hospital, he returned home after a few days. However, he was reluctant to go back to work and stayed at home. As he was unable to earn an income, his wife went to work as a labourer in order to earn and save the family. Listening to his wife's persistent entreaties, Theepan attempted to go back to work. But he was unable to work as before. As soon as he picked up a spade he started to sweat profusely, felt weak and developed a severe headache. As a result he would stop working and return home. For some time he was not able to sleep properly. He would have nightmares of digging with the spade when a landmine would explode, injuring him badly. He would wake up suddenly trembling and sweating profusely. He also would become fearful on seeing a spade. He experienced exhaustion and headaches. Due to economic problems at home, there were frequent quarrels with his wife. Family disturbances also increased. When we heard about his situation, we went to visit him. In the beginning he denied that he had any problems and refused to talk. However, as a result of our persistence and the supportive environment we provided, he began to share his feelings with us. He confessed that he was very afraid that a landmine would explode when he went back to work. He also shared his family

(Box 5A.4 Conted.)

(Box 5A.4 Conted.)

problems. He was at a loss about what he could do. We were able to persuade him to come and talk to a psychiatrist. After examining him, the psychiatrist prescribed some medication and counselling. Theepan took his medication and went for counselling regularly. He was soon able to sleep well and go back to work. We followed up on and arranged for appropriate psychosocial support in the village.

Source: T. Thushyanthan (PST).

Challenges

To function with neutrality amidst the many political and armed forces influencing life in the community was quite risky. The influence of powerful forces involved in the distillation and sale of illicit alcoholic brews in the absence of the police, a scourge in the community, was a threat to our interventions.

The most formidable impediment to our interventions was the abuse of alcohol and caste discrimination. Hospitals were short of resources for the treatment of patients with mental illnesses. Though there was a consultant psychiatrist, he lacked service providers such as mental health and psychosocial professionals to complement him.

There was a lack of privacy when counselling in a home environment, making both the counsellor and the client uncomfortable.

Experience Learnt

As trainee PSTs, grass-roots level experience in the field progressively gave muscle to our theoretical knowledge. This was reflected in the training programmes that we conducted and gauged by the feedback of supervisors during the training. The message was that practical field experience added quality to a psychosocial and mental health trainer.

Learning and practising during a crisis amidst many threats strongly influenced the capacity for psychosocial service delivery; they were experiences worthy of sharing with others in similar situations the world over. The training was a good example of the cumulative impact of a community-based multidisciplinary psychosocial approach with the support of other service providers.

Phase Three—Training of Community Workers

Trainees conducted several trainings for various people in the community such as leaders, volunteers, traditional resources, preschool teachers, government staff (teachers, GSs, Samurdhi officers, health workers) and NGO staff. One objective was to train the core groups in the study villages. The core group was selected from socially oriented youths, village leaders and others with aptitude and interest in psychosocial issues. In each core group there were between eight and twelve members. They were given a weekend's basic training in psychosocial well-being, psychosocial problems and identification, functioning as befrienders, referral and networking. The core group was found to be sustainable in the villages to help people solve their problems at the village level.[7]

Outcome

The TOT programme commenced in July 2001 and ended in April 2002. Sixteen candidates passed out as PSTs. These PSTs functioned under Shanthiham in the war-affected areas with UNICEF support. PSTs trained another batch of trainers, and most have found permanent jobs in government sectors, where they continue to use the psychosocial and counselling skills.

Training of Teachers[8]
Continued by *Daya Somasundaram*

By 1995, in the north-east 173 schools had stopped functioning while 232 were displaced, often functioning in temporary accommodation or with other schools. Some children had classes outdoors, sitting on bare ground under trees. Teachers were in short supply, particularly in specialized subjects like science and English. Over 30 per cent of the students had lost years of education ([basic education for children in disadvantaged areas] BECAre 2003).

---

[7] Since the TOT, twenty-six core groups have been established at the community level and are presently functioning successfully. More than 320 community leaders and members have been taught basic psychosocial issues through the core groups.

[8] Modified from Prof. K. Sinnathamby Felicitation Volume (2010), Prof. K. Sinnathamby Felicitation Volume Committee, Vavuniya.

Teacher Counsellors and Befrienders

As a result of the poor state of education in the north-east, the North East Province Education Ministry and the GTZ Basic Education Sector Programme (BESP) began a massive restoration programme for the school sector in the north-east through buildings, equipment and infrastructure development. However, despite the huge investment in physical improvements of educational facilities, the performances of the students lagged.

Following an appraisal mission of the GTZ in November 1999, workshops and discussion with different stakeholders, visits to other projects and a thorough study of the international and national literature on healing traumatized children, the Basic Education for Children in the Disadvantaged Areas (BECAre) was started in Vavuniya in 2001 under GTZ/BESP. According to the BECAre project director (Divakalala, pers. comm.), Vavuniya district was chosen as it then had highest number of refugee camps, students attending the schools from the camps and untrained teachers. About fifteen thousand displaced children in Vavuniya were living mostly in fifteen camps. It was found that the children with psychological issues were 'punished' by the parents and teachers without knowing the gravity of the problem. Female orphans were often exploited as housemaids and had no chance of going to school. The children had immense problems learning.

The most effective way to reach the largest number of students would be to train the teachers in basic mental health and psychosocial knowledge, skills and attitude to identify and tackle problems within the school, classrooms and where necessary, family and community environment. Students with more difficult, complex problems or those not responding to interventions could be referred to senior, experienced teachers or mental health professionals in the district. Accordingly, it was hoped to train two tiers of teachers: one group with a more intensive, deeper training to function as (master) *teacher counsellors* who would be based in the bigger schools (with over three hundred students) with a commensurate number (two or three) for each educational zone. The second group would be a more basic, general training in psychosocial identification and simple interventions for *befrienders*, usually one or two teachers for each school. There were also general awareness seminars, workshops and discussions for principals, educational zonal directors and teachers throughout the North East Province. With the peace process beginning in 2002 and the war-ravaged North East Province opened up for restorative work, the school-based psychosocial programme was enlarged to include the whole north-eastern provincial educational structure.

Box 5A.5:
Promoting Child Well-being in Schools

- Child-friendly schools
- Joyful learning
- Fun and games
- Creative arts
- Group work
- Field trips
- Less punishment
- More rewards

Source: Author's compilation.

It was planned to build a network of teachers throughout the North-East Province, with the befrienders looking after the simpler problems, carrying out and supervising class- and school-based psychosocial promotional (see Box 5A.5) activities and awareness programmes at the school, while the more difficult issues would be dealt with by the *teacher counsellors* who would visit each school. There were to be more senior, *master counsellors* (more recently called in-service advisors [ISAs] in counselling by the Ministry of Education) at the district level providing a resource centre, regular meetings, follow-up, maintaining records, support and supervising this network (see Figure 5A.2).

Inter-sectorial and multidisciplinary networking and collaboration was to take place between mental health professionals, health, government and NGO sectors at the district MOH, Deputy Provincial Director of Health Service (DPDHS) and GA (Child Protection) levels (see Figure 2A.4).

With initial assessment and research, it was clear that the great majority of teachers did not possess basic knowledge of child psychology or the positive attitudes for child-oriented, child-friendly, well-being perspectives for promotional, class-based psychosocial activities. In fact, the prevalent attitudes were exam- and punishment-oriented, classroom control with traditional, chalk and blackboard style teaching and negative stigma attached to psychological and mental health issues. Teachers themselves were facing considerable stress; many had been traumatized and showed symptoms. In these circumstances, it was thought best to start with a basic child psychology and mental health manual, *Child Mental Health* (Sivayokan et al. 2005); a broad curriculum that tackled ingrained teaching styles, attitudes and perspectives; and a residential training where the problems and trauma of the trainees could be

Figure 5A.2:
District School Psychology Service

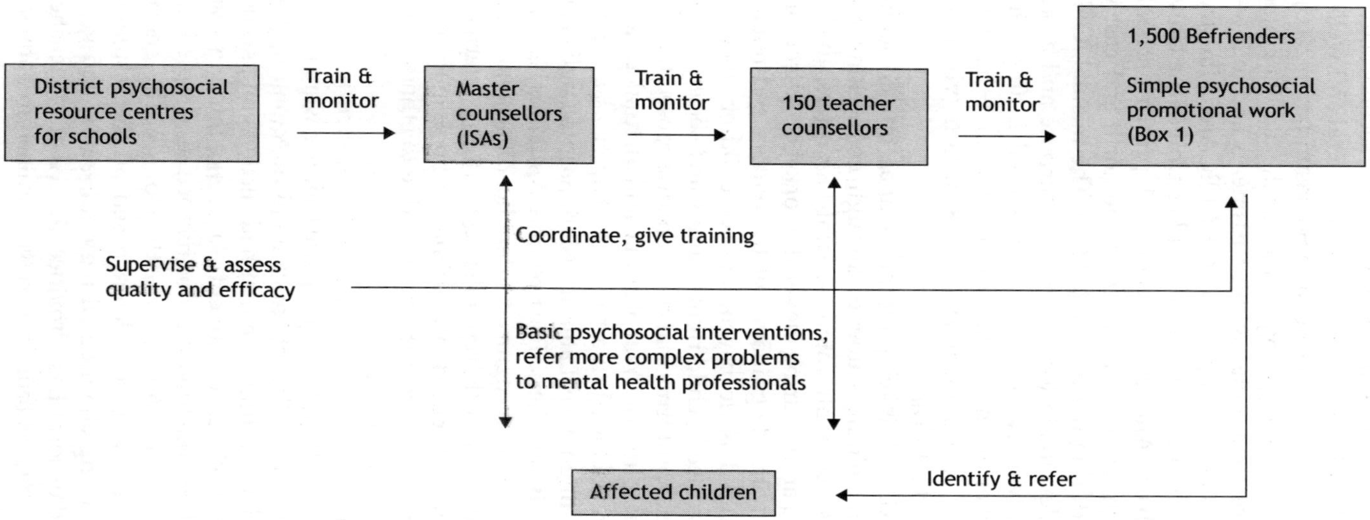

District psychosocial resource centres for schools

Train & monitor →

Master counsellors (ISAs)

Train & monitor →

150 teacher counsellors

Train & monitor →

1,500 Befrienders

Simple psychosocial promotional work (Box 1)

Coordinate, give training

Basic psychosocial interventions, refer more complex problems to mental health professionals

Supervise & assess quality and efficacy

Affected children

Identify & refer

Source: BECAre project, Vavuniya.

addressed collectively and individually. The second, activity-based, structured manual for befrienders was more general and well-being–oriented, called *Joyful Living* (Mahendran and Somasundaram 2003).

A systematic training programme for the teacher counsellors, initially for a period of six months, with assessments and follow-up was carried out with the German-supported GTZ-BECAre; Ministry of Education, North East Province; Extra Mural Studies Unit of the University of Jaffna; and Shanthiham. Altogether around 151 primary school teachers from all three communities selected from the north and east were trained in five batches during the period 2002–05. The manual, *Child Mental Health* (2005), was developed locally for this purpose and a broad curriculum using a wide variety of resources was used in the training. They then received further extensive training in NET (M. Schauer et al. 2005) by a German team from the University of Konstanz (vivo) and a manual for NET translated into Tamil.

In the process of developing the manual, trained senior teachers with experience in helping students through counselling and psychosocial interventions were allocated separate chapters that were prepared initially in Tamil during several workshop discussion sessions at Shanthiham with the guidance of the editors and reference books. The chapters covered basic psychology of children such as development, learning, basic needs, child rights, family and society as well as the variety of psychosocial problems that children are exposed to, their manifestation and possible solutions. War trauma and natural disasters such as the tsunami were included in a separate chapter as a form of severe stress that children might face. Later, translations into English and Sinhala were done separately by others. The first of its kind in Sri Lanka, the usefulness of the manual was recognized after the 2004 tsunami and the manual was accepted by the NIE, republished by PLAN International in all three languages and distributed to all primary schools in the island. The manual was later withdrawn from the schools due to ethnocentric protests in the Sri Lankan Parliament by the JVP.

The teacher counsellor trainees were selected in five groups of thirty each. Teachers willing to undergo the training were recommended by the principal, zonal and district educational directors. Applicants were then administered a questionnaire that had sections on psychosocial aptitude, attitude and intelligence quotient. An intake interview was planned, but for logistical reasons this did not happen as people had to travel from distant areas in the north-east, with poor security and transport conditions. Selections were completed based on the results of the questionnaire and to bring about equal regional, ethnic and gender distribution throughout the North East Province. A total of 143 teachers were selected for training. The first four groups were trained in Tamil at Shanthiham in

Jaffna and the fifth group was trained in Sinhala in Colombo at NIE, with resources from the University of Colombo.

The expected roles and responsibilities of the teacher counsellors are given in Box 5A.6.

Bringing teachers from all over the north-east, accommodating them in Jaffna and then taking them back was a logistically difficult task. On several occasions, travel became impossible due to the local security situation and alternate ways had to be found. Each residential training session lasted between ten and twenty-one days, with four sessions, sixty days in total. Between the sessions, for the rest of the six-month period, teachers were required to do practical work in their schools, such as preparation of case histories and simple psychosocial tasks that were written up as reports and presented during the sessions.

A usual training day's programme began at 8.30 a.m. with *ahaamaithee* (inner calming exercise) which sought to focus the emotions, cognitions

Box 5A.6:
Roles and Responsibilities of Teacher Counsellors

- Helping the child — simple psychosocial help; promotional work; using creative arts and play in groups and class-based activities
- Referral to ISAs for counselling of more severe cases or in case of doubts
- Attending to referrals of students and complaints by other teachers
- Awareness programmes, lectures, discussions for other staff and parents
- Meeting parents regularly, during parents–teachers' association meeting, and individually
- Attending supervision and monitoring meetings in the zone by counselling ISAs
- Promoting co-curricular activities in the school and classrooms; mental health promotional activities, improving the mental health environment in the school, participating arranging community relief, rehabilitation, development programmes, reconciliation and peace building activities
- Protecting child rights
- Helping other teachers
- Recording

Source: Compiled by author for the Teacher Counsellor training.

and behaviour through a meaningful saying for each day followed by silent self-reflection for five minutes. This was followed by singing the teacher's anthem[9] and then the counsellor's anthem.[10] Following the theory from the manual, teachers were trained using a variety of interactive methods in basic skills in building a positive relationship with students; communication skills like listening; using creative artistic activities like play, art, drama, singing and storytelling; relaxation techniques; reaching out to the family and community; interacting with the family to work towards family unity; counselling; and other psychosocial interventions. Apart from specific topics from the manual, there were special lectures on a broad range of subjects from child rights, child abuse, drugs and alcohol and social issues to violence and conflict transformation, which were delivered by a variety of external resources from the university, health, education and civil sectors. The goal was to broaden the outlook of the teachers, increase their psychosocial knowledge base, change attitudes and perspectives. Then there were two or three win-win games (like *palacharu* [fruit salad], sun is burning, green parrot where is your fruit?) played between the regular curriculum programmes. These games were modified from traditional drama games where there is no victor. The games are played joyfully, followed by collective discussions. Teaching methods included didactic lectures, discussions, group work, participant initiatives, narrative methods, role play, drawings, real case presentations,[11] demonstrations and other creative innovations. At night there was opportunity for individual counselling or expression. Many of the teachers had personal problems or had experienced severe trauma due to the ongoing war which were dealt with confidentially.

Assessment and evaluation of each teacher was done by continuous assessment; periodic, unannounced exams using oral questions or a few written questions; final written exam consisting of multiple-choice, structured and compulsory essay questions; viva voce; microteaching practicals; and ten testimonies of students they had helped. Results were graded at first class, upper and lower second, ordinary pass and failure. Those who failed had to repeat parts of the training and undergo the assessment again until they passed to receive the certificate. Certificates were given during a ceremony at the University of Jaffna auditorium or Shanthiham by the vice-chancellor, GTZ national director and other community leaders. Teachers had to take the teacher counsellor oath, which was followed by creative performances like songs and dramas by the teachers and dinner.

[9] Created with musical score by Vamathevan.

[10] Created with musical score by Paheerathy Ganeshathurai.

[11] With the children and parents present, and after discussion, suggestions made to the parents and teacher for future actions.

It is noteworthy that despite the ongoing ethnic conflict, teachers from Tamil, Sinhala and Muslim communities and Hindu, Christian, Islamic and Buddhist religions participated. Muslims were given extra time on Fridays for their customary prayers. Special meals were provided and other cultural needs taken care of.

Those who obtained first class became assistant resources for the next training. The quality of the training increased with each group due to the lessons learnt and experience gained. There were between five and eight dropouts in each group. Travelling difficulties, local security concerns, stress factors, difficulties with the subject that some could not resolve, female Muslim teachers facing special difficulties regarding accommodation, food and travel were some of the reasons for the dropouts. Two became ill, one with psychotic illness; two were unwilling to continue and one had migrated. Two were not able to pass the final exam and repeats. Some who attained first class did not continue in the programme while some who had a second class excelled in their subsequent service at school (counselling, psychosocial activities, supervision and support to befrienders).

Monitoring of the work of the first batch of thirty-four teacher counsellors, once they had returned to their schools, found that they continued to help students who were referred to them by fellow teachers and the principal. In the first few months, altogether 207 children had been helped using counselling, family counselling, relaxation exercises (mainly yoga), art and play therapy, working with the family and colleagues (see Table 5A.4).

Table 5A.4:
Types of Psychosocial Intervention (Per Teacher)

Type of Intervention	Average	Range
Counselling (Sessions)	07	02–30
Family Counselling	02	01–07
Other Family Interventions	–	–
Relaxation Exercises	14	01–106
Art Therapy	06	01–34
Play Therapy	23	02–110
Classroom/School Motivation	11	01–110
Socio-economic Help to Family (Referral)	01	01–06
Social Interventions		
Advice	02	01–20
Support	0.4	01–06
Other	03	01–48

Source: Monitoring and evaluation of the training by the author.

The outcome of the teachers' intervention showed favourable results in 61 per cent of the students (see Table 5A.5).

Table 5A.5:
Outcome of Psychosocial Interventions

Outcome	Total	Average Number Per Teacher	Percentage for Each Teacher
Improved	128	05	61
Same	30	01	14.5
Worse	00	00	00
No information	49	–	24

Source: Monitoring and evaluation of the training by the author.

The teachers also helped fellow teachers, worked with their colleagues and the community to increase awareness and knowledge through discussion and lectures as well as undertaking a variety of community-level preventive and psychoeducation initiatives (see Tables 5A.6 and 5A.7)

Table 5A.6:
Psychosocial Interventions for Colleagues

Type of Intervention	Total	Average Per Teacher
Counselling	71	03
Advice	60	02
Support	54	02
Other	17	0.6

Source: Monitoring and evaluation of the training by the author.

Table 5A.7:
Other Psychosocial Activities

Activity	Total	Average Per Teacher
Discussions		
Teachers	162	06
Parents	59	02
Society	30	01
Other	–	–
Lectures		
Teachers	61	02

(Table 5A.7 Contd.)

(Table 5A.7 Contd.)

Activity	Total	Average Per Teacher
Parents	14	0.5
Society	05	0.2
Other	45	02
Child Rights		
Parent–Teacher Meetings	34	01
Anti-alcohol	20	0.8
School		
Play	115	04
Drama	28	01
Yoga	13	0.5
Art	63	–
Gardens	61	02
Teachers' Meetings	46	02
Library	57	02
Other	07	0.3
Socio-economic		
Economic Help to Family	34	01
Other Help to Family	07	0.3
Economic Help to Society	34	01
Food or Development	01	00
Community Library	06	0.2
Social Justice	02	00
Human rights	04	0.2
Network with Government or NGO	17	0.7
Joint activities	07	0.3

Source: Monitoring and evaluation of the training by the author.

The monitoring showed what can be achieved by adequately trained and motivated teachers. However, it was clear that teachers found it difficult to find time for the type of psychosocial work they had been trained for. As they had not yet been officially appointed to such a post nor allocated time for psychologically helping the child, they had to use whatever free time they had. Many stayed after school to help children in need. Under these circumstances, teachers showed lack of confidence in their ability to do counselling and engage in other psychosocial interventions. The course time of six months and practical training in the skills involved may not have been sufficient. One of the lessons learnt from the study was to organize the practical aspect of actually doing the interventions under supervision. Official recognition and appointment or allocation of time for psychosocial work would help the teachers use and develop their skills.

In order to evaluate and learn from the first training programme so as to improve and change the training course as necessary, an impact study by the North East Province Education Ministry was undertaken two months after the completion of the training (BECAre 2003). The study attempted to assess the activities and attitudes of the teachers during their regular responsibilities once they had returned to their schools after the training. The methodology involved school visits, observation of teachers in the classrooms, discussion with principals, teachers, their colleagues and students, group interviews and individual questionnaire responses. The results were analysed using comparisons and statistical methods.

Overall the course appeared to have changed the activities of the teachers for the better. Attitudes to children, mental health, teaching, human rights, peace and a wide variety of other issues showed a marked improvement. At the school, as well as at home and in society, the teacher counsellors had better relationships, showed more respect and understanding for others and participated in extracurricular activities. The trained teachers had been actively involved in creating awareness about the needs of children, their rights and healthy family life. They interacted with their students in a more positive way, used a variety of teaching methods that helped each child to develop their own skills and creative abilities. They also helped fellow teachers and many managed to bring about changes in the school atmosphere as well as reduce the negative behaviour of colleagues. Many had worked with dysfunctional families to improve their situation. Some had developed socio-economic programmes for the school, family and community.

However, the study found that under direct observation, the knowledge and attitudes imparted to the teachers did not always result in changes in their classroom teaching style and behaviour when compared to a control group who had not received the training. Since all primary school teachers in the north and east had undergone the training in *Joyful Learning* initiated by the GTZ, these non-specific characteristics of good teaching may have been adopted by all teachers and not shown up as a difference due to this training. The teachers may have found it difficult to give up their old habit of the chalk-and-talk method of teaching and rigid control of the classroom environment. Expectations of fellow teachers, principals and parents may have also been a hindrance in their adapting the newer, creative child-centred methods. Direct observation did find that teacher counsellors were emotionally balanced, democratic and accessible to the students and had stopped using physical and punitive punishment. They were observed to attentively listen with empathy to the students.

The teachers with additional resources like the master counsellors were involved in the training of around 1,500 befriender primary school teachers from all over the north-east in simple psychosocial issues using the manual, *Joyful Living*, prepared for this purpose (Mahendran and Somasundaram 2003). Senior master counsellor teachers and the editors prepared the manual which had three chapters on a 'Healthy Child', 'Children Needing Help' and 'Helping Children Return to Normality'. The topics were addressed in a simple, structured, user-friendly format that included many practical exercises and activities. The residential training was held over six days, two days for each chapter, in a school of that area. Apart from some didactic lecture-type teaching, most of training was done in a participatory manner with discussions, singing, play activities, drama, drawing, dancing and narrations that went on long after hours. There was no exam at the end, and everyone received a participation certificate. An evaluative discussion at the end with written and verbal suggestions provided feedback of the training and means to improve the next training. Many, who did well in the course and later functioned with interest and motivation at school, subsequently applied for and followed the teacher counsellor course. A follow-up of the activities of the befrienders showed that they had helped a vast number of students from all over the north-east, apart from improving the classroom and school atmosphere, interactions with pupils and colleagues and introducing more child-centred and creative activities into the schools.

Regular follow-up and local supervision was carried out. Yet, the whole programme faltered after the GTZ changed its programme focus from 2005. This brings up the prickly issue of sustainability of foreign-funded INGO programmes that may create dependence on regular payments of incentives. However, some teachers continued their counselling and psychosocial activities despite having no official support (for example, after hours).

Another advantage of all the training that had been done during the war period became apparent when the tsunami struck in 2004. The trained teachers were mobilized to assist the affected students throughout the north-east. The benefits of this programme became evident nationally. Copies of the manual in Sinhala and Tamil were made available in all the schools in the island through the efforts of PLAN International, and psychosocial training was given for teachers in the tsunami-affected areas. The need for psychosocial assistance was recognized after the tsunami for the first time, the so-called tsunami wisdom due to the obvious psychological and mental health consequences that was evident (Catani et al. 2009), and there were several national and local programmes to help those mentally affected (see Chapter 3A).

However, the training and experience of teacher counsellors from the north-east did not gain official recognition nationally, possibly due to reasons discussed in Chapter 1A. Following the tsunami, a specialized unit to deal with psychosocial work by teachers was set up in the Ministry of Education as the Guidance and Counselling (later changed to Psychosocial Intervention) Unit, under UNICEF direction. The prior training and experience of teacher counsellors from the north-east was devalued and ignored. During their retraining, they were asked to 'forget' all their past learning and skills, a form of 'deskilling' (Harrell-Bond 1986), and undergo re-education in more basic psychosocial work if they wanted to continue in this field. Apparently, it was deemed by the authorities at the centre, possibly at the behest of the new advisors from the West with a more social background, that the training and conceptualization in the north-east had been too clinical, based on a medical model, that concentrated on mental health and pathology.[12] That assumption was made because a psychiatrist had been involved in designing the programme. They did not actually look at the curriculum or at what the teacher counsellors were doing and their capacity. Admittedly, there may have inadvertently been too much emphasis and interest placed on case identification, diagnosis, 'treatment' and different methods of psychological intervention rather than on more general well-being promotion. There was particular criticism of the NET approach that was part of the training by a German team. As a result, many of the teacher counsellors and befrienders were not officially appointed while the others underwent the humiliating retraining in Colombo. The emphasis was shifted to teacher guidance and counselling model, although there was to be no counselling as such. They have happily been reinventing the wheel in Colombo! A separate organization, Aaruthal, was formed to continue with their psychosocial work outside the official mainstream while others continue on their own. However, official recognition and mobilization is needed at this critical time for the work with the Vanni resettlement programme.

Structured Activity

With the aim of the DRC implemented in Sri Lanka, in a collaborative programme involving the Ministry of Education, DRC and SLRC and Shanthiham, 150 teachers and 118 volunteers were trained during 2004–06, to implement structured activity in badly affected schools in the Jaffna

---

[12] This has been the traditional bone of contention between the WHO and UNICEF approaches: the difference between so-called health and well-being models (see also Chapter 5B).

peninsula using a manual titled *We Are Little Children* (Somasundaram et al. 2005) prepared for this purpose. The aim was to promote psychosocial well-being through play, art, dancing, stories, yoga, creative and emotional expression and involvement of the parents. Based on similar manuals prepared in conflict situations in other parts of world where the DRC was implementing school psychosocial programmes, the manual was adapted to the Tamil culture. In the Tamil version, particular attention was paid to use a family and community perspective rather than the individualistic orientation in the Western manuals (for example, emphasizing the name and relationship in the family rather than the child's own name, personality and wishes). Traditional games, art forms, songs and stories were used. Yogic postures were taught as means of relaxation. The manual was divided into chapters on family, relationships, communication, creativity, expression, conflict, peace, values, faith and positive thoughts. The theme in each chapter was developed by the activities undertaken in each session, lasting for two hours. Staring with a song on the theme, thought for the day, traditional exercise (yoga), games, creative activities to express emotion like singing, dancing, acting, drawing, playing, imagining and relaxing were all designed to develop the central theme of that particular chapter and session. Each chapter ran for five sessions; the last session was with parents where a special programme was designed to promote family unity, networks between families and child–parent interaction and understanding. A nutritious midday meal was cooked and served to the students at the beginning of each session. The programme also included health education and programmes, sports activity and excursions.

With the acceptance of this methodology by the NIE in the aftermath of the tsunami, the manual was then translated into Sinhalese and distributed to all schools nationally. The programme ran for two years in selected schools, but had to be stopped in the third year. The whole programme collapsed when the DRC decided to pull out of Jaffna after the resurgence of the war in 2006.

Class-based Intervention

A similar classroom-based intervention, the Child Thematic Project, developed by Robert Macy and colleagues at the Centre for Trauma Psychology, Boston, conducted in conflict-affected countries (Sri Lanka, Burundi, Sudan, Indonesia and Nepal) was implemented in Jaffna together with HealthNet–TPO and Shanthiham, using structured play activity over five weeks for fifteen sessions where students aged between eight and twelve years from fourteen schools underwent this programme from 2004 to 2007. Initially a master training course was organized in September 2004, followed by training and refresher courses to strengthen weak areas and update skills of facilitators and counsellors. There were awareness programmes for directors of education, principals, teachers and parents. The central component was the classroom-based psychosocial intervention, mainly group activities (including games, music, art and drama). The classroom-based intervention aimed to reduce the risk of maladaptation; facilitate resiliency, return to normalcy, empowerment and mastery; and use a natural learning environment while screening for high-risk youth (Macy et al. 2004b).

Children identified as having special needs were provided psychosocial care such as individual counselling for specific child mental health problems, family and parental support, case management, public awareness and youth groups (minimal psychosocial care package—MPCP). In addition, the project networked with existing services and programmes. Research (through a randomized controlled trial for effectiveness and qualitative studies) was conducted at the same time (Tol et al. 2012). The project was carried out in a rapidly deteriorating security situation (with the restart of hostilities in 2005–06) and the logistics proved difficult. The classroom-based intervention activities in the schools were highly appreciated at all levels and well supported by the directors of education of the respective zones and principals of the schools involved.

In time, it is hoped that the school system will incorporate psychosocial well-being and services within their normal function and these subjects would become part of the curriculum in teacher education institutions. Psychosocial knowledge, skills and attitude should be part of a teacher's normal capability.

It is important in training and implementing psychosocial work that one is mindful of the potential effects on the workers themselves of working in such difficult situations. The following section will look at the possible costs and rewards of working with people who have been through traumatic events based on a research study conducted in Sri Lanka in 2007.

Vicarious Trauma
By *Kuhan Satkunanayagam*

Mental health workers in virtually all settings work with clients who are survivors of trauma of some kind and degree. The impact of being in a caring and therapeutic relationship with a survivor of trauma may be expressed very differently depending on context. Vicarious trauma is a relatively recent notion that has emerged in the field of mental health work with survivors of trauma, encompassing man-made trauma such as torture, rape and sexual abuse and to a lesser extent natural traumas such as earthquakes, tsunamis and hurricanes. There are several different terms within the literature that describe its effects on mental health workers, with vicarious trauma being a term given to phenomena uniting various definitions. A central principle is that repeated exposure to client's traumatic experience can cause a shift in the way those working with survivors of traumas perceive themselves, others and the world (McCann and Pearlman 1990).

More commonly practitioners talk about burnout and countertransference. Burnout is a result of frustration, powerlessness and inability to achieve work goals which can lead to psychophysiological arousal such as sleep disturbance, headaches, irritability and aggression, but also physical and mental exhaustion. It has been suggested that burnout may occur in individuals in any profession while vicarious trauma occurs only among those who work specifically with trauma survivors (McCann and Pearlman 1990). Countertransference describes the unconscious attunement to and absorption of people's stresses and traumas. Countertransference tends to refer to a therapist's emotional reaction to a client as a result of the therapist's own personal life experiences, while vicarious trauma refers to the direct reaction to traumatic client material (Figley 1995). Countertransference refers specifically to a therapist's experiences during or around therapeutic sessions, while the effects of vicarious trauma can transcend the session and affect all aspects of a mental health worker's life.

It has, however, been argued that the concept of vicarious trauma can be viewed as an unhelpful and inappropriate pathological descriptor for normal distress that is a consequence of hearing traumatic material within a caring role (Sabin-Farrell and Turpin 2003). Nevertheless, there is an underlying shared recognition that trauma work is difficult, challenging and frequently exhausting for those who undertake it, no matter their profession, gender, age or level of training and experience. In order to minimize the impact of trauma work and lessen one's potential vulnerability to vicarious trauma, it is important to examine constantly the toll that conducting the work takes on the self. Practitioners need to keep monitoring feelings of frustration and hopelessness as well as feelings of joy and accomplishment (Saakvitne and Pearlman 1996). At a deeper psychological and existential level mental health workers need to try and ascertain how the work has touched their personal beliefs and expectations concerning safety, trust, power, esteem and intimacy with self and others (McCann and Pearlman 1990). This awareness comes through training and reflective practice.

A recent study looking at the experience of mental health workers working with survivors of trauma in Sri Lanka used questions about vicarious trauma as a way of tapping into the participants' own understandings and culturally specific ways of managing and withstanding the (dis)stress of trauma work (Satkunanayagam 2008). The study showed that the impact of being in a caring and therapeutic relationship with a survivor of trauma is indebted to prevalent cultural meanings and practices but at the same time it may be experienced as well as expressed differently, and the coping strategies employed may also show great variation.

All the participants acknowledged the negative impact of trauma work. As participants said: 'It has affected me ... I felt that I was also looking at the world in a distorted way not a realistic way ... I felt that my perception was changing and I caught myself at it' (Amila). According to Thilini:

> Most of the people believe that this kind of profession is not good for long time, likewise, because always we are listening to the sorrowful situations and their problems. And it may be a problem for our lives, our family and everything. But I think we should have an ability to make them balance.

For Amila and Thilini there is an awareness that the effects of trauma work are not just on them as professionals but have repercussions in terms of their private and family life. This highlights the contextual nature of listening and the contextual solutions that have to be found to bring balance. However, not all the participants agreed with the term vicarious trauma. According to Balan:

> I don't agree with the term vicarious trauma. You know, trauma is trauma .... You know in our Hindu culture, Tamil, Sinhala, or whatever, Christian or Muslim, the system is this ... it is quite difficult to later compensate. When husband loses the wife or the wife loses the husband, it is more than losing a husband or wife in our context. If the family loses children, it is more than losing kids or children, it has the impact that people cannot explain sometimes. Later on it adds to various things in their life. I would rather call it like a thing that goes like a chain, attached to the other like that, secondary trauma, collective trauma.

Balan rejects the necessity of two terms and differentiating secondary trauma from trauma. For him trauma and its consequences occur at multiple levels, not just primary and secondary with a ripple effect based on kinship and community. Implicit in the notion of vicarious trauma is an emphasis on individual reactions to caring and helping a survivor of trauma. However, in a collective society like Sri Lanka and where survivors of trauma are in the majority, it may be more useful to talk of secondary trauma in more collective terms rather than focusing on the individual.

This broader, holistic perspective becomes paramount in cultures such as Sri Lanka which have traditionally been family- and community-orientated, with the individual tending to become submerged in the wider concerns (Somasundaram 2007a). In collectivist societies the individual becomes embedded within the family and community, so much so that traumatic events are experienced through the larger unit and the impact will also manifest at that level.

The accounts of the participants showed how in spite of the negative social circumstances, mental health workers in Sri Lanka can construct useful coping practices through positive engagements with their successful experiences of treatment interventions. In this study mental health workers seemed to find positive ways of coping with distress using culturally appropriate methods of reflection and sensing togetherness in a community-orientated society (Satkunanayagam 2008).

The importance of reflective practice was highlighted and many of the participants talked about the self-monitoring strategies they used and the self-awareness they cultivated through meditation. Jegan said, 'I do meditation. And I feel I am the best counsellor to me.' Selvan said, 'When I travel by motorcycle, I work through my memory of what happened today.'

The analysis also highlighted the importance of self-care. In their own individualized ways, the participants were able to find and maintain a balance of work, play and rest. As Phoebe said:

> I take care of myself. Sometimes I go for a walk. If it is too much stress for me I walk for a mile in the evenings, get out from the bus and I try to walk. And sometimes just playing music…. So that's how I take care of myself.

Selvan said, 'I will read, or I might go to the temple, or I want to hear music, that's what I do, hearing music and watering plants.'

Vigna said:

> The problem is that in conflict situations and things like that there is a tendency to feel very guilty when there are so many people suffering, can you be listening to music, can you be reading stories, go cycling and stuff like that. You need to get out of that mould, that is dangerous, you go into that and you just get burned out, and you are not useful to anybody.

As Vigna indicates the imperative to engage in self-care and self-nurturing becomes paramount, not just an indulgence when working with survivors of trauma. It is an essential part of the mechanism of working with trauma survivors.

Another important theme was the importance of peer supervision, support and accountability, together, which seemed to help maintain a sense of hope: 'We share our feelings. I share my experiences of work' (Jegan).

The level of supervision available to the participants varied and for many it was through peer supervision and case consultation. Balan explained: 'We work in a punctual way and we have case conferences and supervision. It is a huge team we are working with and we discuss this, every week after every session.'

There is an increasing recognition of the transformative nature of trauma work and that individuals are changed by the work they do with survivors of trauma. For mental health workers these changes can be both positive and negative and there is a belief that the rewards of trauma work can balance the painful effects of vicarious trauma (Saakvitne and Pearlman 1996). The energy, empathy and creativity which are called upon in undertaking work with trauma survivors need to be nurtured, safeguarded and replenished in some way. Mental health workers take seriously the impact of trauma in the lives of the individuals they serve, and are aware of the need to extend the same level of commitment and compassion to themselves (Saakvitne and Pearlman 1996).

Much of the research on the impact of trauma has focused on *negative* responses and unhelpful cognitive processes. However, there is an emerging body of work showing that individuals are also able to apprehend a stressful event or traumatic exposure in ways that render new, helpful meanings out of unpleasantness; post-trauma growth as a possible outcome with salutogenic effects of caring for distressed people is one example of this (Figley 1995). This body of empirical work encourages researchers to adopt a view which recognizes that the experience of traumatic events can have positive as well as negative consequences (Calhoun and Tedeschi 2006; Joseph and Linley 2006; Linley and Joseph 2004; Williams and Joseph 1999).

Several studies have shown how, following the experience of a traumatic event (for example, bereavement, chronic illness, cancer, rape, sexual abuse, hostage taking), many survivors emerged from their ordeal with a belief that they had benefited in different ways and degrees from their experience (Calhoun and Tedeschi 1999; Tedeschi and Calhoun 1995). Irrespective of the specific trauma, similar personal transformations tended to be reported. Tedeschi and Calhoun (1995) suggest that the process of struggling with crises provides opportunities for personal growth that would not have been possible without the challenge of the traumatic event, coining the term 'posttraumatic growth' to describe such an outcome. More theoretical and empirical work is now being carried out looking closely at the human capacity for 'growth through adversity' as an alternative paradigm (Joseph and Linley 2005, 2006; Linley and Joseph 2005).

Very little research seems to have been done on the collective and communal aspects of resilience and growth through adversity. Vázquez et al. (2008) suggest that collective traumas can promote positive social changes with extreme situations providing opportunities for collective action. It appears that terrorist attacks such as the 9/11 attacks in the United States and the 11 March attacks in Madrid, originally planned to weaken society, have acted as catalysts to develop interpersonal strengths, improved social and community aspects and even philosophical or spiritual domains (Ai et al. 2006; Vázquez Valverde 2005). There is an acknowledgement that in addition to the collective negative impact of trauma there can be a collective sense of resilience and growth. In Sri Lanka the collective growth through adversity from over twenty years of civil conflict may have reflected the resilience with which Sri Lanka as a nation faced the Indian Ocean tsunami of 2004.

Community Interventions
Continued by *Daya Somasundaram*

Some community-level interventions that evolved organically from the needs of the situation, the limited resources available, what was being done in other parts of the world and continuing experience and feedback of effectiveness are described below. A few have already been mentioned in Chapter 3A.

Traditional Coping Strategies

Indigenous coping strategies that have helped the local population to survive were encouraged. Culturally mediated protective factors like rituals and ceremonies were researched and promoted where appropriate. For example, funerals and anniversaries were found to be powerful ways to help in grieving and finding comfort. They were a source of strength, support and meaning for the members of the grieving family and community. The extended family and community came together at these occasions and supported each other.

Teaching of the culturally appropriate relaxation exercises like yoga to large groups in the community was undertaken. Yoga and traditional relaxation methods are routinely used in combination with other interventions by the multidisciplinary team functioning in the psychiatric units at General Hospital in Jaffna, Kilinochchi, Vavuniya; Base Hospital in Tellippalai, Point Pedro, Chavakachcheri and other health institutions. Most community-level workers trained by us carry out various forms of traditional relaxation therapy where appropriate. They were particularly useful in the treatment of somatization and related minor mental health disorders namely anxiety disorders, somatoform disorders, minor depression, psychosomatic illnesses and PTSD (Somasundaram 2002b). In torture survivors with musculoskeletal pain and distorted body image issues, relaxation methods, massage and yoga have been found to be beneficial. Similarly in landmine victims and others with amputation experiencing phantom limb problems, these methods have been used to restore a feeling of wholeness. In the long-term management of alcohol and drug abuse, yoga was introduced as a method of changing lifestyles.

Yoga practices include breathing exercises, stretches, posture, relaxation techniques and meditation to balance the body's energy centres. Instructors adapted these range of exercises to meet the needs of patients and their physical and psychological capacity.

Yoga has been recognized as contributing to peace building initiatives. A community-based revival of using traditional relaxation methods could act as a calming, countervailing force against the social chaos and violence of a chronic war. When people come together to learn and practise culturally familiar methods the atmosphere can be reassuring and socially cohesive. Apart from the actual practice of the methods, people will interact in a healthy way, support each other, find meaning for their problems and suffering through the religious doctrines on karma and suffering as well as structure their time and energy in a constructive, non-detrimental way.

In the case of Jaffna, attempts have been made to revive the use of yoga by providing regular instructions to the public and in schools.

Group Therapy

Groups for survivors, affected families, widows, ex-detainees, torture survivors, landmine victims and other similarly affected persons were formed. A psychosocial worker organized and facilitated the formation and interactions within these groups, which in time developed their own momentum in their own healing and caring processes.

An example was a widows' support programme in a particularly badly affected fishing village, Chavatkaddu, which was found to have a significantly high number of war widows. Initially the group was organized and started in 2001 by the first batch of PSTs during their field experience (see previous sections). Later, it was funded as a regular programme by the government of Finland and expanded to other badly affected villages as well. The widows met as a group to support each other, exchange their stories and recount experiences. They were able to organize themselves into a powerful group to overcome stigma and exclusion in their village, undertake joint economic ventures, obtain relief and rehabilitation projects, arrange for education and tuition for their children, go on tours together, celebrate religious and cultural festivals and observe death anniversaries. In time they were able to expand their programmes to other villages, training their counterparts and helping them to organize themselves. A description of the programme follows.

Tharaka—Centre for Blossoming Widows ('Tharaka Vidavaikalukkana Malarvu Myyam')[13]

With contributions from *Thedsanamoorthy Vijayasangar* and *Vijayasangar Sivajini*

A baseline survey of the village of Chavatkaddu indicated a high incidence of young widows. Among the multiple psychosocial problems encountered by them, the significant one was that their basic needs were not being met. Though many governmental organizations and NGOs were working in the area, this need was not effectively addressed. The organizations that were helping were looking at their material needs outside the context of their psychosocial needs.

During our need assessment of the village, widows appeared as the most vulnerable, neglected and ostracized. Hence, our activities primarily targeted this cluster. Basically, we encouraged them to come together and empowered them to seek the support of other institutions to collectively address their needs. It is noteworthy that there were women-based CBOs in the village at the time of our arrival, but they did not include the widows. The widows were marginalized, stigmatized, rudderless and inactive. Some Christian priests had helped individual widows, which brought some amount of displeasure among others but had advised them to function collectively as a group to garner support.

Assessment

The village of Chavatkaddu was selected based on the criteria for the selection of vulnerable villages evolved by Shanthiham mentioned above. Basic information of the village was obtained from the GS and from the divisional secretariat of Sandilipay and also from government officers such as the PHI and PHW.

Chavatkaddu had 750 families with 1,700 women, of whom 119 were widows. Sixty-two of them were young, with forty-two being widowed

[13] Translated by C. Wijeyaratnam.

Box 5A.7:
Case Study 2

> The husband who went out to sea in 1996 did not return home.
> They said that those at sea were arrested. We believed them and
> went in search. On the forty-first day we heard that some bod-
> ies were washed ashore with clothes and skeletons. I rushed to
> the shore and identified my husband by his clothes. I could not
> perform the last rites of my husband. As the body was badly
> mutilated, my relatives buried him on the shore. I lost my father
> during the 1987 war situation and was given in marriage at the
> age of 17. I was widowed when I was 19 and I have a daughter.
> There are many like me in our village and those deserted by their
> husbands.
>
> Shanthiham brought women like us together and organized us
> as a group in 2002 and that is how 'Tharaka—Centre for Blossom-
> ing Widows'.

Source: Abstract of an interview given by Idayaraj Sahila, published in the *Namadhu Ella Nadu*
newspaper on 24 January 2003.

by the war. Amongst them were girls as young as sixteen and seventeen.
Most of them had been widowed after a marriage of six months to one
year. Eight of the families had more than one widow. Most of them had
not remarried. Most of the widowed families had more than four children. Box 5A.7 presents the case of a young woman widowed at the age
of nineteen.

The number of widows in the village had increased dramatically during
the period between 1987 and 2000. Some of the attributed reasons were
high number of men being killed by the IPKF during 1987. Many men
went out to sea for fishing where they were shot and killed by the navy.
Some went missing after being arrested at sea. Others died at sea due to
natural causes. Many men had died during 1995 due to aerial bombing
of this village. Some were arrested and went missing during the army's
roundup and search operations. Then there were deaths due to alcoholism, suicides and sicknesses, mostly cancer.

Findings

The findings are broadly divided into common problems and psychosocial and mental health related problems of the widows.

Identified Common Problems

1. Poverty and lack of livelihood.
2. Being ostracized by the family and community (*kedda sagunam'*— bad omen).
3. Many children in the family (between four and six) and children being uncared for.
4. Increase in family responsibilities.
5. Being unable to function in a male-dominated society, for example, attending to matters in a government offices, markets and dealing with authorities.
6. Harassed by alcoholic men and being sexually abused.
7. Gossip about sexual misdemeanours of widows.
8. Lack of security at home, especially during times of war.
9. Hesitation to seek help from men due to fear of being misinterpreted (sexual connotation).
10. Disallowed from participation in auspicious (good) events (marriage, temple festivals) in the community. However, participation in 'bad' events (funerals) is permitted.

Psychosocial and Mental Health-Related Problems

The inability of many widows to go through the normal process of grief is having repercussions in their mental health and psychosocial well-being, especially young war widows.

Common minor mental health problems identified included depression, anxiety, somatization, suicidal tendencies and PTSD.

Many did not seem to be aware of their suffering and distress while other denied emotional problems that were evident to other villagers. The case in Box 5A.8 illustrates this.

Box 5A.8:
Case Study 3

A mother, aged forty-eight, had two daughters and a son. Her husband died in 1995 during the height of the conflict. One of the daughters attended our children's group activities. She complained that the mother reprimanded her even for a small mistake by beating her and at times using burning firewood. We visited her home and met the mother and found the mother to be suffering from somatization. She refrained from speaking about the

(Box 5A.8 Contd.)

(Box 5A.8 Contd.)

circumstances that led to her husband's death. She mentioned that bringing up the children was a strain on her and she was a sick person. She often said, 'He gave [me] the children and put them on my head while he has peacefully reached his destination. I am now suffering and I get angry when I see them.' She was counselled for three months and referred to the psychiatric and medical units of the Teaching Hospital, Jaffna. They ruled out any organic cause for her many physical complaints. After the three-month-long intervention there was a remarkable change in her attitude and behaviour. She regretted the way she had treated her children and understood the reason for her behaviour.

Source: Case history of widow helped by the PSTs.

Psychosocial Interventions for the Widows and the Community

Building Trust and Rapport with the Widows and the Community

The war and those associated with the war were responsible for the predicament of the widows. Hence it was a Herculean task to build a trusting relationship. Building a trusting relationship during post-tsunami interventions was easier than confidence building with this group of widows.

During visits to local and international organizations that were there to help, this group was shy and drew back from speaking out or participating (perhaps owing to cultural reasons, fear of being ostracized and of those associated with the conflict). However, there were some exceptions that were bold and came forward.

Individual Intervention

Most of those identified as needing intervention were suffering from minor mental disorders and to day-to-day life stresses. PSTs visited the homes of identified individuals and provided psychoeducation, befriending, counselling, yoga and relaxation as appropriate and referred to specialist care where necessary. There were ground problems during interventions as, for example, during counselling sessions family members would linger and inquisitive villagers became a nuisance. To overcome this we had to educate the family and the neighbourhood about the intervention. Over time we overcame this problem by establishing a secluded place in the village to meet clients.

Family and Social Level Intervention

When widows are socially isolated and ostracized by their family and the community or the widows themselves acquiesce to these societal norms, they get withdrawn from the social mainstream. One widow grumbled, 'During weddings a *sumangali* (a married lady living with her husband and having children) will be called upon to bless the couple while widows, spinsters, those separated from their husbands are taboo.' There was resistance from within the society for the empowerment of widows and having them function as a group. It is noteworthy that key people of the village, the GS and president of the fishermen's society, did not support our work to empower the widows. Hence, we had to bring about an attitudinal change at different levels of the community though awareness and group discussions. It was easy to bring about a change of attitude among the youth and disseminate it within the community. The youth were responsible for running the community centre. Its president, a boy who had been admitted to the university, was very supportive. He was influential in gaining the support of key persons in the community to support our activities. The constructive support of the divisional secretary of Sandilipay was another critical factor.

Widows' Group Activities

Forming widows into a group was rendered easy and effective due to the similarities of the problems they faced; the fact that people with similar problems were naturally supportive of each other and were empathetic.

The widows' society met twice a month for empowerment and capacity building programmes. Group activities for those in need of psychological support were normally held two days a week in the evenings as most of them were engaged as manual labourers.

Usually empowerment and capacity building programmes have to be encouraged and participants motivated. However, the widows took the initiative in their own empowerment and capacity building and withstood opposing forces within the community. Normally two PSTs facilitate the discussion while two PSTs support the process. Though most of the discussions revolved around distressing events and involved sad emotions, they were interspersed with hilarity, happy events and jokes.

One widow who lost her husband in 1991 had this to say: 'It is after eleven long years that I had an opportunity to share my distress and even joke and laugh.'

Programmes for children of the widows were conducted simultaneously to bring out their creativity and expression.

Initially, activities were of a therapeutic nature where opportunities were provided for widows to meet in a group to share their feelings and gain insight. Once their mental well-being was taken care of through psychological interventions, the need arose to empower them to demand their rightful help from the state and NGOs. The Tharaka[14] Widows Society gained official recognition by fulfilling the many legal necessities required to function as an organization. This made it easier to receive assistance from the state and other institutions.

Tharaka Widows Society was officially inaugurated on 16 January 2002 in the presence of INGOs and national NGOs, with government representation, under the patronage of Shanthiham. It was somewhat of a revolutionary occasion for the community.

Networking

While providing psychosocial support within our capacity, the society was empowered through role plays and other tools to meet and talk to organizations in the state such as the social service department, women development officers and INGOs such as UNICEF and CARITAS to meet their material needs.

The society was able to convince the late M. Maheswaran, minister of Hindu cultural affairs, to provide the society money for the purchase of a building to function as their centre. Meanwhile, a Christian priest was also motivated to support this venture.

Integrated Psychosocial Support

On a visit to Jaffna, a representative from the government of Finland learnt of the Tharaka Widows Society and offered to help the widows in the whole of Jaffna district. Apart from psychosocial support for widows, avenues for livelihood, vocational training for young widows and youth, evening classes for children were offered over a five-year period. Four women were selected from families of widows to run the Tharaka Widows Society centre and programme; they were trained in basic mental health and psychosocial skills. The programme was expanded to two other villages with high numbers of widows participating.

Under this programme, widows in Jaffna district went on an excursion to the rest of the country, leaving the peninsula, during a respite in the

---

[14] It was the wish of the widows that a respectful Tamil name be chosen for their group. A Tamil scholar at the University of Jaffna was consulted and he suggested the name Tharaka, which according to Tamil mythology is the name of a star that glows with light in the sky. He advised the group be called *Tharaka-Vidavaikalukkana Malarvu Myyam*. However, there was criticism from some sections about the word withawaigal (widows), and it was suggested that it should be replaced. The scholar was consulted again and he opined that the mindset of the critics was not well inclined towards widows; hence, it would be good to bring about a change in their outlook towards widows. He also added that the word 'widow' gives a descriptive nuance to the group.

conflict. It was unfortunate that the bus carrying these Tamil widows was stoned in Ampara.

Capacity Building and Empowerment

After they had been relieved of mental health problems, the organization required capacity building. Various forms of training programmes on human rights, women rights and feminism, child rights and peace, CBO management, basic life skills, problem solving, decision-making, empathy, interpersonal relationships, non-violent communication, basic psychosocial and mental health were carried out.

Progress of Tharaka

After the widows had been empowered, they gradually started to function independently.

They organized similar widows' groups in other villages and facilitated their functioning as self-help groups. With experience they rendered psychosocial assistance to others through home visits, befriending, family and social support. They arranged livelihood assistance for women-headed families through NGOs. They motivated women-headed families of the other villages, such as Kopay, Anaikoddai and Madduvil. It was remarkable that at one time these groups were expecting assistance from others, but following empowerment programmes, they have initiated actions to help themselves and others. The local and foreign media have covered their activities, which has encouraged them. The president of the organization, Idayaraj Sahila, was nominated for the Nobel Peace Prize in 2005 along with one thousand other leading women worldwide for their services, by an international women's group.[15] She had lost her grandfather to the Sri Lankan army, her father to the Indian army and her husband to the Sri Lankan navy. But despite her losses, grief and precarious economic situation, she had been involved in peace building activities in the country (Chawade 2011), visiting women and widows from all three communities in the south with whom she had developed a remarkable rapport and understanding. She said:

> Earlier we hated Sinhalese and thought that their sons and husbands, the Sri Lankan Navy, shot and killed our husbands. As we begin to have reconciliative exchanges, we are seeing that pain and familial loss were felt on both sides. We understand how terrible war is and we want peace.

> (Quoted by Chawade 2011: 147)

---

[15] PeaceWomen Across the Globe. See http://www.1000peacewomen.org/eng/friedens-frauen_biographien_gefunden.php?WomenID=1046

Various organizations functioning at Chavatkaddu, NGOs and other CBOs requested members of Tharaka to conduct training programmes and to share their experiences and knowledge. The society was quite busy with day-to-day activities; conducting vocational training, savings groups, play activities for children, lending library, income generation through home industry products and other activities. They have also been documenting their activities and keeping accounts.

In the initial stage, the community and the other CBOs opposed the functioning of this organization, but gradually, from 2005 they have supported its continuation. Though many CBOs had been functioning over many years in Jaffna, the successful growth of the Tharaka Widows Society stands as a paradigm of empowerment and the transformation of socially and culturally marginalized women to live with dignity.

Challenges

When we began psychosocial interventions in the latter part of 2001, the war was going on and we were forced to face lot of security problems. Even the community was suspicious of our activities, hindering our work. When we started to select widows and implement psychosocial activities through them, the community was opposed. Cooperation was not extended to us from the GS officers and others. Since they understood that no material support would be given except for the psychosocial activities, the community did not appreciate our efforts. Though we have been requested by other NGOs for various kinds of assistance, there were difficulties.

Present Situation

The society holds monthly and weekly discussions and provides assistance to widows who have returned from Vanni areas. The president and group members have visited Poonakerrry village at Kilinochchi and formed six groups of 350 widows to function independently. They visit the widows once a month and empower and encourage them. They extended the same methodology, organizing widows in three villages at Madduvil and at Koolavady, Manipay to form groups, facilitating their meetings and activities on a regular weekly basis. Psychosocial support in the form of counselling, income generating projects, sessions for further education and capacity building with appropriate resources, referral to other NGOs and hospitals where necessary, activities for children and youth programmes were undertaken on a regular basis.

In this section describing community-based approaches, family-based interventions take on importance in a culture where the family bonds are still very strong.

Family Support
Continued by *Daya Somasundaram*

The family was used as an essential resource in therapy. Efforts were taken to keep the family together and united. Other agencies like the ICRC were contacted to trace missing relatives and unite the family. During community work, the family and the extended family were treated as a unit, involving them in all the discussions, decision-making and activities. Where there were misunderstandings, conflicts or separation, attempts were made to repair the damage and re-establish the family unity and dynamics. Family cohesion was promoted and strengthened. Vocational training, income generation projects, microcredit facilities, donation of essential items and other assistance were sought and arranged with appropriate governmental organizations and NGOs through networking. Family members were encouraged to re-assume traditional roles, responsibilities and mutual support. Situations of gender-based violence and child abuse were handled sensitively, attempting as much as possible to keep the family together. Where this was not possible, protection and alternate accommodation were found for members at risk through appropriate NGOs working with women and children. Long-term follow-up was done to look after the interests of the affected members and their families.

Expressive Methods

Art, drama, storytelling, writing poetry or novels (testimony), singing and dancing were used (Wilson and Drozdek 2004). Activities based on expressive and creative arts were organized for children in particular. Structured play activity for children was arranged on a regular basis as mentioned above.

Drama
With *Sambasivamoorthy Sivayokan*[16]

Psychological and socio-dramas can go a long way in creating awareness about trauma among the public and help traumatized individuals ventilate their emotions or seek treatment. In common with other creative and artistic productions, drama also has a variety of inherent psychosocial dynamics. Reisner (2002) envisions theatre in post-conflict situations as a profound instrument of social communication, as an attempt at creatively

---

[16] Apart from being a psychiatrist, Sambasivamoorthy Sivayokan is a dramatist in his own right.

transforming trauma in the public and artistic spheres, to affect healing where avoiding the trauma can be destructive. He sees it as offering

> an active outlet for the energy stirred by the memory of the trauma. The theatre is physical, it engages the body and the voice; it returns the energy to the world in the form of performance, as a creative, interactive force, rather than in the form of disconnected destructive discharge. In fact, in theatre, the expression of the stirred passions can be magnified, their meanings can be enhanced and their effects can be profound. In this way art offers not simply the sustaining of the trauma through memory, but the mode of its transformation.... Art, and in particular, theatre, provides a series of relatively safe spaces for exploration of trauma, analogous to the therapeutic space ... as shared experience, appropriate to a public forum ... [the traumatized] as having experienced something terrible which shakes human values. The space of theatre is safe, symbolic and communal ... [that] provide[s] a forum for testimony, witnessing, symbolization, and transformation of experience that had heretofore been unsymbolizable, because of the very nature of trauma. (Reisner 2002: 16–17)

In northern Sri Lanka, dramas produced during the war had several aims. Beyond entertainment, dramas attempted to educate, inquire, resonate emotionally and provide an opportunity to express concepts. They were performed on different stages, streets and other environments to fulfil needs of the time. With increasing awareness about the effects of war on individuals and their families, it was reflected in the dramatic productions and performances. In some way the impact of war was shown in many dramas. Deaths, destruction, displacement, disappearance, detention, refugee life, psychological suffering and other consequences found their way into dramas.

Initially the psychosocial dramas were produced in Jaffna by Kulanthai Shanmugalingam, with Sambasivamoorthy Sivayokan, Professor Sivathamby, other drama personnel, medical students[17] and the socially conscious general public. Kulanthai Shanmugalingam did not create his dramas from imagination. He would observe what was happening in society closely. He would then discuss these observations and issues with persons with specialist knowledge in that field. After collecting individual case histories, he constructed common roles from this background. As a result many in the audience identify with his characters. The production of the first such psychosocial drama, *Annai idda thee*,[18] included the process of

---

[17] Traditionally, Jaffna medical students produce a socially oriented drama with Kulanthai Shanmugalingam each year.

[18] *Annai idda* comes from the Tamil saint, Paddinathar's *Munnam idda thee. Annai idda thee* connotes the armed struggle as something that the motherland (*annai*) herself created. It was the theme song set to music for the play.

going through case histories, key informant interviews, literature survey, focus group discussions and regular reviews to bring out traumatization.

The drama was produced in the midst of war to portray the psychological consequences of traumatic events like aerial bombing, displacement, torture and disappearances. Though there was resistance from the LTTE in Jaffna to highlighting adverse effects of war (since the militant line had been to promote 'heroic' aspects), the drama proved revolutionary. There was immediate social resonance and empathetic response from the public. Some reacted immediately during the performance, in a kind of cathartic release (and had to be supported and followed up) while others did later. As a consequence, at the social level, it led to public acknowledgement and acceptance of the negative consequences of the war.

Most subsequent social dramas of Kulanthai Shanmugalingam had a prominent psychological theme or dimension. For example, *Velvi thee* (Sacrificial pyre) explored the psychosocial consequences of (and individual, family and social reactions to) rape in the war context and there were several plays on displacement. Isolation in old age from children gone abroad—in *Enthayum thayum* (My father and mother), misunderstandings and conflict in the life of those displaced—in *Yarukeduthuraipom* (To whom shall we tell), the loss of organic relationship with home—in *Narekodu svarkam* (Hell along with heaven) and destructive repercussion due to retributive feelings—in *Yarkalo sathurar* (Who has won) are some other examples.

Nevertheless Shanmugalingam has not succeeded yet in producing a drama on collective trauma as its theme. Although he held many discussions with medical students and started writing initial scenes, he could not continue with it. The continuing events in the country could have affected his creative ability or he could have faced difficulties in dramatizing the concept of collective trauma.

Drama also became very much involved in the developing political and ethnic conflict. It was able to create awareness on current issues. Shanmuglingam's *Mann sumantha maniar* (The embodied man who bore the soil) was a radical departure from ordinary plays in trying to create social consciousness about the situation of Tamils. Dramatists, like Sithamparanathan, went further in directly portraying the ethnic repression in dramatic performances like *Uyirthamanithar koothu* (Dance of the reborn man) and ethno-national emotions in the grand spectacle, *Pongu thamil* (Resurgent Tamil). Thus, drama, which held a powerful position in the creative arts among the Tamil community, was used for political purposes. Those in power during war time began to regard drama with suspicion. As a result, the field had to face many direct and indirect threats and went into disrepute. It lost its vigour and effectiveness.

Drama was also used in the psychosocial programmes after the tsunami. These dramas went beyond strict audience boundaries to involve observers, particularly children, in the performance. The dramatists attempted to teach, ventilate emotions, modify behaviour and bring about other reactions in the audience.

Similarly, *koothu*, the native version of drama, which usually does not need a picture frame stage to perform has been effectively performed in the congested welfare centres after the last phase of Vanni war and later, in resettled villages. People welcomed it and participated in the process since it was culturally familiar (Jeyasankar 2011) and portrays a known story. It also provided ways for the artists and audience to meet and support each other and develop communality. Some of the themes in the *koothu* would have helped them ventilate their feelings and to build lost hopes.

Drama workshops were a powerful tool to provide opportunities not only to understand the elements of drama but also to learn various psychological principles and experiences. They provided a chance for the development of participants' personalities. There were psychological games, concentration exercises, group works, cathartic experiences, mind- and body-related expressions and a feeling of cohesiveness. The drama workshops have been systematically conducted during the conflict and post-tsunami periods. These types of workshops were initially pioneered by Kulanthai Shanmugalingam and his colleagues but later used by many leading artists like Sithamparanathan, Jeyasankar and others.

The time is not ripe yet to use drama as a practical medium for realistic treatment purposes. In the early 2000s the mental health multidisciplinary team had used drama in the long-term treatment of alcoholics. Drama has the potential for being constructively used in psychosocial programmes.

Rehabilitation
Continued by *Daya Somasundaram*

Attempts were made to rebuild social networks and sense of community by encouraging and facilitating formation of organizations, CBOs, rural societies, schools and the like. Social mobilization was promoted by tapping local resources, re-establishing traditional relationships, practices and engendering leadership from among the community. Networking with governmental organizations and NGOs involved in relief, rehabilitation, reconstruction and development work was attempted. The network was used to obtain relief, socio-economic rehabilitation, legal aid, shelter, nutrition, water and sanitation, human rights, protection and other assistance for affected communities, families and their members. A holistic integrated approach was advocated with governmental and NGO aid agencies emphasizing the need for planning that included due consideration for the psychological processes that promote individual, family and social healing, recovery and integration.

In the polarized and totalitarian political situation with competing loci of power and parallel governments, community organization, mobilization and empowering was only allowed to proceed up to a point. When the organization or mobilization started to become effective, political forces took over, infiltrated or interfered in the process. In the Tamil areas no independent large-scale organization or activity was allowed. Perhaps it was taken as a challenge to the existing social arrangements, control, dispensation and loyalties. There was a need for the political organization to be seen as the one doing the construction, channelling the aid, receiving credit and legitimacy as well keeping control of community-level dynamics. Cooperation with the political forces on the ground was the only realistic option available and this was the route taken by the governmental organizations, NGOs and INGOs. But ultimately, political and military priorities took precedence. Independent social activity, particularly beyond a critical, effective level, carried an intrinsic risk. Thus, in such situations, workers need, in addition to cultural competency, political competency as well where every act took on a political significance.

Village-level Psychosocial Interventions

Villages badly affected by the war and later by the tsunami were selected for psychosocial work. The steps taken in the intervention programme in each village are listed in Table 5A.1 and the psychosocial interventions in Table 5A.2. Although broken up as steps, they were in reality all ongoing processes, with the monitoring, evaluation and assessment feedback of the programme to adjust and modify the design and implementation based on lessons learnt and contextual factors. For example, after the tsunami the interventions had to be made more appropriate for the widowers or some areas or aspects of programmes changed due to developing security concerns.

Consequent to the tsunami of December 2004, the WHO developed a strategy of training CSOs to address the mental health needs of the affected families throughout Vadamarachchi East, Maruthankerny, Kilinochchi and Mullaitivu devastated by the Tsunami in northern Sri Lanka as described in Chapter 3A.

Organization

In a situation where there was no official recognition of the need for psychosocial support nor any effective structures in the region to implement programmes or training, an organization had to be developed. One such organizational structure that developed in Jaffna is described below.

Shanthiham
By *Rachel Tribe*

Shanthiham (which means House of Peace) was set up by Anna Doney, Father Damian and members of the medical community in 1987 to train counsellors and psychosocial workers. It quickly became established as a vital resource for many people living in the north of Sri Lanka. Its offices are located within the area where the civil war was taking place, so that carrying out its work was often difficult and bombing could frequently be heard from the central office during the civil war. The first office was completely destroyed by bombing. Shanthiham has undertaken training of a variety of workers as described above and supported several generations of families affected by the twenty-six-year civil conflict, the South Asian tsunami and the flooding of 2011. Working in a country which lived through a civil war for twenty-six years, and which was won militarily by the Sri Lankan government on 19 May 2009, may present a challenge for the future to all parties. More recently, Shanthiham has been helping people deal with the transition to peace time. For many, this has been a complicated process, as the civil war had defined the parameters of their daily lives for over two and a half decades. Secrecy and lack of trust may become functional strategies in a civil war situation (Tribe 2007). People became fearful of trusting anyone, normal social bonds and community life were challenged, and, as Somasundaram (2007a) has discussed, collective trauma was widespread.

Shanthiham undertook some extremely innovative and cutting-edge work, often in very difficult circumstances, and later set up a number of outreach centres throughout the Jaffna region. Its active role and community focus meant that it was able to respond to needs as they arose. Shanthiham decided to move from a counselling agency model to a community-based model as they found this was what people wanted, was more resource effective and minimized possible stigmatization for people attending for counselling. During the civil conflict, travel was not always easy, as there were multiple checkpoints and travelling could be misinterpreted by both sides in the conflict.

Many of the staff trained by Shanthiham subsequently left to take up jobs in the government sectors, and national and international organizations within Sri Lanka and overseas, and the impact of the training work undertaken by Shanthiham can be located across the country and abroad. Their work was particularly important given the dearth of trained mental health staff in the country, many having left to escape the conflict and settled elsewhere. In 2009, there were twenty-six psychiatrists and a handful of psychologists, the majority working in the south of the country, to serve a population of nearly twenty-one million. There was in addition a range of indigenous healers using practices which included Ayurveda and Siddha medicine. The civil war often made the carrying out of traditional rituals difficult, and this may have been detrimental to emotional well-being at the individual and community level. The staff of Shanthiham have produced a range of books. These notably included the innovative *Mental Health in the Tamil Community* (2001), which linked sociocultural factors and traditional healing practices widely used within this community to psychosocial interventions from a range of countries in the service of improved well-being and health. This provided a useful handbook for mental health workers practising both within Sri Lanka and elsewhere among members of the Sri Lankan Tamil diaspora.

After the tsunami, Shanthiham was able to use its community focus to good effect and carried out the only needs assessment conducted in the Jaffna district. In addition they were able to work collaboratively with a number of other agencies, including the WHO. They have also collaborated with the UK Sri Lanka Trauma Group,[19] which was formed in 1996.

Prevention, Policy, Planning
Continued by *Daya Somasundaram*

Tragically, much of the death and destruction caused by natural disasters could have been avoided. In trying to prevent war, ahimsa, peaceful coexistence, conflict resolution, reconciliation and other values were advocated and passed on wherever possible. However, it is sobering that despite all this effort and training, the country was once again returned to full-scale hostilities from December 2005.

Memberships at various committees at the local, district, regional and national levels provided the opportunity to make some contribution towards prevention and alleviation of the effects of individual and collective trauma. The problems of putting psychosocial and mental health concerns on the agenda and the general stigma associated with mental health were quite evident at these committees. Although there was wide acceptance of psychosocial problems due to the tsunami and there were considerable effort to address these by the state, militants, NGO and INGO sectors, the state is still to accept or take responsibility for the psychosocial

---

[19] See http://www.uksrilankatrauma.org.uk/ (retrieved on 8 October 2013).

problems arising from the war. As such it was left to INGO and LNGOs to carry out psychosocial interventions and programmes. The national discrimination, inequity in distribution of resources and programmes and exclusion of the north and east continued to be insurmountable hurdles (Somasundaram 2005a). This has become more acute after the Vanni battle where MHPSS activities are generally not allowed (see Chapter 5C). As of 2012, the country, the politico-military establishment in particular, has not successfully transitioned from a post-war context to a post-conflict phase so that genuine reconciliation and appropriate psychosocial interventions can be implemented. Ironically, Sri Lanka was at the forefront of developing MHPSS interventions, rich experiences and innovative practices that are in danger of being lost.

B.

Trauma and Beyond

The Evolving Field of Mental Health and Psychosocial Work in Sri Lanka*

By *Ananda Galappatti*

The field of post-emergency mental health and psychosocial support is commonly represented as being about the provision of psychological support to people in terrible emotional distress after experiencing a traumatic event. The images in the popular imagination and in the media often are of counsellors or psychiatrists compassionately listening to or treating victims of violence, or survivors of disaster. Whilst these forms of help are still crucial to the field of mental health and psychosocial support in the context of conflict and disaster, they are now by no means the only way in which it seeks to assist people affected. This chapter attempts to sketch some of the key shifts that have taken place in this field over the past decade in Sri Lanka, which has been affected by chronic conflict over several decades and a major disaster in December 2004. These will be illustrated through examples from work that I have been a part of since I entered the field in 1996. At that time, because of the continuing war between the government of Sri Lanka and separatist militants in the north and east of the country, and also a recent failed but bloody insurrection in south, western and central Sri Lanka, numerous services had arisen to deal with the psychological consequences of this violence — mostly provided by NGOs and to a lesser extent by the state. Due to the globalized nature of the field (i.e., in terms of knowledge, technical expertise and financial resources typically flowing from North America and western

* Some of the material in this chapter derives from the public lecture delivered by the author on 2 September 2008 at Manila (Galappatti 2008) and was also previously published (Galappatti 2010).

Europe to poorer conflict-affected countries), the approaches in Sri Lanka closely mirrored those in other similar contexts. Whilst this trend continues today, the development of local expertise and consolidation of experience within the island is beginning to change this dynamic.

The Clinical Model

If we examine the popular stereotype in the field of post-emergency MHPSS work, the representation has its roots in the origins of work in this area. When the field of mental health work with refugees first emerged in the 1980s, as part of the new professionalized humanitarian interventions with refugee populations affected by war and disaster in the developing world, the perspective that dominated this work was that of psychiatry and clinical psychology. It was recognized that civilians affected by the terrible events of war or disaster often had consequences that went beyond material loss or physical injury. Psychological problems like depression, overwhelming grief reactions, anxiety and post-traumatic stress were identified as key issues to address. As a result, the psychotherapeutic and medical approaches that had been developed in Europe and North America to address these same issues in civilian and war-veteran populations were deployed through clinics or community mental health programmes in conflict-affected countries. In Sri Lanka, this meant the establishment of programmes to train counsellors and medical staff to identify people with the symptoms of particular mental disorders and provide them with talk therapies or drug treatment. Their services were provided through hospitals, centres in the community and home visits.

With respect to children, there was an added concern that their stressful experiences might impair their psychosocial development and predispose them to later mental health problems, or that exposure to violence could lead to antisocial or violent behaviour in the future. In Sri Lanka, this again led to the development of programmes for children to work through their experiences using art or play, as well as to many training initiatives for teachers to better help their conflict-affected pupils.

These approaches often took the form of 'stand-alone' psychologically oriented programmes or sometimes deployed a 'psychosocial plus' structure where other practical services were delivered in conjunction with those that were explicitly therapeutic. In the stand-alone or vertical model, psychological or socially oriented interventions are delivered with explicit therapeutic objectives. In the psychosocial plus model, exclusive psychosocial interventions were offered in conjunction with other services (for example, credit schemes or legal aid) that met other pressing needs.

Typically there was limited coordination or cooperation between service providers for the different components.

In the early 1990s, an intervention for women whose husbands had been killed or disappeared during the recent 'southern' insurrection often sought to identify women who suffered from unresolved grief or intrusive post-traumatic symptoms such as nightmares or recurring disturbing memories. The grass-roots counselling services that were offered in response involved basic psychoeducation and reassurance that symptoms were normal reactions, and not signs that they were going 'mad'. Occasionally, mental health professionals from Colombo would conduct clinics in affected districts, providing advice on managing symptoms through relaxation exercises and referring people with psychiatric disorders to the nearest government mental health clinic (which often involved several hours travel to another district). Clients were also encouraged about positive coping strategies they had evolved and encouraged to communicate more effectively about their problems with their family members and others close to them.

In the east of the country in the mid-1990s, the Butterfly Garden project to support children affected by war focused on bringing routine to children's lives through regular activities at village play centres. These activities, facilitated by locally recruited animators, used art to help process traumatic memories and engage children about fears they had of aerial bombing or fighting between armed actors. Cooperative games were also employed to encourage pro-social behaviour. Children were also given a daily snack to improve their nutritional status.

When I first entered this field in 1996, as a volunteer with an organization supporting survivors of torture in Sri Lanka, this was very much the paradigm within which we worked. Our clients were provided with sessions with counsellors to help them talk through the various emotional, existential, relational and practical problems that they encountered. Although the model of care was relatively progressive in that it recognized that our clients and their families had many difficulties beyond the purely psychological, and attempted to provide a 'holistic' care package, these services were all compartmentalized. Medical care and physiotherapy for physical injuries, provision of assistance in job seeking or grants for income generation, legal assistance in seeking justice and counselling for psychological difficulties were each delivered separately and with little interaction with each other. What we did not see at the time was that many of the different problems of torture survivors were actually interrelated, and that our attempts to assist them could have been more meaningfully integrated.

Although clinical and psychologically oriented interventions continued to dominate the interventions in the field in the mid-1990s, these had also begun to draw criticism internationally. One argument was that they focused too narrowly on trauma and individual psychological states and ignored the broader social circumstances and problems that produced and shaped distress. It was also claimed that the 'medicalized' approach emphasized the role of external experts, failed to recognize or make use of the local resources available to affected persons and communities and undermined survivors' roles in effecting their own recovery. The focus on 'vertical' specialist services targeting small well-defined groups (such as torture survivors, people with PTSD, survivors of sexual violence) was also argued to be at the cost of more 'horizontal' general support that could be provided to entire populations, and which would avoid the stigmatization or differentiation of particular individuals. Lastly, there was a suggestion that the Euro-American concepts such as PTSD were not appropriate to use in capturing or addressing the suffering of people in non-Western settings.

The debate this criticism provoked between what has been described as the 'trauma' and 'resilience' camps was quite vigorous and at times even bitter. Whilst these exchanges were mostly conducted in European and North American academic and humanitarian policy arenas, their effects were felt in terms of the design and financing of programmes in conflict-affected countries. In Sri Lanka, whilst practitioners were aware of the specific disagreements taking place, their concerns about the clinical model were first shaped by the practical experiences of implementing it. Clients were not always comfortable with or convinced of the value of talking treatments, preferring practical interventions around the concerns associated with their psychological distress. Often there was divergence in the way that clients and service providers conceptualized or prioritized problems. Limitations in resources for training and supervision meant that the quality of 'barefoot' counselling or 'psychiatry-lite' being offered was often low. The fact that most clients continued to live in communities that continued to be afflicted by violence, social conflict and deprivation also presented challenges to therapeutic progress.

Understanding Social Suffering and Integrating MHPSS

By the end of the 1990s, I had joined a few colleagues in trying to articulate alternative visions of what support to individuals and communities might look like. We drew inspiration and insight from our unsatisfactory experiences with the institutional and theoretical elements of the clinical model, from snippets we read of the Euro-American debates within the field or the emerging work of medical anthropologists on social suffering and most

significantly from research and reflection on the nature of women's suffering Sri Lanka's conflict zones.

Whilst conducting research and being involved with service delivery,
my colleague Gameela Samarasinghe and I were confronted with the
realities of women's lives under conditions of ongoing war in northern
Sri Lanka and also in the disadvantaged south-eastern part of the island
where an armed insurrection had been suppressed some years earlier.
The impacts they described caused us to look beyond purely psychological disorders and effects and adopt a more 'psychosocial' perspective
that aimed to acknowledge how events and circumstances shaped both
their inner psychological and external social worlds, and how these two
domains continued to interact with each other. For instance, the murder
of her husband might not only cause a woman grief, a sense of powerlessness and existential doubts, but also new challenges in terms of material and economic survival, increased vulnerability to sexual violence or
exploitation and changes in social identity and relationships with her children, relatives and neighbours. It was clear also that these impacts had
knock-on effects many years down the line, and that the suffering of conflict laid on a continuum with other forms of violence and hardship that
women experienced even when the fighting was over. The powerful way
that poverty undermined women's abilities to cope with losses or threats
was also evident. The lack of disposable assets like jewellery or savings to
mobilize in a crisis, not owning land or livestock from which to make a
living, the lack of salaried income and the absence of skills or connections
to be able to find work and negotiate the public domain were all often
associated with greater difficulty and distress. The insights gained from
these women's lives were crucial in our understanding of the contours
of the suffering of adults and children in disadvantaged and chronically
affected communities.

If the psychosocial consequences of conflict were mediated and shaped
by the social and structural conditions of people's lives, it seemed to follow
that our interventions to support survivors had to engage with these, and
not simply the individuals affected. In a 1999 manifesto, a small group
of practitioners declared its intention to integrate approaches conducive
to enhancing psychosocial well-being into mainstream development and
humanitarian work, and since then has worked to put this into practice.
Happily, the team of colleagues with whom I began this work was not the
only group to converge on this objective in Sri Lanka around this same
time, and we have enjoyed some rich collaboration and exchange of parallel
ideas and approaches as a result. From 2002, MHPSS practitioners began
to dialogue with and lobby policy-makers and mainstream development
practitioners, whilst also striving to better understand the linkages between
long-term and large-scale development processes and the well-being of

individuals and groups affected by these. This work also fit into a broader trend within the field globally, as illustrated by authoritative guidelines on mental health and psychosocial support interventions in situations of emergency issued by the IASC (the key humanitarian coordination forum established by the UN General Assembly) in 2007, which emphatically argues for the need to support individuals and populations through activities directly related to provision of shelter, education, food and information — but which impact strongly on psychosocial well-being and mental health.

The integration of MHPSS objectives into other aspects of humanitarian and development work can take place in many different ways, using several popular models (adapted from International Federation of the Red Cross 2009). In an integrated model, MHPSS services are delivered in ways that are closely coordinated and related to other side-by-side interventions. Therapeutically oriented activities are bundled together with several other services or interventions (for example, loan schemes, shelter provision, water and sanitation facilities) that address key requirements for human well-being. It is similar to the psychosocial plus model, but is more closely coordinated with other services in implementation. The foundational model sees the use of MHPSS services as the basis for organizing or guiding the provision of other required services. Psychosocial activities and perspectives provide the platform upon which all other needs are identified, prioritized and responded to. In the holistic model, the mental health and psychosocial objectives are achieved through the provision of other services in ways that promote well-being. Psychosocial principles and objectives are integrated seamlessly into other activities that can address key factors for psychosocial well-being (such as loan scheme processes, shelter allocation and construction procedures, reform of community governance systems, establishment of water and sanitation facilities). The psychosocial interventions are integrated to the extent that they are no longer explicit. In the complementary model, implicit psychosocial approaches in other activities are complemented by stand-alone therapeutic interventions to meet explicit psychosocial needs that require targeted services.

This incarnation of mental health and psychosocial support work looks remarkably different from the popular image that I invoked at the start of this contribution. Whilst it still retains and values the individual therapeutic workers doing one-to-one or group work with affected people, increasingly the emphasis is also on less obviously therapeutic processes. These might typically involve any of the following: the way in which people being resettled are well informed about the place to which they will go, their ability to choose their neighbours (relatives or people they knew before as opposed to strangers) or influence the layout of their house;

ensuring that orphans can find foster homes within their own communities (rather than be institutionalized), helping teachers prevent discrimination against orphaned children in school or reuniting siblings who have been separated after the loss of their parents; helping widowed women become more skilled in running home businesses, ensuring a match between their products and market demand and creating opportunities for new friendships and partnerships between them and other women in the community; establishing clear complaint and advocacy mechanisms in refugee camps, ensuring that camp administrators do not privilege particular individuals and groups; or coordinating the way different agencies interact with and provide assistance to a single camp.

In January 2005, after the Indian Ocean tsunami disaster, there were many people who were left searching for family members who had been swept away by the waves. The process of searching through the photographs of the dead at local police stations was extremely distressing. In two districts, it was arranged for special identification tents to be set up to give family members a private and calm environment to view the pictures of the often damaged bodies of tsunami victims. Counsellors accompanied families throughout the process—from preparing them to view the upsetting photos, to explaining the legal process for confirming a death, to arranging for follow-up emotional support if necessary.

In the early 2000s, a resettlement programme in northern Sri Lanka appointed a psychosocial worker as the team leader and primary liaison with the newly established community. Whilst the programme included components of housing construction, starting of new livelihoods and building community governance mechanisms, it was the psychosocial practitioner's interactions and work with individuals and groups that guided the direction and process of all development activities.

Another intervention in 2002 engaged a rural children's club in a social service project at their local hospital, where they read newspapers to bedridden patients. Amongst the club's members were many orphaned children for whom this was a rare opportunity to be valued as helpers, rather than being viewed socially only as being dependent on others. The project also expanded the children's social networks and connections, for example, giving them direct access to hospital staff outside clinic hours in case of illness.

A few years ago, a task force for gender-based violence in eastern Sri Lanka integrated the services of several government (mental health support and policing) and non-government agencies (safe shelter, legal aid, livelihood assistance and community-based support) through cross-agency casework systems that placed psychosocial considerations at the centre of efforts to support affected women.

Learning to Integrate

The new approaches described earlier now have their own challenges. The greatest of them is that these new strategies require new skills on the part of those who wish to intervene — who continue to make use of the clinical techniques offered by the professions of psychiatry and psychology, but need to go beyond these. There is a need to draw in persons with skills in the areas of poverty-alleviation and microcredit, community building and social mobilization, local social and healing practices, camp management, protection and legal aid, education, health care and shelter, and provide them with new understandings of how their actions in these fields can contribute to enhancing psychosocial well-being and mental health. People who wish to specialize in this increasingly multidisciplinary area of work require broad training and must have a willingness to innovate and collaborate. In Sri Lanka, as in other locations around the world, we have started running courses on mental health and psychosocial support for professionals and community workers, both in our universities and in affected areas. There are attempts to ensure that the learning that emerges from new initiatives and developments in the field, especially in our own contexts, is quickly reflected in the curricula of the training on offer.

Working in relatively unmapped territory also requires that practitioners continue to rethink and critique their assumptions about the field, even as they try to consolidate and formalize our learning into concrete guidelines on good practice. At the moment, there is renewed interest in Sri Lanka to better understand local sociocultural frameworks of psychosocial well-being, as well as to find better ways of measuring the impact that our interventions have on the dimensions that affected communities consider to be priorities. Practitioners are challenged to improve the quality of the dialogue with the individuals and groups that they are trying to assist, and to give them greater opportunities to participate in the decisions that shape interventions. There are also attempts, exemplified by this book, to find ways of understanding and responding to suffering and difficulties on a collective level, exploring whether the overall impact may be greater than merely the sum of their parts.

There have also been attempts to build interdisciplinary alliances and better partnerships with other sectors of the humanitarian response and development practice. These linkages and collaborations need to take place at the level of front-line service provision, but also at those of regional or national programmes and policy. At an individual case level, a psychosocial worker may work together with a primary health midwife to support a displaced woman suffering from postpartum depression; at the level of local programmes, psychosocial practitioners and school administrators may collaborate in getting school dropouts to re-enter education;

local government and humanitarian managers may be encouraged at a regional level to adopt standard policies and processes for consulting with affected populations; interventions at the level of central government may include working with the Ministry of Education to develop national curricula and training for teachers on supportive classroom practices for disaster-affected students, or helping to frame policy that diverts children from incarceration within the justice system.

The experience after the tsunami disaster of 26 December 2004 has taught Sri Lankan practitioners many valuable lessons about coordinating services within and across sectors in an emergency context. Granted, what we learnt in the context of the tremendous and unruly post-tsunami response was as much from our mistakes and narrow misses as from our more successful efforts. Still, valuable skills and experience in cooperative action have been developed within the field, which can be harnessed for future work.

New Challenges for the Field in Sri Lanka

At the end of the long and brutal war between the Sri Lankan state and armed Tamil nationalist movements in 2009, the field of MHPSS faces several challenges. In many ways, the field has grown beyond its roots as a response to the suffering caused by armed conflict and disaster, becoming relevant to wider social problems within and beyond conflict zones, such as child abuse or violence against women. However, in the north of the country, where the field first emerged in Sri Lanka, psychosocial interventions have for the first time become politically 'sensitive' to the extent that they are discouraged or restricted by state officials. This situation is both unfortunate and ironic, given that most MHPSS interventions in Sri Lanka have historically avoided overtly political approaches (in contrast, for example, with the field in Latin America) in order to be able to provide services under difficult conflict conditions.

The sustainability of innovations and multidimensional systems of support that developed during the years of conflict and disaster is currently threatened by a decline in the grants available for financing community services. As international donors withdraw emergency-specific funding, or redirect resources towards building of major infrastructure, livelihoods and economic regeneration, the networks of services have begun to dwindle — in the non-government sector, and crucially in terms of adjunct services to the public sector (which so far do not receive government financing). Alternate models for sustaining and extending these services are urgently required.

Regrettably, the momentum within the field of MHPSS intervention to engage other larger areas of development and humanitarian practice has dwindled in recent years. Following the Indian Ocean tsunami, the field expanded very rapidly with a wide range of non-specialist agencies entering this area of work. Unintentionally, this has brought about what I would characterize as a 'bureaucratization' of the field in Sri Lanka — with administrative and management imperatives increasingly overshadowing technical or professional concerns within the sector. The emphasis within coordination and management is often on compliance with guidelines, minimum standards and stereotyped modes of intervention, rather than on substantive learning, innovation and thoughtful extension of a still young field. In the mainstream of development work too, there appears to be a reduction in responsiveness to beneficiaries at the front line. Bureaucratic tendencies are seen within the new arrangements for service delivery, with grass-roots providers often acting as short-term contractors for larger organizations or the state, with increasingly centralized administrative and regulatory systems. A renewed emphasis on large-scale infrastructure development at a national level and a return to internationally set development goals at the global level also create new challenges for horizontal integration of MHPSS concerns. There is a need for ongoing empirical data gathering and critical theoretical work to monitor the status of individual and collective psychosocial well-being, to measure the efficacy of MHPSS interventions and to direct developments in both policy and practice.

Even as we try to enhance the technical capacity of practitioners, adopt new financing mechanisms and develop the institutions and structures to deliver psychosocial and mental health support, we have to remain doubly aware of the human element that is integral to this area of work. Most of what we do is ultimately not very complicated, but our success often hinges on the ability to maintain sensitive and genuine relationships between the persons providing support and those who receive it. Experienced practitioners who were important mentors for me as a novice, as well as key colleagues to whom I look for guidance, demonstrate a remarkable personal capacity to identify with the priorities in the lives of their clients, and allow this to inform their professional interventions in addressing these. It often seems impossible for any of them to treat this work as something simply routine, or to fail to connect with the essential humanity of the people they encounter. Yet, whilst this work requires that practitioners engage closely with survivors and their suffering, this often takes an emotional toll that can easily result in workers feeling ineffective, jaded or disinterested (see the section titled 'Vicarious Trauma' in Chapter 5A), which can spell disaster for our clients. Maintaining healthy, ethical and committed relationships with the people we aim to assist can be greatly aided by the building of small teams and networks of practitioners who reinforce positive professional value practices, as well as provide personal support. In my own experience, this has often been the most important ingredient for successful services.

Changing Relations with the Global Field

In the beginning of psychosocial work around the mid-1990s, the flows of knowledge and expertise were almost exclusively unidirectional, from outside the island. At its best, this meant that services in Sri Lanka benefited from wise and influential international advisers sensitively transferring insights and successes from other parts of Asia, Africa, Europe or North America. At its worst, it meant that initiatives were introduced in Sri Lanka with little attention to how they would interact with local structures, social practices or knowledge systems. However, the longstanding and sometimes pioneering work in Sri Lanka has now meant that a level of experience and expertise has been built up in relation to post-emergency mental health and psychosocial work. This is bringing an increased sophistication and coherence to Sri Lankan MHPSS work, which is increasingly shaped by local practitioners. This is also true for other similar contexts of disaster and chronic conflict, with the result that practitioners from these arenas are beginning to make their mark on the field globally. It is no longer uncommon to have practitioners from Jaffna working in Cambodia, or from Gampaha guiding interventions in the Democratic Republic of Congo. That there is increasing direct exchange between practitioners from emergency contexts is very exciting, considering that this was sorely lacking in the past. It is encouraging to note that initiatives with roots in local practice are seeking to improve global participation in knowledge exchange.

The journal *Intervention* (www.interventionjournal.com) that actively seeks contributions from practitioners working in situations of adversity was founded in Sri Lanka, but now has a global reach. Similarly, the online platform for the Mental Health and Psychosocial Network (www.psychosocialnetwork.net) connects practitioners around the world, but is maintained by 'hosts' based in Sri Lanka and Zimbabwe, amongst other places. A full 'democratization' of the field is still far off, but the voices and priorities of those who live and work in situations of war and adversity are increasingly shaping a dialogue between practitioners and thinkers in affected countries and beyond. This book is a part of this process, and I hope it will move us, and the entire field, forward in our ability to provide appropriate and effective services to the huge numbers of men, women and children affected by violence and disaster. Tragically, the post-war context has proven a step backwards, a curtailment of much-needed MHPSS.

C.

Psychosocial Interventions in Sri Lanka[*]

Challenges in a Post-war Environment

By *Gameela Samarasinghe*

> Victims are a permanent testimony to the ill will that exists in our world and of our own eventual vulnerability.
>
> — Ronnie Janoff-Bulman, *Shattered Assumptions* (1992)

Introduction

As discussed in Chapter 2A, it is now established that the impacts of war, violence and conflict cause disruptions to the emotional, physical and material well-being of individuals and communities (Summerfield 1999).

The need for psychosocial work in Sri Lanka became evident during the conflict, resulting in the gradual development of psychosocial services by humanitarian organizations in conflict-affected areas. Initially inspired and trained in the Western model of treatment, many local organizations provided counselling. However, more recently, organizations have become engaged in a wide range of activities that they describe as psychosocial initiatives (Galappatti 2003: 5; also see Chapters 2A, 5A and 5B).

* This chapter is based on the findings of research undertaken for the International Conflict Research Institute (INCORE), University of Ulster, and funded by the International Research Development Centre (IRDC) (project number 105691). I wish to acknowledge and thank INCORE and IDRC. I also wish to especially thank Priya Thangarajah, who helped with the data collection and editing, and research assistants, Geethika Dharmasinghe and Chamathka Devasirie. I also thank the heads and staff of the organizations for participating in the research.

The Post-war Environment in Sri Lanka

The thirty-five-year-long civil war arising out of ethnic tensions between the majority Sinhalese and the Tamil minority in the north and east of the country ended in May 2009 with the decisive military victory over the LTTE. While this victory was historic, and should have brought about stable peace and normality in the lives of people of all ethnic communities and an end to their suffering, the country is still as divided along ethnic lines as it was during the Eelam war.

In his victory speech on 19 May 2009, President Mahinda Rajapaksa declared that terrorism had been defeated and that 'there are only two peoples in the country. One is the peoples who love this country. The other comprises the small groups that have no love for the land of their birth'. Rajapaksa's new politics of patriotism (Wickramasinghe 2009) in its political reforms does not address the concerns of the minority communities.

However, many positive changes took place after this victory. For example, places that were inaccessible in the north and east have become open and people, particularly from the south, are able to travel to these areas. In the north and east security has been relaxed, roads and bridges are being repaired and land that has been idle for over two decades is being occupied. Schools and hospitals are being renovated and communities in more distant places are able, for the first time in years, to obtain access to some basic necessities such as health care and schooling. The government, supported by international organizations and loans, has launched massive development projects in the provinces where the main focus is on mobility and access. The purpose is to improve the lives of people through better infrastructure and the increased production of goods and services.

However, for the country to move forward and reconciliation to take place, uncomfortable issues of torture, trauma, disability and the resultant depression and psychological distress of the hundreds of affected people, particularly in the north and east, should also be considered. It has been more than three years since the end of the war. People continue to suffer the consequences of the war. Families of the disappeared, those with children and relatives in custody and widows are facing the stress of uncertainty and hopelessness with little support or redress. The people of the north and east have undergone multiple displacements over the last thirty years, leaving behind their lands, homes, possessions and belongings. Along the way each family lost many members, while many were injured. Most people living in these areas have been directly affected with a majority of them having witnessed violent death.[1]

---

[1] Based on information from quarterly reports of the Asia Foundation.

In the last months of the war many people in the north suffered, as they ran for survival before reaching the camps in Vavuniya. It can be estimated that one million people in the north and east are affected. After nearly twenty years many of these families have returned to their original homes in these two provinces. Officially, seventy-eight thousand people have returned to Jaffna alone. It is also expected that several thousands of those who fled to India too will be returning in the near future. Although these families are back, they have survived traumatic events, a life on the move, torture at the hands of armed persons, detention without charges, death of loved ones due to shelling and crossfire. A special case must also be made of the many thousands of Muslims who were forcibly evacuated from the Northern Province in October 1990. With just a few belongings they left behind their comfortable homes and lucrative businesses, religious and educational establishments to refugee camps in Puttalam (Citizens Commission 2011). After twenty years several of these families have begun to return to their homes. However, in many locations they come back only to find that there are other families living in their homes or completely vandalized buildings which are inhabitable. Many of them perceive that their needs and wishes are being ignored in the development and resettlement process, and that they have been left to fend for themselves. Nevertheless in this often hostile environment, families are beginning to live, schools are functioning and homes that were boarded up and decaying from neglect are being renovated.

The Eastern Province has had relatively more time than its northern counterpart to recover and rebuild. Although the war has been over for a considerable period of time there continue to be camps in the Trincomalee district, particularly in and around the areas of Muttur. In the Eastern Province too there are a large number of families either returning from or being relocated from the Vanni region. Nonetheless people in both provinces continue to face similar hardships and traumatic events which were recently compounded by the devastating floods that submerged a greater part of the Eastern Province. Another phenomenon that is characteristic of these areas is the concept of 'border villages' which were in close proximity to the conflict areas. Here the mainly Sinhalese community faced many unprovoked attacks by rebel forces and several bus bombs killed and maimed many hundreds. Several of these families also fled their homes to other parts of the country or remained in isolation as other organizations and state services failed to reach them due to remoteness and fear. Today they have returned to their homes and are attempting to rebuild their lives but they too suffer from reliving past experiences.

Both in the north and east began a spate of armed robberies which led to an overall sense of unease and stress amongst the people. Unexplained killings as well as disappearances have also brought back unhappy memories of past events, which they thought they had seen the end of. Continued military presence — locations are being increasingly fortified — is also a cause of anxiety for those who are seeking to put the past behind and get on with their lives.

ER and the PTA have been enforced in Sri Lanka for over thirty years and have been criticized by international human rights agencies. Many human rights activists and journalists have been arrested and detained and sentenced. The laws ensure that not only 'terrorist' activities but any dissent against the current repressive government is seen as a criminal activity and arrested. The ER lapsed on 31 August 2011. The government has however expressed that it has no intention of repealing the PTA. As a result of the PTA being in operation, conditions for arrests, detention and trial remain unchanged.[2]

In addition, the government's development and reconstruction initiatives in the north and east of the country are contributing to minority fears and alienation. According to Wickramasinghe (2009):

> The lack of accountability and justice for the thousands of civilians killed in the last few months of the war, the collapse of the rule of law, the political killings and impunity for abuses by state officials are grave concerns for people especially for the minority communities.

Listening to the grievances of the affected communities and alleviating their suffering was not a priority in the aftermath of the end of the war.

Psychosocial programmes continued to operate as the numbers of those needing psychosocial care increased. Soon these interventions were perceived by the government as challenging the victory discourse. Victims were perceived as 'a testimony' to what had happened. As a result, the political security environment in contemporary Sri Lanka has restricted psychosocial programmes, compelling some to try and continue their efforts under the guise of other activities.

---

[2] The ICJ report of 2009, describing the substantive implication of the PTA, states:

> It provides for the detention for up to 18 months, without trial and without access to lawyers or relatives, of any person suspected of a wide range of offences including murder, kidnapping, criminal intimidation, robbery of state property, possession of unlicensed weapons, incitement to communal disharmony, mutilation of street signs, etc. In a significant departure from ordinary criminal law, the Act allows confessions made to the police admissible in evidence and shifts the burden of proof in certain cases to the defendant. (Available online at http://icj.wpengine.netdna-cdn.com/wp-content/uploads/2012/06/Sri-Lanka-mass-detention-LTTE-analysis-brief-2010.pdf, retrieved on 13 February 2013)

See also Weliamuna (2011a).

Objectives

This chapter attempts to understand how psychosocial programmes are continuing to operate in a post-war environment. With general observations of the prevailing context and common psychosocial problems, the study which forms the basis of this chapter questions how problems are being conceptualized, trauma in particular. It looks at the different types of psychosocial interventions and whether they can in fact be sustained in such an environment. It also explores whether these interventions make a difference in terms of peace building and development, or more broadly, social transformation.

Psychosocial interventions do have an opportunity to impact on social transformation. Whether they intend to do so through their programmes or they do so indirectly will be studied. According to Castle (2000), 'Social transformation does not imply any predetermined outcome, nor that the process is essentially a positive one .... Generally it implies an underlying notion of the way society and culture change in response to such factors as economic growth, war, or political upheaval.'

Given the post-war environment where psychosocial interventions are perceived as operating against national interest, this chapter will also investigate how these interventions manage to provide services through innovative strategies in order to support the groups they work with. The chapter questions how affected populations can continue to receive meaningful and culturally appropriate psychosocial care in spite of the changed sociopolitical and cultural environment.

Methodology

The study described and discussed in this chapter is based on general observations, survey of media, institutional and organizational reports, semi-structured and key informant interviews and focus group discussions of managers of psychosocial programmes who were involved in the conceptualization of the psychosocial intervention (one or two per location), direct service providers (one or two per psychosocial programme) and a few key informants (lawyers, counsellors, PSWs). In the focus group discussions, participants were asked whether they felt that there was a contextual difference after the end of the war and what were, according to them, the factors that contributed to the shifting context. The last session was an open discussion about their plans to sustain psychosocial activities in the current context, what challenges they might face and how they planned to overcome them (conceptualization changes, reduction or risks, safety methods).

The individual interviews of key informants and managers and staff of psychosocial programmes were semi-structured with guiding questions to find out about the work they were engaged in, their thoughts on the changed situation in the country, the difficulties they faced in doing their work and how they thought their activities impacted on social transformation.

There are evident limitations to the research. At the time when the research was being conducted, NGO activities were under close scrutiny by the government in some locations (Mannar and Jaffna in particular). This constraint resulted in the near-elimination of Mannar as one of the locations to be studied. In order to retain Mannar, the methodology for data collection had to be changed. The researcher was able to conduct individual interviews at the location, but the focus group discussion took place in Colombo to ensure the protection of the programme, participants and of their clients.

The focus group discussions consisted of small groups with seven programme managers who conceptualized the psychosocial programme for their organization and service providers who had direct contact with their clients in different sites. These participants as well as other key informants including lawyers and counsellors were interviewed individually at the locations. The findings therefore cannot be generalized.

Given the politico-military context and the mandate of the PTF at the time the research was carried out, it was decided that researchers would not talk to clients of the programmes in order prevent drawing attention on them. The specific names of the organizations are not disclosed for the present to protect their staff and ongoing work.

Selection and Description of Psychosocial Programmes

The psychosocial initiatives were identified as 'any project incorporating activities that are clearly intended to alleviate or mitigate psychological distress due to conditions of conflict or war'. The sample consisted of four psychosocial programmes, one from each location, Mannar, Kurunegala, Anuradhapura and Jaffna. They are involved in mental health and psychosocial activities and community development programmes. Two of the programmes focused specifically on issues related to gender. The participants belonged to all ethnic groups.

In Mannar, a women's organization that works with Tamil and Muslim women was identified. It is a project for women who have been abused or whose husbands have been abducted. The organization has obtained approval from the PTF to set up shelters for domestic violence cases but is also involved in psychosocial interventions.

In Kurunegala, a national women's organization dedicated to the cause of preventing domestic violence and other forms of violence against women was selected. Its main activities are the promotion of human rights, advocacy/lobbying, research/conflict analysis, trauma counselling and legal services with centres in several districts in Sri Lanka, including Kurunegala. Some of the people who come for counselling and other support include ex-combatants, their families and widows of armed personnel.

In Anuradhapura, a national organization working in the districts of Colombo, Batticaloa, Ampara, Trincomalee, Anuradhapura, Vavuniya, Mannar and Jaffna on issues related to torture and trauma was chosen. It has a centre-based approach where the clients visit the offices and a counsellor along with a medical team attends to their needs. They are supported by field officers who visit the clients' homes and villages for identification and follow-up. It also conducts mobile clinics in some locations where a medical team visits the locations once a month. The organization commonly relies on village-level volunteers and individual one-on-one counselling. Along with these core functions it also conducts awareness raising and community empowerment programmes. It works with NGO consortiums in the districts and also participates in the local psychosocial forums coordinated by the Ministry of Health.

In Jaffna a centre that favours counselling as well as a community-based approach where psychosocial workers spend extensive time at the village locations was picked. The counsellors' work is complemented by psychosocial as well as other services such as medical clinics with a doctor, physiotherapist, regular yoga classes and relaxation methods. Fieldworkers work closely with community volunteers. As the volunteers are selected with the help of *Grama Niladaris* (or GSs) and other community leaders they are also accepted and trusted within the community. They play a significant role in the overall approach by being conduits between the organization and the community. They also play a critical role with follow-up of clients.

Findings and Discussion

The post-war contextual change of the ground situation has not necessarily led to the reconceptualizing of psychosocial intervention either by the state or by service providers. However, service providers have had to face the change in context either directly or indirectly when providing psycho-social interventions to clients and through this grapple with the need for a methodological change.

The Conceptualization of Psychosocial Programming

The psychosocial interventions conducted in Anuradhapura, Mannar, Kurunegala and Jaffna mainly consisted of individual, group and family counselling as well as social work of various types. Following the medical model, counselling focused on the psychological state of the client as an effective intervention for individuals distressed by the conflict. The individual was treated as part of a group or a family but remained the focus of the intervention. The psychosocial workers of these organizations did field visits to follow up on the clients. The participants stated that in addition to doing individual, group and family counselling: 'We have to go further with the new developments in psychosocial intervention and the changes in the context and it is how to incorporate this that is very difficult because there is a mixture of needs in the community.'

As such, these organizations do recognize other needs of their clients, as clients do mention those needs. The psychosocial interventions are conceptualized with the objective of reducing the impact of trauma on the people affected by war or any other situation of violence. After the war ended, there were many people with enormous losses to family, land, property and assets. In dealing with these kinds of cases, the organizations strive to provide clients with necessary services to assist them and to empower them. Interventions would essentially take the form of counselling and are accompanied by medical services, legal assistance, financial aid or even healing services conducted with the cooperation of religious institutions, aimed at reducing the impact of trauma, protecting the victims and their rights. They are mostly designed to support the individual and their families, while keeping in mind that apart from the psychological treatment that may be required, there are other needs that have to be met.

To respond to their other needs, the participants stated that their organizations network with other service providers to ensure holistic care for their clients. Thus, they worked with hospitals, individual doctors, rehabilitation centres, governmental organizations, other NGOs, GSs (village leaders), heads of religious institutions, orphanages, women development officers, social workers, the police, senior police authorities, prisons, HRCSL and legal aid.

Most organizations conduct awareness programmes to inform clients, governmental and non-governmental officers on issues related to human rights, gender, reproductive rights, sexual health and domestic violence.

For example, one organization trains Samatha Mandala officers (mediation board officers) island-wide, on aspects related to gender and domestic violence. Through their awareness programmes these organizations create awareness about legal and psychosocial aspects as well. One participant stated that the objective of their organization is to go into communities to create awareness. They talk about agriculture, bio-agriculture, other developmental activities and cultural and religious aspects through these awareness programmes.

Some organizations have empowerment programmes where they help clients with their financial needs through loan schemes and encourage clients to engage in earning and saving. They also provide clients with legal assistance. Some provide shelter or housing for single women.

Few organizations form support groups amongst clients to encourage them to solve their problems by talking to one another, and also to assist one another in financial matters through loan schemes. The clients are grouped according to the similarity of their situation; for example, widows in one group and women who have been victims of domestic violence in one group, in order to make it easier for clients to find solutions to their own problems by talking amongst group members.

Research in Sri Lanka has revealed that most people living in conflict areas seldom understood their suffering in psychological terms. Instead, they tended to recognize that the material and social conditions of their lives had a bearing on their psychological well-being (Perera 1999; Samarasinghe and Galappatti 1999). Consequently, programmes employed strategies to support psychosocial resilience and well-being through making qualitative improvements in the social and material environment of communities affected by conflict (G. Samarasinghe 2002).

Though approaches to alleviating distress in conflict-affected regions such as Sri Lanka initially depended on concepts of trauma from an Euro-American perspective and interventions such as counselling which do not necessarily address issues that are central to the community, psychosocial workers have started their own debates on the cultural validity and effectiveness of exclusively Western, medical models (see Chapters 5B and 2A). For example, they have questioned the practicability of counselling in the field (G. Samarasinghe 2002) and whether private counselling sessions risk being seen as secretive activities and could cause dangerous intrigues in a village context (Bracken and Petty 1998a; Galappatti 2003). Many organizations have developed a variety of innovative community-based psychosocial interventions through their experiences of working in the war and post-tsunami contexts (see Chapter 3A).

However, the government's current understanding of how to meet the psychosocial needs of the affected population is by training large numbers of persons in counselling. Many ministries have undertaken to conduct training programmes throughout the country and every few months, batches of thirty or forty counsellors qualify, with a three-month certificate in counselling. While this is a very encouraging initiative, there are concerns about how appropriate the training is to meet the varied and specific needs of people.

These changes in contexts and methodologies show that psychosocial interventions cannot be a one-pronged approach, especially in cases of post-war where communities have faced violence, in most cases prolonged violence, and human rights violations.

The common and most pressing psychosocial problems that the communities in the north and east have to face, which was brought out by the study as well as the methods in which the organizations have responded can be categorized for ease of presentation as (a) common problems across all the sites and (b) site-specific problems, though there is considerable overlap.

Common Problems and Responses across the Sites

Almost the entire population in the north and east has undergone traumatic incidents in the last few decades that range from minor to severe trauma. For many, it has been prolonged trauma compounded by the last months of the military offences which directly affected over five hundred thousand citizens.

Even though the numbers would indicate that there are a significant number of persons who have undergone torture and trauma at the hands of various armed groups, the current rules and regulations imposed by the government have made it particularly challenging for organizations offering psychosocial or counselling services to reach their clients. This requires organizations to develop innovative strategies and new partnerships with other INGOs and LNGOs and state structures to enable them to reach their clients and provide much needed services.

Years of war, displacement and the lack of development have also resulted in high levels of poverty in these areas. A majority of the clients served by organizations belong to the poorest of the poor and this situation of vulnerability has a negative effect on their healing process. In this context, it has often been accepted that psychosocial work should take on a more integrated and holistic approach, in which livelihood needs as well as other aspects such as life skills are provided through networking (see Chapter 5A). Partnerships with development organizations should be established.

The participants talked about the contextual differences that have taken place in these areas since the end of the war. One is the caste issue in the north. Tamil society is a stratified society and its practice of caste and the struggle against it by lower castes have been written about in many articles. While the LTTE did away with caste practices and was seen as a harbinger of change, its manner of discipline and punishment for those who practised caste is to be criticized, this control repressed caste practices rather than bringing about real social change. The participants talked about the contextual differences that have taken place in these areas since the end of the war. The return of such practices post war is to be noted. Certain organizations stated that caste-related practices such as dowry, resistance to inter-caste marriages, etc., have led to an increase in violence against women and domestic violence within the family.

According to the participants at the discussion, due to the war which prevailed for thirty years, the values and morals of the people living in those areas have deteriorated. They state that rape cases and teenage pregnancies have increased. Children's education had been neglected due to the situation of war and displacement.

Another issue is, since the end of the war more people have been coming into these areas to settle down. This has caused tension between the Tamil and Muslim communities on matters relating to occupation of land.

In the north, the end of the armed conflict has led to other significant changes. Initially, during the war, people were more concerned about day-to-day survival and safety and security: 'wondering if they would live to see the next day'. However, now people want to earn, collect assets, educate their children, and there is a long-term plan that is visible in peoples' lives, which was not apparent before. With the opening up of access to other parts of the country, people's needs and wants have also increased and with it the need to be economically capable of providing for these needs. These pressures burden those living in war-torn areas and they find it difficult to cope with daily life when they are faced with unemployment and lack of basic facilities. The inability to move ahead in other spheres of life plays a role in how trauma is dealt with.

Last year the phenomena of attacking of '*greaseputham/yaka*' (grease devils) on several women in the north and the east brought out the vulnerability of women and the fragility of communities in the north and the east. Grease yakas are mythical characters in Sinhala folk tales. The yaka or devil is a man who was covered in grease to evade capture and would attack villagers and enter their homes to steal. Underage marriages, young widows and the social ostracism, 'rehabilitated' women cadre and their struggles to integrate into society, access to land and economic empowerment, safety and the right to know about their loved ones either dead, missing, abducted or detained are some of the challenges women in the north and east face.

In the Sinhala-dominated areas there has been a palpable difference in terms of people's mobility. 'They are not scared to come to the city centre, and there are more people coming to the city centres for education and jobs. And the reduction of military presence has given a feeling that the war is really over.' However, the increased number of disabled soldiers and the constant presence of soldiers at home due to prolonged leave have led to social problems at the community and household level. As one participant stated, 'Now they (soldiers) are always home, the wife isn't used to it. The man wants to be able to drink and so there are increased chances for domestic violence.'

For example, in Ibbagamuwa there is a village where soldiers, including those with injuries, live. In those villages there are many problems related to extramarital affairs and domestic violence. The soldiers do not even like it when men from outside come into their village. In such a scenario, interventions had to be reconceptualized and the support of the GS, the head monk of the temple or head priest was taken to conduct programmes and training in that village.

The end of the armed conflict has also meant that Sri Lankans are able to enjoy themselves. As a participant stated, most clients say they 'are involved with more leisure activities, and are relaxed and enjoying and are also not scared to stay longer during the day and even overnight'.

With the end of the war, these organizations have had to provide for various needs of the people and a large number of people affected by the war needed psychosocial support. One representative said that since the loss some of these people suffered was so massive, sometimes they, as counsellors, could not do much more than just listen.

Women and Their Vulnerability While the government tries to implement its 'reconciliation' plans, the realities on the ground in the north and east are ominous. Many households are now headed by women, who are extremely vulnerable under military rule. According to the Ministry of Child Development and Women's Affairs, the number of female-headed households in the north and east is estimated to be 59,501, with 42,565 of them living in the Eastern Province and 16,936 in the Northern Province.[3]

---

[3] Report dated 21 September 2011 received from the Ministry of Child Development and Women's Affairs as cited in the LLRC in http://slembassyusa.org/downloads/LLRC-RE-PORT.pdf (retrieved on 14 February 2013).

[7] http://kafila.org/2011/07/16/two-years-on-no-war-but-no-peace-for-women-still-facing-the-consequences-of-the-war-cmtpc/; 'Two Years On: No War but No Peace for Women still facing the Consequences of the War', CMTPC (retrieved on 13 February 2013).

Women are facing new kinds of conflicts in the north. The control by the LTTE and the conflict led to a control of women and the need to establish traditional (patriarchal) Tamil culture. Now with the end of that control, women are also trying to access the new kind of culture that is coming in. Due to resettlement, they have access to the outside world. As a result, women find themselves having to negotiate between the traditional and the new culture. This has led to a negative reaction from the community in terms of the change that is happening in women's lives. For example, the explanation given for sexual violence has been attributed to the attire more commonly worn in the south (that is, skirt). However, one positive factor is that women have more access to civil administration such as the police and the courts.

According to statements issued by women's organizations working in the north (Kadirgamar 2011) and the recent ICG report (2011c), violence against women has been on the rise in the north and the east or at least has become more visible. While it can be contended that women are now able to access the legal system and organizations, it is also to be noted that in many instances the inaction of the police has also led to a sense of impunity within the community with regard to violence against women.

The lack of adequate shelter, the breakdown in the village and community structures and increased militarization have all led to women's vulnerability. The Sri Lankan state's reluctance to acknowledge sexual violence by state apparatus's in the Menik camp or by its soldiers during the war leaves women without a mechanism for redress.

Before, in cases of domestic violence in the north, the LTTE would deal with the perpetrator immediately and end the violence; however, with the civil administration in place, procedure and law take precedence. Women are also afraid to complain to the police fearing the lack of support. Participants stated that they have had several cases where the police have sided with the man. Women's organizations providing counselling have had to then work with the police and sensitize them on issues of gender so as to ensure that women's rights violations are taken seriously. One representative explained that in such situations they had to rethink how to do the intervention and accordingly they had formed a group of fifty woman leaders from each divisional secretariat who would keep contact with the police, the magistrate, legal aid services and the hospitals when dealing with cases of violence against women. Organizations have also initiated preventive methods such as gender sensitization, lobbying for legal change and working with the police to reduce the violence so that psychosocial interventions are not required.

As the ICG report rightly notes, while the LLRC dealt with the vulnerability of women, it ignored the possibility of sexual violence apart from mentioning the infamous Channel 4 programme (ICG 2011: 17). Last year, the phenomena of grease *putham* or *yaka* attacks on several women in the north and the east brought out the vulnerability of women and the fragility of communities in the north and the east. Underage marriages, young widows and their social ostracism, 'rehabilitated' women cadre and their struggles to integrate into society, access to land and economic empowerment, safety and the right to know about their loved ones, either dead, missing, abducted or detained are some of the challenges women in the north and east face.

A significant aftermath of this war has been the high number of widows with several children. In some cases although they have been 'married', there is no legal proof and many women along with their children have been abandoned by the men, leaving them helpless and at the mercy of relatives. The Tamil culture enforces strong restrictions on these young women, preventing them from taking part actively in social and religious functions. They are not in general considered suitable marriage partners. They also feel particularly vulnerable and at risk since they have to depend on a man for assistance with several tasks.

A critical issue faced by a number of families in the north, particularly women in the north and the east, is that of missing family members — husbands, sons, daughters and others (see Chapter 3C).

Psychosocial Interventions for Women and Social Transformation While providing counselling related to domestic violence, counsellors try to talk to both the wife and the husband to make them understand that they need to be flexible and that both of them need to cooperate and work together to build their lives. Participants said that they focus on these aspects in their awareness programmes as well. During counselling they talk about gender roles and responsibilities while at the same time stressing that these should not be forced. They also emphasize that in certain situations it is important for the husband and wife to be flexible enough to help each other and even fulfil the duties that are conventionally done by the other partner.

They believe that empowering the women is important. They say that in some instances when the husband gets to know that there are places the wife could go and complain against him, he becomes apprehensive and changes his aggressive behaviour.

In severe cases the counsellors talk to the husband to make him understand that he has no right to hit his wife, and they also assure the wife that, if she decides to file a case against the husband, her safety and security would be ensured and that there are organizations willing to assist her in such situations.

The participants stated that during their awareness programmes they had realized that most police officers and other government officers are quite ignorant about the Prevention of Domestic Violence Act, 2005. One of the representatives said that when they went to file a complaint in one instance, the police station did not even have a copy of the statute. Then the counsellors had to make a copy of it for the police.

These interventions contribute towards changing the attitudes of the people and the authorities towards issues related to gender-based violence, which could lead to better understanding of the importance of gender equality and the protection of human rights.

Participants do feel that they need to advocate the rights of the victims if there is to be a long-term solution. That advocacy, lobbying and questions on inequalities at a broader level are important aspects of psychosocial intervention. For example, a participant said:

> If the counsellor is not gender sensitive, and does not believe in gender equality, then the counsellor would look at the client and say, 'why did you open your mouth and say this kind of thing, that is why you got slapped'; at that point the psychosocial intervention fails.

Women are a vulnerable group, having faced the brunt of the war, living to tell the story and carry the loss and trauma. Women are forced in the post-conflict situation to look for the missing and also support economically and socially the family that is left behind. Women not only bear the burden of ethnicity and caste but also gender and thus patriarchy. In such a situation, psychosocial interventions must not only be holistic, providing women shelter, legal aid and economic stability, but must also break down the traditional structures of patriarchy. Reconciliatory measures and peace have to obtain active participation of women if they are to be successful. In the Sri Lankan context, where women are large in number and have been mothers of soldiers or cadre themselves or daughters and wives of those killed, the need for a different method in dealing with her collective trauma and violence is the only manner in which the cycle of violence can end.

Ex-combatants   Among the population in the north and east there are many thousands of ex-combatants, ranging from those who were involved in minor tasks within the LTTE organizational structure (as well as other militant groups) to those who fought on the front lines. They face an uncertain future, still subject to surveillance from the military and have the daunting task of reintegrating themselves into 'normal' society and dealing with their own traumas. They have had experiences at different stages of their lives both as perpetrators and as victims of violence. Informed sources have said that sixteen thousand ex-combatants were released (they are different from the eleven thousand who are in detention centres) at the end of the war during late 2009. Often, these were persons who were involved in minor tasks in the LTTE or were injured. Of those who were retained in detention centres many have been sent to rehabilitation centres where they have been given basic training in different vocations. As of January 2011 it is estimated that around five thousand combatants remain at the detention centres, while the remaining have already been released to their families. The International Organization for Migration (IOM) has been mandated with the task of assisting this group of young persons with training and employment. It is not clear to what extent they are being helped with psychosocial needs. There is no clear plan to reintegrate these young persons into the community. They are often looked at with suspicion, have no friends and are still subject to surveillance, which causes them much anxiety and stress.

There is no evidence that all detainees were subjected to physical torture, but all those interviewed reported threats of physical harm, lack of water, proper clothing and regular taunting from the guards. Once released, they continue to be constantly monitored and cannot lead normal lives. But more importantly, there is a culture of harassment that comes with this form of monitoring. For women there are additional issues. Female ex-cadres and women arrested 'under suspicion' under the ER and PTA are constantly asked to report to military camps. There is a systemic harassment of women who have been detained and subsequently released in the new resettlement areas.

A participant recounting a case stated that one client was an ex-LTTE cadre and due to his high rank within the LTTE, the service providers had to take into account his status so that other clients are not intimidated or made to feel vulnerable. The client was also unable to deal with the change in his status and his life in the IDP camp. In this instance different counselling methods had to be undertaken to deal with the client and the change in context.

Participants also spoke about the hesitance among the people when it comes to reintegrating ex-combatants or the people who were living in camps into the society: to offer them jobs, or even to integrate them into the community through marriage.

Site-specific Observations and Identified Problems

As discussed in the previous section, common characteristics and psychosocial problems for Sri Lanka as a whole were identified. During the study it was also found that different geographical locations had some special and different properties that were of interest to researchers, who also wanted to study them for the purposes of comparison. Some local developments reflect on overall patterns and dynamics in the region as well as nationally.

Mannar   Mannar is a primarily Tamil Catholic area, but had a significant number of Muslims who were ousted in 1991 by the LTTE. Certain areas of Mannar were under the control of the LTTE (UTHR-J 1993c) with most ending up in IDP camps when the state retook these areas in 2008 (see Chapter 3B).

Many IDPs who are resettling have also had to face either the 'Buddhization' of their villages or the constant military presence in their villages apart from the loss of property and lack of basic amenities. Public spaces such as hospitals and schools have become military bases. Post war, a small number of Muslims have returned; however, the relationship with neighbouring Tamil villages has been strained due to land conflicts.

Under LTTE control Mannar saw significant social changes such as an increase of underage marriages due to a fear of recruitment and in the last stages of the war there was a rise in numbers of non-legal marriages for the safety of men from the Sri Lankan army.

With the end of the war, the return of the 'white van' and abductions has increased in Mannar. The year 2011 saw eleven abductions.[4] While police complaints have been made and there are army checkpoints all over Mannar, the abductions have not ceased.

There is heavy militarization in Mannar with many army camps being set up in the town and around Mannar district. There is constant flow of army personnel. Even though checking has reduced, the presence of the military is strongly felt especially by organizations working in Mannar. There is a constant threat, real and imagined, due to the constant surveillance of the state and military presence of the army. As discussed in Chapter 1B, the PTA and structural arrangements ensure that not only dissent is quelled and freedom of expression curtailed but also protection of human rights is prevented and organizations working on empowerment, war-related counselling and humanitarian work and collapse of the rule of law are criminalized.

Recently, Mannar police hired Tamil police officers which enable the locals to communicate and address their grievances through the police station. However the numbers recruited are far from sufficient to provide sufficient personnel at each police station to ensure that people's grievances are understood and no rights are violated.

Mannar has a gender-based violence desk and a mental health unit at the Mannar base hospital. These desks have been intervening and providing counselling to people who have faced violence due to war or domestic violence cases. However, as this is a state-based intervention,

---

[4] RukiFernando, Human Rights Activist, Law and Society Trust, http://groundviews.org/2012/02/26/new-wave-of-abductions-and-dead-bodies-in-sri-lanka/?doing_wp_cron=1375418580.9339900016784667968750 (retrieved on 31 July 2013).

its conceptualization of war-related trauma and effectiveness are being questioned by local organizations in Mannar.

One researcher in the study attempted to interview the person in charge of Mannar's women's organization. She was advised to change locations. She talked to a number of other psychosocial organizations and everyone advised the same. The current situation with the PTF permission regime and the constant surveillance of organizations engaged in rehabilitation, resettlement and conflict resolution places organizations in Mannar in a vulnerable position. Many organizations are reluctant to speak, especially about psychosocial intervention, as the state is particularly interested in that area to ensure that various war-related atrocities do not come to light. Under these circumstances (PTF, PTA, breakdown of the rule of law, etc.) a study of psychosocial interventions post-war in the Mannar district seemed impossible as most organizations refuse to speak or share information regarding the interventions they have conducted.

Jaffna   The population of Jaffna consists of a majority of Tamils and also of Muslims and a few Sinhalese. The majority religions are Hinduism and Islam. There are Christians as well in small numbers. The Muslims evicted by the LTTE in 1990 have been returning in large numbers to Jaffna. People in Jaffna survive on fishing, agricultural daily wage, home gardening and remittances from abroad. There are also shopkeepers, businesses and small-scale tourism. There are seventeen police stations; however, only one police station has a women's desk. The police is primarily Sinhala-speaking even though 95 per cent of the population speaks only Tamil.

Jaffna functioned as the headquarters and political base of the LTTE's Ealam state for a period. It was also viewed as a place of Tamil art and culture, academic excellence and great infrastructure. However, subsequent events brought down the status of Jaffna.

In 1987, the IPKF was brought down under an accord between the Indian and Sri Lankan governments, with the aim of ending the rule of the LTTE and the civil war. However, not only did the IPKF fail to bring a cessation, it also perpetrated gross human rights violations that led to the strengthening of the LTTE and the final exit of the IPKF in 1990 (UTHR-J 1993c).

The Muslims were seen by the LTTE to have collaborated with the IPKF and the state and were evicted in 1990. It is stated that the LTTE evicted over seventy-five thousand Muslims from Jaffna with only hours of notice (*LankaNewspapers.com* 2011).

The hold of the LTTE on Jaffna was lost in 1995 after a brutal battle between the LTTE and the army.[5] Since then Jaffna has been under the control of the Sri Lankan state with a heavy military presence. Under army

[5] http://articles.cnn.com/keyword/jaffna/featured/6

control disappearances, abductions and killings have been rampant. Paramilitary organizations, with the support of the government, were able to keep various groups of people and dissent in control.

With the end of the war, there has been a large influx of Sinhala tourists and also the return of evicted Sinhalese and Muslims. The continuation of high military presence and the construction of permanent military bases have meant that the military will be amongst the permanent populace of Jaffna rather than a temporary presence. The tip of the Jaffna peninsula remains an HSZ that is heavily militarized without the public given access to it. This means that people displaced from that area will not be able to return to their broken homes and land. There has also been no talk of compensation.

Even though the government has claimed that civilian administration has been given power, it has been noted in several human rights reports and by the Tamil political parties that power still remains with the military and permission to engage in any activity or decision-making must come from the military.

Resettlement of Muslims in Jaffna, like in Mannar, has been slow, haphazard and without an overall, holistic plan. There has been no package offered to the Muslims who have returned and the lack of land for the large number of returnees has not been addressed. Muslims in Jaffna town are returning to old Moor street, a street they occupied before they were evicted. Ad hoc citizens' committees have been established to deal with land disputes.

In the months of June–September 2011 the alleged grease *putham* attacks created tensions between the military and the Jaffna populace, reflecting the continuing discomfort the people have with the military. The villagers claimed that some of these attacks have been done with the support of the military and the police.

There is currently a gender-based violence desk at the general hospital in Jaffna town. It is well connected with the mental health unit of the hospital and has a referral system. The desk states that the numbers of domestic violence and child abuse cases have tripled in the last two years.

There is a popular belief that the influx of the 'outside' world into the conservative Jaffna society has led to these abuses. There is also an impression that the LTTE ensured an ideal form of culture and that the opening of society has allowed for 'loose' Sinhala culture to perpetuate in Jaffna. Therefore, community engagement with such problems as teenage pregnancies has been problematic.

There has also been a rise in child trafficking and child abuse.[6] Around eighty-two cases were reported within the first five months of 2011.

[6] http://www.bbc.co.uk/sinhala/news/story/2012/03/120309_jaffna_child_abuse.shtml (retrieved on 31 July 2013).

There is a perception that like in the rest of the north dissent is not an option. While in the rest of Sri Lanka there have been high numbers of protests and demands for higher pay, better laws regarding labour, in Jaffna, like elsewhere in the north, there is little engagement with 'democratic' structures. There have also been tensions between the resident Tamils and returning Muslims as well as the Tamils who have returned after several years.

Anuradhapura Anuradhapura was chosen as a site of study due to its location as a border district and also due to its population being primarily Sinhala. Anuradhapura is one of the ancient capitals of Sri Lanka famous for its well-preserved ruins of ancient Lankan civilization, which date the city back to the fifth century BC according to some records. It is the largest district. The population in Anuradhapura consists of Sinhalese (91.4 per cent), Sri Lankan Moors (6.7 per cent), Sri Lankan Tamils (1.5 per cent) and others (including Burghers and Malays—0.24 per cent).[7]

People living in Anuradhapura suffered during the war because of the district's location. The LTTE attacked Anuradhapura in 1985. The massacre was considered the largest on Sinhalese civilians. The villages in the Kebithigollewa divisional secretariat area in particular were subjected to many attacks. Kebithigollewa, a village in the interior of the Anuradhapura district, is a Sinhalese village situated twenty-three miles south-east of Vavuniya, on the Vavuniya–Horawapatana road. The villages first came under LTTE threat during the third Eelam war and these threats intensified and several villages were attacked in the 1990s. Many other villages in the Padaviya divisional secretariat area, the northern most villages of the Anuradhapura district, which were bordering the Vavuniya district, were the first to be attacked by the LTTE during the second Eelam war and several hapless villagers were hacked to death. These threats and attacks were extended southwards and many villages were abandoned. Border villages in Anuradhapura bore the brunt of the war; they provided a buffer for the Sri Lankan military and faced constant attacks by the LTTE. While the Sri Lankan state has provided compensation for the loss of family members and acknowledged their 'sacrifice', it has been reluctant to provide them with trauma counselling or any form of psychosocial intervention.

People in the Anuradhapura district depend on agriculture—rice cultivation—for survival. But with the war, many of the men became soldiers and home guards.

As per the statistics of the government, women from Anuradhapura are far more economically active than in other parts of the country. However,

---

[7] http://www.dmc.gov.lk/DistrictSection/Anuradhapura/06_Anuradhapura_Divi-sionalInformation.htm, 2011 (retrieved on 31 July 2013).

this access to employment has not meant financial independence or a reduction of violence faced by women. Anuradhapura also formed the transit point for soldiers either returning to service or going on leave, due to which the sex industry was a primary form of employment for women, even though soliciting and all other related activities with regard to sex work is an offence in Sri Lanka.

Kurunegala   Kurunegala is a district in the North Western Province of Sri Lanka. It was chosen for the study because it was not directly affected by the conflict and a majority of its people are Sinhala. However, the impact of conflict was felt in Kurunegala due to the high number of soldiers hailing from there. It seemed interesting to assess whether psychosocial programmes would consider impacts of the conflict in their programme designs and interventions. Due to its ethnic majority being Sinhala there was also a need to understand if psychosocial intervention in these non-conflict areas dealt with larger question in regards to peace and reconciliation, issues that face the north and east of Sri Lanka. The study assessed the kinds of issues faced by civilians in Kurunegala due to its high military participation, the impact that violence has in the society and reintegration of soldiers and trauma of soldiers. There is also a segment of population in Kurunegala who have migrated from the areas that were affected by war. These segments of community are often economically weak and face several social issues due to poverty.

Challenges Faced by the Psychosocial Programmes

The end of the three-decade-old civil war in May 2009 has brought new challenges as well as opportunities for those working on rehabilitation and reconciliation. The changing context from war to post-war has meant that a critical assessment of the current working practices and approaches is needed.

Over the past twenty years or so, several thousands of persons living in the so-called uncleared areas were not able to access counselling and other psychosocial services in their locations. Now back in their own homes after many decades, they are in a position to access these services that can enable them to leave the past behind and rebuild their lives.

Contrary to the belief that there might be less torture victims in a post-war situation, the numbers coming for treatment have increased. This was attributed not to the rise in incidents in the current context, but because victims who have been afraid until now to come forward are beginning to feel more secure in seeking help. Since the end of the war, torture victims are increasingly being referred to these organizations from prisons, courts and other services. When organizations conduct group counselling sessions, although it would have been easier to group everyone together because there was a large number of people who needed counselling, they had to facilitate different sessions for Tamil and Sinhala people. One representative, explaining their experience, said that the way family members of torture victims understood and talked about the issue was different due to the cultural differences, which made it difficult to form them into one group in counselling sessions.

In the case of border areas there is also the need to provide psychosocial interventions in both languages. While such services are provided ensuring that clients of both ethnicities share a group space, it is not always easy given the complex and often violent histories they share.

Common to northern and eastern provinces is also the severe reduction in the number of NGOs, both local and international, operating in these areas. This can be attributed to many factors such as government restrictions on foreign funding, as well as refusal of visas and permission to enter locations. This reduction of NGOs is very evident in the east and in Mannar which used to be well served by NGOs in the past. This means that if the government is to be one of the main psychosocial care providers, it needs to initiate discussions and debate on theoretical issues and implementation strategies. The problems of importing the North American or European discourse on 'counselling' to non-Western societies need to be explored. While it is very helpful to recognize the linkages between global knowledge bases and local interventions, it is also important to note that both knowledge and its effects are transformed within the context of each specific conflict situation. It is equally imperative to recognize the developments in the psychosocial field that have already taken place in the north and east during the war (see Chapters 5A and 5B) and post-tsunami response (see Chapter 3A) to draw on the rich experience, knowledge base and human resources in rebuilding the community in the post-war context.

There also seems to be a lack of awareness regarding the need for psychosocial intervention in post-war situations. Some participants said that the PTF believes there are enough government offices to do the required counselling in these areas. The understanding is that all that is needed is 'counselling', if at all. Although ground-level officers recognize the need of the work that is done by these organizations, ministries and the provincial administration do not. This is one reason why, they say, the NGOs are finding it difficult to get PTF approval.

With the increase in the government sector offices established in these areas after the war, there are new processes which these organizations have to go through in order to implement their psychosocial work. For example, government officers require an official invitation to participate at a training programme conducted by these organizations to be sent through the ministry, which was not the case earlier. The participants say that it is more difficult and more time-consuming now to implement their programmes because they have to work within these new frameworks. Earlier, when the A9 highway was closed, they could work directly with local government officers without obtaining permission from the ministry in Colombo, because they had very little contact with the ministry. But now they must go through these authorities in order to go ahead with their psychosocial activities.

They say that even when handling individual cases they need to be aware of the political connections of the perpetrators of violence or the abusers, in order to ensure that no harm would come to the clients. Because of the political, military and paramilitary influences, these organizations have had to change their usual methodologies and use different tactics in psychosocial interventions to ensure that the safety and rights of the clients are protected.

Due to the wide military presence, PTF and the reluctance to acknowledge the loss of human life at the end of the war, people of the north were unable to openly grieve. Service providers were also unable to deal with this huge loss directly. In Mannar, the service providers brought the people together, and conducted a funeral service following the rituals of the Christians and the Hindus. According to one participant in the study, 'There was a lot of crying, they were all together sharing this moment, and lot of people were able to admit that "yes, my father or my brother or my mother or my sister died."' They also purchased a coffin and got people to write the name of their loved ones who had died and put it into the coffin, and then the coffin was buried. This was the deviation in methodology and the participant stated that they were not able to use the usual methodologies they were aware of to deal with the kind of mass loss and trauma that was felt at the end of the war. However, while a different method was used in this instance, counselling post the grieving ceremony returned to an individual basis.

Breakdown of Rule of Law

The lack of separation of powers (executive, legislative and judicial), the use of excessive state power and the prevalence of armed paramilitary groups have contributed to a breakdown of law and order in the North and Eastern Provinces. Karuna's breakaway LTTE group and other paramilitary groups, which were low-key during the war, have also returned. With this return, abductions and killings of opposition members have increased. People from other parties and politics have been under constant threat.

The fear felt among the community is for two reasons—the law that is against any form of dissent and the extrajudicial mechanisms in place. Torture and detention without being taken to the magistrate's courts, abductions and disappearances have been a part of the state mechanism as much as the PTF, PTA and the ER.

This breakdown of the rule of law ensures that organizations are suspicious even of other organizations and its members. State penetration of some organizations to gather information on civil society members has been a reality that these organizations have faced. Many organizations and activists have been forced to work alone, which may ensure short-term safety but increases the feeling of isolation and a lack of security in the long run.

Many organizations are reluctant to talk to outsiders, especially regarding projects undertaken and interventions they have conducted due to the fear of coming under the radar of the state, especially when these interventions have been related to the war. As the state is at its repressive best and the laws are grey in terms of what activities come under 'against national interest', this fear is one to be expected. Information sharing may not only put these organizations under threat but also individuals who have come to these organizations seeking help. Thus, organizations and individuals are afraid and extremely cautious in sharing information regarding their work in the north and the east.

PTF

The PTF was set up in 2009 for 'Resettlement, Development and Security in the Northern Province' (PTF 2013). It is mandated to prepare strategic plans, programmes and projects to resettle IDPs, rehabilitate and develop economic and social infrastructure of the Northern Province. Under the PTF, civil society organizations need permission to undertake activities such as housing, rehabilitation, development, income-generating programmes, industries and other projects.[8] While the PTF could have ensured a streamlining of NGO functioning and that foreign funding is regulated in an equitable manner, what it has become is yet another instrument of control and surveillance by a state that wishes to keep certain information hidden and unaddressed.

Heads of all the NGO and INGO operating projects in Northern Province were asked to register all the officials of such organizations with the PTF with immediate effect[9] and special permission was to be taken

---

[8] http://www.defence.lk/new.asp?fname=20090514_03 (retrieved on 31 July 2013).

[9] http://www.humanitarian-srilanka.org/CKC/DailyInfo/Circular%20-%20New%20 Procedure%20for%20granting%20approval%20to%20operate%20projects%20in%20North-ern%20and%20Easterna%20Province.pdf (retrieved on 2 August 2013).

to undertake certain activities. Many organizations, therefore, have been forced to work both by providing full information and with constant surveillance (usually by the military) of their projects or to work without stating some of their projects. The state and the PTF have made it abundantly clear that certain activities that it deems 'against national interest' will not be granted permission. Providing psychosocial intervention or documenting human rights violations is part of this list. This denial of a basic health-care service for people who have undergone severe trauma and faced violence as a result of the war is deplorable and unjust. The government has mental health units at the government hospitals. However, these are neither safe nor gender-sensitive spaces for women to talk regarding the war, violence faced during the war, rape, detention or the disappearance of their loved ones.

Many organizations do not have permission to enter the resettlement areas and engage in counselling or psychosocial interventions. Those who have been allowed to enter have to agree to the stringent conditions laid down by the PTF. While some provide psychosocial interventions, they are provided in the office and unknown to the task force to avoid the surveillance. This is not to say that psychosocial interventions and violation of human rights documentations are not being conducted but that the civil society engaged in such activities is under constant threat and fear.

The PTF was subsequently extended to the Eastern Province but repealed due to protest from the chief minister of the Eastern Province — Sivanesathurai Chandrakanthan (Pillayan) — an ex-LTTE commander of the east.

The civilian administration and local elected bodies continue to be circumvented by the central government.

Militarization

Post-war, there has been an increase of the military's presence in the north and the east. Every road has a military checkpoint and there are about 160 military camps alone in Mannar district. These camps cover large acres of land, some of which belonged to the Tamil and Muslim people. From Mangkulam to Iyenkankulam in Killinochchi there are sixteen army checkpoints. The distance between the two places is thirty kilometres, making it approximately two checkpoints per kilometre. In Jaffna, from Jaffna town to Thirunelveli, there are ten checkpoints and twenty-seven checkpoints around Jaffna town. In Jaffna district, in the town and surrounding areas there are ten main army camps (Weliamuna 2011b).

High military presence and the PTA create an environment that does not allow people to form associations or raise any concerns in the north. Most meetings are attended by military personnel as a form of participation in civilian affairs; however, given the role of the military in the past this participation leads to fear and an inability to return to normalcy. For example, in Sannar (in Mannar district) where there is a conflict between the Muslim and Tamil community over land, military brigadiers are brought in by politicians to the mediation meetings. Civilian administration has been overtly and covertly handed over to the military. There were several instances where the army attended village meetings to assess the needs of the village. In Killinochchi and Mullaitivu the police often refuse to take any action against criminal activity unless the complaint is made to the military and forwarded to the police. The refusal of the government to demobilize a large part of the army or to acknowledge the military personnel too needs to be reintegrated into society post their participation in a brutal war has implications on the society at large and its engagement with violence.

Development

While there has been a substantial amount of aid provided for development, the focus of the government has been on infrastructure. While this is an important aspect of development, people in the north and east continue to struggle with basic necessities such as shelter, food, health care and education. Even though most displaced civilians interned in the north at the end of the war have been sent home, they lack most basic amenities. Around 180,000 of those and others displaced in previous stages of the war are still in temporary shelters.

The responses of the participants showed that they were keen on encouraging their clients to engage in the developmental processes in order to upgrade their living standards. Through their counselling sessions and awareness programmes, the counsellors attempt to encourage and prepare their clients mentally to reap the benefits of the development process and to boost a morale that has been adversely affected by the war.

Reconciliation and Peace Building

Although reconciliation and peace building are the top priorities of the government, their progress in this environment is likely to be difficult. With the emergency and anti-terrorism laws still in place, the media and political opponents are being to some extent repressed. In addition, elections are being manipulated (K. Ratnayake 2010) and civil society silenced. Northern areas once ruled by the LTTE are now dominated by the military, which has taken over civil administration and controls all aspects of daily life, undermining what little remains of local capacity (Sumanthiran 2012).

The government established the LLRC as a mechanism for both accountability and reconciliation. While the commission itself has been criticized and has limitations, the recommendations of the commission, if implemented, may provide the base for the long and arduous journey towards rehabilitation and reconciliation. It must also be noted that the LLRC did, albeit minimally, provide a legitimate and official space for people to air their grievances and talk about their losses and for their loss to be acknowledged.

In its chapter on principal observations and recommendations, the LLRC (Commission of Inquiry 2011) states that appropriate redress to the next of kin of those killed and those injured as a humanitarian gesture would help the victims to come to terms with personal tragedy must be provided. It recommends further investigations to be conducted into such specific allegations as those of disappearances after surrendering to the military and prosecution and punishment of the wrongdoers, a comprehensive approach to address the issue of missing persons to be found and previous recommendations of commissions to investigate human rights violations to be implemented. The issuance of death certificates and monetary recompense where necessary are to be done. It further recommends taking necessary measures to ensure that arrests and detentions are within the legal framework and to protect those arrested. It calls for prioritizing the needs of vulnerable groups such as women and women-headed households in all the government's developmental measures, to provide safety and security for those who are vulnerable, that is, women, children and the disabled, and necessary legislative measures to be taken for the realization of the rights of disabled people. Devolution of power in a people centric manner, addressing the legitimate grievances of minority communities, implementation of the language policy, ensuring equality of access and opportunity and active measures towards reconciliation are other important recommendations made by the LLRC (Commission of Inquiry 2011).

The elaborate report of the LLRC reviewed the thirty-year war, tracing its history and acknowledging the systemic exclusion of minority communities. While the LLRC lays the burden of the war crimes committed on the LTTE, holding the army in high regard, it does call for the individual prosecution of 'wayward' army personnel engaged in human rights violations. The report in its whole acknowledges trauma and the prolonged suffering people have faced. The commission recognizes that this suffering needs to be addressed through counselling, justice mechanisms, compensation and acknowledgement, if reconciliation is to take place. The commission also noted that reconciliation and peace can only be achieved through systemic changes in law and state structures and though a process of integration (Commission of Inquiry 2011).

The LLRC did provide many from the north and the east a space to air their grievances, which proves that people are keen for redress and justice. Many civilians attended the LLRC sessions in various parts of the country, narrating their stories, providing at least a partial view of the last stages of the war. The recommendations made by the commission, while limited due to its mandate, have called upon the state to undertake further investigation and also called for the rule of law, separation of powers and devolution.

Another developing issue with psychosocial dimensions is the return of Muslims who were expelled from the north or relatives of those murdered in the east by the LTTE. A recent statement made by Tamil civil society members calling on the Tamil community and Tamil politicians to right the wrongs committed against the Muslims and ensure that reconciliation occurs sets in place a mode of acknowledgement and reconciliation at the community level which is important (Commission of Inquiry 2011). While state acknowledgement of wrongs is important, reconciliatory steps have to be taken at the community level if lasting peace is to be ensured.

Impact of Psychosocial Programming on Reconciliation

The organizations who participated in the study try to bring people of different ethnicities together and provide a chance for them to communicate with one another when conducting their awareness programmes. Other services they provide, such as housing facilities, require the clients to work together; for example, Tamil women helping to build houses for the Muslim women and vice versa in Mannar. Although it may not be an anticipated outcome of the intervention, the holistic support provided by these organizations assures this kind of reconciliatory process. Some organizations also attempt to encourage people to get involved in the national development processes and to encourage them to think of themselves as Sri Lankans.

The representatives from these organizations stated that there is a general lack of research based data related to psychosocial and gender aspects in Sri Lanka, especially in the north and the east. They also complained about the difficulties they face when trying to get such information from governmental authorities. They mentioned that even NGOs are reluctant to share information and data with other organizations.

When they counsel widows, for example, whose husbands were killed by the LTTE, they attempt to make the clients understand that this injustice was done not by the Tamil community but by a terrorist group. These counsellors make the clients look at war not as a conflict between the Tamil and Sinhala communities, but as a dispute between two armed groups: the LTTE and the armed forces. Thus, in instances where clients may develop feelings of hatred or hostility towards the people of the other community, the counsellors try to reduce these kinds of misunderstandings through their intervention.

The limited nature of the intervention and the relatively short term in which service providers work with clients pose a challenge to building long-lasting reconciliation or even initiating such measures. However, in certain cases these organizations, through other project programmes, have integrated these clients into various peace and reconciliatory actions, that is, building houses for women from other ethnicities.

One other aspect mentioned which all representatives agreed was an important way to bridge the gap between the different ethnicities was language. Some organizations encourage their staff to be competent in both languages, Tamil and Sinhala, which in turn would lead to better understanding between the people of different ethnicities.

Addressing the Past

The greatest challenge, as stated by the LLRC, UN experts' panel on Sri Lanka and ICG, is the search for those who are missing. Sri Lanka has a long history of abductions, enforced disappearances and arbitrary arrests and detention. Families in the north and east require accountability, acknowledgement and redress. This is an important aspect of dealing with trauma and building towards peace and reconciliation.

Land is and has always been an area of contestation and could be placed in the centre of self-determination struggles, the ability to control a territory, its resources and its people. Post-war disputes regarding land, exacerbated by the conflict, have increased. However, little has been done to design sustainable solutions devoid of political interference, ensuring equal access to land, proper resettlement and provision of land titles and deeds. People returning to the north have also had to face the acquisition of land for military camps and bases or for multinational industries such as the Sampoor power plant.

Impact of Psychosocial Programmes at a Broader Level

The psychosocial interventions of organizations that were studied help in creating awareness in the society and sensitizing people about broader issues such as gender equality, human rights and reconciliation. Even when psychosocial workers deal with individual cases, there is awareness created in the broader sense among people, particularly among the men, the police and other officers about issues of patriarchy and rights of the people. If a case of domestic violence is being dealt with, the psychosocial intervention that is implemented gives the message that a rights violation has occurred, which needs to be addressed, and that there are places where women could go to seek assistance to free themselves from that situation of violence. These organizations go to the police station and fight for justice for each individual case, which in turn has influenced the police officers to change their attitude towards gender issues and domestic violence. The participants stated that because of this the police are more cooperative than before when dealing with cases of domestic violence. When it comes to torture victims, the main two areas that are being focused on are the prevention of torture and advocating protection of the rights of the victims. These organizations try to introduce concepts like 'do no harm' in the society through their awareness programmes.

Although organizations would wish to ensure justice for the clients by filing a court case against the abuser, sometimes this is not an option, because it would put the client and the client's family in danger. Especially in cases where the abuser is connected to some group with political power or military power, these organizations have to work against the concept of justice in order to take care of the victim's immediate needs, such as safety and security. Participants provided examples of cases when the police would not file a complaint of the wife in a domestic violence case, if the husband has political affiliations. In such instances they would refer clients to the senior police authority and follow up to ensure that the women's rights are protected.

As one participant stated:

> Even though there is a desire to ensure justice, sometimes that is not an option. For example, you have to take care of the safety and the security of the woman, her needs at that point, if she doesn't want to take the case to the court. If it is a rape case, she might not want to talk about it, she might be pregnant, and she needs a place to have the child safely and maybe give the child for adoption. So those kinds of concerns come into play even though you would like to do justice.

However, this is not to say that justice is not one of the aims of the interventions provided by these specific organizations. All four organizations studied have broader mandates of social justice, human rights and equality, but deal with each case according to its specific requirements.

At times, they have had to change their tactics to make sure that the client is safe, for example, in a domestic violence situation, the counsellors have had to use different methods to involve the husband in the counselling process, because if he gets to know that the wife has complained to these organizations about him, her safety would be at risk. In some cases where the husband posed a threat to the wife's life, the counsellors have had to do more than what they would usually do for a client, in order to make sure that no harm would come to her. One strategy they use to get the husband to come to the organization for counselling is stressing on a possible flaw in the wife when talking to him, in order to make the husband feel that the counsellor is impartial. These participants said that they are not always led by what the woman says, and that they also try to get the husband's side of the story when dealing with a domestic violence case. Sometimes they even talk to the children or relatives to find out what is causing the violence in order to find the best solution.

When these counsellors talk to women, they inform them about their duties towards society and to their family and, at the same time, they work towards making the men understand that they cannot abuse the women just because they are their wives. They also work to empower women financially and to create awareness among women that there are places that they could go to in order to get assistance to protect herself from a situation of violence. In situations where wives are reluctant to 'get their husbands into trouble', these organizations assist them in obtaining other types of relief; for example, if the men are neglecting their duties towards the family, they would assist in obtaining economic assistance such as help file a case seeking maintenance.

The service providers stated that their organizations strive to create awareness among the police and society about the fact that people do not have the right to inflict torture on others. However, one participant was of the view that if it was a case of grave importance the police have the right to use torture on the suspects in order to get the necessary information, as long as it is not inhuman torture. The participant said that since the police have the right to do that, the organization cannot do anything about it. She further explained that other than talking to the client and providing him with whatever services they could provide, there is not much they could do. She explained that even when the organization makes the intervention they do not go to institutions (of the state) with a case, pointing out to them the kind of injustice that has happened to the client. She believed that the organizations' role was only to deal with the client and his family in order to reduce the effects of trauma.

However, other representatives believed that it is important that the staff and service providers are sensitive to the broader issues like human rights, patriarchy, torture prevention, injustice, peace and reconciliation during their interventions. One representative was of the view that peace begins in the mind of the psychosocial worker and that this is important in order to ensure that the rights of clients are protected, irrespective of linguistic differences, caste or ethnicity. One representative said that if the counsellor is not gender sensitive then the intervention made into a domestic violence case will not ensure the rights of the woman. Therefore, they think that it is imperative to incorporate these broader concepts in their planning and strategizing in order to train their staff to be sensitive towards these broader issues.

Long-term Sustainability of Psychosocial Interventions

Since the branches of the organizations studied would have to move out of the selected locations once the projects are completed, they had to think about ways of ensuring that the outcomes they worked so hard to achieve last even after they were gone. One participant said that her organization would involve the government officers in their psychosocial interventions in hope of sensitizing them towards these issues, since the government officers would be operating in the areas longer than they would.

One problem the participants mentioned as an obstacle to the sustainability of the impact of the interventions is that psychosocial activities are not valued in society, sometimes not even by the people who come to obtain their services. There is a perception in society that instead of solving problems counsellors create more problems. Therefore, getting recognition through government involvement is one strategy that the representatives said would help in the long term.

Conclusion

As indicated in this paper, the sociocultural and political context has changed in Sri Lanka since the end of the war. Many psychosocial programmes are operating despite the restrictions of the PTF. In addition to counselling, it is evident that they are providing very useful psychosocial services to communities affected by the war. Counselling is an intervention that requires clients to speak about their problems. Inevitably, clients share their experiences during the war and how they survived the terrible events that struck them, their family members and friends. Stories of their losses, violence, abuses of human rights and power, alcoholism and corruption are testimonies of the experiences they underwent and the situation of the country when these took place. But Sri Lanka is 'celebrating' the victory over the LTTE. Such stories could very well blacken the picture that the state wants to depict to its citizens and the international community, that of complete power, control and euphoria, minimizing the suffering of those who survived the war. However, these stories need to be heard if one wants to provide people with appropriate psychosocial care as well as address the broader need of national reconciliation. In listening to the grievances of the people and studying their coping mechanisms, psychosocial programmes would be able to design interventions that would help them adapt to the post-conflict environment. It is often assumed that counselling is all they need. While counselling may be useful for some individuals, this intervention may not necessarily meet the needs of others (such as education of children, shelter, economic assistance, legal issues, vocational training) or families and communities. However, it is important that the government hears what people think of how they can be assisted to improve their well-being. This initiative would acknowledge people's ability to identify their needs and suggest ways of responding to these needs that would be meaningful to them. Of course doing this would mean recognizing one's own vulnerability, and that those in power do not necessarily know better than the victims and what is best for them.

This chapter has attempted to point out that many psychosocial programmes operating in conflict-affected areas in Sri Lanka used counselling but also developed a variety of other interventions to meet the psychosocial needs of their clients. The individual-oriented therapeutic approaches based on a Western, psychiatric approach to mental health attempt to alleviate the suffering of victims by encouraging them to talk about their experiences and their feelings resulting from these.

These programmes have responded to broader issues such as family, gender, economic and physical needs, human rights, justice, reconciliation and peace building in a creative way to address the needs of the community within the prevailing context and available resources. Most of the programmes studied had not in their mission envisaged a need for a larger impact nor had the designers of such programmes thought about the potential to have an impact on social transformation, but had ended up doing so.

These programmes were very concerned about their own survival and how they could sustain psychosocial support to their clients. The PTF was indeed a threat to the continuation of their work as it restricted the implementation of the psychosocial components of the programmes.

A comprehensive programme should be developed by the government in consultation with the different organizations providing psychosocial services in order to respond appropriately to the psychosocial needs of individuals and communities affected by the war. The role of the government would be crucial in ensuring the sustainability of the services, while the NGOs would be able to share their knowledge of the lives and experiences of such individuals and communities to develop meaningful and culturally appropriate interventions. These interventions should ideally strive to make a difference in terms of peace building and development, or more broadly, social transformation.

Epilogue

And the end of all our journeying[1]
Will be to arrive where we started
And know the place for the first time.

—T. S. Elliot, 'Little Gidding'

After the end to the bitter fighting and the horrors of civil war, it appears that we are back to where we started from, back to square one. Are we any wiser? The painful and costly experiences of the past few decades should have given us the maturity and willingness to act, to put things right. Sadly, post-war national reconciliation, recovery and development are yet to materialize. Unfortunately, golden opportunities to address the root causes of the ethnic conflict have not been seized and the possibility of further strife in different forms, a sickening repetition of the karmic cycle, looms large on the horizon. Hopefully some rationality and good sense will prevail. The narrow ethnocentric perceptions through which people are manipulated for short-term political power will need to be overcome, and transcended. This book tries to create awareness in that direction, but a process of psychoeducation among post-war communities will need to be done. For this to happen, there has to be political will, a concerted effort by the media, educators and public opinion leaders. Eventually, there will have to be an expansion in consciousness, a deeper understanding and a change in perceptions and attitudes. Without disentangling the knot of ethnic consciousness, it may not be possible to ensure social justice and equity in the distribution of resources and opportunities for reconciliation and peace.

The Asian tsunami and Sri Lanka's civil war have taught mental health workers important lessons. After massive disasters, we have learnt that it is not effective merely to treat affected individuals. The Western medical model of individual psychotherapy may not be feasible in a resource-poor country with few trained professionals or indeed may not be culturally appropriate in a collectivistic non-Western society. We have to also take into consideration the impact on families and communities in order to

---

[1] 'Exploring' in the original.

intervene in ways that re-establish their functioning. We should make maximum use of the available local resources and try to promote their own healing potential, resilience and adaptive capacity. We have had the experience of using a range of community-level psychosocial interventions that evolved from responding to their needs. Active participatory feedback evaluated our approaches, allowing us to make modifications. This work is of relevance in similar situations elsewhere in the world, as well as more generally, in generic mental health approaches. There is a need to establish an evidence base for the effectiveness of community-level interventions that would have to use fairly sophisticated multilevel statistical analysis. The phenomenon of collective trauma will have to be operationalized with clear guidelines so that public mental health workers can identify its repercussions in a disaster-stricken community.

In the meantime, the people of Sri Lanka who have been affected by this terrible war need to be able to recover, reconcile and return to their 'life plan'. We desperately need to progress from a post-war to a post-conflict ecology, from the victor-and-vanquished mindset to peaceful coexistence, from a repressive to an enabling ecology, to heal the collective trauma and move towards a healthy future.

The collective trauma has affected all the communities, and the society and nation as a whole. At the national level, high defence expenditure, continuing military deployment, Prevention of Terrorism Act and virtual martial law in the north and east are all manifestations of the continuing war mindset and stifling ecology. They must change if we are to go into a post-conflict, national reconciliation mode so that recovery from the collective trauma can take place. Dealing with the plethora of social ills that manifest in post-war communities is rendered more difficult owing to the lack of functioning family and community structures, processes and systems that would normally provide a high level of immunity from trauma or support mechanisms for repair.

In the vacuum created by missing normal community-based support structures, a host of social pathologies are emerging in post-war society. We have to recognize these pathological changes, such as increasing numbers of suicides, violent incidents and sexual abuses that are escalating in the affected communities. Protective factors like existing family ties, female nurturance and creative arts have to be promoted. The whole range of risk factors like depletion of social capital and governance-related issues need to be addressed for the rehabilitation and recovery of communities. This can only be done by finding meaning in what has happened, putting it to rest and strengthening healthy community functioning, networks and creating opportunity structures.

The critical transition process towards post-conflict peace will need to navigate the repercussions of decades of violence, governance issues,

military demobilization, while also introducing responsible role modelling for future generations and a rehabilitation–reconciliation programme
for the current 'missed out' generation. The education system, which has
become archaic and dysfunctional in its entirety, requires rejuvenation
and must be made accessible to all marginalized rural communities. The
imposition of a dominant historical narrative distorted by ethnocentrism
must end; the narrative has to broaden and become more inclusive so that
it listens to the perspective of those affected. A political culture that merely
promotes economic growth runs the risk of deteriorating into consumerism and materialistic craving that find easy ingress in a post-war vacuum.
Resources and effort need to be equally channelled into a more enrich-
ing revival of arts, faith systems, belief in social justice and basic institutions, civic engagement and responsibility, mutual trust and hope in the
future for a vibrant recovery. Some of these mental health and psychosocial issues can be tackled by raising awareness and advocating them with
service providers and their managers, administrators and policy-makers.
Communities can be rebuilt by training teams of psychosocial workers to
work among the community in constructive ways.

The methods used, their effectiveness and lessons learnt in Sri Lanka
will have implications for other communities facing similar situations,
struggling to find their feet, direction, meaning, motivation and hope in a
post-war environment. As T. S. Elliot says in 'Little Gidding':

> And what the dead had no speech for, when living,
> They can tell you, being dead: the communication
> Of the dead is tongued with fire beyond the language of the living.
> Here, the intersection of the timeless moment
> Is Lanka[2] and nowhere. Never and always.

[2] 'England' in original.

References

Abeyratne, S. 2004. 'Economic Roots of Political Conflict: The Case of Sri Lanka', *The World Economy*, 27 (8): 1295–1314.

Abramowitz, S. A. 2005. 'The Poor Have Become Rich, and the Rich Have Become Poor: Collective Trauma in the Guinean Languette', *Social Science & Medicine*, 61(10): 2106–18.

ADBI. 2007. *Economic Challenges of Post-Tsunami Reconstruction in Sri Lanka*. Tokyo: Asian Development Bank Institute. Available online at http://www.adbi. org/discussion-paper/2007/08/31/2354.sri.lanka.post.tsunami.recon-struction/

Agger, I. and S. B. Jensen. 1996. *Trauma and Healing under State Terrorism*. London: Zed Books.

AHRC. 2007. *Sri Lanka: A Disappearance Every Five Hours Is a Result of Deliberate Removal of all Legal Safeguards against Illegal Detention, Murder and Illegal Disposal of Bodies*. Hong Kong: Asian Human Rights Commission.

Ai, A. L., T. Evans-Campbell, L. Santangelo and T. Cascio. 2006. 'The Traumatic Impact of the September 11, 2001 Terrorist Attacks and the Potential Protection of Optimism', *Journal of Interpersonal Violence*, 21 (5): 689–700.

AI. 1993. 'Sri Lanka: "Disappearance" and Murder as Techniques of Counter-Insurgency', in *"Disappearances" and Political Killings: Human Rights Crisis of the 1990s – A Manual for Action*, pp. 23–32. Amsterdam: Amnesty International.

———. 1998. *Sri Lanka: Implementation of the Recommendations of the UN Working Group on Enforced or Involuntary Disappearances Following Their Visits to Sri Lanka in 1991 and 1992*. London: Amnesty International.

———. 2007. *A Crucial Opportunity to End Enforced Disappearance*. Report No. IOR51/055/2007. London: Amnesty International.

———. 2009. 'UN Security Council: Demand Immediate Access and Accountability in Sri Lanka', *Press Releases*, 4 June. Available online at http://www. amnesty.org/en/for-media/press-releases/un-security-council-demand-immediate-access-and-accountability-sri-lanka (retrieved on 12 January 2010).

Allport, G. W. 1954. *The Nature of Prejudice*. Reading, MA: Addison Wesley Publishing. Fig. 1.1 modified from Fig. 2, p 43 with permission of Pearson Education Inc., Upper Saddle River, NJ.

Alston, P. 2008. 'Report of the Special Rapporteur, Philip Alston, Mission to Sri Lanka (28 November to 6 December 2005)', *Addendum to the Report on Civil and Political Rights, including the Question of Disappearances and Summary Executions: Extrajudicial, Summary or Arbitrary Executions*, No.

E/CN.4/2006/53/Add.5, 27 March. Available online at http://daccess-dds-ny.un.org/doc/UNDOC/GEN/G08/134/74/PDF/G0813474.pdf?OpenElement (retrieved on 29 July 2013).

Amato, E. J. 2002. 'Tail of the Dragon: Sri Lankan Efforts to Subdue the Liberation Tigers of Tamil Eelam'. Master's degree thesis presented to the U.S. Army Command and General Staff College, Fort Leavenworth, Kansas. Available online at http://stinet.dtic.mil/cgi-bin/GetTRDoc?AD=ADA406370&Location=U2&doc=GetTRDoc.pdf (retrieved on 29 July 2013).

American Psychiatric Association. 1980. *Diagnostic and Statistical Manual of Mental Disorders: DSM-III*. Washington, D.C.: American Psychiatric Association.

———. 1994. *Diagnostic and Statistical Manual of Mental Disorders: DSM-IV*. Washington, D.C.: American Psychiatric Association.

Anderson, B. 2006. *Imagined Communities: Reflections on the Origin and Spread of Nationalism*, rev. ed. London: Verso.

Anonymous. 2009. 'What Happened in the Vanni? A Testimony of an Experience from the Field', *Kalachuvadu*. Available online at http://www.kalachuvadu.com/issue-116/page47.asp (retrieved on 29 July 2013).

Arasaratnam, S. 1964. *Ceylon*. Upper Saddle River: Prentice-Hall.

———. 1979. 'Nationalism in Sri Lanka', in M. Roberts (ed.), *Collective Identities, Nationalism and Protest in Modern Sri Lanka*. Colombo: Marga Institute.

———. 1998. 'Nationalism in Sri Lanka and the Tamils', in M. Roberts (ed.), *Sri Lanka: Collective Identities Revisited*, Vol. 2, pp. 295–314. Colombo: Marga Institute.

Ardrey, R. 1967. *The Territorial Imperative: A Personal Inquiry into the Animal Origins of Property and Nations*. New York: Atheneum.

Arnestad, B. and M. Daae. 2007. *My Daughter the Terrorist*. Documentary film, 60:00, DVD. Oslo: Oslo Dokumentarkino, Snitt film production.

Arnold, E. 2000. 'Intercultural Social Work', in J. Kareem and R. Littlewood (eds), *Intercultural Therapy*, pp. 171–79. London: Blackwell Science.

Arulanantham, K. 2007. Unpublished MS. 'Sivaram's Views on Counter-Insurgency and International Collaboration in Counter-Insurgency in Sri Lanka'.

Arunakirinathan, T., A. Sasikanthan, R. Sivashankar and D. J. Somasundaram. 1993. 'A Study of Psychological Consequences of Traumatic Stress in School Children Under 12 Years', paper presented at the Ninth Annual Scientific Sessions, Jaffna Medical Association, Jaffna, 27 August.

Assagioli, M. 1975. *Psychosynthesis: A Manual of Principles and Techniques*. New York: Viking Press.

Atkinson, J. 2002. *Trauma Trails, Recreating Song Lines: The Transgenerational Effects of Trauma in Indigenous Australia*. Melbourne: Spinifex.

Australian Centre for Posttraumatic Mental Health. 2007. *Australian Guidelines for the Treatment of Adults with Acute Stress Disorder and Posttraumatic Stress Disorder: Practitioner Guide*. Melbourne: Australian Centre for Posttraumatic Mental Health.

Balakrishnan, N. 1992. 'Statism', Selvanayagam Memorial Lecture, University of Jaffna, Jaffna.

Balasingham, A. 2004. *War and Peace: Armed Struggle and Peace Efforts of the Liberation Tigers*. Mitcham: Fairfax Publishing.

BECAre. 2003. *Impact Study of Counsellor Training at Shantihiham*. Vavuniya: Basic Education for Children in Affected Areas Project.

Bastiampillai, B., R. Edirisinghe and N. Kandasamy (eds). 2010. *Prevention of Terrorism Act (PTA): A Critical Analysis*. Colombo: Centre for Human Rights and Development.

Bastian, S. 1994. 'Liberalised Policies and Regional Autonomy', in S. Bastian (ed.), *Devolution and Development in Sri Lanka*, pp. 143–97. Colombo: International Centre for Ethnic Studies and New Delhi: Konark Publishers.

———. 2007. *The Politics of Foreign Aid in Sri Lanka: Promoting Markets and Supporting Peace*. Colombo: International Centre for Ethnic Studies.

Baykal, T., C. Schlar and E. Kapkin. 2004. *International Training Manual on Psychological Evidence of Torture*. Istanbul: Human Rights Foundation of Turkey.

BBC. 2005. 'Police to Probe PM Tsunami Fund', *BBC News*, 15 September. Available online at http://news.bbc.co.uk/1/hi/world/south_asia/4250190.stm

———. 2009. 'Six Arrests at Tamil London Demo', *BBC News*, 7 April. Available online at http://news.bbc.co.uk/1/hi/uk/7986838.stm (retrieved on 23 July 2010).

———. 2010. 'War Crimes Probe Call Reiterated', *BBC*, 12 February. Available online at http://www.bbc.co.uk/sinhala/news/story/2010/02/100212_war_crimes.shtml (retrieved on 8 March 2010).

Bernal, G., J. Bonilla and C. Bellido. 1995. 'Ecological Validity and Cultural Sensitivity for Outcome Research: Issues for the Cultural Adaptation and Development of Psychosocial Treatments with Hispanics', *Journal of Abnormal Child Psychology*, 23 (1): 67–82. doi: 10.1007/BF01447045

Bettelheim, B. 1979. 'Trauma and Reintegration', in B. Bettelheim (ed.), *Surviving and Other Essays*, pp. 19–37. New York: Knopf.

Beverley, J. 2005. 'Testimonio, Subalternity, and Narrative Authority', in N. K. Denzin and Y. S. Lincoln (eds), *The SAGE Handbook of Qualitative Research*, 3rd ed., pp. 547–58. Thousand Oaks, CA: SAGE Publications.

Bhugra, D. and K. Bhui (eds). 2007. *Textbook of Cultural Psychiatry*. Cambridge: Cambridge University Press.

Blaauw, M. and V. Lähteenmäki. 2002. '"Denial and Silence" or "Acknowledgement and Disclosure"', *International Review of the Red Cross*, 84 (848): 767–83.

Bloom, S. L. 1998. 'By the Crowd They Have Been Broken, By the Crowd They Shall Be Healed: The Social Transformation of Trauma', in R. G. Tedeschi, C. L. Park and L. G. Calhoun (eds), *Posttraumatic Growth: Positive Changes in the Aftermath of Crisis*, pp. 179–208. Mahwah: Lawrence Erlbaum Associates, Inc.

Borland, C. and G. Landrith. 1976. 'Improved Quality of City Life through Transcedental Meditation Program: Decreased Crime Rate', in D. W. Orme-Johnson and J. T. Farrow (eds), *Scientific Research on the Transcendental Meditation Program: Collected Papers*, Vol. 1, pp. 639–48. Rheinweiler: Maharishi European Research University Press.

Boscarino, J. A. and R. E. Adams. 2009. 'PTSD Onset and Course Following the World Trade Center Disaster: Findings and Implications for Future Research', *Social Psychiatry and Psychiatric Epidemiology*, 44 (10): 887–98.

Boss, P. 2004. 'Ambiguous Loss Research, Theory, and Practice: Reflections after 9/11', *Journal of Marriage and Family*, 66 (3): 551–66.

Bowcott, O. 2009. 'Westminster Bridge Closed after Tamil Ceasefire Protest', *The Guardian*, 7 April. Available online at http://www.guardian.co.uk/uk/2009/apr/07/tamil-protest:westminsterbridge (retrieved on 23 July 2010).

Bracken, P. J. 2000. 'Rethinking the Trauma of War', in C. Becker (ed.), *Psychosocial and Trauma Response in War-Torn Societies: The Case of Kosovo*, pp. 53–59. Geneva: International Organization for Migration. Available online at http://publications.iom.int/bookstore/free/PTR_Kosovo_EN.pdf

Bracken, P. J. and C. Petty. 1998a. 'Deconstructing Posttraumatic Stress Disorder', in P. J. Bracken and C. Petty (eds), *Rethinking the Trauma of War: A Critical Analysis of Western Trauma Counselling in Areas of Conflict and Emergencies*, pp. 10–38. London: Save the Children with Free Association Books.

Bracken, P. J. and C. Petty (eds). 1998b. *Rethinking the Trauma of War: A Critical Analysis of Western Trauma Counselling in Areas of Conflict and Emergencies*. London: Save the Children with Free Association Books.

Bracken, P. J., J. E. Giller and D. Summerfield. 1995. 'Psychological Responses to War and Atrocity: The Limitations of Current Concepts', *Social Science & Medicine*, 40 (8): 1073–82.

BRC. 2009. Unpublished MS. 'Vulnerable Women's Project Statistics'.

Brett, R. and I. Specht. 2004. *Young Soldiers: Why They Choose to Fight*. Boulder, CO: Lynne Rienner Publishers.

Bronfenbrenner, U. 1979. *The Ecology of Human Development: Experiments by Nature and Design*. Cambridge: Harvard University Press.

Browde, S. 1988. 'The Treatment of Detainees', in C. Owen (ed.), *Proceedings of the 1987 National Medical and Dental Association Annual Conference*, pp. 105–10. Cape Town: National Medical and Dental Association Publications.

Brown, Derek. 1988. 'Colombo Prison Breakout Raises Chances of Poll being Postponed', *The Guardian* (1959–2003), London, 15 December.

Brown, R. 1965. *Social Psychology*, 1st ed. New York: Macmillan.

———. 1986. *Social Psychology*, 2nd ed. New York: The Free Press.

Buddhaghosa. ~500. *Visuddhimagga* [The path of purification] (B. Nanamoli, Trans., Fifth ed., 1991). Kandy: Buddhist Publication Society.

———. 1991. *The Path of Purification*. Translated by B. Nanamoli, 5th ed. Kandy: Buddhist Publication Society.

Bullman, T. A. and H. K. Kang. 1994. 'Posttraumatic Stress Disorder and the Risk of Traumatic Deaths among Vietnam Veterans', *Journal of Nervous & Mental Disease*, 182 (1): 604–10.

Burke, A. and A. Mulakala. 2011. 'An Insider's View of Donor Support for the Sri Lankan Peace Process, 2000–2005', in J. Goodhand, B. Korf and J. Sepencer (eds), *Conflict and Peacebuilding in Sri Lanka: Caught in the Peace Trap?* pp. 150–167, London: Routledge.

Burvill, P. W. 1980. 'Changing Patterns of Suicide in Australia 1910–1977', *Acta Psychiatrica Scandinavica*, 62 (3): 258–68.

Bush, K. D. and D. Salterelli (eds). 2000. *The Two Faces of Education in Ethnic Conflict: Towards a Peacebuilding Education for Children*. Florence: UNICEF.

Bustos, E. 1992. 'Psychodynamic Approaches in the Treatment of Torture Survivors', in M. Basoglu (ed.), *Torture and Its Consequences: Current Treatment Approaches*, pp. 333–47. Cambridge: Cambridge University Press.

Byman, D. L. 2002. *Keeping the Peace: Lasting Solutions to Ethnic Conflicts*. Baltimore, MD: The John Hopkins University Press.

Calhoun, L. G. and R. G. Tedeschi. 1999. *Facilitating Posttraumatic Growth: A Clinician's Guide*. Mahwah: Lawrence Erlbaum Associates, Inc.

Calhoun, L. G. and R. G. Tedeschi (eds). 2006. *Handbook of Posttraumatic Growth: Research and Practice*. Mahwah: Lawrence Erlbaum Associates.

Camus, A. 1971. *The Rebel*. Translated by A. Bower. London: Penguin Books.

Caspers, P. 1987. *Plantation Economy and Labour, Saturday Review* (6 June 1987; 13 June 1987; 27 June 1987). Jaffna: New Era Publications.

Castle, S. 2000. Development, Social Transformation and Globalization, given at a Centre for Asia Pacific Social Transformation Studies workshop, 23–25 June, 1999. Centre for Asia Pacific Social Transformation Studies, University of Wollongong, Australia.

Catani, C., M. Kohiladevy, M. Ruf, E. Schauer, T. Elbert and F. Neuner. 2009. 'Treating Children Traumatized by War and Tsunami: A Comparison between Exposure Therapy and Meditation-Relaxation in North-East Sri Lanka', *BMC Psychiatry*, 9 (22). doi: 10.1186/1471-244X-9-22

Centre for Policy Alternatives. 2009. 'A Profile of Human Rights and Humanitarian Issues in the Vanni and Vavuniya'. Available online at http://www.cpalanka.org/a-profile-of-human-rights-and-humanitarian-issues-in-the-vanni-andvavuniyamarch-2009/ (retrieved on 30 July 2013).

Ceylon Parliament Hansard, June 1956.

Chamberlain, G. 2009. 'As the Shells Fell, We Tried to Save Lives with No Blood or Medicine', *The Guardian*, 15 September. Available online at http://www.guardian.co.uk/world/2009/sep/15/sri-lanka-war-on-tamil-tigers (retrieved on 27 April 2010).

Chandra, K. 2005. 'Ethnic Parties and Democratic Stability', *Perspectives on Politics*, 3 (2): 235–52.

Chandraprema, C. A. 2012. *Gota's War: The Crushing of Tamil Tiger Terrorism in Sri Lanka*. Colombo: Ranjan Wijeratne Foundation.

Chandrasekaran, R. 2006. *Imperial Life in the Emerald City: Inside Baghdad's Green Zone*. London: Bloomsbury.

Chatterjee, P. 2004. *The Politics of the Governed: Reflections on Popular Politics in Most of the World*. New York: Columbia University Press.

———. 2010. *Empire and Nation: Selected Essays*. New York: Columbia University Press.

Chawade, D. A. 2011. 'Women's Initiative in Building Peace: The Case of Northern Sri Lanka', in K. Stokke and J. Uyangoda (eds), *Liberal Peace in Question: Politics of State and Market Reform in Sri Lanka*, pp. 141–56. London: Anthem Press.

Chen, Y.-H. 2006. 'Coping with Suffering: The Buddhist Perspective', in P. T. P. Wong and L. C. J. Wong (eds), *Handbook of Multicultural Perspectives on Stress and Coping*, pp. 73–90. New York: Springer.

Cheran, R., D. Ambalavanar and C. Kanaganayakam (eds). 2007. *History and Imagination: Tamil Culture in the Global Context*. Toronto: TSAR Publications.

Christy, L. 2009. 'On the Spot Report'. Available online at http://tamilnational.com/world-news/asia/440-on-the-spot-report.html

Chun, C. A., R. H. Moos and R. C. Cronkite. 2006. 'Culture: A Fundamental Context for the Stress and Coping Paradigm', in P. T. P. Wong and L. C. J. Wong (eds), *Handbook of Multicultural Perspectives on Stress and Coping*, pp. 29–54. New York: Springer.

Citizens' Commission. 2011. *The Quest for Redemption: The Story of the Northern Muslims*. Colombo: Law & Society Trust.

Clarance, W. 2007. *Ethnic Warfare in Sri Lanka and the UN Crisis*. Colombo: Vijitha Yapa Publications.

Cohn, B. S. 1987. *An Anthropologist among the Historians and Other Essays*. New Delhi: Oxford University Press.

Colletta, N. J. and M. L. Cullen. 2000. *Violent Conflict and the Transformation of Social Capital: Lessons from Cambodia, Rwanda, Guatemala, and Somalia*. Washington, D.C.: World Bank.

Commission for Historical Clarification. 1998. *Guatemala: Memory of Silence*. Guatemala: Commission for Historical Clarification. Available online at http://shr.aaas.org/guatemala/ceh/report/english/toc.html

Commission of Inquiry. 2011. *Report of the Commission of Inquiry on Lessons Learnt and Reconciliation*. Colombo: Government of Sri Lanka. Available online at http://www.priu.gov.lk/news_update/Current_Affairs/ca201112/FINAL%20LLRC%20REPORT.pdf

Committee for Rational Development. 1984. *Sri Lanka: The Ethnic Conflict: Myths, Realities and Perspectives*. New Delhi: Navrang Press.

Conte, L. 2002. *The Missing: Action to Resolve the Problem of People Unaccounted for as a Result of Armed Conflict or Internal Violence and to Assist Their Families: Support for Families of People Unaccounted For: Final Outcome and Report of the Workshop held in Geneva, 10–11 June*, pp. 37–39. Geneva: International Committee of the Red Cross. Available online at http://www.icrc.org/eng/assets/files/other/icrc_themissing_082002_en_4.pdf

Cooke, M. C. 2011. *The Lionel Bopage Story: Rebellion, Repression and the Struggle for Justice in Sri Lanka*. Colombo: Agahas Publishers.

Coomaraswamy, A. 1977. *Selected Papers: Metaphysics*. Edited by Roger Lipsey. Princeton, NJ: Princeton University Press.

Cordell, K. and S. Wolff. 2010. *Ethnic Conflict: Causes–Consequences–Responses*. Cambridge: Polity Press.

Council of NGOs. 1992. *Nutritional Status of the People of Jaffna District: 1992*. Jaffna: NGO Council.

―――. 1999. *Socio-Economic Degradation: Jaffna Peninsula*. Jaffna: NGO Council.

Crotty, M. 1998. *The Foundations of Social Research*. Crows Nest: Allen & Unwin.

Cullen, M. and H. Whiteford. 2001. 'The Interrelations of Social Capital with Health and Mental Health', Discussion Paper, Commonwealth Department of Health and Aged Care, Canberra.

Curry, A. 1964. 'Myth, Transference and the Black Psychotherapist', *Psychoanalytic Review*, 51: 547–54.

Dalton, J., M. Elias and A. Wandersman. 2007. *Community Psychology: Linking Individuals and Communities*, 2nd ed. Belmont: Thomson Wadsworth.

Damian, S. 1994. *Ula vallathrurai* [Counselling]. Jaffna: S. Damian.

Daniel, E. V. 1984. *Fluid Signs: Being a Person the Tamil Way*. Berkeley, CA: University of California Press.

———. 1996. *Charred Lullabies: Chapters in an Athropography of Violence*. Princeton, NJ: Princeton University Press.

Danieli, Y. 1980. 'Countertransference in the Treatment and Study of Nazi Holocaust Survivors and Their Children', *Victimology*, 5 (2–4): 355–67.

———. 2007. 'Assessing Trauma Across Cultures from a Multigenerational Perspective', in J. P. Wilson and C. S. Tang (eds), *Cross-Cultural Assessment of Psychological Trauma and PTSD*, pp. 65–90. New York: Springer.

Danvers, K., S. Sivayokan, D. J. Somasundaram and R. Sivashankar. 2006. 'Ten Months On: Qualitative Assessment of Psychosocial Issues in Northern Sri Lanka Following the Tsunami', *International Psychiatry*, 3 (3): 5–8.

de Jong, J. T. V. M. 1997. *TPO Program for the Identification, Management, and Prevention of Psychosocial and Mental Health Problems of Refugees and Victims of Organized Violence within Primary Health Care of Adults and Children*. Amsterdam: Transcultural Psychosocial Organization.

———. 2002. 'Public Mental Health, Traumatic Stress and Human Rights Violations in Low-Income Countries: A Culturally Appropriate Model in Times of Conflict, Disaster and Peace', in J. T. V. M. de Jong (ed.), *Trauma, War, and Violence: Public Mental Health in Socio-Cultural Context*, pp. 1–92. New York: Kluwer Academic/Plenum Publishers.

———. 2004. 'Public Mental Health and Culture: Disasters as a Challenge to Western Mental Health Care Models, the Self, and PTSD' in J. P. Wilson and B. Drozdek (eds), *Broken Spirits: The Treatment of Traumatized Asylum Seekers, Refugees, and War and Torture Victims*, pp. 159–78. New York: Brunner-Routledge.

———. 2011. '(Disaster) Public Mental Health', in D. Stein, M. J. Friedman and C. Blanco (eds), *Post-traumatic Stress Disorder*, pp. 217–62. Oxford: Wiley-Blackwell.

de Jong, J. T. V. M., I. H. Komproe, J. Spinazzola, B. A. van der Kolk and M. Van Ommeren. 2005. 'DESNOS in Three Postconflict Settings: Assessing Cross-cultural Construct Equivalence', *Journal of Traumatic Stress*, 18 (1):13–21.

de Jong, J. T. V. M., I. H. Komproe, M. Van Ommeren, M. El Masri, M. Araya, N. Khaled, W. van de Put and D. J. Somasundaram. 2001. 'Lifetime Events and Posttraumatic Stress Disorder in 4 Postconflict Settings', *Journal of American Medical Association*, 286 (5): 555–62.

de Mel, N. 2007. *Militarizing Sri Lanka: Popular Culture, Memory and Narrative in the Armed Conflict*. New Delhi: SAGE Publications.

de Silva, D. 2001. *Mental Health Care of Torture Survivors*. Colombo: Family Rehabilitation Centre.

de Silva, H., C. Hobbs and H. Hanks. 2001. Conscription of Children in Armed Conflict — A Form of Child Abuse. A study of 19 former child soldiers. *Child Abuse Review*, 10: 125–34.

de Silva, D. and S. Jayasinghe. 2003. 'Suicide in Sri Lanka', in L. Vijayakumar (ed.), *Suicide Prevention: Meeting the Challenge Together*, pp. 178–90. Hyderabad: Orient Longman.

de Alwis, M. 2009. 'A Double Wounding? Aid and Activism in Post-Tsunami Sri Lanka', in M. de Alwis and E-L. Hedman (eds), *Tsunami in a Time of War: Aid, Activism & Reconstruction in Sri Lanka & Aceh*, pp. 121–38. Colombo: International Centre for Ethnic Studies.

———. 2010. 'The China Factor in Post-War Sri Lanka', *Inter-Asia Cultural Studies*, 11 (3): 434–46.

de Alwis, M. and E.- L. Hedman (eds). 2009. *Tsunami in Time of War: Aid, Activism & Reconstruction in Sri Lanka & Aceh*. Colombo: International Centre for Ethnic Studies.

De Silva, K. M. 1981. *A History of Sri Lanka*. Colombo: Vijitha Yapa Publications.

———. 2005. *A History of Sri Lanka*. Colombo: Vijitha Yapa Publications.

———. 2012. *Sri Lanka and the Defeat of the LTTE*. Colombo: Vijitha Yapa Publications.

Demographic Training and Research Unit. 1976. *Population Problems of Sri Lanka*. Kattubedda: Sri Lanka University Press.

Denzin, N. K. and Y. S. Lincoln (eds). 2000. *Handbook of Qualitative Research*, 2nd ed. Thousand Oaks, CA: SAGE Publications.

———. 2005. *The SAGE Handbook of Qualitative Research*, 3rd ed. Thousand Oaks, CA: SAGE Publications.

Department of Census and Statistics. 2005. *Census of Public and Semi-Government Sector Employment 2002: Final Report*. Colombo: Department of Census and Statistics, Government of Sri Lanka.

Derges, J. 2009. 'Eloquent Bodies: Conflict and Ritual in Northern Sri Lanka', *Anthropology & Medicine*, 16(1): 27–36.

———. 2013. *Ritual and Recovery in Post-Conflict Sri Lanka*. London: Routledge.

DeVotta, N. 2004. *Blowback: Linguistic Nationalism, Institutional Decay, and Ethnic Conflict in Sri Lanka*. Stanford, CA: Stanford University Press.

———. 2007. *Sinhalese Buddhist Nationalist Ideology: Implications for Politics and Conflict Resolution in Sri Lanka*. Washington, D.C.: East-West Center.

Dharmadasa, K. N. O. 1996. 'The Roots of Sinhala Ethnic Identity in Sri Lanka: The Debate on the "People of the Lion" Continued', *Ethnic Studies Report*, 14 (2): 137–70.

Dharmadasa, Y. V. 2002. *The Missing: Action to Resolve the Problem of People Unaccounted for as a Result of Armed Conflict or Internal Violence and to Assist Their Families: Support for Families of People Unaccounted For: Final Outcome and Report of the Workshop held in Geneva, 10–11 June*, pp. 44–46. Geneva: International Committee of the Red Cross. Available online at http://www.icrc.org/eng/assets/files/other/icrc_themissing_082002_en_4.pdf

Dillbeck, M. C., K. L. Cavanaugh, T. Glenn, D. W. Orme-Johnson and V. Mittlefehld. 1987. 'Consciousness as a Field: The Transcendental Meditation and TM-Sidhi Program and Changes in Social Indicators', *The Journal of Mind and Behaviour*, 8 (1): 67–104.

Dissanayake, S. A. W. and W. P. De Silva. 1974. 'Suicide and Attempted Suicide in Sri Lanka', *Ceylon Journal of Medical Science*, 23 (1–2): 10–27.

Doney, A. 1998. 'The Psychological After-Effects of Torture: A Survey of Sri Lankan Ex-Detainees', in D. Somasundaram, *Scarred Minds: The Psychological Impact of War on Sri Lankan Tamils*, pp. 256–87. New Delhi: SAGE Publications.

Du Bois, W. E. B. 1989. *The Souls of Black Folk*. New York: Bantam.

Duran, L. 2011. 'Hari Sivanesan in Jaffna', in *World Routes Academy, 2011: The Music of South India*. Lucy Duran (producer, director & writer). Broadcast Sat 23 July 2011. London: British Broadcasting Corporation. Available online at http://www.bbc.co.uk/programmes/b012r89m (retrieved on 29 July 2013).

Durgom-Powers, J. E. 2002. 'Unexpected Family Crisis', in *The Missing: Action to Resolve the Problem of People Unaccounted for as a Result of Armed Conflict or Internal Violence and to Assist Their Families: Support for Families of People Unaccounted For: Final Outcome and Report of the Workshop held in Geneva, 10–11 June*, pp. 47–50. Geneva: International Committee of the Red Cross. Available online at http://www.icrc.org/eng/assets/files/other/icrc_themissing_082002_en_4.pdf

Durkheim, E. 1951. *Suicide*. Translated by J. A. Spaulding and G. Simpson. New York: The Free Press.

Eisenbruch, M. 1991. 'From Post-Traumatic Stress Disorder to Cultural Bereavement: Diagnosis of Southeast Asian Refugees', *Social Science and Medicine*, 33 (6): 673–80.

Elbert, T., M. Schauer, E. Schauer, B. Huschka, M. Hirth and F. Neuner. 2009. 'Trauma-related Impairment in Children: A Survey in Sri Lankan Provinces Affected by Armed Conflict', *Child Abuse & Neglect*, 33 (4): 238–46.

Ellason, J. W. and C. A. Ross. 1997. 'Childhood Trauma and Psychiatric Symptoms', *Psychological Reports*, 80 (2): 447–50.

Eller, J. D. 1999. *From Culture to Ethnicity to Conflict: An Anthropological Perspective on International Ethnic Conflict*. Ann Arbor, MI: The University of Michigan Press.

Ellis, C. 1991. 'Sociological Introspection and Emotional Experience', *Symbolic Interaction*, 14 (1): 23–50.

Ellis, C. and A. P. Bochner. 2000. 'Autoethnography, Personal Narrative, Reflexivity: Researcher as Subject', in N. K. Denzin and Y. S. Lincoln (eds), *Handbook of Qualitative Research*, 2nd ed., pp. 733–68. Thousand Oaks, CA: SAGE Publications.

Erikson, E. H. 1963. *Childhood and Society*. New York: W. W. Norton & Company, Inc.

———. 1968. *Identity, Youth and Crisis*. London: Faber and Faber.

Erikson, K. T. 1976. 'Disaster at Buffalo Creek: Loss of Communality at Buffalo Creek', *American Journal of Psychiatry*, 133 (3): 302–5.

———. 1979. *In the Wake of the Flood*. London: Allen Unwin.

Erikson, K. T. and C. Vecsey. 1980. 'A Report to the People of Grassy Narrows', in C. Vecsey and R. W. Venables (eds), *American Indian Environments: Ecological Issues in Native American History*, pp. 152–61. New York: Syracuse University Press.

Esman, M. J. 2004. *An Introduction to Ethnic Conflict*. Cambridge: Polity Press.

Esman, M. J. and R. J. Herring (eds). 2001. *Carrots, Sticks, and Ethnic Conflict: Rethinking Development Assistance*. Ann Arbor, MI: The University of Michigan Press.

Evans, C. 2012. *The Right to Reparation in International Law for Victims of Armed Conflict*. Cambridge: Cambridge University Press.

Evans, G. 2007. 'The Limits of State Sovereignty: The Responsibility to Protect in the 21st Century', Eighth Neelam Tiruchelvam Memorial Lecture by Gareth Evans, President, International Crisis Group, International Centre for Ethnic Studies (ICES), Colombo, 29 July. Available online at http://www.crisisgroup.org/en/publication-type/speeches/2007/evans-the-limits-of-state-sovereignty-the-responsibility-to-protect-in-the-21st-century.aspx (retrieved on 29 July 2013).

————— 2008. *The Responsibility to Protect: Ending Mass Atrocity Crises Once and for All.* Washington, D.C.: Brookings Institution Press.

Fanon, F. 1967. *Toward the African Revolution.* New York: Grove Press.

—————. 2004. *The Wretched of the Earth.* New York: Grove Press.

Farmer, B. H. 1963. *Ceylon: A Divided Nation.* London: Oxford University Press.

Fassin, D. and R. Rechtman. 2009. *The Empire of Trauma: An Inquiry into the Condition of Victimhood.* Woodstock: Princeton University Press.

Fernando, S. R. 2008. 'Gajanayake, 3 Others Indicted', *Daily Mirror*, online edition 12 July 2008, Colombo. Available online at http://archives.dailymirror.lk/# (retrieved on 12 July 2008).

Figley, C. R. 1995. 'Compassion Fatigue as Secondary Traumatic Stress Disorder: An Overview', in C. R. Figley (ed.), *Compassion Fatigue: Coping with Secondary Traumatic Stress Disorder in Those Who Treat the Traumatized*, pp. 1–20. New York: Brunner-Routledge.

Flood, G. 2006. *The Tantric Body: The Secret Tradition of Hindu Religion.* London: I.B. Tauris.

Foley, D. and A. Valenzuela. 2005. 'Critical Ethnography: The Politics of Collaboration', in N. K. Denzin and Y. S. Lincoln (eds), *The SAGE Handbook of Qualitative Research*, 3rd ed., pp. 217–34. Thousand Oaks, CA: SAGE Publications.

Fonseka, S. 2009a. 'Full text of speech of General Fonseka in Washington DC', *Lanka E News.* Available online at http://www.lankaenews.com/English/news.php?id=8567 (retrieved on 29 July 2013).

—————. 2009b. 'Sarath Fonseka Hints, About His Future Political Plans in Washington' [Electronic Version]. Sri Lanka Guardian, October, 27, 2009. Available online at http://www.srilankaguardian.org/2009/10/sarath-fonseka-hints-about-his-future.html (retrieved on 6 June 2010).

Foster, D. 2006. 'Evaluating the Truth and Reconciliation Commission of South Africa', *Social Justice Research*, 19 (4): 527–40.

Freire, P. 1972. *Pedagogy of the Oppressed.* Harmondsworth: Penguin Books.

Frerks, G. and B. Klem. 2005. *Tsunami Response in Sri Lanka: Report on a Field Visit from 6–20 February 2005.* Wageningen: Disaster Studies, Wageningen University and The Hague: Conflict Research Unit, Clingendael Institute.

—————. 2011. 'Muddling the Peace Process: The Political Dynamics of the Tsunami, Aid and Conflict', in J. Goodhand, B. Korf and J. Spencer (eds), *Conflict and Peacebuilding in Sri Lanka: Caught in the Peace Trap?*, pp. 168–82. London: Routledge.

Freud, S. 1991. *New Introductory Lectures on Psychoanalysis.* London: Penguin Books.

Frykenberg, R. E. 1993. 'Constructions of Hinduism at the Nexus of History and Religion', *Journal of Interdisciplinary History*, 23 (3): 523–50.

Fountain, S. 1999. 'Peace Education in UNICEF', Working Paper, Education Section, Programme Division, UNICEF. New York: United Nations Children's Fund.

Galappatti, A. 2003. Unpublished MS. 'Our Views of the Field: Perspectives of Psychosocial Personnel in Sri Lanka', *Report on the Psychosocial Policy Project, Consortium of Humanitarian Agencies and Psychosocial Support Programme*.

———. 2005. 'Psychosocial Work in the Aftermath of the Tsunami: Challenges for Service Provision in Batticaloa, Eastern Sri Lanka', *Intervention*, 3 (1): 65–9.

———. 2008. 'Beyond Trauma: Addressing Psychosocial Suffering', Public Lecture at the Ramon Magsaysay Center, Manila, 2 September.

———. 2010. 'Research to the Rescue? 'The Need for Empirical and Theoretical Work on Wellbeing to Shape MHPSS and Development Interventions in Sri Lanka', In Social Policy Analysis and Research Centre (SPARC) (ed.), *Wellbeing and Development in Sri Lanka*, Colombo: University of Colombo.

Ganesvaran, T. and R. Rajarajeswaran. 1989. 'Attempted Suicide in Jaffna', *Jaffna Medical Journal*, 24: 3–9.

Ganesvaran, T., S. Subramaiam and K. Mahadevan. 1984. 'Suicide in a Northern Town of Sri Lanka', *Acta Psyhiatrica Scandinavica*, 69 (5): 420–25.

Garbarino, J. and K. Kostelny. 1996. 'The Effects of Political Violence on Palestinian Children's Behavior Problems: A Risk Accumulation Model', *Child Development*, 67 (1): 33–45. doi: 10.1111/j.1467-8624.1996.tb01717.x

Geertz, C. 1983. *Local Knowledge*. New York: Basic Books.

Geevathasan, M. G. 1993. 'Psychological Consequence of War on Adolescents'. Unpublished thesis submitted to the University of Jaffna, Jaffna.

———. 1995. 'Follow-up of Counselling at Shantiam'. III MBBS research project submitted to the Department of Community Medicine, University of Jaffna, Jaffna.

Gilroy, P. 1993. *The Black Atlantic: Modernity and Double Consciousness*. Cambridge: Harvard University Press.

———. 2000. *Between Camps: Race, Identity and Nationalism at the End of the Colour Line*. London: Allen Lane.

Gladwell, M. 2008. *Outliers: The Story of Success*. Camberwell: Allen Lane.

Gokhale, N. A. 2009. *Sri Lanka: From War to Peace*. New Delhi: Har-Anand Publications.

Gombrich, R. and G. Obeyesekere. 1988. *Buddhism Transformed: Religious Change in Sri Lanka*. Princeton, NJ: Princeton University Press.

Goodhand, J. 2005. *The European Union and Sri Lanka: Tsunami Response and Long-Term Policy*. London: London School of Economics.

Goodhand, J., B. Klem, D. Fonseka, S. I. Keethaponcalan and S. Sardesai. 2005. *Aid, Conflict, and Peacebuilding in Sri Lanka 2000-2005*. Netherlands Ministry of Foreign Affairs, Swedish International Development Cooperation Agency, The Asia Foundation, Government of the United Kingdom of Great Britain and Northern Ireland and World Bank.

Goodhand, J. and B. Korf. 2011. 'Caught in the Peace Trap? On the Illiberal Consequences of Liberal Peace in Sri Lanka', in J. Goodhand, B. Korf and J. Spencer (eds), *Conflict and Peacebuilding in Sri Lanka: Caught in the Peace Trap?*, pp. 1–15. London: Routledge.

Goodhand, J., B. Korf and J. Spencer (eds). 2011. *Conflict and Peacebuilding in Sri Lanka: Caught in the Peace Trap?* London: Routledge.

Goodhand, J., D. Hulme and N. Lewer. 2000. 'Social Capital and the Political Economy of Violence: A Case Study of Sri Lanka', *Disasters*, 24 (4): 390–406.

Goonewardena, K. 2007. "National Ideology' in a Buddhist State', *Himal Southasian*, 20: 10–11. Available online at http://himalmag.com/component/content/article/1333-.html

Gourevitch, P. 1998. *We Wish to Inform You That Tomorrow We Will Be Killed With Our Families: Stories from Rwanda.* New York: Picador.

Government of India. 2011. 2011 Census data. Ministry of Home Affairs, The Registrar General & Census Commissioner: New Delhi. Available online at http://www.censusindia.gov.in/2011census/PCA/pca_highlights/pe_data.html (retrieved on 27 July 2013).

Government of Sri Lanka. 2005. *Tsunami Disaster Figures as of 5 April 2005.* Colombo: Emergency Operation Room of the National Disaster Management Centre, Ministry of Women's Empowerment and Social Welfare, Government of Sri Lanka.

Gray, M. J., H. G. Prigerson and B. T. Litz. 2004. 'Conceptual and Definitional Issues in Complicated Grief', in B. T. Litz (ed.), *Early Intervention for Trauma and Traumatic Loss*, pp. 65–86. New York: The Guilford Press.

Green, B. L. 1994. 'Psychosocial Research in Traumatic Stress: An Update', *Journal of Traumatic Stress*, 7 (3): 341–62.

Green, B. L., M. J. Friedman, J. T. V. M. de Jong, S. D. Solomon, T. M. Keane, J. A. Fairbank, B. Donelan and E. Frey-Wouters (eds). 2003. *Trauma Interventions in War and Peace: Prevention, Practice, and Policy.* New York: Kluwer Academic/Plenum Publishers.

Green, L. 2004. 'Living in a State of Fear', in N. Scheper-Hughes and P. Bourgois (eds), *Violence in War and Peace: An Anthology*, pp. 186–95. Malden: Blackwell Publishing.

Greenfield, S. 2000. *The Private Life of the Brain.* London: Penguin Books.

Greiger, W. 1964. *The Mahavamsa.* London: Pali Text Society, Luzac and Company Ltd.

Grewal, M. K. 2006. *Approaches to Equity in Post Tsunami Assistance: Sri Lanka: A Case Study.* Colombo. Department for International Development and London: Office of the UN Special Envoy for Tsunami Recovery. Available online at http://www.alnap.org/pool/files/ApproachestoEquity.pdf

Guatemalan Indian Children and the Sociocultural Effects of Government-Sponsored terrorism', published in the *Social Science and Medicine*, 34(5): 533–48.

Gunaratnam, H. R., S. Gunaratnam and D. J. Somasundaram. 2003. 'The Psychosocial Effects of Landmines in Jaffna', *Medicine, Conflict and Survival*, 19 (3): 223–34.

Gunasekara, T. 2011. 'Resisting the Rajapaksa-Yoke, Psychologically', *The Sri Lanka Guardian*. Available online at http://www.srilankaguardian.org/2011/04/resisting-rajapaksa-yoke.html (retrieved on 29 July 2013).

Gunasinghe, N. 1984. 'The Open Economy & Its Impact on Ethnic Relations in Sri Lanka', in Committee for Rational Development (ed.), *Sri Lanka: The Ethnic Conflict: Myths, Realities and Perspectives*, pp. 197–214. New Delhi: Navrang Press.

Goonatilake, S. 2006. *Recolonisation: Foreign Funded NGOs in Sri Lanka*. New Delhi: SAGE Publications.

Gunawardena, R. A. L. H. 1990. 'The People of the Lion: The Sinhala Identity and Ideology in History and Historiography', in J. Spencer (ed.), *Sri Lanka: History and the Roots of Conflict*, pp. 45–86. London: Routledge.

Hamber, B. 2009. *Transforming Societies after Political Violence: Truth, Reconciliation, and Mental Health*. London: Springer.

Hanh, T. N. 2008. *Understanding Our Mind*. New Delhi: HarperCollins.

Haritayana. 2008. *Tripura Rahasya* [The mystery beyond the trinity]. Translated by Swami Ramananda. Tiruvannamalai: Sri Ramanasramam.

Harrell-Bond, B. E. 1986. *Imposing Aid: Emergency Assistance to Refugees*. Oxford: Oxford University Press.

Harrison, F. 2012. *Still Counting the Dead: Survivors of Sri Lanka's Hidden War*. London: Portobello Books.

Harvey, M. R. 1996. 'An Ecological View of Psychological Trauma and Trauma Recovery', *Journal of Traumatic Stress*, 9 (1): 3–23.

Hassan, R. 2008a. *Suicide Bombings: An Analysis of Global Trends 1981–2006*. Adelaide: Flinders University.

———. 2008b. *Suicide Bombings: Homicidal Killings or a Weapon of War*. Adelaide: Flinders University.

Health Reach. 1996. *The Health of Children in Conflict Zones of Sri Lanka*. Hamilton: Centre for International Health and the Centre for Peace Studies, McMaster University.

Hellmann-Rajanayagam, D. 2008. 'Female Warriors, Martyrs and Suicide Attackers: Women in the LTTE', *International Review of Modern Sociology*, 34 (1): 1–25.

Hendin, H., and A. Haas. 1984. 'Posttraumatic Stress Disorders in Veterans of Early American Wars', *Psychohistory Review*, 12 (4): 25–30.

Heppner, P. P., M. J. Heppner, D. Lee, Y. Wang, H. Park and L. Wang. 2006. 'Development and Validation of a Collectivist Coping Styles Inventory', *Journal of Counseling Psychology*, 53 (1): 107–25.

Herman, H. 1992. *Trauma and Recovery: The Aftermath of Violence: From Domestic Abuse to Political Terror*. New York: Basic Books.

Herring, R. J. 2001. 'Making Ethnic Conflict: The Civil War in Sri Lanka', in M. J. Esman and R. J. Herring (eds), *Carrots, Sticks, and Ethnic Conflict: Rethinking Development Assistance*, pp. 140–74. Ann Arbor, MI: The University of Michigan Press.

Hinton, A. 2007. 'Terror and Trauma in the Cambodian Genocide', in L. J. Kirmayer, R. Lemelson and M. Barad (eds), *Understanding Trauma: Integrating Biological, Clinical, and Cultural Perspectives*, pp. 433–50. Cambridge: Cambridge University Press.

Hitchens, C. 2007. 'China Stands Guard for Goons in Rangoon', *Weekend Australian*, 6 October 2007, New South Wales.

Hobbes, T. 1651. *Leviathan*. Adelaide: The University of Adelaide Library, eBooks@ Adelaide. Available online at http://ebooks.adelaide.edu.au/h/hobbes/thomas/h68l/ (retrieved on 29 July 2013).

Hobfoll, S. E. 1998. *Stress, Culture, and Community: The Psychology and Philosophy of Stress*. New York: Plenum Press.

Hobfoll, S. E., P. Watson, C. C. Bell, R. A. Bryant, M. J. Brymer, M. J. Friedman, M. Friedman, B. P. R. Gersons, J. T. V. M. de Jong, C. M. Layne, S. Maguen, Y. Neria, A. E. Norwood, R. S. Pynoos, D. Reissman, J. I. Ruzek, A. Y. Shalev, Z. Solomon, A. M. Steinberg and R. J. Ursano. 2007. 'Five Essential Elements of Immediate and Mid-Term Mass Trauma Intervention: Empirical Evidence', *Psychiatry*, 70 (4): 283–315.

Hofstede, G. and G. J. Hofstede. 2005. *Cultures and Organizations: Software of the Mind: Intercultural Cooperation and Its Importance for Survival*. New York: McGraw-Hill.

Hofstede, G., G. J. Hofstede and M. Minkov. 2008. *Cultures and Organizations: Software of the Mind: Intercultural Cooperation and Its Importance for Survival*. New York: McGraw-Hill.

Holstein, J. and J. Gubrium. 2005. 'Interpretive Practice and Social Action', in N. K. Denzin and Y. S. Lincoln (eds), *The SAGE Handbook of Qualitative Research*, 3rd ed., pp. 483–506. Thousand Oaks, CA: SAGE Publications.

Honwana, A. 2005. *Child Soldiers in Africa*. Philadelphia, PA: University of Pennsylvania Press.

Hoole, R. 2001. *Sri Lanka: The Arrogance of Power: Myths, Decadence and Murder*. Colombo: University Teachers for Human Rights (Jaffna).

Hoole, R., D. J. Somasundaram, K. R. Sritharan and R. Thiranagama. 1988. *The Broken Palmyra: The Tamil Crisis in Sri Lanka – An Inside Account*. Claremont: Harvey Mudd College Press.

Hoole, S. R. H. 2007a. 'Education and the Ethnic Conflict', Lecture at University of Toronto, Toronto, 21 April.

———. 2007b. 'A Time for Tamil Introspection and Reassessment in the Midst of Myth and Propaganda', The Appapillai Amirthalingam Eightieth Birth Anniversary Memorial Lecture, London, 26 August.

Horowitz, D. L. 1980. *Coup Theories and Officers' Motives: Sri Lanka in Comparative Perspective*. Princeton, NJ: Princeton University Press.

———. 2000. *Ethnic Groups in Conflict*, 2nd ed. Berkeley, CA: University of California Press.

Horowitz, M. J. 1986. *Stress Response Syndromes: PTSD, Grief, and Adjustment Disorders*. Lanham: Jason Aronson Inc.

Hoshmand, L. T. 2007. 'Cultural–Ecological Perspectives on the Understanding and Assessment of Trauma', in J. P. Wilson and C. S. Tang (eds), *Cross-Cultural Assessment of Psychological Trauma and PTSD*, pp. 31–50. New York: Springer.

Hovens, J. E., W. Op den Velde P. R. Falger, E. Schouten, J. H. M. de Groen and H. van Duijn. 1992. 'Anxiety, Depression and Anger in Dutch Resistance Veterans from World War II', *Psychotherapy and Psychosomatics*, 57 (4): 172–79.

HRCSL. 2003. *Report of the Committee on Disappearances in the Jaffna Region*. Colombo: Human Rights Commission of Sri Lanka.

HRW. 2006. 'Funding the "Final War": LTTE Intimidation and Extortion in the Tamil Diaspora', *Human Rights Watch*, 18 (1C): 1–47. Available online at http://hrw.org/reports/2006/ltte0306/ltte0306web.pdf

———. 2011. *Sri Lanka: Military Conference to Whitewash War Crimes*. New York: HRW. Available online at http://www.hrw.org/news/2011/05/23/sri-lanka-military-conference-whitewash-war-crimes

HRW. 2008. 'Recurring Nightmare: State Responsibility for "Disappearances" and Abductions in Sri Lanka'. Available online at http://www.hrw.org/reports/2008/08/27/recurring-nightmare (retrieved on 29 July 2013).

———. 2009a. 'Sri Lanka: Domestic Inquiry into Abuses a Smokescreen', 27 October. Available online at www.hrw.org/en/news/2009/10/27/sri-lanka-domestic-inquiry-abuses-smokescreen (retrieved on 16 November 2009).

———. 2009b. *War on the Displaced: Sri Lankan Army and LTTE Abuses against Civilians in the Vanni*. New York: Human Rights Watch. Available online at http://www.hrw.org/en/reports/2009/02/19/war-displaced (retrieved on 9 March 2010).

Huntington, S. P. 1993. 'The Clash of Civilizations?', *Foreign Affairs*, 72 (3): 22–49.

Husain, F., M. Anderson, B. Lopes Cardozo, K. Becknell, C. Blanton, D. Araki and E. Kottegoda Vithana. 2011. 'Prevalence of War-Related Mental Health Conditions and Association with Displacement Status in Postwar Jaffna District, Sri Lanka', *The Journal of the American Medical Association*, 306 (5): 522–31. doi: 10.1001/jama.2011.1052

IASC. 2007. *IASC Guidelines on Mental Health and Psychosocial Support in Emergency Settings*. Geneva: Inter-Agency Standing Committee.

ICC. 2002. *The Statute of the International Criminal Court*. The Hague: International Criminal Court. Available online at http://www.icc-cpi.int/library/about/officialjournal/Rome_Statute_English.pdf

ICG. 2010a. 'The Sri Lankan Tamil Diaspora after the LTTE', *Asia Report No. 186*, 23 February. Brussels: International Crisis Group. Available online at http://www.crisisgroup.org/en/regions/asia/south-asia/sri-lanka/186-the-sri-lankan-tamil-diaspora-after-the-ltte.aspx (retrieved on 24 April 2010).

———. 2010b. 'War Crimes in Sri Lanka', *Asia Report No. 191*, 17 May. Brussels: International Crisis Group. Available online at http://www.crisisgroup.org/~/media/Files/asia/south-asia/sri-lanka/191%20War%20Crimes%20in%20Sri%20Lanka.ashx (retrieved on 21 May 2010).

———. 2011. 'Sri Lanka: Women's Insecurity in the North and East', *Asia Report No. 217*, 20 December. Brussels: International Crisis Group.

———. 2012a. 'Sri Lanka's North I: The Denial of Minority Rights', *Asia Report No. 219*, 16 March. Brussels: International Crisis Group.

———. 2012b. 'Sri Lanka's North II: Rebuilding under the Military', *Asia Report No. 220*, 16 March. Brussels: International Crisis Group.

ICRC. 2003a. *The Missing: The Right to Know*, ICRC video, 4:45. Geneva: International Committee of the Red Cross. Available online at http://www.icrc.org/eng/resources/documents/audiovisuals/video/00758a-missing-right-to-know-video-2003.htm

———. 2003b. *The Missing: End the Silence*. ICRC film, 14.00, Ref. V-F-CR-F-00758-B, released on 31 December, DVD. Geneva: International Committee of the Red Cross.

———. 2009. *Families of Missing Persons in Nepal: A Study of Their Needs*. Kathmandu: International Committee of the Red Cross.

Ilfeld, F. W. and R. J. Metzner. 1970. 'Alternatives to Violence', in D. N. Daniels, F. G. Marshall and F. M. Ochberg (eds), *Violence and Struggle for Existence*, pp. 129–63. Boston, MA: Little Brown & Co.

Imtiyaz, A. R. M. and B. Stavis. 2008. 'Ethno-Political Conflict in Sri Lanka', *Journal of Third World Studies*, 25 (2): 135–52.

Indrapala, K. 2007. *The Evolution of an Ethnic Identity: The Tamils in Sri Lanka C. 300 BCE to C. 1200 CE*, 2nd rev. ed. Colombo: Vijitha Yapa Publications.

Institute of Medicine. 2008. *Treatment of Posttraumatic Stress Disorder: An Assessment of the Evidence*. Washington, D.C.: National Academies of Sciences.

Internal Displacement Monitoring Centre. 2007. 'Civilians in the Way of Conflict: Displaced People in Sri Lanka'. Available online at http://www.internal-displacement.org/8025708F004BE3B1/(httpInfoFiles)/53A197CF6F0A92E3 C1257362002C1F9A/$file/Sri+Lanka+-September+2007.pdf

Iqbal, M. C. M. 2011. 'Still Waiting for Justice in Sri Lanka', in K. Lauritsch and F. Kernjak (eds), *We Need the Truth: Enforced Disappearances in Asia*, pp. 28–32. Guatemala: Equipo de Estudios Comunitarios y Accion Piscosocial - ECAP.

Irwin, C. 2010. *'War and Peace' and the APRC Proposals*. Liverpool: University of Liverpool. Available online at http://www.peacepolls.org/peacepolls/documents/001173.pdf

Isaacs, H. R. 1989. *Idols of the Tribe: Group Identity and Political Change*. Cambridge: Harvard University Press.

Ismail, Q. 1995. 'Unmooring Identity: The Antinomies of Elite Muslim Self-representation in Modern Sri Lanka', in P. Jeganathan and Q. Ismail (eds), *Unmaking the Nation: The Politics of Identity and History in Modern Sri Lanka*, pp. 55–105. Colombo: Social Scientists' Association.

———. 2000. 'Constituting Nation, Contesting Nationalism: The Southern Tamil (Woman) and Separatist Tamil Nationalism in Sri Lanka', in P. Chatterjee and P. Jeganathan (eds), *Community, Gender and Violence*, pp. 212–82. New Delhi: Permanent Black.

Ivan, V. 2003. *An Unfinished Struggle: An Investigative Exposure of Sri Lanka's Judiciary and the Chief Justice*. Colombo: Ravaya.

———. 2008. 'The Harvest of 60 years of Independence', *Montage*, 2 (2): 14–15.

Jacobson, E. 1938. *Progressive Relaxation*. Chicago, IL: The University of Chicago Press.

Janoff-Bulman, R. 1992. *Shattered Assumptions: Towards a New Psychology of Trauma*. New York: The Free Press.

Jayathilaka, M. 2008. *Alimankada Parajayayen Pasu Sri Lankava Saha Indiyava*. Jayathilaka.

Jayatunge, R. M. 2004. *PTSD Sri Lankan Experience*. Colombo: ANL Publishers.

———. 2005. *Combat Stress*. Colombo: Godage Publishers.

———. 2011. 'Post Combat Reactions among the Sri Lankan Soldiers'. Available online at http://www.lankaweb.com/news/items/2011/08/07/post-combat-reactions-among-the-sri-lankan-soldiers/ (retrieved on 20 January 2012).

Jayawardena, K. P. and J. C. Weliamuna. 2007. 'Corruption in Sri Lanka's Judiciary', *Global Corruption Report 2007: Country Reports on Judicial Corruption*, pp. 275–78. Available online at http://issuu.com/transparencyinternational/docs/global_corruption_report_2007_english?e=2496456/2664845 (retrieved on 29 July 2013).

Jayawardena, K. 1986. *Ethnic and Class Conflicts in Sri Lanka: Some Aspects of Sinhala Buddhist Consciousness over the Past 100 Years*. Dehiwala: Centre for Social Analysis.

Jazeel, T. 2009. 'Reading the Geography of Sri Lankan Island-ness: Colonial Repetitions, Postcolonial Possibilities', *Contemporary South Asia*, 17 (4): 399–414. doi: 10.1080/09584930903324138

Jeganathan, P. 1995. 'Authorizing History, Ordering Land: The Conquest of Anuradhapura', in P. Jeganathan and Q. Ismail (eds), *Unmaking the Nation: The Politics of Identity and History in Modern Sri Lanka*, pp. 106–36. Colombo: Social Scientists' Association.

———. 2000. 'A Space for Violence: Anthropology, Politics and the Location of a Sinhala Practice of Masculinity', in P. Chatterjee and P. Jeganathan (eds), *Community, Gender and Violence: Subaltern Studies XI*, pp. 37–65. New Delhi: Permanent Black.

Jeganathan, P. and Q. Ismail (eds). 1995. *Unmaking the Nation: The Politics of Identity & History in Modern Sri Lanka*. Colombo: Social Scientists' Association.

Jensen, S. B. 1996. 'Trauma and Healing in Families of the Disappeared and Killed: A Mental Health and Human Rights Issue', in WHO (ed.), *Mental Health and Human Rights under War Conditions*. Geneva: WHO/PAR/EURO.

Jesse, N. G. and K. P. Williams. 2011. *Ethnic Conflict: A Systematic Approach to Cases of Conflict*. Washington, D.C.: CQ Press.

Jeyanthy, K., N. Loshani and G. Sivarajini. 1993. 'A Study of Psychological Consequences of Displacement on Family Members'. III MBBS research thesis submitted to the University of Jaffna, Jaffna.

Jeyaraj, D. B. S. 2008. 'Army Breaks through Tiger Defences in Three Key Areas', *transCurrents*, 30 August. Available online at http://transcurrents.com/tc/2008/08/army_breaks_through_tiger_defe.html (retrieved on 4 April 2010).

———. 2010. 'Will There Be a Violent Resurgence of the LTTE Soon?', 5 November. Available online at http://dbsjeyaraj.com/dbsj/archives/1792 (retrieved on 29 July 2013).

Jeyasankar, S. 2011. *Koothu Transformation: A New Dimension of Eela Koothu*. Chennai: Meaning=community.

Jones, R. 2008. *International Day of the 'Disappeared': A Focus on Sri Lanka*. Toronto: The Association for Women's Rights in Development.

Joseph, S. and P. A. Linley. 2005. 'Positive Adjustment to Threatening Events: An Organismic Valuing Theory of Growth through Adversity', *Review of General Psychology*, 9 (3): 262–80.

———. 2006. *Positive Therapy: A Meta-theory for Positive Psychological Practice*. Hove: Routledge.

Jung, C. G. 1931. Commentary. In Lu-tsu (~800) *T'ai I Chin Hua Tsung Chih* [Secret of the Golden Flower], Translated by Wilhelm, R. (1929), San Diego, CA: Hartcourt Brace, pp. 112–13.

———. 1947. *Essays on Contemporary Events*. London: Kegan Paul.

———. 1969. *The Archetypes and the Collective Unconscious*. Princeton, NJ: Princeton University Press.

———. 1996. *The Psychology of Kundalini Yoga: Notes of the Seminar Given in 1932 by C. G. Jung*. Edited by S. Shamdasani. Princeton: Princeton University Press.

Jurcević, S. and I. Urlić. 2002. 'Linking Objects in the Process of Mourning for Sons Disappeared in War: Crotia 2001', *Crotian Medical Journal*, 43 (2): 234–39.

Kadirgamar, A. 2011. 'Two Years On: No War but No Peace for Women Still Facing the Consequences of the War – CMTPC', *Kafila*, 16 July. Available online at http://kafila.org/2011/07/16/two-years-on-no-war-but-no-peace-for-women-still-facing-the-consequences-of-the-war-cmtpc/ (retrieved on 13 February 2013).

Kakuma, R., H. Minas, N. van Ginneken, M. R. Dal Poz, K. Desiraju, J. E. Morris, S. Saxena and R. M. Scheffler. 2011. 'Human Resources for Mental Health Care: Current Situation and Strategies for Action', *The Lancet*, 378 (9803): 1654–63.

Kanapathipillai, V. 1990. 'July 1983: The Survivor's Experience', in V. Das (ed.), *Mirrors of Violence: Communities, Riots and Survivors in South Asia*, pp. 321–44. New Delhi: Oxford University Press.

Kapferer, B. 1988. *Legends of People Myths of State: Violence, Intolerance, and Political Culture in Sri Lanka and Australia*. Washington, D.C.: Smithsonian Institution Press.

———. 1997. *The Feast of the Sorcerer: Practices of Consciousness and Power*. Chicago, IL: The University of Chicago Press.

Karmi, O. 2007. 'Feeding the Tiger: How Sri Lankan Insurgents Fund Their War', *Jane's Intelligence Review*, 1 September. Available online at http://www.janes.com/products/janes/defence-security-report.aspx?id=1065926725

Kaufman, S. J. 2001. *Modern Hatreds: The Symbolic Politics of Ethnic War*. Ithaca, NY: Cornell University Press.

Kawachi, I. and S. V. Subramanian. 2006. 'Measuring and Modeling the Social and Geographic Context of Trauma: A Multilevel Modeling Approach', *Journal of Traumatic Stress*, 19 (2): 195–203.

Keefe, A. 2008. 'The Refugee Council Therapeutic Casework Model: Addressing Asylum Seekers External and Internal Issues within a Helping Relationship', *Context*, August (98): 20–22.

Keefe, A. and E. Hage. 2009. *Vulnerable Women's Project Good Practice Guide: Assisting Refugee and Asylum Seeking Women affected by Rape or Sexual Violence*. London: Refugee Council.

Keenan, A. 2007. 'The Trouble with Evenhandedness: On the Politics of Human Rights and Peace Advocacy in Sri Lanka', in M. Feher (ed.), *Nongovernmental Politics*, pp. 88–117. Cambridge: Zone Books.

Keethaponcalan, S. I. 2011. 'The Indian Factor in the Peace Process and Conflict Resolution in Sri Lanka', in J. Goodhand, B. Korf and J. Spencer (eds), *Conflict and Peacebuilding in Sri Lanka: Caught in the Peace Trap?*, pp. 39–53. London: Routledge.

Keiner, E. M. 2002. 'Families and Death', in *The Missing: Action to Resolve the Problem of People Unaccounted for as a Result of Armed Conflict or Internal Violence and to Assist Their Families: Support for Families of People Unaccounted For: Final Outcome and Report of the Workshop held in Geneva, 10–11 June*, pp. 54–56. Geneva: International Committee of the Red Cross. Available online at http://www.icrc.org/eng/assets/files/other/icrc_themissing_082002_en_4.pdf

Kemper, S. 1990. 'J.R. Jayewardene: Righteousness and Realpolitik', in J. Spencer (ed.), *Sri Lanka: History and the Roots of Conflict*, pp. 187–204. London: Routledge.

Kernjak, F. and K. Lauritsch. 2009. *Introduction to The First Asian Conference on Psychosocial Support in the Search for Enforced Disappeared, in the Struggle for Truth and Justice and in Exhumation Processes*, 9–11 November, Manila.

Kincheloe, J. and P. McLaren. 2005. 'Rethinking Critical Theory and Qualitative Research' in N. K. Denzin and Y. S. Lincoln (eds), *The SAGE Handbook of Qualitative Research*, 3rd ed., pp. 303–42. Thousand Oaks, CA: SAGE Publications.

Kinston, W. and R. Rosser. 1974. 'Disaster: Effects on Mental and Physical State', *Journal of Psychosomatic Research*, 18 (6): 437–56.

Kirmayer, L. J. 1996. 'Confusion of the Senses: Implications of Ethnocultural Variations in Somatoform and Dissociative Disorders for PTSD', in A. J. Marsella, M. J. Friedman, E. T. Gerrity and R. M. Scurfield (eds), *Ethnocultural Aspects of Posttraumatic Stress Disorder: Issues, Research, and Clinical Applications*, pp. 131–63. Washington, D.C.: American Psychological Association.

Kitson, F. 1971. *Low Intensity Operations: Subversion, Insurgency and Peacekeeping*. London: Faber and Faber.

———. 1977. *Bunch of Five*. London: Faber and Faber.

Kleinman, A. 1977. *The Illness Narratives: Suffering, Healing and the Human Condition*. New York: Basic Books.

Kleinman, A. M. 1980. *Patients and Healers in the Context of Culture*. Berkeley, CA: University of California Press.

Kofoed, L., M. J. Friedman and R. Peck. 1993. 'Alcoholism and Drug Abuse in Patients with PTSD', *Psychiatric Quarterly*, 64 (2), 151–71. doi: 10.1007/BF01065867

Kostelny, K. 2006. 'A Culture-Based, Integrative Approach: Helping War-Affected Children', in N. Boothby, A. Strang and M. G. Wessells (eds), *A World Turned Upside Down: Social Ecological Approaches to Children in War Zones*, pp. 19–38. Bloomfield: Kumarian Press.

Krieg, A. 2009. 'The Experience of Collective Trauma in Australian Indigenous Communities', *Australasian Psychiatry*, 17 (Suppl 1): S28–32. doi: 10.1080/10398560902948621

Krishnakumar, G., S. Sivayokan and D. J. Somasundaram. 2008. 'Coordination of Psychosocial Activities at the Jaffna District Level in Sri Lanka', *Intervention*, 6 (3–4): 270–74.

Landau, L. and J. Saul. 2004. 'Facilitating Family and Community Resilience in Response to Major Disaster', in F. Walsh and M. McGoldrick (eds), *Living Beyond Loss: Death in the Family*, pp. 285–309. New York: W. W. Norton & Company.

LankaNewspapers.com. 2011. 'Sri Lanka's Evicted Muslims Return to Their Original Places in Jaffna', *LankaNewspapers.com*, 18 January. Available online at http://www.lankanewspapers.com/news/2011/1/63843_space.html

Large, J. 1997. 'Considering Conflict', Concept Paper for the First Consultative Meeting on Health as a Bridge for Peace, 30–31 October, Les Pensières, Annecy.

Lawrence, P. 1999. 'The Changing Amman: Notes on the Injury of War in Eastern Sri Lanka', in S. Gamage and I. B. Watson (eds), *Conflict and Community in Contemporary Sri Lanka: 'Pearl of the East' or the 'Island of Tears'?*, pp. 197–215. New Delhi: SAGE Publications.

Lawrence, P. 2000. 'Violence, Suffering, Amman: The Work of Oracles in Sri Lanka's Eastern War Zone', in V. Das, A. Kleinman, M. Ramphele and P. Reynolds (eds), *Violence and Subjectivity*, pp. 171–204. Berkely, CA: University of California Press.

Lee, M. R. 2009. 'Sri Lanka's ""Bloodbath on the Beach" Made the UN's Ban Ki-mute Moot: Now What?', *School of Advanced International Studies (SAIS) Review*, 29 (2): 39–49.

Lennon, J. 2005. *Imagine*, in D. L. Wopler and A. Solt (eds), *John Lennon. A Film*. London: Warner Bros.

Lewer, N. and M. Ismail. 2011. 'The Genealogy of Muslim Political Voices in Sri Lanka', in J. Goodhand, B. Korf and J. Spencer (eds), *Conflict and Peacebuilding in Sri Lanka: Caught in the Peace Trap?*, pp. 119–31. London: Routledge.

Lewis, J. P. 1895. *Manual of the Vanni Districts*. Colombo: H. C. Cottle, Acting Government Printer.

Liamputtong, P. 2009. *Qualitative Research Methods*. Melbourne: Oxford University Press.

Library of Congress. 2013. 'Library of Congress: Country Studies: Sri Lanka'. Available online at http://lcweb2.loc.gov/frd/cs/lktoc.html

Linley, P. A. and S. Joseph. 2004. 'Positive Change Following Trauma and Adversity: A Review', *Journal of Traumatic Stress*, 17 (1): 11–21.

———. 2005. The Human Capacity for Growth through Adversity. *American Psychologist*, 60: 262–264.

Lipkin, J., A. S. Blank, E. R. Parson and J. Smith. 1982. 'Vietnam Veterans and Posttraumatic Stress Disorder', *Hospital and Community Psychiatry*, 33 (11): 908–12.

Lochner, K. 2000. 'Operationalization and Measurement of Social Capital', *Social Capital and Mental Health Workshop*. Washington, D.C.: World Bank.

Lock, C. 2006. *Nothing in the World: In Tsunami-affected Southern Sri Lanka: A Journey of the Spirit*. Colombo: Vijitha Yapa Publications.

Loganathan, K. 1996. *Sri Lanka: Lost Opportunities*. Colombo: CEPRA, University of Colombo.

Logeswaran, K. C. (ed.). 1982. *Pandaravanniyan Memorial Flower*. Vavuniya: Vavuniya District Development Assembly.

Lorenz, K. Z. 1963. *On Aggression*. New York: Harcourt, Brace and World, Inc.

Losi, N. 2000. 'Understanding the Needs of the Displaced: Some Elements on the Kosovo Case', in C. Becker (ed.), *Psychosocial and Trauma Response in War-Torn Societies: The Case of Kosovo*, pp. 11–20. Geneva: International Organization for Migration.

Ludden, D. (ed.). 1996. *Contesting the Nation: Religion, Community and the Politics of Democracy in India*. Philadelphia, PA: University of Pennsylvania Press.

Lyons, H. A. 1979. 'Civil Violence — the Psychological Aspects'. *Journal of Psychosomatic Research*, 23: 373–79.

Machel, G. 1996. *Impact of Armed Conflict on Children*. New York: United Nations and UNICEF.

Macrae, C. 2011. 'Sri Lanka's Killing Fields', first part of the series *Sri Lanka's Killing Fields*, presented by J. Snow, first broadcast on Channel 4 on 14 June 2011. London: Channel 4.

Macrae, C. 2012. 'Sri Lanka's Killing Fields: War Crimes Unpunished', second part of the series *Sri Lanka's Killing Fields*, presented by J. Snow, first broadcast on Channel 4 on 14 March 2012. London: Channel 4.

Macy, R. D., L. Behar, R. Paulson, J. Delman, L. Schmid and S. F. Smith. 2004a. 'Community-based, Acute Posttraumatic Stress Management: A Description and Evaluation of a Psychosocial-Intervention Continuum', *Harvard Review of Psychiatry*, 12 (4): 217–28.

Macy, R. D., D. J. Macy, S. Gross and P. Brighton. 2004b. *Child Thematic Project*. Boston, MA: Centre for Trauma Psychology.

Maercker, A., C. R. Brewin, R. A. Bryant, M. Cloitre, G. M. Reed, M. Van Ommeren, A. Humayan, L. M. Jones, A. Kagee, A. E. Llosa, C. Rousseau, D. J. Somasundaram, R. Souza, Y. Suzuki, I. Weissbecker, S. C. Wessely, M. B. First and S. Saxena. 2013. 'Proposals for Mental Disorders Specifically Associated with Stress in the International Classification of Diseases-11', *The Lancet*, 381 (9878): 1683–85.

Mahendran, K. and D. J. Somasundaram (eds). 2003. *Joyful Living*. In Tamil, English and Sinhalese. Trincomalee: GTZ/BECAre-Shanthiham.

Mahoney, J., V. Chandra, H. Gambheera, T. de Silva and T. Suveendran. 2006. 'Responding to the Mental Health and Psychosocial Needs of the People of Sri Lanka in Disasters', *International Review of Psychiatry*, 18 (5): 593–97.

Majumdar, D. 2007. 'Tamil Groups Tackled from Within', *BBC News*, 26 February. Available online at http://news.bbc.co.uk/2/hi/uk_news/england/london/6380817.stm (retrieved on 29 July 2013).

Malathy, N. 2012. *A Fleeting Moment in My Country: The Last Years of the LTTE De-Facto State*. Atlanta: Clear Day Books.

Manchanda, R. 2001. 'Where are the Women in South Asian Conflicts?' in R. Manchandra (ed.), *Women, War and Peace in South Asia: Beyond Victimhood to Agency*, pp. 9–41. New Delhi: SAGE Publications.

Mangrove. 2006 'The Mangrove: Psychosocial Support and Coordination Network, Batticaloa'. Available online at http://www.themangrove.blogspot.com/ (retrieved on 29 July 2013).

Manogaran, C. 1994. 'Colonization as Politics: Political Use of Space in Sri Lanka's Ethnic Conflict', in C. Manogaran and B. Pfaffenberger (eds), *The Sri Lankan Tamils: Ethnicity and Identity*, pp. 84–125. Boulder, CO: Westview Press.

Markus, H. and S. Kitayama. 1991. 'Culture and the Self: Implications for Cognition, Emotion, and Motivation', *Psychological Review*, 98 (2), 224–53.

Marshall, M. G. and B. R. Cole. 2008. 'Global Report on Conflict, Governance and State Fragility 2008', *Foreign Policy Bulletin*, 18 (1): 3–21.

McCann, I. L. and L. A. Pearlman. 1990. 'Vicarious Traumatization: A Framework for Understanding the Psychological Effects of Working with Victims', *Journal of Traumatic Stress*, 3 (1): 131–49.

McClean, D. (ed.). 2010. *World Disasters Report 2010: Focus on Urban Risk*. Geneva: International Federation of Red Cross and Red Crescent Societies. Available online at http://www.ifrc.org/Global/Publications/disasters/WDR/WDR2010-full.pdf

McGilvray, D. B. 2008. *Crucible of Conflict: Tamil and Muslim Society on the East Coast of Sri Lanka*. Durham: Duke University Press.

Mckenzie, K. and T. Harpham (eds). 2006. *Social Capital and Mental Health*. London: Jessica Kingsley Publishers.

Melville, M. and M. B. Lykes. 1992. 'Guatemalan Indian Children and the Sociocultural Effects of Government-Sponsored terrorism', *Social Science and Medicine*, 34 (5): 533–48.

Mendis, G. C. 1963. *Ceylon Today and Yesterday: Main Currents of Ceylon History*. Colombo: The Associated Newspapers of Ceylon Ltd.

Military debacle at Elephant Pass. Available online at http://www.lankalibrary. com/phpBB/viewtopic.php?t=676

Miller, K. E. and L. M. Rasco. 2004. 'An Ecological Framework for Addressing the Mental Health Needs of Refugee Communities', in K. E. Miller and L. M. Rasco (eds), *The Mental Health of Refugees: Ecological Approaches to Healing and Adaptation*, pp. 1–67. New York: Lawrence Erlbaum Associates, Inc.

Milroy, H. 2005. *Australian Indigenous Doctors' Association (AIDA) Submissions on the Consultative Document: Preventive Healthcare and Strengthening Australia's Social and Economic Fabric*. Canberra: National Health and Medical Research Council.

Ministry of Defence. 2012. 'Lies Agreed Upon'. Colombo: Ministry of Defence, Government of Sri Lanka. Available online at http://www.defence.lk/new. asp?fname=20110801_LAUvdo (retrieved on 29 July 2013).

Ministry of Finance and Planning. 2012. 'Appropriation: A Bill', *Part II of Supplement, Gazette of the Democratic Socialist Republic of Sri Lanka*. Colombo: Author.

Minority Rights Group International. 2011. *No War, No Peace: The Denial of Minority Rights and Justice in Sri Lanka*. London: Minority Rights Group International.

IRIN. 2010. 'Sri Lanka: Conflict Over, But Not for Widows', *IRIN*, 26 October. Available online at http://www.trust.org/item/20101026092200-oxg8k/? source=search (retrieved on 29 July 2013).

Monin, R. Z. 2007. 'The Missing: Preventing Disappearances and Finding Answers', *ICRC Resource Centre*, 27 August. Geneva: International Committee of the Red Cross. Available online at http://www.icrc.org/eng/resources/documents/interview/missing-interview-270807.htm

Moore, M. 1990. 'Economic Liberalization versus Political Pluralism in Sri Lanka?', *Modern Asian Studies*, 24 (2): 341–83.

Mulligan, M. and Y. Nadarajah. 2010. *Rebuilding Community in the Wake of the 2004 Tsunami: Lessons from Sri Lanka and India*. Melbourne: Globalism Research Centre, RMIT University.

Nandy, A. 2009. 'Narcissism and Despair', *The Little Magazine*, 7 (3 and 4). Available online at http://www.littlemag.com/security/ashisnandy.html (retrieved on 7 July 2010).

Narendran, R. 2010. 'Sri Lanka: Indomitable Life Sprouts in the North', *transCurrents*, 16 July. Available online at http://transcurrents.com/tc/2010/07/ sri_lanka_indomitable_life_spr.html (retrieved on 22 July 2010).

Natali, C. 2008. 'Building Cemeteries, Constructing Identities: Funerary Practices and Nationalist Discourse among the Tamil Tigers of Sri Lanka', *Contemporary South Asia* 16: 287–301.

National Aboriginal and Torres Strait Islander Health Council. 2003. *National Strategic Framework for Aboriginal and Torres Strait Islander Health Context*. Canberra: National Aboriginal and Torres Strait Islander Health Council.

National Commission on the Disappearance of Persons. 1984. *'Nunca más'* [Never again]. Buenos Aires: National Commission on the Disappearance of Persons (CONADEP). Available online at http://web.archive.org/web/20031004074316/nuncamas.org/english/library/nevagain/nevagain_001.htm

National Education Research and Evaluation Centre. 2004. *National Assessment of Achievement of Grade four Pupils in Sri Lanka – 2003.* Colombo: Faculty of Education, University of Colombo.

National Institute for Clinical Excellence. 2005. *Post-traumatic Stress Disorder (PTSD): The Management of PTSD in Adults and Children in Primary and Secondary Care.* London: National Institute for Clinical Excellence.

National Peace Council and Marga Institute. 2001. *The Cost of War: Economic, Social, Human Costs of the War in Sri Lanka.* Colombo: National Peace Council of Sri Lanka.

Neeleman, J. 2002. 'Beyond Risk Theory: Suicidal Behavior in its Social and Epidemiological Context'. *Crisis*, 23: 114–20.

Nehru, J. 1985. *The Discovery of India.* New Delhi: Oxford University Press.

Nesiah, D. 1997. *Discrimination with Reason? The Policy of Reservations in the United States, India and Malaysia.* New Delhi: Oxford University Press.

———. 2012. *Tamil Language Rights in Sri Lanka.* Colombo: Centre for Policy Alternatives.

Nesiah, V. 2002. 'Overcoming Tensions between Family and Judicial Procedures', *International Review of the Red Cross*, 84 (848): 823–44.

Neuner, F., E. Schauer, C. Catani, M. Ruf and T. Elbert. 2006. 'Post-tsunami Stress: A Study of Posttraumatic Stress Disorder in Children Living in Three Severely Affected Regions in Sri Lanka', *Journal of Traumatic Stress*, 19 (3): 339–47.

Nikapota, A. and Samarasinghe, D. 1995. *Helping Children in Situations of Armed Conflict.* Colombo: Ministry of Health and UNICEF.

Nisbett, R. E. 2003. *The Geography of Thought: How Asians and Westerners Think Differently...and Why.* New York: The Free Press.

Nissan, E. 1989. 'History in the Making: Anuradhapura and the Sinhala Buddhist Nation', *Social Analysis*, 25: 64–77.

———. 1990. *Sri Lanka: A Bitter Harvest.* London: Minority Rights Group.

Nissan, E. and R. L. Stirrat. 1990. 'The Generation of Communal Identities', in J. Spencer (ed.), *Sri Lanka: History and the Roots of Conflict*, pp. 19–44. London: Routledge.

Nordstrom, C. 1994. 'Warzones: Cultures of Violence, Militarisation and Peace', Working Paper No. 145, Peace Research Centre, Australian National University, Canberra.

———. 2004. *Shadows of War: Violence, Power, and International Profiteering in the Twenty-First Century.* Berkeley, CA: University of California Press.

Norris, F., H. S. P. Stevens, B. Pfefferbaum, K. F. Wyche and R. Pfefferbaum. 2008. 'Community Resilience as a Metaphor, Theory, Set of Capacities, and Strategy for Disaster Readiness', *American Journal of Community Psychology*, 41 (1–2): 127–50.

Nutt, D., J. R. T. Davidson and J. Zohar (eds). 2000. *Post-traumatic Stress Disorder: Diagnosis, Management and Treatment.* London: Martin Dunitz.

Obermeyer, Z., C. J. L. Murray and E. Gakidou. 2008. 'Fifty Years of Violent War Deaths from Vietnam to Bosnia: Analysis of Data from the World Health Survey Programme', *British Medical Journal*, 336 (7659): 1482–86. doi: 10.1136/bmj.a137

Obeyesekere, G. 1984. *The Cult of the Goddess Pattini.* Chicago, IL: The University of Chicago Press.

———. 1988. *A Meditation on Conscience.* Colombo: Social Scientists' Association of Sri Lanka.

Orme-Johnson, D. W., C. N. Alexander, J. L. Davies, H. M. Chandler and W. E. Larimore. 1988. 'International Peace Project in the Middle East: The Effects of the Maharishi Technology of the Unified Field', *Journal of Conflict Resolution*, 32 (4): 776–812.

Osofsky, J. D. 1995. 'The Effects of Exposure to Violence in Young Children', *American Psychologist*, 50 (9): 782–88.

Ostrovsky, V. and C. Hoy. 1990. *By Way of Deception: The Making and Unmaking of a Mossad Officer.* New York: St. Martin's Press.

Oxfam. 2005. *The Tsunami's Impact on Women: Oxfam Briefing Note.* Oxford: Oxfam International. Available online at http://www.oxfam.org/en/policy/bn05 0326-tsunami-women

PADHI. 2009. *A Tool, a Guide, and a Framework: Introduction to a Psychosocial Approach to Development.* Colombo: Psychosocial Assessment of Development and Humanitarian Interventions.

Pandey, G. 1990. *The Construction of Communalism in Colonial North India.* New Delhi: Oxford University Press.

Papadopoulos, R. K. 2002. 'Refugees, Home and Trauma', in R. K. Papadopoulos (ed.), *Therapeutic Care for Refugees: No Place like Home*, pp. 9–39. London: Karnac. www.tandfonline.com

———. 2007. 'Refugees, Trauma and Adversity-Activated Development', *European Journal of Psychotherapy & Counselling*, 9 (3): 301–12.

Paranavitana, S. and C. W. Nicholas. 1961. *A Concise History of Ceylon.* Colombo: Ceylon University Press.

Partners. 1999. 'Sri Lanka: The Forgotten War', *World Mission Partners*, 11 (1): 14.

Patel, V. and G. Stein. 2007. 'Cultural and International Psychiatry', in G. Stein and G. Wilkinson (eds), *Seminars in General Adult Psychiatry*, pp. 782–810. London: Royal College of Psychiatrists.

Pearlman, L. A. and K. W. Saakvitne. 1995. 'Treating Therapists with Vicarious Traumatization and Secondary Traumatic Stress Disorders', in C. R. Figley (ed.), *Compassion Fatigue: Coping with Secondary Traumatic Stress Disorder in Those Who Treat the Traumatized*, pp. 150–77. New York: Brunner-Routledge.

Peel, M., A. Mahtani, G. Hinshelwood and D. Forrest. 2000. 'The Sexual Abuse of Men in Detention in Sri Lanka', *The Lancet*, 355 (9220): 2069–70.

Peiris, P. and K. Stokke. 2011. 'Liberal Peace and Public Opinion', in K. Stokke and J. Uyangoda (eds), *Liberal Peace in Question: Politics of State and Market Reform in Sri Lanka*, pp. 157–82. London: Anthem Press.

Perera, A. 2010a. 'How China and India Displaced the West in Sri Lanka', *Time*, 3 October. New York: Time, Inc. Available online at http://www.time.com/time/world/article/0,8599,2023178,00.html (retrieved on 29 July 2013).

———. 2010b. 'Sri Lanka and the U.N. in a Confrontation', *Time*, 9 July. New York: Time, Inc. Available online at http://www.time.com/time/world/article/0,8599,2002739,00.html (retrieved on 29 July 2013).

Perera, S. 1999. *Stories of Survivors: Socio-Political Contexts of Female Headed Households in Post-Terror Southern Sri Lanka*. New Delhi: Vikas Publishing House Pvt. Ltd.

Phadnis, U. 1979. 'Ethnicity and Nation-Building in South Asia: A Case Study of Sri Lanka', *Indian Quarterly*, 35 (3): 329–50.

Philp, C. 2009. 'The Hidden Massacre: Sri Lanka's Final Offensive against Tamil Tigers', *The Times*, 29 May. Available online at http://www.timesonline.co.uk/tol/news/world/asia/article6383449.ece (retrieved on 29 May 2009).

Philp, C. and M. Evans. 2009. 'Times Photographs Expose Sri Lanka's Lie on Civilian Deaths at Beach', *The Times*, 29 May. Available online at http://www.timesonline.co.uk/tol/news/world/asia/article6383477.ece (retrieved on 30 July 2013).

Pieris, A. 2010. 'Avian Geographies: An Inquiry into Nationalist Consciousness in Medieval Lanka', *South Asia: Journal of South Asian Studies*, 33 (3): 336–62. doi: 10.1080/00856401.2010.520647

Piyadasa, L. 1984. *Sri Lanka: The Holocaust and After*. London: Marram Books.

Pojskic, M. 2002. 'Families & Death', in *The Missing: Action to Resolve the Problem of People Unaccounted for as a Result of Armed Conflict or Internal Violence and to Assist Their Families: Support for Families of People Unaccounted For: Final Outcome and Report of the Workshop held in Geneva, 10–11 June*, pp. 69–71. Geneva: International Committee of the Red Cross. Available online at http://www.icrc.org/eng/assets/files/other/icrc_themissing_082002_en_4.pdf

Pratap, A. 2002. *Island of Blood: Frontline Reports from Sri Lanka, Afghanistan and Other South Asian Flashpoints*. New Delhi: Penguin Books.

Prigerson, H. G. and S. C. Jacobs. 2002. 'Traumatic Grief as a Distinct Disorder: A Rationale, Consensus Criteria, and a Preliminary Empirical Test', in M. S. Stroebe, R. O. Hansson, W. Stroebe and H. Schut (eds), *Handbook of Bereavement Research: Consequences, Coping and Care*, pp. 613–45. Washington, D.C.: American Psychological Association.

Psychosocial Forum of CHA. 2008. 'A Community-based Model for Mental Health Services', *Reflections*, 5 (2): 1–2.

PTF. 2013. *From Conflict to Stability: Northern Province, Sri Lanka*. Colombo: Presidential Task Force for Resettlement, Development and Security in the Northern Province. Available online at http://www.defence.lk/news/pdf/From_Conflict_to_Stability_20130128_04.pdf

Puvimanasinghe, S. and I. Price. 2010. 'Healing through Giving Testimony: An Empirical Study with Sri Lankan Torture Survivors'. B.A. Honours thesis submitted to the University of New England, Armidale, New South Wales.

Rajanayagam, D. H. 1994. 'Tamils and the Meaning of History', in C. Manogaran and B. Pfaffenberger (eds), *The Sri Lankan Tamils: Ethnicity and Identity*, pp. 54–83. Boulder, CO: Westview Press.

Rajasingham-Senanayake, D. 2001. 'Ambivalent Empowerment: The Tragedy of Tamil Women in Conflict', in R. Manchanda (ed.), *Women, War and Peace in South Asia: Beyond Victimhood to Agency*, pp. 102–30. New Delhi: SAGE Publications.

Rangani, T. 2009. 'Psychosocial Status of the Spouses of Men Subjected to Enforced Disappearance in the District on Hambantota, Sri Lanka'. Thesis submitted to Postgraduate Institute of Medicine, University of Colombo, Colombo.

Raphael, B. 1986. *When Disaster Strikes: How Individuals and Communities Cope With Catastrophe*. New York: Basic Books.

Ratnayake, J. and N. de Mel. 2012. *Sri Lanka Budget 2013: Increasing Assistance and Vulnerability*. Colombo: Verité Research.

Ratnayake, K. 2010. 'Sri Lankan Election Sets Stage for Deep Political Crisis', *World Socialist Web Site*, 26 January. Available online at http://www.wsws.org/articles/2010/jan2010/sril-j26.shtml (retrieved on 30 July 2013).

Read, H. M. Fordham and G. Adler (eds). 1954. *The Collected Works of C.G. Jung*. London: Routledge Kegan Paul.

Reddiar, K. A. 1997. 'Shout and Plea from Trincomalee', *Tamil Times*, 14 (5): 22–23.

Reisner, S. 2002. 'Staging the Unspeakable: A Report on the Collaboration Between Theater Arts Against Political Violence, the Associazione Culturale Altrimenti, and 40 Counsellors in Training in Pristina, Kosovo', in M. Losi, S. Reisner and S. Salvatici (eds), *Psychosocial and Trauma Response in War-Torn Societies: Supporting Traumatized Communities Through Arts and Theatre*, pp. 9–30. Geneva: International Organization for Migration.

Reporters Sans Frontières. 2007. 'Life of Journalist Iqbal Athas in Danger after His Revelations about Purchase of Ukrainian MiGs', *Reporters Sans Frontières*, 29 August. Available online at http://en.rsf.org/sri-lanka-life-of-journalist-iqbal-athas-in-29-08-2007,23466.html (retrieved on 30 July 2013).

Roberts, M. 1982. *Caste Conflict and Elite Formation: The Rise of a Karava Elite in Sri Lanka, 1500-1931*. London: Cambridge University Press.

———. 1994. *Exploring Confrontation: Sri Lanka: Politics, Culture and History*. Chur: Harwood Academic Publishers.

———. (ed.). 1997. *Collective Identities Revisited*. 2 Vols. Colombo: Marga Institute.

———. 2003. 'The Agony and the Ecstasy of a Pogrom: Southern Lanka, July 1983', *Nçthra*, 6 (April–September): 199–213.

———. 2004. *Sinhala Consciousness in the Kandyan Period 1590s to 1815*. Colombo: Vijitha Yapa Publications.

———. 2005. 'Saivite Symbols, Sacrifice, and Tamil Tiger Rites', *Social Analysis*, 49: 67–93.

———. 2007. 'Suicide Missions as Witnessing: Expansions, Contrasts', *Studies in Conflict*, 30: 857–887.

Robins, S. 2009. 'Potential Interventions to Assist Wives of the Missing in Bardiya'. Report to the Transcultural Psychosocial Organisation (TPO-Nepal) and Advocacy Forum, Katmandu Nepal. Available online at http://www.simon-robins.com/NepalMissingReport-Robins.pdf (retrieved on 30 July 2013).

Rogers, J. D. 1990. 'Historical Images in the British Period', in J. Spencer (ed.), *Sri Lanka: History and the Roots of Conflict*, pp. 87–106. London: Routledge.

Rosenbeck, R. 1985. 'The Malignant Post-Vietnam Stress Syndrome', *American Journal of Orthopsychiatry*, 55 (2): 166–76.

Ross, M. H. 2007. *Cultural Contestation in Ethnic Conflict*. Cambridge: Cambridge University Press.

Ruki. 2010a. 'Celebrating War Victory and Banning Commemoration of Dead Civilians: This is 'Home Grown & Indigenous' Reconciliation and Freedom in Sri Lanka?' *Groundviews*, 18 June. Available online at http://www.groundviews. org/2010/06/18/celebrating-war-victory-and-banning-commemoration-of-dead-civilians-this-is-%E2%80%9Chome-grown-indigenous%E2%80%9D-reconciliation-and-freedom-in-sri-lanka/ (retrieved on 22 July 2010).

———. 2010b. 'Vanni in the Year after War: Tears of Despair and Fear', *Groundviews*, 26 May. Available online at http://www.groundviews.org/2010/05/26/vanni-in-the-year-after-war-tears-of-despair-and-fear/ (retrieved on 2 June 2010).

Rutnam, J. T. 1981. *The Tomb of Elara at Anuradhapura*. Jaffna: Jaffna Archaeological Society.

Ruzich, M. J., J. C. Looi and M. D. Robertson. 2005. 'Delayed Onset of Posttraumatic Stress Disorder among Male Combat Veterans', *American Journal of Geriatric Psychiatry*, 13 (5): 424–27.

Ryecroft, C. 1995. *A Critical Dictionary of Psychoanalysis*. London: Penguin Books.

Saakvitne, K. W. and L. A. Pearlman. 1996. *Transforming the Pain: A Workbook on Vicarious Traumatization for Helping Professionals Who Work with Traumatized Clients*. New York: W.W. Norton & Company.

Sabaratnam, T. 2004. 'Manal Aru Becomes Weli Oya', *Pirapaharan*, chap. 23, Vol. 2. Available online at http://www.sangam.org/articles/view2/?uid=633 (retrieved on 29 July 2013).

Sabin-Farrell, R. and G. Turpin. 2003. 'Vicarious Traumatization: Implications for the Mental Health of Health Workers?', *Clinical Psychology Review*, 23 (3): 449–80.

Sackur, S. 2010. 'Sri Lankan Defence Secretary, Gotabaya Rajapaksa on Hardtalk', *Hardtalk*, Part 4. Available online at http://www.bbc.co.uk/programmes/b00sr2wx (retrieved on 29 July 2013).

Said, E. W. 1995. *Orientalism*. London: Penguin Books.

Samarasinghe, D. 2006. 'Different Disasters, Different Needs', *International Psychiatry*, 3 (3): 8–11.

Samarasinghe, G. 2002. 'Counselling vs. Community-Based Approaches', paper presented at National Conference on Mental Health, Sahanaya, Colombo, 4–7 April.

Samarasinghe, G. and A. Galappatti. 1999. Unpublished MS. 'Report on the PSE Survey and the Exploratory Phase of the War-Trauma & Psychosocial Support Programme of the IWTHI Trust'. Colombo: International War-Trauma & Humanitarian Intervention Trust.

Samaraweera, V. 1997. 'Report on the Abused Child and the Legal Process of Sri Lanka'. Submitted to the National Monitoring Committee on the Children's Charter, Colombo.

Saraceno, B. and H. Minas. 2005. *Mental Health Situation in Aceh*. Geneva: World Health Organization. Available online at www.who.int/entity/mental_health/resources/Summary%20Indonesia%20Strategic%20plan%20revised%2027%20Jan.pdf

Sartre, J. P. 1963. *Saint Genet: Actor and Martry*. Translated by B. Frechtman. New York: Brziller.

Sarvananthan, M. 2006. 'Informal Economy in the Conflict Region of Sri Lanka: An Exploration', Working Paper No. 6, Point Pedro Institute of Development, Point Pedro. Available online at http://pointpedro.org/index.php?option=com_content&task=blogsection&id=6&Itemid=63

————. 2011. 'Sri Lanka: Putting Entrepreneurship at the Heart of Economic Revival in the North, East, and Beyond', *Contemporary South Asia*, 19 (2): 205–13.

Satkunanayagam, K. 2008. 'The Realities of Caring: A Qualitative Exploration of Mental Health Professionals' Experience of Working with Survivors of Trauma in Sri Lanka'. Unpublished doctoral thesis submitted to the University of East London, London.

Satkunanayagam, K., A. Tunariu and R. Tribe. 2010. 'A Qualitative Exploration of Mental Health Professionals' Experience of Working with Survivors of Trauma in Sri Lanka', *International Journal of Culture and Mental Health*, 3 (1): 43–51.

Saukko, P. 2005. 'Methodologies for Cultural Studies: An Integrative Approach', in N. K. Denzin and Y. S. Lincoln (eds), *The SAGE Handbook of Qualitative Research*, 3rd ed., pp. 343–56. Thousand Oaks: SAGE Publications.

Saul, J. and S. Bava. 2008. 'Implementing Collective Approaches to Massive Trauma/Loss in Western Contexts: Implications for Recovery, Peacebuilding and Development', paper presented at the Trauma, Development and Peacebuilding conference, International Conflict Research Institute (INCORE) and International Development Research Centre (IDRC), New Delhi, 9–11 September. Available online at http://www.incore.ulst.ac.uk/pdfs/IDRCsaul.pdf (retrieved on 30 July 2013).

Savundaranayagam, T. 2006. 'Bishop of Jaffna Urges Co-Chairs to Prevail upon GoSL to open A9, Implement CFA', *TamilNet*, 19 November. Available online at http://www.tamilnet.com/art.html?catid=13&artid=20324 (retrieved on 30 July 2013).

Scarry, E. 1985. *The Body in Pain: The Making and Unmaking of the World*. New York: Oxford University Press.

Schalk, P. 2003. 'Beyond Hindu Festivals: The Celebration of Great Heroes' Day by the Liberation Tigers of Tamil Eelam (LTTE) in Europe', in M. Baumann, B. Luchesi and A. Wilke Wurzburg (eds), *Tempel und Tamilien in Zweiter heimat*, p. 396. Keesburgstr: Ergon Verlag.

Schauer, E., M. Ruf, C. Catani, P. L. Onyut, S. Gotthardt, M. Schauer, B. Rockstroh, T. Elbert and F. Neuner. 2005. 'Symptoms of PTSD in Sri Lankan Children Affected by the Tsunami', paper presented at the 9th European Conference for Traumatic Stress Studies, Stockholm, 18–21 June.

Schauer, M., F. Neuner and T. Elbert. 2005. *Narrative Exposure Therapy (NET). A Short-Term Intervention for Traumatic Stress Disorders after War, Terror, or Torture*. Gottingen, Germany: Hogrefe & Huber.

Schwarz, W. 1988. *The Tamils of Sri Lanka: The Minority Rights Group, Report No. 25*. London: Minority Rights Group.

Scott, D. 1996. 'Religion in Colonial Civil Society: Buddhism and Modernity in 19th-century Sri Lanka', *Cultural Dynamics*, 8 (1): 7–23.

————. 2000. 'Toleration and Historical Traditions of Difference', in P. Chatterjee and P. Jeganathan (eds), *Community, Gender and Violence*, pp. 283–304. New Delhi: Permanent Black.

Selladurai, A. 2007. *Adangapattu (Vanni) History Part IV*, Vol. 4. Colombo: Aruna Publications.

Selye, H. 1976. *The Stress of Life*. New York: McGraw Hill.

Senanayake, D. R. 2005. 'Humanitarian Assistance and the International Aid Architecture after the Tsunami: Lessons from Sri Lanka and India', paper presented at the ASEAN Roundtable 2005, The Asian Tsunami: Implications for Regional Development and Security, Institute of South East Asia Studies, Singapore, 17–18 November.

Senewiratne, B. 2006. 'The Bombing of Tamil School Children in Sri Lanka'. Available online at http://sangam.org/taraki/articles/2006/08-21_Bombing_of_Children.php?uid=1897 (retrieved on 29 July 2013).

Shanthiham. 2008. *Waiting*. Jaffna: Association for Health and Counselling.

Shaw, J., M. Mulligan, Y. Nadarajah, D. Mercer and I. Ahmed. 2010. *Lessons from Tsunami Recovery in Sri Lanka and India: Community, Livelihoods, Tourism and Housing*. Melbourne: Monash University and RMIT University.

Short, D. (2010). 'Australia: A Continuing Genocide?', *Journal of Genocide Research*, 12 (1): 45–68. doi: 10.1080/14623528.2010.508647

Silove, D. 2007. 'Adaptation, Ecosocial Safety Signals, and the Trajectory of PTSD', in L. J. Kirmayer, R. Lemelson and M. Barad (eds), *Understanding Trauma: Integrating Biological, Clinical, and Cultural Perspectives*, pp. 242–58. Cambridge: Cambridge University Press.

Silove, D. and Z. Steel. 2006. 'Understanding Community Psychosocial Needs after Disasters: Implications for Mental Health Services', *Journal of Postgraduate Medicine*, 52 (2): 121–25.

Silva, N. (ed.). 2002. *The Hybrid Island: Culture Crossings and the Invention of Identity in Sri Lanka*. London: Zed Books.

Silverman, G. K., S. C. Jacobs, S. V. Kasl, M. K. Shear, P. K. Maciejewski, F. S. Noaghiul and G. H. Prigerson. 2000. 'Quality of Life Impairments Associated with Diagnostic Criteria for Traumatic Grief', *Psychological Medicine*, 30 (4): 857–62.

Sims, A. C. P. 1983. *Neurosis in Society*. London: Macmillan Press Ltd.

Siriwardena, R. 1984. 'National Identity in Sri Lanka: Problems in Communication and Education', in Committee for Rational Development (ed.), *Sri Lanka: The Ethnic Conflict: Myths, Realities and Perspectives*, pp. 215–29. New Delhi: Navrang Press.

Sivarajah, N. 1993. *Nutritional Status of the Children in Jaffna*. Jaffna: Department of Community Medicine, University of Jaffna.

Sivaram, D. 1990. 'Karunanidhi's Novel: Payum Puli Pandara Vanniyan', *Sri Lanka Island*, 18 February. Available online at http://tamilnation.co/forum/sivaram/900218.htm

Sivathamby, K. 2005. *Being Tamil and Sri Lankan*. Colombo: Aivakam.

Sivathas, S. 2006. *Nalamudan* [Wellbeing]. Colombo: Nihari Publishers.

Sivayokan, S. 2010. 'The Psychological Impact of Disappearance: A Preliminary Study among Wives of the "Disappeared" persons'. Master's degree thesis submitted to the Postgraduate Institute of Medicine, University of Colombo, Colombo.

Sivayokan, S. and D. J. Somasundaram (eds). 2001. *Muthumai* [Elderly]. Jaffna: Shanthiham.

Sivayokan, S., K. Mahendran and D. J. Somasundaram (eds). 2005. *Child Mental Health*, rev. ed. In English, Tamil and Sinhalese. Colombo: GTZ-PLAN International.

Smith, A. D. 1986. *The Ethnic Origin of Nations*. New York: Basil Blackwell.

———. 1998. *Nationalism and Modernism: A Critical Survey of Recent Theories of Nations and Nationalism*. London: Routledge.

Smith, S. D. 2006. 'Global Families', in B. B. Ingoldsby and S. D. Smith (eds), *Families in Global and Muliticultural Perspective*, pp. 3–24. Thousand Oaks, CA: SAGE Publications.

Social Indicator. 2001–08. *Peace Confidence Index (PCI) Reports: Waves 4–30*. Colombo: Centre for Policy Alternatives.

Somasundaram, D. J. 1993a. 'Child Trauma', Dr. A. Sivapathasundaram Third Memorial Lecture, 30 March, University of Jaffna, Jaffna.

———. 1993b. *Mana vadu* [Psychological trauma]. Jaffna: University of Jaffna.

———. 1993c. 'Psychiatric Morbidity Due to War in Northern Sri Lanka' in J. P. Wilson and B. Raphael (eds), *International Handbook of Traumatic Stress Syndromes*, pp. 333–48. New York: Plenum Press.

———. 1996. 'Post-Traumatic Responses to Aerial Bombing', *Social Science & Medicine*, 42 (11): 1465–71.

———. 1997a. 'Abandoning Jaffna Hospital: Ethical and Moral Dilemmas', *Medicine, Conflict and Survival*, 13 (4): 333–47.

———. 1997b. 'Treatment of Massive Trauma due to War', *Advances in Psychiatric Treatment*, 3: 321–30.

———. 1998. *Scarred Minds: The Psychological Impact of War on Sri Lankan Tamils*. New Delhi: SAGE Publications.

———. 2000. *Psycho-social Needs: A Report for the Framework for Relief, Reconciliation and Rehabilitation*. Colombo: World Bank.

———. 2001. 'War Trauma and Psychosocial Problems: Out Patient Attendees in Jaffna', *International Medical Journal*, 8 (3): 193–97.

———. 2002a. 'Child Soldiers: Understanding the Context', *British Medical Journal*, 324 (7348): 1268–71.

———. 2002b. 'Using Traditional Relaxation Techniques in Minor Mental Health Disorders', *International Medical Journal*, 9 (3): 191–98.

———. 2002c. 'Collective Trauma', Professor K. Balasubramaniam Gold Medal Lecture, Jaffna Science Association Annual Sessions, University of Jaffna, Jaffna, 3 April.

———. 2003a. 'Strategies for Dealing with Collective Trauma', paper presented at the Conference on Psychological Impact of Trauma titled 'Trauma and the Future', UK Sri Lanka Trauma Group and Sri Lanka Medical Association, Colombo, 21–23 August.

———. 2003b. 'Addressing the Psychosocial Problems of Women in a War Ravaged Society', at the People's Forum: Integration of Women in the Peace Process, University of Jaffna, *Lines*, February. Available online at http://www.lines-magazine.org/Art_Feb03/Daya.htm

———. 2004. 'Short- and Long-Term Effects on the Victims of Terror in Sri Lanka', *Journal of Aggression, Maltreatment & Trauma*, 9 (1–2): 215–28.

Somasundaram, D. J. 2005a. *Health and Human Rights in the Jaffna Peninsula*. Colombo: Human Rights Commission of Sri Lanka.

———. 2005b. 'Motivation for the Tamil Militancy', paper presented at the workshop on Sacrificial Devotion in Comparative Perspective, Department of Anthropology, University of Adelaide, Adelaide, 5–7 December.

———. 2006. 'Collective Trauma: A Multi-Level Social-Ecological Perspective', paper presented at 'Brainwaves', Australian Society for Psychiatric Research (ASPR) Annual Meeting, Sydney, 6–8 December. Abstract published in *Acta Neuropsychiatrica*, 18 (6): 270–71.

———. 2007a. 'Collective Trauma in Northern Sri Lanka: A Qualitative Psychosocial-Ecological Study', *International Journal of Mental Health Systems*, 1: 5. Available online at http://www.ijmhs.com/content/1/1/5; doi:10.1186/1752-4458-1-51

———. 2007b. 'Community Level Interventions for Collective Trauma', presentation made at the UK Sri Lanka Trauma Group Conference titled 'Renewal and Regeneration', Colombo, 11–13 May.

———. 2008. 'Psycho-social Aspects of Torture in Sri Lanka', *International Journal of Culture and Mental Health*, 1 (1): 10–23.

———. 2009. 'Collective Violence and War', in N. Loucks, S. S. Holt and J. R. Adler (eds), *Why We Kill: Understanding Violence Across Cultures and Disciplines*, pp. 155–78. London: Middlesex University Press.

———. 2010a. 'Collective Trauma in the Vanni: A Qualitative Inquiry into the Mental Health of the Internally Displaced Due to the Civil War in Sri Lanka', *International Journal of Mental Health Systems*, 4 (22): 1–31. Available online at http://www.ijmhs.com/content/4/1/22

———. 2010b. 'Collective Trauma', presented at the UK Sri Lanka Trauma Group and the Department of Health Service and Population Research, Institute of Psychiatry, King's College London, London, 15 September.

———. 2010c. 'Complex Mental Health Problems of Refugees', in D. Bhugra, T. Craig and K. Bhui (eds), *Mental Health of Refugees and Asylum Seekers*, pp. 73–86. Oxford: Oxford University Press.

———. 2010d. 'Ethnic Consciousness: The Case of Sri Lanka', *McGill Foreign Affairs Review*, 2 (1): 59–66.

———. 2010e. 'Parallel Governments: Living Between Terror and Counter Terror in Northern Lanka (1982–2009)', *Journal of Asian and African Studies*, 45 (5): 568–83. doi: 10.1177/0021909610373899

———. 2010g. 'Preliminary Thoughts on Psychosocial Rehabilitation after Mass Atrocities', in F. Freyenhagen and C. Ferstman (eds), *Rehabilitation as a Form of Reparation Opportunities and Challenges*, pp. 3–4. London. Colchester: REDRESS & Transitional Justice Network.

———. 2010h. 'Using Cultural Relaxation Methods in Post-Trauma Care among Refugees in Australia', *International Journal of Culture and Mental Health*, 3 (1): 16–24.

———. 2010i. 'Suicide Bombers of Sri Lanka', *Asian Journal of Social Science*, 38 (3): 416–41.

———. 2011. 'Collective Trauma', in D. Bhugra and S. Gupta (eds), *Migration and Mental Health*, pp. 149–58. Cambridge: Cambridge University Press.

Somasundaram, D. J. 2012. 'Rebuilding Community Resilience in a Post-war Context: Northern Sri Lanka', paper presented at the University of Jaffna International Research Conference titled 'Capacity Development in a Post-war Context', University of Jaffna, Jaffna, 20–22 July.

Somasundaram, D. J. and C. S. Jamunanantha. 2002. 'Psychosocial Consequences of War: Northern Sri Lankan Experience', in J. T. V. M. de Jong (ed.), *Trauma, War, and Violence: Public Mental Health in Socio-Cultural Context*, pp. 205–58. New York: Kluwer Academic/Plenum Publishers.

Somasundaram, D. J. and S. Rajadurai. 1995. 'War and Suicide', *Acta Psychiatrica Scandinavica*, 91 (1): 1–4. doi: 10.1111/j.1600-0447.1995.tb09733.x

Somasundaram, D. J. and S. Renol. 1998. 'The Psychosocial Effects of Landmines in Cambodia', *Medicine, Conflict and Survival*, 14 (3): 219–36.

Somasundaram, D. J. and S. Sivayokan. 1994. 'War Trauma in a Civilian Population', *British Journal of Psychiatry*, 165 (4): 524–27.

———. 2013. 'Rebuilding Community Resilience in a Post-war Context: Developing Insight and Recommendations: A Qualitative Study in Northern Sri Lanka', *International Journal of Mental Health Systems*, 7: 3. Available online at http://www.ijmhs.com/content/pdf/1752-4458-7-3.pdf

Somasundaram, D. J. and S. Sivayokan (eds). 2001. *Mental Health in the Tamil Community*. In English and Tamil. Jaffna: Shanthiham and TPO.

———. 2005. *Mental Health in the Tamil Community*, 2nd ed. Jaffna: Shanthiham.

Somasundaram, D. J., K. Kall, W. A. C. M. van de Put, E. Eisenbruch and L. Thomassen. 1997. *Community Mental Health in Cambodia*. Edited by J. T. V. M. de Jong. In English and Khmer. Phnom Penh: IPSER/TPO.

Somasundaram, D. J., K. Mahendran and T. Gadmapanathan. 2005. *We Are Little Children*. In Tamil, Sinhalese and English. Colombo: Sri Lanka Red Cross.

Somasundaram, D. J., W. A. C. M. van de Put, M. Eisenbruch and J. T. V. M. de Jong. 1999. 'Starting Mental Health Services in Cambodia', *Social Science & Medicine*, 48 (8): 1029–46.

Spencer, J. 1990. 'Introduction: The Power of the Past', in J. Spencer (ed.), *Sri Lanka: History and the Roots of Conflict*, pp. 1–18. London: Routledge.

———. 2011. 'Reflections on an Illiberal Peace: Stories from the East', in J. Goodhand, B. Korf and J. Spencer (eds), *Conflict and Peacebuilding in Sri Lanka: Caught in the Peace Trap?*, 201–12. London: Routledge.

Sri Lanka Army. 2011. *Seminar on 'Defeating Terrorism – The Sri Lanka Experience*. Colombo: Sri Lanka Army. Available online at http://www.defseminar.lk/defseminar_2011/index.php see particularly, keynote address: http://www.defence.lk/new.asp?fname=20110613_Keynote and annual ongoing Seminars: http://www.defseminar.lk/

Stein, D. J., S. Seedat, D. Kaminer, H. Moomal, A. Herman, J. Sonnega and D. R. Williams. 2008. 'The Impact of the Truth and Reconciliation Commission on Psychological Distress and Forgiveness in South Africa', *Social Psychiatry and Psychiatric Epidemiology*, 43 (6): 462–68.

Stein, G. 2010. 'War Stories', *SBS One: Dateline*, 28 February. Available online at http://www.sbs.com.au/dateline/story/transcript/id/600331/n/War-Stories (retrieved on 8 March 2010).

Stewart, F. 2001. 'Horizontal Inequalities: A Neglected Dimension of Development', Working Paper No. 1, Centre for Research on Inequality, Human Security and Ethnicity (CRISE), University of Oxford, Oxford.

Stewart, K. 2009. 'Offering an Ear to Fleeing Sri Lankans'. Available online at http://www.msf.org.uk/article/offering-ear-fleeing-sri-lankans (retrieved on 30 July 2013).

Strategic Foresight Group. 2006. 'Cost of Conflict in Sri Lanka'. Available online at http://www.strategicforesight.com/ccinsrilanka.htm (retrieved on 10 April 2011).

Sumanthiran, M. A. 2012. 'Militarization of the North and East: Most Serious Problem Faced by People in the North-East on a Day to Day Basis is that of Militarisation', *The Sri Lanka Guardian*, 28 January. Available online at http://www.srilankaguardian.org/2012/01/militarization-of-north-and-east.html (retrieved on 29 July 2013).

Sumathipala, A. and N. Mendis. 2002. 'Floor Discussions: Psychological Trauma', in T. Varagunam, V. Basanayake, T. Munasinghe, S. Sujeevan and N. Mendis (eds), *Community Mental Health Care: Issues and Challenges, 2002*, pp. 165–66. Colombo: National Council for Mental Health - Sahanaya.

Summerfield, D. 1996. *The Impact of War and Atrocity on Civilian Populations: Basic Principles for NGO Interventions and a Critique of Psychosocial Trauma Projects*. London: Relief and Rehabilitation Network.

———. 1998. 'The Social Experience of War and Some Issues for the Humanitarian Field', in P. J. Bracken and C. Petty (eds), *Rethinking the Trauma of War: A Critical Analysis of Western Trauma Counselling in Areas of Conflict and Emergencies*, pp. 9–34. London: Save the Children with Free Association Books.

———. 1999. 'The Nature of Conflict and the Implications for Appropriate Psychosocial Responses' in M. Loughry and A. Ager (eds), *The Refugee Experience: Psychosocial Training Module*, pp. 28–56. Oxford: Refugee Studies Centre.

Sundram, S., M. E. Karim, L. Ladrido-Ignacio, A. Maramis, K. A. Mufti, D. Nagaraja, N. Shinfuku, D. J. Somasundaram, P. Udomratn, Z. Yizhuang, A. Ahsan, H. R. Chaudhry, S. Chowdhury, R. D'Souza, Z. Dongfeng, A. H. M. Firoz, M. A. Hamid, S. Indradjaya, S. B. Math, R. A. H. M. Mustafizur, F. Naeem and M. A. Wahab. 2008. 'Psychosocial Responses to Disaster: An Asian Perspective', *Asian Journal of Psychiatry*, 1 (1): 7–14.

Suntharalingam, S. 2009. 'Sri Lanka: Health as a Weapon of War?' *British Medical Journal*, 338: b2304. doi: http://dx.doi.org/10.1136/bmj.b2304

Swamy, N. M. R. 2003. *Inside an Elusive Mind: Prabhakaran: The First Profile of the World's Most Ruthless Guerrilla Leader*. New Delhi: Konark Publishers.

———. 2008. 'India's Covert Role in Sri Lanka's Ceasefire', *Thaindian News*, 17 February. Available online at http://www.thaindian.com/newsportal/world-news/indias-covert-role-in-sri-lankas-ceasefire_10018328.html

———. 2010. *The Tiger Vanquished: LTTE's Story*. New Delhi: SAGE Publications.

Tajfel, H. 1978. *The Social Psychology of Minorities*, Vol. 38. London: Minority Rights Group.

Tambiah, S. J. 1986. *Sri Lanka: Ethnic Fratricide and the Dismantling of Democracy*. Chicago, IL: The University of Chicago Press.

Tambiah, S. J. 1992. *Buddhism Betrayed? Religion, Politics, and Violence in Sri Lanka.* Chicago, IL: The University of Chicago Press.

Tamilnet. 2004. 'Integrate Psychological Counseling with Relief Effort- Prof Somasundaram', *Tamilnet.* Available online at http://www.tamilnet.com/art.html?artid=13788&catid=13 (retrieved on 30 July 2013).

Taussig, M. 2004. 'Culture of Terror—Space of Death: Roger Casement's Putumayo Report and the Explanation of Torture', in N. Scheper-Hughes and P. Bourgois (eds), *Violence in War and Peace: An Anthology,* pp. 39–53. Malden: Blackwell Publishing.

Tedeschi, R. G. and L. G. Calhoun. 1995. *Trauma and Transformation: Growing in the Aftermath of Suffering.* Thousand Oaks, CA: SAGE Publications.

Tedlock, B. 2000. 'Ethnography and Ethnographic Representation', in N. K. Denzin and Y. S. Lincoln (eds), *Handbook of Qualitative Research,* 2nd ed., pp. 455–86. Thousand Oaks, CA: SAGE Publications.

Terr, L. C. 1991. 'Childhood Traumas: An Outline and Overview', *American Journal of Psychiatry,* 148 (1): 10–20.

Thabet, A. A. and P. Vostanis. 2000. 'Post Traumatic Stress Disorder Reactions in Children of War: A Longitudinal Study', *Child Abuse & Neglect,* 24 (2): 291–98.

Thangarajah, Y. 1995. 'Narratives of Victimhood as Ethnic Identity among the Veddas of the East Coast', in P. Jeganathan and Q. Ismail (eds), *Unmaking the Nation: The Politics of Identity and History in Modern Sri Lanka,* pp. 191–218. Colombo: Social Scientists' Association.

Thapar, R., H. Mukhia and B. Chandra. 1969. *Communalism and the Writing of Indian History.* New Delhi: People's Publishing House.

The Psychosocial Working Group. 2003. 'Psychosocial Intervention in Complex Emergencies: A Conceptual Framework', Working Paper, The Psychosocial Working Group, Edinburgh.

The Sphere Project. 2004. *Sphere Handbook: Humanitarian Charter and Minimum Standards in Disaster Response.* Geneva: The Sphere Project.

Thiranagama, S. 2010. 'In Praise of Traitors: Intimacy, Betrayal, and the Sri Lankan Tamil Community' in S. Thiranagama and T. Kelly (eds), *Traitors: Suspicion, Intimacy, and the Ethics of State-Building,* pp. 127–50. Philadelphia, PA: University of Pennsylvania Press.

———. 2011. *In My Mother's House: Civil War in Sri Lanka.* Philadelphia, PA: University of Pennsylvania Press.

Thiranagama, S. and T. Kelly (eds). 2010. *Traitors: Suspicion, Intimacy, and the Ethics of State-Building.* Philadelphia, PA: University of Pennsylvannia.

Thomas, L. 2000. 'Racism and Psychotherapy; Working with Racism in the Consulting Room; An Analytic View', in J. Kareem and R. Littlewood (eds), *Intercultural Therapy,* pp. 146–60. London: Blackwell Science.

Tol, W. A., I. H. Komproe, M. J. D. Jordan, A. Vallipuram, H. Sipsma, S. Sivayokan, R. D. Macy and J. T. V. M. de Jong. 2012. 'Outcomes and Moderators of a Preventive School-based Mental Health Intervention for Children Affected by War in Sri Lanka: A Cluster Randomized Trial', *World Psychiatry,* 11 (2): 114–22.

transCurrents. 2009. 'My Life in Menik Farm IDP Camp from March to July 2009: A Personal Account', *transCurrents*, 3 October. Available online at http://transcurrents.com/tc/2009/10/my_life_in_menik_farm_idp_camp.html

Transparency International. 2006. '2006 Annual Report – Special Asia Pacific Section'. Available online at http://www.transparency.org/publications/publications/annual_reports/ar_2006_special_asia_pacific

———. 2008. 'Corruption Perception Index 2007'. Available online at http://www.transparency.org/policy_research/surveys_indices/cpi/2007

Trawick, M. 1999. 'Reasons for Violence: A Preliminary Ethnographic Account of the Tamil Tigers', in S. Gamage and I. B. Watson (eds), *Conflict and Community in Contemporary Sri Lanka: 'Pearl of the East' or the 'Island of Tears'?*, pp. 139–63. New Delhi: SAGE Publications.

———. 2007. *Enemy Lines: Warfare, Childhood, and Play in Batticaloa*. Berkeley, CA: University of California Press.

Tribe, R. 2004. 'A Critical Review of the Evolution of a Multi-level Community-based Children's Play Activity Programme Run by the Family Rehabilitation Centre (FRC) Throughout Sri Lanka', *Journal of Refugee Studies*, 17 (1): 114–35.

———. 2007. Health Pluralism: A More Appropriate Alternative to Western Models of Therapy in the Context of the Conflict and Natural Disaster in Sri Lanka?', *Journal of Refugee Studies*, 20 (1): 21–36.

Tribe, R. and Family Rehabilitation Centre Staff. 2004. 'Internally Displaced Sri Lankan War Widows: The Women's Empowerment Programme' in K. E. Miller and L. M. Rasco (eds), *The Mental Health of Refugees: Ecological approaches to Healing and Adaptation*, pp. 161–86. New York: Lawrence Erlbaum Associates, Inc.

Tribe, R. and P. De Silva. 1999. 'Psychological Intervention with Displaced Widows in Sri Lanka', *International Review of Psychiatry*, 11 (2–3): 184–90. doi: 10.1080/09540269974366

Tumarkin, M. 2005. *Traumascapes: The Power and Fate of Places Transformed by Tragedy*. Melbourne: Melbourne University Press.

UKBA. 2010. 'Asylum & Immigration Statistics, 2005-2009'. Available online at http://webarchive.nationalarchives.gov.uk/20110218135832/http://rds.homeoffice.gov.uk/rds/immigration-asylum-publications.html (retrieved on 23 July 2010).

UN. 1984. 'Convention against Torture and Other Cruel, Inhuman or Degrading Treatment or Punishment'. Available online at http://www.hrweb.org/legal/cat.html (retrieved on 24 March 2011).

———. 2011. *Report of the Secretary-General's Panel of Experts on Accountability in Sri Lanka*. New York: United Nations. Available online at http://www.un.org/News/dh/infocus/Sri_Lanka/POE_Report_Full.pdf

———. 2012. *Report of the Secretary-General's Internal Review Panel on United Nations Actions in Sri Lanka*. New York: United Nations. Available online at http://www.un.org/News/dh/infocus/Sri_Lanka/The_Internal_Review_Panel_report_on_Sri_Lanka.pdf

UN General Assembly. 2005. 'Basic Principles and Guidelines on the Right to a Remedy and Reparation for Victims of Gross Violations of International Human Rights Law and Serious Violations of International Humanitarian Law', *Resolution 60/147*. New York: UN General Assembly.

UNHCR. 2006. 'Increasing Intimidation Exacerbates Displacement in Sri Lanka'. Available online at http://www.unhcr.org/cgi-bin/texis/vtx/news/opendoc.htm?tbl=NEWS&id=44523f134 (retrieved on 28 January 2013).

———. 2010. *2009 Global Trends: Refugees, Asylum-seekers, Returnees, Internally Displaced and Stateless Persons*. Geneva: United Nations High Commission for Refugees. Available online at http://www.unhcr.org/4c11f0be9.html

UNOCHA. 2009. 'Sri Lanka: Vanni Emergency: Situation Report No. 18', 27 May. Available online at http://ochaonline.un.org/srilanka/SituationReports/EmergencySituationReport/tabid/5487/language/en-US/Default.aspx (retrieved on 20 May 2010).

United States Army. 2006. *Counterinsurgency: Field Manual No. 3-24*. Washington, D.C.: Department of the Army, Department of the Navy, United States Marine Corps. Available online at http://www.fas.org/irp/doddir/army/fm3-24fd.pdf

——— United States Department of State. 2009. 'Report to Congress on Incidents during the Recent Conflict in Sri Lanka'. Available online at http://www.state.gov/documents/organization/131025.pdf (retrieved on 30 July 2013).

UTHR-J. 1993a. 'From Manal Aaru to Weli Oya and the Spirit of July 1983', *Special Report No. 5*, 15 September. Colombo: University Teachers for Human Rights (Jaffna). Available online at http://www.uthr.org/SpecialReports/spreport5.htm (retrieved on 29 July 2013).

———. 1993b. 'Sullen Hills: The Saga of Up Country Tamils', *Special Report No. 4*. Colombo: University Teachers for Human Rights (Jaffna). Available online at http://www.uthr.org/SpecialReports/spreport4.htm (retrieved on 29 July 2013).

———. 1993c. 'A Sovereign Will to Self-Destruct: The Continuing Saga of Dislocation & Disintegration', *Report 12*, 15 December. Colombo: University Teachers for Human Rights (Jaffna). Available online at http://www.uthr.org/Reports/Report12/Report12.htm (retrieved on 29 July 2013).

———. 1995a. 'Exodus from Jaffna', *Special Report No. 6*, 6 December. Colombo: University Teachers for Human Rights (Jaffna). Available online at http://www.uthr.org/SpecialReports/spreport6.htm

———. 1995b. 'Children in the North-East War: 1985–1995', *Briefing No. 2*, 20 June. Colombo: University Teachers for Human Rights (Jaffna).

———. 1999. 'Gaps in the Krishanthy Kumarasamy Case: Disappearances & Accountability', *Special Report No. 12*, 28 April. Colombo: University Teachers for Human Rights (Jaffna). Available online at http://www.uthr.org/SpecialReports/spreport12.htm

———. 2000. 'The Sun God's Children and the Big Lie', *Bulletin No. 23*, 11 July. Colombo: University Teachers for Human Rights (Jaffna).

———. 2006b. 'The Second Fascist Front in Sri Lanka – Towards Crushing the Minorities and Disenfranchising the Sinhalese', *Special Report No. 29*. Colombo: University Teachers for Human Rights (Jaffna). Available online at http://www.uthr.org/SpecialReports/spreport29.htm

———. 2007a. 'Can the East Be Won through Human Culling? Special Economic Zones – An Ideological Journey Back to 1983', *Special Report No. 26*, 3 August. Colombo: University Teachers for Human Rights (Jaffna).

UTHR-J. 2007b. 'Scripting the Welikade Massacre Inquest and the Fate of Two Dissidents', *Supplement to Special Report No. 25*. Colombo: University Teachers for Human Rights (Jaffna). Available online at http://www.uthr. org/SpecialReports/spreport251.htm

———. 2009. 'Let Them Speak: Truth about Sri Lanka's Victims of War', *Special Report No. 34*, 13 December. Colombo: University Teachers for Human Rights (Jaffna). Available online at http://www.uthr.org/SpecialReports/ Special%20rep34/Uthr-sp.rp34.htm

Uphoff, N. T. 2001. 'Ethnic Cooperation in Sri Lanka: Through the Keyhole of a USAID Project' in M. J. Esman and R. J. Herring (eds), *Carrots, Sticks, and Ethnic Conflict: Rethinking Development Assistance*, pp. 113–39. Ann Arbor, MI: The University of Michigan Press.

Uthayan. 2007. 'News on Scholarship Results', *Uthayan Daily*, 24 September.

Uyangoda, J. 1994. 'The State and the Process of Devolution in Sri Lanka' in S. Bastian (ed.), *Devolution and Development in Sri Lanka*, pp. 83–120. Colombo: International Centre for Ethnic Studies and New Delhi: Konark Publishers.

———. 2008. 'Politics of Sri Lanka in 2007: Trajectories of Conflict Escalation', *Polity*, 4(4): 3–15.

———. (ed.). 2007. *Religion in Context: Buddhism and Socio-Political Change in Sri Lanka*. Colombo: Social Scientists' Association.

Valkyrie. 2011. 'Jaffna and the Vanni Today: The Reality beneath the Rhetoric', *Groundviews*, 17 March. Available online at http://groundviews.org/ 2011/03/17/jaffna-and-the-vanni-today-the-reality-beneath-the-rhetoric/ (retrieved on 20 March 2011).

Van de Put, W. A. C. M., D. J. Somasundaram, M. Eisenbruch, K. Kall, R. Soomers and L. Thomassen. 1997. *Facts and Thoughts on the First Years 1995-1996*. Phnom Penh: Cambodia: Transcultural Psychosocial Organization.

Van de Put, W. A. C. M. and M. Eisenbruch, M. 2002. 'The Cambodian Experience', in J. T. V. M. de Jong (ed.), *Trauma, War, and Violence: Public Mental Health in Socio-Cultural Context*, pp. 93–156. New York: Kluwer Academic/Plenum Publishers.

Van der Kolk, B. A., A. C. McFarlane and L. Weisaeth (eds). 1996. *Traumatic Stress: The Effects of Overwhelming Experience on Mind, Body, and Society*. New York: The Guilford Press.

Van der Veen, M. and D. J. Somasundaram. 2006. Responding to the Psychosocial Impact of the Tsunami in a War Zone: Experiences from Northern Sri Lanka', *Intervention*, 4 (1): 53–57.

van der Veer, G. 1992. *Counselling and Therapy with Refugees: Psychological Problems of Victims of War, Torture, and Repression*. Chichester: John Wiley & Sons.

Van der Veer, P. 1994. *Religious Nationalism: Hindus and Muslims in India*. Berkeley, CA: University of California Press.

Vázquez, C., P. Pérez-Sales and G. Hervás. 2008. 'Positive Effects of Terrorism and Posttraumatic Growth: An Individual and Community Perspective', in S. Joseph and P. A. Linley (eds), *Trauma, Recovery and Growth: Positive Psychological Perspectives on Posttraumatic Stress*, pp. 63–92. Hoboken: John Wiley & Sons, Inc.

Vázquez Valverde, C. 2005. 'Stress Reactions of the General Population after the Terrorist Attacks of S11, 2001 (USA) and M11, 2004 (Madrid, Spain): Myths and Realities', *Annuary of Clinical and Health Psychology*, 1: 9–25.

Vickery, M. 1984. *Cambodia: 1975–1982*. Boston, MA: South End Press.

Vijayasiri, R. 1999. 'Critical Analysis of Sri Lankan Counterinsurgency Campaign'. Master's degree thesis presented to the U.S. Army Command and General Staff College, Fort Leavenworth, Kansas. Available online at http://cgsc.cdmhost.com/cdm/singleitem/collection/p4013coll2/id/664/rec/2 (retrieved on 29 July 2013).

Villalba, C. S. 2009. *Rehabilitation as a Form of Reparation under International Law*. Edited by C. Ferstman. London: REDRESS.

Vittachi, T. 1958. *Emergency '58: The Story of the Ceylon Race Riots*. London: Andre Deutch.

Volkan, V. D. 1988. *The Need to Have Enemies and Allies: From Clinical Practice to International Relationships*. Northvale: Jason Aronson, Inc.

———. 1997. *Blood Lines: From Ethnic Pride to Ethnic Terrorism*. Boulder, CO: Westview Press.

———. 2006. *Killing in the Name of Identity: A Study of Bloody Conflicts*. Charlottesville: Pitchstone Publishing.

Walters, J. S. 1995. 'Multireligion on the Bus: Beyond "Influence" and "Syncretism" in the Study of Religious Meetings' in P. Jeganathan and Q. Ismail (eds), *Unmaking the Nation: The Politics of Identity and History in Modern Sri Lanka*, pp. 25–54. Colombo: Social Scientists' Association.

Watts, A. (1973) *Psychotherapy East & West*. Harmodsworth: Penguin.

Wax, E. 2009. 'New Reports, Imagery Contradict Sri Lankan Government on Civilian No-Fire Zone', *Washington Post*, 30 May. Available online at http://www.washingtonpost.com/wp-dyn/content/article/2009/05/29/AR2009052903409.html?nav=emailpage (retrieved on 30 May 2009).

Weinstein, H. M. 2002. 'Where There is Not Body: Trauma and Bereavement in Communities Coping with the Aftermath of Mass Violence', in *The Missing: Action to Resolve the Problem of People Unaccounted for as a Result of Armed Conflict or Internal Violence and to Assist Their Families: Support for Families of People Unaccounted For: Final Outcome and Report of the Workshop held in Geneva, 10–11 June*, pp. 72–76. Geneva: International Committee of the Red Cross. Available online at http://www.icrc.org/eng/assets/files/other/icrc_themissing_082002_en_4.pdf

Weiss, G. 2011. *The Cage: The Fight for Sri Lanka and the Last Days of the Tamil Tigers*. Sydney: Picador.

Weliamuna, J. C. 2011a. 'Lifting of Emergency: Exposing the Sham Exercise', *Groundviews*, 16 September. Available online at http://groundviews.org/2011/09/16/lifting-of-emergency-exposing-the-sham-exercise/ (retrieved on 13 February 2013).

———. 2011b. 'Peace, Military and People: Are Non-Military Engagements of the Military Valid?', *Groundviews*, 4 November. Available online at http://groundviews.org/2011/11/04/peace-military-and-people-are-non-military-engagements-of-the-military-valid/

Weliamuna, J. C. 2012. 'Discovering the White Van in a Troubled Democracy: An Analysis of Ongoing "Abduction Blueprint" in Sri Lanka', *Groundviews*, 28 April. Available online at http://groundviews.org/2012/04/28/discovering-the-white-van-in-a-troubled-democracy-an-analysis-of-ongoing-abduction-blueprint-in-sri-lanka/(retrieved on 29 July 2013).

Wessells, M. and A. Strang. 2006. 'Religion as Resource and Risk: The Double-edged Sword for Children in Situations of Armed Conflict', in N. Boothby, A. Strang and M. G. Wessells (eds), *A World Turned Upside Down: Social Ecological Approaches to Children in War Zones*, pp. 199–222. Bloomfield: Kumarian Press.

Whitaker, M. P. 1990. 'A Compound of Many Histories: The Many Pasts of an East Coast Tamil Community', in J. Spencer (ed.), *Sri Lanka: History and the Roots of Conflict*, pp. 145–63. London: Routledge.

———. 2007. *Learning Politics from Sivaram: The Life and Death of a Revolutionary Tamil Journalist in Sri Lanka*. London: Pluto Press.

WHO. 1948. *The Constitution of the WHO*. Geneva: World Health Organization.

———. 1992. *Mental Disorders: Glossary and Guide to their Classification in Accordance with the Tenth Revision of the International Classification of Diseases (ICD-10)*. Geneva: World Health Organization.

———. 2001. *The World Health Report 2001*. Geneva: World Health Organization.

———. 2003. *Mental Health in Emergencies: Mental and Social Aspects of Health of Populations Exposed to Extreme Stressors*. Geneva: World Health Organization.

———. 2005a. *The New Mental Health Policy of Sri Lanka*. Colombo: World Health Organization, Country Office for Sri Lanka. Available online at http://www.whosrilanka.org/LinkFiles/Press_Releases_New_Mental_Health_Policy.pdf

———. 2005b. 'Tsunami Affected Areas'. Available online at http://www.whosrilanka.org/en/section15.htm

WHO and UNHCR. 1996. *Mental Health of Refugees*. Geneva: World Health Organization.

Wickramage, K. 2006. 'Sri Lanka's Post-Tsunami Psychosocial Playground: Lessons for Future Psychosocial Programming and Interventions Following Disasters', *Intervention*, 4 (2): 167–72.

———. 2010. *Mental Health in Sri Lanka: Evaluation of the Impact of the Community Support Officers (CSO) in Mental Health Service Provision at District Level*. New Delhi: World Health Organization.

Wickramasinghe, N. 2006. *Sri Lanka in the Modern Age: A History of Contested Identities*. Honolulu: University of Hawaii Press.

———. 2009. 'After the War: A New Patriotism in Sri Lanka?', *The Journal of Asian Studies*, 68 (4): 1045–54.

Wikipedia. 2013. 'Map Showing Countries Affected by the 2004 Indian Ocean Earthquake'. Available online at http://en.wikipedia.org/wiki/File:2004_Indian_Ocean_earthquake_-_affected_countries.png

Williams, R. M. and S. Joseph. 1999. 'Conclusions: An Integrative Psychosocial Model of PTSD', in W. Yule (ed.), *Post-Traumatic Stress Disorders: Concepts and Therapy*, pp. 297–314. Chichester: John Wiley & Sons.

Wilson, A. J. 1994. 'The Colombo Man, the Jaffna Man, and the Batticaloa Man: Regional Identities and the Rise of the Federal Party', in C. Manogaran and B. Pfaffenberger (eds), *The Sri Lankan Tamils: Ethnicity and Identity*, pp. 126–242. Boulder, CO: Westview Press.

———. 2000. *Sri Lankan Tamil Nationalism: Its Origins and Development in the 19th and 20th Centuries*. New Delhi: Penguin Books.

Wilson, J. P. 1989. *Trauma, Transformation, and Healing: An Integrative Approach to Theory, Research and Post-Traumatic Therapy*. New York: Routledge.

———. 2004. 'The Broken Spirit: Posttraumatic Damage to the Self', in J. P. Wilson and B. Drozdek (eds), *Broken Spirits: The Treatment of Traumatized Asylum Seekers, Refugees, and War and Torture Victims*, pp. 109–158. New York: Brunner-Routledge.

———. 2007. 'The Lens of Culture: Theoretical and Conceptual Perspectives in the Assessment of Psychological Trauma and PTSD', in J. P. Wilson and C. S. Tang (eds), *Cross-Cultural Assessment of Psychological Trauma and PTSD*, pp. 3–31. New York: Springer.

Wilson, J. P. and C. S. Tang (eds). 2007. *Cross-Cultural Assessment of Psychological Trauma and PTSD*. New York: Springer.

Wilson, J. P. and B. Drozdek (eds). 2004. *Broken Spirits: The Treatment of Traumatized Asylum Seekers, Refugees, and War and Torture Victims*. New York: Brunner-Routledge.

Wind, T. R. and I. H. Komproe. 2012. 'The Mechanisms That Associate Community Social Capital with Post-Disaster Mental Health: A Multilevel Model', *Social Science & Medicine*, 75 (9): 1715–20.

Winter, I. 2000. 'Towards a Theorised Understanding of Family Life and Social Capital', Working Paper No. 21, Australian Institute of Family Studies, Melbourne.

Wong, P. T. P. and L. C. J. Wong (eds). 2006. *Handbook of Multicultural Perspectives on Stress and Coping*. New York: Springer.

Woodward, B. 2002. *Bush at War*. New York: Simon & Schuster.

———. 2004. *Plan of Attack*. New York: Simon & Schuster.

Yeh, C. J., A. K. Arora and K. A. Wu. 2006. 'A New Theoretical Model of Collectivistic Coping', in P. T. P. Wong and L. C. J. Wong (eds), *Handbook of Multicultural Perspectives on Stress and Coping*, pp. 55–72. New York: Springer.

Young, A. 1980. 'The Discourse on Stress and the Reproduction of Conventional Knowledge', *Social Science & Medicine*, 14 (3): 133–46.

Index

About the Author and Guest Contributors

Author

Daya Somasundaram is a senior professor of psychiatry at the Faculty of Medicine, University of Jaffna, and a consultant psychiatrist working in northern Sri Lanka for over two decades. He has also worked in Cambodia for two years in a community mental health programme with the Transcultural Psychosocial Organisation. Apart from teaching and training a variety of health staff and community-level workers, his research and publications have mainly concentrated on the psychological effects of disasters, both man-made wars and natural tsunami, and the treatment of such effects. His book *Scarred Minds: The Psychological Impact of War on Sri Lankan Tamils* describes the psychological effects of war on individuals. He has co-authored *The Broken Palmyra: The Tamil Crisis in Sri Lanka: An Inside Account*.

Somasundaram received the Commonwealth Scholarship in 1988 and the fellowship of the Institute of International Education's Scholars Rescue Fund in 2006–07. He is a fellow of the Royal College of Psychiatrists, Royal Australian and New Zealand College of Psychiatrists and Sri Lanka College of Psychiatrists. He has functioned as co-chair of the subcommittee on PTSD formed under the WHO working group on stress-related disorders during the ICD-11 revision process. Currently on an extended sabbatical in Australia, he is working as a consultant psychiatrist at Glenside Hospital, supporting Survivors of Torture and Trauma Assistance and Rehabilitation Service (STTARS), and is a clinical associate professor at the University of Adelaide.

Guest Contributors

Ananda Galappatti is a medical anthropologist and a practitioner in the field of MHPSS in emergency settings. His work in this field over the past seventeen years has mostly been in Sri Lanka, where he has been involved in the development and coordination of services in situations of conflict and disaster. His interests span the provision of MHPSS emergency responses, integration of support into post-emergency reconstruction and development, care and protection of vulnerable children, responses to gender-based violence and services for people with serious mental illness. He co-founded the journal *Intervention* and the online MHPSS Network to improve knowledge exchange amongst service providers, academics and policy-makers, especially in low- and middle-income countries. He was awarded the annual Ramon Magsaysay Award for Emergent Leadership in 2008.

Ruwan M. Jayatunge graduated from the National Medical University, Vinnytsia, Ukraine, and joined the Ministry of Health, Sri Lanka. He worked predominantly in the field of mental health. From 2002 to 2006 he worked with Neil J. Fernando, consultant psychiatrist at the Military Hospital, Colombo, profoundly studying the impact of combat-related PTSD. He underwent residential training in EMDR in Philadelphia, United States, under the renowned psychologist Susan Rogers. He has written several books that narrate the psychosocial effects of combat trauma in Sri Lanka. He has published several research articles on PTSD and the therapeutic effect of EMDR. At present he is pursuing further studies in psychology at the York University, Toronto.

Andrew Keefe is the director of national clinical services at Freedom from Torture (Medical Foundation for the Care of Victims of Torture), a rehabilitation service for survivors of torture in the United Kingdom, and is a psychodynamic psychotherapist. During 2000–2010, he was Mental Health Lead at the British Refugee Council.

Gameela Samarasinghe is Associate Professor in psychology in the Department of Sociology and the Director of studies, Faculty of Arts, University of Colombo, Sri Lanka. She is a clinical psychologist by training. She has been the recipient of research grants such as the Fulbright–Hays Senior Research Scholar Award and the Fulbright Advanced Research and Lecturing Award. She has collaborated in many research projects with universities such as the University of Ulster, Northern Ireland and Sydney University, Australia. She holds a bachelor's in psychology and a master's degree in clinical psychology from the University of Paris, Sorbonne. She has a doctorate in psychology from the Université de Bretagne Occidentale, Brest.

Kuhan Satkunanayagam is a Sri Lankan–born chartered counselling psychologist. His main research interest is secondary trauma and his doctoral thesis at the University of East London was entitled 'The Realities of

Caring: A Qualitative Exploration of Mental Health Professionals' Experience of Working with Survivors of Trauma in Sri Lanka'. He is an active member of the UK Sri Lanka Trauma Group, having undertaken training of mental health workers in Sri Lanka. He is now an ordained priest in the Church of England.

Vijayasangar Sivajini holds a bachelor's from the University of Jaffna and a postgraduate diploma in education from the Open University, Sri Lanka. She also has a diploma in counselling from the National Institute of Social Development (NISD), Sri Lanka. She was a psycho-social trainer for teacher counsellors from the North East. Presently she is employed as a teacher, and is a counsellor and resource person in the field of psychosocial work. Her experience involves working with women with a special interest in war widows and children.

Sambasivamoorthy Sivayokan is the consultant psychiatrist at Teaching Hospital, Jaffna. He completed his MBBS in 1992 at the University of Jaffna and obtained his MD in psychiatry from the Postgraduate Institute of Medicine, Colombo, in 2001. He was the co-editor and a contributor for the following books: *Mental Health in Tamil Community* (in Tamil and English), *Child Mental Health* (in Tamil and English), *Muthumai* (Elderly) and *Uyirppu: An Introduction to Reproductive Health* (in Tamil). He is interested in drama and music and has taken an active role in producing various dramatic and musical productions.

Rachel Tribe is a fellow of the British Psychological Society and a registered psychologist with the Health Professions Council. She has many years of experience in training, developing clinical services and conducting research, both in the United Kingdom and abroad. She is active in national and international consultancy and training work with a range of organizations. She is on the executive committee of the UK Sri Lanka Trauma Group. She has worked in the private, public, charitable and academic sectors. She has co-edited two books: *Handbook of Professional and Ethical Practice* (2005) with Jean Morrissey and *Working with Interpreters in Mental Health* (2003) with Hitesh Raval. She has also published over forty peer-reviewed journal papers and thirteen book chapters.

Thedsanamoorthy Vijayasangar is the president-elect of Shanthiham, the premier psychosocial service provider and training centre in the north of Sri Lanka. Vijayasangar is from Jaffna and holds a postgraduate degree in psychosocial work and counselling from the University of Colombo, in addition to subject matter training within Sri Lanka and abroad. His experience spans over twelve years in the war-ravaged northern and eastern parts of the island. He is the author of many articles and research findings. He worked as a psychosocial trainer after the tsunami of 2004, and was sought after as a trainer in resource development. He has developed his own 'model steps for community-based psychosocial intervention' to suit the local context. Mrs. Vijayasangar Sivajini holds a BA from the University of Jaffna and Post graduate Diploma in Education from the Open University, Sri Lanka. She also has a Diploma in counselling from the National Institute of Social Development (NISD) Sri Lanka. She was a psycho-social trainer for Teacher counselors from the North East. Presently she is employed as a Teacher, and is a counselor and resource person in the field of psychosocial work. Her preference is working with women with special interest in war widows and children.